THE INSIDERS' GUIDE TO

Cincinnati

THE INSIDERS' GUIDE TO

Cincinnati

by
Skip Tate
and
Felix Winternitz

Insiders' Guide
105 Budleigh St.
P.O. Box 2057
Manteo, NC 27954
(252) 473-6100
www.insiders.com

Sales and Marketing:
Falcon Publishing, Inc.
P.O. Box 1718
Helena, MT 59624
(800) 582-2665
www.falconguide.com

•

THIRD EDITION
1st printing

•

Copyright ©1998
by Falcon Publishing, Inc.

•

Printed in the United States
of America

•

Publications from The Insiders' Guide®
series are available at special discounts for
bulk purchases for sales promotions,
premiums or fundraisings. Special editions,
including personalized covers, can be
created in large quantities for special
needs. For more information, please write
to Karen Bachman, Insiders' Guide, P.O.
Box 2057, Manteo, NC 27949, or call
(800) 765-2665 Ext. 241.

ISBN 1-57380-064-3

Insiders' Guide

Publisher/Editor-in-Chief
Beth P. Storie

Advertising Director/
General Manager
Michael McOwen

Creative Services Director
Giles MacMillan

Art Director
David Haynes

Managing Editor
Dave McCarter

Project Editor
Pat von Brook

Project Artist
Bart Smith

Insiders' Guide
An imprint of Falcon Publishing Inc.
A Landmark Communications company.

Preface

If you haven't seen Greater Cincinnati in, say, the past 10 years, you wouldn't recognize the place.

The downtown is in the midst of a retail renaissance, with a new department store just opened and a second soon to come. There's the thriving downtown Tower Place mall, a new Tiffany's and the recently opened Aronoff Center for the Arts, a mighty state-funded theatrical complex bringing a taste of Broadway to the city. The Backstage area now sprouting up around the Aronoff features shops and restaurants open late into the night, defying the city's longstanding reputation that we roll up our sidewalks at 7 PM.

Down on the riverfront, plans call for a National Underground Railroad Freedom Center and the new Paul Brown Stadium for the Bengals. The Reds, too, may soon be leaving Cinergy Field for a new urban ballpark.

Look, too, across the river, where hotels are sprouting up in anticipation of the new Northern Kentucky Convention Center. Plans on the "south side of Cincinnati," as Northern Kentucky labels itself in this era of regional cooperation, also call for a $40 million aquarium and the opening of the Millennium Monument, to be the world's 11th largest tower, by the year 2000.

The Cincinnati/Northern Kentucky International Airport, for its part, is now one of the busiest in the country. And to the west, the new powerhouse presence of riverboat casinos is changing the face of rustic river towns and bringing millions more travelers to the region.

Of course, with prosperity comes change — and confusion. That's where *The Insiders'® Guide to Cincinnati* comes in. We approached this book as if we were putting our arm around our visiting uncle or aunt's shoulder, whispering inside information and offering them advice about this river city that only a local could possibly know.

Greater Cincinnati is a city of neighborhoods. That's the first thing you should learn if you're a newcomer, especially if you hail from a city that's one great metro government such as Columbus, Indianapolis or the like. Greater Cincinnati crosses three state lines and is composed of some 200 quite individual villages, townships, hamlets, boroughs, towns and cities individual in character and in content.

Even the city of Cincinnati proper is split into dozens of urban neighborhoods, and believe us, residents know EXACTLY where the borders are. Don't confuse Mount Adams with Mount Airy, or you'll appear the dunce. Such urban neighborhoods as Price Hill, Westwood, Avondale, Walnut Hills, the East End, Hyde Park and Mount Lookout have distinct cultures and quasi-governmental councils. You'll be amazed to find families who were born, lived and died in the same neighborhood for generations.

If you've just moved to Cincinnati — or even if you're visiting — be careful. You may just get stuck here for the rest of your life because you'll never want to leave. This happens to unsuspecting folks who think they've been transferred to some backwater burg only to find that the burg has just about everything they liked about bigger cities, such as premier arts institutions and terrific restaurants, without so many of the things they didn't like, such as rampant crime and other pronounced forms of urban decay. It's a surprisingly small town for such a large city, too. Walk down any downtown street and, like as not, you'll run into somebody you know. Nobody ordered locals to be as friendly and well-mannered as they are, that's just the way they were raised.

Cincinnati is a great place to rear a family. It offers many choices of safe neighborhoods and schools, both urban and suburban. It's also a beautiful city with a varied collection of grand mansions and vintage buildings because it was the second-biggest city this side of Alleghenies in the mid-1800s. Thanks to the handiwork of Ice Age glaciers, Cincinnati also offers a variety of stunning views atop its Seven Hills. Cincinnati, in fact, spends more money on hillside reclamation and erosion control than any city in America, including San Francisco.

If you're a tourist, you are not alone. Some 4.5 million tourists, convention delegates and other visitors traveled to Greater Cincinnati during 1997, pumping $3 billion into the local economy. Convention traffic was up nearly 21 percent over 1996 totals. And leisure hotel stays were up 59 percent over the previous year, due largely to the presence of the new gambling casinos in nearby Indiana as well as mainstays such as Paramount's Kings Island amusement park, the Reds and the Bengals.

If you're moving to town, welcome to perhaps the happiest city in Ohio. Headlines in 1998 announced "Housing Sales Soar," "Serious Crime Drops in City for Fourth Year of Decline," "Local Inflation at Record Low," "Conventions Thrived in 1997." Indeed, going into the first months of 1998, the news seemed almost TOO good. At least a half-dozen corporations committed to major expansions, most notably DHL Worldwide Express at the international airport, which announced a $170 million expansion of the cargo carrier's operations that will create 700 jobs. With all this economic vitality — and with the state of Ohio's Bicentennial celebration on the horizon — it's an exciting time to be living and working in Greater Cincinnati.

What follows is an attempt to give newcomers a guide to this unique place. Kick up your feet, lean back and give us a read. *The Insiders'® Guide to Cincinnati* is written by two guys who moved here years ago from out of town, fell in love with the city and stayed. Let us know your comments about the guide and what ought to be added in the fourth edition. Address your suggestions to Insiders' Guide, 105 Budleigh St., Manteo, N.C. 27954. Or check out our website at www.insiders.com — sign on and e-mail us your thoughts.

About the Authors

Skip Tate

Skip Tate is a longtime Cincinnati resident who got to know the ins and outs and the back roads of the city the hard way — by moving around a lot. He is now settled in a home in Bellevue, Kentucky, just across the river from downtown Cincinnati, and joined the staff of *Cincinnati Magazine* in February 1996 after two years as a full-time freelance writer. His freelance work appeared in more than a dozen magazines locally, regionally and nationally.

Skip graduated from Ohio University in 1984. Journalism degree in hand, he set out on search of news, working at several newspapers around Ohio. For five years, his main agenda was sports news, and he wrote about everything from the pros to youth bowling. Looking to broaden his horizons, Skip made the radical jump to writing business news in 1989, which he did for five years at two business newspapers in Cincinnati. His work has been honored by the International Association of Business Communicators, Cleveland Press Club, the Cincinnati Editors Association, American City Business Journals, Society of Professional Journalists and the Associated Press.

When he's not working his fingers to the bone, Skip serves on several nonprofit boards as well as on several committees within his church. He can also be found chugging around the local exercise path impersonating a jogger.

Felix Winternitz

Felix Winternitz has lived in Greater Cincinnati since 1986. The Texas native also resided in Philadelphia, New England, California, and Washington, D.C. before deciding, well ahead of the experts, that Cincinnati was about the best place to live in America.

Felix attended Temple University and quickly moved from reporting stints at midsize dailies in Wilmington, Delaware; Savannah, Georgia; and Rochester, New York, to deputy features editor and entertainment editor at *The Cincinnati Enquirer*. For six years, he served as editorial director at *Cincinnati Magazine*, chronicling the highlights and lowlifes of the city. A freelance writer since 1995, he currently teaches journalism at the University of Cincinnati and is a contributing editor at the urban weekly *Cincinnati CityBeat*.

The author of one other book, *America's Best Headlines — And the People Who Write Them*, Felix's articles have appeared in *USA Weekend*, *Aloft Inflight Magazine*, *Quill Magazine*, and numerous newspapers across the nation.

Felix lives with his wife, *Cincinnati Post* reporter Connie Yeager, and their daughters Katie and Abby in Anderson, just a few paces from the Cincinnati city line. When not working, he is found frequenting the Celtic and folk music festivals of the region.

Acknowledgments

Skip . . .

I thought I knew Greater Cincinnati. Thought I knew it like an old, comfortable pair of Nikes — the ins, the outs, the holes in the toes. Then I sat down to write this book. Wow, was I surprised! I knew Greater Cincinnati had a lot to offer, but until I began seeing it all compiled in one place I never realized exactly how much fun, culture, nostalgia and talent can be found here. I guess the area just keeps a low profile. It was an eye-opening experience for me, and I can only hope that reading *The Insiders' Guide® to Greater Cincinnati* is an equally eye-opening experience for you.

For you, the eye opening comes with the flip of a few pages. For me, it took a lot of help from a lot of people. And for that I am grateful, specifically to the following: Jim Borgman, for allowing me to squeeze into his already jam-packed schedule and John Ruthven, for allowing me to squeeze into *his* already jam-packed schedule. The Greater Cincinnati Film Commission for not only bringing movies here but for sharing its resources. Rich Boehne at E.W. Scripps Co. for *Days In History*.

All the familiar faces at the library who have helped me over the years. The Convention and Visitors Bureau for being so well-organized. The Greater Cincinnati Chamber of Commerce for its business knowledge. The Cincinnati Historical Society for its vast knowledge and resources of Cincinnati past, stored in its wonderful library at the Museum Center at Union Terminal and in the pages of its Bicentennial publications. John Clubbe, whose book, *Cincinnati Observed*, provided previously unknown insights into the area's vast array of historic places for those of us who are armchair architects.

Molly Perkins and Pat von Brook for their patience, guidance and editing skills. Jack Neff, who originally wrote the other half of the book, and Felix Winternitz for seamlessly taking over the updates.

As well as the cast and crew in the Tate family and all my friends who lent their support and cared enough to ask at least 1,395 times, "Got that book done yet?"

With all of the help from the people above I can finally say, "Yep."

Felix . . .

On my first day in Cincinnati, oh those many years ago, I landed at the airport, walked off the jet, and was shocked to discover I'd somehow wound up in the wrong state. The greeting signs welcomed me to KENTUCKY. I panicked until a fellow passenger informed me that, strange as it may seem, Greater Cincinnati's international airport isn't even located in the State of Ohio, but in Kentucky.

This, I discovered, is quintessential Cincinnati. Confused and perplexed. In desperate need of a guidebook. Here it is.

Thanks to the dozens of writers and journalists I've worked with along the way since that first day, people who've taught me more about Greater Cincinnati than is imaginable: John Bryan, Linda Cagnetti, Jim DeBrosse, Sacha DeVroomen, John Fox, Patricia Gallagher, Jon C. Hughes, Jim Knippenberg, Gail Madden, Mary McCarty, Dale Parry, Laura Pulfer, Larry Thomas and many more. To Beth Charlton of the Greater Cincinnati Convention & Visitors Bureau, who was always armed with the correct answer and the stunning photograph. To Jay and Judy Yeager, for all your support and love. To Bernard Adelsberger, Mike Brehm, Doug Scott and Paul Suszynski for twenty years of friendship. And to the memory of my late mother Josephine, the wittiest woman I ever knew.

Thanks to coauthor Skip Tate and to editors Molly Perkins and Pat von Brook and the rest of the folks at The Insiders'® Guide for making this book a reality. And to my predecessor in previous editions, Jack Neff, who laid much of the groundwork in these pages.

Special thanks go to my wife, Connie Yeager, and our daughters Kathryn Ann and Abigail Grace. They lived this project as much as I did and aided at every turn. (Well, except the day Abby ate two pages of a chapter.)

Table of Contents

Directory of Maps

Greater Cincinnati

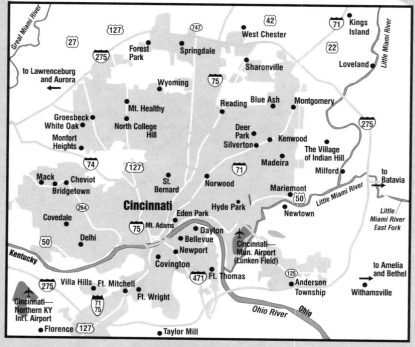

Downtown Cincinnati

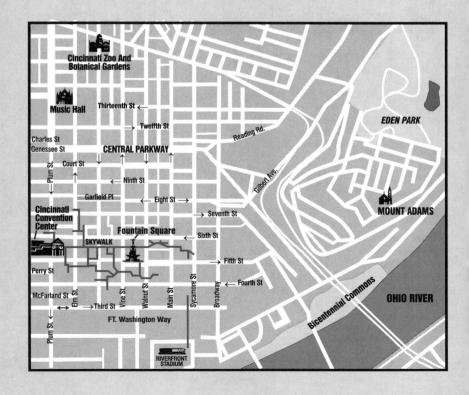

Northern Kentucky

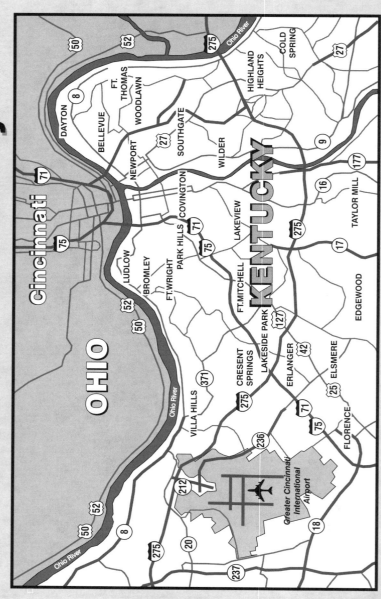

Photo: Skip Tate

The Tyler Davidson Fountain graces the center of Fountain Square in Downtown Cincinnati.

How to Use This Book

Unlike some aspects of Greater Cincinnati, there is a logical order to this book. A method to its madness, if you will. Because the book deals with so many topics and each topic covers three states, eight counties and numerous independent cities, we had no choice but to put some order to it — if not for you, at least for ourselves.

As you work your way through, you may begin to notice some of the patterns and tendencies we've employed. Some are fairly obvious; others are more subtle. They all have their reason for being and their importance, except perhaps for chapter order. We arranged the chapters so that each one has some connection with the chapter before and the chapter after, kind of like the JCPenney catalog. Truly, though, it makes absolutely no difference in what order you read this book. It isn't a novel. Start in the front, in the back, in the middle, with Attractions, with Restaurants, with History or even with the Insiders' Tips. If you happen to read it in order, we hope the order will make the trip smoother.

Otherwise, to help you along, here's what we've done.

Many chapters are organized geographically. On a large scale, they begin with the city of Cincinnati and Ohio counties, then head to Northern Kentucky and then Southeastern Indiana. Within the boundaries of Cincinnati and the Ohio counties we generally subdivided it this way: First, the City, which is the heart of the area, including downtown; then the central suburbs, which are the communities squeezed between Interstates 75, 71 and 275; then the East, West and North. The East comprises those communities east of I-71, the West those west of I-75 and the North those north of I-275. Some references may be made to Northeastern suburbs, an area that is rapidly expanding and developing its own unique characteristics, but has yet to fully bloom. This area is generally east of I-71 and north of I-275.

Some chapters, for logical reasons, are arranged in categories, such as types of food or attractions. No matter how the chapters are arranged, the listings in each section are arranged alphabetically.

The area code for all telephone numbers in this book is assumed to be 513 unless shown otherwise. A word about area codes, however, and that word is "confusion." The phone company split the Southern Ohio region last year into two area codes, 513 and 937. Now sometimes, but not always, you can't connect to a 937 number from the 513 area code without having the operator direct dial the number for you. And it's quite possible to be within the 513 area code and still have to dial 513 to reach your number, especially in the farflung northern towns such as Oxford. That's the Ohio side of things. In Southeastern Indiana, there's yet another area code, 812. And in Northern Kentucky, the area code is 606. Wait, things get better. Sometimes, but not always, you can dial Kentucky from Ohio without using the 606 prefix. In fact, if you DO use the 606 prefix, you'll often get a "sorry, we can't connect, please check your number" recording. There's no rhyme or reason to this. It's the phone company. Just because.

We hope this guide will help you newcomers feel at home and you natives discover something you may have missed. Although

we have made every effort to ensure accuracy and to include all the best of Cincinnati, we're only human. We update this guide every year, so if you find a mistake, if you disagree with something we've written or if you'd like to see additions or changes in future editions, please take the time to let us know. We'd love to hear any suggestions or comments that will help us improve our effort to make the most of your time in Cincinnati. Write to us in care of Insiders' Guide, P.O. Box 2057, Manteo, North Carolina 27954.

Cincinnati is one of the
few cities to rank in the
top 5 percent of
America's Most Livable
Cities through five
consecutive editions of
Places Rated Almanac.

Area Overview

One of the easiest ways to get to know Cincinnati is to have lunch at Fountain Square on a warm, sunny afternoon. Look around and you will see a microcosm of the diversity and uniqueness that prompted *Places Rated Almanac* to rate Cincinnati as America's Most Livable City in 1993. You'll see myriad people — young and old, black and white, rich and poor, white collar and blue collar — intermingling. You'll see the symbol of Cincinnati, the Tyler Davidson Fountain. You'll see new shiny office towers adjacent to well-kept, architecturally rich buildings that are more than 100 years old. You'll see the Carew Tower, Cincinnati's tallest building, which was built in less than a year during the height of the Great Depression by hundreds of hands eager for the work.

A few blocks away you'll see the Ohio River, which gave birth to the city and made Cincinnati at one time the second-largest city west of the Alleghenies and the sixth-largest city in the nation. You'll see traces of the strong German heritage that is still at the root of the conservative, hard-working philosophy adhered to by a majority of the city's residents. You'll see friendly, Midwestern people who, if you ask, will give you the time of day and not tell you to buzz off or push up their coat sleeve and ask you if you want to buy a watch. In fact, you'll more than likely see one or two police officers on horseback or bicycle go by, maintaining Cincinnati's position as the sixth-lowest in crime rate among major U.S. cities.

Is Cincinnati special? Is it truly America's most livable city? When the 1996 version of *Places Rated Almanac* came out, the city dropped from No. 1 to No. 19, but it is one of the few cities that has managed to stay in the top 5 percent of America's Most Livable Cities through five consecutive editions of the publication. *Employment Review* also rated the city in 1996 as one of the 20 best cities in the country in which to live and work, and *Fortune*

magazine ranked it seventh among cities balancing business and quality-of-life. In October 1996, *Entrepreneur* magazine ranked Cincinnati seventh on its list of the 30 best cities for small business development, citing its diverse economy, new zoning laws for home-based businesses and eager-to-lend banks.

That's plenty of proof for some people that Cincinnati is truly a special place to live. It has the amenities of a big city, they will point out, without most of the urban problems. Others, though, will argue that new ideas are met with cynicism, that the city is so conservative and set in its ways that it can easily be described as dull. Mark Twain, who lived in Cincinnati for six months and left unimpressed, wrote, "If the world would end, I would come to Cincinnati, for everything happens here 10 years later."

Mostly, though, the city is typical. Psychographically, *American Demographics* ranks the area as the ninth most typical metro area in the United States, as measured by a number of attitudinal issues. It is also the 11th most typical city demographically and one of only four cities nationwide to rank in the top 25 in both categories. A strong showing overall — that's typical of Cincinnati.

Demographically, the city of Cincinnati squeezes 364,000 people into just 77.62 square miles. Geographically, it is at the midpoint of the 981-mile-long Ohio River and sits 540 feet above sea level. The Cincinnati area is more than just the city, though. It is a region that encompasses three states, eight counties and dozens of smaller cities, unincorporated townships, incorporated villages and tiny, one-horse towns. Collectively, the area is better known as the Tri-state or Greater Cincinnati.

Put it on a map and Greater Cincinnati engulfs the southwesternmost portion of Ohio, the northernmost portion of Kentucky and the southeasternmost portion of Indiana. As a whole, this Tri-state region takes up 3,810 square miles and includes 1.7 million people, making it the second-largest city in Ohio and the 23rd largest in the country.

Despite its size, the area is easily accessible. Even the most distant suburbs are reachable within 25 minutes, affording residents the opportunity to live fairly deep in the country yet still within easy driving distance of downtown. And despite the city's efforts to develop more housing downtown, most of the area's residents live in the suburbs.

Neighborhoods at a Glance

Greater Cincinnati can be divided into seven geographic areas: the city, central suburbs, East Side, West Side, Northern suburbs, Northern Kentucky and Southeastern Indiana. Ask someone where they live, though, and most won't answer with a geographic area but with a very specific community. It's a social thing.

The geographic areas of Greater Cincinnati are vastly different and so are the specific communities within those areas. Where you live automatically brings with it an unspoken commentary about who you are. *The Cincinnati Enquirer* editorial cartoonist Jim Borgman once poked fun at the vast differences between the East Side and the West Side of Cincinnati, for instance, equating Vine Street (the dividing point) with the Berlin Wall. On the Western side were blue-collar people with bowling balls and kegs of Hudepohl beer, listening to the Reds game on the radio while flipping burgers on the grill. On the East Side were white-collar sorts, playing tennis, drinking Perrier, walking poodles and shopping at Kenwood Towne Centre. ''Gorbachev would have less of an identity crisis settling in California than most

of us would have moving across town,'' Borgman jokes. Sort of.

The City

Downtown, which sits in the river valley and is wrapped on three sides by steep hills, is the anchor of the city. It's been said that Cincinnati is built on seven hills, like Rome, but no two Cincinnatians agree on which seven hills. Cincinnati has 15 "Hill" communities (Bond Hill, College Hill, Crestview Hills, Greenhills, Indian Hill, North College Hill, Oak Hills, Paddock Hills, Park Hills, Price Hill, Seven Hills, Villa Hills, Walnut Hills, Western Hills and Winton Hills) and nine "Mount" communities (Mount Adams, Mount Airy, Mount Auburn, Mount Carmel, Mount Healthy, Mount Lookout, Mount Repose, Mount Washington and Mount Zion). Many of the hills and mounts make for wonderful vistas of the city.

City leaders are trying to attract more residents to the city by building affordable dwellings around downtown. Mostly, though, those who live in the city can either afford to live in one of the few upscale developments or can't afford to move. The city also includes the low-income Over-the-Rhine district and Laurel Homes, the nation's largest public housing project.

Central Suburbs

The central suburbs encompass the greatest array of neighborhoods, from low-income areas such as Lincoln Heights to wealthy communities such as Glendale and Amberley Village. And many of the communities, despite their economic differences, exist side by side. Most of these neighborhoods are well-established, and little new development occurs. The central suburbs include Norwood, which is a separate city surrounded on all sides by the city of Cincinnati, and Blue Ash, which was listed in *Places Rated Almanac* as one of the best places in the country to raise a family. The central suburbs offer the best access to all parts of Greater Cincinnati, with Interstate 71, Interstate 75, Cross County Highway and the Norwood Lateral (Ohio Highway 562) within easy reach.

East Side

The East Side contains the largest collection of affluent neighborhoods in Greater Cincinnati, including Anderson, Mariemont, Hyde Park, Mount Lookout, Madeira and Greater Cincinnati's most luxurious neighborhood, Indian Hill. Much of the East Side's affluence is the result of the population explosion of young, dual-income families looking for nice places to live. Previously undeveloped farmlands are sprouting new subdivisions, and the outlying edges of what once defined the East Side are now spilling over into rural Clermont County.

Most of the business activity on the East Side is retail, with many small, quaint, upscale shopping districts such as Hyde Park Square and Mount Lookout Square, in addition to some large malls, such as Beechmont Mall, Eastgate Mall and the most popular mall in the area, Kenwood Towne Centre. Thousands of stores also line popular roadways such as Beechmont Avenue and Montgomery Road. Interstates 275 and 71 are the two main access routes for the East Side and become crowded during rush hours.

West Side

Older, well-cared-for homes make up most of the West Side. In Cincinnati's early years, when the affluent first headed for the hills to escape the smoke and pollution of the industrial valley that is now downtown, they moved to the West Side. Many of their homes still exist. Most of the homes on the West Side are one-timer homes — lived in by the same family for generations. Homes feature front porches and small yards, and neighborhoods have a Catholic church every few blocks and a small tavern on just about every corner. A few upscale subdivisions are also being built on the West Side, some with fantastic river

views. The West Side also has some of the area's nicest parks, including Mount Echo Park and Mount Airy Forest.

Northern Suburbs

Residential growth is a new concept here, with large, upscale homes built on what only a few years ago were large farm fields. The area includes West Chester, Fairfield, Mason, Landen and Symmes. Growth in this area is so great that the school districts are being forced to create makeshift classrooms in trailers or, in several instances, build more schools. Lakota School District in West Chester had to close its high school, build two new ones and split up its students. The area is close to three major shopping malls -— Tri-County, Northgate and Forest Fair — and hundreds of stores along Colerain Avenue and U.S. Highway 4 (commonly called Route 4 or Dixie Highway) but is only about a 30-minute drive from downtown on I-75.

A large number of businesses are also located along the I-75 corridor in the Mason area. The area's annual Homearama event, in which home builders and designers build dream homes and show off their most outrageous ideas, is frequently held on farmland in the Northern suburbs. Kings Island, the Beach Waterpark, and the ATP tennis tournament and PGA Seniors golf tournament facilities are nearby.

Northern Kentucky

Northern Kentucky likes to call itself the southern side of Cincinnati. It is the area's largest suburb, and growing. To a certain extent, residents (at least longtime residents) still feel a loyalty to one side of the river or the other. Kentucky, to some, is another world. Newcomers, though, usually don't care — what they find so attractive about this area is a lot of affordable homes, including many large Victorian-era homes that are still in good condition, as well as newly built homes on the Bluegrass State's rolling hillsides.

When *Cincinnati Magazine* conducted a study of the area's top neighborhoods a few years ago, the top three were in Northern Kentucky. However, Northern Kentucky is a vast

Famous Folks Call Greater Cincinnati "Home"

Greater Cincinnati is the home of — or the place once called home by — many of the nation's most famous citizens, from five presidents to stars of the silver screen to great sports legends to corporate leaders. We've compiled a list of some of the better-known citizens we claim, or at one time claimed, as our own. Some of them, we must admit, we claim begrudgingly. Even the sun has its dark spots.

Famous Folks Who Live Here

Neil Armstrong, the first man on the moon, owns a large, very private farm in Lebanon.

Dr. Henry Heimlich, best known as the inventor of the Heimlich Maneuver that is used to save choking and drowning victims, is a professor of advanced clinical medicine at

Close-up

Xavier University and president of the Heimlich Institute. He also developed a method of constructing a new esophagus, was the first doctor ever to replace an internal organ and developed a method to help stroke victims swallow so they don't have to be tube fed.

Oscar Robertson, the "Big O," arguably the greatest basketball player ever, can frequently be seen at University of Cincinnati basketball games.

Johnny Bench, Hall of Fame catcher for the Reds, is frequently seen around town and on commercials for Fifth Third Bank.

Suzanne Farrell, at 15, was the youngest ballerina to join the New York City Ballet. She performed solo at age 18 and later became a principal dancer for the company. She now helps the Cincinnati Ballet.

Steve Cauthen, the jockey who rode Affirmed to the Triple Crown, owns a 300-acre farm in Boone County and is a vice president at Turfway Park.

Erich Kunzel, the conductor, is known worldwide for his direction of the Cincinnati Pops, which he founded in 1977. He also conducts the national orchestra in Washington on the Fourth of July.

Anthony Munoz, the NFL Hall of Fame tackle, is very active in community events.

Jim Bunning, the baseball Hall of Fame pitcher, is now a congressman from Northern Kentucky.

Jack Twyman, the NBA Hall of Famer, is now president of a regional food distribution company.

Lilias Folan popularized yoga through her long-running television show *Lilias, Yoga and You*.

Ken Griffey was a former key player in the Reds Big Red Machine day.

Aaron Pryor, "The Hawk," was a former middleweight boxing champion.

Famous Folks Who've Moved On

Leaders

Five U.S. presidents called the city home: **William Henry Harrison**, who was born in Virginia but moved to North Bend after marrying the daughter of John Cleaves Symmes, the river city's founder; **Ulysses S. Grant**, born in the Clermont County village of Point Pleasant; **Rutherford B. Hayes**, who practiced law in Cincinnati and was the city solicitor from 1858 to 1861; **Benjamin Harrison,** William Henry Harrison's grandson, born in North Bend; and **William Howard Taft**, who was born in Cincinnati.

— continued on next page

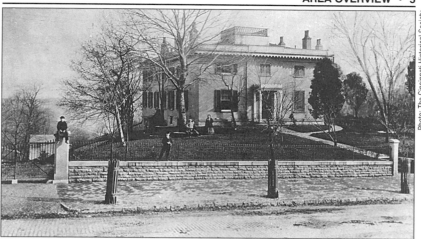

Photo: The Cincinnati Historical Society

William Howard Taft was born in this Cincinnati house, now a museum run by the National Park Service.

Also, inventor **Thomas Edison**, who worked as a telegraph operator at the local Western Union office as a teenager and received the message that Lincoln was assassinated (he spent most of his time studying at the Apprentice Library of the Ohio Mechanics Institute on Central Parkway and apparently learned a thing or two); onetime Republican presidential candidate **Robert Taft**; **Solomon P. Chase**, a lawyer who defended runaway slaves and later became governor, senator, Secretary of the Treasury and Chief Justice of the U.S. Supreme Court; U.S. Supreme Court Justice **Potter Stewart**; inventor of the oral polio vaccine **Dr. Albert B. Sabin**; hardline judge and baseball commissioner **Kenesaw Mountain Landis** (born in Millville, between Cincinnati and Oxford); businessman **Ted Turner**, whose father owned a billboard company in town; *The New York Times* publisher **Adolph Ochs**, who coined the phrase, "All the news that's fit to print"; 1960s activist **Jerry Rubin**; Boy Scouts founder **Daniel Carter Beard**; kook **Charles Manson**, a native and a leader of a different sort, although not one of our favorite claims to fame; and savings and loan convict **Charles Keating**.

Artists

Mark Twain, who lived here six months, left unimpressed and learned to pilot a steamboat after leaving Cincinnati for a trip to New Orleans; *Uncle Tom's Cabin* author **Harriet Beecher Stowe**, who lived here 18 years while her father, the Rev. Lyman Beecher, was a preacher here; naturalist **John James Audubon**, a taxidermist before he set out drawing nature scenes; composer **Stephen Foster**, who moved here when he was 19, wrote "Oh, Susanna" and a few other ditties and then left; Pulitzer Prize-winning poet **Nikki Giovanni**; writer **Earl Hamner**, author of the Waltons saga (good night, John Boy); "Calvin and Hobbes" cartoon creator **Bill Watterson**, former editorial cartoonist for *The Cincinnati Post*; painters **Robert S. Duncanson, Frank Duveneck** and **Henry Farney**; Metropolitan Opera musical director **James Levine**; opera star **John Alexander**; dancer **Lee Roy Reams**; conductors **Thomas Schippers** and **Leopold Stokowski**; and **William Holmes McGuffey**, author of the McGuffey Readers textbooks for children.

— continued on next page

Entertainers and Athletes

George Clooney, better known as the rakish Dr. Ross of the TV show *ER* as well as Batman; baseball great **Pete Rose**, still believed by many residents to be an innocent man; former heavyweight champion **Ezzard Charles**; singer **Rosemary Clooney**, in *White Christmas* with B-b-bing Crosby; movie producer **Steven Spielberg**, who was born and raised here and learned about Schindler's List in Cincinnati; actress **Doris Day**, born here as Doris von Kappelhoff; actors **Hugh O'Brien, Edward G. Robinson** and **Tyrone Power**, who was born and raised on Taft Road in Walnut Hills; singer **Andy Williams**, who attended Western Hills High School; jockey **Eddie Arcaro**, who won the Kentucky Derby five times and the Preakness and Belmont six times each; football legend **Paul Brown**; basketball Hall of Famer **Dave Cowens**, from Newport; basketball coach **John Wooden**, who coached at Dayton High School in Northern Kentucky; baseball Hall of Fame catcher **Buck Ewing**; head Mousketeer **Jimmy Dodd** (sang the M-I-C . . . song); former lightweight boxing champion **Bud Smith**; singer **Libby Holman**, who left the area for fame in the 1920s and scandal followed her; singer/cowboy **Roy Rogers**, born Leonard Slye where Cinergy Field now stands; silent movie actress **Theda Bara**, born Theodosia Goldstein in Avondale; *Twilight Zone* creator **Rod Serling** (imagine, if you will . . . Serling in Cincinnati); TV personality **Durward Kirby**, born in Covington; tennis stars **Bill Talbert** and **Tony Trabert**; comedian and former *Family Feud* host **Ray Combs**; two-time Olympic gold medal archer **Darrell Pace**; football stars **Roger Staubach, Jack "Hacksaw" Reynolds** and **Jim O'Brien**; and TV talk show host **Jerry Springer**, who was once the city's mayor and later a news anchor on a local television station.

---

area lumped into one package, so categorizing it can be tricky. It includes everything from the very rural to the very upscale urban. Access to the western half is limited to the always-clogged I-75/I-71. The eastern half is accessible from I-471, with I-275 cutting through the southern portion.

As an aside — a personal opinion — one of Greater Cincinnati's nicest residential areas is the Historic Riverside District in Covington. It's a tree-lined throwback to another era.

Southeastern Indiana

Many of Cincinnati's workers live in Southeastern Indiana and endure the 30- to 45-minute commute into downtown for one main reason: to take advantage of the rural setting and vast acres available for those who prefer to get away from the city. The homes in areas such as Hidden Valley Lake are large and secluded on wooded tracts.

This area could be in for more development, as riverboat gambling was recently legalized and casinos have already opened in Lawrenceburg and Rising Sun, both off U.S. Highway 50 in Southeastern Indiana.

Economy and Government

Economically, living in Greater Cincinnati is a blessing. The median price of a house in the area is 14 percent cheaper than the U.S. average. A home that costs $172,000 in Boston or $177,000 in San Diego is only $92,000 here.

Recessions tend to have less of an impact on the area, too, because of the diversity of local businesses. No single company employs more than 3 percent of the area's population, helping unemployment stay between 4 and 5 percent. Many major corporations are located here. Greater Cincinnati is the headquarters of six Fortune 500 companies (most notably the consumer products giant Procter & Gamble) and home to 11 other companies on *Fortune*'s list of the country's 500 largest service companies. Plus, more than 370 other Fortune 500 companies have operations in Greater Cincinnati.

Look around and you'll see the headquarters of many famous businesses that moved here: Chiquita, Star-Kist, Heinz Pet Products, Kroger, Federated Department Stores, Scripps-Howard, Totes, Kenner, Gibson Greetings.

Cincinnatians must like government at least a little because we sure have a lot of it, and it can be a confusing mess. Laws and politics don't cross the borders as easily as workers do. The Greater Cincinnati area has nearly 200 local political jurisdictions, including cities, villages, townships and counties, and what holds true for one may not hold true for another. And this patchwork of local government can become downright absurd at times. Columbia Township in Hamilton County, for instance, is split by municipal boundaries into several noncontiguous parcels — "God's little half-acres," as a township trustee once wryly put it. Overseeing this Lilliputian state is a township administrator earning more than $100,000 a year.

Not surprisingly, many longtime residents don't even know which local government they belong to. The City of Cincinnati gets a small windfall each year from suburbanites who think they live in the city limits and thus send the local portion of their license tag fees downtown.

Once in a while, some ambitious civic leader, politician or other sort of do-gooder talks about consolidating some of these governments for the sake of efficiency or sanity. One need only look toward nearby Indianapolis or Lexington to see the benefits of metro government. But such talk is generally short-lived in Cincinnati. Don't look for local governments from Madeira or Delhi to willingly surrender power to anyone downtown anytime soon.

In Cincinnati, the government is actually run by a city manager. The city elects a weak, part-time city council (the top vote-getter is named mayor) to set policies that the city manager is to implement. Theoretically, that's how it works anyway. Realistically, council members and the city manager regularly engage in power struggles.

They toss barbs, wrestle egos, point fingers and make the public access channel that broadcasts council meetings one of the most entertaining in the area. Tensions run so high that Cincinnati recently went through four city managers in six years.

Ohio and Indiana counties operate with a three-member commission and a county administrator. In Kentucky, the highest elected county official is the judge executive, who oversees the Fiscal Court. An Ohio-Kentucky-Indiana Regional Government also exists for problems that overlap the three states.

No discussion of government in Cincinnati, of course, would be complete without mentioning the Cincinnati Business Committee. This is a group of top executives from the major public and private companies in the city that takes an active advocacy — and in many cases advisory — role in government affairs. It is the unofficial fourth branch of Cincinnati government, and some might say more than that.

The terms "star chamber" and "shadow government" spring to many minds when you mention the CBC. In 1995, when the CBC got fed up with the increasingly ineffective city council, it proposed a "strong mayor" ballot initiative that was set up to give Republicans their best possible shot at taking control of the city. What looked to be a well-planned hostile leveraged takeover of Cincinnati's municipal government, however, proved to be a Waterloo. City council designated the initiative for an August special election. In that setting, the CBC learned that all the money and TV advertising in the world were no substitute for the grass-roots organization of the Democratic party. The issue failed badly.

Actually, even before its troubles became public, there wasn't anything all that shadowy about the CBC. Most of its work was right out in the open. The Cincinnati City Council and the Cincinnati School Board often have called on the business community for answers to troublesome situations. City council asked former Procter & Gamble chairman and CBC member John Smale to lead a study of the

FYI

Unless otherwise noted, the area code for all phone numbers listed in this guide is 513.

city's infrastructure needs in the 1980s, so he did. When the Cincinnati public schools faced a financial crisis in the early 1990s, they turned to the CBC for help, and many of the recommended ways to improve school efficiency and performance were ultimately implemented.

More recently, city council turned to CBC members and other business leaders to help create a development plan for downtown. The downtown reform project, which includes two new sports stadiums, is still under way and is one of the most debated subjects regionally. Efforts are also being made to add to the shopping, cultural, residential and entertainment aspects of downtown.

www.insiders.com

See this and many other **Insiders' Guide®** destinations online — in their entirety.

Visit us today!

Arts and Culture

The $82 million Aronoff Center for the Arts, opened in the fall of 1995, showcases Broadway Series performances, the Cincinnati Ballet, the Cincinnati Opera and dozens of smaller productions.

Dozens of small theaters also stage regular performances, including Emery Theater, Taft Theater, Showboat Majestic, Playhouse in the Park, University of Cincinnati College Conservatory of Music and, of course, Music Hall.

Individuals with a good set of vocal cords can be part of the May Festival Chorus, the oldest chorus in the country (see our Arts chapter). Annual auditions are held for the chorus' 200 spots. Individuals with an attraction to the silver screen can also find themselves in the movies locally, as filmmakers regularly flock to Cincinnati with cameras in hand and hire extras by the score.

Several top-notch museums cater to lovers of the visual arts. These include the recently renovated Cincinnati Art Museum, Contemporary Arts Center and Taft Museum. The area has more than 100 art galleries and annually stages several outdoor arts exhibitions downtown. (See our Arts chapter for lots of information on museums and art galleries.)

For those who prefer cuisine with their culture, adjacent to the Aronoff Center is the five-star The Maisonette restaurant, and two

blocks west is the four-star Palace restaurant in the luxurious Cincinnatian hotel. Greater Cincinnati has more top-rated restaurants than any other city its size (see our Restaurants chapter).

If you have a taste for something different, Cincinnati chili is an area favorite. The chili is sweet, not hot like Texas chili, and is served over a plate of spaghetti or a hot dog and smothered in cheese. The area's beer manufacturing is still a reminder of Greater Cincinnati's strong German heritage. The lone surviving brewery is Hudepohl-Schoenling, which makes Little Kings and Christian Moerlein (the only American beer to pass Germany's purity test). The area is booming with microbreweries, including the Oldenberg microbrewery in Northern Kentucky, which also houses a beer museum.

At one time, one-quarter of the area's population were German immigrants. Although Greater Cincinnati's heritage remains primarily European, there is some ethnic diversity among area residents; 87.2 percent are white, 11.6 percent African-American and 1.2 percent Asian or Hispanic. The median age is 32.8 years.

Greater Cincinnati's strong German background is still evident, though, in the odd usage of the word "please." When Greater Cincinnatians say "please?" they really mean "pardon me?," "come again?" or "what?" This linguistic quirk dates back to German settlers who would say "*bitte*?" — German for "please?" — when they didn't get your drift. The direct English translation became everyday parlance for most residents. Today, you can still identify lifelong Cincinnatians by their use of the word "please?" The usage gets rarer the farther you get from the city and is virtually unheard outside of the eight-county area.

The "please?" thing can cause confusion for newcomers, too. One woman from South Carolina, a place renowned for its attention to manners, was taken aback when she asked to make a transaction at a bank and the teller responded "Please?" The woman mistakenly thought she was being chastised for rudeness because she didn't say "please" when she addressed the teller. The two finally overcame the language barrier sufficiently to complete the transaction, but the customer left nearly in tears and only realized what had happened when a friend explained it to her later.

Another local cultural oddity is Parrothead frenzy. Each year when singer Jimmy Buffett performs at Riverbend Music Center, the town becomes crazed and starts wearing bright flowered shirts, grass skirts and funky hats decorated with parrots, cheeseburgers, sharks, Margarita glasses, salt shakers and anything else associated with one of Buffett's songs. Cincinnati is where the singer began calling his fans Parrotheads, and the area is perversely proud of that fact.

Otherwise, musical preferences are varied. Country music and hip-hop are just as popular as rock music. Numerous musical groups bring their tours through Greater Cincinnati each year, playing at Riverbend Music Center, The Crown, Cinergy Field or even smaller venues such as Bogarts, Kings Island and the Cincinnati Zoo.

In addition to staging concerts, the zoo is world-renowned as "the sexiest zoo in the country," according to *Newsweek* magazine, because of its successful breeding of wild animals. You'll see plenty of wildlife outside of the zoo, too, particularly in area parks. Bald eagles occupy some Hamilton County parks. Hawks, falcons, blue heron and pheasants are spotted frequently. And the 800-acre Cincinnati Nature Center is a 20-minute drive from downtown. The area has 16,700 acres of parkland, including several city parks that offer an escape from the concrete jungle so typical of most downtowns.

Greater Cincinnati has more than 60 public golf courses and 34 private clubs and plenty of other sporting activities, too, most notably Reds baseball, Bengals football and Cyclones hockey. The University of Cincinnati and Xavier University basketball teams are nationally ranked. The ATP tennis tour stops in Greater Cincinnati each year. So does the PGA Seniors golf tour. Two major horse racing tracks are in the area, and the Kentucky Derby and Indianapolis 500 are both about two hours away. Other annual events such as the World Figure Skating Championships and the NCAA basketball tournament are frequently held here.

For those whose favorite sport is shopping, Greater Cincinnati has more malls than other areas its size, plus smaller shopping centers and traditional retail storefronts.

The Public Library of Cincinnati and Hamilton County has 41 branch libraries and has the second-highest per-capita circulation figures in the nation. Surrounding counties have a total of 29 additional libraries.

A few cultural items won't be found in Cincinnati, though. There are no strictly-adult book stores (with the glaring exception of Larry Flynt's Hustler bookstore downtown), no peep shows and no red-light districts. The recent establishment of several exotic dance businesses set the vice squad scurrying.

The latest First Amendment fight involves the Internet, with a new regional task force raiding several local bulletin board operators and seizing their computer equipment because it was believed they were providing access to pornographic material. The case is now being fought in the courts. A few years ago, the vice squad invaded the Contemporary Arts Center and charged its director with pandering obscenity for showing a traveling exhibit of photographs by Robert Mapplethorpe. That effort earned Cincinnati the nickname "Town Without Pity," thanks to an article in *GQ* magazine. The whole issue left a scar on the city, and it remains a touchy subject with the citizens, who are split on whether all this censorship is good or bad.

Tourist Information

For information about the area, including lodging and attractions plus discounts on attractions and hotels, these local convention and visitors bureaus can help.

Clermont County Convention and Visitors Bureau, 4440 Glen Este-Withamsville Road, Glen Este, 753-7211

Greater Cincinnati Convention and Visitors Bureau, 300 W. Sixth Street, Cincinnati, 621-2142

Northern Kentucky Convention and Visitors Bureau, 605 Philadelphia Street, Covington, (606) 655-4155.

Because of its fertile soil and abundance of rivers, settlers began arriving in what would become the Cincinnati area as early as 1788.

History

It's hard to believe, but Cincinnati — firmly entrenched in the Midwest — once sat in the heart of the Northwest Territory. In the 1700s, this area was the wilds, the untamed and unknown frontier. British policy up through the Revolutionary War, when we were nothing more than "the colonies" to the queen, was to leave the area to the Indians, who were already angry about being pushed from their eastern territories.

Native Americans were very prominent here, and their influence is seen in many of the names and historic sites found in the area. Native American artifacts, in fact, are still being discovered during excavations for new buildings. Burial grounds and serpent-shaped mounds are scattered throughout the region. While digging to expand a runway at the Cincinnati/Northern Kentucky International Airport, workers unearthed a 2,700-year-old Indian site and 7,000 artifacts.

Shortly after the Revolutionary War, the newly victorious American government declared the territory available for settlement. Ohio and all points west had nothing more to offer settlers than opportunity, although that was plenty to entice explorers, range rovers and wide-eyed gamblers looking for a chance to strike it rich in real estate.

The westward movement began, and it didn't take long for people to find the area that would become Cincinnati. Because of its rich soil and abundance of rivers, which were vital to the transportation and livelihood of the day, settlers started arriving as early as 1788. Most of the city's early settlers arrived by putting several weeks worth of food and their life's possessions on a flatboat — basically a small log cabin sitting on a modified Huck Finn-style raft — and drifting down the Ohio River. The current was their source of power, and travel was slower than on an L.A. freeway during rush hour.

John Filson, one of the area's first settlers, originally named the area Losantiville, a compilation of Latin, Greek, French and Delaware Indian meaning "town opposite the mouth of the Licking River." Shortly after coming up with the name, Filson wandered into the nearby woods and was never heard from again.

As a base for Northwest Territory exploration and a defense against Indian attacks, Fort Washington was built in 1789. The fort, demolished in 1808, was located on what is now Third Street, on a hill just above the river basin. A small park near the intersection of Third and Broadway marks the site. A plaque on a nearby parking garage on Broadway notes the site of the fort's powder magazine. The five-sided, 15-foot-deep magazine was discovered when the garage was being built in 1952.

The name Losantiville lasted about as long as Filson in the woods. In 1790, two days after Gen. Arthur St. Clair arrived to assume command of Fort Washington and the Northwest Territory, he invoked his newly given powers and renamed the area Cincinnati in honor of the Society of Cincinnati, an organization of Revolutionary War officers to which he belonged. The society drew its name from Lucius Quintus Cincinnatus, a farmer who rescued the Roman army after it became trapped by the Aequi during the early period of the Roman Empire. After Cincinnatus saved the army (and possibly the Roman Empire), he decided he didn't like military life and returned to farming.

Gen. St. Clair didn't have as much success militarily as Cincinnatus, however. After recruiting a militia in Pittsburgh, he set out to take on the Indians. Desertion and illness depleted St. Clair's army, and the Miami Indians, led by Chief Little Turtle, whupped him, inflicting upon the U.S. Army its worst defeat ever. The boys in Washington summoned "Mad" Anthony Wayne in relief and he eventually defeated the Indians.

Steamboatin' and Pork Packin'

Meanwhile, settlers kept flowing into the area. When the *Orleans* steamed into port on October 27, 1811, though, the city became more than just a flotation destination. The steamboat changed Cincinnatians' lifestyle almost as much as the apple changed Adam's. People were shocked and mystified by the fact that it took the *Orleans* just 45 hours to make the 180-mile trip upriver — against the current — from Louisville.

The steamboat not only made trade and transportation upriver easy for the farmers plowing the area's rich soil, it gave Cincinnati a new industry. The area produced more than a quarter of all steamboats built in the United States during the next decade, about 30 a year.

On the other side of the Ohio River, Northern Kentucky got its start when three Cincinnatians — John and Richard Gano and Thomas Carneal — crossed the river and plotted the city of Covington in 1814. Neighboring Newport was recognized as a city in 1834.

Inland transportation was still rough and slow, however, and in order to expand the city's commerce center, the Miami-Erie Canal was conceived and built, connecting the Ohio River with the Great Lakes. The section between Cincinnati and Dayton opened in 1829.

With more and more immigrants coming to America and better transportation methods getting them off the East Coast, Cincinnati boomed. Between 1830 and 1850 the city's population grew by 40 percent, faster than that of any other city in the country. It became known as the Queen City of the West, developing into the country's sixth-largest city and its third-largest manufacturing center.

Cincinnati's major industries during this period included metalworking, woodworking and, most importantly, pork packing. Ummm, good eats. By 1835, the city was the nation's chief pork-packing center and would later become the largest such center in the world. Slaughterhouses were in such abundance the city was given the moniker Porkopolis. Pigs were herded through the streets hundreds at a time on their way to the slaughterhouses. Small companies sprang up to process pork by-products such as lard, which was turned into soap and candles. One of these companies, started in 1837, was called Procter & Gamble.

Residents fully expected Cincinnati to become the largest city in the country. However, city leaders failed to plan adequately for the introduction of the railroad. When river transportation was replaced, Cincinnati quickly found itself being bypassed for cities such as St. Louis and Chicago.

Rhineland Revisited

Perhaps because the area reminded them of their homeland, German immigrants flocked to Cincinnati, forming communities such as Over-the-Rhine and building breweries and beer gardens by the dozens. Cincinnati's German population more than doubled between 1840 and 1850, eventually comprising 25 percent of the city's population. German language classes were taught in city schools. Four German newspapers were published. And the strong, no-nonsense work ethic the Germans brought with them formed a foundation for what is to this day the area's employment philosophy.

The potato famine in Ireland also brought thousands of Irish immigrants and greater ethnic diversity to Cincinnati. Racial diversity was more limited, as few free blacks chose to live so close to the Mason-Dixon Line. Thousands of blacks passed through the area, however, because Greater Cincinnati played a major part in the Underground Railroad, providing a crucial path for escaped slaves to reach freedom. Homes and businesses with hidden rooms can still be found on both sides of the river. The city also played an important role in the antislavery movement; Harriet Beecher Stowe penned *Uncle Tom's Cabin* based on her Cincinnati experiences.

Although Cincinnati was a border city during the Civil War, it wasn't as affected by the war as other cities in nearby Pennsylvania, West Virginia and Kentucky. Only once was the city in grave danger of a Confederate invasion, and then Gen. Lew Wallace, better known for writing *Ben Hur*, rallied 72,000 squirrel hunters and ordinary citizens to its defense.

Upward and Onward

The 4 square miles of the river valley (surrounded by hills on three sides and the river on the fourth) that is now downtown Cincinnati were becoming increasingly crowded, with as many as 30,000 people living in each square mile. It was like New York City without the attitude. The solution to the problem came in 1872, with the opening of the Mount Auburn incline, which used steam-powered motors and cables to raise and lower platforms carrying people, horses, wagons and, later, electric street trolleys to the nearby hills. By 1876, inclines encircled the basin like giant escalators.

As soon as they could, the more affluent residents of the city fled to the hills, placing themselves above the smoky industrial valley — and the less affluent. They moved first to the west side, upwind from the smoke. (Many Victorian homes from this period are now being restored.) The middle class followed shortly, moving farther away from the basin and creating new communities and early versions of the suburbs. The last incline closed in 1948.

It was also during this period that many of the historic landmarks that define Cincinnati today were developed: Findlay Market in 1852, the Suspension Bridge and Isaac Wise Temple in 1866, the Tyler Davidson Fountain in 1871, Hebrew Union College in 1875, the Zoo in 1875, Music Hall in 1878, the Rookwood Pottery in 1880, the Art Museum in 1886 and City Hall in 1893.

Cincinnati's most famous landmark, the Tyler Davidson Fountain, was a gift from businessman Henry Probasco in honor of his deceased brother-in-law. Probasco toured several foundries in Europe to find the fountain's statue. The city tore down a market house in the center of Fifth Street to make way for the fountain, which, 100 years later, was moved to what is now Fountain Square.

The Industrial Revolution

In addition to residential areas, industrial areas began developing outside of the basin as the City of Cincinnati expanded its borders through annexation. Avondale, Norwood and the Millcreek Valley blossomed with industrial businesses, forcing the basin to become less industrialized and more focused on retail, banking and other services.

Up on the hills or down in the basin, the manufacturing and service industries that now form the core of Cincinnati's business community were founded during this time: Cincinnati Gas & Electric in 1843, Fifth Third Bank in 1858, U.S. Playing Card Co. in 1867, the Cincinnati Reds in 1869, Cincinnati Bell in 1873, Kroger Co. in 1883, Children's Hospital in 1883, Cincinnati Milacron in 1884, LeBlond-Makino Machine Tool Co. in 1887, Western and Southern Life Insurance Co. in 1888, The Christ Hospital in 1888 and Bartlett & Co. in 1898.

The rapid changes brought about by the Industrial Revolution and general labor conditions, however, were unsettling to many workers. In May 1886, their unrest peaked and laborers organized a strike. In early May, 12,000 workers walked off their jobs. By the end of the month, 20,000 more had joined them. Businesses, hit hard by the lack of employees, eventually agreed to their demands, including limiting workdays to just eight hours.

Rolling on the River, Rioting in the Streets

Cincinnati had a rough year in 1884. In February, the Ohio overflowed its banks and didn't stop until it crested at 71.9 feet, flooding much of the downtown basin and not receding for two weeks. A few weeks later, when a local resident was murdered, the city's temper got almost as high as the river. When the killer was found guilty only of manslaughter, people began venting their anger.

A crowd of 20,000 gathered, threw stones, called for a lynching and twice rushed the jail, which at the time was attached to the courthouse. Unable to find the murderer, they then rushed the courthouse, claiming injustice and setting the courthouse afire. The Ohio National

Guard was called in to clear the streets. By the end of the riot, almost 60 people had died and more than 200 were injured.

With the courthouse in ashes and the jail ransacked, city leaders laid plans for better protection against such acts. They hired architect Samuel Hannaford to design a municipal building/jail that was riot- and fireproof. His work is now City Hall, with its steep slate roof and stone exterior.

www.insiders.com

See this and many other **Insiders' Guide®** destinations online — in their entirety.

Visit us today!

Boss Cox

As in many other cities across the country, a single, strong political voice dictated the operations of Cincinnati in the late 1800s. That voice belonged to George B. Cox, a hard-drinking, rough businessman better known as Boss Cox. He sat on the city council for just a few years, but he virtually controlled the political scene for 30 years from his office above a saloon. Cox helped hold together and build certain parts of the city — albeit mostly for self-serving purposes — until 1910, when he "retired" shortly before the election of reformer Henry Hunt as mayor.

During Cox's "tenure," the city's debt was among the country's highest, taxes were outrageous, and *McClure's* magazine found Cincinnati to be the worst-governed city in America. Hunt offered a reasonable alternative to Cox's measures; however, Hunt's plans were costly, and the people hated expense more than they hated inefficiency. Hunt wasn't reelected and, fuming with frustration, he left the city and returned only once. Cox died of a stroke in 1916. Reform was underway, though, and in 1956 Cincinnati was called the best-run big city in America by *Fortune* magazine.

War at Home

The onset of World War I was a major story in Cincinnati, even more so than in other cities because of its huge German population. At the start of World War I, the city still published German newspapers, taught German in schools and was decidedly populated with German immigrants, who defended their native country and published attacks on America's position on the war.

By the time America joined the war in 1917, anti-German sentiment had become so intense that the city changed the names of streets, banned German books from the library, required German newspapers to be censored and eliminated the teaching of German in city schools. It wasn't until 1996 that the city got over this, adding secondary signs to the renamed streets noting their original German names.

Roaring '20s, Depressing '30s

The Roaring '20s hit hard at one of the cornerstones of Cincinnati's foundation: beer. At one time, 32 breweries operated in Cincinnati. It was a drunkard's dream. Prohibition forced the closing of more than two dozen local breweries and hundreds of pubs.

The 1930s didn't bring much more good news, as the Great Depression hit and the city's worst flood ever struck in 1937. The river rose to 79.9 feet, more than 25 feet above flood stage. Forty-five square miles of the city were under water. The water works and electric generators were put out of commission. More than 60,000 people were left homeless. The Suspension Bridge was the only bridge open along the entire Ohio River. Even Crosley Field, which sat several miles outside of downtown, was under 20 feet of water. Some jocular fans circled the bases in rowboats. The city remained flooded for 19 days.

The second great wave of development occurred during this time, though, and many

From Baseball to Boy Scouts: Cincinnati's "Firsts"

Cincinnati is well known for having baseball's first professional team, formed in 1869 and known as the Red Stockings. In the ensuing years, the team has often been in the forefront of the sport's innovations. Catcher Douglas Allison was the first to wear a glove, cutting the fingers off an old winter glove to protect his sore left hand. The Reds initiated the double play, the seventh-inning stretch, the doubleheader, the uniform number, shin guards and season tickets. The team was also the first to fly to a game, play a night game and play a televised game.

Baseball is not the only area where Cincinnati has forged a new trail, though. Some of the city's other "firsts" include:

• First to have a high-rise building built of reinforced concrete: the Ingalls Building, built in 1902 and still standing at Fourth and Vine streets.

• First to use airmail, lifting a bag of mail by balloon in 1835.

• First to produce Catawba wine in 1828.

• First to publish greeting cards in 1850 by Gibson Greeting Cards.

• First to establish a Jewish Hospital in 1850 and a Jewish theological college, known as Hebrew Union College, in 1875.

• First to have a Jewish congregation west of the Alleghenies, formed on January 8, 1830, at what is now the Rockdale Temple.

• First to establish a municipal fire department, use a steam fire engine and set up a fireman's pole in 1853.

• First to establish a weather bureau in 1896. (And they still don't know what the weather is going to be like.)

• First to establish a municipal university, the University of Cincinnati in 1870, and the first city to offer cooperative education in 1906.

— continued on next page

Photo: David Nelson

Cincinnati is home to the world's largest permanent half-dome, Union Terminal.

•First to have a woman, Maria Longworth Nichols Storer, begin and operate a sizable manufacturing operation, Rookwood Pottery, in 1880.

•First to hold an industrial exposition in 1870.

•First and only city to build and own a major railroad. The track from Cincinnati to Chattanooga, Tennessee, was built in 1850 (too late to save Cincinnati's dream of becoming the largest city in America) and is still owned by the city, although it is now leased to the Southern Railway System. The real Chattanooga Choo-Choo ran on the tracks from Cincinnati.

•First to have a licensed public television station, WCET, in 1954.

•First heart-lung machine, developed by Children's Hospital in 1952, allowing open-heart surgery.

•First to hold a municipal song festival in 1849.

•First Boy Scout troop, started by Daniel Carter Beard. At the time it was called the Sons of Daniel Boone.

•First woman to be seated on a U.S. Appeals Court, on March 27, 1934, when Franklin Roosevelt appointed Florence Allen to the 6th Circuit Court of Appeals. She was also the first woman to serve as a chief judge in that court.

•First Cesarean section performed in Newtown on April 22, 1827, by Dr. John Lambert Richmond.

•First library to be established west of the Alleghenies, April 18, 1835. The Mercantile Library was only the third library in the country.

•First female rabbi in 1946, when Sally Priesand was ordained at Hebrew Union College.

•First credit cards in August 1959. The "Charga-Plates," as they were known, were made of metal and were good at any of the city's major department stores.

. . . And "Largests"

In addition to a number of "firsts," Greater Cincinnati is also home to a number of the world's "largests," including:

•Soap manufacturer, Procter & Gamble;

•Cosmetic factory, Avon Products in Springdale;

•Permanent half-dome, Union Terminal;

•Collection of nonreligious murals, which are divided between Union Terminal and the Cincinnati/Northern Kentucky International Airport;

•Swinging bell, at St. Francis de Sales Church in Evanston;

•Pediatric training program, at Children's Hospital Medical Center;

•Stained-glass window, at Cathedral Basilica of the Assumption;

•Manufacturer of church bells, the Verdin Co.;

•Number of chili parlors per capita;

•Collection of ventriloquist dolls, at the Vent Haven Museum of Ventriloquism in Fort Mitchell;

•Beer memorabilia, at Oldenberg Brewery.

of the landmarks that define how Cincinnati looks today came about: The Dixie Terminal in 1921, the Doctor's building in 1923, the Cincinnati Club in 1924, the Queen City Club building in 1927, the Masonic Temple in 1928, the CG&E building in 1929, the Carew Tower in 1930, the Cincinnati Bell Telephone building in 1931, the Times-Star building in 1933 and Union Terminal in 1933.

As a result of the construction, much of which was privately financed, Cincinnati was cushioned, temporarily at least, from the impact of the Great Depression. At one point in 1933, however, the economy caught up with

Photo: Skip Tate

The controversial winged pigs and flood monument
mark the entrance to Bicentennial Commons.

the city and only half of the city's work force was employed full time.

Back at War

Even before the United States entered World War II, Cincinnati was involved in the war effort. The city converted its abundance of manufacturing businesses into production facilities for military supplies. Procter & Gamble, LeBlond-Makino Machine Tool Co., Cincinnati Milacron, even the U.S. Playing Card Co. shifted gears to stock the troops. Although it was top secret at the time, U.S. Playing Card produced maps of Germany on the back of its cards, which were then distributed to prisoners of war to help with escapes.

After the war, Union Terminal was the country's main transfer station for soldiers heading to their homes in the west. And as part of the country's effort to clean out its war chest, the federal government deeded its aircraft training centers in Boone County, Kentucky, to the neighboring Kenton County Airport Board, which turned them into what is now the Cincinnati/Northern Kentucky International Airport.

Modern Times

Following World War II and into the 1950s, area residents once again fled to the outskirts of the area, creating newer suburbs. As automobiles became more affordable, people didn't need to live as close to where they worked.

As in the rest of the country, the '60s brought strife and unrest to the Cincinnati area. A weeklong race riot, in fact, broke out in the suburb of Avondale in 1967, prompting the calling of the National Guard.

On the brighter side, that same year the city was awarded a professional football team, the Bengals, who began playing in 1968 under the guidance of the legendary Paul Brown. Three years later the team made the playoffs. Another 1960s sports milestone occurred in the city: Pete Rose played in his first game as a Red in 1963.

Very little downtown development took place between the 1930s and the 1960s, but in the 1970s a third major development phase occurred. Riverfront Stadium, now Cinergy Field, was built, opening in 1970. Fountain Square was built and dedicated in 1971, 100 years and 10 days after the fountain was originally dedicated. The first segment of the skywalk system — a second-story elevated sidewalk that weaves its way through much of downtown — opened. Riverfront Coliseum, now The Crown, opened in 1975. The Serpentine Wall was completed in 1976. This concrete riser at the base of the downtown area is actually a floodwall, but it also has steps down to the river and serves as a place to sit and watch the activity on the river. The serpentine design makes it architecturally interesting. Throughout the 1980s and early 1990s, more modern skyscrapers were built as the real estate market boomed, creating much of the familiar skyline the city has today.

In order to make room for the new buildings, many old, historic, architecturally rich buildings were destroyed, despite the efforts of many angry citizens to save them. The animosity continues today; Cincinnati's most recent addition, the Aronoff Center for the Arts, met with resistance because of the destruction of historic buildings on the site. Cincinnatians hate change, especially when old, architecturally interesting buildings are replaced with bland structures that lack personality.

The area had the pleasure — and, oh, was it a pleasure! — of recording another piece of history in the 1970s: snow and cold. The mercury dipped to an area record of 25 degrees below zero on January 18, 1977. A year later a blizzard hit, dumping more than 50 inches of snow and completely freezing the river, sinking boats and allowing Cincinnatians whose brains apparently had frozen, too, to walk across to Kentucky. As they walked, they later said, they could hear the ice cracking and feel the river flowing beneath the ice.

The Big Red Machine (the Cincinnati Reds to the uninitiated) dominated baseball in the 1970s and is still the greatest team ever. Two of the most notable dates in Reds history occurred in 1985. On February 7, Marge Schott became the team's managing partner, buying out partners William and James Williams. On September 11, Pete Rose got his 4,192nd hit, becoming baseball's all-time hits leader. The whole city saw the sold-out game except for a few poor souls with incredibly bad timing who were in the restroom when Rose got the hit — and TV reporter Michael Collins filed a special report on those unfortunate fans.

Also in 1985, Cincinnati opened the floodgates for what would become the nation's savings and loan disaster. Depositors made a rush to withdraw their savings from Home State Savings after learning of the bank's bad investments. State officials later closed the bank and 70 others for three days to stop the onslaught of withdrawals.

In 1988, the city celebrated its 200th anniversary and dedicated the $15 million, 22-acre Bicentennial Commons park along the riverfront. The park reflects upon much of Cincinnati's past. Winged pigs on top of smokestacks at the entrance speak of the steamboats and slaughterhouses. A 100-foot-high pole notes the heights of the city's worst floods. A portion of the old stone Water Works building was turned into an amphitheater. And Cincinnatus, now bronzed and 10 feet tall, stands in Yeatman's Cove, where the first settlers landed, welcoming you to his city.

To help keep area highways flowing smoothly, an electronic system called ARTIMIS uses 1,100 pavement sensors, 60 television cameras, and radar units mounted on poles to monitor traffic.

Getting Around

Greater Cincinnati sits at the north-south intersection of the eastern half of the United States. It's a crossroads for planes, trains and automobiles. Five major highways form its automotive arteries, an airline calls the area its hub, a river runs through it and eight bridges keep it connected. Buses and boats, trolleys and taxis, river ferries and horse-drawn carriages all weave their way in and out and keep the area's 1.7 million people on the move.

Despite Greater Cincinnati's diversity and complexity, its many highways make it easy to get wherever you are going. In fact, traffic usually moves so quickly that the afternoon traffic reports may include warnings of "sun delays." To outsiders coming from cities where traffic generally doesn't move fast enough to be slowed down by the sun shining in drivers' eyes, this is quite a novelty. Most newcomers are also surprised by the fact that even the most distant suburbs are reachable from downtown within 25 minutes, meaning golfers can leave work at 5:30 on a summer evening, drive to the suburbs and still squeeze in nine holes before dark.

And much to the joy of many business people and families looking for a quick getaway, flights from the Cincinnati/Northern Kentucky International Airport can put travelers on just about any point on the globe daily.

There's much talk about expanding the area's transportation options. A light-rail system running from the airport to Kings Island is being discussed. Pedal-pushers regularly lobby for bike lanes (which are virtually non-existent) so bikers won't have to do a daily joust with cars. There is even pie-in-the-sky talk about canals through downtown and sky trams connecting downtown with Mount Adams. Mostly, though, the transportation methods in the area are pretty basic — nothing fancy, nothing exotic, just roadways, runways and rivers.

If you have a problem finding your way around, check out the back of the Yellow Pages. There's a map and a listing of all the streets in the area. Or just ask. Most locals are friendly enough, or at least courteous enough, to gladly help you with directions.

Roadways and River Crossings

Highways and Interstates

Five major highways — Interstates 75, 71, 275, 471, and 74 — run through the area, creating a maze of roadways that either keep the populace moving at a rapid pace or, in the unfortunate event of an accident, jam up to create large parking lots. Two crosstown arteries, the Norwood Lateral and the Cross County Highway, act as major roadways as well, connecting the parallel sections of I-75 and I-71 and allowing traffic to cut across town with ease. U.S. Highways 22, 27, 42, 50, 52 and 127 also run through the area, as do the statewide AA Highway in Kentucky and the James Rhodes Appalachian Highway in Ohio.

I-75 runs north/south from Detroit to Miami and right through the heart of Greater Cincinnati. This interstate is constantly busy, particularly around rush hour, on any given Friday, and on holidays. I-75 serves as the main thoroughfare for people living in West Chester and much of the northern suburbs. The Northern Kentucky section of the road includes "Death Hill," a steep section of highway that — thank goodness — no longer includes the sharp S-curve it once had. Like clockwork, a truck traveling down the hill would go too fast, be unable to negotiate the curves and wipe out, causing massive traffic jams. Or trucks going up the hill would chug like the little red caboose ("I think I can, I think I can") up the hill at 15 mph, causing a massive tie-up in that direction. A truck lane was added headed up the hill and the S-curve was straightened in 1996. Still, the section keeps its moniker and its reputation as a place to avoid, particularly if you are in a hurry.

I-71 runs northeast/southwest from Cleveland to Louisville and actually merges with I-75 around downtown before splitting again 20 miles south into Northern Kentucky. The highway is the primary access for commuters working in Blue Ash, the area's second-largest business district, as well as for residents of Landen, Loveland and other northern suburbs.

FYI

Unless otherwise noted, the area code for all phone numbers listed in this guide is 513.

I-275 is the beltway that encircles the area, running through six counties in Cincinnati, Northern Kentucky and Southeastern Indiana. At 83 miles, it is the longest full-circumferential beltway in the nation. The northern section around the Tri-county area and the eastern section between I-71 and I-471 are the busiest on a daily basis. The highway also leads to the airport and southeastern Indiana.

I-471 runs from the eastern part of I-275 in Northern Kentucky to downtown. The highway is only about 5 miles long, but it's highly traveled by commuters from Northern Kentucky and eastern Cincinnati.

I-74 begins at I-75 just northwest of downtown, runs west through Indianapolis and ends in Quad Cities, Iowa. The highway serves the western suburbs and southeastern Indiana and is only moderately traveled.

The **Norwood Lateral** (a.k.a. Ohio Highway 562) provides a crosstown shortcut, running east/west inside the I-275 beltway between I-71 and I-75. It should be noted, however, that there are no signs in the city that say "Norwood Lateral." It's just a given name, and everyone assumes everyone else knows what it is. The signs actually say "Norwood" and "Ohio 562." Ask Cincinnatians, though, where Ohio 562 is and they probably won't know.

The **Cross County Highway** is the Norwood Lateral's crosstown companion and is now living up to its name by actually crossing the whole county. It runs east/west parallel to the Norwood Lateral, only farther north. It starts at I-71 to the east and stretches all the way west to U.S. Highway 27, better known as Colerain Avenue. It should also be noted that the Cross County Highway is officially named the Ronald Reagan Cross County Highway after the former president, although Reagan never stepped foot in the county. It's a political thing. Don't ask.

The **AA Highway** (Alexandria, Kentucky, to Ashland, Kentucky) connects Greater Cincinnati with Interstate 64 in eastern Kentucky, which stretches southeast to Norfolk, Virginia.

Bridges

For some, the river isn't a playground but an obstacle. To, well, bridge that obstacle there are eight main bridges between Cincinnati and Northern Kentucky. With the exception of the Roebling Suspension Bridge, named after builder John Roebling, the bridges carry the names of famous Kentuckians. Most are better known by nicknames, though. In either case, here are the bridges from east to west.

The **Combs-Hehl Bridge**, named for a former governor and a former Campbell County judge, is the eastern half of the I-275 loop and connects the eastern portions of Cincinnati and Northern Kentucky. Many travelers from the eastern half of Cincinnati cross the bridge and jump onto I-471 to get into downtown.

The **Daniel Beard Bridge** is named in honor of the founder of the Boy Scouts. It is better known as the "471 Bridge" because I-471 crosses it or the "Big Mac Bridge" because of its yellow arches. The bridge joins I-471 in Northern Kentucky with Columbia Parkway, Fort Washington Way, Sixth Street downtown or I-71 in Cincinnati.

The **L&N Bridge** connects the eastern

Photo: Greater Cincinnati Convention and Visitors Bureau

Getting around Cincinnati was first done by boat.

portion of downtown along Pete Rose Way with Third Street in Newport, Kentucky. This very old bridge has railroad tracks on one side and two very small lanes on the other. Because of its age, it has a weight capacity of 5 tons.

The **Taylor-Southgate Bridge** is brand new. The light gray bridge is next to The Crown arena and connects downtown with Newport, Kentucky.

The **Roebling Suspension Bridge** is right next to Cinergy Field and connects downtown with Covington, Kentucky. This two-lane bridge is instantly recognizable for its stone piers, gold crowns and lights tracing its blue suspension cables. The bridge ends at the Covington Landing entertainment complex. Pedestrian walkways flank each side of the bridge.

The **Clay Wade Baily Bridge** is named after a noted *Kentucky Post* political reporter. The under-used bridge connects western

downtown at Third Street with Covington, Kentucky.

The **Brent Spence Bridge** is named for a well-known Kentucky congressman. It is also known as the "I-75 Bridge" or the "Car-Strangled Spanner." I-71 connects with I-75 just before the bridge on the Cincinnati side and creates monumental traffic jams during rush hours. The bridge is a double-decker, with northern traffic moving under southern traffic.

I-275 Bridge West connects Southeastern Indiana with Northern Kentucky on the western side of Greater Cincinnati and completes the loop.

Ferries

Bridges aren't the only way of getting a car across the river. Two ferries operate in the area, taking cars back and forth the old-fashioned way. The **Anderson Ferry** has been transporting cars and people since

1817. It operates an eight-car ferry boat between Boone County, Kentucky, and Delhi on the western side of Cincinnati. The boat lands on the Kentucky side just north of the airport and is a more scenic and historic way of getting across the river. The cost is $2.50 per car.

The smaller **Augusta Ferry** runs cars from U.S. 52 on the Ohio side to Augusta, Kentucky (about 50 miles upriver from Cincinnati). Ferry hours are 8 AM and 6 PM and the cost is $5 per car (see our Daytrips chapter).

Commuting

Whether you'll be commuting on a regular basis or just making a pass or two through town, help is available.

ARTIMIS

In an attempt to keep traffic moving even more smoothly than it already does and avoid massive tie-ups when accidents happen, a $37 million electronic "smart highway" messaging system was constructed on 88 miles of the busiest highways throughout Greater Cincinnati. The Advanced Regional Traffic Interactive Management and Information System, known as ARTIMIS, uses 1,100 pavement sensors, 60 television cameras, and radar units mounted on poles to monitor traffic. The information is relayed to a central operator, who dispatches information to 44 electronic message boards that hang over the highways, informing drivers about conditions ahead. The signs are obvious and informative, but try not to spend so much time reading them that you stop watching where you're going and what the car in front of you is doing.

SmarTraveler

SmarTraveler traffic service provides up-to-the-minute traffic information for eight specific roadways in the area, along with a direct link to TANK, Metro, JetPort Express, RideShare (more on these below), and details on transportation to special events.

For information about a specific highway, call 211 and then push the highway number and the star button. For instance, to get information on I-275, call 311 and push 275*. For the Cross County Highway push 774*. For the Norwood Lateral push 562*. For information about downtown push 1*. Metro is 91*, TANK 92*, JetPort Express 93*, RideShare 94*, and transportation to special events 99*.

Tips to Make the Drive Easier, Safer, and Legal

• New residents have 15 days to get new license plates in Kentucky, 30 days in Ohio and 60 days in Indiana.

• To comply with Clean Air Act standards, E-Check emissions tests are required for obtaining new license plate stickers in southwestern Ohio counties, although only every other year, depending on the year in which your car was manufactured

• The speed limit on most interstate roads that go through Greater Cincinnati is generally 65 mph, although there are sections on each highway in which the speed limit will suddenly drop to 55 for no apparent reason, so pay attention to the signs.

• You can turn right on red unless otherwise posted. And a left turn on red is permis-

---

INSIDERS' TIP

The suspension bridge between Cincinnati and Covington was built by John Roebling and was the prototype for the larger Brooklyn Bridge in New York City, which he built 17 years later. The suspension bridge took 10 years and $1.5 million to build, and when completed in 1866, the 2,252-foot bridge was the world's longest. The second day after its opening, 120,000 people — half the city's population — walked across the bridge.

Close-up **Getting Out of Town**

City	Miles	Drive Time	Flight Time
Atlanta	373	9 hours	1:09
Boston	752	17 hours	1:52
Chicago	265	6 hours	1:02
Cleveland	221	5 hours	:50
Columbus	116	2 hours	:36
Detroit	230	5 hours	:51
Indianapolis	98	2 hours	:32
New York	589	13 hours	1:34
Philadelphia	507	11 hours	1:24
Washington, D.C.	411	10 hours	1:04

sible from a one-way street onto another one-way street.

•Wear your seat belt during the daily commute. Not only is buckling up a state law, but it's also highly recommended, particularly if your drive happens to take you onto I-75 or I-71 during rush hour. Whenever a little space opens up, some yahoo in an urban-assault vehicle will fill the gap and go zipping off. Generally, though, the area is free of inconsiderate drivers, especially the gun-and-run variety prevalent in some large cities — a dirty look or a single-digit salute is about as bad as it gets.

•Although motorcycle drivers are not required to wear helmets, all motorcycle passengers are.

•A child 3 or younger, under 40 pounds, or less than 40 inches tall must be strapped into a child safety seat.

•Inevitably, the highways back up during rush hours. Expect slowdowns or delays from 7 AM to 9 AM and 4 PM to 6 PM each day. Between the speeders and the slowdowns, commutes can be so upsetting to some people that popular bumper stickers proclaim "I survived a trip down Death Hill" and "I-75 (uh, makes like a vacuum)."

•Many major streets have center lanes — sometimes referred to as "chicken lanes" or "suicide lanes" — where cars travel in alternate directions depending on the time of day. During the morning rush hour, the lanes are open for drivers heading into downtown; in the afternoon, the lanes are open

for drivers heading away from downtown. Lights above the lanes use green arrows or red Xs to indicate which way traffic is allowed to travel.

•Traffic problems are magnified when precipitation, particularly snow, falls. Cincinnati straddles the north/south weather border, so county highway departments find it difficult to justify purchasing a lot of snow-removal equipment. The county's general philosophy on clearing the streets is to spread some rock salt and let the cars drive over it until the snow clears. Salt trucks have snow plows, but don't often use them. As a result, when it snows our roads can become borderline bad, and our driving becomes out-and-out awful. Drivers become overly cautious. Even if just a few flakes fall and the streets are just wet, drivers here slow way down.

•Spring brings its own problems. Melting snow and ice create giant potholes, and the roadways become like the moon with all the craters. So be prepared to make sudden swerves to avoid the holes, some of which have been known to flatten tires, knock off hubcaps and even break an axle.

•A unique springtime sickness known as the Orange Barrel Blues also afflicts area drivers. Every spring, some portion of one of the major interstates or driving routes undergoes repair, and traffic flow becomes restricted by the placement of orange barrels. It's as inevitable as death and taxes. In order to help ease the congestion, the Ohio-Kentucky-Indiana Regional Council of Governments came up with a Beat The Jam information line, 483-5800, which offers information and updates on construction sites and a chance to provide feedback.

• If driving is too much for you, RideShare, 241-RIDE and Van Ohio, (800) VAN-RIDE can arrange for car or van pooling from outlying communities. Also, in conjunction with Metro, Cincinnati has multiple Park and Ride locations (see below).

Getting Around Downtown

By car or by foot, getting around downtown is easy. Streets running east/west are numbered, starting at the river (Second Street, though, was renamed Pete Rose Way). Streets running north/south have your typical downtown street names (in order, from east to west): Broadway, Sycamore, Main, Walnut, Vine, Race, Elm, Plum, and Central. A silly saying that uses the first letter of the street names helps people remember the order: Big Strong Men Will Very Rarely Eat Pork Chops. Vine Street is the dividing point between east and west addresses.

Cincinnati's downtown isn't so big that it can't be walked from one end to the other. And in some parts, walking through downtown is possible without exposure to the outside elements. Cincinnati has a 20-block skywalk, a maze of elevated walkways connecting many buildings in the heart of downtown. Only Minneapolis' second-story walkway is as complex.

One of the more difficult aspects of walking downtown, though, is getting from the business district to the riverfront. Even though the riverfront is considered part of downtown, a great automotive chasm known as Fort Washington Way separates the two. Just a handful of bridges over the roadway act as connectors to the riverfront, although a great deal of planning and money are being spent on ways to improve access. A plan to narrow Fort Washington Way and create a new Second Street is on the books, with construction set to begin in 1998.

Parking is a big problem for downtown drivers. Plenty of lots and garages are available, but many are full or costly on weekdays. There are a number of larger lots on the perimeter of downtown, but you're in for a several-block walk to get into the heart of downtown. Some downtown parking lots offer 3-hours-for-$1 incentives. While you're shopping downtown, you can get "Park and Save" coupons with your purchases, which cut down or eliminate the cost of parking.

Public Transportation

Because of the geographical configuration of Greater Cincinnati, the area's public transportation system is divided among three operations: **Metro**, a bus line serving Hamilton County and parts of Clermont, Warren and Butler counties; the Transit Authority of Northern Kentucky, or **TANK**, a bus line that covers Northern Kentucky and downtown Cincinnati; and the Clermont Area Rural Transit, or **CART**, which offers service by reservation in the more rural parts of eastern Clermont County. And even though they are totally separate businesses, and in some cases overlap each other's area of operation, there is a working relationship between the three systems that benefits riders by offering reduced transfer rates from one to another.

Both Metro and TANK have rules of the road for riding their buses, such as no smoking, drinking, eating, playing of audio devices, cursing, swearing or causing disruptive behavior.

Metro
120 E. Fourth St. • 621-4455

Metro is the main bus service for Cincinnati and the most populated suburbs. It serves more than 70,000 people a day and covers three zones: (1) within the city, (2) outside of the city but still in Hamilton County, and (3) surrounding counties. There are 45 express routes into downtown daily and an additional 44 local bus routes that simply make loops around different sections of town. All buses that head into downtown make a stop at Government Square, Metro's main stop at the corner of Fifth and Walnut streets. Maps of all Metro routes can be picked up at an informa-

Photo: Greater Cincinnati Convention and Visitors Bureau

The sternwheeler paddles past one of Cincinnati's busiest landmarks, Cinergy Field.

tion booth at Government Square, in special racks on the buses, or at various bus stops that offer indoor shelter spaces, such as at Kroger grocery stores or mall department stores.

Metro also runs special express routes from various pickup locations throughout the area to deliver passengers to Bengals games, River Downs racetrack, Riverbend Music Center, and downtown for special occasions such as Riverfest. It also has 16 Park and Ride locations throughout the area. Or, if you're just looking to cut across downtown, Metro offers a shuttle that runs around downtown all day for 25¢.

Rates for riding the Metro vary. Fares are 65¢ during non-rush hours, but jump to 80¢ from 6 AM to 9 AM and 3 PM to 6 PM. Transfers cost 10¢, and a 30¢ additional charge is added to the fare if the bus changes zones. Individuals 44 inches or shorter pay only 40¢ on Metro, as do riders transferring from TANK

to Metro. Riders who are 65 and older, or on Medicare, or have a disability receive Fare Deal discounts, in which rides are also 40¢. Exact change is required for all Metro rides. Monthly passes on Metro are $32 for one zone, $44 for two zones and $56 for all zones.

Five Metro routes feature buses equipped with a wheelchair lift. For those with a more severe disability who cannot ride Metro buses, Metro offers the curb-to-curb Access Shuttle within the I-275 beltway.

TANK
3375 Madison Pike, Fort Wright, Ky.
• (606) 331-8265

TANK covers all three Northern Kentucky counties, operating as far south as Florence, Grants Lick and Independence. TANK also has routes that lead to the airport and the popular Florence Mall. Many of the routes lead into downtown Cincinnati, with stops as far north as Sixth Street.

Fares for all TANK trips are 75¢, although children 5 and younger ride for free, students ride for 50¢ between 6 AM and 6 PM, and senior citizens and those with disabilities ride for 35¢. Exact change is required and transfers are free. Unlimited-ride monthly passes cost $30, weekly ticket books for 10 rides cost $7.25. A monthly pass for unlimited rides on both TANK and Metro is available for $45. For those with a more severe disability who cannot ride its buses, TANK offers a Regional Area Mobility Program, or RAMP.

In January 1998, TANK also began operating a shuttle around the riverfront cities and into downtown Cincinnati for 25¢ per rider.

CART
915 W. Main, Williamsburg Twp.
• 724-7433

The highly rural parts of Clermont County not covered by Metro are served by CART, a small bus service operated by the county. Because so much of the county is so rural, CART does not operate regular schedules, but is available through reservation only. Reservations must be made 24 hours in advance, although CART tries to accommodate those in need of immediate or emergency transportation, like when your car breaks down as you're leaving for work. CART does cross over into Hamilton County to make trips to Anderson-Mercy, the closest hospital to Clermont County. Fares are $3 for adults, $1.50 for handicapped individuals, children and senior citizens, and $2 for high school students.

Taxis

There are more than 20 taxi companies in Greater Cincinnati. Taxis aren't used in this area as widely as they are in, say, New York, but they can easily be found lined up on downtown streets, in front of hotels, at the airport or spread throughout the suburbs. Cabs cost $1.50 to $2 for the drop of the flag and $1.20 per mile, plus 20¢ a minute.

A more luxurious, but still affordable, alternative to a taxi is **Cincinnati Corporate Cab**, 388-3808 or (800) 701-8964, which offers a fleet of Lincoln Town Cars and nine-passenger vans with uniformed drivers.

To make sure you have a cab waiting for you, call one of the following or check the Yellow Pages for a complete listing: **Yellow Cab**, 241-2100; **Veteran Cabs**, 531-9300; **Skyline Taxi**, 251-7733; **Suburban Cabs**, 471-2222; **Community Cab**, (606) 727-2900.

Limousines

If you wish to arrive in Greater Cincinnati in style, you can hire a limousine from one of more than 50 companies that operate in the area. Most offer the traditional six-seat stretch or 10-seat ultra-stretch limousines that include a color TV, VCR, stereo, cellular phones and a wet bar. Use of the phone is an extra cost, and Ohio law prohibits stocking a limo's bar with alcohol.

Rates vary by company and destination — and in some cases, by the time of the year. Rates tend to increase during high school prom season. Generally, though, standard limousines rent for around $150 for three hours and $40 to $50 for each additional hour. Ultra-stretch limos rent for around $180 for the first three hours.

Or, if you want something a little different, check out **The Great White**, 658-1959. The Great White is the last known 1959 Cadillac stretch limousine. The 24-foot-long white Caddy, with six doors and giant tail fins, seats six comfortably in its two full-size back seats, which sit four feet apart. The Great White rents for $177 for three hours and $59 for each additional hour.

Schworer's Beverly Hills Limousine Service, 356-6255, rents not only traditional limos but also a 1964 Rolls Royce Silver Cloud, which is identical to the cars used in the Grey Poupon commercials. But, of course.

The car has a large moon roof, leather seats, a cellular phone, a television and wooden tables that unfold from the backs of the front seats. The Rolls rents for $195 for three hours and $65 per hour thereafter. Mustard not included.

Check the Yellow Pages for a complete listing, but some of the most popular limousine companies include **Washington Limousine Service**, 221-0074; **Cincinnati Limousine**, 388-3808; **Queen City Limousine**, 861-9949; **Gold Coach Limousine Service**, 851-8801; **Park Avenue Limousines**, 984-5466

Carriage Rides

Horse-drawn carriage rides through downtown are available all year, although during the summer there seems to be a carriage at every turn. The rides offer a good way to tour downtown, and the drivers are usually knowledgeable about different aspects of the area and generally love to answer questions. Several carriage companies operate downtown and are very competitive.

You can privately rent a horse-drawn carriage. Basic prices for a single-horse carriage are between $300 and $400 for an hour, and prices increase from that point. Some operators require a deposit of as much as 50 percent at the time reservations are made.

Carriage companies include **Ambassador Carriage**, 341-6085; **Camelot Carriage**, 352-5882; **Cincinnati Carriage**, 941-4474; **Midwest Carriage**, 523-7523; **Royal Carriage**, 553-3383.

Trolleys

Parking Company of America
250 West Court St. • 241-0415

Parking Company of America offers not only a place to park, but also a means of getting around the city in a unique manner. The business operates four motorized trolleys, which look vaguely like the old street cars that once ran around the city. The 40-seat vehicles do not run on regular schedules but are available for rent for special occasions. The cost is $80 an hour, with a three-hour minimum. Call in advance.

Car Rentals

Greater Cincinnati has more than 25 car rental agencies spread throughout the area. Those at the Cincinnati/Northern Kentucky International Airport include **Alamo**, (800) 327-9633; **Avis**, (606) 283-3773; **Budget**, (606) 283-3100; **Dollar**, (606) 283-3607, **Hertz**, (606) 283-3535; and **National**, (606) 283-3655. For something a little less expensive, try **Rent A Wreck**, 242-1800, or **Rent-A-Heap Cheap**, 631-0099.

River Travel

The Ohio River fills up once the weather turns nice. Boaters, water-skiers, jet-skiers, barges and bridges all compete for space, and the river becomes very congested, particularly around downtown. A piece of advice to boaters: keep an eye out for bridges and barges. Barges take a mile or more to stop; they always have the right of way and they can sink a boat in seconds. So can bridge piers. It sounds like common sense, but every year a boater hits one or the other and always loses.

You can set sail on the river in one of two ways: unhitch a trailered boat at a launch ramp or rent a slip at a local marina. Cincinnati has three main public launch ramps. On the east side, the ramp is at Schmidt Playfields along Eastern Avenue in the East End, about 4 miles from downtown. On the west side, the ramp is in Riverside on Southside Avenue, also about 4 miles from downtown. And downtown, the ramps are at the Public Landing. A small fee is charged for launching from Riverside or Schmidt Playfields.

The area also has 12 local marinas for docking. Many of the marinas offer winter storage areas. Most restaurants along the riverfront also offer piers for boat docking.

For non-boat owners looking for river excursions, eight local charter companies offer trip packages (see our River Fun chapter). The boats feature indoor or outdoor seating, catering, wet bars, and even gambling — OK, pretend gambling, since the real thing is still illegal in Ohio and Kentucky. For that you'll have to go to southeastern Indiana. Boat trips are popular for office parties and weddings. The largest charter company is **BB Riverboats,** (606) 261-8500, with boats that hold from 20 to 900 people. Several luxury yachts that ply the river are also available for rent.

Be aware that if a boating excursion takes you more than 35 miles in either direction of downtown, you'll have to get in line with barges and every other boat for a trip through a set of dam locks. And it's important to know that most of the river is actually under the control and responsibility of Kentucky, according to a U.S. Supreme Court decision, but both states as well as the Coast Guard patrol the river and enforce boating laws.

Airports

Cincinnati/Northern Kentucky International Airport
I-275 and S.R. 212 • (606) 283-3151

It's puzzling to many passengers flying into Greater Cincinnati for the first time when they realize the airport isn't in Cincinnati or even Ohio, but Kentucky. The Cincinnati/Northern Kentucky International Airport is a prime example of how the area overcomes state boundaries and works together to form a cohesive unit.

Since the federal government deeded it to the Kenton County Airport Board in 1945, the airport has proved to be ideally located to serve the region's air transportation needs. The rural setting, about 12 miles south of downtown Cincinnati, allows the airport to acquire space and slowly grow to meet the area's changing transportation needs without butting heads with residential expansion. Its rural setting also keeps it away from the bulk of daily traffic, so travelers don't have to mix with commuters in the fight to make a flight.

Fifteen commercial carriers operate at the airport, which also serves as the headquarters for DHL, the world's largest air courier. The other airlines are Air Canada, AirTran, American, American Eagle, British Airways, Comair, Continental Connection, Continental Express, Delta, KLM, Northwest, Swissair, TWA, and United.

> **FYI**
>
> Unless otherwise noted, the area code for all phone numbers listed in this guide is 513.

One of the most amazing facts about the airport is that it is one of the world's busiest. The airport has more than 510 nonstop flights departing daily to 104 cities and an additional 30 direct flights. Nonstop international flights leave daily for Frankfurt, London, Paris, Munich and Zurich. And the 20 million passengers it handles each year makes the airport the world's 41st busiest for commercial operations. Add cargo operations and it jumps to the 24th busiest airport in the world, ahead of those in such major destinations as Toronto, JFK and LaGuardia in New York, Orlando, Amsterdam, Honolulu, Houston, Seattle and Charles DeGaulle in Paris.

And there's no foreseeable slowdown . . . the airport remains one of the nation's fastest growing, both in terms of passengers and physical size. It recently built a new runway, extended another runway, and is in the beginning stages of adding yet another new runway, which will be its fifth.

Plus, more renovation and expansion plans for the parking and terminal areas are in the works. These plans come after a $500 million expansion, completed in 1995, that included a new terminal, a new road system, a new control tower, an automated baggage system that carries 21,000 bags an hour, an underground train that carries passengers to the terminal, and three new concourses. The airport now has all of the major conveniences of a small city — a wide variety of stores and bars, a barber shop, a chapel, two banks and its own police station, fire department and post office.

The airport is one of the most vital players in the region's economy. Every time a plane takes off from the airport, $19,000 are contributed to the local economy through direct and indirect expenditures, for a daily average of $8.3 million and an annual impact of $3 billion.

Because the airport sits within an hour's flight of 62 percent of the nation's population and 65 percent of its manufacturing facilities, numerous businesses relocating to the area from other parts of the country cite the airport as a primary factor in their decision. Because of its popularity, though — and the fact that

Photo: Greater Cincinnati Convention and Visitors Bureau

The Delta Queen passes beneath one of the
many bridges across the Ohio River.

it's a Delta hub, so Delta sets costs and stifles competition — the airport is not always the cheapest place to catch a flight. In fact, it's one of the most expensive. If the money factor outweighs the time factor, cheaper flights can easily be found in Columbus, Dayton, Louisville or Indianapolis. All four airports are about a two-hour drive from Cincinnati. In fact, Columbus' airport even advertises in Cincinnati in an attempt to lure travelers.

What you won't find at other airports, though, is more on-time flights. The Cincinnati/Northern Kentucky International Airport ranked first in the nation for on-time arrival performance in 1995, with 82.3 percent of arrivals landing on time.

Because of the increase in flights, nearby residents, some of whom were there long before the airport was and now sit immediately under a flight path, continually sound off about the nonstop noise. The airport board is buying as many nearby houses as it can, sound-insulating others and trying to route planes over less populated areas. It's still a battle between "progress" and people, though.

Getting from the airport to downtown or a suburban destination is easy. Cabs are available with a set fee of $22 for one to four passengers (five if you want to squeeze) to downtown. Flat fees are also available for a variety of suburban locations, such as $54 to the Kings Island Inn and $6 to the Radisson Inn Airport. Rides otherwise are $1.25 a mile.

Direct phone lines to all major car rental agencies are located in the baggage claim areas of each terminal, and buses go directly from outside these areas to the on-site rental companies. The Transit Authority of Northern Kentucky has a route that makes stops at the airport and will take riders downtown, although not without making a few stops first.

Two commercial shuttle services operate at the airport. **JetPort Express**, 767-3702, provides a shuttle bus to and from downtown ho-

tels every half-hour every day between 6 AM and 10 PM for $10 one way and $15 round trip. It also has a suburban service that operates four 10-passenger minivans that go to suburban destinations inside the I-275 loop for $10 to $25 one way and $15 to $35 round trip, depending on the length of the trip. **Royal Coach Transportation**, 662-0400 or (800) 998-4040, has six 10-passenger minivans that will travel up to 10 miles outside of the I-275 loop between 5 AM and midnight. Rides cost $24.50 for up to four people within I-275 and $29.50 outside of I-275. Each additional person is $5.

Lunken Airport
Kellogg and Wilmer Aves. • 321-4132

The City of Cincinnati owns and operates Lunken, which was the area's primary airport in the early days of aviation. The airport is in the Little Miami River valley, about 15 minutes east of downtown. Because of its positioning in the valley, the airport often becomes enshrouded in fog or floods during the spring thaw, thus earning itself the nickname Sunken Lunken. As airplanes became bigger, the airport became too small, and Sunken Lunken also became Shrunken Lunken. It now serves private, corporate and air cargo commercial planes and is the landing spot for the Goodyear blimp when it is in town and for helicopters from the Army National Guard when they are on training or maneuvers. Flight schools, hangars, major and minor maintenance and tiedowns are available here. Also, several fixed-base operations, executive jet management and jet charter companies operate out of the airport. Car rentals are available.

Blue Ash Airport
Plainfield and Glendale-Milford Rds.
• 984-8603, 791-8500

Blue Ash Airport, located about 25 miles north of downtown, is operated jointly by the City of Cincinnati and the Hamilton County

Regional Airport Authority. It sits adjacent to a 500-acre industrial park and near the area's second-largest business district, making it convenient for corporate planes. A small, private collection of World War II vintage military planes known as the War Birds is housed at the airport. Tours of the planes are free.

Clermont County Airport
Old S.R. 74, Batavia • 732-2336

The Clermont County Airport is a small airport serving mostly private planes. It is located about 30 miles east of downtown. It is also the home of Sporty's, a well-known international retail and catalog merchandise business aimed at the aviation industry. The airport is privately owned and managed by Eastern Cincinnati Aviation.

Long-Distance Bus Lines

Greyhound Bus Lines
1005 Gilbert Ave. • 352-6012
2583 E. Sharon Rd. • 771-1151
Fifth St. and Madison Ave., Covington, Ky. • (606) 431-2254, (800)231-2222

Greyhound operates a modern bus station on the northeastern edge of downtown and a suburban station in Sharonville, about 20 miles north of downtown on I-75. The downtown station offers regular daily departures to cities across the country in addition to package express and charter services.

Trailways Bus Systems
1005 Gilbert Ave. • 352-6020

Trailways shares space with Greyhound Bus Lines at Greyhound's downtown station. It also offers package express and baggage shipments.

Trains

Amtrak
1301 Western Ave. • 651-3337,
(800) 872-7245

For years, Union Terminal, the giant half-dome that sits just northwest of downtown, was center stage for one of the areas most common forms of transportation, the trains. The terminal's importance has mostly faded now, with the introduction of air travel; however, Amtrak keeps part of the legacy alive by operating a limited service. Three trains a week depart from the station heading east to New York or Washington, D.C. Eastbound trains depart at 5 AM on Sunday, Wednesday and Friday. Westbound trains heading to Chicago depart at 3:30 AM on Monday, Thursday and Saturday.

The Greater Cincinnati
area abounds in
tasteful, comfortable,
delicious eateries,
nearly all
reasonably priced.

Restaurants

Cincinnati's dining scene is rife with baffling contradictions. We're far from the Texas border but known worldwide for our chili. We're populated largely by settlers of German extract but claim relatively few German restaurants. We've hardly any settlers from France but boast the country's top-rated French restaurant, The Maisonette.

These contradictions are in perfect keeping with Cincinnati, a city of delightful discrepancies. The only constant on the town's dining scene is that Cincinnati restaurants, whether they serve haute cuisine or eclectic eats, are a solid value. Cincinnatians are noted penny-pinchers (Abe Lincoln, on occasion, has been heard to scream aloud), and they tolerate neither fools nor pricey food gladly. This is terrific news for the visitor or newcomer, who will find that the area abounds in tasteful, comfortable, delicious eateries, nearly all reasonably priced.

Price Code

The following ratings are based on the average price of two entrees, excluding tax, tip, appetizers, desserts and beverages.

$	Less than $20
$$	$20 to $35
$$$	$35 to $50
$$$$	$50 and more

If you are the kind of diner who likes to immediately sample the regional cuisine and scenery, head first to any Skyline Chili outlet for Cincinnati chili, slightly sweet rather than spicy (some say the secret ingredient is cinnamon or cocoa) and served atop spaghetti. The other lunch landmark you shouldn't miss is Arnold's, the city's oldest

bar and grill — it fairly drips with the essential flavors of Cincinnati.

Come dinner, choose The Maisonette for a formal Continental meal or, for more casual fare, head to the trendy and wonderful Pigall's Cafe. And for a late dessert or snack, indulge in raspberry chocolate chip at any Graeter's ice cream parlor.

Like to stroll and gaze at menus in windows before making a decision? The streets with the highest density of diverse restaurants per block are Ludlow Avenue in Clifton, St. Gregory Street in Mount Adams, Mount Lookout Square in Mount Lookout, Fourth and Sixth streets downtown, and Main Street in Over-the-Rhine. (A caution: Main Street is . . . how shall we put it . . . a gritty area more suited to the urban pioneer.)

This isn't to say you can sample the full flavor of Cincinnati by simply stopping at this handful of eateries. At last count, there were some 700 restaurants in the region. You could dine out for a full year and not savor the entire range of Queen City fare.

You'll find that most restaurants in Greater Cincinnati are fairly kid-friendly. You probably won't want to take kids to The Maisonette or other fine downtown restaurants, but there are few other places where bringing a child would be inappropriate.

City of Cincinnati law requires restaurants to provide a nonsmoking section. Outside the city limits nonsmokers aren't quite as lucky, and your chance of finding a smoke-free restaurant decreases mightily if you drive south into Kentucky, a big-time tobacco farm state. We've noted those restaurants that don't have a nonsmoking section in the listings. Greater Cincinnati does offer 289 smoke-free restaurants, by last count. The local American Lung Association will happily mail you a list of them — call 985-3990.

We chose to break this chapter down by culinary categories rather than by neighborhood or some other geographical listing. Frankly, Cincinnati is a small enough place that you are never more than a stone's throw from a delightful discovery. If you've read other chapters in our book, you know by now that Cincinnati is a city of neighborhoods, dozens and dozens of them. And while we generally don't list neighborhoods in our addresses if those neighborhoods are within Cincinnati city limits, we thought it would be helpful to do so in the restaurant chapter because so many newcomers and tourists seek out restaurants. If there's just a street address, it's downtown Cincinnati.

We offer a mix of the venerable establishments and the newest trend-setting bistros. These are the places to take Aunt Maude and Uncle Dale when they visit town (as well as a new boss or a first date you're trying to impress), and you'll be equally charmed. As a rule, we don't list chain restaurants unless they offer something unique or exceptional from what you can expect to find at the chain's other outlets elsewhere in the country.

Here are a few other tips about how to use this chapter and on dining in general in Greater Cincinnati. Dress in Cincinnati restaurants is usually casual, even more so the farther you get from downtown. But as a rule, don't wear jeans, shorts or tennis shoes to restaurants with a $$$ or above rating. Restaurants with dress codes are noted, as are those that are particularly kid-friendly or that confound expectations one way or the other.

Unless otherwise noted, assume the restaurants listed here accept major credit cards. Even so, check before you order if you don't have the cash. And, unless otherwise noted, all restaurants are open Monday through Sunday and serve both lunch and dinner. Restaurants that serve breakfast or brunch are so noted.

Finally, please remember that it's impossible for even us to go everywhere in one year. Cincinnati just has too many terrific restaurants. So if you don't see your favorite place listed below, stay tuned for future editions.

African

Bintimani
$ • 1178 W. Kemper Rd., Forest Park
• 674-0315

If plantain with liver and onions is to your liking, or curried goat or jerk chicken, this is the place. African fare as well as Caribbean and Filipino dishes are all expertly cooked.

American Contemporary and Eclectic

Arthur's
$ • 3518 Edwards Rd., Hyde Park
• 871-5543

This popular neighborhood spot just off Hyde Park Square dishes up some of the best burgers in town. Wood-paneled elegance and good, simple food make this one of the area's better dining values.

Behle Street Cafe
$ • 50 E. RiverCenter Blvd., Covington, Ky. • (606) 291-4100

Settle down to comfort foods, including pork chops and the town's tastiest Shepherd's Pie, in a casual setting. It's certainly one of the few places to still offer Blue Plate Specials on its menu.

Bistro Gigi
$$ • 6904 Wooster Pk., Mariemont
• 272-2444

A casual French restaurant from the same folks who bring us The Maisonette, it's located in

Mariemont (pronounced Mary-mont), a Tudor-style town and planned community well worth a visit in itself. Next door to Bistro Gigi, the renovated Mariemont Theater shows art films. Gigi serves dinner only and is closed on Monday.

Blue Wolf Bistro
$ • 801 Elm St. • 621-6512

The place is subtitled "Innovative Healthy Dining," and that's what this charming little downtown luncheonette delivers. Plenty of salads, a black bean soup with curry and raisins, and a polenta pizza are just some of the vegetarian offerings. Plus there's mahi-mahi and salmon. Dinner only is served Thursday through Saturday, and the restaurant is closed Sunday.

Cafe Joseph-Beth
$ • 2692 Madison Rd., Norwood
• 396-8966

You'd think that when a business tries to be a bookstore, music store, toy store and restaurant all at the same time, it wouldn't do a good job at all of them. Guess again. The cafe at this popular Rookwood Pavilion bookstore is terrific, offering everything from a tasty Bleu Cheese and Mushroom Polenta to Walnut and Roasted Garlic Linguini. Lunch and dinner are served Monday through Saturday, and there's a Sunday brunch. Buy the latest issue of your favorite magazine and lounge around here.

Cafe at the Palm Court
$$-$$$ • 35 W. Fifth St. • 564-6465

The trendy downtown Mediterranean menu is popular with the downtown lunch crowd at this, the less formal of the restaurants at the Omni Netherland Hotel in the Carew Tower. Piano music nightly and most weekdays and a jazz quartet on the weekends give this already beautiful bistro some added ambiance. Breakfast and Sunday brunch are also served.

Carol's on Main
$ • 825 Main St. • 651-2667

This brick-walled bistro is where the city's literati and theatrical types hang out. And, thanks to the opening of the nearby Aronoff Center for the Arts, you are likely to spot Carol Channing or some other touring Broadway celebrity. Regulars opt for the signature Custer's Last Pasta with cilantro pesto and tangy chipotie red pep-per sauce. Upstairs is, predictably enough, "Upstairs at Carol's," a cabaret room featuring local entertainers. Sunday brunch is served.

Chateau Pomije
$$ • 2019 Madison Rd., O'Bryonville
• 871-8788

Try the Chateau Chicken (with caramelized onions, mushrooms and sherry) or the gourmet pizza du jour at this relaxed, moderately priced spot. It's also known for its wine, which is produced at an Indiana vineyard. On Saturday there's dinner only, and the restaurant is closed on Sunday.

Ciao Cucina
$$ • 700 Walnut St. • 929-0700
$$ • 11834 Montgomery Rd., Symmes
• 489-7373

The nouvelle Italian menu here is among the most innovative in Cincinnati. Do make reservations for dinner at the downtown location on Walnut Street, which is usually very crowded with theatergoers and the like. Some of the best choices on a menu filled with creative cuisine include the proscuitto and fennel pizza and the roast duck pasta. The Symmes location is fairly noisy, thanks to the bar-like layout and acoustics, yet it's also surprisingly kid-friendly. There's no lunch on weekends at the downtown location.

Coco's
$$ • 322 Greenup St., Covington, Ky.
• (606) 491-1369

This intimate neighborhood spot with exposed brick walls and Southwestern accents is the kind of place you'd expect to find in Mount Adams, only it's in the increasingly rejuvenated Covington. Don't pass up the appetizers, which include a good selection of tapas and soups. You'll also find nice touches such as fried oysters and blackened tuna. Coco's is closed on Sunday.

Dee Felice Cafe
$$ • 529 Main St., Covington, Ky.,
• (606) 261-2365

A Cajun restaurant playing Dixieland jazz may be a little incongruous with surrounding Mainstrasse Village, but never mind the culture clash. Good gumbo and jambalaya combined with Dixieland and classic jazz seven nights a week make this one of the top restaurants and nicest low-key nightspots south of the river. It's also a popular place for lunch away from the hustle and bustle. No lunch on weekends.

deSha's
$$-$$$ • 11320 Montgomery Rd., Symmes • 247-9933

This restaurant at the Shops of Harper's Point shopping center is among the best midrange restaurants around, with well-prepared dishes such as prime rib and rainbow trout. Don't miss the house corn bread.

diJohn
$-$$ • 724 Madison Ave., Covington, Ky. • (606) 581-5646

Just reopened and under new management, this is a smartly decorated cafe featuring everything from comfort food such as meatloaf to Greek-style fried mussels. Lunch is served Monday through Friday and dinner Tuesday through Saturday.

FYI
Unless otherwise noted, the area code for all phone numbers listed in this guide is 513.

The Diner on Sycamore
$$ • 1203 Sycamore St., Over-the-Rhine • 721-1212

This is an honest-to-goodness diner with the '50s railcar-dropped-from-space motif you may remember from your own youth or vicariously through the movie *Diner*. The Diner on Sycamore, in fact, was manufactured by The Mountain View Diner Car Co. of Singac, New Jersey, in 1955 and served for 28 years as the Tiger Town Diner in Massillon, Ohio. The food, however, is anything but retro. A wide variety of eclectic offerings includes Caribbean crab chili, tomato shallot Brie and a tremendous Seafood Diablo. Parking is across the street on Sycamore.

First Watch
$ • 2692 Madison Rd., Norwood • 531-7430
$ • 8118 Montgomery Rd., Kenwood • 891-0088
$ • 11031 Montgomery Rd., Symmes • 489-6849
$ • 700 Walnut St. • 721-4744

If the business breakfast meeting hadn't already become a staple by the time First Watch opened, it would have had to be invented. These restaurants are the breakfast destination of choice for many Cincinnatians who live on the Interstate 71 corridor from Hyde Park to Symmes — and a good ways beyond. They're always good, always reasonably priced and always packed. Specialties include the turkey dill "crepegg" and great pancakes. Breakfast is served all day, but they also have a lunch menu, a selection of light fare and salads. First Watch is open for breakfast and lunch daily.

Geri Christine's
$$ • 6923 Miami Ave., Madeira • 561-4707

Housed in a charming little building in equally charming Madeira, this cozy cafe has a challenging menu. How challenging? Try Eggplant Napoleon — grilled eggplant, spinach and goat cheese in puff pastry. Art by local photographers adorns the walls. Dinner is served every day.

Grand Finale
$$ • 30 E. Sharon Ave., Glendale • 771-5925

Set in a century-old Victorian tavern, this is the perfect place to bring your visiting parents or that hard-to-please maiden aunt. The house specialty is Chicken Ginger marinated in soy, sherry and honey, then grilled with ginger and walnuts. The apple cinnamon cheesecake is not to be missed. Or try one of the four flaming desserts. It's closed on Monday.

The Heritage Restaurant
$$-$$$ • 7664 Wooster Pike (U.S. Hwy. 50) between Terrace Park and Mariemont • 561-9300

These folks introduced Cincinnatians to wild game and blackened redfish, and the menu is always good for new twists on traditional cuisine. The Heritage dares to be politically incorrect each year with a late-winter menu that includes super-exotic meat dishes, which always draws a crowd of diners and animal rights activists. Some of the dinners are pricey, but lunches are a good value for

Fine dining is made even more special by the view of the city's lights reflected in the Ohio River.

the quality of food. Built in a restored 1827 manor house, the restaurant's decor is Early American hunt-club. It's posh, but it does have a children's menu. Lunch is served Monday through Friday only.

Hotel Discovery
$$ • 7800 Montgomery Rd., Kenwood • 792-9499

This isn't a theme restaurant, it's a theme park restaurant that encourages adventure and exploration. A huge saltwater aquarium and giant visuals from the Hubble telescope are just two of the attractions at this imagination odyssey. And, oh yes, they serve food too. Try the filet mignon fajita.

Jake's American Cafe
$$ • 622 Riegert Sq., Fairfield • 868-8492

If you live around here, you've seen Jake's TV cooking show on Channel 9. This way-above-average eatery is hidden in an unassum-

ing Fairfield shopping center. Among the Cajun and American specialties to try are the Caribbean jerk pork appetizer, Nawlins gumbo and berry cobbler. Lunch is served Monday through Friday, dinner Thursday through Saturday.

Jeckle's in Hyde Park
$$ • 3724 Paxton Ave., Hyde Park • 531-1600

Locals go for the London broil and the diverse appetizer and drink menu. This is a popular singles spot, yet an inviting family restaurant, too.

LeBoxx Cafe
$$ • 819 Vine St. • 721-5638

This downtown cafe's peculiar name is a reminder that they deliver boxed lunches to those hard-working, chained-to-the-desk types downtown, but it's a cut above your usual we-deliver deli. The budget member of the Phoenix Group (which includes Plaza 600 and the

Phoenix), LeBoxx seems to be thriving in a spot where others have failed by offering creative touches on old favorites. Some of the best dishes include the white chili, Portobello sandwich and Fountain Square burger. Leboxx serves lunch only, Monday through Friday.

Maya's Restaurant and Pastry Shop
$-$$ • 9749 Kenwood Rd., Blue Ash • 791-5005

This is another of Greater Cincinnati's hidden treasures, tucked away in a strip shopping center in Blue Ash. They take eclectic to new extremes with a menu that includes American, Italian, Bolivian and German cuisine. El Boliviano is a spicy Bolivian sampler plate worth a try both for its novelty and its taste. Don't skip dessert. The shop is open for breakfast too.

www.insiders.com

See this and many other **Insiders' Guide®** destinations online — in their entirety.

Visit us today!

The Melting Pot
$$ • 11023 Montgomery Rd., Milford • 530-5501
$$ • 3520 Edwards Rd., Hyde Park • 871-7773

If you didn't get enough fondue during the '70s, this is the place for you. We'll break the chain rule here because this Florida-based chain has sites mainly in the Southeast and some people may not be familiar with it. It has fondue everything, from filet mignon to dessert. It's open for dinner only.

Mullane's Parkside Cafe
$, no credit cards • 723 Race St. • 381-1331

This New Age diner specializes in seafood and vegetarian dishes such as veggie burgers and spinach saute. Any entree can be made-to-order vegetarian. If you don't get there by 11:45 AM, however, forget about getting in for lunch on a weekday. Paintings by trendy local artists line the walls. Dinner only on Saturday. Closed Sunday.

The Palace
$$$$ • 601 Vine St. • 381-6006

This top-rated restaurant just off the lobby of the century-old Cincinnatian Hotel (originally The Palace) has all the trappings of its rank: mahogany paneling, fresh flowers, sterling silver serving trays and formally attired servers. The menu combines traditional four-star hotel fare with more adventuresome offerings, including tempura quail with wilted spinach salad; tuna medallion pyramid with red pepper sauce, cilantro, crisp potatoes and vegetable salad; and breast of chicken with pesto couscous. This is no place to dine alone because the synchronized lifting of the serving domes is something of a tradition. Dinner dress code calls for jacket (tie optional) for men. Lunch is not served on weekends.

Petersen's Restaurant
$ • 308 Ludlow Ave., Clifton • 861-4777 (carry-out only)
$ • 700 Elm St. • 723-1113
$ • 1111 St. Gregory, Mount Adams • 651-4777

Petersen's offers special-occasion dining for the budget-minded. The three locales provide some of the best all-around values in town, with understated but attractive decor and carefully prepared and beautifully presented dishes that you'd expect at a much finer hotel restaurant at an accordingly steep price. Novel twists with spices and preparation make even the commonplace something of an adventure. Try the black bean burritos and the spicy pasta dishes. The Mount Adams location offers jazz six nights a week in the adjoining Promontory. Petersen's is closed on Sunday.

Pigalls Cafe
$$ • 127 W. Fourth St. • 651-2233

Pigalls is one of downtown's most popular dining spots and a hangout for journalists (*The Cincinnati Enquirer* is practically next door). The ambitious menu includes Calypso coconut shrimp, pineapple and macadamia nut pizza, sauteed tilapia and feta. Lunch is not served Saturday. It's closed Sunday.

Plaza 600

$$ • 600 Walnut St. • 721-8600

Adjacent to the Aronoff Center for the Arts, Plaza 600 is known for its smoked salmon burrito and the savory sea bass with sun-dried tomato hollandaise. It's also known for being loud, especially on busy nights at the Aronoff. Plaza 600 doesn't serve lunch on Saturday and it's closed Sunday.

The Restaurant at the Phoenix

$$$-$$$$ • 812 Race St. • 721-8901

This highly rated restaurant is a landmark and one of the most beautiful places to eat downtown. It's a good, slightly out-of-the-way place to impress out-of-town friends or business associates without taking them to The Maisonette. The menu includes an interesting mix of American, Asian and Caribbean cuisine plus an extensive wine list. It serves dinner only and is closed Sunday and Monday.

South Beach Grill

**$$$ • 14 Pete Rose Pier, Covington, Ky.
• (606) 581-1414**

This is Cincinnati's all-around glitziest restaurant, a place for special occasions and a regular hangout for athletes and other celebrities, some of whom are part owners (including former Bengal Cris Collinsworth and Boomer Esiason and some guy named Pete Rose, along with restaurateur-to-the-stars Jeff Ruby). In addition to the same selection of steaks (and to a large extent, clientele) you'll find at Ruby's The Precinct in Columbia-Tusculum, this riverfront institution offers seafood and other entrees.

What's For Dinner?

**$ • 3009 O'Bryon Rd., O'Bryonville
• 321-4404**

Tucked just off the main drag (Madison Road) of O'Bryonville, this restaurant answers its own question astutely. You can eat in or carry out the wide array of gourmet mom food, which is either packed cold or heated in the microwave. Whatever you do, save room for a Carmellita, a rich and gooey treat that is well worth the assault it will make on your arteries and waistline. It's closed on Sunday.

York Street Cafe

**$ • 738 York St., Newport, Ky.
• (606) 261-9675**

A genteel little cafe, York Street Cafe has the look and feel of a Victorian parlor, complete with sofas where you can eat your meal over coffee tables. Bookcases line the walls. Reasonably priced dishes include a wide selection of tasty sandwiches, focaccia creations and "conversational" meals of appetizer-size portions of several dishes for two or more.

American Traditional

The Albee

$$ • 21 E. Fifth St. • 852-2740

Overlooking Fountain Square in the Westin Hotel downtown, The Albee boasts a tremendous view of the square and the horse-drawn carriages that come and go all evening. Built on the site of the old Albee movie theater, silver screen memorabilia line the restaurant walls. The establishment's pork loin with apricot glaze is as good as it gets. Superb service rounds out the experience, as does a trip before or after to the Albee Bar, the newly opened hors d'oeuvres bar.

Arnold's Bar and Grill

$-$$ • 210 E. Eighth St. • 421-6234

Time for only one quick meal in Cincinnati? To soak up as much local color as possible, head immediately downtown to Arnold's, the oldest tavern in town (established 1861). The cost of beer and sasparilla may have changed, but not the ambiance. Prohibition finally forced Arnold's into the restaurant business, but the bathtub (for brewing illegal gin) on the second floor remains. This is where the town's politicos and newspaper types, as well as local law enforcement, judges, radio DJs — you name it — hang out. Just sit at the long bar and you'll get a crash course in "Cincy speak." Jim Tarbell, Arnold's ebullient proprietor, is one of the town's most colorful characters and the genius behind many a civic campaign, such as the one to establish a Broadway Commons old-time ballpark. The house specialty is Greek Spaghetti Deluxe, bathed in olive oil, butter, garlic sauce, then topped with sauteed olives, bacon and vegetables. The enclosed courtyard offers outdoor dining, and some of the town's finest folk and bluegrass musicians appear on stage. Arnold's is closed on Sunday.

Cinema Grill
$ • 3187 Linwood Ave., Mount Lookout
• 321-3211

Nestled in enchanting Mount Lookout Square, the Cinema Grill occupies an old movie theater and, guess what, really shows movies. The casual fare is headlined by an excellent chicken teriyaki grill. Films are generally second-run, after they've cleared the mainstream movie houses. There's also a Cinema Grill in Covedale, but we prefer the original location.

Dion's
$ • 3173 Linwood Ave., Mount Lookout
• 871-9282

One of Mount Lookout Square's newest restaurants is also its most innovative. Housed in an unpretentious storefront along the square's restaurant row, Dion's challenging menu includes salmon croquettes, sautéed Portobello mushrooms, New Zealand rack of lamb with rosemary/blueberry sauce and other regional favorites. Dion's serves lunch and dinner Wednesday through Sunday.

The Glass Onion
$$$ • 1 Madison Ave., Covington, Ky.
• (606) 491-6692

Located atop Covington Landing, a floating entertainment palace, The Glass Onion offers everything from veal to elk on its menu — and, of course, a splendid view of the river and cityscape. Boasting a self-described "San Francisco look," the decor includes lots of windows and white tablecloths. The house specialty is the Onion Grillade, filet mignon and South African lobster tail in a cognac blend. It serves dinner only and is closed Monday.

The Golden Lamb
$$-$$$ • 27 S. Broadway, Lebanon
• 932-5065

Talk about staying power, The Golden Lamb's been here for 180 years and still packs 'em in. Under the ownership of The Maisonette Group, a.k.a. the Comisar family, the tradition rests in good hands. The Golden Lamb is to traditional American cuisine what The Maisonette is to French cuisine. Some specialties here include the roast leg of lamb (natch'), roast stuffed Ohio pheasant breast with champagne sauce, Shaker spiced apple pudding and fillet of Ohio smoked trout. Rooms are named after famous guests, such as Charles Dickens and Mark Twain. Greater Cincinnati's top antique stores are located nearby, so make a day of shopping and fine dining. Lunch is not served on Sunday.

Grafton's Restaurant
$ • 7314 Montgomery Rd., Silverton
• 891-2380

Look up "neighborhood restaurant" in the dictionary and you'll find a picture of this place. It's been around forever, and a member of the Grafton family is still in charge. Peppercorn filet and crab cakes are among the standouts on the menu. It has comfy booths, an intimate bar and terrific service. It's closed Sunday and Monday.

The Green Derby
$ • 846 York St., Newport, Ky.
• (606) 431-8740

A Newport fixture, the Derby is supervised by the third generation of the family that opened it a half-century ago. This is where to find home cooking, be it a comforting chicken noodle soup, fried halibut sandwich, catfish with hush puppies or savory pan-fried chicken livers. The main dining room is bright and cheery, the walls painted with vines and ferns. It's closed Sunday.

Hathaway Restaurant
$, no credit cards • Carew Tower Arcade
• 621-1332

This favorite of the downtown lunch crowd is good enough to draw crowds from the 'burbs, too. Expect friendly first-name service at a lunch counter where the decor reminds you of the great cars of the 1930s, when this place opened. Whatever you do, don't pass up the chocolate ice cream soda from the old-time soda fountain. Like the far posher Omni Netherland restaurants nearby,

Hathaway's is a very welcome blast from the past. Breakfast and lunch are served Monday through Saturday.

James Tavern
$$ • 4200 Cooper Rd., Blue Ash • 891-8300

If you like history dished up with your food, James Tavern is the place. Lots of fireplaces and a cozy atmosphere make for a relaxing dining experience. Patrons come from everywhere for the tavern's specialty, Bourbon Pecan Pork Loin with sun-dried cherry apple dressing. Lunch is not served on Sunday.

La Normandie
$$-$$$ • 118 E. Sixth St. • 721-2761

Despite the French name and being owned by the same folks as The Maisonette upstairs, La Normandie is a less formal, less expensive and decidedly un-French restaurant. Moderate prices, a semi-posh atmosphere with the feel of a Medieval English dining hall, and hearty food make this one of downtown's most popular spots. There's free parking at Century Parking across the street. Lunch is served Tuesday through Friday. It's closed Sunday.

National Exemplar
$$ • 6880 Wooster Pike, Mariemont • 271-2103

This spot, operated by the same folks who run the wildly popular local chain of First Watch restaurants, is renowned for great breakfasts that feature giant omelets, gourmet pancakes, fritattas and crepes. But they want you to know they also serve lunch and dinner — steak, seafood and pasta — at this beautifully appointed restaurant at the Best Western Mariemont Inn.

Nick & Tom's Restaurant & Bar
$$ • 5774 Bridgetown Ave., Bridgetown • 574-4242

Here's a popular, friendly casual west side spot that serves good steaks, chops, chicken, burgers and pasta; the french dip is a standout. It's one of the few locally owned west side favorites that's open on Monday.

Orchids at the Palm Court
$$$-$$$$ • 35 W. Fifth St. • 564-6465

This is the more formal of the restaurants at the downtown Omni Netherland Hotel in the Carew Tower and one of the highest-rated restaurants in the area. The art deco surroundings and variety of well-prepared regional American cuisine make this historic downtown restaurant a great place for a special occasion. It has what is probably the city's most extensive wine list. Orchids serves lunch on weekdays and brunch on Sunday.

Quality Inn Riverview
$$$ • 668 Fifth St., Covington, Ky. • (606) 491-5300

For some, a culinary tour of any city must include a visit to a revolving restaurant. So be it. Riverview is our choice, not only because it offers a splendid panorama of the skyline and environs, but because the menu would move you even if the floor didn't. Particularly worth sampling is the Pork Rio Grande and the Veal Riverview.

Rookwood Pottery
$$ • 1077 Celestial Ave., Mount Adams • 721-5456

This historic pottery sits high atop Mount Adams. Housed in a Tudor-style structure, the giant kilns are still here, but now they've got tables and chairs in them. Locals know to specifically ask to be seated in one of them. Run your finger down the menu and it's like a lesson in local history: McGuffeyburger, Boss Coxburger, Shillitoburger. But it's best known for its Idaburger (bacon, mushrooms and cheddar). There's a great downtown view (from the parking lot).

Symphony Hotel
$$-$$$ • 210 W. 14th St., Over-the-Rhine • 721-3353

Opened in the former Clyde Hotel, a gracious Victorian stone mansion, this is a distinctly upscale establishment that offers five-course meals. Hours are odd — dinner is only offered on nights when there is a performance at nearby Music Hall.

The Syndicate
$$-$$$ • 18 E. Fifh St., Newport, Ky. • (606) 491-8000

Newport was once a gambling mecca. Al Capone and his cronies are long gone, but the newly opened Syndicate pays homage to Newport's gangster era. Waiters wear fedoras, there is plenty of gambling memorabilia, and the menu features such cute dishes as Chicken Corleone and Death by Chocolate. Leave your machine gun at home.

The White House Inn
$$ • 4940 Muhlhauser Rd., West Chester • 860-1110

A huge restored farmhouse with fireplaces and a gazebo, the inn is surrounded by herb gardens and outdoor patios. The house specialty is Steak Lynchburg, a strip steak studded with peppercorns and bathed in Jack Daniel's sauce. Also excellent is the Farmhouse Duck in peach and cherry sauce.

Asian and Oriental

Ambar India
$ • 350 Ludlow Ave., Clifton • 281-7000

Ambar India is a perennial winner as best Indian restaurant in the seemingly endless restaurant polls conducted by the city's newspapers and magazines. The title, however, is well deserved. Vegetarians flock to this Ludlow Avenue haunt, long known for its northern India oven dishes and exotic curries. Meat lovers will find plenty of choices, too, from a savory lamb curry to chicken tikka. Don't miss the mango milk shake. Lunch is not served on Saturday, and the restaurant is closed Sunday.

Aralia
$, no credit cards • 815 Elm St. • 723-1217

The best and, dare we say, only Sri Lankan restaurant in Cincinnati, Aralia would merit a visit even without that distinction. Triset De Fonseka, author of *Cooking With Herbs*, a self-published cookbook widely distributed locally, puts her recipes into practice in this cozy brownstone off the beaten path downtown. Her very reasonably priced (all entrees less than $10) Sri Lankan fare is similar to Indian cuisine, but with some added zing and a smokier roasted flavor for some dishes. The ginger beer made on the premises is excellent. Breakfast is served on Sunday only.

Arloi Dee
$ • 18. E. 7th St., • 421-1304

This Thai restaurant is the darling of the town's restaurant critics, and for good reason. They also dabble in Japanese and Chinese — and do it all well. Bargain prices apply even to the seafood dishes, including the honey jumbo shrimp with honey sauce (we recommend the whole ginger fish). Decor is funky hole-in-the-wall chic. Closed Sunday.

Cheng-1 Cuisine
$$ • 203 W. McMillan St., Clifton • 723-1999

Cheng-2 Gourmet
$$ • 11296 Montgomery Rd., Symmes • 489-2388

Unlike movies, Cincinnati restaurants usually have to be good to warrant a sequel. Cheng's serves good Szechwan and Hunan food along with more modern California-style dishes in modern decor. Ask for the Chinese-language menu (with translations), which has a broader selection. Cheng-2, the fancier suburban restaurant in the Shops at Harper's Point, has an elegant neon and black-lacquer look.

China Gourmet
$$$ • 3340 Erie Ave., Hyde Park • 871-6612

Cincinnatians like their Chinese restaurants pretty, and this Hyde Park establishment is

> **FYI**
>
> Unless otherwise noted, the area code for all phone numbers listed in this guide is 513.

Rookwood Pottery Has A Distinguished Past

Today, the kilns are cool. Air conditioning, in fact, is pumped into the stone cylinders that once cooked some of the world's most prized clay. Tables sit in the center of the ovens and waiters and waitresses breeze in and out. The Rookwood Pottery is now a restaurant.

Not long ago, however, Cincinnati's Rookwood Pottery was a different place. It was one of the centers of Cincinnati, an obligatory stop for every visiting dignitary and VIP.

The artistic pottery that came out of the kilns was compared to art glass from Tiffany. It was also a place that helped put Cincinnati on the international art map.

While Cincinnati's foremost artists and art institutions were still in their infancy or just developing their reputation, the Rookwood was creating masterpieces that were recognized worldwide for their brilliance. In such prestigious international competitions as the 1900 Exposition Universelle in Paris, the 1901 Pan American Exposition in Buffalo and the 1901 Exposition International de Ceramique et de Verrerie in St. Petersburg, Russia, Rookwood pottery swept the awards.

Even today, the embodiment of Maria Longworth's work and dreams are still recognized as treasures and are highly sought by museums and private collectors. In fact, in 1980, 100 years after the Pottery's founding, a piece of Rookwood sold for $23,000 at an auction at Christie's in New York, setting a world record price for pottery.

Rookwood Pottery was born on Thanksgiving Day 1880 when Maria Longworth pulled the first of thousands of pieces of pottery from her kiln. The granddaughter of Nicholas Longworth and daughter of Judge Joseph Longworth, Maria formed the business after being snubbed by a group of 11 other women who had formed a pottery club. Her father bought her an old schoolhouse along Eastern Avenue near the river, which she named "Rookwood" after her family's Walnut Hills estate.

Rookwood was conceived as a place where she and other women could enjoy their

— continued on next page

Photo: The Cincinnati Historical Society

Workers at Rookwood turned out some of the finest pottery ever made in the United States.

hobby of decorating pottery, but Longworth's aspirations quickly rose beyond dabbling in pottery as a hobby. With money from the homefront to help her along the way, she made Rookwood Pottery one of America's first major industries to be owned and operated by a woman.

And business quickly developed. The pottery was instantly recognized for its quality craftsmanship and glazing. She immediately hired Henry Farny, a well-known painter of American Indian subjects, as a full-time decorator. Three years later she named William Watts Taylor as manager of the pottery. An astute businessman, it was under Taylor's leadership that the pottery reached its peak. He reorganized sales methods and made Rookwood the first pottery to hire a chemist to develop the unique glazes the pottery is known for. He encouraged innovation and risk-taking and paid special attention to the pottery markings, which added to its appeal to collectors. He brought in professional artists and let them build a career around painting pottery. One of his artists, Kataro Shirayamadani, worked as one of the pottery's outstanding painters from 1890 until his death at age 93 in 1947.

Always on the forefront, Rookwood developed innovative techniques, one of the first of which was the use of an atomizer, which operated much like an airbrush, for application of the glaze. The glazing techniques were closely guarded and sometimes patented secrets. The distinctive green and golden tints of the Rookwood glazes came from blending base pigment with Ohio Valley clay.

In 1891, the old schoolhouse near the river flooded and a massive new Tudor building was constructed on the edge of Mount Adams. At the time, Rookwood employed more than 50 artists. By then, Longworth had married Bellamy Storer Jr. and had begun showing less and less interest in the business, eventually transferring ownership to Taylor, although still maintaining a studio for herself. Taylor continued running the business until his death in 1913.

A commercial architecture department was added to the pottery in 1902 to produce the decorative flatware pieces used in commercial buildings across the country. Rookwood tiles decorate the Carew Tower, Union Terminal and Dixie Terminal in Cincinnati and the Vanderbilt Hotel, Grand Central Station and several subway stops in New York City. Master Rookwood potter Earl Menzel even created a plaque for the cornerstone of Procter & Gamble's world headquarters, inscribing the first line of the Bible in 43 languages. Many of the flat pieces were also used around fireplaces in homes in Greater Cincinnati and can still be found in older houses.

The pottery tried to balance the two divisions: the commercial one to pay the bills and the art one to build the name. The 1920s were highly prosperous years for Rookwood. The pottery employed about 200 workers, and 4,000 to 5,000 visitors made the trip to the Mount Adams business each year. Almost every local bride had a piece of Rookwood among her wedding gifts. Even Mark Twain, who admittedly was not an art collector, visited the pottery and went on a shopping spree.

Most of the pottery's products were expensive, although it did make some inexpensive mass-produced items. When the Depression hit, though, it didn't matter what the price was. The company was hit hard. Architects couldn't afford Rookwood tiles and mantels. Mass production potters churned out cheap look-alikes. By 1934, the company showed its first loss, and by 1936 it was operating an average of just one week a month. On April 17, 1941, it filed for bankruptcy.

The pottery went through a series of salvations by hopeful owners. A group of businessmen led by Walter Schott (father-in-law of Marge) bought the pottery and gave it to the Institutium Divi Thomae, a scientific, educational and research foundation under the jurisdiction of the Archdiocese of Cincinnati. The commercial operation was split off and transferred to Sperti Inc., a company operated by Dr. George Sperti,

— continued on next page

director of the Institutium. Sperti later sold it to local businessmen William MacConnell and James Smith. None of them could make Rookwood profitable.

Herschede Hall Clock Co. bought the business in 1959 and, in a final revival attempt, moved it to Starkville, Mississippi, in 1960. By 1967, though, it was out of business for good.

The legacy of Rookwood lives on, however. Pottery is still sold at auctions locally. The Art Museum occasionally holds special Rookwood exhibits. And, if nothing else, the building has turned into a darn good restaurant.

one of the most attractive and popular in town. It's been voted Best Chinese by *Cincinnati Magazine* readers for so many years it might as well stop counting. For some tastes, the food is on the mild side, but it's always well-served and beautifully prepared. It's closed on Sunday.

Lemon Grass
$-$$ • 2666 Madison Rd., Hyde Park • 321-2882

Named favorite restaurant by the readers of *CityBeat* alternative newspaper, this Thai find serves up a spicy Panang Chicken Curry and other fare. Emphasis is on the attractive display of dishes as well as taste. Lunch is served on weekdays only.

LuLu's Noodles and Rice Shop
$, no credit cards • 135 W. Kemper Rd., Springdale • 671-4949

LuLu's occupies an unpretentious storefront in a shopping strip, but it's gaining critical acclaim. Noodle bowls generously overflow with plump shrimp or chicken and exotic Asian vegetables. It's closed on Sunday.

The Pacific Moon Cafe
$$ • 8300 Market Place Ln., Montgomery • 891-0091

Be sure to allow ample time to peruse the voluminous menu, which includes dishes from throughout the Pacific Rim. Chef Alex Chin has long been producing some of the city's finest Asian fare. Some of his specialties include ginger scallops (delivered table-side in a sizzling wok) and a steamed pike that's out of this world.

Song Phung
$$ • 637-A Northland Blvd., Forest Park • 825-9292

Fast becoming our favorite Vietnamese restaurant, this wonderful find is ensconced in a strip shopping center. No matter. There is no better Bun Ga in the region, the prices are fair, and the service prompt.

Ta Han Mongolian Bar-B-Q
$-$$ • 11483 Chester Rd., Sharonville • 772-5855

They call the fare authentic Mongolian cuisine. And you almost can picture Ghengis and the boys, after a hard day of terrorizing Eurasia, filing out of their yurts, filling up their plates with chopped meat, veggies and Ta Han's combination of nine sauces, and then gathering around the 48-inch-diameter steel conical woks as they share ribald tales of conquest. OK, not quite. But the food is superb, and the self-serve stir-fry concept is a winner. Ta Han is closed on Monday.

Tandoor India Restaurant
$$-$$$ • 8702 Market Place Ln., Montgomery • 793-7484

This casual, brightly decorated spot in a somewhat out of the way retail strip special-

INSIDERS' TIP

Want to try The Maisonette, the city's top-rated restaurant, without paying The Maisonette prices? Head to the downstairs La Normandie, a more casual restaurant that shares The Maisonette's kitchen and many of its same wonderful sauces.

izes in northern Indian cuisine, which is creamier and milder than dishes from the south side of the continent. Some of the best bets from an abundant menu include the Dal and Mulligatawny soup, the shish kebab and the tandoori mixed grill. A lunch buffet — always a good bet with relatively unfamiliar ethnic foods — is available weekdays, but lunch is not served on Saturday. Tandoor's is closed on Sunday.

Teak Thai Cuisine
$$ • 1049 St. Gregory St., Mount Adams
• 665-9800

Just when you thought Mount Adams didn't really need another great restaurant, another one comes along. The decor, including a giant mural, and the inventiveness of the dishes have quickly made Teak's one of the most popular Asian restaurants in town. Among the specialties are crab spring rolls and Thai sweet-and-sour pork. Lunch is served weekdays only. The restaurant is closed Monday.

Barbecue Joints

Cincinnati isn't exactly a rib capital along the lines of Memphis, but it does have a strong collection of distinctive ribs restaurants. Here are some favorites.

The Boathouse
$$ • 925 Eastern Ave. • 721-7427

Owner Ted Gregory is the undisputed Ribs King of Cincinnati. Indeed, comedian Bob Hope has a slab of Gregory's pork loin ribs flown to his California estate on a weekly basis, along with the special barbecue sauce. The Boathouse is our favorite of the Montgomery Inn ribs outlets (see the Montgomery Inn listing below) because of its striking view of the river, colorful sports memorabilia and nearby Bicentennial Commons riverfront park. The restaurant is bright with plenty of wide windows. The hustle and bustle, however, may discourage large groups or those with young kids. For dessert, indulge in another Cincinnati culinary tradition: Graeter's black raspberry chip ice cream. On your way out, purchase a bottle of the barbecue sauce at the gift shop to bring home.

Burbank's Real Bar-B-Q
$ • 11167 Dowlin Dr., Sharonville
• 771-1440
$ • I-75 and Buttermilk Pike (at Drawbridge Inn), Ft. Mitchell, Ky.
• (606) 341-2806
$ • 211 Forest Fair Dr., Forest Fair Mall
• 671-6330

Burbank's would be worth a visit if only to take in a little of the schtick of Cincinnati's most popular radio personality, Gary Burbank. Here's where you can buy the voluminous collections of annual Burbank tapes, featuring such popular characters as Earl Pitts and Gilbert G-N-A-R-L-E-Y. The menus are newspapers featuring Burbankesque humor. You can even catch Burbank's routines playing on the sound system in the bathroom. But don't overlook the food, which is still the main attraction. Besides ribs, other specialties include the pulled (shredded) pork platter and sandwich, smashed potatoes (with the skins) and super-sweet cornbread and sweet potatoes. The barbecue sauces also tend to the sweet side, harkening to Burbank's Memphis roots. They come in three levels of hotness, from mild to "911," which isn't really unbearably hot. Doc Wolfe, Burbank's former radio sidekick and now a successful cookbook author, concocted all the sauces.

Montgomery Inn
$$ • 9440 Montgomery Rd., Montgomery
• 791-3482

This is Cincinnati's most popular rib joint and must be counted among the area's culinary institutions. Ribs King Ted Gregory only lets the Ribs Queen know the secret recipe of the sauce, lest it slip into enemy hands. The sauce (also available in grocery stores throughout the region) is a somewhat less-sweet recipe that Cincinnatians simply love. The uncompromising quality of the ribs themselves also keeps 'em coming back. Other specialties include Saratoga chips (extra-thick potato chips with barbecue sauce on the side for dipping) and Pigs in a Pocket (rib meat with sauce in pita bread). You can also find Montgomery Inn ribs and sauce at such diverse locations as The Boathouse, Paramount's Kings Island and Coney Island.

Burger Joints

The high-end burger chains — Johnny Rockets, Fuddrucker's and Max & Erma's — are well-represented in the Greater Cincinnati area, with new ones popping up seemingly overnight. But you've probably been there, bun that. Besides, Cincinnati has some hometown burger joints that can compete with the best of the chains. See also Rookwood Pottery (American Traditional) and Arthur's (American Contemporary and Eclectic); these two establishments are a little too versatile to be labeled burger joints, but great hamburgers are one of their specialties.

City View Tavern
$, no credit cards • 403 Oregon St., Mount Adams • 241-8439

Finally, a place that lives up to its name. The City View Tavern has one of the finest views of the city anywhere, yet prices are dirt cheap. This no-frills Mount Adams bar and grill (they prefer the term "dive") serves burgers and, well, burgers. But what burgers they are! We've whiled away many an hour on the breezy patio. The "dive" is hard to find, so call for directions first. No lunch Monday through Wednesday.

Quatman Cafe
$, no credit cards • 2434 Quatman Ave., Norwood • 731-4370

There's nothing the least bit fancy about this place. Just good — and cheap — half-pound hamburgers and quick service. It's closed Sunday.

Zip's Cafe
$ • 1036 Delta Ave., Mount Lookout • 871-9876

An Insider hesitates even to mention Zip's because this place needs another customer like the Cincinnati city council needs another publicity hound. Every additional person who finds out about this local favorite burger joint is an additional person ahead of us in line. Alas, sense of duty prevails. Zip's offers some of the juiciest hamburgers this side of your backyard grill at reasonable prices in a cozy, quaint neighborhood diner. You can entertain yourself while you wait by watching sports on TV and entertain the little ones with the electric train that runs nonstop along the wall near the ceiling. This is no place for an intimate conversation, though. The booths and tables are crammed together.

Cincinnati Chili

If a Cincinnatian offers to take you out for a three-way, he's not making an improper suggestion. A three-way is Cincinnati chili in its most basic form — spaghetti below, grated cheddar cheese above and the chili in the middle. A four-way adds chopped onions on top. A five-way also mixes in kidney beans.

Blue Ash Chili
$, no credit cards • 9565 Kenwood Rd., Blue Ash • 984-6107

Get a glimpse of Blue Ash from before the days of sprawling, shimmering glass office buildings at this down-home chili and sandwich parlor. The restaurant is known for its huge double- and triple-deckers and a good rendition of Cincinnati-style chili. Closed Sunday.

Skyline Chili
$, no credit cards • 3822 Glenway Ave., Price Hill • 471-2445
$, no credit cards • Seventh and Vine Sts. • 241-2020
$, no credit cards • 290 Ludlow Ave., Clifton• 221-2142

There are 101 Skylines, but we've listed the original on Glenway Avenue (opened in 1949) and two other popular locations. We recommend Skyline over some other chains as Gold Star and Empress. Why? By popular consensus, it's the winner, selling 3,800 tons of the stuff a year. The recipe is still a closely guarded secret, but locals suspect cinnamon or cocoa gives the recipe its slightly sweet tinge. Skyline is a mandatory stop for campaigning presidential candidates as well as tourists; every four years, the Secret Service calls and asks to scout locations. Be aware: the original ambiance has given way to yuppified decor in the new Skylines.

Delis

Floyd's
$, no credit cards • 129 Calhoun St., Clifton • 221-2434

Floyd's serves some excellent roasted chicken marinated in Mediterranean spices, in addition to dolmas, falafel, hummus, tabouli and other well-prepared Middle Eastern staples. Extremely reasonable prices make this one of the better deals on the university-area strip, or anywhere in town. Floyd's is open weekdays only.

Izzy's
$, no credit cards • 819 Elm St. • 721-4241
$, no credit cards • 610 Main St. • 241-6246

This Cincinnati culinary institution is famous for its kosher sandwiches piled high with corned beef, pastrami and other meats. It's also known for the large, thick and delectable potato pancakes that come with every sandwich, great fresh kosher dill pickle slices and sauerkraut condiments, and its lively kitchen banter. "You're only a stranger once," is one of the late Izzy Kadetz's mottos. And even strangers get treated pretty well. Payment is on the honor system, so you just tell the cashier what you ate and pay for it. Izzy's is closed Sunday.

Italian

With all due apologies to Italians, we've taken some liberties here by including under the Italian heading some restaurants with a decidedly American twist.

No Anchovies Pizza
$, no credit cards • 324 Ludlow Ave., Clifton • 221-2277

An impressive array of toppings (includ-ing, despite the name, anchovies) and the hand-tossed pizza dough make this a popular choice for the University of Cincinnati crowd. A ham and pineapple pizza and the Groovy Pizza (spinach and feta) are the most popular choices.

New York Noodles
$, no credit cards • 633 Vine St. • 421-2220

A wonderful spot for a quick lunch, this no-frills pasta joint serves cafeteria style. Downtowners love the Rigatoni à la Vodka and the Sun-Dried Pesto with Bowties. It's open weekdays only.

Pomodori's Pizzeria and Trattoria
$ • 121 W. McMillan St., Clifton Heights • 861-0080

Fans come from far and wide to sample the delectable wood-fired pizzas, especially the leeks pancetta and goat cheese, the gorgonzola walnut, and Pomodori's famous apple pizza. There's also now a Pomodori's outlet in Montgomery, but this one is the original and still champ. The brick and copper decor and unusual offerings make this pizzaria several cuts above your typical college pizza joint.

Pompilio's
$ • 600 Washington St., Newport, Ky. • (606) 581-3065

Dustin Hoffman, Tom Cruise and the gang from *Rain Man* made this Newport institution famous, but it should have been anyway. The now-named Rain Man Sampler, which includes spaghetti, lasagna and eggplant parmesan, was a favorite of the movie crew, and it's still a good choice for an overview of the delicious, reasonably priced Italian fare. An intricately carved wooden bar and large circular mirrors make the decor a throwback to many periods past. You can also play bocce ball (Italian lawn bowling) out back.

INSIDERS' TIP

Downtowners with a sweet tooth know to head to Fred and Gari's, a tiny takeout joint at Sixth and Vine that sells the most delicious pies in town — by the slice or whole pie. (Take the whole pie and run.)

Photo: The Cincinnatian Hotel

The Cincinnatian Hotel offers elegant dining in the luxurious Palace Restaurant

Primavista
$$$ • 810 Matson Pl., Price Hill
• 251-6467

Primavista offers one of the most striking views of downtown of any restaurant in Cincinnati, and fantastic northern Italian cuisine as well. The Salmone in Sacco (salmon in a paper bag) is a standout. Primavista serves dinner only.

Scalea's Ristorante
$$ • 318 Greenup St., Covington, Ky.
• (606) 491-3334

Anita Hirsch-Cunningham is perhaps the city's best-known chef, so when she chose to go out on her own (she has worked at the prestigious Precinct and Palace restaurants) and open Scalea's Ristorante, the critics took notice. The chef is known for her innovative twists on traditional fare as well as her daring fusion cuisine. Scalea's is a reference to nearby Scalea's Italian Market, which first opened in 1925 and has a long history in the city.

Spazzi
$$-$$$ • 14 W. Pete Rose Pier,
Covington, Ky. • (606) 291-9025

This latest upstairs addition to the Waterfront complex adds liberal doses of culinary imagination to Northern Italian cuisine at what's already one of Cincinnati's favorite dining destinations. Owners include Tommy Lasorda, the former Los Angeles Dodgers' manager well-known for his love of pasta. This casual and somewhat loud riverfront restaurant offers an antipasto bar well-stocked with great appetizers, pizzas baked in wood-fired ovens and other Italian meat and seafood dishes. Spazzi serves dinner only and is closed Sunday.

Tony Palbino's Pizzeria and Cucina
$$ • 7791 Cooper Rd., Montgomery
• 985-0505

Wood-roasted pizza pies are generously topped (a 10-inch comfortably feeds two). The Greco is our favorite — tomato pesto with grilled chicken, feta, olives and mozzarella. Gourmet salads also put Palbino's a cut above most similarly priced family restaurants.

Mexican and Tex-Mex

Amigo's
$ • 8111 Cincinnati-Dayton Hwy., West Chester • 777-9424

The Leal and Rodriguez families, who own this restaurant, bill it as having 100 percent authentic Mexican food, and we have no reason to doubt them. The menu even includes a section of Mexican soft drinks. This is also one of the best dining deals in town, with good food in huge quantities at very reasonable prices. Like most of the best ethnic food spots in town, it's hidden in a nondescript strip shopping center. But it towers above chain Mexican fare and even beats some locally owned competitors. The atmosphere is informal and shopping-centerish, but the investment here has obviously been made in the food. The menu is complete, both in offerings and descriptions for the uninitiated. Lunch is not served on Sunday.

Blue Cactus Grill
$$ • 7846 Cincinnati-Dayton Rd., West Chester • 779-6826

Thanks to its location in West Chester, Blue Cactus has been named best Mexican restaurant in both Cincinnati and Dayton by various publications. It's also been named twice as one of the top 50 Hispanic restaurants in the United States by *Hispanic* magazine. The salsa here is tasty, with unusually thick chips. Fruta con queso — fresh peach slices with chopped onion, jalapeño and cheese between tortillas — is an original twist worth trying. Carnitas are another specialty you can order as hot as you wish. Lunch is not served on Saturday, and the restaurant is closed Sunday.

Burrito Joe's
$, no credit cards • 364 Ludlow Ave., Clifton • 751-2911
$, no credit cards • 39 E. Court St. • 381-5637
$, no credit cards • 328 E. Fourth St. • 721-5637

Pick from chicken, beef or black bean burritos, with a mix of toppings that includes a range of veggies, three types of salsa, sour cream and guacamole. They've also got imaginative burritos-of-the-day, including Jamaican, Thai and Cajun versions, as well as a fish burrito. Lunch only is served, Monday through Friday.

Cactus Pear
$$ • 3215 Jefferson Ave., Corryville • 961-7400

They may be short on Tex-Mex authenticity, but they're long on imagination at this popular university-area restaurant. Don't miss the chunky salsa. Other specialties include the fajitas, red pepper noodles with pasta and grilled chicken with vegetables. Lunch is served on weekdays.

El Coyote
$$ • 7404 State Rd., Anderson • 232-5757

One of three El Coyotes in the region, but this one is the original. Nothing beats their pork tenderloin fajitas, though the empanada — a baked pastry pie stuffed with shredded beef, cheese and onions — is a close second. It's always packed, and no, they don't take reservations. Nonsmokers may be discouraged by the absence of a nonsmoking section. No lunch is served during the week.

Microbreweries

A year ago, we didn't even need this category. Now there are close to a dozen microbreweries/restaurants at all points of the compass. Here's a sampling.

BrewWorks
$$ • 1115 Main St., Covington, Ky. • (606) 581-2739

Housed in the abandoned Bavarian Brewing Factory, BrewWorks offers an aggressive menu that includes pan-seared shrimp in barbecue sauce and cornmeal crusted trout. Ambiance is early-American factory — lots of steel and rust. Locals favor Mephistopheles Metamorphosis, brewed the first Friday of each month. It's closed on Sunday.

Main Street Brewery
$$ • 1203 Main St., Over-the-Rhine • 665-4677

At the hub of the Main Street renaissance in Over-the-Rhine, Main Street Brewery touts its Main Street Meatloaf with garlic mashed potatoes as a signature dish. But the lobster chimichanga is not to be missed. Front and center, of course, are the brews. Regulars are also partial to the 5-Layer Oyster Shooter, an oyster with layers of mustard, cocktail sauce, horseradish, sour cream and a shot of pepper vodka. It's closed Sunday and Monday.

Rock Bottom Brewery
$$ • 10 Fountain Square • 621-1588

If the Tyler Davidson Fountain is the city's most recognizable landmark (the lady with her outspread hands on the cover of this book), then what trip would be complete without a visit to Fountain Square? And the Rock Bottom Brewery. Five microbrews are made on site, but only one is pure Cincinnati — the malty Crosley Field Pale Ale. We also like the Alder Smoked Fish & Chips, a beer-battered cold smoked salmon.

Teller's of Hyde Park
$$ • 2710 Erie Ave., Hyde Park • 321-4721

This trendy Hyde Park Square establishment opened inside a savings and loan bank building, and it even uses old safety deposit box drawers as centerpieces. You'll find plenty of real bankers to go with the theme. Teller's serves up tasty yuppie chow, such as gourmet Portobello pizza and grilled tuna, along with plenty of handcrafted microbrews.

Watson Bros. Brewhouse
$$ • 4785 Lake Forest Dr., Blue Ash • 563-9797

Yet another entry in Cincinnati's growing microbrewery wars, this one offers lakeside dining and an outdoor patio. The varied menu offerings include Shepherd's Pie and spaghetti Carbonara. But the brewskies are the stars, mellow and magnificent.

Northern European

At the risk of rekindling ancient continental animosities, we'll lump the French and German restaurants together here.

Chez Alphonse
$$$ • 654 Highland Ave., Fort Thomas, Ky. • (606) 442-5488

Alphonse Kaelbel, for decades the maitre d' at The Maisonette, went to the Hotel Ritz in London a few years ago. Now he's back in Greater Cincinnati, opening the first new formal dining restaurant the town has seen in years. Jacket and tie are required, 'natch. Crystal, linen and tuxedoed staff await you. Menu is traditional French (terrine of foie gras, breast of duck, dover sole), though the standout entree in our mind is the seabass in a dark sauce of truffles. Dinner only. Closed Sunday. Reservations are required on weekends.

The Celestial
$$$-$$$$ • 1071 Celestial St., Mount Adams • 241-4455

The Celestial offers one of the best views from any restaurant in Greater Cincinnati. The menu's in French, the cuisine is continental European with some American twists, and the atmosphere is formal — jacket and tie required for men at dinner, no jeans or shorts anytime ('natch). Favorite dishes include rack of lamb, poached scallops in curry sauce and delicious desserts. Complimentary valet parking is available. Lunch is not served on Saturday. The Celestial is closed on Sunday.

Forest View Gardens
$$ • 4508 North Bend Rd., Monfort Heights • 661-6434

We'll set the scene with wiener schnitzel served by the Garden's famous singing waitresses. Specialties at this German restaurant include sauerbraten and brats, plus German raspberry mousse torte and double-chocolate mousse desserts. It's closed Monday through Wednesday; lunch is served Tuesday through Friday only.

The Maisonette
$$$$ • 114 E. Sixth St. • 721-2260

They stopped making superlatives large enough to describe this landmark French restaurant a few years back. Undoubtedly, it's the best restaurant in Cincinnati. Bigger-city snobs might say "So what," but it's also one of the dozen highest-rated restaurants in the United States and the only one to maintain that rating for 34 consecutive years. Impeccable service, Old World charm and the lighter, contemporary cuisine of chef Jean-Robert de Cavel are what currently earn The Maisonette its reputation. Menus change based on what's fresh and what suits Chef de Cavel's fancy. Some favorites you'll usually find include the lobster bisque, New Zealand rack of lamb and a chef's sampler menu that also changes seasonally. The most popular drink is their Maisonette Cocktail (champagne and framboise), the most popular appetizer is lobster bisque, and the most called-for dessert is their signature white chocolate mousse.

Old-fashioned phone jacks along the wall (now painted over in The Maisonette's salmon hue) point out that this was a venue for the most powerful of power meals long before the cell phone came along. But some tradition has given way to modern demands in this most traditional of restaurants. Men are no longer required to wear ties, though they must wear jackets. And the menu is now in English, though the French influence remains in most dishes.

Like to look for famous faces at the next table? Spotted dining here recently were Andy Rooney, Vidal Sassoon, Susan Lucci, Suzanne Somers, Jerry Lewis, Rod Stewart and Woody Harrelson (a local boy made good). You can forget getting in on a Saturday night without a reservation. Partner Michael E. Comisar estimates that while Bill and Hillary would post 1-to-2 odds and Ohio's governor might earn even odds of getting a table unannounced on a Saturday, the rest of us should make reservations a month in advance.

Do make reservations for dinner or lunch, which moves at a leisurely pace and includes only two seating nightly. Lunch is served Tuesday through Friday only. It's closed Sunday.

Mecklenberg Gardens
$$ • 302 E. University Ave., Corryville • 221-5353

The rebirth of this once-great restaurant, which closed in the 1980s, marks a welcome comeback to what had become a rundown corner of Corryville. The German-influenced cuisine, including tasty chicken and pork schnitzel, is rife with creative touches, from creamy gorgonzola salad dressings on way-above-average garden salads to the citrus cheesecake or Black Forest cake for dessert.

The Sherman House
$$ • 35 S. Main St., Batesville, Ind.
• (812) 934-2407, (800) 445-4939

One of the better German restaurants in the area is this out-of-town, beautifully decorated Old World-style inn, established in 1852. Try the schnitzel, which is especially good. Breakfast is also served.

Scottish

Nicholson's Tavern & Pub
$$ • 625 Walnut St. • 564-9111

Cincinnati's only Scottish restaurant, Nicholson's opened to much newspaper fanfare in 1998. It deserves the attention. Step inside and you're positive you've been transported to a British Isles pub, right down to the menu of Scotch eggs, bangers and mash, and sticky toffee pudding. The bar features 67 single-malt Scotches and 16 British Isle beers on draft. There's no lunch on weekends.

Seafood

For being a thousand miles from the nearest ocean, Cincinnati has an ongoing love affair with fresh seafood. Perhaps it's BECAUSE we are a thousand miles from the beach.

Arboreta
$$ • 1133 Sycamore St. • 721-1133

The succulent Thai-flavored seabass, lobster/shrimp rolls and the Autumn Salad (with dried fruits, nuts, goat cheese and apple fritters) top a diverse menu. Arboreta is open every day for dinner.

Dockside VI
$$ • 4747 Montgomery Rd., Norwood • 351-6000

A nautical theme with lots of fish tanks makes this a fun trip for the entire family.

Booths are cozy and private. The house specialty is the mixed grill of beef, shrimp and the catch of the day. Lunch is not served on weekends.

The E Room
$$ • 10 E. RiverCenter Blvd., Covington, Ky. • (606) 261-8400

The E Room at the Embassy Suites Hotel is our favorite hotel restaurant for two reasons: It's reasonably priced — for what you get and considering the terrific river view — and it hasn't been discovered yet by locals, so there's rarely a crowd. Top-notch seafood includes the blackened salmon fillet with five-onion sour cream. Lunch is not served on Sunday.

Four Seasons Restaurant
$-$$ • 4609 Kellogg Ave., California • 871-1820

East side families flock to the Four Seasons for its reasonable prices and river ambiance. A New England nautical theme livens up this marina restaurant. There's a predictable selection of lobster and crab, but the breaded, deep-fried walleye is the tastiest in town. The restaurant is closed Monday.

J's Fresh Seafood
$$-$$$ • 2444 Madison Rd., Hyde Park • 871-2888

This award-winning restaurant with its amazingly fresh fare enjoys about the best reputation a seafood place can have in Cincinnati. It's in the *Cincinnati Magazine* hall of fame and has received an Award of Excellence from *Wine Spectator*. The antipasti table includes 20 appetizers, and the wine list has 250 entries. It's closed on Monday.

Michael G's
$$ • 4601 Kellogg Ave., Columbia-Tusculum • 533-3131

Overlooking the Rivertowne marina and swimming in elegance, Michael G's offers live jazz and a dish not often seen in Cincinnati: conch chowder. There is a full selection of ocean and freshwater fish, including catfish, tilapia and the finest lake trout in town. Lunch is not served on Saturday, but do try the Sunday brunch.

Mount Adams Fish House
$$$ • 940 Pavilion St., Mount Adams • 421-3250

Cincinnati diners can get a different spin on seafood at this Asian-influenced restaurant. Some of the better offerings include the swordfish steak, planked salmon in Pinot Noir sauce cooked on a cedar board to give it a woodsy flavor, and a sushi bar with a wide array of offerings. It's open for lunch Monday through Friday and for dinner Monday through Saturday.

Pelican's Reef
$ • 7261 Beechmont Ave., Anderson • 232-CLAM

A delight you'd never expect to find in a strip mall, Pelican's Reef is more reminiscent of those friendly little fish 'n' beer shacks you find along Florida's coast. A sea motif and casual atmosphere (no napkins, just rolls of paper towels at each table) make this a nifty place. The calamari is consistently voted best in town by local restaurant polls, but we like the grilled halibut. The prices can't be beat either.

Seafood 32
$$$ • 150 W. Fifth St. (at the Regal Hotel) • 352-2160

Some of Cincinnati's best seafood comes with a revolving view atop the Regal Hotel downtown. Actually, the menu offers as much steak, lamb and duck as it does fresh fish. Still, there's a full selection, from crayfish to snapper. Dinner is served Monday through Saturday.

Sloppy Joe's
$$ • 101 Riverboat Row, Newport, Ky. • (606) 581-2800

No visit to Cincinnati is complete without driving across the Ohio River and onto Riverboat Row in neighboring Kentucky. Kentucky is blessed with the most outstanding view of the city skyline. The theme at Sloppy Joe's is tropical, with lots of Ernest Hemingway puns. This casual seafood house (butcher paper on the tables) is a reasonable deal, by Riverboat Row standards anyhow.

Sweeney's Seafood House
$ • 8372 Reading Rd., Reading • 821-3654

Residents know to head here for the most

reasonably priced seafood in town. The owners tout their Lemon Parmesan Tilapia, though the Norwegian salmon can't be beat either. A New England coastal motif rounds out the nautical experience. It's closed on Monday.

Steakhouses

Cincinnati has the full complement and ever-growing numbers of chain steakhouses, including Outback, Longhorn, Lone Star, Mountain Jack's and so on. Below is a review of some homegrown steakhouses worth noting.

Morton's of Chicago
$$$-$$$$ • Tower Place at Carew Tower • 241-4104

We've violated the "no chain restaurants" rule here because (1) there are very few of these chain restaurants nationwide and (2) it's one of the better steakhouses in town. You'd better be hungry if you plan on eating dinner here, as the portions are huge. Try the double filet with béarnaise sauce or, for non-steak lovers, the chicken oregano. Morton's serves dinner only.

The Precinct
$$$$ • 311 Delta Ave., Columbia-Tusculum • 321-5454

Located in a converted police precinct house, The Precinct is Cincinnati's most prestigious — and priciest — steakhouse. Steaks are named after local sports celebs, and you're as likely to see those same sports celebs dining at the next table as not. A popular entree is the Steak Collinsworth, a filet crowned with crabmeat and sauce béarnaise. Heaven. Open for dinner only.

Ice Cream Parlors

So they're not exactly restaurants — we didn't want you to miss them!

Aglamesis Brothers
$ • 3046 Madison Rd., Oakley • 531-5196
$ • 9887 Montgomery Rd., Montgomery • 791-7082

Aglamesis is Cincinnati's little secret. The Aglamesis brothers, like those other Greek immigrants, the chili-making Lambrindes brothers, have graced the city with one of its culinary landmarks. Most Cincinnatians will tell you Graeter's is the best ice cream in Cincinnati, maybe even the world. But only one Cincinnati ice cream parlor has been featured in *Bon Appetit* and the *Mobil Travel Guide*, and it's not Graeter's. Make no mistake: Graeter's is great, but Aglamesis really has the best ice cream in Cincinnati.

The ambiance of the original Aglamesis Oakley store also scores points. Aglamesis Brothers still operates the same quaint, old-fashioned ice cream parlor where it all began in 1908. Aglamesis chocolates, made at the same location, are nothing to sneeze at either.

Graeter's
$ • 2704 Erie Ave., Hyde Park Square, Hyde Park • 321-6221
$ • 332 Ludlow Ave., Clifton • 281-4749
$ • 6918 Wooster Ave., Mariemont • 272-0859
Multiple additional locations

Graeter's is the oldest surviving ice cream manufacturer in America (125 years) and the only one left that still makes ice cream using the French pot method. The huge dark chocolate chunks in Graeter's chip flavors — the best being black raspberry chip and chocolate mocha chip — are where Graeter's enjoys clear superiority to every ice cream on earth. Another big advantage for Graeter's is its abundance of locations — 14 of them, including one in just about every major suburban area and several places where people are found taking leisurely strolls on summer afternoons and evenings, such as the town squares in Clifton, Hyde Park and Mariemont. You also can buy Graeter's by the pint at Kroger stores. Graeter's is a Cincinnati institution akin to Skyline Chili, available democratically to persons of all creeds and neighborhood origins.

United Daily Farmers
$ • 1124 St. Gregory St., Mount Adams • 723-1900
$ • 1301 Western Ave., Queensgate (inside Museum Center) • 721-4985
Multiple additional locations

United Daily Farmers, UDF for short, is a Cincinnati staple. The convenience stores are found on practically every block, but the ice cream parlors within are particularly notable. Try a cone with the UDF brand's signature cookies 'n' creme first.

Although there are a hundred UDFs spread around the area, we've listed two above that are particularly notable. The Mount Adams UDF is sparkling new with all the yupscale amenities (it's a big hangout for WLW and WEBN radio types who work across the street, too). The Queensgate location is actually located inside the Museum Center, housed in a Rookwood tile-lined ice cream parlor. If you go to another location for a milkshake, however, be aware that not every UDF has a soda fountain.

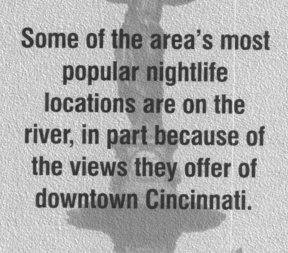

Some of the area's most popular nightlife locations are on the river, in part because of the views they offer of downtown Cincinnati.

Nightlife

Like any vibrant metropolitan area, Greater Cincinnati has an abundance of nightlife. There's a place here for everybody, regardless of musical preference, age or social status. You can boot scoot, disco, line dance, slam dance, sumo wrestle, arm wrestle, rub elbows with celebrities, watch five games at once, drink alcohol, drink Perrier, play pinball, play volleyball, sing along, sail, laugh, cry or even do your laundry all in the name of nightlife.

And like other vibrant metropolitan areas, the segments of nightlife seem to be congregated into certain areas. We've broken down our listings by those areas.

It would be impractical, however, to list in this chapter all the bars, nightclubs and other such entertainment establishments in the area. There are simply too many, and they change too fast. So rather than list every joint, pub, saloon, club and lounge from the Du Drop Inn on Eastern Avenue to Big Mama's on Compton Road, we just mention those institutions that are a tried-and-true part of the area's social scene.

And it should be duly noted that there's more to nightlife than just bellying up to a bar. This chapter examines some different nocturnal options as well. Other types of nightlife, though, may overlap with other chapters in this book. Concerts by the Cincinnati Symphony Orchestra or Pops, for instance, are listed in the Arts chapter. Sports events are in the Spectator Sports chapter. Restaurants often feature bands and other types of entertainment. (Conversely, if a nightspot listed in this chapter serves food, chances are you'll find a write-up about it in our Restaurants chapter.) We encourage you to check out these other chapters as well.

You will find that most of the nightspots listed in this chapter have a cover charge, particularly those that have live bands performing. Most cover charges will be a minimum of $3, although they can get as high as $8 or more, so be prepared. Also be prepared to be carded no matter where you go. The legal drinking age in Ohio, Kentucky and Indiana is 21, and many bars won't let anyone in — even older adults with graying hair who haven't been younger than 21 in many years — without some sort of identification. And even though some bars cater to those 19 and older, that doesn't necessarily mean they serve liquor to those customers. Bars shut down at 2 AM, and it is very illegal to drink and drive anything — including boats and bicycles — with a blood-alcohol level of more than .10.

Oh, and one final note regarding this chapter: Despite the attempts by local law enforcement agencies to purify the area from certain, shall we say, not-so-morally-correct forms of dancing, such entertainment clubs do exist. It is not our position here, however, to inform you of the locations of such establishments, despite arguments that they are rightfully considered nightlife. If you want to frequent such places, you can find them easily enough without our help.

Cinemas

If you want to catch a movie, Greater Cincinnati has nearly 20 multi-screen megaplex theaters that feature first- and second-run films, in addition to a couple of drive-ins and numerous smaller cinemas that feature foreign, art, classic or cult films.

Discount Cinemas

Central Parke 11
4600 Smith Rd., Norwood • 531-7655

Central Parke, which sits at the Montgomery Road exit off the Norwood Lateral, offers 11 screens showing recent releases. All seats for all shows are $2.

Danbarry Dollar Saver Cinema
5190 Glencrossing Way, Western Hills
• 451-2300

All seats at Danbarry's 12-screen cinema are $1.75 at all times. All of the movies are either blockbusters at the tail-end of their showings or lesser-known titles. Matinees are shown daily and late shows are offered Friday and Saturday nights.

Marianne Theater
607 Fairfield Ave., Bellevue, Ky.
• (606)291-6666

Located in the heart of historic Bellevue, the Marianne Theater is a leftover from the days of community movie cinemas. The theater has just one screen and has just one showing a night except on weekends, when the movie is shown twice. The movies are second run, but tickets are only $1. And you can't beat the old-time ambiance.

Midway Theater
210 W. Plane, Bethel • 734-2278

The Midway Theater is a discount cinema in price only, as it somehow manages to offer first-run blockbuster movies for only $4. It's not well-advertised outside of Bethel but it's worth the effort to find out what's showing and make the drive.

SuperSaver Cinemas
601 Forest Fair Dr., Forest Park
• 671-1710
Biggs Place, Eastgate • 753-6588

The SuperSaver Cinemas are a great alternative if you're not in a hurry to see a film as soon as it comes out. The cinemas offer recently introduced movies for only $2, although not for a month or so from the initial release date. Each of the cinemas offers seven or eight movie options and a $1 special before noon on weekdays.

Turfway Park 10
7650 Turfway Rd., Florence, Ky.
• (606) 647-2828

Turfway Park 10 is the sister cinema to Central Parke 11. It offers three blockbuster first-run movies at discount prices. The selected blockbusters can be seen for $6.50 at night and $4.35 during matinees; children 10 and younger and senior citizens 65 and older get in for $4.25. All other shows are $2.

Alternative Film Theaters

Emery Theatre
1112 Walnut St. • 721-2741

The Emery is a Cincinnati treasure. This old-time theater not only serves as a place for plays, but shows movies as well. Concerts are given on the theater's Wurlitzer organ — a leftover from the silent movie days — at intermission. The Marx Bros., Laurel & Hardy and such older classics are the types of movies shown. The theater is located in the Ohio College of Applied Science building at the corner of Walnut Street and Central Parkway. Showings are Saturday at 7:30 PM, Sunday matinee at 2:30 PM. Adult admission is $4, children $2.

FYI

Unless otherwise noted, the area code for all phone numbers listed in this guide is 513.

Esquire Theater
320 Ludlow Ave. • 281-8750

The Esquire is a small, three-screen theater that offers art and alternative films. It was, for instance, the only place in Greater Cincinnati to show the Academy Award-winning *Shine*. The theater is a bit of a throwback in that it sits in the heart of the quaint Clifton business district, just as it did in the 1940s. Its location allows moviegoers a great variety of after-movie dessert, coffee or drink options. Matinees are shown daily, and Tuesdays are Bargain Days, with movies $3.50 all day.

Mariemont Theater
6910 Wooster Pike, Mariemont
• 271-8887

The Mariemont Theater is a sister theater to the Esquire and also offers alternative movies. Like the Esquire, it has matinees daily and Bargain Tuesdays with films all day for $3.50. The theater, which dates back to 1938, sits in the middle of the upscale Mariemont Square, a replica of an English Tudor village with shops, restaurants and plenty of after-movie options.

Drive-Ins

Oakley Drive-In
5033 Madison Rd. • 271-4600

For a blast from the past, put down the rag top, slick back your hair and cruise to Oakley Drive-In. It shows first-run movies for a fraction of the cost of cinemas, and can actually be very inexpensive if you pay by the carload. A warning, though: It fills up very fast on warm summer nights.

Starlite Drive-In
2255 Ohio Pike, Monroe • 734-4001

The Starlite also shows first-run movies for a fraction of the cost of indoor theaters, and it, too, fills up very fast on warm summer nights. And for a real throwback of a day, check out the flea market that sits adjacent to the Starlite.

Cinema Grills

Covedale Cinema Grill
4990 Glenway Ave. • 251-2000

The cinema grill concept was so popular in Mount Lookout, the owners decided to open one on the West Side in January 1998. Diners here have three movies to choose from. Tickets are $2.50 and $1.50 for matinees, with Mondays being Movie Madness days and admission only $1 and Tuesdays being Two-for-One nights. No one under age 18 is admitted without a guardian.

Mt. Lookout Cinema Grill
3187 Linwood Ave. • 321-3211

The owners of Mt. Lookout Cinema Grill took out the traditional movie seats from the old theater on Mount Lookout Square and replaced them with tables and chairs where moviegoers can sit and be served dinner while watching a movie. Diners have the option of one of four movies. Tickets are $3.50

and $2.00 for matinees, plus you pay for whatever you decide to eat. Mondays are Movie Madness days and admission is $1. No one under age 18 is admitted without a guardian.

Comedy Clubs

Go Bananas
8410 Market Place, Montgomery • 984-9288

Go Bananas features top-of-the-line comics from around the country, many of whom are regularly seen on HBO or Showtime. Generally, you can find out who is performing by listening to local radio stations — the comics get on the morning shows and rattle off a few gags in hopes of boosting attendance. Call for reservations.

Concert Venues

Bogart's
2621 Vine Street • 281-8400

Bogart's, which is located in University Village, brings in many smaller national acts to its 1,300-seat venue, but occasionally has a major act that's looking for a cozier setting. Carly Simon, for instance, kicked off her nationwide tour here in 1995. Bogart's likes to bill itself as one of the Midwest's premier rock halls, and that's not far from the truth. B.B. King, George Thorogood, Megadeath, Johnny Land and Warren Zevon have performed here. The telephone number above is a 24-hour concert line.

Coyote's
400 Buttermilk Pike, Fort Mitchell, Ky. • (606) 341-5150

On the country side, Coyote's brings in small- to medium-size country acts. Coyote's is located in the Drawbridge Estate, along I-75 at Buttermilk Pike.

INSIDERS' TIP

Coffeehouses with dozens of exotic blends are popular in the area and a great way to cap off an evening. Many also feature bands or musicians.

The Crown
Broadway and Pete Rose Way
• 721-1000

During the winter, concerts head indoors, and the major shows are held at the 16,000-seat The Crown. The Crown — formerly Riverfront Coliseum — was purchased in 1996 and underwent extensive renovation. The facility is now much cleaner and has plush seats and additional concession stands, including some where you can buy microbrewed beer made in vats in the arena's lower level. And some really good news for female concertgoers — the number of women's restrooms was doubled. The new owners also brought in the Michigan-based Nederlander Group to manage the facility. Nederlander books major concerts throughout the country, including those at Riverbend during the summer months.

As a concert facility, the Crown is generally like any other indoor arena, with the stage at one end of an oval and concertgoers wrapped around the stage. Tickets for all concerts have assigned seating.

Peacock Pavilion
Cincinnati Zoo, 3400 Vine Street
• 281-4701.

Another concert setting with an interesting backdrop is the Peacock Pavilion at the Cincinnati Zoo. The zoo books medium-size national acts, many (but not all) of which are jazz acts that perform as part of the annual Jazzoo series. Recent acts performing as part of Jazzoo have included the Doobie Brothers and Big Head Todd & The Monsters. Pay for a concert and admission to the zoo is included.

Riverbend Music Center
I-275 and Kellogg Avenue, Anderson
• 232-6220

Riverbend is the primary site of Greater Cincinnati's musical mania each year. This outdoor amphitheater seats roughly 5,000 in its covered pavilion and another 13,000-plus on its sloping grass lawn area.

Every major musical act eventually performs here. There's some kind of concert on virtually every night during the spring, summer and early fall — when the river allows. Riverbend, as its name suggests, sits along a bend in the Ohio River. Each spring when April showers are bringing May flowers, the river tends to overflow its banks and put the stage and half the pavilion seats under water. So if you're planning to attend a concert in the spring, don't be surprised if it's canceled and rescheduled for a date later in the summer.

The venue, which shares space with Coney Island, Sunlite Pool and River Downs racetrack, has two 10-by-14 video screens to the back of the pavilion structure and turns a camera on the stage, so those with lawn seats can get a close-up of the performers. It's a nice addition. Riverbend also just began letting kids 4 and younger sit on the lawn for free with an adult who has a lawn ticket.

Riverbend does have its drawbacks. Because of a lawsuit a few years ago, it now lets cars park for "free" in the parking lot, but adds a $2 surcharge for parking to each ticket, so it doesn't pay to carpool because you're paying for parking whether you drive or not. Also, because shows are held rain or shine, the lawn tends to get torn up during the spring rains and has a hard time recovering the rest of the summer. As a result, it can sometimes become quite muddy, despite efforts to keep it repaired.

For some concerts, lawn chairs are allowed. If the lawn is packed, though, and those in chairs block the view of those behind them, forget it. Generally, blankets are recommended for all shows. Also, umbrellas are not allowed, nor are bottles, cans, alcohol or drinks of any kind. Bringing your own food, though, is allowed but not in coolers. A stack of forbidden goodies is usually piled outside the entrances where people drop them rather than haul them back to their cars.

Timberwolf Amphitheater
Paramount's Kings Island, Kings Mill
• 573-5700

The 10,000-seat Timberwolf Amphitheater is another popular concert venue. The theater is inside the amusement park but is a sepa-

Photo: Greater Cincinnati Convention and Visitors Bureau

The city's riverfront is a lively spot come nightfall.

rate entity. Tickets to the park do not get you into the theater, nor do tickets to the theater get you into the park. The screams from the riders on the nearby roller coasters make an interesting backdrop for shows, however. The general feeling — or hope — of the developers was that performers who record on the Paramount label would stage shows at the park because of the common ownership, although to date that hasn't proven true.

Entertainment Districts

Corryville/Clifton

The Corryville/Clifton entertainment district is populated mostly by college students from the nearby University of Cincinnati, and as a result the clubs tend to be geared toward the interests of today's twenty-something crowd. Alternative, punk and hard rock music are popular, along with moshing, black clothes, boots, body piercing and tattoos, although that is not the limit of the nightspots in Corryville.

Clifton Bay Yacht Club & Reggae Lounge
115 W. McMillan St. • 559-9863

All right, so Cincinnati doesn't exactly sit on a bay or have a lot of yachts, it's the atmosphere that counts. Clifton Bay provides that by serving up reggae, mon, to go with the pool on the front deck, a tiki bar on the back deck, fooseball, dancing and Caribbean cuisine.

Corinthian Restaurant & Lounge
3253 Jefferson Ave. • 961-0013

Although the name conjures up Greek images, Corinthian spans the globe for entertainment and dance music. It becomes a particularly popular place on Fridays, when it has Latino nights. Patrons jam the club, with its abundance of tropical plants spread about, including a canopy of plants hanging from the ceiling, and dance to the sounds of Latino music. Another great benefit is that the restaurant, which offers Greek, Italian and American food, doesn't close until 11 PM.

Fries Cafe
3247 Jefferson Ave. • 281-9002

Fries is two and sometimes three bars in one. Its first floor bar is as basic as it gets, with tables and a bar for sitting and a jukebox, fooseball and shuffleboard tables as entertainment. Upstairs is a pool lounge with nothing but pool tables. During the warm months, an outdoor patio makes a third bar, with two bocci ball courts and an outdoor grill.

Mad Frog
1. E. McMillan St. • 784-9119

Mad Frog is one of the newer bars in Corryville, taking the longtime spot of Cory's on the highly traveled corner of E. McMillan and Vine streets. Mad Frog is two bars in one — a front bar section that is a traditional bar, and a larger, more open back room with a stage on one side of the room and a second bar on the other. Mad Frog's focus is blues, with the area's top blues acts playing in the bar. And for a long evening, the pool table is free from 4 PM to 8 PM before the bands start playing.

Mecklenburg Gardens
302 E. University Ave. • 221-5353

Mecklenburg Gardens, located at the corner of E. University and Highland avenues, is a 130-year-old German biergarten that served German immigrants at the turn of the century. Mecklenburg has opened and closed twice, but this time it is placing a stronger emphasis on the beer part, with 60 different beers in bottles and 16 on tap. And half of the 60 wines are available by the glass. It is a bit too far off the beaten path for university students to cram into, which offers a respite from the rowdiness. Its patio in the summer is built around trees that have long grown there and a vine-covered arbor.

Murphy's Pub
2329 Clifton Ave. • 721-6148

Darts is the king of the bar games at Murphy's, which offers two pool tables, sev-

eral video games and five dart boards. At different times of the year the pub holds tournaments and leagues for those with enough skill to hit the bull's eye. The bar, which opened in 1970, offers a wide selection of draft beers inside, and has a small courtyard outside that is open during the warmer months. Cookouts are common in the courtyard.

Perhaps its most distinguishing characteristic is its "Wall of Shame," a space reserved for embarrassing moments in the lives of bar patrons captured on film by one of the bar's employees. It costs a donation to a cystic fibrosis foundation to get the picture down.

Ripley's
2507 W. Clifton Ave. • 861-6800

Ripley's jams with a wide variety of live bands playing reggae, jazz and rock. It is very strict about its "21 and older" admission requirement, so it attracts more than just students from UC.

Sudsy Malone's Rock & Roll Laundry and Bar
2626 Vine St. • 751-9011

Sudsy's is one of the most unusual nightspots in town, giving people a chance to down some suds while cleaning their duds. The laundry/bar has live rock and alternative music nightly, 365 days a year, and an instant solution to spilling your beer down the front of your shirt. But it isn't just the uniqueness of the concept that makes Sudsy's so popular, it's the quality of the bands it brings in. Sudsy's has turned into one of the area's top destinations for small regional and national acts.

Top Cat's
2822 Vine St. • 281-2005

Top Cat's can be found in University Village and is one of the most popular bars for UC students, in part because it welcomes those age 18 and older. The club has live alternative rock on weekends and has a large number of dart boards, pool tables and pinball machines.

Uncle Woody's
339 Calhoun St. • 751-2518

There aren't many fancy attractions to Uncle Woody's — no games or bands or DJs

— and that's an attraction unto itself. The patio is open year round and the front porch is extremely popular during warm weather, when you can enjoy a beer and watch the activity on the streets. In the winter, in front of the fireplace is the place to be. It's a great place to mingle without having to scream over a band. You can sit in one of the booths or on one of the couches in the sunken living room portion of the back bar area and actually hear what's being said on the giant screen TV.

Vertigo
1 W. Corry St. • 751-2642

Vertigo bills itself as an altered state of mind for those who need to dance. Not to mention those looking for cheap beer, with $1 drinks all night Fridays and Saturdays. The club, which is located in the University Plaza, is widely popular among UC students because it welcomes those age 19 and over, is open seven nights a week and doesn't close until 4 AM on weekends. Alternative music from the 1980s is the choice on weekends, with disco and funk nights during the week.

Downtown

The city is trying to revive nightlife downtown the hard and expensive way — by forcing it. It is upgrading the area around the new Aronoff Center for the Arts by tearing up streets and sidewalks and replacing the concrete with brick pavers. It is offering incentives to entrepreneurs to buy old buildings, sweep out the old tenants, rip down or repair the structures and bring in new, upscale, glitzy occupants. It may work; the jury is still out. The area that is being called the "Backstage Entertainment District" is off to a good start, though.

All of the hotels downtown, of course, offer entertainment venues, and a few other notable nightspots are located downtown.

Arnold's Bar and Grill
210 E. Eighth St. • 421-6234

Arnold's is the oldest bar in town, dating back to 1861, and doing quite well. Once the restaurant crowd clears out, traditional jazz, blues, folk and other types of acoustic music fill the air. Arnold's is relatively small, but offers one of the quaintest patios in the city,

where you can escape from the crowd on nice evenings. The patio is enclosed except for a wrought-iron gate that leads to the street, and features trees growing up through the floor, lights strung on wires overhead, ivy on the brick walls and giant Coca-Cola memorabilia from the 1940s nailed to old barn boards. The bar doesn't pay for bands, but allows each group to pass a hat during the shows.

The Blue Wisp
19 Garfield Place • 721-9801

The Blue Wisp is one of those classic dark, smoky bars with unbelievably good jazz. Although it has moved around a few times, the tiny basement bar, with such a nondescript front entrance that it's easily missed, remains arguably the best jazz club in town. Many of the acts that play at the club are top regional and national draws, such as Cal Collins. The club, which offers jazz seven nights a week, has a different act each weekend. During the week it has two house jazz bands that play several nights a week and its own Big Band that plays on Wednesdays. The club doesn't require a cover charge on Tuesdays.

Champs
151 W. Fifth St. • 579-1234

Located in the Hyatt Regency Hotel, Champs offers fine Italian dining and then puts away its good china and turns into a nightclub, offering patrons dancing or just a place to relax and watch one of the seven TVs in its Tree Trunk Bar.

Ciao Cucina
700 Walnut St. • 929-0700

This upscale Italian restaurant is located across the street from the Aronoff Center and stays open late on show nights for those in search of an after-show drink.

The Cricket Lounge
601 Vine St. • 381-3000

The Cricket Lounge is in the Cincinnatian Hotel and is one of the most elegant settings in the city. It most frequently offers piano music or jazz. Guests of the hotel — Billy Joel, for example — have been known to come down to the Cricket and start playing the piano.

Elevation Dance Club
1005 Walnut St. • 621-9828

Elevation is a new club (opened in mid-1997) that caters to the over-21 crowd that likes to dance. The stylish, modern deco decor could easily have been transplanted from clubs in South Miami, with white lycra stretched above the dance floor, creating a cloud-like look when the club's dazzling array of lights hits it. The music is strictly cutting-edge dance music, and played very loud. DJs from all over the country are brought in to spin records each Thursday.

High Spirits Lounge
150 W. Fifth St. • 352-2160

The High Spirits Lounge is on the 31st floor of the Regal Hotel, offering a great view of downtown and live jazz all week long.

Oscar's
700 Pete Rose Way • 421-3007

Oscar's is located in the eastern end of the massive Longworth Hall and frequently caters to the college crowd by offering drink specials to those with a college ID and by staying open until 3 AM each night. It is now the only bar in what was once a small entertainment district along Pete Rose Way, but the construction of the new Bengals stadium forced all of the others to close.

Oscar's is a bit off the beaten path. Follow Pete Rose Way west past Cinergy Field and under the bridge that carries I-75 traffic over the river. Longworth Hall, a onetime railroad warehouse that has been converted into an office and entertainment complex, sits on the right.

The Palm Court
35 W. Fifth St. • 421-9100

The Palm Court is the lounge in the Omni Netherland Plaza Hotel and is one of the most elegant spots in Cincinnati with its marble and rich wood decor. A jazz trio plays in the lounge on weekends in this relaxing environment.

Plaza 600
600 Walnut St. • 721-8600

Plaza 600, located immediately adjacent to the Aronoff Center, is mostly a restaurant, but stays open late on performance nights and provides an upscale post-show retreat. Theatergoers can enjoy a drink at the small bar near the entrance or find a seat and enjoy one of the many wonderful desserts.

Rock Bottom Brewery
10 Fountain Square • 621-1588

The 10,000-square-foot microbrewery pub and restaurant sits right in the heart of downtown and offers a great setting to enjoy one of its six home-brewed beers or any of the items on its menu. During the warm months, a patio facing Fountain Square opens, offering fresh air and the sounds of water cascading off the fountain as a backdrop. It's located one-half a block away from the Aronoff Center.

Main Street

The Main Street entertainment area evolved in the early 1990s when two or three bars opened just north of the downtown central business district in the Over-the-Rhine neighborhood. Although most people used to shy away from that area, which was run down and crime-ridden, the opening of the bars began to change that. Soon the crowds started rushing into Over-the-Rhine. Club owners, attracted by the availability of empty space and the relatively low rent, quickly followed. Before anyone knew it, the Main Street area became its own entertainment district.

The area is now the main hangout for Greater Cincinnati's singles crowd. More than one million visitors a year make it the second-leading entertainment destination in the city (behind the Reds' games). That translates into thousands of people packing the area each weekend, streaming north from downtown after work or driving in from other parts of the city.

Although the streets and bars are jammed, this poor residential neighborhood didn't change when the bars moved in. Police patrol the area quite heavily at night, but the occasional safety problem does occur. The hit-up for money from beggars happens quite frequently, and every so often it might expand to an offer to purchase some merchandise at a discounted price that is so hot asbestos gloves are needed to handle it. So it pays to lock your car and pay attention to your surroundings when visiting Main Street.

BarrelHouse Brewing Company
22 E. 12th St. • 421-2337

BarrelHouse is one of the area's many microbreweries and slightly off the Over-the-Rhine Main Street entertainment district's beaten path — about two blocks away from Main Street on 12th Street — but not far enough to keep the crowds away. Located in a renovated print shop, the pub features a large copper bar and a Day-Glo mural of Cincinnati's skyline. It serves up eight home-brewed beers, which are cooking and cooling in giant stainless steel containers behind the bar, as well as live music and a wide variety of outstanding gourmet pizzas and specialty sandwiches. Hand-rolled cigars are also available.

Carol's on Main
825 Main St. • 651-2667

Carol's has been a longtime favorite among the alternative crowd. Under its founder, Carol, the facility grew from a tiny corner cafe into a larger two-story restaurant/nightclub that was decorated as if it were the headquarters of the Betty Boop fan club. Carol sold the restaurant in early 1998 and took her Betty Boop collection with her. The facility's new owners swear, though, that nothing else is going to change. Each night after dinner the restaurant will make a slow transition into a nightclub, it will still cater to a wide variety of customers, and the kitchen will continue to remain open until 1 AM.

Courtyard Cafe
1211 Main St. • 723-1119

The Courtyard Cafe is a classic little Over-the-Rhine saloon that offers free weinerwurst on Fridays with the purchase of a beer and — here's a switch — root beer on tap. It has a cozy courtyard in the back that overlooks a small, cobblestone-paved courtyard with plants and trees and features live music.

DV8/Renaissance
1120 Walnut St. • 665-6575

DV8 and Renaissance are two of the newest clubs in Over-the-Rhine and are becoming popular as places to go after the other bars close, since neither closes until 4 AM. Although slightly off the beaten path of the Main Street entertainment district — about one block south and one block west — the clubs are serving to expand the district. DV8 is a cutting edge dance hall, cocktail bar and billiard hall that offers club music. Upstairs from DV8 is Renaissance, a dance hall that offers a retro dance mix. Both cater to the 21-and-older crowd and offer garage parking to avoid any problems created by parking on the street.

Japp's
1134 Main St. • 684-0007

Japp's, a longtime Main Street establishment, was recently purchased, underwent a renovation and shifted its focus. Rather than being a straightforward rock and blues bar, it is now aiming toward an older audience by becoming a New York-style salon with an added cigar section and a wine and martini menu. The club's site was once the home of a wig shop and offered wigs from "virgin nun's hair."

Jefferson Hall
1150 Main St. • 723-9008

Jefferson Hall is one of the newer bars in Over-the-Rhine. It took the owners five months to bring the 130-year-old building up to code, and the bar now brings in highly popular regional and national blues acts, who perform every Tuesday through Sunday on the hall's stage, which sits in the front window. The bar's atmosphere is big on history, with black-and-white photos and old colored postcards of Cincinnati hanging on the unpainted brick walls. Word has it the bar's name came from the original building, which was an assembly hall for secret societies.

Kaldi's Coffeehouse and Bookstore
1204 Main St. • 241-3070

Kaldi's paved the way for the coffeehouse/bookstore craze in the area and remains highly popular with the area's artists, literati and bohemians. The club offers poetry and play readings as well as jazz and bluegrass music with its specialty coffees and assorted drinks. It is small, awkwardly shaped and often very crowded. The furniture is mismatched and paintings by local artists adorn the walls where shelves upon shelves of dusty books can be found.

Local 1207
1207 Main St. • 651-1207

This long, alley-thin bar in Over-the-Rhine was one of the premier entertainment spots along Main Street and is still surviving after all these years. From its stage in the back, live bands entertain patrons on weekends.

The Loft
1338 Vine St. • 421-6270

The Loft is an Over-the-Rhine pool bar and lounge that attracts a wide variety of the over-21 crowd from the area's arts and alternative scene. It is basic, with checkered tile floors and brick walls, but the works of local artists decorate the walls.

The Loft, which sits two blocks west of the heart of the Main Street entertainment district, is open seven days a week and offers dollar drafts on Monday nights and Grape Night on Thursdays, meaning wines are the featured drink. Secured parking is available one-half block south on Vine Street, and if there's something about the bar you like or don't like, a suggestion box hangs by the door.

FYI

Unless otherwise noted, the area code for all phone numbers listed in this guide is 513.

Main Street Blues
1427 Main St. • 241-6111

There's no getting out of control at Main Street Blues, as its three owners are former Cincinnati police officers. But that doesn't mean patrons don't have a good time. In fact, they do, jamming to — as one might imagine — live blues music on the weekends. This northernmost bar on Main Street is distinguishable from other establishments in the district by the three little pigs that sit on the sidewalk out front. The concrete pigs aren't a commentary on the owners' former occupations (so they say), but were there when they bought the place. The owners laugh about the irony, though, and consider it a good omen. Rumor has it the pigs were being led to slaughter during Cincinnati's Porkopolis heyday and when they heard where they were going they became petrified on that very spot.

Main Street Brewery
1203 Main St. • 665-4677

Main Street Brewery was the area's first microbrewery and one of the bars that helped launch the Main Street entertainment district. It brews five of its own beers in giant kettles in the bar, and the place is nearly impossible to get into on weekends. There's live swing music in its new upstairs loft area known as The Swing Room on weekends, but it mostly relies on taped music, the quality of its beers and its foods, which go beyond the usual pub fare. Although most of the tables are reserved for those wishing to eat, items from the menu can be ordered from the bar and eaten anywhere, even at the large window that looks out on all of the activity taking place in the entertainment district.

Neon's
208 E. 12th St. • 721-2919

Neon's was one of the original hot spots in the Over-the-Rhine Main Street entertainment district, and it still packs in the patrons with its single-malt scotches and upstairs cigar bar, complete with walk-in humidor. Neon's occasionally has live bands but mostly sticks with the stereo or juke box. During the warmer months, Neon's doubles its size thanks to a huge outdoor patio.

Rhino's
12th and Clay Sts. • 241-8545

Rhino's was one of the first bars into Over-the-Rhine and remains a popular hangout. It's basic as bars go — a long bar stretching along the length of a long, thin room — but separates itself from other bars through its huge selections of beers and its equally vast collection of rhinoseros memorabilia. Its motto: "Butt ugly, but we like to drink." And if you like to sing, the place is also well known for its karaoke nights.

Rhythm & Blues Cafe
1142 Main St. • 684-0080

RBC is the newest bar to open on Main Street in Over-the-Rhine. The new owner bought out once-popular Stow's and converted it. Despite its name, the live music played at the bar is not limited to rhythm and blues but includes all types of high-energy acts.

Sycamore Gardens
1133 Sycamore Ave. • 621-1100

Sycamore Gardens has quickly established itself as a prime Over-the-Rhine concert venue by bringing in a wide variety of bands ranging from Blessid Union of Souls to Manhattan Transfer. The cavernous club has a large stage and dance area, and its outdoor patio is second to none in the Main Street district. The adjacent Arboreta restaurant is one of the best places to grab a nice meal along Main Street.

Westminster Billiard Club
1140 Main St. • 929-4400

Westminster is upscale, uptown and upstairs from the popular Japp's and Rhythm & Blues Cafe. The club is different from most of the nightclubs in Over-the-Rhine in that it does not depend so much on bands or beer to survive — although it does offer plenty of both — and generally does not attract the bar-hoppers. Rather, it's main attraction is pool, including snooker, which can be played until 2:30 AM. Lessons are available and all of your pool-shooting equipment can be found in the pro shop. A $25 membership fee gets you discounts on hourly rates. Highly competitive darts is also popular at Westminster.

Mount Adams

Mount Adams has been one of the area's main sources for nightlife for a long time. Mount Adams residents, as diverse a group as you will find in any one area in Greater Cincinnati, choose to live up on the hill as much for the nightlife as for the location and views. The nightlife crowd is a bit of a melting pot of Greater Cincinnati — a little of this crowd, a little of that crowd.

If any one group can be pinpointed as most frequently visiting Mount Adams, it would be the arts crowd. They leave their cars at the nearby Playhouse in the Park or the Art Museum and walk down into Mount Adams, partly because the arts buildings are so close and partly because one of the problems with Mount Adams is finding a place to park. It's virtually all on-street parking, and finding a vacant slot to slide into can be a tough chore. And, don't be surprised if your journey to and from your car takes you up or down a hill or two.

Blind Lemon
936 Hatch St. • 241-3885

Blind Lemon, named after blues singer Blind Lemon Jefferson, is a small but outstanding bar. It features a partially covered, fenced-in brick garden with wrought-iron chairs and tables. It's a peaceful place to sit and listen to a band during the summer. The bonfires on cold nights are also a great attraction. Jazz and folk are the most common types of music offered.

City View Tavern
403 Oregon St. • 241-8439

City View Tavern is your classic dive, with a small balcony and a great view of downtown and the riverfront. Postcards and memorabilia from guests line the walls of the tiny bar, including signs such as "Children left unattended will be sold." The bar is squeezed between two homes — if it wasn't a bar it would probably be someone's house — and more signs out on the balcony remind guests not to get too loud for this reason. Food is available, although it's served on paper plates and the menu is limited.

The Incline Lounge
1071 Celestial St. • 241-2121

The Incline Lounge sits in the Highland Towers on the edge of the Mount Adams hillside and offers patrons live jazz and a great view of the city below. It's a bit more expensive and dressier than some of the Mount Adams bars, but it's a great place to end the evening. Its name comes from its location, which is where the old streetcar that chugged up the incline made its stop.

Longworth's/The Attic
1188 St. Gregory St. • 579-0900

Bar patrons get two bars for the price of one at Longworth's/The Attic. A DJ plays rock from the '70s, '80s and '90s upstairs in The Attic, while live bands play downstairs in Longworth's. During the warmer months, reggea, folk and acoustic music are added to the list of players on the patio overlooking downtown. Dinner from Longworth's can also be ordered until 10 PM daily — a reason to go there in itself. On Thursdays, The Attic serves "big-ass beers at half-ass prices."

Mt. Adams Bar & Grill
939 Hatch St. • 621-3666

The Mount Adams Bar & Grill is popular with a lot of the radio and television personalities, but it attracts all types, from yuppies to granolas, the salt-of-the-earth to guys in ties. It's a bit more upscale than what you might find on Main Street, but the atmosphere remains very down to earth. It is also one of the few bars that stays open until 2:30 AM every night.

The Promontory
1111 St. Gregory St. • 651-4777

The Promontory is located upstairs from Petersen's Restaurant and serves up jazz with no cover charge. It's a bit more upscale than what you'll find scattered throughout the rest of Mount Adams, although the atmosphere is certainly relaxed. It's a good place to have dessert after eating downstairs at Petersen's.

Northern Kentucky

While a great deal of Northern Kentucky's nightlife centers around the long row of bars, restaurants and nightclubs that sit along the river, there are many hundreds of corner bars and popular gathering places that aren't on the waterfront.

Bobby Mackey's
44 Licking Pike, Wilder, Ky.
• (606) 431-5588

Bobby Mackey's specializes in country music, although the main attractions of the bar, which is part of a national chain, are the mechanical bull and an arm-wrestling machine. The bull gives cowboy-wannabes the ride of their life, and the arm-wrestling machine can break even the strongest of challengers.

BrewWorks
12th St. and I-75, Covington, Ky.
• (606) 581-2739

BrewWorks opened in 1996 in the renovated Bavarian Brewery and is the largest nightspot in Northern Kentucky. Inside of the historic five-story building, which underwent an $11 million renovation and is run by Wynkoop of Denver, one can find a brewery, bistro, billiards, banquet and beer garden. A cigar bar was also recently added. In addition to its own wide selection of microbrewed beers, BrewWorks offers more than 1,000 other beers for sale. And if the party continues, BrewWorks is adjacent to The Party Source, the area's largest party supply store. The massive yellow building is easily spotted off I-75.

Coco's
322 Greenup St., Covington, Ky.
• (606) 491-1369

Coco's is a longtime Northern Kentucky nightspot, offering an eclectic mix of jazz, blues, folk and reggae in an intimate setting with exposed brick walls. During the day it serves up American fare as a restaurant. The food stops at 7 PM, though, and the music starts at 9 PM.

Coyote's
400 Buttermilk Pike, Ft. Mitchell, Ky.
• (606) 341-5150

Coyote's, which is located in the Drawbridge Estate just off I-75, features a 3,000-square-foot dance floor, making it the largest country music and dance hall in the Midwest. It books regional and national acts, and when major acts aren't performing, a DJ puts on some CDs and the dancing continues. You can also get free dance lessons if you show up before the crowd gets too heavy, so when the music starts you can scoot your boots with the rest of the gang. Huge video screens and pool tables are available for those whose idea of line dancing is having to wait to get into the restroom when you really have to go bad.

Dee Felice Cafe
529 Main St., Covington, Ky.
• (606) 261-2365

Stepping into Dee Felice is like stepping into the heart of New Orleans. The cafe, in Mainstrasse Village, has live jazz every night and even has its own band, Dee Felice Sleep Cat Dixieland Jazz Band, which performs on weekends. All bands play on an elevated stage, making it easy to catch the acts. Because of the popularity, you're asked to or-

Photo: Greater Cincinnati Convention and Visitors Bureau

The Ohio River gave birth to Cincinnati, and its waters still largely influence the city's culture and commerce.

der something to eat and are limited to two hours during dinner hours. Reservations are suggested.

Lucille's
3715 Winston Ave., Covington, Ky.
- **(606) 431-8086**

Lucille's picked up its name from B.B. King's famous guitar, and the intimate bar in the heart of Covington serves up the blues.

Mansion Hill Tavern
502 Washington St., Newport, Ky.
- **(606) 581-0100**

Mansion Hill is a small neighborhood bar that is big on dishing out the blues. It's the home of the Greater Cincinnati Blues Society, a group of blues fans. Some of the finest blues bands in the area can be found on stage here. During the warm months, Mansion Hill has a small outdoor courtyard.

September's Cafe
921 Monmouth St., Newport, Ky.
- **(606) 779-9462**

September's just opened in 1997 and is fast becoming a popular night spot. The restaurant/nightclub has an elevated stage along the wall next to the bar that patrons can see from both the downstairs dining room or the upstairs loft. The club brings in a variety of acts, from blues to contemporary.

Southgate House
24 E. Third St., Newport, Ky.
- **(606) 431-2201**

The Southgate House is actually an historic site in Northern Kentucky — it's the birthplace of James Thompson, who invented the Tommy Gun — but it has since become one of the liveliest bars in Northern Kentucky. Many local and regional bands play at the club, but it occasionally hosts a smaller national act. The bands here, which range from country to rock, usually keep the beat uptempo and the volume loud.

York Street Cafe
738 York St., Newport, Ky.
• **(606) 261-9675**

York Street Cafe is a coffeehouse and nightclub and is gaining quite a reputation for bringing in well-known soloists and smaller acts from all over the country. The music selection is very eclectic; acts include solo jazz guitarists, instrumental quartets and blues bands. Listeners can sit at tables or on couches and overstuffed chairs and put their drinks on the coffee tables.

On the River

Some of the area's most popular nightlife locations are on the river, in part because of the views they offer of downtown Cincinnati. Many of the restaurants located on the river also have bars or offer limited entertainment options after dinner hours.

Barleycorn's
201 Riverboat Row, Newport, Ky.
• **(606) 292-2978**

Barleycorn's is primarily a restaurant, but it also offers a long indoor bar and an outdoor patio during the summer months, both with a great view of the river and downtown. Barleycorn's also has a free Reds Shuttle that carries patrons to and from Cinergy Field before and after Reds games.

Gator's Sports Cafe
1 Madison Ave., Covington, Ky.
• **(606) 491-6692**

Gator's is one of the newest sports bars in the area, opening in 1997 on one of the barges that are part of the Covington Landing entertainment complex. Gator's has your traditional sports bar look, with nine televisions to keep patrons tuned into what's happening in the world of sports and oak-fired pizza to keep them filled. The bar sits directly across from Cinergy Field, and shuttle

boats carry patrons to and from Reds and Bengals games. Its outdoor pavilion is known as The Swamp and offers live bands on weekends and pregame parties before Bengals games.

Hooters
301 Riverboat Row, Newport, Ky.
• **(606) 291-9191**

Hooters, as you might expect, offers plenty of wonderful things to look at. No, no, no, not that. We're talking about the views of the river and downtown that can be seen from the giant windows on the floating restaurant and nightclub, which sits across from downtown Cincinnati. During the summer months, the patio area that connects Hooters and its sister restaurant, Remington's Roadhouse, becomes an outdoor tiki bar that offers live music. Waitresses from Hooters and Remington's offer drinks and food from both places.

Howl At The Moon Saloon
101 Riverboat Row, Newport, Ky.
• **(606) 581-2800**

The highly popular dueling-pianos bar moved in late 1997 to a spot on the second floor of the floating complex it now shares with Sloppy Joe's restaurant. The move added more room so the crazies looking to laugh aren't packed in quite as tight. A trip to Howl at the Moon is a must experience, with its two piano-playing comics singing goofy songs, razzing patrons, starting singalongs and encouraging fun and controlled chaos.

Tickets
100 W. Sixth St., Covington, Ky.
• **(606) 431-1839**

Tickets is one of the top sports bars in Northern Kentucky. Located in a restored firehouse, the facility offers a variety of big- and small-screen TVs spread over two floors. Downstairs offers booth seating and a full menu for those who are hungry, while upstairs pub grub is available at the bar or at tables sitting on a floor that is painted like a basketball court.

FYI

Unless otherwise noted, the area code for all phone numbers listed in this guide is 513.

The Waterfront
14 Pete Rose Pier, Covington, Ky.
• **(606) 581-1414**

Owners Boomer Esiason, Cris Collinsworth, Pete Rose and others, have made this is a great place to catch sports and entertainment celebrities. The five-part Waterfront complex includes South Beach Grill, an upscale restaurant; Spazzi, a casual Italian restaurant; Fusion, an upscale dance club; The Lookout Bar, a 150-seat balcony with an island theme that overlooks the Cincinnati skyline; and Las Brisas, an outdoor club with a truly tropical setting. Las Brisas has been one of the most popular warm-weather night spots in the area for the past 11 years, with live bands and partyers mingling around a waterfall, palm trees and a swimming pool.

Yucatan Liquor Stand/Bogus Brewery/Barber Shot
1 Madison Ave., Covington, Ky.
• **(606) 261-0600**

These bars are located in Covington Landing, just west of the Suspension Bridge on the first floor of the large floating entertainment complex. While other bars on the first floor of the complex have struggled over the years, Yucatan Liquor Stand, which bills itself as the "world's most notorious beach bar" with its tropical atmosphere, has always done well, and its owner decided in 1997 to take over the entire first floor. He subdivided the space into minibars and now allows customers to wander from bar to bar as they please.

Bogus Brewery offers a huge selection of microbrewed beers from all over the country, while Barber Shot is a barber shop bar that allows patrons to drink while sitting in barber chairs. More bars are planned.

The upstairs portion of the Landing also includes TGI Fridays and Applebee's restaurants. A smaller, sister barge also floats next door and includes The Glass Onion restaurant and Gator's Sports Bar.

Other Places

Not every popular nightlife spot in Greater Cincinnati is located in a defined entertainment district. Here are a few that are spread throughout the city.

Allyn's Cafe
3538 Columbia Pky. • 871-5779

Allyn's has any kind of beer you might want, tangy Cajun food and a great sound system for the live blues music it offers seven nights a week. Allyn's is also, how should we say, intimate. Its patio offers a break from the crowds during the warmer months, though.

Annie's
4343 Kellogg Ave. • 321-0220

Annie's is highly popular with the area's younger crowd, as it is one of the few places that actively welcomes those age 19 and older. Plus it frequently teams up with local alternative radio stations to bring in medium-size national acts. Those with a college ID get in for half price every night. Fridays are Dance Party night, Wednesdays are Party Band night and Sundays become Sunday Night Fever disco nights.

The Blue Note Cafe
4520 W. Eighth St. • 921-8898

The Blue Note is actually three bars in one and almost always has two live bands playing at the same time. One bar sits at the main entrance with a stage near the door, while a smaller, more quiet bar with a grill that offers hamburgers and other traditional bar fare sits in the middle and a third bar and stage are in the back. Although it does book some of the area's best blues bands, the music isn't limited to just blues.

Bourbon Street
Forest Fair Mall, Forest Park • 671-4433

Bourbon Street is a five-bar nightclub located in the entertainment wing of the massive Forest Fair Mall, just off I-275 in Forest Park. One cover charge gets you into four of the five bars: the Bonzi Pipeline, a 1970s-1980s disco dance club; Aftershock, an alternative and progressive music dance hall; O'Mally's Sports Pub, with 30 TVs so you don't miss any of the action from any of the games; and the Rock It Room, which offers live rock bands, games and big screen TVs. The fifth bar, Cheyenne Cattle Co., offers live country music, and a separate cover charge is required. Line dancing lessons are available.

The Breakroom Lounge
8809 Beechmont Ave., Cherry Grove
• 528-2601

The Breakroom combines live blues music with its dozens of pool tables. Although the bar is a popular spot, it can be hard to find. It sits on the heavily traveled Beechmont Avenue on the second floor of a nondescript building, and the entrance and much of the parking is in the back, so it doesn't appear as if there's a lot going on.

Dave & Busters
11775 Commons Dr., Springdale
• 671-5501

By far the largest "adult playground" in Greater Cincinnati at 65,000 square feet, this massive club just off I-275 at State Rt. 747 offers a little bit of everything: play-for-fun blackjack casino, a grand dining room, four bowling lanes, four bars, a party room, custom-made billiard tables, a golf simulator, a 130-seat special event theater, shuffleboard, and an arcade room with more than 150 games and simulators, including virtual reality games.

In the arcade room, rather than plug coins into the machines, you purchase credit on a special card that slides into the machines. Food from its restaurant can be ordered from the pool tables or Midway Bar. And while it sounds like some sort of carnival arcade that's going to be overrun by kids, anyone under the age of 21 must be accompanied by a legal guardian and must stay with an adult. Only three kids per guardian are allowed, and they must leave by 10 PM.

East End Cafe
4003 Eastern Ave. • 871-6118

The East End Cafe is popular with young East Siders. Located in a restored building near Mount Lookout, the bar has a large stage and space enough to pack in several hundred patrons to hear the different live bands who perform there each weekend. The music is generally modern rock or cover tunes, and it's usually loud.

Extra Innings
8325 Colerain Ave., Colerain • 741-7768

Former Reds second baseman Tommy Helms now serves up doubles at his own sports bar, which, as one might expect, has plenty of Reds memorabilia. The bar is a great place to catch Reds games, and there's a good chance of seeing Helms behind the bar.

Forest View Gardens
4508 North Bend Rd., Monfort Heights
• 661-6434

Forest View Gardens combines German and American food with Broadway musical performances. Three hours of dining and entertainment are offered, including singing waitresses, and the night is topped with highlights from hit musical revues.

Joseph-Beth Booksellers
2692 Madison Rd., Norwood • 396-8960

Located in the Rookwood Pavilion, Joseph-Beth offers jazz or acoustical music to entertain patrons while they browse through the vast selection of books for sale. The combination of books and music, along with something to drink from the adjoining Cafe Joseph-Beth, makes a wonderfully relaxing way to spend an evening.

O'Bryon's Irish Pub
1998 Madison Rd. • 321-5525

O'Bryon's attracts a lot of the sports-minded single sorts with sand volleyball courts and plenty of beer. The atmosphere is laid back, and the TVs are usually tuned in to a ball game of some sort. It offers a deck up on the roof with nine umbrella-covered tables during warm weather. The pub used to be known as Foley's Irish Pub, but other than the name nothing has changed.

Shady O'Grady's
9443 Loveland-Madeira Rd., Symmes
• 791-2753

Shady O'Grady's offers a place to rock to live music out in Symmes. It offers more than 150 imported, domestic and microbrewed beers.

Sorrento's
8794 Reading Rd., Norwood • 821-6666

For die-hard sports fans, Sorrento's is like hanging out at Sotheby's. We're talking serious memorabilia here, not this nickel-and-dime stuff you can get today. If you show up at Sorrento's and want to talk sports, you had better know your stuff.

Willie's

5054 Glencrossing Way, Western Hills
• 922-3377
401 Crescent Ave., Covington, Ky.
• (606) 581-1500
8470 Montgomery Rd., Kenwood
• 891-2204
8188 Princeton-Glendale Rd., West
Chester • 860-4243

These restaurants/bars are owned by the loud and boisterous radio talk show host Bill Cunningham and are favorite hangouts for local sports celebrities, particularly the Covington, Kentucky, location. Several basketball and football coaches around the area broadcast their radio shows live from the bars. Several giant-screen TVs and dozens of smaller sets pack the facilities, offering views of several different games at one time. In addition to the decor, sports games such as Pop-a-Shot can be played.

If you want an authentic Cincinnati experience, your best bet is to stay downtown or across the river in Covington or Newport.

Hotels and Motels

There's a story that Mark Twain, on one particularly lamentable visit to Cincinnati, stayed in a hotel with such pitiful room service that the author remarked he hoped to be staying in that same establishment when the world ended, "because there, everything arrives 10 years late." Yes, Twain later modified the barb to refer to the entire city rather than a single lodging house, but the damage to our town's innkeeping reputation was already done.

Whether this tale is apocryphal or not, Twain's turn-of-the-century critique shouldn't reflect badly on today's terrific accommodations. Cincinnati, like many places, has seen an explosion of hotel and motel development in the past decade. In all, the area has 18,000-plus hotel rooms. In this chapter, we present a range of options, with amenities and rates to suit most travelers' needs.

Among the all-around best places to stay in town are two historic downtown hotels — The Cincinnatian and the Omni Netherland Plaza — plus the more modern downtown Westin and the Embassy Suites at the Covington RiverCenter. Two historic inns — The Best Western Mariemont Inn and The Golden Lamb Inn in Lebanon — are among a handful of country-style inns that offer a nice break from the routine. And for pure hedonistic enjoyment, it's hard to beat the Wildwood Inn Tropical Dome and Spas in Florence. The spate of modern suite hotels that have sprung up in the past decade, mainly in the suburbs, also offer numerous cozy homes-away-from-home.

Northern Kentucky hospitality gets short shrift from major national travel guides, although it has 5,000 rooms all its own. Not only are most Northern Kentucky lodgings not included with Cincinnati listings, they don't even appear in the same book because regional lines are drawn at the Ohio River. But hotels in Covington and Newport are extremely convenient to downtown, and boast the best views of the Cincinnati skyline and Ohio River. Most offer transportation across the bridges, although you can certainly make the 10-minute walk on a nice day.

Know, too, that these waterside hotels book up early and fast for such major Ohio River events as the Riverfest fireworks and the Tall Stacks steamboat celebration. Reserving a room a year in advance is not unheard of. Some hotels are also taking reservations for the turn of the millennium. Party down!

The majority of attractive Greater Cincinnati hotels and motels are clustered in four areas: downtown and just across the river in Covington and Newport; the northeastern Interstate 71 corridor; the North Central area intersected by Interstates 75 and 275; and the Florence area in Northern Kentucky. The east and west suburbs of Cincinnati have only a handful of hotels and motels, though that may change eventually on the West Side due to the advent of casino gambling in Lawrenceburg, Indiana.

If you want an authentic Cincinnati experience, your best bet is to stay downtown or across the river in Covington or Newport. If you eschew urban congestion and would rather stay at a quiet hotel with a lot to see within walking distance, head to the Best Western Mariemont Inn, a grand Tudor structure along Mariemont's delightful town square. You can catch an art film, munch on Graeter's ice cream and dine at the area's most talked-about new cafe, Bistro Gigi, all within a few steps of the hotel.

Whatever you do, don't book a hotel near Kings Island amusement park on the north side of town, unless of course, all you plan to do during your stay in Cincinnati is ride rollercoasters. During the summer, you end up paying a premium for the convenience of easy access to the theme park (not to mention the ATP), a pointless cost if Kings Island or pro tennis tournaments aren't your primary tourist destinations.

The listings below don't cover every hotel, motel and inn. They're meant to cover a choice of the best-quality and best-value hotels in each area. You can expect that the newer suburban hotels offer great accommodations and plenty of free parking. But they generally are in areas that are hard to distinguish from most other suburban commercial districts around the country. We include descriptions of room interiors for the more unique hotels; expect the chain motels to offer four walls and a bed unless otherwise noted. Most hotels do not allow pets, but we'll let you know of those that do. All hotels and motels listed here accept major credit cards unless otherwise noted.

Price Code

Keep in mind that the pricing guides below are for weekday rates, double occupancy. You can undoubtedly find better deals through group bookings, travel discounts or other special packages.

$	Less than $50
$$	$50 to $75
$$	$75 to $100
$$$$	$100 to $150
$$$$$	$150 and more

Downtown

The Cincinnatian Hotel
$$$$$ • 601 Vine St. • 381-3000

This historic hotel was built in 1882 and elegantly restored in 1987. It's within easy walking distance of downtown attractions — the new Aronoff Center for the Arts, shopping at Tower Place, and the new Lazarus/Tiffany's are only a block or two away. It's also home to the exquisite Palace Restaurant and the popular Cricket Lounge, with a good selection of lesser-priced offerings.

This is Cincinnati's most expensive hotel, with rates for double occupancy at $210 and up, but such is the price of elegance. It has 146 rooms, meeting halls and a well-equipped exercise room. Personal computers, in-room safes, secretarial services and data ports are available for business travelers. Amenities for all guests include Roman-size tubs, bathroom phones, terry cloth robes, 24-hour room service, complimentary overnight shoeshine, turndown service, and twice-daily maid service. The rooms, as you might expect, are stunning, with intricate wood cabinets, high ceilings, impressive vase lamps, lush quilt comforters and roomy desk space.

If you choose what might be the city's most expensive hotel room, the Emery Presidential Suite, you'll fork over $1,500 per night. For that, you get two bedrooms, a living room, a dining room and two baths. The decor is warm tones of beechwood and stately marble, accented by two fireplaces, a wet bar, whirlpools and surround-sound stereo system. Heck, what's an expense account for?

Famous guests have included Billy Joel, who stayed here and played the hotel lobby's baby grand at 2 AM, plus Ronald Reagan, Margaret Thatcher, Tom Cruise, Dustin Hoffman, Frank Sinatra, Cher and the Rolling Stones. Not long ago, Fleetwood Mac's Stevie Nicks thrilled guests by serenading Lindsey Buckingham in the Cricket Lounge.

Another of the hotel's claims to fame is its English tea at the Cricket Lounge, for which people make reservations weeks in advance. Besides a great selection of specialty teas, you get live harp music and pastries made daily by the hotel's pastry chef.

Crowne Plaza Cincinnati
$$$ • 15 W. Sixth St. • 381-4000

The lobby of this attractive downtown hotel is actually on the eighth floor of the building — the first seven floors and also some of the higher floors are office space. The 270 rooms are elegantly appointed in beige and white, with blond wood cabinets and lush carpeting; some have bars, coffee makers and refrigerators. The outstanding services and facilities for business travelers include meeting rooms, personal computers, secretarial services, room service and irons and ironing boards in all rooms. Child care also is avail-

The place to stay for work and play...

Best Western

BLUE ASH HOTEL
CONFERENCE CENTER

800-468-3597

Whether you are attending a conference or just want to get away for an exciting weekend adventure, the Blue Ash Hotel and conference Center has the amenities you are looking for. Within a few minutes of the hotel, you can be at any one of these fabulous

attractions. Scream all you want on America's favorite rides at

Paramount's Kings Island; battle the four-footers in the wave pool at the Beach Waterpark; try your luck at the Argosy Casino; or take in 18 holes at the Golf Center, the course Jack Nicklaus built. You might want to mingle with the monkeys at the

Cincinnati Zoo, walk through the Ice Age of 19,000 years ago at

the Museum Center or enjoy the beautiful Ohio River and Cincinnati skyline aboard a riverboat. We're easy to get to, located just 15 minutes from downtown Cincinnati and just minutes from all major highways.

Exit 15 at I-71, Cincinnati, OH
513-793-4500

Visit us at our web site: http://www.blueashhotel.com

able for a separate fee. There's complimentary HBO, a free *USA Today*, and a concierge on duty on the 19th floor.

A well-equipped exercise room, sauna and whirlpool are among the other on-site creature comforts. The hotel offers a dining room and cocktail lounge, in addition to being within walking distance of a number of fine downtown restaurants. It's certainly one of the closest hotels to the Aronoff Center for the Arts.

The Garfield Suites
$$$$$ • 2 Garfield Pl. • 421-3355

This is one of the sleepers, if you'll pardon the pun, among downtown hotels. It's only a few blocks off Fountain Square adjacent to Piatt Park, across the street from the main library. In addition to an on-site restaurant, LeBoxx Cafe, the Garfield House has a small grocery store on the premises for essentials. For more adventuresome fare, Mullane's Parkside Cafe, Petersen's and the Blue Wolf Bistro are nearby.

Two- and three-bedroom penthouse suites are available at an appropriately lofty price of $450 a night. The 153-room hotel includes 76 two-bedroom suites plus some two- and three-bedroom penthouse suites on the 16th floor. Weekly and monthly rates are available. All rooms have kitchens, microwaves, refrigerators and safes, and a coin laundry is on the premises. Some rooms have coffee makers and whirlpools. Small pets are allowed.

Holiday Inn-Downtown
$$$$ • 800 W. Eighth St. • 241-8660

They say downtown, but to avoid confusion, know that this 12-story, 244-room hotel is slightly north of downtown (in the Queensgate neighborhood, a mixture of office parks and light industry). A popular spot for business meetings and seminars, it's also the closest hotel to the Museum Center at Union Terminal. A $5 million renovation of the interior was completed in 1998. On-site amenities include meeting rooms, an outdoor pool, Simmering Pot restaurant, Top of the Inn rooftop cocktail lounge and a coin laundry. Many rooms have bars, coffee makers, refrigerators and whirlpools. All rooms have free Showtime. They offer free parking, unlike many of the downtown hotels.

Hyatt Regency Cincinnati
$$$$$ • 151 W. Fifth St. • 579-1234

This 485-room hotel in the heart of downtown is adjacent to Saks Fifth Avenue, with shopping at Tower Place nearby via the Skywalk system. The popular Champs Italian Chop House restaurant is on the ground floor, and the 22-story hotel is also a short walk from many other downtown restaurants. This is one of the few downtown hotels with a heated indoor pool, and it also has saunas and a whirlpool.

Omni Netherland Plaza
$$$$$ • 35 W. Fifth St. • 421-9100

This stately old art deco-style hotel is a National Historic Landmark. Notice the intricately carved moldings and unusual art deco accents in the Omni's large ballrooms. This is a well-preserved hotel, but because it's an older building, some rooms are cramped by modern standards. Still, they are grand enough, with lots of walnut, lush carpeting and comfortable beds. Many rooms have bars, coffee makers, microwaves, refrigerators and whirlpools, plus a selection of free and pay in-room movies.

Downtown's shopping mall, Tower Place, is adjacent to the hotel (through Carew Tower), and Saks Fifth Avenue is within easy walking

---

INSIDERS' TIP

If money is no object, head first to The Cincinnatian Hotel. Cincinnati's most expensive hotel is also its most ritzy, holding high English teas and treating guests to glimpses of the Hollywood stars who often stay here. The hotel restaurant, The Palace, is simply stunning.

distance via the Skywalk. Right across the street is the city's brand new Lazarus and Tiffany's. Tower Place itself features shops such as Banana Republic, the Nature Company and Brentano's bookstore. A food court on the ground floor also is popular with the downtown lunch crowd (try the bourbon chicken at the Big Easy).

Amenities in the 619-room, 31-story hotel include a heated indoor pool, saunas, a whirlpool and privileges at the Carew Tower Health & Fitness Club in the same building. Among the two on-site restaurants is Orchids, one of downtown's finest.

Regal Cincinnati Hotel
$$$$ • 150 W. Fifth St. • 352-2100

Formerly the Clarion Hotel, this is a large convention hotel and popular meeting spot that, while a notch below the plushness of the luxury-class downtown hotels, is still nicely appointed and comfortable. It's certainly convenient enough for convention-goers, since the Regal is directly across from the Albert B. Sabin Convention Center via the Skywalk. The Regal also has a revolving rooftop restaurant upstairs, Seafood 32, with a good selection of well-prepared seafood flown in daily. Down on terra firma, the Elm Street Grill offers breakfast, lunch and dinner.

With 888 rooms in its 31 stories, the Regal is by far the largest hotel in the center city, so you shouldn't have trouble finding a room most of the time. Off-site health club privileges, secretarial services and personal computers are available. Some rooms have bars and refrigerators. Small pets are allowed.

Westin Hotel Cincinnati
$$$$$ • Fifth and Vine Sts. • 621-7700

Centrally located directly across Fifth Street from Fountain Square, the 450-room Westin is a modern, nicely decorated hotel in line with the high standards set by Westin nationwide. This is a newer hotel opened in 1981 and renovated in 1990, with another $4 million renovation planned for 1998, improving the lobby, all rooms and the health club. The Westin may not have the historical character of the Omni Netherland Plaza or The Cincinnatian, but it compensates with other amenities, such as a spacious restaurant, The Albee, convenient access to parking in an underground garage, an interesting collection of boutiques and specialty shops, and a commanding view of Fountain Square. (Be forewarned, however, that a view of Fountain Square in 1998 may not be all that inviting; the Square is slated for a long-awaited reconstruction project and makeover.) There's an indoor pool and fitness center. The Westin's rooms are among our favorites, with comfy sofa chairs, sizable desks, immaculate carpets and conservative color schemes.

Near Downtown (North)

Quality Hotel Central
$$$ • 4747 Montgomery Rd., Norwood • 351-6000, (800) 292-2079

Approximately a 10-minute drive from downtown Cincinnati, the Quality Hotel Central is a popular business meeting location, with some nice amenities and a good hotel restaurant, Dockside VI, which does a fairly brisk lunch trade with non-guests. This value-priced eight-story, 146-room hotel has a heated outdoor pool and free in-room movies plus a bar, coffee maker, microwave and refrigerator in some rooms. Free continental breakfasts come with all rooms. Airport transportation is available, and pets are allowed. Parking is ample.

Vernon Manor Hotel
$$$$ • 400 Oak St. • 281-3300

Built in 1924, the dignified Vernon Manor Hotel was the site of a scene in the Academy Award-winning movie *Rain Man* and the subject of several mentions in the movie. This is by far the best hotel that's convenient to both the Pill Hill hospital district and the University of Cincinnati.

The hotel also has two fine restaurants downstairs that are popular for business lunches and great Sunday brunches. The lounge, Beagles, is a friendly spot the hotel manager describes as "a lounge where you'll still be married when you leave." The hotel's authentic reproduction of an English manor includes a panoramic view of the city from its rooftop garden. And rare is the Saturday when there aren't multiple wedding receptions going on here.

Its old-world dignity aside, the Vernon Manor in many ways has the look and feel more of an apartment building than a hotel. Fifty-six of its 168 rooms have kitchens with refrigerators and microwaves, so it's well-suited for extended stays. The staff prides itself on providing friendly, informal, first-name service for folks who may have loved ones at nearby hospitals or who just like to loosen their ties after a long day of work. There's an on-site massage therapist and hair salon, and a fitness center and business center have just been added. Monthly rates are available.

Northern Kentucky Riverfront (Just South of Downtown)

Comfort Suites Riverfront
$$-$$$ • 420 Riverboat Row, Newport, Ky. • (606) 291-6700

Cincinnati's newest riverfront hotel features six floors with 124 rooms and is certainly one of the most economical hotels in the downtown area (especially since each room comes with complimentary continental breakfast). A fully equipped business center is open 24 hours, offering copier, fax, laser printer and computers, plus there's a fitness room with Lifecycles, stair steppers, treadmills and Nautilus equipment. It's an all-suite hotel, with each room boasting fridge, microwave, ironing board and more. A sample room we saw is done up tones of white and green, with vaulted ceilings, framed flower prints and dark-stained walnut cabinetry. The sofa, coffee table and dining table were nice touches.

The Chart House restaurant is immediately adjacent, as is Don Pablo's. You may wonder why this hotel even exists in sleepy Newport. It's because Newport won't be sleepy for long. Plans call for a marina, a $40 million aquarium and a $43 million entertainment district on Third Street (a short walk from the hotel) featuring a multiscreen movie theater, interactive video arcade and wild animal venue.

Embassy Suites Rivercenter
$$$$-$$$$$ • 10 E. RiverCenter Blvd., Covington, Ky. • (606) 261-8400

OK, it's not Cincinnati. It's not even Ohio. But it does have a breathtaking view of Cincinnati across the riverbank. And it's one of the city's nicest hotels, combining the convenience of being a bridge away from downtown with the more relaxed feel and readily available covered parking of a top suburban hotel. This hotel also combines the two-room suites and monthly rates of an extended stay hotel with the look and amenities of a luxury-class downtown hotel. A towering atrium lobby has marble floors and a splashing fountain that lead to glass-enclosed elevators.

The eight-story, 226-room hotel includes six two-bedroom units, meeting rooms, business center, heated indoor pool, sauna, whirlpool, sun deck for the summer months, well-provisioned exercise room and complimentary evening beverages. Guests also receive a free full breakfast. All rooms have two TVs, honor bars, coffee makers, microwaves, refrigerators and a choice of free or pay movies. A room we saw was spacious, with dining room table (complete with four chairs), sofa, coffee table and more, all done in tones of beige and light blue.

The hotel restaurant, The E Room, is one of our favorite seafood restaurants. Nearby are also several fine restaurants and shops, including the Behle Street Cafe and several restaurants and specialty shops at MainStrasse Village in Covington.

Hampton Inn
$$ • 200 Crescent Ave., Covington, Ky. • (606) 581-7800

This brand-new hotel, opened in 1997, features 151 rooms in a six-story complex. Amenities include an indoor pool, plus free Disney and HBO. The rooms feature king-size beds, writing desks and plush carpeting, all done in a color scheme of beige and white.

Hannaford Apartments
$-$$ • 803 E. Sixth St., Newport. Ky. • (606) 491-9600

Hannaford offers one- and two-bedroom unfurnished and furnished corporate suites for

extended stays or for newcomers looking for a home. Located in Newport's Mansion Hill Historic District just minutes away from downtown, the complex has a swimming pool, clubhouse and private parking on site. Monthly rates are available. The rooms are antique traditional, with lots of cherry finish and nicely appointed touches.

Holiday Inn-Riverfront
$$$ • 600 W. Third St., Covington, Ky.
• (606) 291-4300

Only a half-mile from the brand-new Northern Kentucky Convention Center, this hotel balances nicely the needs of the corporate and the leisure traveler. The 153 newly remodeled rooms are tastefully furnished and each is outfitted with color TVs and computer data ports, There's a new outdoor pool, fitness facilities, multiple meeting rooms and the Greenery restaurant and lounge. Covington Landing and Riverboat Row are just a few minutes' walk away, and the free parking lot is ample.

Riverview Hotel
$$ • 668 W. Fifth St., Covington, Ky.
• (606) 491-1200, (800) 292-2079

The giant scalloped cylinder in Covington is the Riverview Hotel. A rotating restaurant, the Riverview, on the top (18th) floor provides a panoramic view of downtown Cincinnati and Northern Kentucky. Just a brief walk from MainStrasse Village, this Covington landmark gives you ample opportunity to get out and enjoy the fine shops and restaurants there. Or you can make the quick trip across the bridge to more attractions in downtown Cincinnati. Many rooms have commanding views of the Cincinnati skyline, which is just across the river. Most others have nice views of beautiful 19th-century homes in Covington.

The rooms seem ample; decor is light pastel, with floral print bedspreads, vertical striped wallpaper and geometric shaped tiles. Handsome lithograph portraits hang on the walls. Each of the 236 rooms has its own recliner, data port and coffee maker. Some rooms have microwaves and refrigerators. Jacuzzi and wet bar suites also are available. (There are an impressive four floors devoted to non-smoking rooms.) Other amenities include a heated indoor/outdoor pool, exercise room with sauna and tanning bed, platform tennis court, whirlpool, room service and valet laundry service. There's a casual English pub, Kelly's Landing, on the first floor. Courtesy transportation is available to downtown and the airport. Barber and beauty shops are on-site, and plenty of free parking is available above or below ground.

Northern Kentucky (Suburbs and Airport)

Commonwealth Hilton
$$$$ • 7373 Turfway Rd., Florence, Ky. • (606) 371-4400

One of the nicer suburban hotels in Greater Cincinnati, the Commonwealth Hilton has larger-than-average rooms and better-than-average furnishings. A fairly wide assortment of rooms includes some suites and others with king-size beds. Convenient to shopping at Florence Mall, the Turfway Park horse track and a variety of restaurants in Florence, it's also only 5 miles from the airport. The Grand Cafe restaurant features a wine cellar, bakery on the premises and live entertainment.

Amenities of the five-story, 211-room hotel include a heated outdoor pool, sauna, lighted tennis court and exercise room, plus computer hookups for business travelers. Special services include valet laundry and free airport transportation. Some rooms have honor bars, microwaves, refrigerators and whirlpools. One room we saw featured a high ceiling, comfy armchair, dining table for two, a six-foot tree and a restrained tan and white decor. The executive concierge service package includes a free continental breakfast, evening drinks and hors d'oeuvres.

Cross Country Inn
$ • 7810 Commerce Dr., Florence, Ky. • (606) 283-2030

Dependable chain quality, comfortable rooms and a value price make this a good choice. It's convenient to Florence Mall and

Turfway Park, and an array of dining choices await nearby. The 112-room, two-story inn has a heated outdoor pool. Weekly rates are available.

Cross Country Inn
$ • 2350 Royal Dr., Fort Mitchell, Ky. • (606) 341-2090

Another good choice for dependable quality and value prices, this 106-room, three-story motel just off Buttermilk Pike is near a variety of dining options. It's also just 5 miles from downtown and 5 miles from the airport. Amenities include a small, heated pool. Weekly rates are available.

Drawbridge Estate
$$-$$$$ • 2477 Buttermilk Pike, Fort Mitchell, Ky. • (606) 341-2800

With 505 rooms, this is one of the largest hotels in the area. Extensive facilities include one of the largest collections of meeting rooms in Greater Cincinnati, the Oldenberg Microbrewery and Brewing Museum next door and a hair salon. There are four restaurants and a lounge here, including Burbank's, Josh's, Gatehouse Taverne and Chaucer's, so you can stay nearly a week without having to go to the same place twice for dinner or leave the grounds. The hotel is 5 miles from downtown and 5 miles from the airport.

Though some rooms are in the value-price range, Drawbridge also has luxury-class rooms, accounting for the higher end of our price rating. A VIP concierge/corporate floor is an all-adult floor with concierge service, continental breakfast and honor bar — and all rooms have queen-size four-poster beds. Throughout the hotel, all rooms are accessible by interior corridors. Some rooms have coffee makers, refrigerators and whirlpools. An elegant room we saw included a walnut writing table, armchairs and small dining table, colorful blue floral quilts and beige wallpaper.

The complex has three swimming pools — including one indoor pool and an outdoor heated pool — a sauna, whirlpool, two lighted tennis courts, exercise room, playground, basketball court and sand volleyball court. Available services include a masseuse, valet laundry, on-site barber shop and beauty salon and on-site car rental. Coin laundry, free airport transportation and children's programs are additional amenities. Ask about a variety of seasonal and year-round special packages.

Fairfield Inn by Marriott
$$ • 50 Cavalier Blvd., Florence, Ky.
• (606) 371-4800

This three-story, 135-room hotel provides dependable quality as well as good value. Some rooms have interior corridors and all have data ports for computers. Numerous dining options are nearby. It's only a few minutes from Florence Mall and Turfway Park, five minutes from the airport and five to 10 minutes from downtown.

Hampton Inn
$$ • 7393 Turfway Rd., Florence, Ky.
• (606) 283-1600

Another great suburban hotel value, the four-story, 117-room Hampton Inn is close to Florence Mall and Turfway Park, five minutes from the airport and five to 10 minutes from downtown. The lobby has a fairly cozy breakfast area with free continental breakfast provided. Each room also gets free movies, and half the rooms are designated for non-smoking guests. A sample room we saw included a comfy sofa, desk and a tasteful beige and brown color motif. Other amenities at the hotel include meeting rooms, an outdoor pool and free airport transportation. All rooms are accessible from interior corridors.

Holiday Inn-Florence
$$$ • 8050 Holiday Pl., Florence, Ky.
• (606) 371-2700

Amenities at this 106-room, two-story hotel include valet and room service, free airport transportation plus an on-site restaurant and lounge and outdoor swimming pool. It's about 6 miles from the airport and 13 miles from downtown and only a few minutes from Turfway Park and Florence Mall. All rooms have safes. Some have refrigerators and coffee makers.

Holiday Inn-Cincinnati Airport
$$$ • 1717 Airport Exchange Blvd.,
Erlanger, Ky. • (606) 371-2233

This airport hotel offers a good combination of convenience and atmosphere. Only 2 miles from the airport and 8 miles from downtown, the six-story 306-room hotel has a plush atrium lobby with comfy chairs, lots of greenery and a fountain. The hotel has all interior corridors, conference facilities, a heated indoor pool, whirlpool, saunas, fitness center, secretarial services, data ports, free airport transportation, coin laundry and the on-site River City restaurant and cocktail lounge. All rooms have coffee makers, irons and ironing boards, voice mail and computer data ports. Some have whirlpools, honor bars and refrigerators. It's one of the closest full-service hotels to the *Argosy VI* riverboat casino and Perfect North ski slopes.

Holiday Inn-South
$$$ • 2100 Dixie Hwy., Fort Mitchell, Ky.
• (606) 331-1500

The Holidome fun center here makes this a good place for families to stay. It includes a children's play area, miniature golf, shuffleboard, electronic game room, table tennis, billiards, a heated indoor pool, sauna, whirlpool and exercise facilities. Other amenities include room service, valet laundry service, free airport transportation and the on-site J.T. Ashley's restaurant and lounge. The restaurant is particularly elegant for a Holiday Inn, with linens, fine china and other nicely appointed table settings. The 214 rooms are attractive and clean, recently remodeled and done up in shades of brown. The hotel is only 3 miles from downtown and 7 miles from the airport. Turfway Park racetrack is just minutes away.

Radisson Inn-Airport Cincinnati
$$$ • Cincinnati/Northern Kentucky
International Airport • (606) 371-6166

You can't get much closer to the airport than this: the hotel is right on the airport grounds (about 15 minutes from downtown). The eight-story, 217-room hotel offers the business traveler secretarial services, valet laundry and dry cleaning, and free airport transportation, plus conference facilities. The plain-Jane exterior belies the plush lobby and open-air atrium, accented by greenery and winding walkways.

On site are a heated indoor pool, whirlpool, exercise room, table tennis, video games, billiards, a children's play area (with mammoth circular slide), gift shop, Clouds restaurant and Bungee's piano lounge. Rooms are tastefully decorated in shades of white and beige, with tan carpeting, framed contemporary art on the walls and 3-foot-high plants, a nice plus. The rooms seem comfortable, with lots of space between the bed and the padded chairs, desk and coffee table. Each soundproof room offers free movies.

Residence Inn Airport
$$$$-$$$$$ • 2811 Circleport Dr., Florence, Ky. • (606) 282-7400

Always a good bet for extended stays or business trips, Residence Inn offers nicely decorated one- and two-bedroom apartment suites. A complimentary continental breakfast is included. Many rooms have fireplaces, some have two baths and each unit has data ports, a refrigerator and a gas grill for cookouts. Other amenities include a heated pool, whirlpool, exercise room, sports court and volleyball court. Video players are available for a fee. Weekly, monthly and seasonal rates are available, and you can bring Fido or Kitty if you are willing to pay the mandatory $100 cleaning fee.

Signature Inn-Turfway
$$ • 30 Cavalier Ct., Florence, Ky. • (606) 371-0081

A nice value, this hotel is nothing fancy but does provide all the basics and then some for a moderate price. It's close to Turfway Park race track and Florence Mall and less than 10 minutes from downtown. The two-story, 125-room hotel has all interior corridors, meeting rooms, an outdoor pool, privileges at a nearby health club and airport transportation. Private office space is free to guests. Every room gets a free *USA Today* and *The Wall Street Journal*, free breakfast, and free movies. Some rooms have microwaves and refrigerators, and VCRs are available for a fee. A sample room we saw included a cozy gray recliner, plush blue carpeting, abundant desk and counter space (they call it a work center) and plenty of room to stretch out. Ask about weekend rates. Weekly and monthly rates also are available.

Super 8 Motel
$ • 7928 Dream St., Florence, Ky. • (606) 283-1221

Dependable chain quality and a value price make this 93-room, two-story motel with interior corridors a winner. On-site services include a coin laundry, and, in some rooms, microwaves, refrigerators and whirlpools. Rooms, predictably enough, are plain. What'd you expect, the Presidential Suite?

Wildwood Inn Tropical Dome and Spas
$$$-$$$$$ • 7809 U.S. Hwy. 42, Florence, Ky. • (606) 371-6300

The Wildwood Inn offers one of the most complete recreation packages in Greater Cincinnati, with something to suit honeymooners, weekend escapees or transferees looking to relocate. The Fabulous Tropical Dome and Tropical Garden Atrium have an indoor heated swimming pool, kiddie pool, sauna, whirlpool, billiards, table tennis, sun deck and video game room. Coffee is on the house.

The 124 rooms range from plush doubles to an assortment of spa rooms featuring heart-shaped tubs surrounded by, ahem, mirrored walls and a choice of king-size waterbeds or standard mattresses. The two-story Champagne Spa room has a spiral staircase and cathedral ceilings. Other spa room choices include the Fitzgerald Elite Suite, Victorian, Contemporary and Safari spa suites that cater to a wide variety of fantasy backdrop needs. The Cave Room and Nautical Boat room are also available. All theme rooms come with big-screen TVs and refrigerators. One- and two-room furnished apartments, which have microwaves, stoves, refrigerators, coffee makers, flatware, dishes and silverware, also make this a good choice for relocators. Ask about weekly or monthly rates and midweek or weekend packages.

New at the Wildwood Inn are the Western-theme suite, the Fifties-theme suite and the African Safari Village with 12 round huts circling a small lagoon. Private entrances and driveways, cathedral ceilings, 6-foot projector TVs, African artifacts, king-size bamboo beds

> ### FYI
> Unless otherwise noted, the area code for all phone numbers listed in this guide is 513.

and bamboo furniture are just some of the amenities of these unusual accommodations. Rooms have spas, refrigerators and microwaves and rent for $200 a night ($250 on weekends).

Northeastern Suburbs

Note that varying rate ranges for these hotels reflect higher rates during the summer months because of demand for Kings Island and other nearby water parks and attractions.

AmeriSuites
$$$-$$$$ • 11435 Reed Hartman Hwy., Blue Ash • 489-3666

One of a host of comfortable suite hotels that have sprung up in the northern suburbs in recent years, AmeriSuites offers a good home away from home for the long-term business traveler or newcomer putting down roots. It's in the middle of the Blue Ash business corridor, which rivals downtown for office space. The hotel is also only 10 minutes or less from shopping at the Kenwood Towne Centre or Tri-County Mall and a host of good restaurants in all price ranges in the Blue Ash area.

Wooded grounds and a luxurious lobby help set this 128-room hotel apart. Offerings include a mixture of king-size-bed and double-bed rooms, all of which have bars, microwaves, free movies, refrigerators and VCRs. Some have coffee makers. Monthly rates and senior discounts are available.

Best Western Blue Ash Hotel & Conference Center
$$-$$$ • 5901 Pfeiffer Rd., Blue Ash • 793-4500

Renovated in 1993, this is a nicely appointed business hotel with 217 rooms in six stories. Amenities include a heated indoor pool and on-site dining room and coffee shop. Also consider breakfast just a few minutes down Kenwood Road at Marx Hot Bagels, a local favorite. The hotel offers a shuttle service to the Blue Ash area business corridor and Kenwood Towne Centre, both of which are only minutes away. Some rooms have bars, coffee makers, microwaves and refrigerators. There's also a game room.

Best Western Kings Island
$$-$$$ • 9847 Escort Dr., Mason • 398-3633

This two-story, 124-room motel is five minutes from Kings Island and only 10 minutes from business areas in Blue Ash or shopping at the Kenwood Towne Centre. Several restaurants are nearby. Little ones will enjoy a playground on the premises. Other amenities include an outdoor pool and coffee makers in some rooms.

Candlewood Suites
$$$-$$$$ • 10665 Techwood Cir., Blue Ash • 733-0100

One of the newest hotels in the northern suburbs, Candlewood opened in mid-1997. Its three floors offer 77 suites, both studio and one-bedroom. Each suite comes equipped with kitchen, VCR, ironing board, hair dryer, work station and computer data ports. The decor is modern, in shades of blue and maroon. The one-bedroom suites also feature a sofa. Room access is via indoor corridors, and amenities include a fitness center and — a rarity among Cincinnati hotels — an on-site grocery. Dining options abound nearby, including the popular Watson Bros. Brewhouse (see our Restaurants chapter). Rates decreases considerably for extended stays (a studio is $45, a one-bedroom suite is $75 nightly).

Cincinnati Marriott-Northeast
$$$-$$$$ • 9664 Mason-Montgomery Rd. (I-71 at Fields Ertel Rd. exit), Mason • 459-9800

This 303-room hotel serves the Kings Island area and Cincinnati's Northeast corridor. It has 13,000 square feet of flexible meeting space, concierge-level business rooms, a workout center, a heated indoor/outdoor pool and many rooms with microwaves, coffee makers, hair dryers, irons and ironing boards. There are seven Jacuzzi suites. Other amenities include an on-site restaurant, Kokomo's poolside lounge and safe deposit boxes.

Comfort Inn-Northeast
$$-$$$ • 9011 Fields Ertel Rd., Mason • 683-9700

Comfort Inn gives you all the basics and is less than 10 minutes from Kings Island. The

Beach and the ATP Tennis Tournament. There's also a brand-new Showcase Cinemas complex with state-of-the-art movie technology nearby. The three-story, 117-room motel has an outdoor pool, interior corridors and meeting rooms. Numerous dining choices are nearby, and there's a complimentary breakfast. Other amenities include same-day dry cleaning service, an on-site laundry facility for guests, and three suites with microwaves and mini-fridges. Guests may use the fitness club across the street at no charge.

Comfort Suites
$$$-$$$$ • 11349 Reed Hartman Hwy., Blue Ash • 530-5999

This 50-room suite hotel has an attractive atrium lobby decorated in a French Quarter motif with cast-iron grills, a fountain and lush vegetation. Rooms are spacious and come with refrigerators and free movies. Some have coffee makers and pullout sofas, and VCRs are available for a rental fee. Other amenities include meeting rooms and an outdoor pool. Its location in the Blue Ash business corridor makes it a popular business hotel.

Courtyard by Marriott
$$$-$$$$ • 4625 Lake Forest Dr., Blue Ash • 733-4334

The Courtyard is a no-nonsense business hotel in the Prudential Business Park. All 149 rooms in the three-story hotel are spacious and have data ports. Some have refrigerators. Other features include indoor corridors, a heated indoor pool, a mini-gym, an on-site restaurant and lounge and a coin laundry.

Days Inn Kings Island
$$-$$$$ • 9735 Mason-Montgomery Rd., Mason • 398-3297

The two-story, 124-room Days Inn provides all the basics for Kings Island visitors and business travelers, including meeting rooms, a pool and playground. Some rooms have coffee makers, and a wide array of restaurants are nearby. A free continental breakfast is provided.

Doubletree Guest Suites
$$$$-$$$$$ • 6300 E. Kemper Rd., Blue Ash • 489-3636

Doubletree is an attractive suite hotel on wooded grounds with a posh lobby and corridors at I-275 and Reed Hartman Highway. The three-story, 151-room hotel has all one-bedroom suites, each with a separate living room and refrigerator and some with coffee makers. Weekly and monthly rates and a breakfast plan are available, as are personal computers and secretarial services for business travelers. Other amenities include a heated indoor/outdoor pool, whirlpool and an exercise room.

Embassy Suites Hotel
$$$$-$$$$$ • 4554 Lake Forest Dr., Blue Ash • 733-8900

Another great Embassy Suites Hotel, this one in the heart of the Blue Ash business corridor makes a nice first impression with a large, luxurious atrium filled with tropical plants. The five-story, 240-room hotel has meeting rooms, a heated indoor pool, sauna, whirlpool, and coin laundry. The on-site restaurant, Cascades, features a waterfall and babbling brook. The spacious suites include two TVs, bars, microwaves, refrigerators and data ports. Some also have coffee makers. Guests get a free full breakfast and complimentary evening beverages.

Harley Hotel
$$$-$$$$ • 8020 Montgomery Rd., Kenwood • 793-4300

Situated amid a vast array of Kenwood shopping and dining choices, this fine hotel also has a good restaurant of its own. The two-story, 152-room hotel has interior corridors, meeting rooms, a putting green, heated outdoor and indoor pools, two lighted tennis courts, shuffleboard, volleyball, a sauna, whirlpool, exercise room and on-site restaurant and cocktail lounge. Secretarial services are available. Some rooms have bars, coffee makers, refrigerators and whirlpools. Ask about package trips to area attractions.

Holiday Inn Northeast-Kings Island
$-$$$ • 10561 Mason-Montgomery Rd., Mason • 398-8015

Another Kings Island-area favorite, this Holiday Inn's rates reflect the seasonal influx for area attractions and events. The two-story, 104-room hotel includes meeting rooms, a playground, an outdoor pool and a game room. Some rooms have coffee makers, and pets are allowed.

Holiday Inn Express

$$-$$$$ • 5589 Kings Mills Rd., Kings Mills • 398-8075

This former Quality Inn, recently renovated and reopened as a Holiday Inn Express, is a good value for visitors to Paramount's Kings Island, The Beach and The Golf Center at Kings Island. The two-story, 210-room complex offers conference facilities, an outdoor pool, a playground, an on-site 24-hour restaurant, a lounge, coin laundry and video game room. There's outdoor recreation and fishing nearby. Some rooms have refrigerators, and VCRs are available for a separate rental fee.

Kings Island Resort

$$$-$$$$ • 5691 Kings Island Dr., Kings Mills • 398-0115

You won't get much closer to Kings Island, The Beach and The Golf Center at Kings Island without pitching a tent on the grounds (not recommended or allowed). This popular conference location has 288 rooms in two stories, with a mix of interior and exterior corridors. A full package of amenities includes two pools — one heated and one indoors — a sauna, whirlpool, putting green, two tennis courts, an exercise room, a coin laundry, playground, free area transportation and an on-site restaurant and lounge. Some rooms have bars, coffee makers, microwaves and refrigerators.

Red Roof Inn

$ • 5900 Pfeiffer Rd., Blue Ash • 793-8811

This motel provides dependable chain quality in a nice location minutes from Blue Ash businesses. There's no on-site restaurant, but plenty of options are nearby, including the popular Marx Hot Bagels a short drive down Kenwood Road.

Residence Inn by Marriott

$$$$ • 11401 Reed Hartman Hwy., Blue Ash • 530-5060

Always a good bet for extended stays or business trips to the Blue Ash business center, Residence Inn offers 118 nicely decorated one- and two-bedroom apartment suites. Many have fireplaces, some have two baths and each unit has data ports, a refrigerator and a gas grill for cookouts. There's also a complimentary breakfast.

The comfortable lobby has a fireplace. But you won't have to just sit around looking at the fire; you can avail yourself of the heated pool, whirlpool, exercise room, sports court and volleyball court. VCRs are available for a fee. Weekly, monthly and seasonal rates are available, and you can bring Fido or Kitty if you also bring a $100 cleaning fee.

StudioPlus
$ • 4260 Hunt Rd., Blue Ash • 793-6750

This 71-room extended-stay hotel beats the price of other extended-stay offerings in the Blue Ash area, albeit with smaller studio apartments. All studios have fully equipped kitchens with microwaves. The hotel also has an outdoor pool, exercise room, a sauna and coin laundry. Weekly rates are available. Several restaurant options are within short driving distance.

North Central

AmeriSuites
$$$ • 12001 Chase Plaza Dr., Forest Park • 825-9035

A great suite hotel, AmeriSuites looks more like a condominium complex than a hotel. It's convenient to Surf Cincinnati, shopping at Forest Fair Mall and Tri-County Mall and a host of fine restaurants. The 126 rooms include a mixture of king-size- and double-bed rooms, all of which have bars, microwaves, refrigerators and VCRs. Some rooms have coffee makers. Monthly rates and senior discounts are available.

Best Western Springdale Hotel
$$$-$$$$ • 11911 Sheraton Ln., Springdale • 671-6600

This 10-story, 268-room hotel offers luxurious rooms and monthly rates for extended-stay travelers. Some rooms have coffee makers and refrigerators. All rooms have data ports. Other amenities include meeting and conference rooms, an exercise room, a heated indoor pool, whirlpool and an on-site restaurant. A movie theater and several popular restaurants are nearby, and Tri-County and Forest Fair malls are only five minutes away.

Cincinnati Marriott
$$$$ • 11320 Chester Rd., Sharonville • 772-1720

Built in the 1970s, this is an older hotel for this area, but it's well preserved and renovated. If you have memories of the big boat next door, the landmark Windjammer restaurant, sorry but it closed in 1997. This hotel is convenient to the many area businesses and Tri-County Mall. The 14-story hotel has an attractive atrium lobby and 352 rooms. Ask for a corner room if you want one of the bigger ones. If you're feeling a little rumpled, all rooms have ironing boards. Some rooms have bars, microwaves, refrigerators and whirlpools. Other features include interior corridors, conference facilities, a heated indoor/outdoor pool, whirlpool, an exercise room and two restaurants on-site in addition to many other choices on the Chester Road strip.

Cross Country Inn
$-$$ • 330 Glensprings Dr., Springdale • 671-0556

This is a good choice for dependable quality and good prices. The 120-room motel is only five minutes away from shopping at Tri-County Mall and a number of closer strip cen-

---

INSIDERS' TIP

Coming to town with the entire brood? Consider the Drawbridge Estate in Fort Mitchell, one of the largest hotel complexes in the region. There's something for everyone in your family: a beer museum, a country dance hall, four restaurants on site, an English pub, three swimming pools, tennis courts, a basketball court, a playground . . . you could spend a week here and never leave the building.

ters and a variety of dining options. Amenities include a heated outdoor pool and coffee makers in some rooms. Weekly rates are available.

Extended Stay America
$$ • 11547 Chester Rd., Sharonville
• 771-7829
$$ • 320 Glensprings Dr., Springdale
• 671-4900

These two extended-stay hotels, opened in 1996, are among the bargain-price entries in the growing market for longer-stay facilities. They include 300-square-foot efficiencies (126 in Sharonville and 128 in Springdale) with fully equipped kitchens and two twin- or queen-size beds. There are guest laundries on site but no exercise facilities. Weekly rates are available.

Fairfield Inn by Marriott-Sharonville
$$ • 11171 Dowlin Rd., Sharonville
• 772-4114

Amenities include an outdoor heated pool, meeting rooms and complimentary continental breakfast. The hotel has a mix of rooms accessed by interior and exterior corridors. Rooms are cheerfully decorated and include data ports.

Hampton Inn
$$ • 10900 Crowne Point Dr., Sharonville
• 771-6888

You get a free continental breakfast, and the inn has all-interior corridors, meeting rooms, an outdoor pool and video players (for an additional fee). The four-story, 130-room hotel has several dining choices nearby.

Holiday Inn Express
$$ • 8567 Cincinnati-Dayton Rd., West Chester • 755-3900

This 61-room budget version of the Holiday Inn includes such amenities as an indoor pool and complimentary continental breakfast. It provides a clean and tasteful choice for business travelers and family guests in the rapidly growing West Chester community. Two of the best Mexican restaurants in town are nearby — Amigo's and the Blue Cactus — in addition to a variety of fast food choices. For shoppers, the brand new Union Centre shopping strip is just at the next exit on I-75.

Holiday Inn I-275 North
$$$$ • 3855 Hauck Rd., Sharonville
• 563-8330

You have no excuse for a sedentary existence in this Holidome facility, which has a heated indoor pool, wading pool and playground, exercise room, sauna, whirlpool and tennis and basketball and volleyball courts. All rooms in this 275-room hotel have been refurbished within the past year, and some have refrigerators. Dining is at the on-site Chase Grille restaurant. You're only 10 minutes from Paramount's Kings Island and other nearby attractions, plus shopping at the Kenwood Towne Centre, Tri-County Mall or Forest Fair Mall. Small pets are permitted at no charge.

Holiday Inn-North
$$$$ • 2235 Sharon Rd., Sharonville
• 771-0700

Another Holidome facility, this one offers a putting green, playground and wading pool for the kids, heated indoor pool, sauna, whirlpool, exercise room and volleyball court. This is one of the largest suburban hotels, with four stories, 409 rooms and all-interior corridors. Monthly rates are available, as are other special packages and deals. Amenities include secretarial services, a coin laundry and an on-site restaurant and lounge with live entertainment. Some rooms have bars, coffee makers and whirlpools.

Homewood Suites-Cincinnati North
$$$-$$$$ • 2670 E. Kemper Rd., Sharonville • 772-8888

Yet another slice of the suite life in the north suburbs, each room at Homewood Suites has a separate bedroom, living room and kitchen area, and you get a free continental breakfast and an evening reception. Weekly, monthly and seasonal rates are available, as are storage facilities — a nice twist for transferees.

Among the 111 rooms in the three-story complex are 12 two-bedroom units. Each room has data ports, an equipped kitchen and a video player. There are interior corridors throughout the hotel. Other amenities include meeting rooms, an outdoor pool, an exercise room, a whirlpool and sports court, plus secretarial services and personal computer availability. Homewood Suites is convenient to north suburban business areas and about 10 minutes from three shopping malls. Pets up to 40 pounds are allowed with an $8 cleaning fee.

Red Roof Inn
$-$$ • 11345 Chester Rd., Sharonville • 771-5141
$-$$ • 2301 E. Sharon Rd., Sharonville • 771-5552

These two motels are only minutes apart. Each has approximately 105 rooms. Both offer standard Red Roof Inn quality and cleanliness, complimentary morning coffee and plenty of off-site dining options nearby. The Chester Road motel is next door to the Sharonville Convention Center.

Residence Inn by Marriott
$$$$ • 11689 Chester Rd., Sharonville • 771-2525

Another good suite option for the Chester Road corridor, this 144-room hotel caters to the business traveler, transferee and other extended-stay guests. It has a mix of studios without kitchens and one- and two-bedroom suites with kitchens in a setting that looks more like a condominium complex than a hotel. All units are comfortably large and tastefully decorated. Other amenities include a heated pool, sports court and whirlpool, complimentary breakfast and evening beverages, and a coin laundry. Should tire of cooking for yourself, numerous dining options are nearby on the Chester Road strip. Pets are allowed for a one-time $75 cleaning fee.

Signature Inn North
$$ • 11385 Chester Rd., Sharonville • 772-7877

This 100-room hotel has all interior corridors and caters to business travelers with large rooms and convenient desks. Some of the rooms, which have queen-size beds, also have sleeper sofas. Complimentary breakfast is available, as is HBO on the house. It's only a short walk from the Sharonville Convention Center and a drive of five minutes or less (rush-hour traffic notwithstanding) to Tri-County Mall. The inn has an outdoor pool, and video players are available for a rental fee.

Signature Inn Northeast
$$-$$$ • 8870 Governors Hill Dr., Landen • 683-3086

It's called Northeast, but it's really in the North Central section on our map. This hotel is just off I-75 near Sharonville and Springdale businesses, Tri-County Mall and the Sharonville Convention Center. The three-story, 130-room hotel with all-interior corridors was created for the business traveler, with a nice atrium lobby, large desks, meeting rooms and data ports and coffee makers in all rooms. Because it's a business hotel, weekend rates are very reasonable. VCRs are available for a fee. Complimentary breakfast is available, as is HBO on the house.

FYI

Unless otherwise noted, the area code for all phone numbers listed in this guide is 513.

StudioPlus
$$ • 11645 Chesterdale Rd., Springdale • 771-2457
$$ • 961 Seward Rd., Fairfield • 860-5733

These extended-stay hotels for the budget-conscious include studios that are smaller than the higher-priced extended-stay hotels in the area. But they have fully equipped kitchens with microwaves, outdoor pools, cable television, an exercise room, a sauna and coin laundry. Weekly rates are available. Several restaurant options are within short driving distance.

Woodfield Inn & Suites
$$$ • 11029 Dowlin Dr., Sharonville • 771-0300

This brand new facility is one of our favorites to the north of town, if only for all it offers at a reasonable price. The 151-room, eight-story complex includes indoor pool, whirlpool, exercise room, interior corridors and all that you'd expect in a suite hotel. Each room features coffee maker, iron and ironing board, hair dryer, fridge and microwave. Add to that a billiards room, complimentary continental breakfast and complimentary cocktails from 5 PM to 7 PM. Many rooms feature a comfy sofa. For a few dollars more, you can get a kitchen suite or whirlpool suite. Next door is Burbank's, a popular local restaurant.

The Cincinnatian Hotel is one of many Tri-state accommodations available to visitors.

Far North

The Alexander House
$$-$$$ • 22 N. College Ave., Oxford • 523-1200

This charming two-story six-room historic country inn was built in 1869. All rooms are furnished with antiques and quilts. There are no TVs, and parking is on the street, but the charm makes this a favorite for visitors to Oxford. There is a fine restaurant here as well. Smoking is prohibited on the premises. Forget getting a reservation during graduation or parents' weekend at nearby Miami University — consider, instead, a bed and breakfast in Oxford (see our Bed and Breakfast chapter).

AmeriHost
$$ • 6 E. Sycamore St., Oxford • 523-0000

AmeriHost is a well-kept 61-room hotel just a short drive from the campus of Miami University. It has all-interior corridors, meeting rooms, a heated indoor pool and whirlpool. Some rooms have bars, refrigerators and whirlpools. Dining is available in nearby restaurants. The same caveat about Miami U. applies as above.

The Golden Lamb Inn
$$$ • 27 S. Broadway, Lebanon • 932-5065

This beautiful historic country inn is the oldest public lodging in Ohio. In fact, it was founded in 1803 only a few months after Ohio became a state. In 1815, a two-story Federal-style brick building replaced the original log tavern and today serves as the lobby and part of the second floor of today's four-story restaurant and inn.

The inn became nationally famous in the 19th century, when it hosted famous literary figures and politicians of the day. Its heyday came during the days of coach travel, when many drivers and travelers who couldn't read were simply told to stop at the sign of the Golden Lamb. One of the travelers — who surely could read — was Mark Twain. He stayed here as he rehearsed for a performance at the Lebanon Opera House. Charles Dickens also stayed here during a tour of the United States in 1842. Presidents William Henry Harrison and Ulysses S. Grant stayed here too, as did Kentucky's famous Sen. Henry Clay.

Today, presidents tend to choose more modern establishments. But there's still plenty to love in the 18 rooms that make up the Golden Lamb Inn, especially for antique lovers. Rooms, each of which is named after a famous guest from the past, double as museum displays until rented, showcasing the Golden Lamb's collection of Shaker furniture and Currier and Ives prints. In fact, the inn is listed as a Shaker museum — one of the few museums you also can sleep in.

You can't buy the antiques in the rooms, but plenty are available for sale at the many antique stores along Broadway in Lebanon or in Waynesville, which is less than 10 minutes away. The gift shop at the Golden Lamb is also a popular place for its collection of reproduction antique merchandise. Fine dining is always nearby, too. The Golden Lamb is probably best known these days as a fine restaurant that attracts diners from throughout the Greater Cincinnati and Dayton areas and is owned by the same group that owns Cincinnati's five-star The Maisonette.

There is, of course, no pool, no exercise room, no refrigerator in the room. And it probably goes without saying that they don't want any pets gnawing on the antiques.

The Hamiltonian Hotel
$$ • 1 Riverfront Plaza, Hamilton • 896-6200

This six-story, 120-room hotel overlooks the Great Miami River in the heart of the historic section of Hamilton. Amenities include an outdoor pool and on-site restaurant, with coffee makers, refrigerators and whirlpools in some rooms.

West

Argosy Casino Resort
$$$-$$$$ • 777 East Eads Pkwy., Lawrenceburg, Ind. • 1-888-ARGOSY7

This 300-room hotel opened in May 1998 with a 200,000-square-foot pavilion decorated in a Mediterranean theme complete with palm trees. The *Argosy VI* floating casino — the world's largest inland riverboat — is docked immediately adjoining the hotel and pavilion complex, and all are serviced by a six-story, 1,800-car parking garage (this is good news for gamblers who previously had to park a mile outside of Lawrenceburg and hop shuttle buses into town).

Argosy spent $200 million on this hotel complex, and it shows. The three-level pavilion is capped with a stained-glass dome designed to look like a map of the earth; inside, hotel guests have the choice of dining in restaurants that include the Outpost Lounge, featuring African themes (including a thatched roof and African baobab trees), Chart Room (which is decorated with an actual cropduster airplane hanging from the ceiling) and Bogart's. The 350-seat Passport buffet area is particularly noteworthy, as it's split into separate rooms decorated in French, Egyptian and other Mediterranean styles, as well as the Lost City of Atlantis. The Walt Disney Co. helped create the stone columns and paintings to offer the illusion of under-the-sea Atlantis. (See the Close-up in our River Fun chapter for more details on the casino itself.)

Hyatt Resort
$$$-$$$$$ • 600 Grand Victoria Dr., Rising Sun, Ind. • 1-800-GRAND11

Hyatt Corporation just opened this theme resort area centered around the *Grand Victoria II* riverboat casino, flashing back to 1890s Indiana with cobblestone streets and gaslights. The 300-acre resort in Rising Sun features a hotel, health club and Wellington's steakhouse, all set in a Victorian motif. In addition to the 200-room hotel/resort itself, there are small motels and a few bed and breakfasts in the area (see our Bed and Breakfasts chapter), but you really shouldn't miss the resort experience. Its concert hall features the likes of Tom Jones and Wayne Newton, plus there are gift shops, the Victoria Pub, Picadilly's delicatessen and other amenities.

Imperial House West-Cincinnati
$$ • 5510 Rybolt Rd. • 574-6000

This five-story, 198-room motel has a mix of interior- and exterior-corridor rooms, plus an outdoor pool, exercise room and a sauna. Meeting rooms and a coin laundry also are available. Small pets are allowed in designated rooms. The hotel includes 32 efficiency units with refrigerators.

Quality Inn
$$ • I-74 and New Haven Rd., Harrison • 367-5200

This hotel provides business travelers and other visitors with a good value. The two-story, 108-room structure has all-interior corridors, plus meeting rooms, secretarial services, a heated outdoor pool, a coin laundry and a coffee shop. Some rooms have bars, and 10 efficiencies have microwaves and refrigerators. Video players are available for a fee.

East

Best Western Mariemont Inn
$$ • 6880 Wooster Rd., Mariemont • 271-2100

A little out of the way from most business destinations and attractions in Greater Cincinnati, the Mariemont Inn is still well worth the trip. Right in the heart of Mariemont, one of Cincinnati's quaintest villages, the Mariemont Inn is the only Cincinnati hotel in the *National Trust Guide to Historic Bed & Breakfast Inns and Small Hotels*, which only includes inns 50 years old or older that have maintained their architectural integrity.

This is also one of the best values among area hotels. Built in 1926, this old English-style inn has 58 rooms and antique furniture, including beds with hand-carved headboards in many rooms. It would almost be more at home in our bed and breakfast chapter — but your hotel stay doesn't include breakfast. Eat breakfast here anyway, though, because the morning fare at the National Exemplar restaurant is among the best you'll find anywhere in Cincinnati. Dinners aren't bad either, though with Bistro Gigi — one of the city's hottest new cafes — right across the street, you certainly aren't going to go hungry.

The hotel doesn't include such modern amenities as pools or exercise rooms, but it's hard to beat for a weekend getaway or change from the usual business-hotel pace.

Cross Country Inn
$ • 4004 Williams Dr., Cherry Grove • 528-7702

Cross Country is a good choice for dependable quality and value prices. The 128-room motel just off I-275 at the Beechmont Avenue exit is close to a variety of dining options, including Shells, The Olive Garden and Chi-Chi's. (If you've stayed here before and remember dining at the locally famous Montgomery Inn, don't be mystified at its disappearance. It burned to the ground in 1997.) The inn is also less than 10 minutes from the Eastgate or Beechmont malls. Amenities include a heated outdoor pool. Weekly rates are available.

Red Roof Inn
$ • 4035 Mt. Carmel-Tobasco Rd. • 528-2741

Another good all-around value with dependable chain quality, this Red Roof is located at the Beechmont Avenue, I-275 interchange. Its 109 rooms include several "business king" rooms with king-size beds, large desks and data ports on the telephones. Small pets are allowed. It's close to several shopping and dining possibilities.

Holiday Inn-Eastgate
$$$ • 4501 Eastgate Blvd. • 752-4400

This six-story, 247-room hotel has spacious, attractive public areas, an on-site restaurant and lounge and extensive conference facilities. The hotel is next to Eastgate Mall, so there's plenty of shopping nearby, including a McAlpin's and Kohl's department stores. Other amenities include a heated indoor pool, sauna, whirlpool and exercise room. Secretarial services are also available. Some rooms have bars, coffee makers, microwaves, refrigerators and whirlpools. Pets are allowed. Call for details on special rates and packages.

Allison House was a stop on the Underground Railroad for escaping slaves in the 1860s.

Bed and Breakfasts

Bed and breakfast inns in Greater Cincinnati provide a relaxing change of pace for travelers. Though they often don't have such modern amenities as swimming pools, exercise rooms or in-room data ports, they more than make up for it in homespun charm and atmosphere. And, as you can gather from the name, breakfast comes with the deal. Here are some of the better bed and breakfast accommodations in the region, though some of the area's well-kept secrets no doubt eluded our writer's net.

Before you visit, here are some words of advice: Don't plan on just dropping in. Reservations are required at all these inns. Keep in mind that phones and TVs in the rooms are the exception rather than the rule. And if you prefer the nameless/faceless treatment, bed and breakfasts are a bad choice. Chances are, you'll spend some time socializing with the owners and guests in the cozy common areas — and maybe make some new friends.

Travelers would do well to contact the two bed-and-breakfast associations serving the region before they book a bedroom. The **Ohio Bed & Breakfast Association**, (614) 868-5567, can provide a list of its Cincinnati members, all of whom are inspected regularly and must meet certain standards. The **Bed & Breakfast Association of Kentucky**, (606) 291-0191, doesn't actively inspect its members, but does require them to provide proof of a state operator's license as well as valid health permit.

Assume that the inns listed here do not allow pets or smoking unless we've noted otherwise. Some inns do not accept credit cards — we let you know which ones — although all accept checks. In some case, children are not allowed — again, we'll indicate when this is the case.

Price Code

Keep in mind that this pricing guide is for weekday rates, double occupancy.

$	Less than $50
$$	$50 to $75
$$$	$75 to $100
$$$$	$100 to $150
$$$$$	$150 and more

Ohio

Allison House
$-$$, no credit cards • 65 S. Third St., Waynesville • 897-6611

Owner Jackie Allison laughingly describes her bed and breakfast as "this big monstrous historic house," and the description says as much about the owner's buoyant personality as it does the home. Nestled among the many antique shops in the heart of Waynesville, Allison House has played many roles throughout its history. Built in 1840, it was a stop on the Underground Railroad for escaping slaves in the 1860s. It served in the 1900s as the private residence of Seth Silver Haines, founder of the Haines Clothing Co. and the first bank in Waynesville. It was a boarding house prior to its current incarnation as an attractive bed and breakfast inn.

INSIDERS' TIP

Keep in mind that the Tri-state's bed and breakfast scene is nowhere near as historical as the East Coast's. That said, Civil War buffs will find lots of fodder, particularly in Ripley (see our listings for Baird House and Signal House bed and breakfasts).

Four guest rooms are available for single or double occupancy, with two and a half shared baths. Jackie personally serves you breakfast in your room. Cable TV and VCRs are available in two living areas. Pets are allowed in some cases.

Amish Country Log Cabin Bed & Breakfast
$$, no credit cards • 2658 Coon Hill Rd., Winchester • (937) 386-3144, (800) 738-3332

Yes, a real log cabin, albeit with its own 800 phone number. Ah, the intermingling of rustic and modern times. The cabin lodge, as you might expect, blends reminders of bygone eras with modern conveniences. There are porches with rocking chairs to while away an afternoon and plenty of hiking, fishing and birdwatching on the 27 wooded acres (which includes a 1-acre pond). Breakfast, in fact, is served on golden pond — or at least overlooking it. (The pecan apple flips are not to be missed.)

Owners Donna and Glen Sorrell are retirees and, indeed, we get the sense that this particular bed and breakfast particularly caters to seniors, although certainly guests of all ages would be welcome. There's a foyer, lounge and great room in addition to two bedrooms with private baths. Antiques line the walls of all. Before you leave, plan a noontime hike. Picnic lunches are available upon request.

Arlene's Stone Porch Bed & Breakfast
$$-$$$$ • 1934 Hopkins Ave., Norwood • 531-4204

This 1889 Victorian home offers three bedrooms as well as a deluxe suite featuring a kitchen and sitting room. Proprietor Helen Arlene Wagner raised all her children in this house, and she's particularly proud of its stylized architectural features, including angled walls, four bay windows to provide plenty of natural sunlight, ceiling fans and hardwood floors. Private baths are available.

Baird House Bed & Breakfast
$$-$$$, no credit cards • 201 North 2nd St., Ripley • (937) 392-4918

One of two terrific bed and breakfasts in the tiny town of Ripley (believe it or not), Baird House Bed & Breakfast is an 1840s Civil War timepiece with a spectacular view of the Ohio River, private baths, porches galore, and an inviting rustic feel. Innkeepers Patty and Glenn Kittles put on a delicious six-course breakfast and even have been known to stage musical shows for lucky guests.

Ripley itself is better known as the tobacco capitol of Ohio, with its Ohio Tobacco Museum, annual tobacco auctions and famous Tobacco Festival. That said, nonsmokers are welcome to sample a bit of rural Americana in a town where little has changed over the decades.

The Dorie IV
$$$$ • Whiteoak Marina, Higginsport (off Route 52) • 553-4382, (937) 375-5444

About 45 minutes from Cincinnati, this new bed and breakfast (opening in May 1998) advertises itself as "the only floating bed and breakfast on the Ohio River." A safe bet. The 65-foot Kelly motor cruiser is captained by Dan and Nancy Henson and features three staterooms (with queen, full and bunk beds), an eat-in galley and a hot tub on the upper deck. There's complimentary wine-and-cheese in the evening, in addition to break-

---

FYI

Unless otherwise noted, the area code for all phone numbers listed in this guide is 513.

INSIDERS' TIP

The Golden Lamb isn't listed in this chapter, but it ought to be. Strictly speaking, it's not a bed and breakfast, so it wound up in our Hotels and Motels chapter. Nonetheless, the Lamb has all the historical significance and charming imagery of the finest bed and breakfast — sans complimentary breakfast. Consider it.

fast. The staterooms don't have complete private baths, but the Hensons only book one couple (or couples that know each other) at a time, so your privacy is ensured. Base price is $139 ($249 for the weekend package). If you can round up friends or family, it's just $45 for each extra couple (up to four couples). Anchors away.

The Duck Pond
$$, no credit cards • 6391 Morning Sun Rd., Oxford • 523-8914

Proprietor Toni Kohlstedt raises white Peking ducks, to answer your question about the name of this place. The bustling duck pond is the first stop for many regulars, and admittedly, some guests stay here with no interest in a bed and breakfast other than it offers an available mattress. This inn fills up quickly, you see, during graduations and parents weekends at Miami University, which is only a couple miles away. Hueston Woods State Park is also only 2 miles from this 1863 house, which has four guest bedrooms, including one with a private bath. The other three guest rooms share two baths. The 5-acre property features a rolling meadow for a leisurely stroll. Kids 12 or younger are not allowed.

Empty Nest Bed & Breakfast
$$-$$$ • 2707 Ida Ave., Norwood • 631-3494

Maryann and Hank Burwinkel welcome you to this 1904 Victorian, with its three bedrooms, two of which are connected and can form a suite. The suite is ideal for two couples traveling together or for parents with older children who'd like some privacy on their trip. Baths are private. Nugget, a Golden Retriever (Nugget, get it?), presides and would appreciate no competition (in other words, no pets). This restful home is adorned with antiques, and outside is Hank's perennial garden and shade trees. Breakfast can be anything from a salmon quiche to vegetable frittata, and there are complimentary snacks and beverage served in the afternoon as well as dessert in the evening. It's within walking distance of Rookwood Pavilion, a shopping center full of neat stores and restaurants (see our Shopping chapter).

Hickory Ridge Bed & Breakfast
$$, no credit cards • 1418 Germany Hill Rd., Manchester • (937) 549-3563

This delightful rustic cottage, surrounded by well over 100 acres of flowers and hickory trees, is home to proprietor Sue Bradley, who prepares all the meals. The two guest bedrooms are cozy, outfitted in white carpet and linens. The one shared bath is downstairs. Lunch and dinner, afternoon teas and snacks are all options. Don't miss a wonderful hiking opportunity, and yes, picnic lunches are provided upon request.

Kings Manor Inn Bed & Breakfast
$$-$$$ • 1826 Church St., Kings Mills • 459-9959

Here's a remnant of the past in the place from which Paramount's Kings Island drew its name. This three-story inn was built in 1903 by Col. George King, whose family owned the King Powder Factory from which the town got its name. The inn is convenient to Kings Island and surrounding attractions. Owner Bob Molinaro offers a spacious living room, cozy library, sun room and giant wraparound porch. Three guest rooms and a two-room suite are available — all with private baths. Furnishings are comfortable and in appropriate turn-of-the-century styles. Smoking is permitted.

Murphin Ridge Inn
$$$-$$$$ • 750 Murphin Ridge Rd., West Union • (937) 544-2263

An hour's drive from downtown Cincinnati, the Murphin Ridge Inn is one of our very favorite bed and breakfasts in the region. Why? It's perfect in almost every respect. The 1810 Virginia-style brick farmhouse and adjoining guest house are adroitly managed by innkeepers Sherry and Darryl McKenney. Its location, on the edge of the Appalachian foothills in Adams County and surrounded by 140 acres of countryside, allows plenty of opportunities for either leisurely strolls or serious hiking. In addition to wooded trails, the bountiful recreation amenities include an outdoor swimming pool, tennis and basketball courts and even a charming croquet court.

Location alone, however, doesn't account for Murphin Ridge's popularity. The dining experience is unparalleled, as chef Natasha

Shishkevish prepares regional American specialties (lunch and candlelit dinners are available, though only breakfast is included in the overnight price). She'll even pack a picnic lunch for hikers. The dozen or so guest rooms are somewhat spartan, though lovingly furnished in custom wood furniture built by the area's best known craftsman, David T. Smith. Each room features a cathedral ceiling and private bath, while some include porches or fireplaces.

Nearby is the historic Serpent Mound as well as the intriguing Amish community and bountiful shopping experiences (see our Adams County listing in the Daytrips chapter). There are plans for adding an organic garden so that guests may better reap the benefits of seasonal garden produce, as well as "Gourmet Getaway" packages featuring cooking classes by chef Natasha.

The Parker House
$$-$$$ • 2323 Ohio Ave. • 579-8236

The Parker House is an historical bed and breakfast inn in the city neighborhood of Clifton, only a short walk from the University of Cincinnati and a brief car trip or walk from "Pill Hill" hospitals. The 7,000-square-foot Queen Anne Victorian mansion was built in the 1870s. The four guest rooms all have private baths, and the first two floors (out of three) are devoted entirely to guests' enjoyment. Breakfast is served in the original music room, with its 12-foot mural ceilings. Parking is free and available, a rare amenity in Clifton. Smoking is OK. Ask about weekly, monthly and seasonal rates.

Prospect Hill Bed and Breakfast
$$$-$$$$ • 408 Boal St. • 421-4408

Built in 1867, this Italianate Victorian townhouse is nestled on a wooded hillside on Prospect Hill, a national historic district in Over-the-Rhine, within 15 minutes walking distance of Fountain Square downtown. Proprietors Gary Hackney and Tony Jenkins oversee the house, which has a spectacular city view and four bedrooms furnished with period antiques. Two of four rooms have private baths, and the other two share a bath. Two rooms have woodburning fireplaces. There's also an outdoor Jacuzzi area. Great pains have been made to preserve the original woodwork, doors, hardware and light fixtures.

Ross B&B
$, no credit cards • 88 Silverwood Circle, Springdale • 671-2645

One of the most affordable bed and breakfasts in town, Ross B&B is hosted by Joan and George Ross in an unpretentious split-level home on a quiet residential street in Springdale. This could be ideal for the business traveler tired of the budget motel life. Two bedrooms are available, a single and a double, with a shared bath. Tri-County Mall and Forest Fair Mall are just minutes away for the shopper in the family. In addition to a full breakfast, Joan serves homemade dessert upon your arrival in the evening. Smoking is permitted.

Signal House Bed & Breakfast
$$ • 234 North Front St., Ripley • (937) 392-1640

This early 1800s Italianate home has been expertly transformed into a quaint bed and breakfast by proprietor Betsy Billingsly. Its history is one of post-revolutionary pedigree: The Signal House was used to signal (get it?) the Rev. John Rankin by lantern that the waterfront was safe to lead slaves to freedom during the heady days of the Underground Railroad. (Why not call it the Rankin House? Because that honor goes to nearby The Rankin House, a museum honoring Rankin and the 2,000 slaves he saved — all immortalized by local Harriet Beecher Stowe in *Uncle Tom's Cabin*.)

Yes, all of Ripley drips with Civil War history, but this bed and breakfast is hardly just for history buffs. Four-poster beds, private baths, romantic views of the Ohio River, and one of the best breakfasts you'll ever enjoy await you in Ripley. Come on down. (For more on attractions in this area, see our Daytrips chapter.)

Photo: Greater Cincinnati Convention and Visitors Bureau

Many area bed and breakfasts offer rustic settings.

Symphony Hotel
$$$$ • 210 W. 14th St. • 721-3353

Occupying the former Clyde Hotel, the Symphony Hotel is a gracious Victorian stone mansion in (unlike most bed and breakfasts) a distinctly urban inner-city neighborhood. Although located the gritty urban pioneer district of Over-the-Rhine near downtown Cincinnati, this is a distinctly upscale establishment. Manager Karen Blatt oversees the accommodations and dining room. The building itself, built in the mid-1800s, is like a trip back in time. It's been totally restored and refurbished, with furniture from the period in each room.

In addition to breakfast, the establishment also offers five-course dinners, though the hours are odd — dinner is only offered on performance nights at nearby Music Hall. The management also offers many ticket packages in conjunction with the Cincinnati Symphony Orchestra, which plays at Music Hall. (Symphony Hotel, get it?)

Three Islands at the Ridge
$$-$$$ • Manchester (call for street directions) • (937) 549-2149

Proprietor Cornelia Dettner says she feels more like a museum curator than an innkeeper, and little wonder. As guests enter the Ridge, built in 1856, they step back in time: The home's original wallpaper still clings to the walls, Dettner proudly notes. Top hats are found in closets, and the library is lined with ancient reading. This Victorian home, overseen by Dr. Dettner (yes, she's a real M.D., in case you're in sudden need of medical attention) features four bedrooms with huge 12-foot ceilings. There's a parlor for, need we say it, parlor games.

Dettner prides herself on the fresh omelets she makes, using vegetables from the garden, as well as her violet jelly. Guests dine at a huge dining room table that seats 18 — come prepared to chat. Nearby is the ancient Indian burial site, Serpent Mound, as well as bountiful shopping opportunities.

Victoria Inn of Hyde Park
$$-$$$$ • 3567 Shaw Ave. • 321-3567

Just two blocks east of great shopping and dining at Hyde Park Square in the city-neighborhood of Hyde Park, this 1909 inn has four guest rooms with feather beds that will soften you up in a hurry. Each room has its own bath, TV and private phone. Owner Tom Possert's establishment has been named the best bed and breakfast in Cincinnati by *Cincinnati Magazine* and listed among the 10 most romantic bed and breakfast inns in the country by *Vacations* magazine. Guests have privileges at the Cincinnati Sports Club about 10 minutes away and an in-ground pool out back. Ask about weekly or monthly rates. Kids 14 or younger are not allowed.

FYI

Unless otherwise noted, the area code for all phone numbers listed in this guide is 513.

Northern Kentucky

Amos Shinkle Townhouse Bed and Breakfast
$$-$$$$ • 215 Garrard St., Covington, Ky. • (606) 431-2118, (800) 972-7012

Built in 1854 by entrepreneur Amos Shinkle, this inn lies in the heart of Covington's historical Riverside District amid courtyard gardens. The Amos Shinkle Townhouse is ornately decorated with rich cornices, an Italianate facade with a cast-iron filigree porch, grand chandeliers, elaborate crown moldings, Italianate mantels and oak floors. This bed and breakfast inn — overseen by proprietors Bernard Morrman and Don Nash — is listed by the National Trust for Historic Preservation, which requires that an inn be at least 50 years old and have maintained its historical integrity.

A long screened porch affords a nice view of the Ohio River and the surrounding historical district. And it's only a short walk or drive to downtown Cincinnati or antique stores and fine dining in Covington's MainStrasse Village.

Among the seven guest rooms is a master bedroom in the main house with a private bath and four rooms in the carriage house, in which horse stalls have been redesigned as imaginative sleeping quarters for kids. All rooms have four-poster Victorian beds, and telephones. Smoking is allowed.

Carneal House Inn
$$$-$$$$ • 405 E. Second St., Covington, Ky. • (606) 431-6130

Built in 1815 by the founders of Covington, this Palladian Georgian-style mansion was featured in *Antiques* magazine as one of the first Federal Period houses in America. At the confluence of the Licking and Ohio rivers, the structure was a stately landmark for early river travelers in the area. The 183-year-old home has been visited by Lafayette, Henry Clay and Andrew Jackson. Today you can stay in one of six guest rooms with private baths and outdoor porches.

Carneal House Inn, managed by Karen and Peter Rafuse, is within sight of Cinergy Field just across the river and a few short blocks from fine dining and entertainment in Covington. With a little advance notice, you can arrange to have a horse-drawn carriage meet you at the door for your night on the town. For business travelers, desk space, a fax and portable phones are available, as are attractive weekday rates for conferences.

The inn is closed December 23 to February 13 for holidays and upkeep. These folks allow smoking and most pets ("not reptiles, please") but no children 12 or younger.

Christopher's B&B
$$-$$$$ • 604 Poplar St., Bellevue, Ky. • (606) 491-9354

This new bed and breakfast is in the most unique of buildings: the former Bellevue Christian Church in the town's historic district. Steve and Brenda Guidugli spent a year stripping the sanctuary to its frame; only the floor, stained-glass windows and painted tin roof remain in the interior. They added a balcony that wraps around three sides of the second story. There are three bedrooms with private baths — one is a suite with a living room and a two-person whirlpool. Each room has a TV with a built-in VCR and cable. An interesting note: The church congregation weighed offers from other churches before deciding that a life as a B&B was a better future for the building.

First Farm Inn
$$$, no credit cards • 2510 Stevens Rd., Burlington, Ky. • (606) 596-0199

Dana Kisor and Jennifer Warner have just opened one of Northern Kentucky's newest bed and breakfasts in a rustic 1870s farmhouse well away from the hustle and bustle of the city. Set among the rolling hills on the bluffs above the Ohio River, First Farm Inn offers a fish pond as well as a full farm complement: horses, cows and goats. Spacious rooms are decorated with century-old hand-crafted oak furniture belonging to Wagner's great-grandparents and have private baths. Lest you think yourself too far from civilization, fax and Internet access are provided. Breakfast itself is anything from Grand Marnier French toast to baked Southwestern eggs. You're welcome to bring your horse (pasture boarding available).

Gateway Bed and Breakfast
$$$ • 326 E. Sixth St., Newport, Ky. • (606) 581-6447, (888) 891-7500

This 1878 Italianate townhouse with floor-to-ceiling windows and decorative plaster moldings is in Newport's East Row National Historic District. Rooms are spacious and beautifully decorated, with many antique musical instruments throughout the house. Owners Ken and Sandy Clift serve a full country breakfast in the dining room. A rooftop deck is a great place to pass a summer evening — especially during the Riverfest fireworks on Labor Day weekend. There are three guest rooms, all with private baths.

Licking Riverside Historic B&B
$$$-$$$$ • 516 Garrard St., Covington, Ky. • (606) 291-0191

Located on the scenic Licking River, a tributary that flows into the Ohio alongside the Covington riverbank, this bed and breakfast caters in particular to the romantic traveler , vacationing honeymooners or couples celebrating anniversaries. Innkeeper Lynda Freeman will even host a small wedding (if you arrange in advance for a justice of the peace) in this three-story, 1868 Greek Revival structure. And romantic is certainly the word to describe the two suites and two rooms, all outfitted with double Jacuzzi baths, candles, refrigerators to chill champagne and even the wine

glasses supplied. A winding hairpin staircase is just one fascinating architectural facet of the home, which includes decks and a bucolic courtyard.

The Mansion
$$$-$$$$ • 1003 North Third St., Bardstown, Ky. • (502) 348-2586

Okay, this is edging more towards central Kentucky but it's well worth noting nonetheless. The Mansion is an 1851 Greek Revival home presided over by Charmaine and Dennis Downs. The gorgeous old antebellum is elegant and, better yet, air-conditioned (unlike many of its contemporaries around the area). Period antiques, hand-crocheted bedspreads and dust ruffles abound here. All guest rooms have private baths. Breakfast is served on no less than china, silver and crystal.

The Mansion was built by a former lieutenant governor of the state and is on the National Register of Historic Places. The estate's grounds are alive with fragrant dogwoods, mimosa, pear and apple trees. Only two hours from Cincinnati proper, this is perhaps our favorite old Kentucky home.

Mansion Hill Manor
$$$$ • 315 E. Third St., Newport, Ky. • (606) 291-1700

Sharon Love welcomes you to this stately mansion, a Queen Anne-style home built in the 1800s and listed on the National Historic Register. There are four bedrooms to rent, with shared baths (Love has hired an architect and is in the process of adding private baths). One room has a balcony with a view of the Ohio River and the Cincinnati skyline. Located in Newport's historic district, Mansion Hill Manor is just a few minutes' walk to the riverwalk and such restaurants as The Chart House. The home also has outside gardens and a porch (where smoking is permitted).

Mary's Belle View Inn
$$-$$$$ • 444 Van Voast St., Bellevue, Ky. • (606) 581-8337

Talk about your truth in advertising. Mary Bickers runs this two-story bed and breakfast, and it certainly does boast a splendid view. The 90-year-old home, with a deck on the second floor overlooking the Ohio River, is booked solid every year for the Riverfest fireworks. The rest of the year, you are more likely to nab a room. There are three bedrooms to rent, one a suite with a Jacuzzi and all with private baths.

Sandford House Bed and Breakfast
$$-$$$ • 1026 S. Russell St., Covington, Ky. • (606) 291-9133

This restored 1820s mansion is in Covington's Seminary Square Historic District. Built in the Federal style, it was refurbished in the Victorian style in the 1880s. The four guest rooms in the house range from a single room to the garden suite or a furnished apartment. Each has color cable TV and a refrigerator. Third-floor apartments have a nice view of Cincinnati. A full breakfast is served either in a dining room or the gazebo of a lovely garden in the warmer months. Pets and smoking are allowed.

Summer House B&B
$$-$$$$ • 610 Sanford St., Covington, Ky. • (606) 365-5141, (800) 365-5141

Proprietor Betty Brown promises a completely different experience from the starchy Victorians you sometimes encounter on the bed-and-breakfast circuit. Her 1865 Second Empire-style home is decorated in a Caribbean/Key West kind of theme, with light, soft colors and an airy decor more appropriate to a Florida beach house than an Ohio riverfront. There's a private bath in each of the four bedrooms as well as cable TV, an in-wall sound system, and (this is a novelty) private phones. If business beckons, there's a fax machine, copier, computer and printer on site. Brown sometimes serves breakfast in the open-air courtyard out back, and for dinner you can head to the nearby South Beach Grill, in keeping with the Summer House's beachy theme. Pets are negotiable, but call first.

Taylor Spinks House
$$-$$$ • 702 Overton St., Newport, Ky. • (606) 291-0092

Kara and John Zinn host guests in this beautiful 1878 Italianate-style residence in Newport's East Row Historic District. Two grand staircases, plaster medallions and restored fireplace mantles greet visitors. There are two bedrooms on the second floor: The Front Room features a Jacuzzi, bidet, and walk-in closet; the Back Room is a suite of two rooms that nicely accommodates families. (A nice plus: Guests in the Back Room have private access via a backstairs to the suite.) There are lots of period antiques and complimentary wine, sodas and snacks.

Weller Haus Bed & Breakfast
$$-$$$$ • 319 Poplar St., Bellevue, Ky. • (606) 431-6829

Mary and Vernon Weller welcome you to this 1880s Victorian gothic homestead in Bellevue's Taylor Daughter's Historic District (only a mile or so from downtown Cincinnati). Church steeples, city streets and stained glass are just some of the attractive sights to see from the windows of the antique-appointed guest and sitting rooms, all equipped with private baths. Weller Haus features original millwork and five spacious antique-furnished guest rooms with cathedral ceilings. A skylit great room and secluded garden are other nice features.

An exquisite breakfast is served among the pattern glass, linens, laces and porcelains of yesteryear. This isn't to say there aren't modern amenities: Consider the Double Jacuzzi Suite, for instance. The location is within walking distance of fine dining along Riverboat Row and five minutes from downtown.

Southeastern Indiana

Folke Family Farm Inn
$$ • 18406 Pribble Rd., Lawrenceburg, Ind. • (812) 537-7025

If you're a nature buff, you'll want to come commune with the wild turkeys, rabbits, coyote and deer. No, they're not in your bedroom, but close enough. The Folke Family Farm Inn is just outside the once-sleepy, but (thanks to riverboat gambling) now bustling town of Lawrenceburg. There are plenty of panoramic views and walking trails to keep your mind off the craps tables, however. The 14-room farmhouse features rooms with private baths, a glassed-in solarium, sitting room and more. Billing itself as an authentic Hoosier Homestead (whatever that means), Folke Family Farm Inn does offer a scenic and relaxed alternative to the hustle and bustle of the nearby gambling and ski slope industries.

Mulberry Inn & Gardens
$$ • 118 South Mulberry St., Rising Sun, Ind. • (812) 438-2206

Less than an hour's drive from downtown Cincinnati, the Mulberry Inn is one of the highlights in the quaint town of Rising Sun. The home is in the heart of the town's residential area. Proprietors Janet and Jim Willis maintain a charming establishment, featuring gardens where you can watch the birds flutter while enjoying a full country breakfast. The back porch offers a bucolic view as well — a world away from urban tensions. Each room includes a private bath and color TV, though certainly the most popular room for a romantic getaway is the Jungle Room, complete with canopy bed, fireplace and whirlpool bath.

Rise N Shine Bed and Breakfast
$-$$ • 412 South High St., Rising Sun, Ind. • (812) 438-2375

Another Rising Sun favorite, the Rise N Shine Bed and Breakfast is an imposing Indiana mansion house with an amiable front porch on which to sit and watch the world stroll by. The rooms are more spacious than in many bed and breakfasts, and private night entry is a nice plus. Free snacks, soft drinks and coffee are available 24 hours a day, and the buffet breakfast (served promptly at 9 AM each day) features Belgian waffles in addition to the standards: eggs, hash browns and bacon.

Rosemont Inn
$$ • Ind. Hwy. 56, Vevay, Ind. • (812) 427-3050

About an hour's drive from downtown Cincinnati, the Rosemont Inn is located on the banks of the Ohio River in the historic town of Vevay. The inn — built in 1881 by James K. and Charlotte Pleasant, members of a wealthy merchant and river shipping family — is a Victorian Italianate with five bedrooms. The home was purchased in 1993 by innkeepers James Abraham and Kenneth Lockridge, who undertook extensive renovations of the interior and exterior.

Each room features interior woodwork with six types of inlaid hardwood and has a private bath and fireplace. Terrycloth robes in each room are a nice touch, and lovely antiques are scattered throughout the household. A full-service breakfast is served in the sunny dining area overlooking the Ohio River, as are late afternoon refreshments and, in winter, a high English tea. The rose garden is particularly stunning.

Just look for the tallest
building and you'll
have found the heart
of downtown
Cincinnati shopping —
Tower Place mall.

Shopping

Shopping opportunities abound in Greater Cincinnati. Three department store chains — McAlpin's, Lazarus and Parisian — permeate the region, plus there's a dizzying variety of discount retailers and everything in between. The northern Interstate 275 corridor alone is a fertile crescent for the shop-'til-you-drop crowd. Here, within about a 15-mile area, are Cincinnati's biggest suburban shopping malls, with nearly 5 million square feet of retail space combined and almost 600 stores. Each mall has plenty of satellite retailers as well, making this one of the most densely shopped areas you'll find anywhere.

Lost in the hubbub of suburban mall development is the fact that downtown Cincinnati is in the midst of a retail renaissance. Witness the first opening of a department store downtown in half a century — Lazarus' huge complex at Fountain Square West (and Maison Blanche just announced it would be opening a second department store in mid-1998, and Nordstrom's confirmed it was negotiating with the city to open yet a third downtown department store). Witness the opening of a ritzy Tiffany & Co. Jewelers in a brand-new complex that also features Brooks Brothers. Witness the newly renovated Saks Fifth Avenue and the thriving Tower Place mall, which boasts the likes of the Nature Company, Banana Republic, Brentano's, The Limited and more. Downtown now has an estimated 1.7 million square feet of retail space with more than 400 shops . . . an embarrassment of riches.

In this chapter you'll find information about area shopping, outlet stores and flea markets, along with our favorite (among Greater Cincinnati's many) specialty food stores and wineries, bookstores, and gift shops.

Try not to blame us too much if one of these stores is gone by the time you get there. We've tried to mention only establishments with staying power, but even bright stars wink out in the fast-changing retail market.

Shopping Areas

What follows is a shopping tour beginning downtown and extending to the neighborhood and village shopping districts and the area's suburban malls and major shopping centers.

Downtown

Looked at collectively, downtown is still the biggest shopping mall in town. Unfortunately, most suburbanites prefer to stick close to home. But they're missing out on a lot.

Anyone who thinks traffic and parking are a problem downtown hasn't been there for a while. It's as easy if not easier to navigate traffic and find a good parking place downtown on a weekend than at virtually any suburban shopping mall and its surrounding traffic tangle. Parking downtown isn't free, but it's close. Metered parking is in fact free on Saturday and Sunday. And parking in city garages is $1 for three hours. Do make sure you don't overstay that three hours without moving your car, though, as the rates escalate quickly after that.

Besides convenience, downtown offers an ambiance that even the most marble-encrusted suburban malls can't: Fountain Square, restaurants that go beyond the usual food court choices, and horse-drawn carriage rides.

Tower Place

Just look for the tallest building downtown and you'll have found the heart of downtown Cincinnati shopping — Tower Place mall, at the base of the Carew Tower, Fifth and Race streets. Try parking either at the Fountain Square Garage, a city garage with entrances on Vine Street north of Fifth Street, Walnut Street south of Sixth Street and beneath the Westin off of Vine Street just north of Fourth Street. This garage usually will serve you well, in fact, no matter where you're going downtown. Downtown isn't so big yet that you can't walk fairly easily most everywhere from one parking garage.

Inside Tower Place you'll find a nicely appointed marble and gold-trimmed mall that looks very much like a suburban shopping mall. Among the stores here are **Banana Republic**, **Brentano's**, a nicely stocked two-story **Nature Company**, the **Gap**, **The Limited** and **Limited Express** nearby at 441 Race Street.

The food court is above average, particularly **The Big Easy**, purveyor of great Bourbon Chicken and other fast Cajun dishes. And not far away in the arcade of the Carew Tower is **Hathaway Restaurant**, a friendly retro excursion to an old-fashioned lunch counter. The Carew Tower arcade is also home to one of Cincinnati's more intriguing specialty stores, **Mahatma**, featuring Indian (not Native American) jewelry, accents and artifacts.

Tower Place itself doesn't have anchor stores, but **Saks Fifth Avenue** at Fifth and Race streets (the only Saks in Greater Cincinnati) is easily accessible directly via Skywalk connection. The new **Lazarus** at Fountain Square West is also accessible via the Skywalk (more on Lazarus below).

Fourth Street

Fourth Street was once the center of downtown shopping until Tower Place and Lazarus shifted it a block north. The art gallery scene, once vibrant on Fourth Street, has shifted even farther north to Over-the-Rhine's Main Street district (see below). Today, the future of Fourth Street retailing is a big concern.

Even so, you'll still find some good stuff here. **A.B. Closson Jr. Co.**, better known as Closson's, is one of the best places in town for fine furniture, art and accessories. Its downtown store at 401 Race Street, on the corner of Fourth Street, is bigger and better-stocked than its Montgomery Store at 10100 Montgomery Road. There are still some noted galleries here, including the **Laura Paul Gallery**, 49 E. Fourth Street.

Fourth Street's main specialty these days is Oriental rugs. Closson's carries them, as do **Dingilian Rugs** across the street at 209 W.

Fourth Street and **Jamshid Rugs** at 151 W. Fourth Street.

Contemporary Galleries, nearby at 221 W. Fourth, offers a nice selection of reasonably priced Mission-style wood furniture. And over a block, **The Bromwell Co.**, 117 W. Fourth Street, has a wide selection of fireplace inserts, door knockers and other brass accessories.

Around Fountain Square

The specialty shops near the lobby of the Westin, south of Fountain Square, are also worth a visit. Jellybean lovers can satisfy their sweet tooth at **Galerie Au Chocolat** with an amazingly broad assortment of flavors, including three varieties of watermelon jelly beans, not to mention chocolates and other goodies.

Just north of Fountain Square, hat aficionados will find a small paradise in **Batsakes Hat Shop**, 605 Walnut Street. Up the street, check out **Walnut Street Popcorn & Sweets**, a beacon for nearby office dwellers who love the fresh-popped popcorn in assorted flavors, including the well-regarded cheese, caramel and chocolate. This shop is smack dab in the midst of the new "Backstage" area surrounding the Aronoff Center for the Arts, with such popular restaurants as **Nicholson's Tavern and Pub**, **Ciao Cucina**, **First Watch** and **Plaza 600** (in the Aronoff Center for the Arts).

Lazarus opened in late 1997 at Fountain Square West (on the block just west of Fountain Square, naturally). And what a department store it is — a $28 million tri-level complex, 184,000 square feet in all, with Italian marble floors and African wood veneers. It's open and bright, with lots of windows. The ground floor is devoted to women's cosmetics, accessories, jewelry, shoes and such. The second floor houses men's, women's and children's apparel. Housewares are on the third floor. In a bid to appeal to women and differ itself from the suburban Lazaruses, services such as a mammography center and vendor shops are also offered.

Tiffany's and **Brooks Brothers** also have stores here.

FYI

Unless otherwise noted, the area code for all phone numbers listed in this guide is 513.

Main Street and Over-the-Rhine

Main Street, both downtown and across Central Parkway in Over-the-Rhine, has become the areas's most vibrant entertainment and gallery district in recent years, and it has some other good specialty stores too. Here you'll also find such popular downtown eateries as **Arnold's Bar and Grill** (just off Main on Eighth Street), **Carol's on Main** and **Izzy's**, along with the newer **BarrelHouse Brewing Company** and **Main Street Brewery** in Over-the-Rhine. One block over on Sycamore Street is an equally hip bistro, appropriately named **The Diner on Sycamore**.

Among the shops to visit on the downtown side of the border are the **Ohio Book Store**, 726 Main Street, with its five stories of used books. Next door is **Erban Earth**, 201 E. Eighth Street, which carries an eclectic collection of objets d'art and knickknacks. On the other side of the street be sure to visit **Greg's Antiques**, 925 Main Street, and **Artistiques**, 633 Main Street, home to fine collections of architectural and other antiques.

You'll need to walk north a few blocks and over Central Parkway (a.k.a. The Rhine) to Over-the-Rhine, site of a whirlwind of boutique and nightclub development in recent years. Keep in mind that this is still one of Cincinnati's poorest neighborhoods despite the influx of urban pioneering, so be careful. At night, it's probably safest to park in a relatively well-lit parking lot or space south of Central Parkway and walk a few blocks rather than wandering the side streets looking for your car in the wee hours.

Among the galleries and boutiques worth visiting here is **Kaldi's Coffeehouse and Bookstore**, 1206 Main Street, a friendly spot with musty used books. **Marta Hewett Gallery**, 1209 Main Street, is known for contemporary glass and other contemporary art. **BASE Art Gallery**, 1311 Main Street, shows the work of an ensemble of area artists. **only artists**, 1315 Main Street, specializes in contemporary primitives. **St. Theresa's Textile Trove**, 1329 Main Street, has a bewildering variety of cloth from around the world. **Classical Glass**, 1333 Main Street, has a wide selection of windows and glass items. **Shadeau Breads**, 1336 Main Street, sells tasty baked goods from a former baker at Cincinnati's most

highly regarded bakery, Bonbonerie. **Celio!**, 1341 Main Street, sells consignment art and vintage curios. **Furniture By Design**, just over a block away at 1622 Vine Street, features furniture built by owner Mark Kessler.

Nearby, also make sure to check out **Carl Solway Gallery**, 424 Findlay; **Machine Shop Gallery**, 100 Central Parkway; and **River City Works**, 532 E. 12th Street.

A shopping trip to Over-the-Rhine really isn't complete without a stop at **Findlay Market**, a few blocks west of Main Street at Race and Findlay streets. This combination indoor and open-air market offers produce, meat and confections at competitive prices. Note: This is not Quincy Market, the very nice Boston tourist trap. It's more like the authentic open-air markets found in Boston's North End. This is a real live market where locals buy fresh food, though suburbanites do flock here on Saturday mornings. Outside, street vendors hawk all kinds of street-vendor stuff. Of special interest is **Saigon Market**, 119 W. Elder Street, just off the main Findlay Market building. Here you can buy an array of Vietnamese foods and spices.

Near Downtown

Clifton, Clifton Heights, Clifton Gaslight District, University Heights and Corryville

This area goes by many names thanks to the district lines of Cincinnati neighborhoods, but it's all part of the University of Cincinnati neighborhood and is much like big university ghettos everywhere, only nicer. The Ludlow Avenue shopping district is the best in the university area — a sort of New Age shopping mall with out-of-the ordinary jewelry, apparel and art offerings. Most shoppers walk here since parking is tough, but you'll find parallel parking along the side streets off of Ludlow Avenue if you cruise around long enough.

Don't miss **Michael's Affordable Art**, 329 Ludlow Avenue, probably the best all-around gift store of any kind in town, offering a wide range of inexpensive reproductions of famous paintings, African-American art, small musical instruments for kids and adults, educational toys, imaginative Christmas ornaments, a broad line of Pooh-related stuffed animals and merchandise, lovely handcrafted blankets, and great posters and T-shirts (including the classic Jim Borgman "How Do You Feel Today?" model in several languages). It's so packed with merchandise, you'll have trouble making your way through. But do.

Across the street is **Mediterranean Foods** at 314 E. Ludlow and **New World Bookshop**, 336 E. Ludlow, one of Cincinnati's few remaining general-interest independent bookstores. (If you're in the area at showtime, stop in at **The Esquire Theatre**, 320 E. Ludlow, to see art, international and other films that are generally free of car chases and Sylvester Stallone.)

Other shops of note include the **Shops at Ludlow Garage**, 344 E. Ludlow, four businesses that operate under one roof (including **Paola** jewelers); **Hansa Guild**, 369 E. Ludlow, for anything from moccasins to Dhurrie rugs; **Semesters**, 313 E. Ludlow, which caters to the fraternity crowd with emblazed fraternity and sorority items; and **Pathways**, 270 E. Ludlow, purveyors of incense, crystals and chimes.

This is also a good place if shopping makes you hungry. Good restaurants here include **No Anchovies Pizza** (an archetypal college pizza joint), **Thai Cafe**, **Thatsa Wrapp**, and a carry-out-only **Petersen's Restaurant**, one of three outposts for the most elegant mid-priced restaurant in Greater Cincinnati. Don't forget to stop at **Graeter's** for dessert. The area also has two fine bakeries: **Big Sky Bakery**, just off Ludlow at 265 Hosea, and **Virginia Bakery**, 286 Ludlow.

Elsewhere in Clifton and Corryville are shops that are mostly of interest to college students, and if you are one, you'll find them soon enough. Standing out among the many used/vintage/offbeat clothing retailers here and elsewhere in the city is **Scentiments/Rock City**, 2614 Vine Street. Nearby, **Duttenhofer's Treasures**, 214 W. McMillan, is an interesting newsstand and bookstore, with a special map store that has the area's most complete selection of maps in addition to a wide selection of travel books.

Covington — MainStrasse Village

The easiest way to find MainStrasse is to look for the Quality Inn Riverview, a tall, scalloped, cylindrical building, and then head south. There's nary a single German-theme store in this German-theme village, but there's still some good shopping to be done. The German cuisine at **Wertheim's** restaurant and the Cajun fare and entertainment at **Dee Felice Cafe** are two big draws here.

Among shops of special interest are **The Doll Clinic**, selling antique and collectible dolls; **Center Field Cards and Collectibles**; **Kaleidoscope Stained Glass**; **Kilims**, a Turkish rug shop; and **The Magic Shop**, purveyors of fake vomit, whoopee cushions and tools of the magician's trade. In the same house as The Magic Shop is **Philadelphia Street Antiques**, home to an impressive collection of military and historical antiques.

Mount Adams

Mount Adams is Cincinnati's trendiest neighborhood and a place that, were it not so darned hilly, would probably have as many joggers per capita as Hyde Park. Even so, it has plenty of good restaurants to make you fat. The best shopping here is along St. Gregory Street. Of special interest: **Mount Adams Bookstore Cafe**, 1101 St. Gregory, an inter-

INSIDERS' TIP

Whether shopping for beer, wine or spirits, know that prices and selection are definitely better on the south side of the Ohio River. Technically, it's illegal for Ohioans to buy on the Kentucky side, but only in quantity — a bottle or two is well within the prescribed limit. And, heck, nobody can remember the last time the Ohio state cops actually staked out a Kentucky liquor store, anyhow.

esting little bookstore and bistro; **Botanicals**, 953 St. Gregory, specializing in plants and home accessories; and **Briani & Miotto** jewelers, 1111 St. Gregory, which carries reasonably priced semiprecious-stone art jewelry. Good places to eat on this strip include **Teak Thai Cuisine**, **Cafe Vienna**, **Cherrington's**, **Adrica's** and **Mount Adams Fish House**. They've also got the nicest **United Dairy Farmers** store around.

East

Beechmont Mall
7500 Beechmont Ave., Anderson
• 232-3438

Just off I-275 at Beechmont and Five Mile Road, this 600,000-square-foot, 57-store mall attracts many Northern Kentucky shoppers. Anchors stores are **Kmart**, **Lazarus** and **Parisian** — a pretty nice range under one roof. Other stores here include **Outdoor Adventures**, **Candles by Chris**, **Planet Wear**, **Gentry Men's Clothing**, **B. Dalton** bookstore and **Victoria's Secret**. New owners promise to spruce up and modernize the mall, though it's certainly clean and attractive as is. The **Pizzeria Uno** and **T.G.I. Friday's** here do a bang-up business, and **Bill Knapp's** is on an outlot. Other good eateries just across Five Mile Road include **Fuddrucker's** and **Outback Steak House**.

Eastgate Mall
I-275 and Ohio Hwy. 32, 4601 Eastgate Blvd., Mount Carmel • 752-2290

This Clermont County mall is in one of the fastest growing shopping areas in town. The mall itself is the area's sixth-largest, with 766,000 square feet and nearly 90 stores. Anchor stores and major attractions here include a newer **McAlpin's** department store, a new **Kohl's**, **Sears**, **JC Penney** and an eight-screen **Showcase** movie theater where parents from throughout the East Side like to do the old dump-and-run with their preteens. Eastgate Mall also has a **Waldenbooks**, **Camelot Records** and **Victoria's Secret**.

Near Eastgate Mall, off Ohio 32 along Eastgate South Boulevard, is a discount shopper's paradise, including a **Bigg's**

hypermarket with a **SuperSaver Cinemas**, a **Meijer** supercenter, **Wal-Mart**, **Sam's Warehouse Club** and probably the world's most varied collection of home electronics retailers, including **Best Buy**, **Circuit City** and **Sun**. If it plugs in and you can't find it here, you probably can't find it anywhere. Also here is one of America's most complete collection of fast-food joints in one square mile, in addition to some great Thai food at **Ban Thai** (across the street from Bigg's) and a delightful **Krispy Kreme** donut shop.

Hyde Park

Welcome to the neighborhood with more joggers and women's apparel stores per capita than any other in Cincinnati. Here's a tour of Hyde Park's three hottest shopping spots, only one of which is actually in Hyde Park.

This is the one: **Hyde Park Square**, at Erie and Edwards streets. It actually is the square of Hyde Park, which was its own city until it was conquered by Cincinnati early in this century. Today, the corner of Erie and Edwards, along with surrounding side streets, makes up the best known and most widely shopped of Cincinnati's neighborhood shopping districts. Here you'll find first-class art galleries, good-to-great midrange restaurants, women's apparel galore and, perhaps best of all, **Graeter's** ice cream.

Art stores and galleries worth visiting include **The Framery**, 3508 Edwards Road, home of Jim Borgman originals; **Miller Art Gallery**, 2715 Erie Avenue, and the **Malton Gallery**, 2709 Observatory Avenue. Next door to the Malton Gallery, check out **Voltage** for modern furniture and accessories. Popular apparel stores on or near the square include **Talbots**, 2771 Observatory; **Wizard Weaver's**, 2701 Observatory; **Acorn**, 2701 Erie; and **Stocks Gentleman's Clothiers**, 2736 Erie. **Willow House**, 3526 Edwards Road at the old Drew's Bookstore, has probably the widest and certainly the best selection of lamps in Greater Cincinnati, in addition to other eclectic home accessories.

You needn't go hungry here either. For at-home gourmet dining, do your shopping at **Hyde Park Gourmet**, 2707 Erie Avenue. You'll also find a branch of the **Great Harvest Bread Company**, sellers of delicious bread baked at the Montgomery store. Or, just eat at the square. Among the selections: **Indigo Casual Gourmet Cafe**, 2637 Erie Avenue, for great gourmet pizza; **The Echo**, 3510 Edwards Road, a longtime favorite mom-food diner; **Arthur's**, next door, for a slightly more modern read on American cuisine; and **Teller's of Hyde Park**, run by the folks at Main Street Brewery in an old bank building.

Next there's **Hyde Park Plaza** at Wasson Road and Paxton Avenue. It's actually in Oakley, but no one really notices except maybe the Oakley Community Council. "Oakley Plaza" doesn't have quite the cachet, if you catch the drift. (Trendy Hyde Park has been successfully extending its borders for years. Parts of Oakley, East Walnut Hills, Norwood, even Evanston have been dubbed "Hyde Park Near" by fast-talking real estate ads.)

Anyway, Hyde Park Plaza is a mix of upscale and discount shopping, including both **Kroger** and **Thriftway** grocery stores, where the skim milk always runs out first. The Kroger here is one of the few in the region that sells hard liquor. Of special interest are the **Barnes & Noble** superstore, **Old Navy Clothing Co.** (the Gap's more budget-minded cousin), **Servatii Pastry** for luscious sweets and **Starbucks**.

The third spot is **Rookwood Pavilion**, at Madison and Edwards roads. OK, Rookwood Pavilion is not in Hyde Park either. But it's so much like Hyde Park that even natives confuse the issue. Actually, Rookwood Pavilion is squarely within the boundaries of Norwood, whose city officials will be quick to fill you in on this fact. This shopping center, converted from an old machine tool factory, is a sign of rejuvenation for a city abandoned by GM and LeBlond Makino plants in the 1980s.

Rookwood Pavilion is today possibly the hottest shopping center in Greater Cincinnati, thanks largely to two very popular spots. The giant **Joseph-Beth Booksellers** book/restaurant/music/toy/food store is probably the all-around nicest bookstore in Greater Cincinnati. Nearby, **First Watch** is the best and most popular place in town for breakfast. This is also a good discount center, with **Stein Mart** apparel and housewares, **HomeGoods** discount housewares and **T.J. Maxx** discount clothing. The center also has a **Coconuts** music superstore, **Smith & Hawken** for finer house and garden supplies, and **Fawn Confectionery** for tasty treats.

Mariemont

A *Cincinnati Magazine* cover story recently anointed Mariemont (pronounced Mary-mont) "the town's trendiest suburb," and indeed, the once-sleepy town square is now hopping. All thanks to the opening of one of the city's most talked about restaurants, **Bistro Gigi**, run by the same family that brings us The Maisonette. Not to mention the opening of an art film house next door, The **Mariemont Theater**. The square is done up in Tudor, as is the entire village (one of the nation's first planned communities), and well worth a visit for a leisurely stroll. Shops and restaurants along the square and nearby "Strand" include **The Villager** (an all-purpose notions shop), **Dilly Deli** (a wine cellar), **Starbucks**, **Eva's Esthetica** cosmetics, **Leslie at the Strand** hair salon, **Graeter's** ice cream, and the **National Exemplar** (a terrific breakfast spot). Stop in the **Mariemont Inn**, a royal hotel done up in medieval grandeur, and catch a drink at its Southerby's Pub.

Mount Lookout Square

A pleasant neighborhood shopping district at Delta and Linwood avenues, the Square caters mainly to locals but has a few attractions that make it worth a visit even if you don't live nearby. **Boardwalk Hobby Shop**, 1032 Delta Avenue, has perhaps the city's most extensive collection of model kits and vintage toys and games. Across the street, check out **Unicorn Miniatures**, 1028 Delta, where miniature houses and furniture are a very big deal. **Confetti Cats**, 3165 Linwood, carries items for the feline in your household (we like the catnip-stuffed Newt Gingrich chew toy). The square also features two upscale consignment shops, **Second Hand Rose** at 1030 Delta and **Champagne Taste** at 821 Delta.

The Square also offers many choices of good and unpretentious dining, including **Dion's**, 3173 Linwood Avenue; **Betta's** (Italian cuisine), 1026 Delta Avenue, where you can eat in or take it home (hot or cold); and **Zip's Cafe**, 1036 Delta, a terrific little hamburger joint and restaurant that may be the hardest place in town to get a seat. You can enjoy some after-dinner coffee or get some java to go from the **Blue Mountain Coffee Co**.

You can also assault your cardiovascular system in other ways here. **Bracke Meats & Produce**, 1010 Delta, is a popular local butcher shop. And if a bang-up combination of first- and secondhand smoke is your thing, join the **Private Smoking Club**, 3195 Linwood Avenue, where the smoking section is always open.

O'Bryonville

Foot for square foot, this little strip in the 2000 block of Madison Road west of Hyde Park is one of the best neighborhood shopping districts in Cincinnati. It includes six of Cincinnati's better antique stores: **Federation Antiques**, **English Traditions**, **Gartell's Antiques**, **Treasures** and **Treadway Gallery**, specializing in Rookwood Pottery. You'll also find the **Toni Birckhead Gallery** and **Rottinghaus Gallery** for fine art.

You'll find good eats here, too, including gourmet pizza at **The Brick Yard**; gourmet mom food for dining in or out at **What's For Dinner?** (on O'Bryon Road, just off Madison); or good wine and eclectic dining at **Chateau Pomije**. Past What's for Dinner off O'Bryonville is the **Bonbonerie** and its Tea Room, which has got to be the best pastry shop in town.

Oakley Square

Like O'Bryonville, Oakley Square doesn't have the reputation enjoyed by Hyde Park Square, but it may be Cincinnati's all-around best shopping district. Just head northeast from O'Bryonville to the 3000 block of Madison and you're there. It's not as attractive on the outside as some other East Side shopping districts, but it's what's inside that counts.

Highlights here include **King Arthur's Court**, the all-around best toy store in town; the **Blue Marble**, one of the best kids' bookstores in town; **Cappel's**, a great place for seasonal decorations, party supplies and Halloween costumes; a good consignment store in **Astute Furnishings**; **Flaggs USA**, offering a variety of those decorative flags plus hilariously inflammatory bumper stickers and other interesting gift items; **Oakley Cycles**, presenting the town's most comprehensive stock of bicycles, and **Bona Decorative Hardware**, a

good place to find replacements for all those little things that break in old houses.

The food is terrific here too. Oakley Square has a **Big Sky Bakery** and the original **Aglamesis Brothers** ice cream store, a genuine old-fashioned ice cream parlor that serves up some of the best ice cream in town. A couple of blocks up the road, check out **The Production Line Cafe**, 3210 Madison Road, where vegetarian meals are always available. It's a great dine-in/carry out lunch spot with superb sandwiches and daily specials.

Northeast

Blue Ash

If you furnished your house strictly with what you could find on Kenwood Road through downtown Blue Ash, you'd have a pretty nice place. The **Rug Gallery**, 9350 Kenwood Road, has probably the best selection of rugs in town, priced from the low three figures to five figures. **Arhaus Furniture**, 9405 Kenwood Road, **Gourmet Furniture**, just north of Cooper, in the Keystone Plaza, and **Montags** on Cooper and Kenwood roads offer good values in contemporary and traditional styles. All three have good prices for high-quality stuff. The **Down Lite International Factory Outlet** store, not far from here at 7818 Palace Drive, also off of Cornell, is a great place for deals on down comforters and winter clothes.

The food around here is pretty scrumptious. Try **Marx Hot Bagels Factory** and **Maya's Restaurant** in Keystone Plaza, and for the biggest double-deckers you ever saw go a few blocks north to **Blue Ash Chili**, Kenwood and Pfeifer roads.

Kenwood Towne Centre
7875 Kenwood Rd., Kenwood • 745-9100

Though slightly smaller (at least for the time being) than Tri-County and Forest Fair Malls, Kenwood Towne Centre generally enjoys the reputation as the top mall in Cincinnati. With about 2,000 fewer parking spaces than those similarly sized malls, it can present a big parking challenge at holiday time. But that doesn't keep people from coming here in droves.

Anchors of this mall, at the corner of Kenwood and Montgomery roads, include

McAlpin's, **Lazarus** and **Parisian**. Other stores among the 180 at the 1.1 million-square-foot mall include the only **Sharper Image** and **Brookstone** stores in town, **Benetton**, **Banana Republic**, the **Nature Company**, **Waldenbooks**, **The Bombay Company**, **The Disney Store**, **Imaginarium**, **Eddie Bauer**, **The Limited** and **Limited Too**.

Don't leave without visiting the one-of-a-kind **Games People Play**, the best grown-up game store in town. **A Show of Hands** features Ohio artisans only. And for the area's best selection of gargoyles — well, all right, the area's ONLY selection of gargoyles — head to **The Museum Company**. In addition to a complete range of stone gargoyles to adorn any refrigerator or bookcase, there are kaleidoscopes, calendars, ties, jewelry, mugs, coasters and pocket watches.

The quality of the surrounding shopping adds to the Kenwood Towne Centre's attraction. Across Kenwood you'll find fine menswear at **Joseph A. Bank Clothiers** and fine eclectic dining at **Trio's**. And across Montgomery Road you'll find Kenwood Towne Centre's discount-oriented alter image, **Sycamore Plaza**. This used to be called Kenwood Mall before Kenwood Towne Centre turned it into a ghost town. In its second life as Sycamore Plaza, it's one of the hottest retail properties in town. Among the 15 stores in this 345,000-square-foot center are a **Barnes & Noble** superstore, **Lazarus Furniture Gallery**, **Men's Wearhouse**, **Toys 'R Us** and **Staples**. It also has some popular restaurants in **Dick Clark's American Bandstand Grille**, **Max and Erma's**, **Hotel Discovery** and **Johnny Rockets**.

Madeira

The "central business district" around the intersection of Miami and Euclid roads is a worthwhile shopping destination, particularly for practitioners of the crafts and other domestic arts. Highlights include **Heart's Desire**, an arts and crafts gallery, and **Peach Mountain Studios**, yarn and knitting supplies, 7010 Miami Ave. Just south at Camargo Station (next to the Kroger store) are **Creative Cottage**, featuring quilting and cross-stitching and other home

FYI

Unless otherwise noted, the area code for all phone numbers listed in this guide is 513.

accessories; the **Family Massage Center**; **Kristin's** kids clothing shop; **Country Manor Ltd.** antiques and American traditional doodads; **Maller's Gourmet Shoppe**, and **The Bead Shop**, a truly focused retail specialty store.

Across the street at Miami Avenue and Goff Terrace is **Ferrari's Little Italy** and the **Italian Bakery**, which, in addition to serving up some fine Italian food, has great bread available for takeout. Nearby at **Madeira Crossing** (7011 Miami Avenue) is **Starbucks** and **Bruegger's Bagels** (for when you're not close to Marx's).

Milford

The small, quirky shopping district in Old Milford is just across the Little Miami River from Indian Hill and Terrace Park, but it's a slice of small-town Clermont County life. Besides several antique and gift stores, shops of note on Main Street include **Fountain Specialists**, purveyors of just about any kind of concrete yard object you could want; **Nature Outfitters**, a store offering a full selection of gear for outdoor sport; and **Anglers' Outfitters**, specializing in fishing supplies and instruction. For dining, try the beautifully decorated **Mill Street Manor** at Main and Water streets.

Montgomery

This historic old town center at the corner of Montgomery and Cooper roads is home to the original **Montgomery Cyclery** and the original **Montgomery Inn** rib restaurant in addition to many other fine specialty stores, particularly for food. Other stores include **Kotsovos Furs**; the cleverly named **Burning Desires**, specializing in gourmet coffee and fine cigars; **Audible Elegance**, with sound equipment suitable for audiophiles; **Botanica**, a nice plant store at 7872 Cooper Road just off the main drag; and just off the other side of Montgomery on Cooper Road you'll find great bread at the **Great Harvest Bread Company** and other good eats at the **Gourmet Bazaar**. Just next door is **Palbino's**, a place for wood-fired pizza. It's also the most elegant place in town that's also kid-friendly.

The **Shops at Harpers Point** and **Harper Station**, on the 11000 block of Montgomery

Road in Symmes, are two of the newest and fastest-growing strip shopping centers in town and among the biggest and most elegant non-malls. The eats alone are outstanding, including four of the best restaurants in the city: **Ciao Cucina**, **Cheng-2 Gourmet**, **deSha's** and **First Watch**. Good shopping here includes fancy digs at **Hollandia Interiors** and **Southwestern Designs**, good secondhand clothes at **Snooty Fox** and nice value-priced housewares at **Paperphanalia**.

North Central

Forest Fair Mall
I-275 and Winton Rd., Exit 39, Forest Park • 671-2882

Forest Fair fell into the retailing industry's hard times shortly after opening its doors in 1989 and lost two of its biggest anchor stores to bankruptcy. But the mall has bounced back with the addition of such stores as **CompUSA** and such popular eateries/nightspots as **Burbank's Real Bar-B-Q**, **Bourbon Street** and **Choice Harvest Bakehouse**. Other major attractions include **SuperSaver Cinemas**, **Bigg's** and the **Time Out** amusement arcade (see our Kidstuff chapter). Other anchor stores include **Elder-Beerman** and **Kohl's**. You'll also find a very nice **Little Professor Book Center**.

Nearby at **Cobblewood Plaza**, 1189 Smiley Avenue, are several huge "category killer" stores, including the **Baby Superstore**, **Joann Fabrics** and **Circuit City**.

Roselawn
Normally, one store and one restaurant wouldn't be enough to warrant placement of a shopping district in this guide, but we'll make an exception because of the quality. The store is **Chapeau Creations**, 7385 Brookcrest Drive, just off of Section Road at its intersection with Reading Road, where one-of-a-kind women's hats are designed by Ruth Kropveld, a past winner of *W* magazine's award for the nation's top hat designer. On Reading Road, just north of the intersection with Section Road is **Song Long**, one of the best Asian restaurants in town, with a 96-item Vietnamese menu and a complete Chinese menu as well.

Tri-County Mall
11700 Princeton Rd., Springdale • 671-0120

Built in 1960, this was Southwest Ohio's first mall and once drew shoppers from a 100-mile-plus radius. By the 1990s, sandwiched by new competition from Kenwood Towne Centre and Forest Fair Mall, it was losing shoppers fast. But remodeling has turned this mall into a vibrant center with more occupied space than any other in the city. Flanked by multilevel parking structures, this place is easy to get into and out of and provides plenty of that covered parking so treasured on hot or rainy days.

Anchors in this 1.37 million-square-foot, 180-store mall include **Lazarus**, **McAlpin's** and **JC Penney**. It's pretty much of a toss-up between Tri-County and Kenwood Towne Centre as to which has the biggest or best McAlpin's. Tri-County's Lazarus store is slightly bigger. Other specialty stores here include **Eddie Bauer**, **The Limited** and **Limited Too**, the **Gap**, **Abercrombie & Fitch**, **Fiedler & Fiedler** menswear, **The Disney Store**, **Brentano's**, **Waldenbooks**, **Imaginarium**, **Compagnie International Express** and **Li'l House Dollhouse Shop**.

West

Northgate Mall
Colerain Ave. at Springdale Rd. off I-275 • 385-5600

A lot of malls might have crumbled when they saw the likes of Forest Fair and

Farms & Orchards

The agriculture industry in Ohio, Kentucky and Indiana is sizable, so it should be no surprise that there are plenty of farms and orchards in the area where you can purchase fresh fruit, vegetables and other produce. At many, you can even pick the stuff yourself. And prices for produce (like eggs) are generally cheaper in the country.

If you are determined to remain downtown, there are two primary urban options: Findlay Market in Over-the-Rhine and Court Street Market on Court Street downtown. And, of course, there are any number of grocers that carry fresh-picked local produce. We particularly recommend Jungle Jim's, Silverglade & Sons or Newtown Farm Market (see the Food Shop section).

Close-up

Autumn is a terrific time to hit the region's many, many harvest festivals (as well as shop for cider or your Halloween pumpkin), though produce-related festivals occur throughout the year. Most notable: Applefest in Lebanon, the Apple Butter Festival in Oxford, the Sauerkraut Festival in Waynesville, and the Honey Festival in Hamilton (don't miss the guy who makes a "mask" on his face from thousands of buzzing honey bees).

Picking it yourself? Know that 'round here strawberry season is early June through mid-October, raspberry season mid-June to early October, blueberry season late June to late September, apple season late June to late October, corn season early July to late October, and the pumpkin harvest late September to late October.

You'll get the best cherries and peas in June; beans in late June and August; broccoli in early July; blackberries and cabbage all through July; cantaloupes, cucumbers, peppers and watermelon in late July; pears and tomatoes in August; grapes in September and October; and turnip and mustard greens, gourds and squash in October. Keep these dates in mind as you plan your visits to the following farms and orchards

It's also wise to bring a basket or plastic bucket, since not all farmers supply containers (and those that do frequently run out). Wear long pants and a long-sleeved shirt as well as light gloves and a hat. Apple pickers will find they gain some one-upmanship on competing pickers if they bring along a small stepladder. Pick in the early morning or late afternoon. Assume that farmers accept cash only. The hours indicated below are during the growing season.

A&M Farm Orchard, 22141 Ohio 251, Midland (875-2500) has grapes, strawberries and apples. Hours are 8 AM to 8 PM Monday through Saturday, 1 PM to 8 PM Sunday.

Barn 'n' Bunk Farm Market, Ohio Highway 73 at Wayne-Madison Road, Trenton (988-9211) sells strawberries, snow peas and stringless beans. Hours are 8 AM to 8 PM Monday through Friday, 8 AM to 5 PM Saturday, noon to 5 PM Sunday.

Barrett's Strawberry Farm, 11434 Fairfield Road, Leesburg [(937) 780-4961] specializes in — yes — strawberries. Hours are 8 AM to dusk daily.

Benton Farms, 11946 Old Lexington Pike, Walton, Kentucky [(606) 485-7000] offers corn, beans and pumpkins. Hours are 10 AM to 6 PM Monday through Saturday, noon to 6 PM Sunday.

Better Farm, 1971 Sicily Road, Mount Orab (446-2593) is all strawberries. Hours are 8 AM to 8 PM Monday through Saturday.

Beiersdorfer Orchard, 21874 Kuebel Road, Guilford, Indiana [(812) 487-2695] sells apples, cherries, peaches and pears, but you can't pick your own. The cider here is tremendous. Hours are 9 AM to 6 PM Monday through Saturday, 1 PM to 6 PM Sunday.

— continued on next page

Apples are but one of the area's abundant crops.

Binning Road Farm, 1302 Binning Road, Milford (831-4282) is a raspberry farm. Hours vary by week of the season, so call first.

Burger's Farm & Garden Center, 7849 Main Street, Newtown (561-8634) carries corn, apples, watermelons, tomatoes and pumpkins (no picking yourself). Hours are 9 AM to 6 PM Monday through Friday, 9 AM to 5 PM Saturday and Sunday.

Dale Stokes Fruit Farm, 3182 Center Road, Wilmington (382-4004) sells strawberries, red raspberries and black raspberries. Hours are 8 AM to dusk daily.

Frank's Farm and Market, 1660 North Ohio Highway 741, Lebanon [(800) 797-1528] has corn, tomatoes and pumpkins. Hours are 10 AM to 7 PM daily.

Freels Strawberry Farm, 7999 Conteras Road, Oxford (523-4413) also sells red raspberries and pumpkins (in addition, of course, to strawberries). Hours are 9 AM to 7:30 PM Monday through Saturday, 9 AM to 1 PM Sunday.

Haase's U Pick, 1132 North Ohio Highway 101, Milan, Indiana [(812) 654-3091] has pumpkins, gourds and squash. Hours are dawn to dusk.

Helton Farm, 1523 Ohio Highway 125, Hamersville [(937) 379-1104] sells beans, corn, tomatoes and pumpkins. Hours are 9 AM to 8 PM daily.

Hidden Valley Fruit Farm, 5474 North Ohio Highway 48, Lebanon (932-1869), is this writer's favorite, as much for its farmer's market and terrific cider as the picking. Produce includes strawberries, cherries, apples, blueberries, blackberries, green beans, pears, corn, grapes and pumpkins. Because of the wide variety, hours vary by the week of the season, so call first.

Hollmeyer's Orchards, 3241 Fiddler's Green Road (574-0663) sells apples. Hours are 9 AM to 6 PM Monday through Friday, 9 AM to 5 PM Saturday and Sunday.

Iron's Fruit Farm, 1640 Stubbs Mill Road, Lebanon (932-2853) carries strawberries, red and black raspberries and pumpkins. Hours are 9 AM to 6 PM Monday through Saturday, noon to 6 PM Sunday.

Maplewood Orchards, 3712 Stubbs Mill Road, Morrow (932-7981) has apples and pumpkins. Hours are 10 AM to 6 PM daily.

McGlassen's Farm, Ohio Highway 8 at Taylorsburg, Kentucky, [(606) 689-5229]

— continued on next page

has beans, tomatoes, turnip and mustard greens. Hours are 9 AM to 7 PM Monday through Friday, 9 AM to 6 PM Saturday and Sunday.

Owens Orchard, 5480 Hamilton-Richmond Road, Oxford (523-5926) sells apples but you can't pick your own. Hours are 9 AM to 6:30 PM daily.

Red Raspberry Acres, 4658 Ohio Highway 222, Batavia (732-1440) has red raspberries and red raspberries. Hours are 8 AM to Noon and 5 PM to 8 PM Monday through Saturday.

Rouster's Apple House, 1980 Ohio Highway 131, Milford (625-5504) is so popular for its Krispy apples that people get on a waiting list to buy them by the bushel and half bushel. Unless there's a bumper crop, most of the Krispys get taken by people on the list, so call by mid-August to reserve your spot. Rouster's also has blueberries, red and purple raspberries and thornless blackberries. Hours are 8 AM to noon Tuesday through Sunday (farmer's market opens at 10 AM).

Schuchter's Farm Market, 2041 U.S. Highway 22, Morrow (899-2595) sells peas, broccoli, green beans, cucumbers, peppers, tomatoes, corn, cabbage, cantaloupes, watermelons and pumpkins. Because of the wide variety, hours vary by the week of the season, so call first.

Valley Orchards, 7029 River Road, Hebron, Kentucky [(606) 689-4992] has strawberries, green beans, peas, tomatoes, apples and pumpkins. Hours are 9 AM to 6 PM daily.

Valley Vineyards, 2276 Ohio Highway 22, Morrow (899-2485) sells only strawberries. Hours are 8 AM to noon and 4 PM to 8 PM Tuesday through Sunday.

Windmill Farm Market, 1454 Ohio Highway 73, Springboro (885-3965) sells strawberries, broccoli, peas, beans, red raspberries and black raspberries. Hours are 10 AM to 6 PM daily.

Kenwood Towne Centre moving in nearby and Tri-County undergoing a major renovation and expansion. But the neighborhood Northgate Mall did some rehabbing of its own to create a megamall in its own right. Anchors of this 1 million-square-foot mall include **McAlpin's** (including a **McAlpin's Big and Tall Men's Store**), **Sears**, **Lazarus** and **JCPenney**. You'll also find such other mall favorites as the **Gap**, **The Disney Store**, **B. Dalton**, **World of Science**, **Bombay Company**, plus unique offerings such as the **Stone Fence** gift shop, **Connections** (selling communication and computer gizmos) and **Kids Footlocker**. A nicely appointed food court includes the area's only **A&W** root beer stand.

Western Hills Plaza
Glenway Ave. and Werk Rd. • 481-0505

This venerable West Side institution has 47 stores in its 450,000 square feet. Major stores include **Media Play**, **Waldenbooks**, **Staples** and **Pier One** imports.

Western Woods Mall
6300 Glenway Ave. • 661-7468

The other West Side mall has 27 stores in 350,000 square feet, including a brand-new **McAlpin's** (formerly up the road in Western Hills Plaza), **Home Depot** and a **Finish Line** outlet store with some great bargains.

Northern Kentucky

Crestview Hills Mall
2929 Dixie Hwy., Crestview Hills, Ky. • (606) 341-5151

This 387,000-square-foot mall is dominated by a large **McAlpin's**, the only one on the south side of the river, as well as the gigantic **Signatures Home Store**.

Florence Mall
I-75 at Exit 180A, 2028 Florence Mall Rd., Ky. • (606) 371-1231

The big kahuna among malls in Northern Kentucky, this 828,000-square-foot center has

133 stores. They include anchors **Lazarus**, **Lazarus Home Store**, **Sears** and **JC Penney** in addition to such mall favorites as the **Gap**, **Victoria's Secret**, **Waldenbooks**, **B. Dalton** and **Babbages**. Chefs in the family will find a great selection of spices and cookware at **The Cookstore**, as well as an impressive selection of recipe books.

Outlet Shopping

Down Lite International Factory Outlet
7818 Palace Dr., Blue Ash
• 489-DOWN

Down Lite is an honest-to-goodness factory outlet, with sometimes deep discounts on goods from some of the nation's top catalog operations (such as **L.L. Bean**) and retailers.

Dry Ridge Outlet Stores
1100 Fashion Ridge Rd., Dry Ridge, Ky. (I-75 at Exit 159) • (606) 824-9516

A little more than 20 miles south of Florence Mall, Dry Ridge Outlet Stores, I-75 at the Dry Ridge exit, is the closest outlet mall to Cincinnati. Among the stores here are **Mikasa China**, **Crystal and Gifts**, the **Nike Factory Store**, **Liz Claiborne**, **Carter's Children's Wear**, **Geoffery Beane**, **Van Heusen**, **L'eggs/Hanes/Bali**, **Nine West**, **Spiegel Outlet Store** and the **Guess Factory Store**.

Entenmann's Bakery Outlet
123 W. Kemper Rd., Springdale
• 671-2722

Ever wonder what happens to those Entenmann's baked goods that don't sell in the grocery? Here's where they go, available at cut-rate prices and still delectable.

Esther Price Fine Chocolates Outlet
7501 Montgomery Rd., Silverton
• 791-1833

Esther Price is Southern Ohio's finest chocolate, and while you can buy a box in the refrigerator section of certain local groceries, nothing beats coming to the factory outlet itself. You get the freshest choice of creams and nougats possible *and* you can handpick your box. All chocolate cherries? No problem.

The Four Seasons Garment Factory Outlet
1111 Western Row Rd., Mason
• 398-3695

The Four Seasons Garment Factory Outlet store is a true manufacturer's outlet, next to the factory, where you can get good deals on nylon jackets, caps, visors, T-shirts, sweatshirts and more.

Jeffersonville Outlet Center
1100 McArthur Rd., Jeffersonville (I-71 at Exit 69) • (614) 426-6992

It's not quite in Greater Cincinnati, but the Jeffersonville Outlet Center is hard to ignore and well worth the hour's drive north. This 70-store megamall has the state's best lineup of designer and name-brand outlets: **Spiegel**, **Liz Claiborne**, **Mikasa China**, **Saks Fifth Avenue Clearing House**, **Reebok** and more.

The Original Mattress Factory
Ohio Hwy. 4 at Muhlhauser Rd., Fairfield
• 860-9988

This factory and showroom was founded by a former Serta exec who wanted to manufacture quality mattresses at outlet prices. He succeeds (we know, we sleep on one). Choose from standard and custom brass, iron and wood beds. And best yet, no haggling — the prices are the same every single day. If a trip

INSIDERS' TIP

The most efficient use of your shopping time may well be to browse the Beechmont Avenue strip in Anderson. Where else, within a mile, can you find a Lazarus, Parisian, Kmart, Target, Sears Hardware, Staples, Home Depot, two (count 'em, two) Super Krogers, Thriftway, plus hundreds of smaller merchandisers. Take Exit 69 off the I-275 loop. Shopping nirvana.

to the Fairfield factory is too far, there are five satellite shops across the Tri-state.

Flea Markets

Peddlers Flea Market
4343 Kellogg Ave. • 871-3700

Peddlers Flea Market in the Columbia-Tusculum neighborhood of Cincinnati (worth a visit in itself for a gander at all those painted beauty Victorian houses) is your best bet for retro and fixer-upper furniture. You're not going to find a better selection of '50s, '60s and '70s authentic furniture outside of your grandma's attic.

Trader's World
601 Union Rd., Monroe (I-75 and Ohio Hwy. 63, Exit 29) • 424-5708

Trader's World, by far the Tri-state's largest flea market, has a little of everything. Some of its major specialties are hardware and supplies (including great prices on dowels, wood knobs and assorted doohickeys coveted by woodworkers), shoes, die-cast cars, trucks and other assorted vehicles (there are three large booths just devoted to these) plus other scattered offerings. Admission to the grounds is 75¢ per vehicle.

Turtle Creek Flea Market
320 N. Garver Rd., Monroe (I-75 and Ohio Hwy. 63, Exit 29) • 539-4497

Specialties at Turtle Creek include some great deals on shoes, a booth specializing in country and bluegrass tapes and CDs, a **Velva Sheen** sportswear outlet booth with some outstanding deals on overstocks of college and other licensed (lots of Disney) clothes, a wig stand, and the **Payless Grocer's Liquidation Outlet**. Admission is free.

Food Shops

The Best of Cincinnati
484 Northland Blvd. • 851-2900

Whether you're new or a native, ordering a catalog from these folks is the quickest way to taste a crash course in Cincinnati cuisine. Anything from the trademark Montgomery Inn barbecue sauce and Skyline chili to Izzy's hot mustard, Graeter's candy, LaRosa's salad dressing and The Maisonette hazelnut liquor cake can be delivered to your door.

Bilker Fine Foods
7648 Reading Rd., Roselawn • 821-6800

Where else to go for your smoked whitefish, nova lox or knishes and blintzes? Or a full line of kosher frozen food products from the likes of Best and Tabatchnick? Don't leave without sampling the chopped chicken liver.

Bonbonerie
2030 Madison Rd. • 321-3399

Bonbonerie and Jenny Craig — never the twain shall meet, but oh well. This is the city's premier bakery, hands down. Scones, cheesecakes, the works — and their trifles are not to be trifled with. There's an adjoining tea room, too.

Bounty Seafood II
6675 Salem Rd. • 232-5959

For the freshest salmon, lobster and crab this side of Maine, try Bounty Seafood II in Mount Washington. Owner Kevin Smith flies in his catch each morning (along with copies of that morning's *Bangor Daily News*, so you know he's not kidding about how fresh-caught everything is). Also the place to find seaweed, alligator and other exotic eats.

Dilly Deli
6818 Wooster Pk. • 561-5233

This relatively new Mariemont gourmet deli offers sandwiches and wine tastings, plus daily takeout dinner specials such as chicken tetrazzini.

Etta's Bakery
4070 E. Galbreath Rd., Deer Park • 793-5100

The last full-service kosher bakery to serve what was once a sizable Orthodox Jewish population in Cincinnati, Etta's continues to cater to some 24,000 customers a year. Rabbi Zelig Sharfstein certifies kosher production at Etta's, which serves Jewish families and synagogues in Deer Park, Roselawn, Amberley Village, Golf Manor and elsewhere in the city. Popular items include challah bread for Sabbath and pareve pastries (which, unlike those prepared with milk, may be eaten with meat).

Fred and Gari's
629 Vine St. • 784-9000

For the best chocolate cream pie in town, try a calorie-laden slice of heaven served at Fred and Gari's, a takeout bakery and lunch spot. Their banana cream pie is no slouch, either.

Gethsemani Monastery
Gethsemani Farms, Trappist, Ky.
• (502) 549-3117

The oldest Trappist monastery in the United States is found across the river in Trappist, Kentucky, but ordering the monks' famous cheese or fruitcake is as easy as picking up your phone — and, Lord yes, the good friars accept credit cards. The monks produce their semisoft creamy cheese based on a centuries-old European formula, available in mild, aged or smoked — or try all three in a sampler box of wedges. Their fruitcake is the real thing, by the way, redolent with Kentucky bourbon and aged cherries, raisins, pineapple, dates and nuts.

Great Harvest Bread Company
7819 Cooper Rd., Montgomery
• 984-9212

Fresh and delicious loaves in all imaginable flavors delight the nose as well as the mouth. You can take a hands-on tour of the baking operations at the main store, which also makes bread for satellite outlets in Anderson (7739 Five Mile Road) and Hyde Park (2727 Erie Avenue).

Hyde Park Gourmet
2707 Erie Rd. • 533-4329

There's something for every palate at this Hyde Park Square gourmet food shop. But not for every pocketbook. It's a bit pricey, right in keeping with its yuppie environs. Among the goodies are imported brie and fancy pasta sauces.

Jungle Jim's
5440 Dixie Hwy., Fairfield • 829-1919

Jungle Jim's is a huge gourmet food store with a small grocery store wrapped around it. It's also, as billed by owner "Jungle" Jim

Bonaminio, "The Most Unusual Store in America." You can't miss the giant, gaudily painted animals, tropical fruits or jungle soundtrack as you walk in. Inside you'll find singing mechanical refugees from Chuck E. Cheese's.

Besides the kitsch, you'll also find great stuff for the kitchen, including what the store claims is Ohio's largest wine collection. You'll also find possibly the city's best all-around cheese, bakery and deli shops, all under one roof. Entire mini-stores here are devoted to Mexican, Indian, Mediterranean and Oriental fresh foods and groceries.

Even if you didn't like eating, this place would be worth a visit just as a food museum. You can easily spend hours just looking around — and some folks do. New at the grocery is local food maven Carol Tabone and her up-tempo cooking school. Sessions feature anything from a Javanese Barbecue to a Six-Foot Burrito and Avocado Caviar class.

Kaffe Klatsch
Inside the Mercantile Building, Fourth and Walnut Sts. • 721-2233

In this era of Starbucks and other coffee chains, downtown's Kaffe Klatsch is still our choice for fresh and exotic coffees. They were doing it first and still do it best. Enjoy a full line of fresh pastries, too.

Marx Hot Bagels Factory
7617 Reading Rd., Roselawn • 821-0103
9701 Kenwood Rd., Blue Ash • 891-5542
316 Northland Blvd., Springdale
• 772-3101

Cincinnati's premier kosher bagelries are owned and run by the flamboyant, provocative — and Catholic — John "Bagelman" Marx. It's worth a visit to the Roselawn shop just to catch a little of Bagelman's act. The bagels? They're the closest thing you'll find to New York bagels, and the atmosphere is pretty Gotham-like too. Placing an order at the Blue Ash store on a Saturday morning can be a little like placing an order at the New York Stock Exchange. But it's well worth the grief. You'll come away with a bag of the best bagels this side of the Alleghenies, and much of the time they'll still be too hot to eat.

Mediterranean Foods
314 Ludlow Ave. • 961-6060

This is the place to go for Arabic, Greek, Italian and Turkish foodstuffs — with Egyptian, Turkish, Moroccan and Lebanese thrown in to boot. More than 1,600 items line the walls, from 10 types of pita bread to rices, nuts, figs and beans. Nifty cheese selection, too. Where else to find that Hungarian kaskaval cheese?

Newtown Farm Market
3950 Roundbottom Rd., Newtown
• 561-2004

These folks grow their own strawberries and corn in the summer, and they carry great produce and specialty foods from around the globe. The waiting list for Michigan cherries can be a long one. Owner Bobby Palmisano, from a Cleveland produce family that goes way back, is the former produce director at Jungle Jim's. Don't miss the deli and the incredible selection of exotic canned foods and salad dressings.

The Party Source
95 Riveria Dr., Bellevue, Ky.
• (606) 291-4007

Right across the Big Mac (I-471) bridge from downtown, this huge outlet has fast become party central for folks on both sides of the river. Besides an extensive selection of wine and other beverages, The Party Source stocks an extensive array of gourmet foods, including some great frozen hors d'oeuvres for the lazy host and hostess. There's also a full plate of other party gear. And we'd be remiss if we didn't remind you that Kentucky liquor prices are quite competitive when compared to Ohio's state store operation, and the selection's far more diverse.

Pasta Supply Co.
2942 Wasson Rd. • 841-1800

Tired of canned spaghetti for dinner? Head to the Pasta Supply Co. in Hyde Park for a complete range of Italian meats and cheeses, homemade sauces, fresh foccacia and delectable pasta. With its 11 flavors of takeout pasta and 13 sauces to go, plus pestos, something is bound to please. (We love the Smoked Salmon Ravioli.)

Saigon Market
119 W. Elder St. • 721-8053

Saigon Market in Over-the-Rhine is the perfect place for the occidental tourist interested in Asian foodstuffs of all sorts. Take a wok on the wild side.

Silverglade & Sons
6660 Clough Pk., Anderson
• 231-6483

Silverglade started with a booth at Findlay Market (which is still there), but this is a full-service grocery with perhaps the most extensive and eclectic choice of cheeses in town, as well as a butcher's shop, deli meats, and (for the busy worker) a half-dozen hot meals prepared daily for take-home.

Spatz Natural Life Health Food
607 Main St. • 621-0347

In a city crammed with health food and vitamin stores, Spatz stands out. First, the downtown fixture is locally owned; second, it offers far more than bottled worts and boosters. There's a cafeteria with plenty of hot vegetarian cuisine, plus a 25-item salad bar.

Tel Aviv
7384 Reading Rd., Roselawn • 631-8808

Tel Aviv offers a wide selection of vegetarian dishes, pizza, pasta and an apple strudel we come back for again and again. There are a few tables and chairs if you want to sit and eat.

INSIDERS' TIP

One of the oddest local traditions is the Busken's Cookie Polls. The chain of local bakeries asks customers to vote on Super Bowl wins and other outcomes by buying cookies decorated with the logo of the team they think will win. Eerily enough, the polls are almost always dead on. The Super Bowl poll has been right 11 of the last 13 years.

Workshops of the Restoration Society
3414 DeCoursey Ave., Latonia, Ky.
• (606) 491-1291

Workshops of the Restoration Society is primarily a furniture restoring outfit, but it also devotes an entire room to goodies fresh from the Amish of nearby Adams County: jams, cheeses, breads, and more. The raspberry pie is not to be missed.

Wineries

Chateau Pomije
2019 Madison Rd. • 871-8788

Chateau Pomije is actually a wine shop; the wine is produced at an Indiana vineyard. A delectable gourmet pizza du jour is also produced at this relaxed, moderately priced spot.

Colonial Vineyards
6222 North Ohio Hwy. 48, Lebanon
• 932-3842

It's worth a drive from Cincinnati for these grapes. Stop for lunch at The Golden Lamb while you're at it.

Henke Winery
701 East Epworth Ave. • 541-3177

Henke Winery is perhaps Ohio's only inner-city winery, located in Winton Place in a c. 1920s structure. Joe and Joan Henke serve up five or more varieties of wine each day made from grapes grown in Virginia, New York and Ohio.

Meier's Wine Cellars
6955 Plainfield Pike, Silverton
• 891-2100

Meier's is Cincinnati's own source for Cream Sherry, LaBrusco or any of the other dozen varieties of wine produced here.

Moyer's Winery
3859 U.S. Hwy. 52, Manchester
• (937) 549-2957

Moyer's is a scenic winery and (just as notably) a restaurant, all with a picturesque view of the river, gazebos and lots of atmosphere. Ken and Mary Moyer have been growing the grapes and serving up regional American cuisine on the Ohio River for a quarter-century.

Vinoklet
11069 Colerain Ave. • 385-9309

Vinoklet is also a winery that's a restaurant. There's a choice of steaks, chicken or seafood (which you can grill yourself). Dinner, wine and dessert for a couple is $38 (cash or check only).

Booksellers and Newsstands

Aquarius Bookshop
831 Main St. • 721-5193

As you might guess from the name, this is a New Age shop, and it is well known to downtowners for its wonderful and eclectic selection of American Indian literature and music. Lesser known is its equally diverse collection of Celtic songs.

B. Dalton Bookseller
Beechmont Mall, 7500 Beechmont Ave., Anderson • 232-2970
Northgate Mall, 9577 Colerain Ave., Bevis • 385-5608
Tri-County Mall, 11700 Princeton Pk., Springdale • 671-3420
Florence Mall, 2028 Florence Mall Rd., Florence, Ky. • (606) 371-3833

B. Dalton is a standard-bearer of mall book outlets. That doesn't mean these shops aren't worth a visit, however. They carry some of the area's largest selections of humor, Hollywood tell-alls, how-to books and other specialties. The Beechmont Mall branch is particularly known for its friendly service and easygoing return policy.

Barnes & Noble
3802 Paxton Ave., Hyde Park • 871-4300
895 E. Kemper Rd. • 671-3822
7800 Montgomery Rd., Kenwood
• 794-9440
7663 Mall Rd., Florence, Ky.
• (606) 647-6400

You get what you'd expect from the Barnes & Noble chain-wide inventory — competent help and comfortable environs. If you have a choice, head to the superstore on Montgomery Road.

Bee Tree
3615 Glenmore Ave., Cheviot • 661-3433

You'll find a terrific selection of children's literature, supplemented by intriguing toys, games and puzzles here. Don't miss signing up for the newsletter, which updates store patrons on the literally dozens of storytime hours and other kids' activities held here each month.

The Blue Marble
3054 Madison Rd.
• 731-2665
1356 S. Ft. Thomas Ave., Ft. Thomas, Ky.
• (606) 781-0602

This local store is among the best children's bookstores in Greater Cincinnati. The Blue Marble has frequent signings by children's authors, readings and other special events.

Books & Co.
350 E. Stroop Rd., Dayton
• (937) 297-6358

This one is worth a special drive, whether you're a book lover, music lover or coffee lover. Folks from across the region flock to Books & Co., which aggressively brings in top-name authors for signings and hosts a highly regarded music series on weekends in the store. The coffee and dessert shop is a must visit, and oh yes, they sell books, too. Lots. The mystery, children's and local interest sections are particularly strong, and the business books department has actually grown into its own adjoining separate shop.

The Bookshelf Inc.
7754 Camargo Rd., Madeira • 271-9140

The Bookshelf is a smaller shop that caters to the interests of area residents, and in this upscale community (which is quite near ritzy Indian Hill), the interests would be art, antiques, fine cooking, history and the like. There's a varied selection of general interest texts, too.

Borders Books & Music
11711 Princeton Rd., Springdale
• 671-5852

Borders is another book megastore with tons of inventory. Beyond the books, however, is a wonderfully esoteric collection of magazines. Where else can you snag the latest copy of *Flatiron News*?

Brengelman's Bookstore
454 W. McMicken Ave. • 621-4865

Here's a quirky place: It's open only on Saturday and Sunday afternoons, and the building is marked only with a small sign that says "Bookstore." Nonetheless, it's delightful to sink into an overstuffed couch and browse the books, both old and new.

Brentano's
Tower Place Mall, Carew Tower
• 723-9656

Downtowners flock to Brentano's book store, especially for its sizable collection of audio books-on-tape and its up-to-date business section.

Channel 48 Store of Knowledge
Kenwood Towne Centre, 7875
Montgomery Rd., Kenwood • 891-2500

Just about any PBS-related product is available here, from books that have been adapted on *Masterpiece Theatre* to British humor plus lots of kid's books.

The Children's Bookery Co.
1169 Smiley Ave., Forest Park
• 742-8822

Specializing in educational products and games as well as resources for teachers in the classroom, this juvenile bookshop also makes a name for itself with author appearances, book talks and storytelling.

The Crazy Ladies Bookstore
4039 Hamilton Ave. • 541-4198

Crazy Ladies has one of the area's largest selection of gay and lesbian studies as well as feminist writings and women's health texts. Also, there are mysteries, poetry, psychology and spiritual works. Crazy Ladies is located in Northside, a diverse community that certainly reflects the alternative nature of the bookstore.

Duttenhofer's Treasures
214 W. McMillan St. • 381-1340

Every city has one of these, or ought to —

FYI

Unless otherwise noted, the area code for all phone numbers listed in this guide is 513.

Findlay Market is one of the oldest open-air markets in the nation and one of the few still active. It's been a center of Cincinnati commerce since 1852.

a dusty, musty, marvelous used book store that prides itself on maintaining a diverse collection, from first editions to campy science fiction, mystery novels to local interest books. A treasure trove, literally.

F&W Publications Warehouse Sale
3637 Woodburn Ave. • 531-2690

Natives are going to be mad that we told you about this one. F&W is the company that publishes *Writer's Digest* magazine, *Writer's Market* yearbook, plus all sorts of graphic arts, sewing, gardening and how-to writing books. Once a year, in early December, remainders are put on sale and priced to go at $1 and up.

Fountain News
Fifth and Walnut Sts. • 421-4049

More than 130 newspapers from all corners of the globe give new meaning to the word newsstand. Be it an Arabic weekly, the *Sunday Times* of London or such mags *as Chicago Gardener*, you'll find it here.

Friends of the Public Library Book & Gift Shop
Public Library of Cincinnati and Hamilton County, 800 Vine St. • 369-6920

There's plenty of local flavor here, with a box of "Doors of Cincinnati" notecards, hologram magnets, Cincinnati coloring books, games, puzzles, ties and — needless to say — books.

Half-Price Books
11389 Princeton Rd., Springdale
• 772-1511
8118 Montgomery Rd., Kenwood
• 891-7170

We're not sure how they do it, but the hard and softcovers here really are half price — and pretty new, too.

The Heritage Shop of the Historical Society
1301 Western Ave. • 287-7000

The Heritage Shop of the Historical Society sells all sorts of nifty literary items, including books, toys, posters and ornaments. Of most local interest, perhaps, is the Cat's Meow line of wood miniature buildings representing Cincinnati's most unique architectural treasures: Findlay Market, Fountain Square, the Art Museum, the Hamilton County Courthouse, Wise Temple, Lunken Airfield and more. The Procter & Gamble headquarters in miniature, for instance, would make a terrific gift for that Proctoid you know.

Joseph-Beth Booksellers
Rookwood Pavilion, 2692 Madison Rd., Norwood • 396-8965

The incredible diversity of the selection as well as the helpful service make Joe-Beth stand out from the crowd. Whether you're in search of the latest copy of *Punch* or an obscure fanzine, you'll find it here — as well as a friendly smile. We like to snuggle in the overstuffed armchairs, listen to the weekly live music by the likes of Kim Cooper or Silver Arm, and enjoy life.

King Arthur's Court
3040 Madison Rd. • 531-4600

This is primarily a toy store with a nicely arranged selection of educational toys and a downstairs department devoted solely to model trains, model cars and other sorts of model projects. However, King Arthur's also carries 3,000 hardback and softcover juvenile titles, making it a substantial player on the local children's bookstore scene.

Little Professor Book Center
Forest Fair Mall, Forest Park • 671-9797

Little Professor features a very extensive selection of titles in books and other media.

It certainly has the best selection of foreign magazines in town. Need the Brit edition of *Esquire* or some elusive French fashion mag? The Little Professor has twice the number of foreign mags (120) as its closest competitor.

Little Professor Book Center
8537 Winton Rd. • 931-4433

This Little Professor is more of a neighborhood store than its big brother at Forest Fair Mall. Hence, we've given it a separate listing. Although it can't offer 100,000 titles like big bro, the shop does stress one-on-one service and caters to its customers with loving care.

Media Play
6174 Glenway Ave. • 481-4775
4488 Montgomery Rd., Norwood
• 531-5250
87 Spiral Dr., Florence, Ky.
• (606) 647-6950

One of the newer additions to the book wars, Media Play is a gigantic complex with an equally gigantic inventory. Lots of software and CD displays here, too, though the magazine rack is our favorite. Whether you're hunting a quarter horse weekly or a monthly devoted to left-handed quilt stitching, these folks probably have it.

Montgomery Book Co.
9917 Montgomery Rd., Montgomery
• 891-2227

Formerly a Little Professor bookshop, Montgomery's is still the friendly, neighborhood kind of bookseller, with one-on-one service and free coffee percolating in back. Not to imply it that the store is tiny — it carries thousands of titles, from cookbooks and mysteries to children's literature and, unusual for any bookstore, a full selection of books on tape that are available to rent.

INSIDERS' TIP

You might not think of an airport as a mall, but the Greater Cincinnati/Northern Kentucky International Airport could qualify as one. The Delta terminal features a Sportsworld, Waterstones Booksellers, The Body Shop, Destination Disney and the area's only duty-free shop. Plus the concourse offers a Cheers bar for nervous passengers.

Mt. Adams Bookstore Cafe
1101 St. Gregory Pl. • 241-9009

Cincinnati's premier wine bar and bookstore features wine tastings, desserts, microbrew beers, espresso, and — oh yes — some books.

New World Bookshop
336 E. Ludlow St. • 861-6100

Located near the University of Cincinnati's Clifton campus, this is definitely *the* bookshop for thinkers and the place to go for New Age and soul-searching works as well as a complete selection of current best-sellers.

Odyssey Learning Center
7791 Cooper Rd., Montgomery • 793-6100

Enrichment and childhood learning is the name of the game here. The store offers a full selection of ABC books, math tutorials and other teacher and parent resources.

Ohio Book Store
726 Main St. • 621-5142

True to its name, this is the area's niftiest display of books on Ohio, Ohio history, Ohio cuisine, Ohio . . . well, you get the point. They've also got thousands of back issues of *Life* and *Look* from 1937 on, plus copies of *National Geographic*, *Sports Illustrated* and more.

Pink Pyramid
907 Race St. • 621-7465

Pink Pyramid is an adult bookstore, or at least the closest thing conservative Cincinnati has to an adult bookstore outside of Larry Flynt's Hustler shop (which we have chosen not to list). Unlike the Hustler shop, Pink Pyramid has much socially redeeming value, with challenging homosexual literature and art books as well as thoughtful philosophical writings. There are also video rentals, and that is what has gotten this shop into trouble with local law enforcement on many occasions lately. The store is becoming something of a cause célèbre among First Amendment absolutists and local literati.

St. Francis Bookshop
1618 Vine St. • 241-7304.

You'll discover anything from handpainted wooden ornaments from El Salvador to glazed ceramic peace signs at the St. Francis Bookshop. But its book collection (crossing all faiths) is notable. The children's book *Can You Find Jesus?*, best described as a Christian version of *Where's Waldo?* (Gospel clues are hidden in the elaborate color illustrations), was one of the area's top-sellers at Christmas.

Significant Books
3053 Madison Rd. • 321-7567

Proprietors Bill and Carolyn Downing know everything about finding obscure books and rare editions. (Case study: We went looking for a novel 30 years out of print. They searched, and found a copy in Dallas within a week.)

The Villager
6932 Madisonville Rd., Mariemont • 271-0523

Not strictly a bookstore, this variety shop offers children's books, general fiction and nonfiction hardcovers and paperbacks and the odd biography among its shelves of art supplies, greeting cards and gift ideas.

Waldenbooks
Eastgate Mall, 4601 Eastgate Blvd., Eastgate • 752-9591
Kenwood Towne Centre, 7875 Montgomery Rd., Kenwood • 791-0011
Northgate Mall, 9483 Colerain Ave., Bevis • 385-5454
Tri-County Mall, 11700 Princeton Pk., Springdale • 671-0777
Western Hills Plaza, 6139 Glenway Ave., Westwood • 662-5837
Crestview Hills Mall, 2929 Dixie Hwy., Crestview Hills, Ky. • (606) 341-0158
Florence Mall, 2028 Florence Mall Rd., Florence, Ky. • (606) 371-0216

If you're inside a mall in Greater Cincinnati, chances are it has a Waldenbooks. This archtypical mall bookstore covers all bases, from sports and biography to fiction and mysteries.

Whatever Works Wellness Center & Bookstore
7433 Montgomery Rd., Silverton • 791-9428

Whatever carries a first-class collection of books relating to the care and maintenance of the spirit, the soul, the karma, or whatever you'd like to call it, plus health texts, aromatherapy, classes and more.

Unique Gift Shops

Aronoff Center for the Arts Gift Shop
650 Walnut St. • 621-2787

Be it a Mona Lisa switchplate or a Felix the Cat magnetic memoboard, you'll stumble across just about anything at the Aronoff Center for the Arts Gift Shop. For budding musicians, there are bongo drums, tin whistles and glockenspiels. For the older set, there are artsy playing cards, jewelry, chimes, stained glass, clocks, Harley Davidson memorabilia, Broadway CDs, cookbooks and jigsaw puzzles.

Cincinnati Art Museum Gift Shop
920 Eden Park Dr. • 721-5204

Surprisingly, this is the best place in town for oddball computer-related gifts. Where else to find a Macintosh CD-ROM with a font suitcase of Egyptian hieroglyphics — write a unique letter to your mummy. Or how 'bout a Dali screensaver, featuring 25 of the artist's most bizarre visions. There's also a selection of mousepads with famous artworks, as well as the expected repertoire of any art museum gift shop: Andy Warhol wristwatches and desk clocks, Dali desk calendars, Museum of Modern Art appointment books, pottery and silver services, Mapplethorpe notecards, artist ties and jewelry.

Cincinnati Zoo Gift Shop
3400 Vine St. • 559-7716

Searching for a gift to please the animal lover in your family? Here you'll find animal jewelry, posters, umbrellas, clocks, music and books. But for a truly unique gift, consider the ADOPT program. For $40, you can adopt a snow leopard, Bengal tiger or whatever and help defray its weekly veterinary care and food bill. You get a packet with a color photo of the adoptee, a fact sheet, a gold ADOPT ornament and a certificate of adoption. (The Ben-

gal tiger, we're told, makes a great gift for any Bengals fan you know.)

Contemporary Arts Center Gift Shop
Mercantile Center • 721-0390

Here you'll find anything from a classy rosewood and silver-plated bottlestopper to less pricey items such as artsy umbrellas, stained glass, color claymation clay, belts, book bags, paint sets, rubber stamp kits, notecards and the ever popular "Fighting Nun" puppet.

Cottage Garden Shop
2715 Reading Rd. • 221-0981

Cincinnati's green thumbs congregate at this shop in the Cincinnati Garden Center in Avondale to share advice and tips. The shop presents lots of seminars, hands-on lessons and the latest in gardening literature and tools.

FYI

Unless otherwise noted, the area code for all phone numbers listed in this guide is 513.

Hebrew Union Gift Shop
3101 Clifton Ave. • 221-1878

You'll find a wide selection of menorahs in silver, ceramic, wood, stone, glass and traditional brass as well as other Jewish items at Hebrew Union College's gift shop. This Clifton shop is also a treasure trove of local Jewish history.

I Love Cincinnati Shoppe
Tower Place Mall, Carew Tower • 651-5772
Tri-County Mall, Springdale • 671-5448
Kenwood Towne Centre, 7875 Montgomery Rd., Kenwood • 792-9215

Are you a fan of the UC Bearcats? A complete line of Bearcats hats, sweatshirts and infant wear bearing the Bearcats logo is available at the I Love Cincinnati Shoppe. As is, of course, anything Queen City-related, from skyline T-shirts to Reds and Bengals merchandise.

Krohn Conservatory Gift Shop
Eden Park • 421-4086

When in dire need of a gift idea for gardeners, turn to our favorite old Krohn. Krohn Conservatory that is, where you'll run across bird feeders, herb plants, baskets, mail box covers, topiary kits, and a nifty ceramic birdhouse in the shape of Noah's ark. An added benefit: This is the only place in town steamy enough that you can do your holiday shopping in T-shirt and Bermuda shorts.

The Meow Mart
6958 Plainfield Rd., Silverton • 984-3312

Cat lovers should head first to The Meow Mart, whose sales benefit the adjoining no-kill cat shelter, The Scratching Post. You'll find a full line of Iams cat food, notecards, jewelry, toys, teaser sticks and more.

Natural History Museum Collectors Shop
1301 Western Ave. • 287-7000

Forget educational toys. Forget boring 'ol books. The gift shop at the Natural History Museum has what your kids REALLY want, say a giant Darth Vader action figure or a kit to help produce special effects like in the Hollywood movies. Of course, there are more sedate gifts, too: fossils, kaleidoscopes, gemstones, Vivaldi CDs, Ruthven animal prints, kids' nature books and American Indian crafts, as well as art items from Africa and Peru. Magnet kits seem to be the most popular scientific item, with no less than seven different kits devoted to the magic of magnetism.

Ohio Star Quilt Shop
8556 Beechmont Ave., Cherry Grove • 474-9355

Ohioans are mad for their quilts, and this is the region's definitive quilting source. Perhaps the passion dates back to our Midwest farming family roots, or the fact that the state boasts as many Amish as Pennsylvania, but whatever the reason, quilting remains a top pastime among the handicraft hobbies 'round here. At Ohio Star, you'll find Ohio-made quilts, fabric, patterns and supplies of all sorts, along with homespun advice. Hey, who says winners never quilt?

Wine World-Baskets Gourmet
7737 Five Mile Rd., Anderson • 232-6611

If you've totally run out of gift ideas, this ambitious shop, located inside a suburban strip mall, is a wonderful source. They can whip up any delectable combination possible for a basket. Smoked salmon pate? Oui. Tangy salsa? Si. Pick and choose from a full selection of nuts, candies and, of course, wine and beers of the world.

If you can't get to
Hawaii any time soon,
you can hang ten in the
half-acre wave pool at
Surf Cincinnati.

Attractions

Life is more than going to work and cutting the grass, and Greater Cincinnati offers lots of leisure-time alternatives — something for everyone, no matter what your taste. In this chapter we talk about major attractions that aren't covered in other chapters (or are covered in less detail or from a different point of interest). For instance, cultural attractions such as the world-famous Cincinnati Symphony Orchestra or the Cincinnati Art Museum are listed in our Arts chapter. The Bengals and Reds get the full treatment in our Spectator Sports chapter. For riverfront entertainment areas, turn to our Nightlife chapter (also see our Parks and Recreation and River Fun chapters).

We've subdivided this chapter into four categories: Pure Fun, Pure Fun Plus (fun with some special interests/education included), Museums and Historical Attractions. All the information was the latest available at the time this guide went to press. As with everything in life, change happens, so some of the hours or admission charges may be different by the time you started flipping through the book. For the absolute latest information, call the locations.

Several recorded messages about current attractions are also available through different services. You may also want to check the numbers below before you go:

Citylink, 333-6888, offers detailed accounts of activities downtown, including parking and transportation, special weekly events, future events, sporting events, dining and shopping, "I Do Downtown" specials, arts and entertainment activities and things for kids and family.

The Talking Yellow Pages, 333-4444, has numerous specialty lines for entertainment and events: a concert line, a points of interest line and a special events line. Check the front of the Yellow Pages for a complete listing.

Pure Fun

Americana Amusement Park
5757 Middletown-Hamilton Rd. (Ohio Hwy. 4), Middletown • 539-7339, (800) 486-3070

It may not be the main event in Cincinnati amusement parks, but this is a good bet if you live close or are just looking for a less-intense alternative to Paramount's Kings Island (more below) at roughly half the price. Americana is a modest-size park that may be more appropriate for smaller kids with shorter attention spans and fuses. This 80-acre park has more than 100 rides, shows and other attractions.

Americana is also under new management, and they've spent a considerable sum to upgrade the premises. The reconditioned Screechin' Eagle is among the state's last classic wooden roller coasters, and fans say it's one of the scariest thrill rides around. A Ferris wheel and other new rides have been added and the waterplay park expanded. Live stage shows, a petting zoo, a log flume and the Jolly Roger play area round out the experience of an 'ole time fun park.

The park is open weekends in April and May (call for hours) then daily from June 1 through Labor Day. Hours during the summer are 11 AM to 9 PM Tuesday through Friday,

---

INSIDERS' TIP

Two of the best places for home landscapers to get inspiration and a look at how various plants do in the Cincinnati climate are the Spring Grove Cemetery and Arboretum and the Cincinnati Zoo and Botanical Garden, a.k.a. the Cincinnati Zoo.

Eden Park

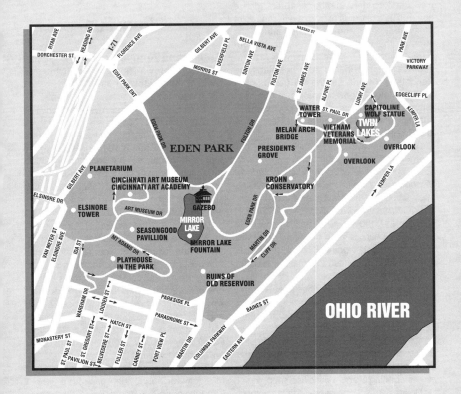

11 AM to 10 PM Saturday and 11 AM to 9 PM Sunday. (At press time, the park was considering opening its doors on Mondays, too. Call first.) Admission is $13.95, $11.95 for folks 60 and older or shorter than 48 inches. Kids 2 and younger get in free. It's on Ohio 4, 5 miles south of Exit 29 on I-75.

Argosy VI
777 East Eads Pkwy., Lawrenceburg, Ind. • (888) ARGOSY7

Just across the Indiana state line — about a 20- to 25-minute drive from downtown Cincinnati — is Lawrenceburg and the *Argosy VI* gambling riverboat. The *Argosy VI* is the largest riverboat casino in the world (the length of a football field). It has 1,746 slot machines and 88 table games, including blackjack, roulette, Caribbean stud, mini baccarat and craps, plus a full array of video poker units. Gaming cruises sail every two hours starting at 9 AM, with the last cruise at 1 AM (3 AM on Fridays and Saturdays). See the Close-up in our River Fun chapter for more details.

The Beach Waterpark
I-71 and Western Row Rd., Mason • 398-SWIM, (800) 886-SWIM

Hey, we're landlocked and easily a thousand miles from the nearest sandy ocean beach. That explains the popularity of Greater Cincinnati's half-dozen waterparks, of which The Beach is perhaps the most notable. The Beach likes to fashion itself as Jamaican cool, as if its 35 acres sit along the coast of Kingston. Yeaaah, mon. You can body surf in the wave pool, hydroplane down the giant slides, take a slow cruise on single or double innertubes, or go for a ride on the thrilling Aztec Adventure water coaster in this H_2O extravaganza. Or, you can kick back on the sandy beaches, play volleyball, scale The Cliff, play in the children's water areas or take in the live entertainment.

The park is open Memorial Day through Labor Day beginning at 10 AM; closing times vary throughout the season. Admission is $85 for a season pass for adults, $32 for senior citizens 65 and older and children 2 and younger and $235 for a family of four. Single-

day admission is $18.95 for adults and $10.95 for seniors and children shorter than 4 feet. It's immediately off I-71, Exit 25, across from Paramount's Kings Island.

Coney Island
6201 Kellogg Ave., Anderson • 232-8230

Located off I-275 at the Kellogg Avenue exit, this laid-back getaway on the banks of the Ohio River offers a fun family outing without all the cost or utter exhaustion of a day at a larger, more frenetic amusement park. Unless you go to its Sunlite Pool, it's no more than a two- or three-hour excursion. Overall, this is a popular attraction for East Siders, although more modern waterparks up north at Surf Cincinnati and The Beach have stolen some of its thunder regionally. Coney is also adjacent to the Riverbend Music Center and RiverDowns racetrack, which makes the area one of the city's entertainment meccas.

Before 1972, Coney was *the* amusement park in Cincinnati. When Coney's owner also opened Kings Island, most of Coney's original attractions were carted off to stock the new park. But Coney was reopened as a low-key amusement park in the mid-1970s under the name "Old Coney." Many longtime residents still call it this, but the PR department discourages this usage now, preferring the current name, Coney Island, and dwelling on what it offers today, which is actually quite a lot.

Sunlite Pool at Coney is billed as the world's largest recirculating pool (200 feet by 400 feet). Although the World Recirculating Pool Council could not be reached for independent verification, suffice it to say there's plenty of room for splashing and swimming. Sunlite Pool also has a 500-foot water slide and 180-foot water coaster.

Pedal boat trips on Lake Como are another popular attraction at Coney. (In another entry from the Cincinnati truth-is-stranger-than-fiction department, police once engaged an assault suspect in a pedal-boat chase here.) The park also offers a fairly wide variety of food services, a miniature golf course and a large, well-equipped playground. Moonlite Gardens is a popular spot for dances that

FYI

Unless otherwise noted, the area code for all phone numbers listed in this guide is 513.

range from teen sock hops to Big Band bashes for the slightly older crowd.

Coney is also an extremely popular site for company picnics, and it hosts two major annual events: the Appalachian Festival in May and Summerfair in June (see our Annual Events chapter).

Sunlite Pool is open Memorial Day through Labor Day 10 AM to 8 PM daily. Park rides are open during this period from 11 AM to 9 PM Saturday and Sunday and noon to 9 PM on weekdays. Admission to Sunlite Pool is $13.95 for adults, $10.95 for children ages 4 through 11 and for senior citizens. An all-day ride ticket costs an extra $3 with pool admission or $7 on its own. Parking is $3. (If the Ohio River is at flood stage, call first. Flood waters sometimes force Coney to close temporarily.)

Paramount's Kings Island
I-71 and Kings Mills Rd., Mason
• **573-5700, (800) 288-0808**

More than three million people jam into Paramount's Kings Island each summer, and most of them are heard to utter two phrases at least once while they are there: "How much longer?" and "Wow, that was fun." Like at most amusement parks, the lines for rides are long. But you can't beat this park for fun.

No matter what kind of entertainment you are looking for, there's a good chance you'll find it at Kings Island. The giant amusement park, which is one of the top 15 parks in the country and the largest in the Midwest, is filled with rides, major stage productions, children's shows, movies, dozens of restaurants, dozens of shops, games, arcades, picnic areas and even its own amphitheater, Timberwolf, that attracts major concerts.

Its 1,600-acres are divided into seven theme areas and centered around a one-third-scale replica of the Eiffel Tower. (After a visit to France, local humor columnist David Wecker remarked that "they've built one of those Kings Island towers in Paris, too.") The observation deck at the top of the tower, by the way, offers spectacular views of the park and surrounding area, particularly in the fall with the colorful leaves.

The park, which opened in 1972, was purchased by movie and entertainment giant Paramount Communications in 1992, and they won't let you forget who the owners are. Paramount signs are everywhere, and the park now packages many of its rides and retail stores around Paramount movies or recordings. Klingons and other *Star Trek* characters walk around the park. Cars from *Days of Thunder* are on display. You can see memorabilia from *Top Gun* around the roller-coaster of the same name, which is designed to look like it takes off from an aircraft carrier.

www.insiders.com
See this and many other **Insiders' Guide®** destinations online — in their entirety.
Visit us today!

Richard Scarry and his Busytown friends are the center of the children's area. A growing family-oriented Nickelodeon area is a huge hit with the kids — particularly Splat City, which allows kids to get "slimed" by gobs of green, gooey glop.

There are hundreds of rides, ranging from easy to intense, and new ones are added on a regular basis. As with all amusement parks, roller coasters are the star attractions. The best Kings Island has to offer, in our experienced and highly opinionated view, is The Beast, the longest and fastest wooden roller coaster in the country. The ride goes through two tunnels, hits 60 mph, makes you swear you're going to fly off the track on a couple of corners and is so bumpy you feel like you've just operated a jack hammer. It's great! The Vortex is a close second, hitting higher speeds and adding two over-the-top loops and a horizontal corkscrew, but it glides on steel rails so the ride is smoother.

Top Gun has the rails on top of the cars so you're left dangling in midair. The cars swing out sideways on corners, and with the rails on top you can't see what's coming up so some of the turns catch you by surprise. King Cobra has you riding standing up. It's a short ride and brakes hard. The Racer offers a different twist, with one set of cars turned backward. Adventure Express is mild, but seems to take corners at 90 degrees. The Space Commander allows you to spin your individual capsule upside down. One of the newest coasters is The Outer Limits: Flight of Fear, which catapults riders from 0 to 65 mph

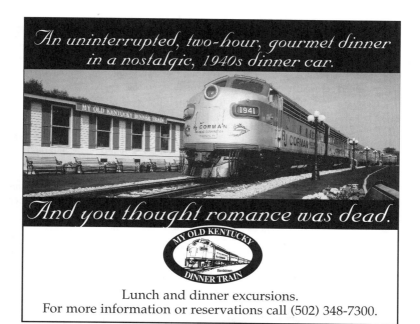
in four seconds and then sends them soaring through a maze of loops, drops and spins — all indoors! The coaster is completely contained inside a building.

With the addition of new coasters and thrill rides, the supply is greater, making the wait in line somewhat shorter on each. Still, be prepared to wait sometimes more than two hours to get on some of the popular rides. Some of the less intense rides have shorter lines but, generally, be prepared to stand in line to get on, or in, everything, including restaurants and food booths. Sometimes, though, two tasks can be carried out at one time. The park's management isn't dumb — they often put food and drink booths adjacent to where people are standing in line. It's common to send one member of the family on a food or drink run, while the rest of the group keeps his/her place in line. (Cutting in line, though, is expressly forbidden, and violators get kicked out of the park. That rule is strictly enforced.) Be prepared to pay a premium if you buy food — or anything else —

in the park. You can bring your own food and drinks, and lockers are available so you don't have to carry it around all day.

During the summer, the solution to baking in the sizzling summer heat is a cup of Homemade brand cherry cordial ice cream from one of the vendors and catching the train to the Water Works area. The area was doubled to 30 acres in 1997, with a 600,000-gallon heated wave pool, a 99,000-square-foot sunning area and a kids waterplay zone that includes a five-slide pirate ship and a kiddie pool with low-intensity slides. For the brave-hearted, The Plunge water slide starts about 70 feet off the ground and drops straight down. For a relaxing ride, try a slow innertube trip down the Lazy Miami.

For a family trip, gather in one of the giant innertubes with seats and roll down Whitewater Canyon, where strategically placed workers with itchy trigger fingers explode bursts of water into the air. Strapped into your seat, there is nothing you can do but watch the water go up, watch it come down, cover your head and get soaked. It's wonderful on steamy summer days, but on chilly or breezy days you leave the ride with chattering teeth and goose bumps the size of golf balls.

If you have very young children, run, do not walk, straight to Hanna-Barbera Land (with its adorable, and tame, miniature roller coaster for tots). This themed park within the park is more than enough to occupy the day. Hanna-Barbera includes pint-size rides and the Enchanted Theater, a haunted house with a sense of humor. (See our Kidstuff chapter for more details.)

Kings Island is open daily during the spring, summer and early fall. It used to stay open into late fall, offering cooler weather and colorful vistas from the abundance of trees in and around the park, but two years ago park management decided to close the park during weekdays after Labor Day because so many of their employees quit when school started. It opens on weekends, though, during September and October.

The park opens at 9 AM, but rides don't start until 10 AM. With the hour difference, it's quite common — and a darn good idea — to see people entering the park when the gates open and go sprinting like they were late for a bus to their favorite roller coaster. Although they still have an hour until the ride opens, it's one of the shorter waits of the day for the popular coasters.

Individual tickets are $30.95 for "adults" 7 through 59 and $16.95 for children 3 through 6 and seniors 60 and older. Children 2 and younger get in free. It's becoming more and more difficult to take in the whole park in one day, especially for first-timers. Knowing this, the park offers two-day passes for $41.95 for adults and $22.50 for children and seniors. Season passes are $64.95 for adults and $37.95 for children and seniors. A season pass for a family of four is $169.95, with $50 for each additional child. Season passes are also good for admission to Paramount's six other amusement parks in the United States and Canada. Parking is $5.

Surf Cincinnati Waterpark
11460 Sebring Dr., Forest Park
• 742-0620

If you can't get to Hawaii any time soon, you can hang ten in the half-acre wave pool at Surf Cincinnati. If rafting is more your style, the park has fast and slow options with body flumes, speed slides and innertubing, either down "rapids" or drifting down the Lazy River. There are two children's pools. If you get waterlogged, volleyball, miniature golf, go-carts and bumper boats are also available. You can buy food here and eat in the picnic areas.

The park is open daily 10:30 AM to 8 PM from early June to late August, with limited hours during select weeks in May and September. Admission prices are based on height. Those 48 inches or shorter pay the lower of the following: $12.95 and $10.50 weekends, $10.95 and $6.95 Monday through Thursday. Reduced rates are available after 3:30 PM. Season passes are $39.95.

Pure Fun Plus

Carew Tower Observation Deck
Fifth and Race Sts. • no phone

It isn't the Sears Tower, but the 49th-floor observation deck atop Cincinnati's tallest building has buckled the knees of a few acrophobics. With an unobstructed view in every direction, you can watch storms roll in from the west, catch spectacular sunsets and even stand above the clouds on some days. To get there, take an elevator to the 45th floor of the Carew Tower and then walk up four flights. Admission is $2 for adults, $1 for children 6 through 11 and free for children 5 and younger. Hours are 9:30 AM to 5:15 PM Monday through Friday, 10 AM to 4:45 PM Saturday and 11 AM to 4:45 PM Sunday.

Cathedral Basilica of the Assumption

Madison Ave. and 12th St., Covington, Ky. • (606) 431-2060

This small-scale replica of Notre Dame is a must-see. The cathedral features a French Gothic design with gargoyles, flying buttresses, mural-size oil paintings by renowned artist Frank Duveneck and 82 stained-glass windows, including the world's largest at 24 feet by 67 feet.

Cincinnati/Northern Kentucky International Airport

I-275 and Donaldson Rd., Hebron, Ky. • (606) 767-3144

More than 40,000 children take a guided tour of the airport each year. The tour includes the airport's aircraft rescue firefighting facility and a demonstration of the rescue equipment, the murals that were taken from Union Terminal, the different concourses and the airport's own airplane, where children can explore the cockpit and instrumentation and receive an explanation of emergency procedures. Tours begin 9:30 AM, 11 AM and 1 PM and they're free. Call the Communications Department for reservations two weeks in advance.

Cincinnati Zoo and Botanical Garden

3400 Vine St. • 281-4700, (800) 94HIPPO

The Cincinnati Zoo is facing some hard times and some hard decisions. The voters of Hamilton County turned down a levy in 1997 that was to provide the operating expenses as well as a new parking garage for the zoo. Now there is talk by zoo directors that the elephants will have to go and that other high-cost animal exhibits may be revamped or eliminated. All this said, the Cincinnati Zoo certainly isn't down for the count. Just keep in mind that any current exhibit noted here may not still exist in 1998 or beyond

Even so, this is among the most respected zoos in the country among its peers. The Cincinnati Zoo, the name by which most people know it, is particularly renowned for its collection of 100 endangered species, including six that are extinct in the wild. Alas, the last passenger pigeon on earth died here in 1914. The memorial to her and the last Carolina para-

keet, which also died here in 1918, is still on the grounds today.

The zoo is also known worldwide for its captive-birth programs with such exotic animals as Malaysian tapirs, okapis, gorillas and white tigers. More than 100 white tigers have been born here. And the zoo is a particularly fecund place for gorillas, which have had a world-record number of captive births here. The annual Zoo Babies event in June, in which newborns of all sorts go on display, is among the zoo's most popular attractions. Newborns are on display all year at the nursery in the Joseph H. Spaulding Children's Zoo, a petting zoo that also includes the zoo's penguins and walrus (orangutans in Pampers climbing the jungle gym are a hit, and check out the subterranean view of prairie dogs and underwater view of the walrus).

Another popular attractions is Jungle Trails, a mock African and Asian rain forest that combines indoor and outdoor displays of rain forest flora and fauna. You won't exactly be convinced you've been whisked off to Sumatra, but it's still quite nicely done. The wait can be as long as 30 minutes during peak times.

The Cat House (an ironic name for squeaky-clean Cincinnati) is a popular indoor exhibit of big cats from around the world in well-lit and nicely decorated glass-enclosed habitats. These vanishing animals are easy to find here.

Some of the other best or most popular displays include **Insect World**, a well stocked insect house teeming with contained creepy-crawlies; **Gorilla World**, home of the zoo's extensive collection of lowland gorillas, headed by Colossus, a male silverback and one of the biggest lowland gorillas in captivity; **Komodo dragons**, with Indonesian lizards that are the world's largest (the zoo also holds the world records for most Komodo dragons to hatch); **The Bear Wall**, home to the zoo's collection of bears, which can be found out of their caves frolicking or sleeping most of the day; **Big Cat Canyon**, home of the zoo's white tigers; **The Nocturnal House**, with everything from aardvarks to vampire bats (complete with bowls of blood for convenient sipping); **Monkey Island**, perhaps one of the most natural-looking habitats in the zoo, where monkeys frolic and otherwise interact, apparently oblivious to the crowds around them; **The Bird House**, home to many exotic and not-so-exotic birds; and the **Bald Eagle**, which can be found majestically perched within a large meshed-in habitat

The Festival of Lights, held during the winter holidays after Thanksgiving, is so popular it helped close down a similar event at Kings Island. More than 1.5 million light bulbs are strung from just about everything that doesn't move and a few things that do. Ice-skating, hayrides and ice carvings also add to a festive holiday mood.

Shows in the zoo's amphitheater during the Memorial Day through Labor Day period are worth a trip all their own. Besides special artistic performances and Jazzoo music concerts featuring near-top-name acts, there are animal shows hosted by zoo staff, including one of the nation's few trained-bird shows.

Kids also enjoy the train rides, which cost an extra $1.50 for adults and $1.25 for kids 12 and younger. They give a good, if brief, overview of the park. Tram rides, which cost the same, last longer and are a good alternative.

What with all the animals, many people forget the Botanical Garden part of the zoo. It contains an extensive collection of flora scattered about throughout the site. In fact, the zoo (along with Spring Grove Cemetery — see the Close-up in our Parks and Recreation chapter) is among the best places in Cincinnati for home landscapers to scope out their options of plants that can survive Cincinnati's climate before shopping the nurseries.

Admission to the zoo is $10 for adults, $5 for children 2 through 12 and $8 for seniors 62 and older, plus $5 for parking. You can buy a family membership for $59 or $50 for single parents; add $24 to include parking. (Metered street parking is also available near the zoo and is a good deal for nonmembers, but it goes very fast.) Admission to the Children's Zoo is another 75¢ for nonmembers. A family membership is $65 and will pay for itself for a family of three if you go to the zoo three times a year or more. It also gives you a first crack at new attractions (which come along fairly frequently), reduced-

FYI

Unless otherwise noted, the area code for all phone numbers listed in this guide is 513.

admission guest passes, 10 percent discount at zoo shops, discounts on Jazzoo music concerts and educational classes, a monthly newsletter, neat-looking stickers for your car and free admission to 100 other cooperating zoos around the country. You can get a credit for your admission toward annual membership if you visit. Warning: Credit cards are not accepted for admission. Strollers can be rented for $3.

The zoo is open daily 9 AM to 5 PM (until 6 PM from Memorial Day weekend to Labor Day weekend). Once in, you don't have to leave until 7 PM. The Children's Zoo is open 10 AM to 4 PM. The Festival of Lights holiday display is open 5 to 9 PM Sunday through Thursday and until 9:30 PM Friday to Saturday from late November through early January.

Fountain Square
Fifth and Vine Sts. • no phone

The square is the heart of Cincinnati. It is where major events take place, such as Oktoberfest and the Reds World Series' victory parties, and it's the place where downtown workers and visitors gather for lunch on warm days.

Krohn Conservatory
Eden Park, access from Kemper Ln., Victory Pky. or Gilbert Ave.• 421-4086

The massive conservatory, which is one of the largest public greenhouses in existence, grows 5,000 of the world's most exotic plants. The Conservatory is divided into five areas: Palm House, Desert House, Tropical House, Orchid House and a seasonal area that changes displays six times a year. The conservatory is especially popular during Easter with its lilies display and at Christmas with its poinsettia display. It's open daily 10 AM to 5 PM. Admission is free, although donations are encouraged.

MainStrasse Village
Covington, Ky. • (606) 491-0458,
(606) 357-6246 24-hour special event line

Cincinnati's German heritage is actually best commemorated south of the river in

Photo: Paramount Parks Inc.

Paramount's Kings Island entertains more than three million people a summer with rides, stage productions, shops and more.

Covington. The six blocks making up MainStrasse Village in Covington is an area of restored 19th-century shops and homes retrofitted in a German motif. The area is home to several antiques shops, a playground for kids and fine restaurants (see listings for Dee Felice Cafe and Werthheim's in our Restaurants chapter).

The Germany portrayed at MainStrasse should be known as "land of many festivals." Area businesses hold a Spring Stroll in late March and early April, a Maifest in May, a Summer Sunfest in late June and an Oktoberfest in September (usually a couple of weeks before Cincinnati's Oktoberfest, also in September. Go figure.) That should help you meet your beer, brat and German puff pastry quota for the year. A Christmas Open House in late November is another popular attraction.

Of particular interest is the Carroll Chimes Bell Tower, a 43-bell carillon. At 7 minutes past each hour, mechanical figures in the bell tower move onto a balcony and act out *The Pied Piper of Hamelin* story. The tower is lighted after dark from April through December.

Another attraction is the Goose Girl Fountain, a life-size sculpture of a German maiden carrying two geese to market. Greek-born sculptor Eleftherios Kardoulias threw away the mold after he made this one, so you won't see any others.

A visitors center adjacent to the Carroll Chimes Bell Tower offers half-hour audiovisual presentations on Northern Kentucky and Cincinnati.

Look for MainStrasse just east of the Quality Inn Riverview, the giant scalloped cylinder just off I-75's first Covington Exit south of the Ohio River.

Meier's Wine Cellars
6955 Plainfield Rd., Silverton • 891-2900
Meier's offers a guided tour explaining how wine is made, with a tasting room as the *pièce*

de résistance. OK, so Ohio wine is not exactly Bordeaux. But the tour is free and interesting. Tours are available June through October, Monday through Saturday on the hour from 10 AM to 3 PM. Take I-71 exit 12 to Montgomery Road, then 1.5 miles west to Plainfield Road.

Mount Lookout Observatory
3489 Observatory Ave. • 321-5186

One of the first observatories in America, Mount Lookout was founded by Ormsby Mitchell in 1842 and remains the oldest fully operational observatory in the nation. It was originally located in Mount Adams, but pollution from the industry-rich river basin upwind forced its move to the appropriately named Mount Lookout. Samuel Hannaford designed the structure, which the University of Cincinnati physics department operates and maintains. It remains a hidden treasure. Only 3,000 visitors tour the Hyde Park facility each year, largely because even locals don't know it exists even though the stately domed structure sits majestically atop Mount Lookout. Tours and children's programs are available, but you need to call first. Resident astronomer Paul Nohr particularly encourages kids 10 and older to take the "star trek" to the Observatory and peek at heavenly bodies through the huge telescope. All programs are free and open to the public.

My Old Kentucky Dinner Train
602 N. Third St., Bardstown, Ky.
• (502) 348-7300

Who says the era of fine dining on the rails is gone? It's worth the drive to climb aboard My Old Kentucky Dinner Train, a diesel engine and three dining cars accommodating 176 passengers, to take the 35-mile roundtrip through the scenic Bluegrass countryside. The train even rolls through the middle of the Jim Beam distillery, for fans of the famous Kentucky bourbon. In the kitchen car, meanwhile, the chef is busy whipping up three-course lunches or five-course dinners; there are prime rib, seafood specials and even entrees for vegetarians.

Lunch trips run for two hours ($34.95 includes your train ticket, meal and parking), and dinner excursions last two-and-a-half hours ($55.95). Children 5 through 11 pay $5 less for lunch, $10 less for dinner. There are no senior rates, and please, no children under the age of 5. Schedules and days of operation vary by the month, but the train does operate year round. There are special packages on most holidays, plus the popular Murder Mystery Tour ($72.95), in which an acting troupe puts on a detective thriller in the train station prior to boarding as well as aboard during the train journey.

OMNIMAX Theater
1301 Western Ave. • 287-7000

This state-of-the-art theater is part of the Museum Center at Union Terminal. Using special technology, OMNIMAX shows movies on a five-story, 260-degree domed screen that wraps around the seats and gives viewers a feeling of being in the picture. Some of the movies shown include a trip on the Space Shuttle, a dive into shark-infested waters, a trip across Alaska and a Rolling Stones concert. A debate rages about which scene is scarier: the sharks attacking or Mick Jagger's lips enlarged on a five-story screen. Tickets are $6.50 for adults and $4.50 for children 3 through 12 and $5.50 seniors 65 and older. Show times vary depending on the day and the movie.

Spring Grove Cemetery & Arboretum
4521 Spring Grove Ave. • 681-6680

There aren't many cemeteries you'd go out of your way to visit if you didn't have a loved one there, but this is one of them. Spring Grove Cemetery is renowned throughout the area for its landscaping and can be a great place for home gardeners to find ideas and information about plants that grow in the area. Maps available at the front office can help you find and identify the wide variety of vegetation. This is not just a spring or summer trip, for the landscaping has been planned for year-round appeal. Grounds are open 8 AM to 6 PM daily.

Turtle Creek Valley Railway
198 S. Broadway, Lebanon
• (513) 398-8584, (513) 933-8014

Formerly known as the Indiana and Ohio Scenic Railway, Turtle Creek provides an enjoyable hour-long, roundtrip train ride through the beautiful rolling countryside of Southwest Ohio. While you're in Lebanon, you can enjoy a meal at the historic Golden Lamb Inn and some boutiquing and antiquing at the bounty of Lebanon's shops (see our Daytrips chapter). Trains run Wednesday, Saturday and Sunday May through June, plus Friday July through October. Only weekend Santa rides are available in November and December. Trains depart at 10:30 AM and noon on Wednesday, Friday and Saturday, plus 1:30 PM and 3 PM on Saturday. Sunday departures are at noon, 1:30 PM and 3 PM. Fare is $9 for adults, $8 for seniors 60 and older and $5 for children 12 and younger.

Valley Vineyards
2401 E. U.S. Hwy. 22, Morrow
• **(513) 899-2485**

You can see the wine-making process from the wine to the bottle and sample some while you're at it. Wine-making can be viewed from late August to early October, but Valley Vineyards is also open the rest of the year, offering tours of storage facilities, wine and food. The tours are free, as is a taste of the wine. But the food isn't. Hours are Monday through Thursday 11 AM to 8 PM, Friday through Saturday 11 AM to 11 PM and Sunday 1 to 6 PM. Take U.S. 22 northeast to 2.5 miles south of Morrow. You can also get here from the Little Miami Scenic River Bike Trail. But beware: Bicyclists have been arrested for DUI in Ohio. No kidding.

Museums

American Museum of Brewing History
I-75 and Buttermilk Pike, Fort Mitchell, Ky. • **(606) 341-2800**

Roll out the barrels. The museum inside the Oldenberg Brewery at the Drawbridge Estate houses the largest collection of beer and brewing memorabilia ever assembled, with nearly one million items on display. Remember when collecting beer cans was the rage? Someone here took it to extremes. Tours are offered on the hour 10 AM to 5 PM. Fees are

$3 for a basic tour and $1 extra for a tastier sampling tour.

Behringer-Crawford Museum
1600 Montague Rd., Covington, Ky.
• **(606) 491-4003**

The setting is fantastic, overlooking the Ohio River valley. The house is rich in character, dating from 1848. And the collection is truly ancient, with items spanning back 450 million years. The museum is packed with natural and cultural memorabilia and artifacts from Northern Kentucky's past: wildlife, 19th-century history, industry, transportation, archaeology and paleontology. Hours are 10 AM to 5 PM Tuesday through Friday and 1 to 5 PM weekends. Admission is $3 for adults, $2 for seniors 65 and older and students. The museum is closed Mondays.

Butler County Historical Society Museum
327 N. Second St., Hamilton
• **(513) 896-9330**

Occupying the 1861 Victorian home of the Benninghofen family, this museum offers period decorations and artifacts gathered in Butler County from the pioneer days until the turn of the century. Admission is $1 for everyone 12 and older. The museum is open 1 to 4 PM every day except Monday.

Chateau LaRoche
12025 Shore Dr., Loveland • **683-4686**

Sir Harry Andrews began building this Medieval-style castle on his heavily wooded estate outside Loveland in 1929. Today it's open to the public through the work of the Knights of the Golden Trail. It's also the perfect locale for a haunted house, which runs in October. This Loveland landmark is open 11 AM to 5 PM daily April through August and the same hours weekends only the rest of the year. With admission of only $1 (kids 5 and younger get in free), it's a bargain of an afternoon excursion.

INSIDERS' TIP

For some free summer refreshment while downtown, go to Yeatman's Cove in Bicentennial Commons for a dip in the wading pool and fountain.

Children's Museum
Union Terminal, 1301 Western Ave.
• 287-7020

Once located in Longworth Hall three blocks from the Ohio River, the Children's Museum of Cincinnati found itself UNDER the Ohio River during the great flood of '97. Don't despair. The museum has found new life inside the Museum Center at Union Terminal. Temporary exhibits are just a hint of future plans for an annex devoted to the Children's Museum, opening in fall 1998. Some exhibits that have been staged at the Children's Museum include "The Works, Where in the World Are You?," "Jungle Moves," and "Toddler Tidepool." Hours are 10 AM to 5 PM Monday through Saturday, 11 AM to 6 PM Sunday. Admission is $5.50 for adults, $3.50 for kids ages 3 through 12 and free for kids 2 and younger. Combination tickets for Union Terminal's other attractions are also available. (See our Kidstuff chapter for more information.)

Cincinnati Art Museum
Eden Park, access from Kemper Ln.,
Victory Pky. or Gilbert Ave. • 721-5204

The recently restored art museum has more than 118 galleries filled with paintings, prints, sculptures, drawings, photos, costumes, musical instruments and other forms of visual arts spanning 5,000 years. (See The Arts chapter for more details.)

Cincinnati Fire Museum
315 W. Court St. • 621-5553

In 1852 Cincinnati became the first city to use a steam fire engine, making it the model for other city fire departments, and it has collected memorabilia ever since. Located in the firehouse built for horse-drawn engines back in 1907, the museum includes a look at fire trucks over the years, the first fire alarm in Cincinnati, helmets, badges, shields and other equipment. Children like the interactive computer displays and the wonderful hands-on displays, including a fire pole they can slide down and the cab of a 1995 firetruck that allows them to operate the sirens and lights. The museum emphasizes teaching fire prevention and includes a safe house where children are taught the stop, drop and roll tech-

nique. Hours are 10 AM to 4 PM Tuesday through Friday and noon to 4 PM weekends. Admission is $3 for adults, $2 for children 2 through 12 and $2 for seniors 65 and older. Older folks are kept from hogging the fire pole so the kids can have fun.

Cincinnati Museum Center at Union Terminal
1301 Western Ave. • 287-7000,
(800) 733-2077

Cincinnati's once-grand railroad station, Union Terminal, has been converted into the area's home of history. Inside the massive half-dome structure are the Museum of Natural History & Science, the Cincinnati Historical Society's Library, the Cincinnati History Museum, the Children's Discovery Center and the Robert D. Lindner Family OMNIMAX Theater.

Within the Museum Center are displays showing the history of Cincinnati and the region, as well as permanent and rotating displays about the history of the world. The museum also makes good use of today's technology with plenty of hands-on, interactive exhibits.

Cincinnati's history can be traced through its various stages, starting at the Ice Age. The Clues Frozen in Time display takes visitors back to the days when ice was carving out our seven hills. Visitors are led through a chilly, mist-enhanced meltwater channel of a replica glacier. Musk ox, woolly mammoths, saber-toothed tigers and other ancient creatures that once roamed the area during that period are amid the displays. A mastodon that got stuck in a salt lock struggles to get free just a few feet from the pathway.

A replica of the Cincinnati riverfront during the early years shows how the city was founded and the importance of the river to its development. The display includes a 94-foot-long replica steamboat, a reproduction of the Public Landing c. 1850 and a 50-foot model of the Miami and Erie Canal.

Visitors can walk through a man-made replica of a Kentucky limestone cave, which is so realistic the temperature stays at a constant 52 degrees. The cave includes a waterfall, dome pit, stalagmites, stalactites and, of

FYI

Unless otherwise noted, the area code for all phone numbers listed in this guide is 513.

Photo: Cincinnati Zoo

A Bengal tiger lies in repose at the Cincinnati Zoo, one of the country's largest zoological parks.

course, just like real caves, live bats. (Okay, so they're blocked off from the inside of the cave with Plexiglas, but they're there.)

The Children's Discovery Center offers hands-on exhibits that introduce children to the human body and demonstrate how humans have adapted to and changed their environment. Various traveling exhibits can also be found at the Museum Center. The Historical Society has one of the nation's largest regional research libraries. Restaurants and shops are available in the outer terminal if you need a break. Or, the OMNIMAX theater offers movies on its giant, domed screen.

The museum is open 10 AM to 5 PM Monday through Saturday and 11 AM to 6 PM Sunday. Three-way combo tickets for the Museum of Natural History, the Historical Society and the OMNIMAX Theater are $12 for adults and $8 for children 3 through 12. Two-way combo tickets are $9 for adults and $6 for children. Tickets to just the Museum of Natural History are $5.50 for adults and $3.50 for children.

Gray Wireless Communications Museum
1223 Central Pkwy. • 381-4033

Cincinnati native Powel Crosley was a pioneer in the broadcast communications industry, manufacturing affordable radios and televisions and then founding WLW radio and WLWT television so buyers had something to tune in to. Crosley was always experimenting, and many of the remnants of his experiments — both the successes and the failures — are displayed in the studios of WCET television. Other artifacts from the early days of wireless communications fill glass cabinets. Admission is free. The museum is open 9 AM to 5 PM during WCET's regular business hours.

Hauck House Museum
812 Dayton St. • 721-3570, 563-9484

Hauck House is a museum on how the other half lived during the late Victorian age. Built during the Civil War, it gives an interpretive tour of how a wealthy family lived in the late 1800s. The house was the home of John Hauck, a German immigrant and prominent Cincinnatian who made a fortune in brewing. (Dayton Street was once known as Millionaires' Row.) The museum is open 1 to 5 PM Friday through Sunday. Group tours are available by appointment. Admission prices are $3 for adults, $2 for seniors 65 and older and $1 for children 12 and younger.

Indian Hill Historical Museum
8100 Given Rd., Indian Hill • 794-1941

Better known as the "Little Red Schoolhouse," this one-room schoolhouse was built in 1874 and used until 1935. It is now a museum for historical material significant to the Indian Hill area. It is open by appointment only.

Loveland Historical Museum
201 Riverside Dr., Loveland • 683-5692

The Loveland displays material relevant to the history of the town, including artwork from local artists. The museum is open Friday through Sunday 1 to 4:30 PM and by appointment. Admission is free.

McGuffey Museum at Miami University
Miami University Art Museum, Patterson Ave., Oxford • 529-2232

This museum is the former home of William Holmes McGuffey and a depository of the works of McGuffey, who taught the world through his innovative *McGuffey Readers*. He was a professor at Miami. Admission is free, and hours are 11 AM to 5 PM Tuesday through Sunday.

Railway Exposition Museum
315 W. Southern Ave., Covington, Ky. • (606) 491-7245

A collection of 50 locomotive and train cars sits in a 4-acre rail yard in Covington, Kentucky, showing how life on the railroad used to be. Included in the collection are a rail post office car, an open platform business car from 1939, a Pullman troop sleeper and a 1939 sleeping car. The museum is open May through November, 12:30 to 4:30 PM weekends. Admission is $4 for adults, $2 for children 12 and younger.

Shawnee Lookout Archaeological Museum
Shawnee Lookout Park, Cleves • 521-7275

Prehistoric Indian artifacts dating back to 14,000 B.C., which were discovered during archeological digs in the area, are on display in the Shawnee Lookout Park. Admission is free, and the hours are 1 to 5 PM on weekends only May through September.

Skirball Museum at Hebrew Union College
3101 Clifton Ave. • 221-1875

Biblical sources of contemporary Jewish celebration and holidays are shown via displays of ancient artifacts and modern objects. The museum is open Monday through Thursday 11 AM to 4 PM, closed Friday and Saturday and open Sunday 2 to 5 PM. Admission is free.

Taft Museum
316 Pike St. • 241-0343

The Taft's massive, 175-year-old home is now a 30-room museum for the family's art collection, one of the greatest private collections in the country. Chinese porcelains from the Qing and Ming dynasties, French enamels and paintings by Rembrandt, Duncanson, Van Dyke, Whistler and Grandma Moses fill the home. (See The Arts chapter for details.)

U.S. Playing Card Museum
Beech and Park Aves., Norwood • 396-5700

The U.S. Playing Card Co., which manufactures cards for everyone from Las Vegas casinos to Aunt Ethel's weekly bridge games, set up a museum of historic playing cards, including some dating back to the 14th century — which is older than Aunt Ethel. The museum is open to the public Thursday only from 1 to 4 PM. Admission is free.

Vent Haven Museum

33 W. Maple Ave., Fort Mitchell, Ky.
• (606) 341-0461

Vent Haven is a museum for dummies. It houses the largest collection of ventriloquist dolls — about 500 — including some that belonged to Edgar Bergen. Sorry, Charlie McCarthy moved to the Smithsonian. The museum is open Monday through Friday May through September by appointment only.

Warren County Historical Society Museum

105 S. Broadway, Lebanon • 932-1817

This three-story museum shows the development of southwestern Ohio from prehistoric days through the 19th century. It includes an award-winning Shaker gallery, as well as an extensive genealogy library, fossil collection, Native-American artifacts and a recreation of an 1860s village. The museum is open 9 AM to 4 PM Tuesday through Saturday and noon to 4 PM Sunday. Admission is $3, $1 for students.

Historical Attractions

Dinsmore Homestead

5654 Burlington Pike, Burlington, Ky.
• (606) 586-6117

The Dinsmore Homestead is a museum of real life, offering no fancy memorabilia, just life on a working farm from its beginnings in 1841 through the five generations who maintained it. The homestead is very visitor-friendly, allowing guests to wander through the main house and outbuildings such as the wagon shed, cookhouse and wine house. The homestead is open April through December, 1 to 5 PM Wednesday, Saturday and Sunday. Admission is $3 for adults, $1.50 for children 17 and younger, $2 for senior citizens 65 and older or $7 for families. Take I-75 to Ky. 18 and go west 12 miles.

Findlay Market

Race and Elder Sts. • 352-6364

This open-air marketplace has been the city's connection to fresh fruits, vegetables, meats and cheeses since 1852. It's like a trip back to the early days of the century — hot dog links strung over wire, whole fish on ice inside a display case, every edible part of a pig, chicken or cow cut up and being hawked by fifth-generation mom-and-pop vendors with long white aprons and pencils stuck behind their ears. The market is open year round on Wednesday, Friday and Saturday. Get there early for the pick of the produce. The market also recently got a $2.3 million renovation and expansion of parking facilities, making it easier to find a place to park as well as a lot less likely to get whacked in the back of the head by someone carrying a giant salami.

Fort Ancient Museum

Ohio Hwy. 350 and Middleboro Rd.,
Lebanon • 932-4421

Fort Ancient is more than just the museum. The 100-acre park features prehistoric earthworks and remains of village sites built by the ancient Hopewell Indian tribe. The circular mounds were used as a sort of sundial calendar. The museum illustrates the religion, culture and customs of the prehistoric Hopewell people. Picnic facilities and hiking trails are available to help make this a well-rounded daytrip.

From Memorial Day weekend through Labor Day, the park is open 10 AM to 8 PM Wednesday through Sunday and on holidays. From April 1 to the day before Memorial Day weekend and between Labor Day and October 31, it's open 10 AM to 5 PM on Saturday and noon to 5 PM on Sunday. The museum closes at 5 PM during the Memorial Day to Labor Day period, but it's open the same hours as the park the rest of the year. Admission is $4 per carload; $3.20 for senior citizens.

INSIDERS' TIP

With all the roller coasters at Paramount's Kings Island, the visual thrills are worth the extra 15-minute wait to get a seat in the front car.

Mark your calendar for June when the annual Kids' Fest enlivens
Sawyer Point with music, demonstrations and booths galore.

Harriet Beecher Stowe House
2950 Gilbert Ave. • 632-5120

Harriet Beecher Stowe lived in Cincinnati for 19 years, and it is here where she became familiar with the concept of slavery and formulated the thoughts and experiences that led to the writing of *Uncle Tom's Cabin*. Her home features family pictures, her journal, manuscripts and a chair once owned by President Grant. Hours are Tuesday through Thursday 10 AM to 4 PM. Donations are accepted.

Procter & Gamble's Ivorydale Plant
5201 Spring Grove Ave., St. Bernard • 983-1100

For a 99.44-percent interesting and educational experience, see how Crisco and Ivory soap are produced and packaged. The tour begins with a movie and slide show about the process and then goes through the old plant. Tours are free. Call for a reservation.

Sharon Woods Village
U.S. Hwy. 42, Sharonville • 563-9484

A 19th-century village has been re-created here, with nine buildings, including a train station, a doctor's office, a church and a jail. All of the buildings are furnished with 19th-century, Ohio-made furniture and decorations. The village is open Monday through Thursday 8 AM to 4 PM, Friday noon to 8 PM, 10 AM to 5 PM Saturday and noon to 4 PM Sunday May through October. The village is decorated for Christmas each December and open on weekends during the month. Admission is $5 for adults, $3 for seniors 65 and older and $2 for children 6 through 12. Take I-275 E. off I-75, or west off I-71 to U.S. 42; go south a mile to the park entrance.

Ulysses S. Grant Homestead
E. Grant and Water Sts., Georgetown • (513) 378-4222

Artist John Ruthven now owns the two-story boyhood home of our 18th president. Memorabilia and period furnishings are displayed throughout. The home is open Tuesday through Saturday 9 AM to 5 PM and Sunday by appointment. Admission is free.

William Howard Taft Home
2038 Auburn Ave. • 684-3262

This 150-year-old home is the birthplace and boyhood home of the 27th president of the United States and the 10th chief justice of the U.S. Supreme Court. Exhibits of his life are displayed. The home is run by the National Park Service and is open 10 AM to 4 PM daily. Admission is free.

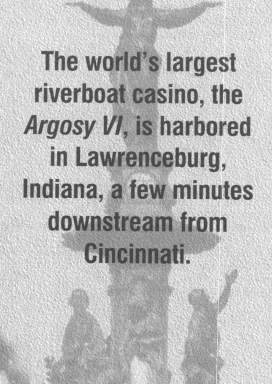

The world's largest riverboat casino, the *Argosy VI*, is harbored in Lawrenceburg, Indiana, a few minutes downstream from Cincinnati.

River Fun

Without the Ohio River, there would be no Greater Cincinnati. Though it may not be steeped in quite as much lore as the Mississippi, the Ohio is what ties the Tri-state area together historically and recreationally.

The average depth of the Ohio in front of Cincinnati is 26 feet. Flood stage is 52 feet. And, boy, we do flood! The Great Flood of 1937 decimated the city. In the spring of 1997, the river spilled millions of gallons of water into the downtown area, wiping out the Children's Museum as well as numerous riverfront businesses — a reminder that the river is never to be taken lightly, even in this age of flood walls.

The river brings good things, too. Since the dams were built in 1929 (ironically, to ensure a minimum water depth), river trade has increased more than 800 percent. You'll see lots of barges slowly plying their way on the Ohio any day of the week. Two-thirds of all river freight is some type of energy-producing commodity: coal, coke, petroleum. Every kilowatt of electricity in the area is produced from coal, which all arrives by river barge.

All that commerce and industry has its down side, of course. The river may be beautiful, but the adjective "pristine" does not apply. "Look but don't touch" might be the best way to approach the Ohio River. Water quality has improved over the last two decades, but let's face it: Cincinnati is downriver from many industrial areas and the city itself contributes more than its fair share of pollution.

Most of the year, swimming in the river is technically OK. But during the summer months, the Cincinnati Health Department frequently issues advisories not to swim in the river because of high concentrations of bacterial nasties. At any time of year, there are hundreds of better and safer places to swim than the Ohio River.

Fishing is OK, too. Fish are more numerous and healthier now than in the '70s, but all three states warn to steer clear of eating walleye, carp, channel catfish, white bass and paddlefish caught in the Ohio. High levels of chlordane and PCBs are sometimes found in these bottom feeders.

A year ago, if you were talking river attractions in the region, you might be talking about boating. Or jet skiing. Or even marine fireworks displays. Today, you're talking casino gambling. In fact, the world's largest riverboat casino, the *Argosy VI*, is harbored in Lawrenceburg, Indiana, a few minutes downstream from Cincinnati. That once-sleepy little town is fast becoming the most popular tourist destination in the region outside of Paramount's Kings Island (see our Attractions chapter) — and the riverboat is certainly the largest river attraction. And a bit farther along the river is the (for now) sleepy burg of Rising Sun, with yet another riverboat casino, the *Grand Victoria II*. (See the Close-up on riverboat gambling in this chapter).

But despite all the attention the gambling riverboats are getting, they are by no means the only attractions on the Ohio River (or the Little Miami, the Great Miami or the Licking Rivers, for that matter). Read on.

INSIDERS' TIP

Although most fishing enthusiasts tend to keep their favorite fishing holes to themselves, a recent poll of local anglers showed their No. 1 spot for fishing in the Tri-state area is Markland Pool, just below the Markland Dam near Warsaw, Kentucky. Striped bass, flathead and smallmouth bass abound.

Riverboat Cruises

Dozens of riverboat cruise lines and charter services offer trips on the waters of the Ohio, from sightseeing tours to romantic moonlight voyages. Some of these charter lines' brochures claim that they require a minimum party of 20 or even 50 people. You should know that there is considerable leeway in these numbers, especially if a charter has empty seats to fill on any given departure date. Call first and negotiate. In all cases, reservations are a must. Here are some of the more popular charters.

FYI

Unless otherwise noted, the area code for all phone numbers listed in this guide is 513.

A La Carte Charter Services
4609 Kellogg Ave., California • 533-0002

Choose a casual or a fine-dining cruise in a 57-foot, wood-hull Chris Craft cruiser. Packages for two- to 30-person parties are available. A La Carte supplies specific price quotes only on request; prices vary with the size of the group, the kind of meal served and other factors such as the time of year.

BB Riverboats
1 Madison Ave., Covington, Ky.
• (606) 261-8500

BB offers dozens of package cruises — day cruises, dance cruises, sunrise breakfast cruises — aboard the open-air barge *RiverRaft*, the large-capacity *FunLiner*, the steamboat-era *River Queen* or an authentic replica of a Mark Twain sternwheeler. Especially popular are the one-day trips to New Richmond, Rabbit Hash and other scenic river towns. Packages and prices vary greatly, depending on the ship, day of the week, season, and age of the ticket-buyer. A sample price for an adult for a Fun Lunch is $19.50. A dinner dance on a Saturday night costs $33.95 for an adult. And an overnight River Hop to, say, Louisville is $375 for an adult.

Celebrations Riverboats Inc.
848 Elm St., Ludlow, Ky.
• (606) 581-0300

The 400-passenger excursion ship *Celebrations* caters to corporate and personal functions as well as the general public. Theme voyages include a lobster bake and tropical and Cajun cruises. A sample two-hour lunch cruise, at $13.95 per person ($14.95 on Saturday), includes a ham dinner with salad and pie. Dinner cruises start at $21.50 Sunday through Thursday and $27.50 Friday and Saturday.

Delta Queen Steamboat Co.
30 Robin St. Wharf, New Orleans, La.
• (800) 543-1949

Although based in New Orleans, the *Delta Queen* and her sisters make frequent stops in the Port of Cincinnati. The company offers trips on the nation's only overnight paddlewheelers, including the *Delta Queen*, the *Mississippi Queen* and the *American Queen* (the world's largest steamboat). There are cruises throughout the year, but all three boats particularly frequent Cincinnati in May, August and October. Cruises range from two to 14 nights and include a champagne reception, meals, dancing, stories and river lore, and calliope concerts. Prices vary greatly depending on the length of the cruise, the boat and the type of stateroom or suite. A two-night cruise can cost anywhere from $390 to $1,290 and a 14-night cruise from $2,290 to $8,660 (all prices per person).

Kap'N Klan Charter
Departs 4 miles west of the I-75 Bridge on Route 8, Villa Hills, Ky.
• (606) 341-8221

A six-passenger, 40-foot houseboat offers a more intimate trip along the river than the huge, glass-enclosed yachts. Customized

---

INSIDERS' TIP

If you enjoy the nautical ambiance of marinas and waterside restaurants, take a drive along Kellogg Avenue around the (aptly named) California neighborhood of the city. Marinas, sea shanties, bait shops and more dot this Ohio River community. It's not Catalina Island, but it'll do.

Photo: Jeff Friedman

The glitter of lights adds to the festive mood when Tall Stacks, a gathering of many American steam-powered riverboats, happens in Cincinnati.

cruises can be as short as three hours or as long as three days. A three-hour cruise is $250 for a party of up to six people. One nice plus — you can bring your own picnic (though meals are available for an extra fee).

Queen City Riverboat Cruises
303 O'Fallon Dr., Dayton, Ky.
• (606) 292-8687

This company offers charter and regular public cruises aboard the *Spirit of Cincinnati* and the *Queen City Clipper* paddleboats. Meals can be anything from a continental breakfast to a formal dinner. Theme cruises include Hawaiian luaus and Italian-American nights. Prices vary. A three-hour cruise on the *Spirit of Cincinnati*, for instance, starts at $16.95 with a buffet ($19.95 on Friday and Saturday).

Satisfaction II Yacht Charter Services Inc.
4609 Kellogg Ave., California • 231-9042

The luxurious, 85-foot *Satisfaction II* is

available exclusively for corporate and private functions and accommodates 10 to 100 guests. Unlike many seasonal charters, the ship is fully enclosed and is in service year round. A typical voyage costs $68.50 per person; the menu might include beef Bourguignonne, wild rice with dates and Santa Fe cheesecake.

Victory Yacht Charters
5975 Boymel Dr., Fairfield • 242-7837, 860-4100

Departing from the Rivertowne Marina, the *Victory* offers a 360-degree panoramic view and meals. This is a great place to hold a wedding or birthday or graduation celebration, although two-person river outings are also available. The charter offers the option of docking at the Serpentine Wall and Bicentennial Commons, the park along the Cincinnati riverfront. Lunch cruises range from $35 to $49 per person. Dinner cruises range from $54 to $59.

Riverboat Gambling

Riverboat gambling is rapidly becoming one of the hottest attractions in the Greater Cincinnati area. Gambling is illegal in Ohio and Kentucky, but not in Indiana. A 20- to 25-minute drive from downtown Cincinnati puts you in Lawrenceburg, Indiana, home of the *Argosy VI*. The *Grand Victoria II* docks in Rising Sun, a bit farther downriver.

Close-up

Lawrenceburg is currently the destination of choice for most gamblers. It's closer to Cincinnati than Rising Sun, and the riverboat operation there is bigger. From downtown Cincinnati, the quickest route to Indiana is (trust us) via Kentucky. Take I-471 south and pick up I-275 west. Immediately upon crossing the Ohio River into Indiana, take the first exit (16). From there, numerous signs point you to Lawrenceburg and the huge parking lots for the casino. Free shuttles take you to the dock area. (From the Cincinnati/Northern Kentucky International Airport, you're even closer — about a 15-minute drive.)

The *Argosy VI* is the length of a football field, with three decks. Not only is it the largest riverboat casino in the world, it's the largest passenger vessel of any kind on America's inland waterways. Passenger capacity is 4,000, with a crew of 400. The gaming areas are certainly roomier and better ventilated than those in most casinos we've seen, riverboat or otherwise. There are 88 table games and 1,746 slot machines. The tables include blackjack, roulette, Caribbean stud, mini baccarat and craps, and there's a full array of video poker units.

In case you want to spend more money than you'd anticipated, you'll find plenty of ATMs on board. High rollers have their own stake on the third deck, the high-denomination area.

Nonsmoking areas are available. A snack shop on the third deck purveys hot dogs and sub sandwiches and free munchies such as cheese cubes and carrot sticks are available.

— continued on next page

Photo: Patrick Hayes

The *Argosy VI* brings riverboat gambling back to the river.

Gaming cruises depart every two hours starting at 9 AM, with the last cruise at 1 AM (3 AM on Fridays and Saturdays). This means you could conceivably gamble 20 out of 24 hours on weekends. Call 1-888-ARGOSY7 for rates and special packages. See our Hotels and Motels chapter (West) for information on the new Argosy Casino Resort. The Dearborn County Convention and Visitors Bureau, (800) 322-8198, can supply you with a list of the half-dozen local motels and hotels, but be aware that most of these date from the pre-casino era and it shows.

Rising Sun is about 45 minutes from downtown Cincinnati (just follow the above directions to Lawrenceburg, then drive west on U.S. 50 for eight miles, then jog onto St. Rt. 56, which takes you into Rising Sun). The *Grand Victoria II* is a replica of a 19th-century Victorian sternwheeler, with 1,900 gaming positions and 1,302 slot machines. Some 80 tables offer blackjack, craps, roulette, Caribbean stud and Let It Ride. Passenger capacity is 2,700, with a crew of 300.

Nearly 3 million visitors hit the gaming tables of the *Grand Victoria II* in its first year of operation (1997). Gaming cruises depart every two hours starting at 9 AM, with the last cruise at 1 AM (3 AM on Fridays and Saturdays). Call 1-800-GRAND11 for rates and special packages.

There's more here than just a casino, though. The Hyatt Corporation just opened an 1890s-Indiana theme resort centered around the casino. The 300-acre resort features a 200-room hotel, a health club, a Wellington's steakhouse, gift shops, the Victoria pub, Picadilly's delicatessen and other amenities, all set in a Victorian motif on cobblestone, gas-lit streets. A concert hall features the likes of Tom Jones and Lorrie Morgan. Rising Sun does have some small motels and a few bed-and-breakfasts, but you really shouldn't miss the resort experience.

Enjoy your day (or night) of gaming. Just don't go overboard.

Ferries

Two water taxis regularly cross the Ohio River in the Cincinnati area. The Anderson ferry is primarily for commuters, but it has some recreational uses. The Augusta ferry is used mostly by tourists and sightseers.

The Anderson Ferry Boat Inc.
4332 River Road, Delhi • (606) 485-9210

The Anderson ferry crosses the river about every 15 minutes between Boone County, Kentucky, and Delhi just below the Trolley Tavern. Hours are 6 AM to 9:30 PM Monday through Saturday and 7 AM to 9:30 PM Sunday. The cost is $2.75 per car each way.

Augusta Ferry
U.S. Highway 52, about 5 miles from the Clermont County line • (606) 756-2464, (606) 756-3291

From just west of Higginsport, about 5 miles from the Clermont County line on U.S. 52, you can catch the Augusta Ferry to Au-gusta, Kentucky. This ferry provides the only river crossing for 63 miles between Cincinnati and Maysville. Keep a keen eye on the road for a sign that points toward the river and says "Augusta, KY, 1 Mile." The ferry runs 8 AM to 8 PM Monday through Friday and 9 AM to 6 PM Saturday and Sunday, with between three and five departures an hour, depending on the number of cars waiting. Crossing time is 10 minutes and the cost is $5 per car.

Riverfest and Tall Stacks

The city's two biggest public celebrations — one annual, the other occurring every three to four years — are Riverfest and Tall Stacks. Appropriately, both are centered around the Ohio River, the lifeline of the region.

Riverfest
On the Ohio River • 352-4000

A half-million people jam the riverbanks every Labor Day weekend for Riverfest, better known to locals as the 'EBN Fireworks. There's music and food, to be sure, but the highlight of the festivities is a half-hour of fireworks, synchronized to rock music broadcast on WEBN (102.7 FM). The fireworks are such a big deal around here that the local TV stations interrupt programming to broadcast the display live. And a fantastic show it is . . . some say unequalled in America. Be sure to read more about Riverfest in the Close-up in our Annual Events chapter.

Tall Stacks
On the Ohio River • 721-0104

Tall Stacks is Cincinnati's version of the East Coast's "Tall Ships" celebrations and is indeed a nautical wonder. This world's largest assembly of steamboats occurs every three to four years (it's next scheduled for October 13 through 17, 1999). A nationally renowned event, it harkens back to the days when steamboats made Greater Cincinnati one of the largest cities in the country. The *Delta Queen*, the *Mississippi Queen*, the *American Queen*, the *Belle of Louisville* and dozens of other paddlewheelers — calliopes tooting — line the banks of the Ohio as if it were 1835 all over again. Replica flatboats, which were floated down the river by settlers before steamboats were invented, also dock at the Public Landing, which itself is set up to look as it did in the early 1800s, with hay bales, storefronts and people in period costumes.

This must-see event draws the attention of all three major television networks and leading newspapers around the county and attracts more than 2 million visitors. Tickets for short-hop cruises and overnight voyages go on sale about a year in advance and sell out quickly, especially for trips on the *Delta Queen* and the *Belle of Louisville*. Separate on-board ticket packages are available, allowing a range of activities, from touring the boats to fun day cruises and ritzy dinner cruises.

More River Attractions

Rivers are repositories of unique places. Here are some interesting sites and backwaters located along our waterways, listed from west to east.

Markland Locks and Dam
U.S. Hwy. 42, 5 miles west of Warsaw, Ky. • (606) 567-7661

This dam offers sightseers the largest drop in pool levels of any dam on the river. Visitors are welcome to an observation room and deck that overlooks the locks. If you wait a while, you should be able to see a barge come through. Displays in the observation room show how the locks work.

Rabbit Hash
Ky. Hwy. 338 at Lower River Rd.

No one knows exactly how this village got its name, but it's a popular summer stop for riverboats. When boats dock, the village blacksmith demonstrates his trade. The main attraction here is The General Store, (606) 586-7744, which opened in 1831. It's a great place to stop for some sarsaparilla between 8 AM and 9 PM Monday through Sunday year round.

Showboat Majestic
At the foot of Broadway on the Public Landing, east of Cinergy Field • 241-6550

The *Showboat Majestic* is a National Historic Landmark. It has an onboard theater that has featured musicals, comedies and dramas for the past 70 years. The season runs April through October. (See our Arts chapter for more information.)

Bicentennial Commons at Sawyer Point and the Serpentine Wall

The snakelike steps of the Serpentine Wall, which stretch from the Public Landing to near Yeatman's Cove park, are a favorite place for kids and adults to while away summer moments along the river. At nearby Bicentennial Commons, surrounding the famous Flying Pigs sculpture at Sawyer Point, is a miniature sidewalk version of the entire Ohio River, providing interesting and not-so-interesting details. Parking is available either at the Public Landing or just off Pete Rose Way, if you're not walking from elsewhere downtown.

New Richmond
U.S. Hwy. 52 at Ohio Hwy. 132
• 553-4146 (City Hall tourist information)

Another pleasant stop on the river, this is the site of an annual Fourth of July festival and River Days, a three-day August event that culminates in a hydroplane race. An amphitheater on Front Street on the east side of town is the site of frequent concerts on summer weekends. Two good places to eat in town are Joe's Place (home of the famous Tex White Chili) and The Landing, both located on the river along Front Street. You'll also find some nice antique stores scattered along Front Street.

Birthplace of Ulysses S. Grant
Point Pleasant • 553-4911

The cottage where general and president U.S. Grant was born is decorated with furniture from the period. It's open April through October, 9:30 AM to noon and 1 PM to 5 PM Wednesday through Saturday and from noon to 5 PM on Sunday. Admission is $1 for adults, 75¢ for senior citizens and 50¢ for children ages 6 through 12.

Moscow
Just off U.S. Hwy. 52, east of Cincinnati

This is the site of the giant cooling towers of the William H. Zimmer power plant. Originally conceived as a nuclear plant, a series of construction problems, unremitting protests and red tape forced the three power companies building the facility to convert it to what is possibly the most expensive coal-burning power plant in history. The cooling towers loom over every house in Moscow, and you can see how property values might have become slightly depressed had the plant gone nuclear. Today, it's a major contributor to employment and taxes for the area.

Captain Anthony Meldahl Locks and Dam
U.S. Hwy. 52 at Chilo • 876-2921

The observation deck here, free and open during daylight hours, lets visitors watch the barges make their way through the locks. The dam is named after the captain who once owned Maple Lane Farm just across the road. He took members of a Congressional committee down the 981 miles of the river in 1905 to prove the need for a system of dams to aid navigation. They agreed, and the project was completed in 1929. Actually, 12 more modern high-level structures were built after World War II to further improve navigation.

Maysville
U.S. Hwy. 52 at Aberdeen
• (606) 564-5534

Cross the bridge into this Kentucky town and you begin to suspect something's up. First, there's Rosemary Clooney Street. Then you see multiple references to actor George Clooney and his dad, American Movie Channel host Nick Clooney. Yes, this is Clooneyville, and the *ER*/Batman star as well as the rest of the famous Clooney clan still hang out here, much to the autograph seeker's delight. They're not the only reason to visit this quaint town, though — it abounds with history (Daniel Boone lived here for a while).

How many kids get a chance to slide down a real fire pole? They can at the Cincinnati Fire Museum.

Kidstuff

It's a familiar story. Cincinnati kids grow to adulthood, move away to one coast or the other to pursue careers, and then — inevitably — return here to raise their own families.

This astounding return rate is no accident. Cincinnati is a terrific place for rearing children, as nurturing and relatively safe an environment as you'd expect to find in any midsize Midwestern town. There's an added emphasis here on play and enrichment, however, and that's largely due to the voters, who diligently keep passing levies for museums and parks. Furthermore, corporate giants such as Procter & Gamble and Chiquita, both headquartered here, wisely invest in any attraction that helps them lure new talent (and their families) to Cincinnati. An aquarium in Newport is currently under construction thanks to corporate dollars.

City and suburban governments also put an unusual emphasis on public parks — in fact, the City of Cincinnati devotes more acreage to urban parkland and green space per capita than any other metropolis in America. A complete listing of parks and recreation centers can be found in our Parks and Recreation chapter, but we've noted the public parks and playgrounds with the best attractions for kids in this chapter as well, along with a kids-eye view of some popular activities that are also written up in our Attractions chapter. Unless otherwise noted, all the attractions listed here accept major credit cards. Whenever available, toll-free 800 and 888 numbers are noted.

We've distinguished those parks and museums you wouldn't want to miss as "major attractions." These are the places to head first if time or money is an issue (although many of these attractions are free, or nearly so).

Major Attractions

Aronoff Center for the Arts
650 Walnut St. • 621-2787

Cincinnati's newest arts complex presents a special family series (bringing in the likes of *Sesame Street Live* and *Magic School Bus*) as well as Saturday workshops where, for instance, children are taught how to juggle or create their own costumes. Local companies such as Child's Play Theatre and Madcap Productions put on zany musicals and puppet performances. Traveling road shows and juggling acrobats also make frequent appearances. Shows cost $6 to $14, workshops $12.

Americana Amusement Park
5757 Middletown-Hamilton Rd. (Ohio Highway 4), Middletown
• (513) 539-7339, (800) 486-3070

Americana is under new management, and the new owners spent a considerable sum to upgrade and refurbish this modestly sized amusement park (see our Attractions chapter for full details). The reconditioned Screechin' Eagle is among the state's last classic wooden roller coasters, and fans say it's one of the scariest thrill rides around. There's a new Ferris wheel, an addition to the waterplay park, and other new rides as well. Live stage shows, a petting zoo, a log flume and the Jolly Roger play area round out the experience of an ol'-time fun park. Although teenagers may prefer the diverse offerings of a Paramount's Kings Island, Americana offers smaller kids a day of play for less than the cost of admission to a giant theme park. Americana is on Ohio 4, 5 miles south of Exit 29 on Interstate 75. It's open weekends in April and May (call for hours), then daily from June 1 through Labor Day. Summer hours are 11 AM to 9 PM Tuesday through Friday, 11 AM to 10 PM Saturday and 11 AM to 9 PM Sunday. (At press time, the park was considering opening its doors on Mondays, too. Call first.) Admission is $13.95, $11.95 for folks 60 and older or less than 48 inches tall. Kids 2 and younger get in free.

The Beach Waterpark
2590 Waterpark Dr., Mason • 398-SWIM, (800) 886-SWIM

This 35-acre waterpark has water slides, inner-tube rides, a wave pool, a thrilling Aztec Adventure water coaster and children's water areas in addition to live entertainment (see Attractions for full details). The park opens daily at 10 AM Memorial Day through Labor Day. Closing times vary throughout the season. All-day passes cost $18.95, $10.95 for kids 4 feet tall or under and seniors of any height. Season passes are $85 for adults, $32 for senior citizens and children younger than 3, and $235 for a family of four. It's immediately off Interstate 71, Exit 25, across from Paramount's Kings Island.

Behringer-Crawford Museum
Devou Park, Covington, Ky.
• (606) 491-4003

The only museum devoted to Northern Kentucky's natural and cultural heritage, Behringer-Crawford boasts a fascinating collection of dinosaur-era fossils and Ice Age artifacts. There are also exhibits on the Civil War. The museum sits atop Devou Park, which has a terrific playground and a sweeping vista of the Ohio River and Cincinnati skyline that's worth a trip in itself. The museum is open Tuesday through Friday, 10 AM to 5 PM, and Saturday and Sunday, 1 PM to 5 PM (closed Mondays). Admission is $3, $2 for kids. Call ahead for schedules of special hands-on programs for kids.

Children's Learning Center
Public Library of Cincinnati and Hamilton County, 800 Vine St. • 369-6900

Housed inside the brand-new, three-story annex to the downtown branch of the public library, the Children's Learning Center has quickly become a treasure for children and their parents. Opened in 1997, the center features dozens of computers loaded with educational games and — get this, parents — free Internet access to select (i.e., safe) Web sites for kids. No irritating waits in line, either; you can reserve a half-hour block of computer usage. The center is about more than computers, of course. A 420-gallon saltwater aquarium features a live coral reef. And because the center is run by librarians, books are a priority. The weekly reading programs are ambitious, from "Library Babies" to "Pre-School Storytimes" to "Family Read-Aloud Time." Everything's free. A library card is required only if you want to check books out. Hours are 9 AM to 9 PM Monday through Friday, 9 AM to 6 PM Saturday, and 1 PM to 5 PM Sunday. See our Libraries chapter for more details.

Children's Museum of Cincinnati
Union Terminal, 1301 Western Ave.
• 287-7020

Once located in Longworth Hall three blocks from the Ohio River, the Children's Museum of Cincinnati found itself UNDER the Ohio River during the great flood of '97. Don't despair. The museum has found new life inside the Museum Center at Union Terminal. Temporary exhibits are just a hint of future plans for an annex devoted to the Children's Museum, scheduled to open in the fall of 1998. Hours are 10 AM to 5 PM Monday through Saturday, 11 AM to 6 PM Sunday. Admission is $5.50 for adults, $3.50 for kids ages 3 through 12 and free for kids 2 and younger. Combination tickets for Union Terminal's other attractions are also available. See the Museum Center at Union Terminal listing below for combo details.

FYI
Unless otherwise noted, the area code for all phone numbers listed in this guide is 513.

Photo: Ron Austing

A stop at Jungle Trails in the Cincinnati Zoo and Botanical Garden is a must for kids.

Cincinnati Fire Museum
315 West Court St. • 621-5553

No family with a budding firefighter should miss this restored, turn-of-the-century firehouse. The museum features firefighting memorabilia and antique engines. Ring the fire bell, see a movie and visit the "safe house" for fire prevention tips. And where else can junior get a chance to slide down a real fire pole? Open 10 AM to 4 PM Tuesday through Friday, noon to 4 PM weekends (closed Mondays). Admission is $3 for adults, $2 for children.

Cincinnati History Museum
Union Terminal, 1301 Western Ave.
• 287-7020

History? Blah, says your youngster. But wait. This history museum, operated inside the town's art deco train station, actually makes the past fascinating. There's a re-created paddlewheeler, a World War II presentation, a working radio studio, and revolving exhibits. The Scripps Howard Newsreel Theatre shows vintage newsreels. During the autumn, Boofest is one of the most frightfully fun haunted houses (the Eerie Express is a new miniature train ride for toddlers), and Holiday Junction features a winter wonderland of trains. Hours are 10 AM to 5 PM Monday through Saturday, 11 AM to 6 PM Sunday. Admission is $5.50 for adults, $3.50 for kids ages 3 through 12, and free for kids 2 and younger. Combination tickets for Union Terminal's other attractions are also available.

See the Museum Center at Union Terminal listing for combo details.

Cincinnati Museum of Natural History & Science
Union Terminal, 1301 Western Ave.
• 287-7020

The Cincinnati Museum of Natural History & Science contains much for the junior paleontologist to love. Of special interest to kids is The Children's Discovery Center, an interactive exhibit, and a real bat cave. The museum also has special programs year-round for preschoolers through teens. Although we're not big gift shop fans, this one is a must. Hard-to-find chemistry and science sets, telescopes, microscopes and other educational stuff abound. Hours are 10 AM to 5 PM Monday through Saturday, 11 AM to 6 PM Sunday. Admission is $5.50 for adults, $3.50 for kids ages 3 through 12, and free for kids 2 and younger. Combination tickets for Union Terminal's other attractions are also available. See the Museum Center at Union Terminal listing for combo details.

Cincinnati Observatory
3489 Observatory Ave. • 321-5186

The oldest fully operational observatory in the nation (since circa 1845), the Cincinnati Observatory is nonetheless a hidden treasure. Only 3,000 visitors tour the Hyde Park facility each year, largely because even locals don't know it exists. The stately domed structure sits majestically atop Mount Lookout. Tours and children's programs are available, but you need to call first. Resident astronomer Paul Nohr particularly encourages kids 10 and up to take the "star trek" to the observatory and peek at heavenly bodies through the huge telescope. All programs are free and open to the public.

Cincinnati Playhouse in the Park
962 Mt. Adams Cir. • 421-3888

The Playhouse is a terrific resource, with family shows such as the magical "Abracadabra" juggling presentations and an annual production of *The Christmas Carol*. The best of these shows is the Saturday morning series just for kids, the Rosenthal Next Generation Theatre Series; anyone — puppets, storytellers, singers, even Winnie the Pooh — may show up. Shows on Saturday at 10:30 AM, 12:30 PM and 2 PM from October through May. Tickets are $2.50 for theatergoers 3 through 18, $4 for adults. Also ask about the creative dramatics classes for kids age 5 through 10.

Cincinnati Zoo and Botanical Garden
3400 Vine St. • 281-4700, (800) 94HIPPO

The second oldest zoo in the country (opened in 1875), the Cincinnati Zoo is a must-see for any family. The magnificent "Jungle Trails" exhibit transports you into the rainforests of Africa and Asia, where you'll discover families of orangutans and chimpanzees lolling about among waterfalls and banks of rolling fog. There's also the popular Komodo dragons, Colossus the gorilla, and an Insect World exhibit that can't be beat. Even very young kids will get a kick out of the Children's Zoo and the tram that runs throughout the complex.

One word of caution: The zoo is facing some hard times and some hard decisions. The voters of Hamilton County turned down a levy in late 1997 that would have provided operating expenses as well as a new parking garage for the zoo. Now there is talk by zoo directors that the elephants will have to go and that other high-cost animal exhibits may be revamped or eliminated. Keep in mind that the exhibits mentioned above may or may not still be here in 1998 — and beyond. Call first.

Buying a family membership for $59 or $50 for single parents will make you feel less pressured to get everything done at once (add $24 if you want to include parking). Plus, membership gives you discounts that encourage use of the many enrichment programs offered for kids on weekends (see our Attractions chapter). Regular admission is $10 for adults, $5 for children ages 2 through 12, and $8 for seniors 62 and older, plus $5 for parking. Strollers can be rented for $3. Admission to the Children's Zoo is another 75¢ for nonmembers. Warning: credit cards are not accepted for admission. Metered street parking is available near the zoo and is a good deal for nonmembers, but it goes very fast.

The zoo is open for admission daily 9 AM to 6 PM from Memorial Day weekend through Labor Day weekend and from 9 AM to 5 PM the rest of the year. Once in, you don't have to leave until 7 PM. The Children's Zoo is open 10 AM to 4 PM. The Festival of Lights holiday display runs from late November through early January; hours are 5 PM to 9 PM Sunday through Thursday and until 9:30 PM Friday and Saturday .

Coney Island
6201 Kellogg Ave., Anderson • 232-8230

Located on the banks of the Ohio River, Coney Island (also see our Attractions chapter) offers a fun family outing without all the cost or utter exhaustion of a day at a larger, more frenetic amusement park. Sunlite Pool at Coney is billed as the world's largest recirculating pool, and parents of small children will like the fact that the shallow section is huge and lifeguards are in abundance. Coney also has a 500-foot water slide and a 180-foot water-coaster. Pedalboat trips on Lake Como are another popular attraction for older kids. And the park has a miniature golf course, a Ferris wheel and a large, well-equipped playground.

Sunlite Pool is open Memorial Day through Labor Day 10 AM to 8 PM. Rides operate from 11 AM to 9 PM on Saturday and Sunday and noon to 9 PM weekdays. Admission to Sunlite Pool is $13.95 for adults, $10.95 for children ages 4 through 11 and for senior citizens. An all-day ride ticket costs an extra $3 with pool admission or $7 on its own. Parking is $3. (If the Ohio River is at flood stage, call first. Flood waters sometimes force Coney to close temporarily.)

Dayton Museum of Discovery
2600 DeWeese Pky., Dayton, Ohio
• (937) 275-7431

The newest player on the children's museum scene is Dayton's Museum of Discov-

ery, part of the city's Natural History Museum complex. It's full of hands-on play exhibits, mazes, giant sandboxes and more. Hours are 9 AM to 5 PM Tuesday, Wednesday, Thursday and Saturday, 9 AM to 9 PM Friday, noon to 5 PM Sunday (closed Mondays). Adult admission is $3, children $1.50.

East Fork State Park
Intersection of Ohio Hwy. 125 and Ohio Hwy. 222, between Amelia and Bethel
• 734-4323

Just a dozen or so miles from Cincinnati is a natural playground that's often overlooked even by longtime residents of the area. The centerpiece is East Fork Lake, which offers bountiful bass fishing and boating opportunities as well as a 200-yard-long beach (a lifeguard is on duty most weekends). There's also a campground, bridle and hiking trails, picnic shelters and seasonal nature programs for kids (see our Parks and Recreation chapter for more details on this and other area parks). The park is open daily May through September.

Eden Park
Mount Adams • no phone

Centered in the heart of Mount Adams, Eden Park has plenty to offer adults, too, like ice-skating in the winter on Mirror Lake. Of particular note is the park's Krohn Conservatory, one of the nation's largest public greenhouses. Wander through a tropical rainforest or dash under the rushing 20-foot waterfall. And although your little ones may not have much interest in orchids or floral displays, they're sure to think the cactus exhibit is pretty darned, um, sharp (see our Parks and Recreation chapter). The conservatory is open daily and admission is free.

Miami Whitewater Forest
9001 Mt. Hope Rd., Harrison • 521-7275

The park's Pirate Cove is a nifty "sprayground," with a cascading waterfall and water cannons. It's open May to October; hours are 11 AM to 9 PM. Admission is free but there's a $1 parking pass unless you have an annual Hamilton County Parks parking sticker ($3) (see our Parks and Recreation chapter).

Museum Center at Union Terminal
Union Terminal, 1301 Western Ave.
• **287-7020**

The Museum Center at Union Terminal is actually three separate museums as well as an OMNIMAX theater, all housed under one roof under a joint agreement. And what a roof it is! One of the world's largest half-domes covers Union Terminal, the classic art deco structure that served as the town's train station for half a century before finding new life as a home for homeless museums.

For clarity's sake, we've listed the three museums — Cincinnati History Museum, Cincinnati Museum of Natural History & Science, and the Children's Museum — and the OMNIMAX under separate headers. But the terminal building itself is worth a visit, if for no other reason than the striking architecture, the giant tile murals, and — hey, kids, listen up — the antique Rookwood ice cream parlor. Order the cookies 'n' creme, a Cincinnati favorite for generations. Also worth noting is the Cincinnati Railroad Club's exhibit in Tower A, with a view of the original tracks, diagram board and dispatcher's desk.

Hours are 10 AM to 5 PM Monday through Saturday, 11 AM to 6 PM Sunday. Admission for each museum is $5.50 for adults, $3.50 for kids 3 through 12, and free for kids 2 and younger. Combination tickets are the preferred choice for most families. Any two combined attractions cost $9 for adults and $6 for children ages 3 through 12. Three combined attractions cost $12 for adults and $8 for children 3 through 12. Parking is an additional $3.

Ohio Renaissance Festival
Ohio Hwy. 73 at Harveysburg
• **897-7000**

This replica of a 16th-century town offers both youngsters and the young-at-heart a charming trip back to a time that was nowhere near as cheery as it's portrayed today. The 30-acre complex comes complete with roving jesters, kings, queens, magicians, singers and the like. The elephant rides are a particular hit with kids (we wonder how many medieval English towns actually had elephants, but no matter), as are the daring displays of swordplay and the knights jousting atop horses and adorned in full armor.

A few cautions: Some of the live stage shows can be a bit, well, bawdy for the very young. And never, ever attempt a day at the Festival if it has rained within the past 24 hours. Instead of being submerged in the medieval, you'll sink in the mud-ieval. The festival is open weekends, August through October, 10:30 AM to 6 PM. Admission is $12.95 for adults, $6 for children 5 through 12, and kids younger than 5 get in free.

OMNIMAX Theater
Union Terminal, 1301 Western Ave.
• **287-7020**

If you've never taken your kids to an OMNIMAX, do it here. Think "movie screen combined with planetarium" and you've got a sense of this intriguing film format, shown above moviegoers' heads on a domed ceiling. The wraparound theater encases the viewer with whatever is showing, from sharks to volcanoes to the Rolling Stones. Warning: The loud sound system may be too intense for the very young, and young children may also be intimidated by the steep tiers of seats. Show schedules vary (and even scheduled shows may be already be booked by a large group), so call first. Tickets are $6.50 for adults, $4.50 for children.

Paramount's Kings Island
I-71 and Kings Island Dr., Kings Mills
• **573-5700, (800) 288-0808**

If you've got young children, run, do not walk, straight to Hanna-Barbera Land (with its adorable, and tame, miniature roller coaster for tots) and Waterworks. These two theme parks-within-the-park are more than enough to occupy the day (see our Attractions chapter). Hanna-Barbera includes pint-size rides and the Enchanted Theater, a haunted house with a sense of humor.

Waterworks includes 16 water slides. Nickelodeon Splat City is also popular with kids: you'll find it at the southern tip of Hanna-Barbera Land, where the gooey goings-on include GAK slime shooting, GAK cooking, "Double Dare" and "What Would You Do?" shows and numerous other ways to get slimed.

Though many rides may be a little rough on young children, there's still more than enough to go around for kids of all ages. If the kids are older, of course, they'll want to queue up for the park's stomach-churning roller coasters. You can monitor your child's development of intestinal fortitude as he/she graduates from the Racer roller-coaster to the Beast (the longest wooden roller coaster in the world), then to the steel Vortex. Two of the newest rides reflect the new ownership by Paramount — The Outer Limits: Flight of Fear (four loops, all inside and in the dark) and Top Gun, a suspended coaster. Other major theme areas include International Street and Coney Mall. The view from the 330-foot replica of the Eiffel Tower is something the whole family can enjoy.

There's a Baby Care Center for changing and feeding, stroller rentals, and first aid stations in both Hanna-Barbera Land and Waterworks. A dining tip: Our favorite of the park's 30 restaurants and snack shacks is Wings Diner because (1) it's a comfortable, roomy cafeteria where the family can spread out, and (2) the menu features Montgomery Inn chicken and ribs, a local favorite. Who needs a burnt burger and pesky gnats at an outdoor shack?

The park is open Memorial Day through Labor Day weekend from 9 AM, but rides don't start until 10 AM. Closing times vary throughout the season (it really is worth staying for the fireworks), as do operating times in the spring and fall. Keep in mind that weekdays may be best for smaller children, as the lines on weekends can try the patience even of older folks.

Individual tickets are $30.95 for people ages 7 through 59 and $16.95 for children ages 3 through 6, people 48 inches or shorter, and senior citizens 60 and older. Children 2 and younger get in free. Parking is $5. Season passes ($64.95) may be a good investment if you want to visit three or more times in one year.

Parky's Farm
Winton Rd. and Lake Forest Dr., Springfield • 521-7275

Parky's Farm at Winton Woods, a combination play farm and petting zoo, is one of the nicest mostly free attractions around, with goats, sheep, chickens, horses and other farm animals in abundance. Pony rides ($1) and a playground inside a barn (admission $1.50)

are also available. Parky's Farm Fair Days in mid-July is a nifty festival featuring kiddie tractor pulls, outdoor movies, lumberjack exhibitions and more. The park is open dawn to dusk all year and admission is free except for a $1 parking pass or your $3 annual Hamilton County Parks parking sticker.

Railway Exposition Company
315 W. Southern Ave., Covington, Ky.
• (606) 491-RAIL

Greater Cincinnati's living museum of trains and rail history features four acres of locomotives, passenger cars, freight cars and memorabilia. Hours are 12:30 PM to 4:30 PM Saturday and Sunday. Admission is $4 for adults, $2 for children.

Seasongood Nature Center
Woodland Mound Park, Nordyke Rd., Anderson • 474-0580

This is a small natural history and nature center with several interesting exhibits. Located on the grounds of Woodland Mound Park, the center is open Wednesday through Sunday 11 AM to 6 PM in March, April, October and November and daily 11 AM to 6 PM from May through September. Admission is free, though parking costs $1 unless you've bought a $3 parking pass good for a year at all Hamilton County parks. (See our Parks and Recreation chapter).

Sharon Woods Park
U.S. 42, Sharonville • 521-7275

Two attractions make this giant park a mile south of Interstate 275, Exit 46, a particularly great place for kids: Sharon Woods Village and a small water park. Sharon Woods Village has restored 19th-century buildings brought from other parts of Southwest Ohio, including a doctor's office exhibiting Civil War medical equipment and a barn with period equipment. On weekends, kids are invited to participate in crafts such as weaving, tin punching, quilt patchworking and candle dipping. It's open Wednesday through Friday 10 AM to 4 PM and Saturday and Sunday 1 to 5 PM from May through October. Admission is $5 for adults, $3 for adults 62 and older, $2 for kids 6 through 12 and free for kids 5 and younger.

The water park, which includes an elephant fountain and pedal-boats, paddle boats and canoes, is free and open the same dawn-to-dusk hours as the park. Admission to the park is free, provided you have a $1 daily parking pass or a $3 annual Hamilton County Park District pass. Go ahead and get the pass. It's the best entertainment investment in Cincinnati. (See our Parks and Recreation chapter).

Stonelick State Park
2895 Lake Dr., just east of Milford
• 625-7544

Want to attempt your first camping trip with the kids but without the investment in all the equipment? Stonelick offers an innovative Rent-a-Camp program. For $26, you get a campsite complete with tent, foam sleeping pads, cots, cooler and other necessities for your first night in the forest. Restrooms with hot water and showers are available so you and Smokey Bear Jr. don't have to rough it entirely. Reservations are a must. The park also offers canoeing, boating and fishing. Nature programs are presented at the park amphitheater. The park is open daily, May through September. (See our Parks and Recreation chapter).

Sunrock Farm
103 Gibson Ln., Wilder, Ky.
• (606) 781-5502

One of the most ambitious petting zoos around, Sunrock Farm allows kids to milk a goat, gather eggs from the chicken coop, and hand-feed the farm animals. Family tours are conducted from 2 PM to 3 PM weekdays ($3) and 2 PM to 4 PM weekends ($5.50). Reservations are required. Ask about the hay rides.

Surf Cincinnati Waterpark
11460 Sebring Dr., Forest Park
• 742-0620

Surf Cincinnati offers a half-acre wave pool, an inner tube ride, a body flume, speed slides,

a small pool and a beach for children. The park has fast and slow options for inner-tubing — you can speed along rapids or simply drift down the Lazy River. Food and picnic areas also are available. The park is open daily 10:30 AM to 8 PM from early June to late August, with limited hours during select weeks in May and September. Admission prices are based on height. Persons 48 inches and shorter pay the lower of the following prices: $12.95 and $8.95 Friday through Sunday and $10.95 and $6.95 Monday through Thursday, with reduced rates after 3:30 PM.

Turtle Creek Valley Railway
198 S. Broadway, Lebanon • 398-8584

Formerly known as the Indiana and Ohio Scenic Railway, the railway continues to offer an hour-long train ride through the beautiful rolling countryside of Southwest Ohio. Trains run Saturday and Sunday in April; Wednesday, Friday, Saturday and Sunday May through October; and Saturday and Sunday through mid-November. Theme trips, including Santa rides, mystery dinners and ice cream socials, are also available. Trains depart at 10:30 AM and noon weekdays, 11:30 AM, 1 PM and 3 PM on weekends. Fare is $9 for adults, $8 for seniors 60 and older, and $5 for children 12 and younger. Grandparents ride free on Grandparents' Day, moms ride free on Mother's Day, dads ride — well, you get the picture.

U.S. Air Force Museum
Gate 28B, Wright-Patterson Air Force Base, Dayton, Ohio • (937) 255-3284

This impressive facility, the oldest military aviation museum in the world, touts itself as Ohio's most popular free attraction. We find it hard to argue. A whopping 10 acres of exhibits relate the history of flight. Among the

FYI

Unless otherwise noted, the area code for all phone numbers listed in this guide is 513.

INSIDERS' TIP

Many visitors and natives overlook, if you'll excuse the pun, the Carew Tower Observatory. The viewing area at the top of the city's tallest skyscraper offers your family an exciting panoramic view of the city and the adjoining rolling hills. Kids pay just a buck, parents $2.

Photo: Greater Cincinnati Convention and Visitors Bureau

The gigantic pool and waterslides are two attractions at Coney Island, an amusement park that's the site of several major events in Cincinnati.

many air/spacecraft are a real British Sopwith Camel, a B-1 bomber, and even an Apollo command module. And don't overlook "Discovery Hangar Five," the newly opened interactive section that teaches youngsters about the varying models of airplanes and jets, as well as essential principles of flight. Kids will love crawling through planes and jets and the show at the six-story IMAX theater. Parents will love the price: free. Hours are 9 AM to 5 PM daily.

Other Fun Places for Kids

Dave & Buster's
11775 Commons Dr., Springdale
• 671-5501

More than 200 interactive and carnival games, a ski simulator and more make this complex a popular destination. The size of a football field, Dave & Buster's also features bowling, simulation golf and an onsite restaurant. In case you're contemplating the old dump-and-run, forget it — the management strictly enforces the rule that all children and teens must be accompanied by an adult over 25. Hours are 11 AM to 1 AM daily (but no one younger than 21 is

allowed in after 10 PM.) There is no admission charge; you pay per game.

Discovery Zone
1140 Smiley Ave., Forest Park
• 851-2292
8057 Beechmont Ave., Anderson
• 474-9099

The cure for the winter and rainy-day blahs, the huge indoor playground with tunnels, nets, slides and balls at Discovery Zone has quickly become a favorite with Cincinnati kids. The low-key room for kids 3 and younger helps keep them from getting roughed up by the big ones. Open Monday through Thursday 11 AM to 8 PM, Friday and Saturday 10 AM to 9 PM, and Sunday 11 AM to 7 PM. Admission is $5.99 per kid. Parents can tag along free or stay in the lounge for some peace of mind or to get some work done. Birthday party plans are available.

Doc Hollidays Game Emporium
6383 Glenway Ave. • 574-2222

The Emporium has great party packages and a wide selection of games, ranging from classic arcade to state-of-the-art electronic. It's open weekdays 10 AM to 11 PM, Saturday and Sunday 10 AM to 12 PM, and you pay per game.

Eastgate Adventure Golf & GoKarts
3232 Omni Dr., Eastgate • 753-8000

This place combines a souped-up version of miniature golf with ever-popular go-cart racing. Adventure golf includes waterfalls and other man-made hazards that make it a little more interesting than Putt-Putt. Eastgate is open April through October 10 AM to 11 PM daily. The cost is $5 for adults and $3.50 for children 12 and younger for Adventure Golf, $4 for adults and children for the go-cart rides. Kids must be at least 56 inches tall to ride the go-carts, but there are small Jeeps for younger kids. Jeeps rides are $2. Birthday packages and other group rates are also available.

Eastgate is easy to see from the road, but can be hard to find once you get off. Take the Eastgate Boulevard Exit off Ohio Highway 32, then head south on Eastgate Boulevard to a right on Aicholtz Road followed by another right onto Omni Drive.

Emery Theatre
1112 Walnut St. • 721-2741

The Emery is a Cincinnati treasure. This old-time movie theater, complete with live Wurlitzer organ concerts at intermission, crams its schedule with family films: The Marx Bros., Laurel & Hardy, and more. Show are Saturday at 7:30 PM, Sunday matinee at 2:30 PM. Adults pay $4, children $2.

Fantasy Frontier
7891 Fantasy Frontier Dr., Florence, Ky. • (606) 371-8228

You'll find a wide range of indoor and outdoor amusements here, including go-carts, 18-hole miniature golf, laser tag, and arcade games. There's also an outdoor picnic area. Birthday party and other special-event plans also are available. Take Exit 180 off I-75. Laser tag costs $4 per person for a five-minute game. Go-carts are $4 for a four-minute ride (for people 56 inches or taller unless accompanied by an adult; smaller Power Wheels are available for smaller kids). Miniature golf is $5 for adults, $3.50 for kids 6 and younger. Hours are Monday through Thursday 3 PM to 10 PM, Friday 3 PM to 11 PM, Saturday 10 AM to 11 PM, and Sunday 11 AM to 10 PM.

FYI

Unless otherwise noted, the area code for all phone numbers listed in this guide is 513.

Great Time Family Fun Center
756 Old Ohio Highway 74, Mount Carmel • 753-6900

This all-indoor amusement center has miniature golf, batting cages, a slam dunk basketball court, a kids' play area, and video and arcade redemption games. Hours are 10 AM to 10 PM Monday through Thursday, 10 AM to midnight Friday and Saturday, and 11 AM to 9 PM Sunday. Miniature golf and 15 minutes of slam dunk basketball cost $2 per person. Batting cages and other games are 25¢ a round. A birthday party plan is available.

Malibu Grand Prix
I-75 at Sharon Rd., Sharonville • 772-1292

Keep both eyes open as you whip around this awesome half-mile Grand Prix track. Three types of vehicles are available. To drive the mini-Grand Prix, the only requirement is a minimum height of 4 feet, 6 inches. For the other two more speedy vehicles, you to be a licensed driver. The track is open Thursday 3 PM to 9 PM, Friday 3 PM to midnight, Saturday noon to midnight, and Sunday noon to 9 PM. The cost is $2.95 per lap.

Putt-N-Fun, Maze-N-Fun and Bank Shot
1192 Ohio Hwy. 28, Mulberry • 575-0455

You can literally lose your kids for a while here. Maze-N-Fun is a sort of cloth version of the Minotaur's lair, a challenging 75-foot by 100-foot maze that kids of all ages can enjoy. Configurations are changed weekly, and, depending on the difficulty, it can take 10 to 45 minutes to get through. This attraction also has three 18-hole miniature golf courses and Bank Shot, a sort of cross between basketball and miniature golf. Every shot must be banked, and every backboard presents a different angle and challenge. The basket is 5 to 8 feet high, so kids 7 and older can play fairly easily.

The park also has a Water Wars water balloon game, ice-cream parlor, snack bar and a small game room. It's open, weather permitting, weekends in April, September and October, and daily June through August. Hours are noon to 9 PM Sunday through Friday, 10 AM to 11 PM Saturday. Cost is $3.50 per game per person, $9 for three-game or three-person tickets, and $30 for 12-game or 12-person tickets.

Sega Time Out Amusement Park
Forest Fair Mall, 1047 Forest Fair Dr., Forest Park • 671-7165

This indoor amusement park is the perfect cure for winter cabin fever. It's also good as a quick stop or bribe for good behavior if you happen to be at the mall anyway. Time Out has something to appeal to kids of all ages, including a two-story Ferris wheel, four types of amusement park rides, a good-size carousel, a miniature golf course, bumper cars, a mini-boat ride and a small race track for trikes. There's also an oversize play set with balls to jump in, nets to climb and tunnels to burrow through. Older kids will enjoy laser tag and Virtuality, a virtual reality fun center. Most attractions cost $1.50 each, or you can purchase an all-day pass for $7.95 or a $4.95 pass that's good weekdays from 10 AM to 2 PM. Parents can come along free with kids young enough to need them there.

Sports of All Sorts Family Fun Center
10138 Transportation Way, Springdale
• 860-4636
5170 Delhi Rd., Delhi • 451-8386
6925 Alexandria Pk., Alexandria, Ky.
• (606) 635-4386
25 Cavalier Blvd., Florence, Ky.
• (606) 371-5511

This chain of indoor family fun centers (formerly known as Funky Dunks) offers basketball, a soft-play jungle gym area for kids, redemption and video games, batting cages and air hockey. The soft-play area costs $2 weekdays, $3 weekends and evenings after 5 PM. Basketball is $2 per 15-minute session per person, though they're not too strict on time during weekdays when it's less crowded and no one is waiting. Other games and batting cage cost 25¢ to $1 per session, with discounts for purchases of 25 tokens or more. The centers are open Sunday through Thursday 11 AM to 9 PM, Friday 11 AM to 10 PM, and Saturday 10 AM to 10 PM.

Outdoor Playgrounds

The best playground generally is the one closest to you, but here's a listing of some other playgrounds in the area. See our Parks and Recreation chapter, too.

Airport Playfield
Corner of Beechmont and Wilmer Aves.
• 321-6500

This playground near Lunken Airport includes several interesting airplane, train and other mechanical-looking devices that double as tunnels and jungle gyms for kids. Admission is 50¢ and well worth it. The adjacent walking/biking trail and airport also help make for an all-around fun and educational outing.

Indian Hill Park
Shawnee Run and Drake Rds.
• no phone

What better time than now for your kid to begin making future business contacts? This public park happens to be in Cincinnati's most affluent neighborhood. All kidding aside, this is a lovely playground in a very nice public park.

Juilfs Park
8249 Clough Pike, Anderson • 474-0003

The playground here is a fully loaded, with numerous climbing, sliding, digging and swinging options. The Anderson Park District also puts on free movies under the stars on some summer evenings here, which make for a great family outing. Call for details.

Megaland
Springdale Rd. at Colerain Ave.
• no phone

A 10,000-square-foot playground just opened by the Colerain Community Playground Commission, Megaland boasts mazes, towers, tunnels and more. The local daily called it "the stuff of a child's imagination gone wild with possibility," and it's right. It's open daily, dawn to dusk, and admission is free.

Sawyer Point
Corner of Pete Rose Way and Eastern Ave.

Look at this park as Cincinnati's Bicentennial gift to its kids. The beautiful and fully equipped playground with separate areas for big- and little-kid play, the Serpentine Wall and historical attractions at the Bicentennial Commons nearby make for a fine outing for the kids.

Woodland Mound Park
Nordyke Rd., Anderson • 474-0580

In addition to several small swing and slide areas, Woodland Mound has a large, fully equipped play area with tunnel slides, jungle gyms and plenty of sand. It also has a nice kid-size nature trail adjacent to Seasongood Nature Center.

Special Events and Enrichment Opportunities

Watch weekend sections in the local newspapers for calendars of upcoming events for children. (The "Harried ... With Children" feature in Friday's *Enquirer* is particularly helpful.) Here are a few regular events and educational programs worth attending.

All About Kids Show
1077 Celestial St. • 684-0501

This annual show at the Albert B. Sabin Convention Center (scheduled for August 7 through 9 in 1998) is aimed at creating some "quality time" for parents and kids by providing numerous interactive play areas, and it also gives vendors a place to sell their services. It was created by developmental psychologist Earladeen Badger, an entrepreneur and local crusader for kids' causes. Watch for details in Badger's monthly *All About Kids* newspaper or daily newspaper calendars.

All About Kids is also a great free resource for parents in the Greater Cincinnati area. It's filled with useful information such as summer camp listings, holiday activity ideas, consignment shops for kids and other more weighty matters. Pick one up at your local public library or at other kids' attractions throughout the area.

Art for Kids
Art Academy of Cincinnati, 1125 St. Gregory St. • 562-8748

You can send your budding artist to the Art Academy for Saturday programs offered in three semesters each year. After-school classes are also offered at satellite locations. Examples of some recent classes include drawing, print making, found-art objects, sculpture and performance art. "While You Wait" classes are available for parents, and special Saturday family tours of the adjacent Cincinnati Art Museum are available on many occasions. Class fees range from $60 to $180 for the general public, with discounts for members of the Academy Circle.

Artrageous Saturdays
Raymond Walters College, 9555 Plainfield Rd., Blue Ash • 745-5705

Five shows each season cover a broad spectrum of performing arts, including classical, contemporary and ethnic dance; folk, orchestral and chamber music; and children's theater. Artists not only entertain but take the time to inform kids about the art form. All shows are presented from 11 AM to 2 PM on Saturday. Call for dates, ticket prices and a season brochure.

ArtReach Touring Theater
3074 Madison Rd. • 871-2300

This professional troupe offers live performances of classic children's stories for schools and groups, plus occasional performances that are open to the public and creative drama classes in the spring, summer and fall.

INSIDERS' TIP

Cincinnati has more than its share of waterparks, but you'll find few free ones. An exception is the "sprayground" at Parky's Pirate Cove in Miami Whitewater Forest, a part of the Hamilton County Park District. Water cannons and a giant squirting octopus are just part of the fun. And yes, mom, the water is chlorinated.

Kids can't get enough of the waterparks in Cincinnati.

Calico College
Clermont College, 4200 Clermont College Dr., Batavia • 732-5263

What could make kids want to go to college on their day off from school? It must be fun. Kids come here from throughout the region for Saturday classes on cartooning, computers, magic, photography, music and more. Sessions run two hours for four weeks twice a year. Each class has a different age range, but there are choices available in each session for kids in kindergarten through 8th grade. The cost is $35, plus materials fees for some classes.

Calico Theatre
Clermont College, 4200 Clermont College Dr., Batavia • 732-5281

Friday evening performances are designed for kids and are offered six times a year. The series cover a range of performing arts, including music, dance, juggling, puppets and illustrated theater. Ticket prices vary by perfor-

mance, but series tickets and group rates of $1 per kid for groups of 25 to 100 are available.

Carnegie Visual and Performing Arts Center
1028 Scott Blvd., Covington, Ky. • (606) 491-2030

The Carnegie provides a place for emerging artists to show their art and perform plays, but it also runs some ambitious childhood learning programs. That includes bringing in volunteer artists to teach classes, and a hands-on arts program in the Biggs Early Learning Center. The Art Stop after-school program, intended for Covington children ages 6-15, allows them to experiment with all forms of painting, drawing, sculpture and ceramics, at no cost.

Chateau LaRoche
12025 Shore Dr., Loveland • 683-4686

This is a one-fifth scale replica of a medieval castle. Really, no kidding. Chateau

LaRoche, also known as the Loveland Castle Museum, offers tours to the public 11 AM to 5 PM daily. Admission is $1 (kids 4 and younger free). Most notable for youngsters, however, are the way-cool overnight sleepers. Scouts, school and other groups populate this place at night, along with the odd ghost and rattling chain. The overnight sleepers are arranged through area schools and Scout groups ($100 for school groups and Scout troops up to 25 people; $150 for any other two people).

Cincinnati Art Museum
920 Eden Park Dr. • 721-5204

The museum offers a variety of programs aimed at kids and families, including two summer programs offered in conjunction with the Public Library of Cincinnati and Hamilton County in June and July for children ages 5 through 12. Curious Kids programs, held on several Sundays from 2 PM to 4 PM, combine a guided gallery experience with storytelling by children's librarians. Call ahead for times and tickets (tickets often sell out). Family Fun Tours geared to children are offered Saturday and Sunday at 1 PM. General admission is free for members and $5 for nonmembers, but anybody younger than 18 always gets in free. Admission is free for adults on Saturday.

Cincinnati Children's Theater
Taft Theatre, Fifth and Sycamore Sts.
• 569-8080

Besides school-day field-trip performances, the Children's Theater also puts on popular weekend family performances in March and November.

Cincinnati Nature Center
4949 Tealtown Rd., Glen Este/Milford
• 831-1711

The nature center offers the best hands-on nature study you'll find in the area, with numerous educational programs for youths, including spring and fall biology programs and summer classes. Besides the 1,425 acres of trails, there's a well-stocked library and an educational building with lots of great stuffed specimens.

Cincinnati Park Board
950 Eden Park Dr. • 352-4080

Several great events, such as Halloween hikes and enrichment classes, are offered at Cincinnati parks through the Park Board. A schedule of events is available.

Cincinnati Symphony Orchestra
Music Hall, 1229 Elm St. • 381-3300

The orchestra presents Young People's Concerts for school field trips and Lollipop Concerts for children ages 4 through 9 on two Saturdays a year. Watch newspaper calendars for details; better still, call ahead for times because tickets go fast. Admission is $4.50 for children and $7 for adults. The Cincinnati Youth Symphony Orchestra, a group of young performers under the leadership of CSO veterans, tours area high schools on a rotating basis to expose students to works of the masters. The Youth Symphony performs one joint concert with the CSO each year.

College-Conservatory of Music Preparatory Program
University of Cincinnati • 556-2595

Among noteworthy graduates of this preparatory program are ballerina Suzanne Farrell, actress Sarah Jessica Parker and Tchaikovsky medalist violinist Alyssa Park. Options in this prestigious program, offered by one of the nation's leading conservatories, include private and group instruction in dance, musical theater, drama and orchestral and chamber music. Among the most popular programs are the Suzuki violin program, Kindermusik and the Children's Choir. A brochure is available.

INSIDERS' TIP

Take your youngster, and yourself, for a nostalgic trip to the last operating Cinerama theater in the nation. The New Neon Movies in Dayton rotates a number of movies filmed in the sweeping three-camera format, including *This Is Cinerama* and *How the West Was Won*. Call for times: (937) 222-7469.

Drake Planetarium
Norwood High School, 2020 Sherman Ave., Norwood • 396-5560

The region's last remaining planetarium in an age of high-tech gimmickry and OMNIMAX spectacles is open to students across Greater Cincinnati. Funded by the National Science Foundation and NASA, this regional gem offers astronomy programs for 40,000 students annually. Admission is $4.50 for students.

Enjoy The Arts
307 Ludlow Ave. • 621-4700

This nonprofit organization provides full-time students of any age with discount and free tickets to sample Cincinnati's many arts offerings. It also presents special events, exhibits and chances to meet performing artists.

Gorman Heritage Farm
3035 Gorman Heritage Farm Lane, Evendale • 831-1711

A 100-acre historical working farm located in the heart of the city, Gorman is operated by the staff of the Cincinnati Nature Center. The site offers a wheelchair-accessible trail and a gift shop and library. Hours are Wednesday through Saturday 9 AM to 5 PM and Sunday 1 to 5 PM. Admission is free during the week; on weekends it's $3 for adults and $1 for children 12 and younger.

Great Harvest Bread Company
7819 Cooper Rd., Montgomery • 984-9212

You and your group can take a hands-on tour of the baking operations at the main store, which also makes bread for satellite stores in Anderson and Hyde Park. Kids get to see how the grain is milled and how the dough is mixed in giant vats. Each kid gets to knead and shape a miniature loaf and gets a free cookie sample. Yum. You need to call to arrange a visit.

Hamilton County Park District
10245 Winton Rd., Greenhills • 521-7275

The county park district hosts special events and classes for kids year-round at parks throughout the area. Animal lore, storytelling, crafts and kite-flying lessons are just a few examples. Most activities are free. Look for the park district's semimonthly "Evergreen" inserts in the Sunday *Enquirer*, or call for times and details.

Kids Fest
Sawyer Point, 950 Eden Park Dr. • 352-4080

This event, held each year in June, is no mere day at the park. There are shows, musical performances, demonstrations, tons of interesting booths and great freebies to be had by all. Watch newspaper calendar listings for details.

The Little Gym
7235 Beechmont Ave., Anderson • 231-9431
60 E. Crescentville Rd., West Chester • 671-9721

This versatile gym offers gymnastics instruction for kids from infants through grade school and karate, sports development and cheerleading for preschoolers on up. The birthday party package here is great. And there's a Friday-night-out drop-off program with pizza and plenty of activities that's popular with kids and parents alike.

Odyssey Learning Center
7791 Cooper Rd., Montgomery • 793-6100

Besides offering a wide range of toys and teaching materials, Odyssey provides educational diagnostic evaluations and tutoring by certified instructors for $30 an hour. And it has a host of enrichment programs, including an ongoing reading incentive club, foreign language instruction and computer education. Saturday Eye-Opener programs focus on literature, art, science, cooking and crafts; many of the sessions have modest fees of $3.50 to $4. Call for details or to get on the mailing list.

Super Saturday Program
5017 Marion Ave., Norwood • 786-6826

This program offers a wide variety of Saturday enrichment classes for gifted children. Children must submit "proof of intelligence," generally a referral from their teacher or school. Classes, most of them held at Xavier University, 3800 Victory Parkway, run from 9:30 AM to 11:30 AM. About 25 classes in several areas of science, foreign language, chemistry, origami and magic are offered to 225 students during three six-week terms each year. Cost is about $55 per class but varies. Free lectures also are available for parents who want to wait for their kids rather than enjoy a blissful two hours of freedom. The program is organized by the nonprofit Parent Association for Gifted Education.

Tall Stacks
Cincinnati Riverfront · 721-0104

Come October 13 through 17, 1999, the city will once again host Tall Stacks, the largest steamboat festival in the world. Dozens of paddlewheelers steam into town and carry the riverfront back to a bygone era. Kids will love the tours and voyages down the Ohio River. Tickets go on sale about a year in advance and sell out quickly, especially for trips on two of the largest boats, *Delta Queen* and *Belle of Louisville*.

YMCAs of Greater Cincinnati

Each Y in the area offers a range of swimming, gymnastics, karate and other education programs for kids. See our Parks and Recreation Chapter for a rundown on all the Ys in the area, as well as assorted youth sports.

Christmas Holiday Tips

Santa, of course, has that uncanny ability to be everywhere at once between Thanksgiving and December 25th. But he makes his presence known a little more dramatically in a few places. Here are some Christmas trips particularly worth making with kids over the holidays.

Downtown at Christmas

Yes, Virginia, there really are some very good reasons to come downtown to shop during the holidays. Although the suburban malls offer plenty of free parking, they'll never quite capture the holiday spirit the way downtown Cincinnati does. If you stay for three hours or less, parking is $1 at any city garage ($1 for each additional hour). Parking at meters is free on weekends. Here are some downtown holiday attractions.

• The annual electric train display in the lobby of the Cinergy/Cincinnati Gas & Electric Co. headquarters, 139 E. Fourth Street.

• An interesting display of caroling beasts at Tower Place Mall in the Carew Tower at Fifth and Race streets (just look for the tallest building in town). The folks behind the controls can actually see the kids and ask them appropriate questions, which makes for a few surprises.

• Christmas lights and ice-skating rink on Fountain Square.

• Horse-drawn carriage rides, available at various prices from independent operators year-round, but especially nice during the holidays.

Festival of Lights at the Cincinnati Zoo

No less than *USA Today* recently called the Festival of Lights one of "the 10 best in the nation." This event is such a hit with children — and the child in all of us — that it bears another mention here (see our earlier listing under Major Attractions in this chapter, or turn to our Attractions chapter). Of special note are the Enchanted Village with its toddler-size train and caboose and the real live reindeer.

Grant Farm and Greenhouses
5552 Bucktown Rd., Williamsburg · 625-9441

They pull out all the Christmas stops here by filling the greenhouse with a Lionel train display, stringing more than 100,000 lights over the property and setting up an animated nativ-

INSIDERS' TIP

If you think there's a lot for your kids to do now, just wait. Ohio celebrates its 200th birthday in 2003, and the Ohio Bicentennial Commission is already making plans for myriad celebrations, festivals and educational programs.

ity scene with live animals. Rudolph the Red-Nosed Reindeer and Santa also appear here nightly. All this is free, but they won't mind, of course, if you buy a Christmas tree, fruit basket or other Christmas items while you're here. Take U.S. Highway 50 13.5 miles east of Milford, then left on Bucktown Road, which is the first street after the Ohio Highway 133 intersection. Hours are 9 AM to 9 PM Sunday through Thursday and until 10 PM Friday and Saturday.

Rudd's Christmas Farm
1205 Cassel Run Rd., Blue Creek • (937) 544-3500

No holiday season is complete without a visit to the Rudd family's Christmas farm. From the day after Thanksgiving through New Year's Day the farm is turned into a spectacular Christmas light show featuring hundreds of thousands of lights and displays. Take Ohio 32 east, turn right on Ohio 247, drive into West Union, take a left on Ohio 125 and follow it into Blue Creek. There's no charge, but expect traffic tie-ups on the remote rural road leading to the Rudd farm.

Toys Stores and Bookstores for Kids

The area has many good conventional toy stores, such as Toys 'R Us, locally based Johnny's Toys chain, and Kay-Bee Toy and Hobby shops in many malls. Bigg's Hypermarkets and Meijer also carry a good selection of toys at good prices. What follows is a list of stores whose offerings go well beyond the usual to include particularly good selections of educational or other high-quality toys and books for children.

Barnes & Noble
3802 Paxton Ave., Hyde Park • 871-4300
895 E. Kemper Rd. • 671-3822
7800 Montgomery Rd., Kenwood • 794-9440
7663 Mall Rd., Florence, Ky. • (606) 647-6400

These stores have great collections of children's books and software, plus ample opportunity to try out software or CDs before you buy. Readings of children's books are offered throughout the year. Call for schedules.

Bee Tree
3615 Glenmore Ave., Cheviot • 661-3433

Here you'll find a terrific selection of children's literature, supplemented by intriguing toys, games and puzzles. Don't miss signing up for the newsletter, which updates store patrons on the literally dozens of storytime hours and other kids' activities held here each month.

Borders Books & Music
11711 Princeton Rd., Springdale • 671-5852

Borders is another book megastore with a great selection of kids' books. "Wee Read" every Monday at 10 AM is for ages 2 through 4, and for older kids there's "Kids Storytime" every Saturday at 11 AM.

The Blue Marble
1356 S. Ft. Thomas Ave., Ft. Thomas, Ky. • (606) 781-0602
3054 Madison Rd. • 731-2665

Among the best children's bookstores in Greater Cincinnati, locally based The Blue Marble has frequent signings by children's authors, readings and other special events. Free weekly storytimes are Thursday at 10 AM. Storytelling, crafts and other group activities are also featured. Get on the mailing list for a monthly flyer with book recommendations and listings of upcoming events.

Channel 48 Store of Knowledge
Kenwood Towne Centre, 7875 Montgomery Rd., Kenwood • 891-2500

Channel 48 (public television) owns 25 percent of this brand new store, and you can find just about any PBS-related product for children you could want here — from *Shining Time Station*'s "Thomas the Train" to *The Big Comfy Couch*'s "Molly" storybooks. There's a full line of grown-up stuff, too. From cartoons to obscure Brit comedy videos, you'll find it all. Furthermore, figure that public television gets a quarter for every dollar you spend.

The Children's Bookery Co.
1169 Smiley Ave., Forest Park • 742-8822

Specializing in educational products and games as well as resources for teachers in the classroom, this juvenile bookshop also makes a name for itself with author appearances, book talks and storytelling.

The Disney Store
Tri-County Mall, 11700 Princeton Rd., Springdale • 671-5905
Kenwood Towne Centre, 7875 Montgomery Rd., Kenwood • 984-4775
Northgate Mall, 9501 Colerain Ave., Bevis • 385-7520
Florence Mall, 2028 Florence Mall Rd., Florence, Ky., • (606) 647-7791

No longer must parents travel all the way to Florida or California to blow a wad on Mickey and friends. These stores have got the goods. Be prepared . . . your kids *will* find these stores and they *will* make you take them there.

Imaginarium
Kenwood Towne Centre, 7875 Montgomery Rd., Kenwood • 984-0890

Another good mall toy store alternative to Toys 'R Us, Imaginarium has a collection of educational and harder-to-find toys.

Joseph-Beth Kids
Rookwood Pavilion, 2692 Madison Rd., Norwood • 396-8965

For a bookstore, this is also one great toy store. It wins hands down in the contest for most comfortable and inviting children's book department, even in a city with three book superstore chains and numerous other kids' bookstores competing head to head. A stair-step amphitheater area gives kids and parents a cozy place to sit and read. The store also has regular readings for kids at 10:30 AM on Wednesday and Saturday. JB Kids After Dark on Friday at 7 PM features spooky fiction for kids 8 and older.

Kinder Haus Toys
7835 Cincinnati-Dayton Rd., West Chester • 759-9100

The source for Brio, GeoSafari, Gund and other yupscale toys, they also have a large array of baby gifts.

Photo: United States Air Force Museum

Exciting exhibits fill the U.S. Air Force Museum — the largest aviation museum in the world.

King Arthur's Court
3040 Madison Rd., Oakley Square
• 531-4600

If you want to take it easy on yourself and your kids, do your Christmas shopping at King Arthur's Court, which has the best selection of high-quality toys in Greater Cincinnati. It also carries some of the usual Sega and Nintendo ware and other conventional toy store merchandise. You will pay more for many comparable items than at Toys 'R Us, but you'll also find a nicely arranged selection of educational toys and a downstairs department devoted solely to model trains, model cars and other sorts of model projects. Plus, The Blue Marble bookstore for kids is just up the street, making this a pretty good one-stop shopping area.

Laugh & Learn
8130 Beechmont Ave. • 474-4888

A solid runner-up for best toy store in Greater Cincinnati, Laugh & Learn also has a very good selection of educational and unusual toys. Look for the Anderson Station shopping center with Blockbuster Video.

Little Professor Kids
Forest Fair Mall, 1047 Forest Fair Dr.,
Forest Park • 671-9797

Little Professor features a very extensive selection of children's titles in books and other media.

Media Play
6174 Glenway Ave. • 481-4775
4488 Montgomery Rd., Norwood
• 531-5250
87 Spiral Dr., Florence, Ky.
• (606) 647-6950

One of the newer additions to the kid bookstore wars, Media Play is a gigantic complex with an equally gigantic inventory. It offers weekly storytime programs, crafts, and one of the largest children's video sections around.

Odyssey Learning Center
7791 Cooper Rd., Montgomery
• 793-6100

Here's a store that may be more popular with parents and teachers than with kids because of its great selection of educational toys, plus books and science and math learning aids. Another section is for teachers' instructional materials, but it's also open for parents interested in home schooling. The store also has a wide selection of parent resources addressing learning difficulties and other issues.

Once Upon a Child
2733 Madison Rd. • 871-8700
5138 Glencrossing Way • 451-7600
9898 Colerain Ave. • 385-3034
8550 Beechmont Ave., Anderson
• 474-5105
8087 Connector Dr., Florence, Ky.
• (606) 282-8922

These stores get our vote for best toy bargains in town. They carry slightly used but hardly dented toys, previously worn but immaculate outfits. Why pay retail for Oshkosh and other premium name brands?

Toby's Toy Outlet
2716 Erie Ave. • 871-1255

Toby's offers a wonderful nostalgia trip if you're looking for yo-yos, balsa wood airplanes or other toys from your own childhood. It's also a great place for educational toys and baby music.

Charles and Anna Taft acquired so much art during their well-traveled lives that their home (now the Taft Museum) contained one of the greatest private art collections in the world.

The Arts

Cincinnati has some of the oldest and most respected cultural institutions in the country, of which we boast with a great deal of pride. The Symphony and Pops are world renowned. The theater community is prominent enough to draw Edward Albee to town to direct. Broadway shows regularly stop here. The Ballet, May Festival Chorus and Cincinnati Boychoir are recognized nationally. And dozens of community theaters and art galleries offer local artists a chance to demonstrate their talents.

For newcomers, trying to take it all in can be a bit overwhelming. We have a suggestion, though. The best way to get a taste of Greater Cincinnati's arts offerings is during the Fine Arts Sampler Weekend in mid-February. It is the biggest and perhaps the most fun arts showcase of the year. More than 70 visual and performing arts events are held for free as part of the kickoff for the annual Fine Arts Fund fund-raising campaign that benefits the city's major cultural institutions. The events are held at 35 locations throughout the area, so it's impossible to take them all in, but going through the full listings of the events that run in the daily and arts papers and carefully planning out your weekend is all part of the fun.

The rest of the year you can become familiar with the arts scene through functions such as TGIF (Thank Van Gogh It's Friday), a party held at the Art Museum on the first Friday of every month. On the last Friday of the month, try Final Friday, a tour and social event that takes place in the abundance of art galleries in Over-the-Rhine.

If you have artistic talent, you can further your education through the University of Cincinnati College-Conservatory of Music or the School for the Creative and Performing Arts. CCM offers more than just music, despite its name. And the SCPA, which stages legendary theatrical productions, offers educational and practical experience for school children in grades 4 through 12 who are interested in vocal and choral music, graphic and visual arts, dance and creative writing. Students from SCPA perform regularly with the Ballet and Pops. SCPA was created as an alternative school for the artistically inclined 20 years ago and is called Cincinnati's most important institution by Pops conductor Erich Kunzel. It has grown in both size and stature in those two decades, with student performances making national tours and graduates heading off to Broadway.

The most important name to know in Cincinnati arts is that of the Corbett family. Ralph and Patricia Corbett's establishment of the Corbett Foundation has resulted in contributions of more than $50 million toward maintaining and improving the arts in Greater Cincinnati.

Arts Organizations

Perhaps because of its lengthy history and continual evolution, Cincinnati is one of just five of the top 50 U.S. population markets that doesn't have a central arts agency. Rather, we have several organizations that help pull together all of the arts efforts in town. For the most part, they get along well, and together they keep the area's arts strong.

Arts Consortium
1515 Linn St. • 381-0645

The Arts Consortium is the city's premier African-American arts organization. It has a dual focus of education and presentation, which it accomplishes through not only theater performances, but also photography, art, theater and dance classes. The center, which also has a gallery, recently reinstated its theater programming and expanded its performance space for more stage and seating room.

Cincinnati Arts Association
650 Walnut St. • 241-SHOW

The Cincinnati Arts Association is the central organizing and operating organization for the area's largest venues: Music Hall, Memorial Hall and the Aronoff Center for the Arts. It keeps the abundance of performing arts shows that fill the city's calendar from becoming a tangled mess and competing against each other.

Cincinnati Institute of Fine Arts
2649 Erie Ave. • 871-2787

The Cincinnati Institute of Fine Arts is the organization behind the annual Fine Arts Fund drive. The drive helps keep the quality of Cincinnati's arts at its high level by collecting more than $6 million annually in contributions that go to the Art Museum, Ballet, Opera, Playhouse in the Park, Symphony, Contemporary Arts Center, May Festival and Taft Museum. A Projects Pool also offers grants to smaller organizations in the area. The institute puts on the Fine Arts Sampler Weekend each February (see our Annual Events chapter).

FYI

Unless otherwise noted, the area code for all phone numbers listed in this guide is 513.

Northern Kentucky Arts Council
Robbins and Scott Sts., Covington, Ky. • (606) 491-2030

The premier arts organization in Northern Kentucky, the Council oversees and coordinates arts events on the south side of the river.

Venues

Aronoff Center for the Arts
650 Walnut St. • 621-2787

After years of planning and construction, Cincinnati got a new cultural core in October 1995 when the $82 million Aronoff Center for the Arts opened to rave reviews and packed houses. Since then, performances of some sort have taken place almost nightly in one of the center's three performance halls: the 2,700-seat Procter & Gamble Hall, the 150-seat Fifth Third Bank Theater and the 450-seat Jarson-Kaplan Theater.

The center is now the performance home for the Ballet, the School for the Creative and Performing Arts and the Contemporary Dance Theater. It's the theater for Cincinnati's stagings of Broadway Series productions.

Many arts lovers wondered if the opening of the Aronoff Center would eventually doom Music Hall and the Taft Theater, which previously hosted the Ballet and Broadway Series shows. But the love of performing arts in Cincinnati has proven great enough that none of the venues is suffering. In fact, Cincinnatians now get to see even more high-quality performances.

And if bringing more arts options to the area wasn't enough, the center is also playing a vital role in resurrecting downtown nightlife. The center sits in the heart of downtown, just a block away from Fountain Square, and because of the number of people it draws to its shows nightly, numerous restaurants and entertainment-oriented businesses are cropping up all around the building in an area known as Backstage. Gourmet coffee shops, Graeter's ice cream and other dessert shops, restaurants of all price levels, and microbreweries are flourishing. The businesses offer enough pre- and post-theater entertainment opportunities that it's now possible to stay downtown after work and not be bored in the few hours until the show starts — or after it ends.

Patricia Corbett Theater
University of Cincinnati • 556-4183

The Corbett Theater recently underwent a major renovation and expansion to modernize the facility, which is the frequent site of musical and theatrical performances by the University of Cincinnati's College-Conservatory of Music as well as regional and national acts.

Abigail Cutter Theater
1310 Sycamore St. • 632-5910

The Cutter Theater is located in the School of the Creative and Performing Arts and is the main center for theatrical and musical performances by the school's students.

Emery Theater
1112 Walnut St. • 721-2741

In addition to being one of the area's oldest and most beautiful theaters, the Emery offers an intimate setting and excellent acoustics, making it a wonderful venue for piano recitals and other musical events. The theater is home of many smaller performances by local and regional acts. It's located on the Walnut Street side of the Ohio College of Applied Science building at the corner of Walnut Street and Central Parkway.

Memorial Hall
1225 Elm St. • 241-7469

Memorial Hall is the smaller sister to Music Hall (see below), sitting next door to the historical facility. Memorial Hall offers a more intimate setting, and it is the home of the Cincinnati Chamber Orchestra.

Music Hall
1241 Elm St. • 721-8222

Music Hall is the grand dame of Cincinnati's arts venues. This architectural masterpiece dates back to 1878 and has seen some of the world's greatest musicians and artists grace its stage. Despite the opening of the Aronoff Center, it remains one of the key arts locations, serving as the home of the Cincinnati Symphony Orchestra and Cincinnati Pops Orchestra. It's also arguably better than ever as a musical venue now that it doesn't have to share its stage with the Ballet and other theatrical organizations. A new acoustic backdrop was recently added, improving the sound in the three-tiered hall.

Playhouse in the Park
Eden Park, access from Kemper Ln., Victory Pky. or Gilbert Ave. • 421-3888

While many of the nation's regional theaters struggle to survive, Playhouse in the Park is thriving and is on the verge of national recognition. The 38-year-old theater, which just underwent a massive renovation and expansion, has more than 18,000 subscribers for its performances.

The Playhouse, which likes to refer to its productions as "Great theater in a great theater," is actually two theaters, the 629-seat Marx Theater and the 220-seat Thompson Shelterhouse Theater. Every seat is a good seat in both theaters. Marx Theater holds six major productions that run three or four weeks each. Thompson Shelterhouse has four or five productions that run about two and a half weeks each.

The Playhouse, sometimes referred to as PIP, tries to offer something each season to please the area's wide variety of theatrical tastes, so the productions range from Shakespeare to modern musicals. The selections are usually well-balanced, though, and theatergoers generally find something they like.

It is also home of the annual debut of the nationally renowned Rosenthal Award winners for new playwriters, as well as the immensely popular annual production of *A Christmas Carol*. Plays run nightly except Monday from September through July. Matinees are on Saturday, Sunday and Wednesday.

Murray Seasongood Pavilion
Eden Park, access from Kemper Ln., Victory Pky. or Gilbert Ave. • 352-4080

This outdoor venue is regularly the site of both theatrical and musical performances. The Pops often performs free concerts in the natural amphitheater, located in the beautiful setting of Eden Park. Some bench seating is available near the stage, which sits down the hill from both the Art Museum and Playhouse in the Park.

Showboat Majestic
Public Landing • 241-6550

The *Showboat* is owned by the city, but is leased to the University of Cincinnati's theater department, which produces plays and musicals on the historic riverboat/floating theater Wednesday through Sunday between July and October. Productions feature some of the best semiprofessional and community theater talent in the area. A performance on the *Showboat* also offers an historical look at theater, as the boat is an authentic riverboat performance hall that was pushed up and down the river by a paddlewheeler 70 years ago to stage performances at different cities along the way.

Taft Theater
Fifth and Sycamore Sts. • 721-8883

When the Taft lost its longtime staple, the Broadway Series productions, to the new Aronoff Center for the Arts, everyone thought the 67-year-old Taft would be in trouble. That hasn't turned out to be the case. The 2,476-seat theater has since staged such notable plays as *Les Miserables* and *Arms Too Short to Box With God*, in addition to concerts, comedy shows and other productions. It hasn't lost stride with the larger Aronoff at all.

Music

Cincinnati Boychoir
322 Wyoming Ave., Wyoming • 948-0100

The 120-member choir is one of the world's largest boys choirs. Members not only perform locally but also sing everywhere from California to Austria and in such hallowed venues as Carnegie Hall and the Crystal Cathedral. When they aren't traveling the world, the Boychoir can be seen performing in concerts at Music Hall each May or brightening the holiday season at various venues each December.

Cincinnati Opera
1241 Elm St. • 621-1919

The Cincinnati Opera is the second-oldest opera company in the country. It presented its first performance on June 27, 1920, in a converted band shell at, of all places, the Cincinnati Zoo. The company's fame and fortune grew during World War II when highly talented European performers from New York's Metropolitan Opera and other large companies couldn't get home and were looking for summer work. The Cincinnati Opera was the only summer opera company at the time, so area residents were treated to the best. Fostering new and young talent became a Cincinnati Opera tradition that continues to this day.

The Opera, which performed at the zoo until moving to Music Hall in 1972, stages four performances a year (all with English surcaps)

with leading national and international performers. It fills Music Hall to 99 percent of capacity for the concerts, so tickets are sometimes difficult to obtain. It also offers an introduction performance for children.

The Opera is now under the artistic direction of the highly acclaimed Nicholas Muni, who replaced James de Blasis, the Opera's artistic director for 28 years.

Cincinnati Pops Orchestra
1229 Elm St. • 381-3300

Conductor Erich Kunzel and the Pops perform nine times a year from September to May in the glorious Music Hall and then mix their spirited music with the sounds of the outdoors 10 times each summer at the Riverbend amphitheater. There is nothing quite like listening to the Pops under a starry summer sky.

No matter what the venue, though, the Pops offers highly entertaining concerts. Entertainers such as Doc Severinsen, Roy Clark, Andrew Lloyd Webber, The Chieftains and Ray Charles team up with the Pops to create a fascinating and most enjoyable mixture of classical and modern sounds. The Pops also entertains audiences by combining its outstanding symphonic music with lasers, projections, fireworks, fire and water and hot-air balloons.

So far, 50 concerts with well-known entertainers have been recorded and released on CDs or tapes. The CDs of the Pops performing with the late Henry Mancini are bestsellers. Kunzel, who was *Billboard* magazine's top crossover artist for three straight years, was recently named top classical album-maker by *Billboard*, and also leads the National Orchestra each Fourth of July during its concert in Washington, D.C. He's so popular the Pops has turned the focus of its advertising campaign into "An Evening with Erich."

INSIDERS' TIP

The Cincinnati Symphony Orchestra first performed on January 17, 1895. Conductor Frank A. Van Der Sticken opened with Mozart's *Symphony in G Minor*. The next evening he became the first conductor to stage an all-American concert by devoting the evening strictly to American composers.

Visual art spanning 5,000 years fills the Cincinnati Art Museum.

Cincinnati Symphony Orchestra
1229 Elm St. • 381-3300

Led by conductor Jesus Lopez-Cobos, the CSO dazzles audiences from September to May with 50 concerts at the elegant Music Hall and then six concerts in the relaxed, outdoor amphitheater at Riverbend during the summer. As a special treat during the summer, a scaled-down version of the Symphony sets up in various city and county parks and gives free concerts.

Since its founding in 1894 (making it the fifth-oldest orchestra in the country), the Symphony has awed music lovers all over the world. It was the first U.S. symphony orchestra to be selected to tour Europe, and it has been invited back numerous times. It was also the first guest symphony orchestra ever invited to the Festival Casals, during the 25th anniversary celebration in Puerto Rico. The CSO also regularly sells out American venues outside of Cincinnati, such as Carnegie Hall during its annual visit to New York.

When the Symphony isn't going to the best places, the best people come to Cincinnati to perform. Guest conductors and performers over the years have included Vladimir Horowitz, Beverly Sills, Benny Goodman, Marian Anderson, Sir Thomas Beecham, Enrico Caruso, Pablo Casals, Arthur Rubenstein, Itzhak Perlman, Yo Yo Ma and Ezio Pinza.

Maestro Lopez-Cobos is widely recognized across Europe, where he served as general music director of the Deutsche Oper Berlin, was principal guest conductor for the London Philharmonic and conducted for the Berlin Philharmonic, L'ochrestre de la Suisse and many other celebrated European orchestras. Under his direction, the Symphony has recorded 12 CDs, including a release of music by Falla in 1987 that was named "Record of the Year" by *Stereo Review*.

The CSO is also in the forefront of new ideas, experimenting with video screens dur-

Ruthven's Wildlife Art
Enriches America's Cultural Landscape

Phyllis Weston remembers it like it was yesterday. When John Ruthven left the first exhibit of his paintings, he was melancholy, with his head down, thinking he was finished before he even began.

Ruthven was fresh from winning the prestigious Federal Duck Stamp competition and eager to establish himself as a full-time wildlife artist. He selected his best paintings, priced them and took them to Weston, the longtime art director at the A.B. Closson Jr. Co., an antique store and art gallery in Cincinnati. She immediately tore up his price tags and made up her own, doubling and in some cases tripling Ruthven's original asking price.

" 'Phyllis, you can't do this to me,'" Weston recalls him saying. "'These prices are so high none of them will sell, and I'll look foolish in front of my friends.'"

Weston laughs at the story. So does Ruthven. It's easy to laugh now. Today Ruthven's works are some of the most highly sought-after wildlife paintings in the world, with early originals selling for $20,000 and more. He has three paintings of eagles hanging in the White House and one of a cardinal in the Hermitage Museum in St. Petersburg, Russia. Crown Prince Henri of Luxembourg commissioned him to paint a wild boar; the painting now hangs in the Palace of Luxembourg. He was commissioned by the former governor of Ohio to paint *Eagle to the Moon* to commemorate the accomplishments of Neil Armstrong; this painting now hangs in Armstrong's museum in Wapakoneta, Ohio.

His work is part of the permanent collection at the Cincinnati Art Museum. He has done work for just about every major corporation in Greater Cincinnati, including the Cincinnati Bengals, who once used his painting on the cover of the team's media guide. John Deere & Co., Bellingrath Gardens in Mobile, Alabama, and the city of Colonial Williamsburg have also commissioned him to do paintings.

Today, Ruthven does most of his painting in Georgetown, Ohio, about 40 miles east of Cincinnati, where he and his wife Judy moved 28 years ago. He has two studios in Georgetown, one in his A-frame house on a hill overlooking the Ohio River Valley and another nearby for larger paintings. The studios sit on Ruthven's 163-acre farm, which includes four ponds, three streams and three barns that attract an abundance of the wildlife that is the subject of his work.

It's a quaint setting in a comfortable little town, which has benefited greatly from the Ruthvens' presence. In addition to bringing notoriety to the town, the couple purchased and restored two homes in the center of town, both of which were built in the early 1800s. One is the boyhood home of Ulysses S. Grant, which the Ruthvens renovated and secured as a National Historic Landmark. The house next door was owned by the Thompson family and is now known as the Thompson House Gallery, Ruthven's personal gallery and business office.

The plaster walls of the old Thompson house are now lined with Ruthven's work. They frame just about everything he does these days: rough pencil sketches, detailed drawings, original paintings, prints. The prices are high, but fair, and probably quite a bargain considering how his previous works have increased in value.

Just looking at his work, it's easy to see what makes the paintings so desirable: the incredible detailing that makes each animal lifelike. But it takes a closer look to really see

— continued on next page

Photo: The Artist

No detail is overlooked in Ruthven's wildlife paintings.

what separates his work from that of other wildlife artists and puts it in the same category as Greater Cincinnati's other famous wildlife artist, John J. Audubon. Beyond his artistic skills, Ruthven is a naturalist, a lover of the outdoors who knows the characteristics and habits of wildlife and brings the accuracy of the animal and the environment to the paintings.

"I don't see how a person could be a wildlife painter without being a naturalist," he says. "A lot of artists paint wildlife and are not naturalists, and I can tell right away because of certain nuances, the little way feathers hang from the muscles, things like that."

Accuracy, he says, is paramount. "I was once commissioned to do a painting of a yellow-billed cuckoo," he says. "I had a dead bird that I used as a model and did a nice painting of it sitting up on a branch singing like a robin. I showed it to a professor at UC and he said it was a nice painting but not realistic because the yellow-billed cuckoo was a slinky bird and didn't sit up like that when it sang. I got home and tore the painting up. I was so discouraged that I did not study it and know it.

"Another time I was at a show in Chicago and this little girl comes up to me and asks how many primary feathers are in a duck's wing. I said 10. She said OK and walked away. A few minutes later she came back and said I only had nine feathers on a duck in one of my paintings. I checked and sure enough there were only nine. I took the painting down, took it home and reworked it so the duck had 10 feathers. That's how technical it can be, and it's important for me as a naturalist to leave no stone unturned."

For his paintings, Ruthven studies the skeletal and muscular structures of animals and uses actual specimens borrowed from the massive collection at the Museum of Natural History or other museums. He also has a salvage permit that allows him to collect road kill. When neighbors find dead animals on their property, they call him, and he tells them to record how and where it died, put it in a plastic bag and put it in the freezer until he can get it. If he needs a tiger or larger animal, he calls Ed Maruska, director of the Cincinnati Zoo, and arranges to have the animal placed in a containment cage. He sits a few feet away and makes sketches. If he needs branches or plant life,

— continued on next page

he calls Spring Grove Cemetery, which has 850 species of trees and bushes, and gets a clipping.

He even goes so far as to travel to an animal's natural habitat to learn how it behaves and maneuvers in the wild, even if it involves trudging to the world's remote corners. Once, while he was on an expedition to the Philippines, a new subspecies of thrush was discovered. It is now named Thrush Ruthveni. "You have to capture the moment," he says. "It immediately captivates the viewer and lets you tell as much of the story as you can tell." He takes notes and makes sketches at remote sites, but uses his memory of the scene to make the actual painting, much like Audubon did.

Since he was in grade school, Ruthven was aware of Audubon and was deeply moved by his works. He began attending the Art Academy of Cincinnati on Saturdays in second grade and continued until high school, spending his summers walking from his family's Walnut Hills home about 10 miles south to the Ohio River. Here he would take out his sketch pad and fishing gear and lounge around thinking about Audubon going up and down the river.

Although you can't tell from his current works, Ruthven was initially drawn to cartooning as much as wildlife drawing and even made money at cartooning early in his career. He drew the first cartoon characters for advertisements for Play Doh. When he was drafted into the Navy in 1943, his assignment was to be the art director of the Subchaser Training Center newspaper and draw cartoons to teach seamen about antisubmarine warfare.

When the war was over, Ruthven took his GI Bill and went back to the Art Academy for a year and to the Central Academy of Art in Cincinnati, which is no longer around, to study commercial art.

"I wanted to get into wildlife art professionally but I didn't know how," he says. "In those days they taught you the basics of how to draw and paint but not how to get a job. The ones making the money back then were illustrators, and I thought that's where the best money was, so that became my bread-and-butter work, and I took the opportunities to do wildlife work as they opened to me."

Ruthven makes as many as 20 rough sketches of a picture that will eventually become a painting, all done on see-through tracing paper so he can compare sketches. A rough pencil sketch is done, followed by a detailed, finished drawing and then the painting.

Paintings may take three weeks to complete but require months of research and preparation for Ruthven. Often he works on more than one at a time, alternating between studios in order to avoid losing the fresh perspective and glazing over an ever-important detail or two.

"There is nothing like a fresh eye. It is a wonderful thing," he says. "I never rush. If I am tired or having a tough time, I quit. And I'm not a temperamental artist. I don't care if people talk to me or watch me work. They can even criticize something about my work because I know that even if they don't know what they are talking about, there is something about it that bothers them and their eye is perceiving it in an unnatural way. I may not agree with it, but I don't forget it either. I will go back later and see if what they had to say is true."

Watercolor and acrylic paints are his two favorite mediums, he says, particularly acrylic because it allows for overpainting, which can create some wonderful effects.

Ruthven's defining moment as a wildlife artist came in 1960 when he won the Federal Duck Stamp competition. The most recent winner of the contest collected a $1 million prize along with the blue ribbon. Ruthven didn't do that well financially by winning the contest, but he earned his keep in recognition as a great wildlife artist.

He was immediately contacted by Abercrombie & Fitch who wanted him to be one

— continued on next page

of its staff artists, which meant they would market his works in their 15 stores and arrange shows. In a few years he had a five-year waiting list for his works. Even now he has a hard time fulfilling all the requests. And he still has a show each November at Closson's downtown, just at the beginning of Christmas shopping season, as he has done for the last 30 years.

"I remember that first show we put his paintings in the back gallery, which was a little more woodsy," says Weston. "Burton Closson Sr. came up to me and said, 'Why did you put a new artist in one of the galleries? This is our prime time.' I knew what would happen once he saw the paintings, so I let him keep talking. All the way to the back gallery he kept saying, 'I can't believe you did this.' As soon as he saw John's paintings he went to the front of the store and made everyone who came in go straight to the back gallery and look at the show. That's how good they are."

ing performances to enhance the visual aspects of the concerts. It is also in the forefront of developing new talent. Violinist Alexander Kerr, who is just 26 years old, became the Symphony's concertmaster in 1996 — the youngest concertmaster of a major orchestra in the country — before becoming the concertmaster of the Royal Concertgebouw Orchestra in Amsterdam, one of the world's most prestigious orchestras. Former associate conductor Keith Lockhart recently become conductor of the Boston Pops.

May Festival Chorus
1241 Elm St. • 621-1919

The oldest choral festival in the nation was formed in 1873 and has become world-renowned. More than 200 average Joes and Josephines with good voices rehearse year round for two weekend performances in May at Music Hall and the Cathedral Basilica of the Assumption. The Chorus also travels and performs in venues such as Carnegie Hall and often hosts world-class guest artists and conductors.

Director James Conlon is also the principal conductor of the Paris Opera and has conducted national telecasts for the Metropolitan Opera and the National Symphony's Fourth of July concert. Conlon, who speaks four languages and "gets along" in several others, recently won France's Bellan Film Prize for his musical direction of the film version of *Madame Butterfly*.

If you miss the May performances, the Chorus offers Carolfest, singing traditional holiday carols and Christmas favorites each December. The annual family holiday concert is presented as a gift to the city from the Chorus.

Auditions are held on a regular basis throughout the year if you have good pipes.

Northern Kentucky University Choirs
NKU, Louis B. Nunn Dr., Highland Heights, Ky. • (606) 572-6399

Under the guidance of Dr. Randy Pennington, Northern Kentucky University has established three choirs, each of which is gaining a reputation as one of the area's most up-and-coming groups in its category. The NKU Chamber Choir, for instance, received an invitation to perform at the prestigious gala for arts patron Patricia Corbett in 1997, as well at the Kentucky Education Association convention. The Chamber Choir is the university's elite choral ensemble and is auditioned at the beginning of each fall semester, along with the nine-member Vocal Jazz Ensemble. The Northern Chorale is the third of NKU's choirs. The groups are made up of NKU students, although not all of them are music majors. Some are just students who like to sing.

University of Cincinnati College-Conservatory of Music
Patricia Corbett Theater, University of Cincinnati • 556-4183

Dating back to 1867, CCM is one of the three oldest schools of music in the United States. It enjoys a strong reputation among the top tier of American conservatories, particularly for its innovative operas and its top-ranked Philharmonic Orchestra. Some of its graduates include Al Hirt, Tennessee Ernie Ford, James Levine, Eddie Albert and Lee Roy Reams. Many concerts are free.

Smaller orchestras

With one of the best music schools in the country at our doorstep and limited opportunities to perform with the Symphony or the Pops, area musicians have formed numerous small- to mid-sized orchestras. Despite not having the budget of the major orchestras, they offer excellent music at a fraction of the admission price in addition to a more casual approach. Their concerts are well-attended, some with several thousand people.

Among the smaller orchestras are the **Northern Kentucky Symphony**, (606) 431-6216, which performs at Northern Kentucky University; the **Blue Ash Symphony**, 248-1584, which performs at various venues in Blue Ash; the **Hamilton-Fairfield Symphony**, 241-0900, which performs at Miami University's Middletown branch; and the **Middletown Symphony**, (513) 424-2426, which also performs at MU-Middletown. The Middletown Symphony is conducted by Carmon DeLeone, who is also the longtime conductor of the Cincinnati Ballet's orchestra.

Dance

Cincinnati Ballet
1555 Central Pky. • 621-5219

One of the nation's top 10 professional companies, the Cincinnati Ballet is known nationally for its diverse repertoire of contemporary and classic dance works. Thirty-five dancers and a full orchestra perform five subscription-series ballets between September and May and 10 highly popular *Nutcracker* performances each Christmas.

The Ballet mixes its performances with such ballet classics as *Swan Lake* and *Romeo and Juliet* and modern dance numbers such as *L*, the tribute to Liza Minelli. The orchestra is led by longtime musical director Carmon DeLeone,

who not only conducts but composes scores for some of the ballet's original works.

In 1997, Victoria Morgan became artistic director of the company, the first female to hold this position. The Ballet has had only seven artistic directors since its founding in 1958, but four of those have come and gone since 1990. The hiring of Morgan is expected to create stability within the company without sacrificing the quality of performances. She was formerly a dancer for Ballet West in Salt Lake City and the San Francisco Ballet and most recently served as resident choreographer and ballet mistress for the San Francisco Opera, the second-largest opera company in the country.

Contemporary Dance Theater
2728 Vine St. • 751-2800

The Contemporary Dance Theater offers a dozen modern dance concerts a year, including numerous touring dance events. Now in its 26th season, the CDT brings in such nationally known companies as the Liz Lerman Dance Exchange and Urban Bush Women. Performances take place at the Jarson-Kaplan Theater in the Aronoff Center for the Arts and at the Dance Hall in Corryville.

Theater

Broadway Series
Aronoff Center for the Arts, 650 Walnut St. • 621-2787

Cincinnati is a regular stop on the travelling productions of popular Broadway shows. Shows that have been performed at the Aronoff Center since its opening in late 1995 include *Miss Saigon, Cats, Grease, Damn Yankees, Stomp, Rent, Phantom of the Opera* and *Hello, Dolly* to name a few. The Broadway Series productions are so popular that tickets are sold in packages, and nearly 15,000 people have become season subscribers.

Cincinnati Shakespeare Festival
639 Rockdale Ave., Avondale • 559-0642

Established in 1995, the Cincinnati Shakespeare Festival offers area residents a taste of Shakespeare five times a year. The CSF performs at the site of the old The Movies Theater downtown and has been well-received in the few years it has been staging the events, with more than 900 annual ticket subscribers now packing the theater. Although the performances are classical Shakespeare, they are sometimes done with a bold twist. The recent performance of *Hamlet*, for instance, the title role was played by a woman. Season tickets are $51. Individual ticket prices vary.

Ensemble Theater of Cincinnati
1127 Vine St. • 421-3555

Cincinnati's professional resident theater performs five or six new works and modern classics with new twists Wednesday through Sunday nights between September and July. The theater, which was founded in 1986, brings in 1,000 subscribers and sells more than 15,000 tickets each season for performances of plays such as Edward Albee's *Three Tall Women* and one-act plays by Woody Allen, Elaine May and David Mamet.

Community Theaters

Dozens of community theaters operate year-round throughout Greater Cincinnati, including 20 that form the Association of Community Theaters. ACT began in 1955 and has been the center for the area's community theaters. All the community theaters use local, unpaid talent and perform an average of four times a year. Despite the lack of high-priced talent, most of the performances are of high quality. Many groups perform in local school or college auditoriums, although the larger groups, including **Footlighters**, **The Mariemont Players**, **Stagecrafters**, and **The Wyoming Players**, have their own theaters. Shows average between $5 and $15 for admission.

College Theaters

University of Cincinnati College-Conservatory of Music
Patricia Corbett Theater, University of Cincinnati • 556-4183

Although CCM is better known for its musical productions, it also offers an array of cultural alternatives, including theater, opera and dance performances. Its Hot Summer Nights repertory theater programs are very popular.

Miami University Theater
Shriver Center, Miami University, Oxford • (513) 529-6031

Students from the school perform a wide variety of musical and theatrical shows during the school year as well as during the summer.

Northern Kentucky University Theater
NKU, Highland Heights, Ky. • (606) 572-5464

The NKU Theater stages numerous theatrical shows during the academic year at the NKU Corbett Theater on the school's campus.

Xavier University Theater
3800 Victory Pky. • 745-3939

Xavier's student theater offers a wide variety of performances in the Xavier University Center Theater on the Xavier campus.

Art Museums

Cincinnati Art Museum
Eden Park • 721-5204

The recently restored Cincinnati Art Museum is one of the best in the country, with more than 118 galleries filled with paintings, prints, sculptures, drawings, photos, costumes, musical instruments and other forms of visual arts spanning 5,000 years. It is also one of the nation's oldest art museums, with the building dating back to 1866 and the museum itself to 1876.

Ironically, what helps make the museum so big is the world's largest collection of miniature art. Other displays include several works by Picasso, Warhol's *Pete Rose*, a 300 B.C. Egyptian mummy, a large collection of native Frank Duveneck's paintings, dozens of pieces of Rookwood pottery, Persian architecture dating to 480 B.C., marble carvings dating to 2500-2400 B.C., an unparalleled collection of Nabataean art and Jin Dynasty wood carvings.

Once a month from October through May the museum holds a Thank Van Gogh It's Friday party, giving art lovers a chance to get a cultural start on the weekend.

Museum hours are 10 AM to 5 PM Tuesday through Saturday and noon to 6 PM Sunday (closed Monday). Admission is $5 for guests, $4 for seniors 60 and older and students. The museum is open free to seniors on Wednesday, free to everyone on Saturday, and free to members and children 17 and younger anytime. Membership, which includes plenty of perks and discounts, starts at $30.

Contemporary Arts Center
115 E. Fifth St. • 721-0390

The CAC will probably never be separated from its showing of the Robert Mapplethorpe exhibit, in which Cincinnati embarrassed itself in front of the world by charging the center and its curator with pandering obscenity. Still, the CAC offers the best in local and international modern visual art, as well as concerts, videos, film, lectures and publications. Displays change regularly. Past exhibitions have included works by Yoko Ono and the founder of the American pop art movement Roy Lichtenstein.

The CAC is building a new facility across from the Aronoff Center for the Arts, but currently maintains a low profile on the second floor of the Mercantile Center on Fifth Street. Look for the contemporary "robot" — with digital message boards for arms, pay phones for legs — sitting out front. Hours are 10 AM to 6 PM Monday through Saturday, noon to 5 PM on Sunday. Admission is $3.50 for adults, $2 for students and seniors 65 and older and free for children 12 and younger. Admission is free for everyone on Monday.

Miami University Art Museum
Sycamore and Talawanda Sts., Oxford
• (513) 529-2232

Rouault's "Miserere" folio is the highlight of the university's museum, which also displays an extensive camera collection, sculptures, paintings, 1840s textile and wallpaper designs and 20th-century American art. The museum, which is located in Millet Hall, also houses an international collection of folk, pre-Colombian and African art. Admis-

sion is free and hours are 11 AM to 5 PM Tuesday through Sunday.

Taft Museum
316 Pike St. • 241-0343

Rather than tie up their money in real estate or bonds, Charles and Anna Taft invested in art. They collected so much of it during their well-traveled lives, in fact, that their longtime residence became home to one of the greatest private art collections in the world. An ivory carving of the Virgin and Child, dated from the 13th century and once lost from the Abbey Church of Saint-Denis, became part of their collection. Chinese porcelains from the Qing and Ming dynasties, French enamels and paintings by Rembrandt, Duncanson, Van Dyke, Whistler and Grandma Moses filled their home.

In 1932, the Tafts, who intended their collection to become public, gave it all to the city — a giant gift — including the house. The massive, 175-year-old home, where Charles' half-brother, William Howard Taft, accepted the Republican nomination for president, now has 30 exhibit rooms for the Tafts' art collection. Hours are 10 AM to 5 PM Monday through Saturday and 1 to 5 PM Sunday. Admission is $4 for adults and $2 for seniors 65 and older and students. Children 17 and younger and museum members get in free. Admission is free for everyone on Wednesdays.

FYI

Unless otherwise noted, the area code for all phone numbers listed in this guide is 513.

Galleries

Greater Cincinnati has dozens of galleries featuring local, regional and national artists. Although the west end of Fourth Street was once the gallery area, artists now flock to the historical-but-somewhat-rundown Main Street area in Over-the-Rhine.

Not all local art is hanging in a gallery or museum, though. Downtown is filled with more than two dozen sculptures, statues and fountains, all displayed in the name of public art. Many sit in front of office buildings or in the downtown parks. A self-guided Public Art Walk tour brochure of the works is available at the downtown library.

Yelena Pankova and Kirill Melnikov perform a pas de deux during a performance of *Le Corsaire* by the Cincinnati Ballet.

Hollywood on the Ohio

Aaaaaand action!

The cry of movie directors everywhere is becoming familiar in Cincinnati, where cameras roll on such a regular basis that the area sports the nickname "Hollywood on the Ohio." Tear-jerkers, shoot-'em-ups, comedies — movies of all sorts find their way to the screen sporting Greater Cincinnati scenery.

Since 1987, 12 feature films and two made-for-TV movies have been shot in the area, where the diversity and well-kept condition of the architecture (that's another way of

Close-up

saying our streets still look like the 1930s) keep directors walking around with their thumbs together framing shots. When the directors of *Eight Men Out* went looking for buildings reminiscent of Chicago in 1919, they set up shop on Fourth Street downtown. When the directors of *A Rage in Harlem* wanted to reproduce the look of New York City neighborhoods during the 1930s, they headed to Over-the-Rhine. When *Tango and Cash* needed a jail to break out of, actors scaled the walls of the old Hamilton County Workhouse.

The area's architecture is combined with a little lobbying by the Greater Cincinnati Film Commission, a nonprofit agency that lures filmmakers to the area. And when they are here, you know it. Local papers run star sightings and daily shooting location updates. TV and radio stations jockey to get the stars on the air. It's a big deal here.

Financially, it's a big deal too. Filming has grown the area's economy by $38 million since 1987. That's how much film crews have spent on props, extras, hotels, transportation and related items.

In some of the movies, Cincinnati's presence is obvious. In others, the contribution is more subtle and you have to know what to look for. For your viewing pleasure and to help you spot Cincinnati, we've compiled a list of movies and their Cincinnati locations.

Eight Men Out, a 1987 film about baseball's Black Sox scandal, stars Charlie Sheen and was directed by John Sayles. Cincinnati was, in part, where the real tragedy took place, when the Reds played the Chicago White Sox in the 1919 World Series. Some recognizable locations from the movie include the former Cincinnati Club building on Garfield Place, which is supposed to be a Chicago hotel; store fronts on Fourth Street; and the row houses on Elizabeth Street in Queensgate, where the famous line, "Say it ain't so, Joe," is uttered.

Rain Man, the Academy Award-winning film starring Dustin Hoffman and Tom Cruise, was filmed here in 1988. Cincinnati is mentioned 17 times in the movie. The most recognized locations include Pompilio's Restaurant in Newport, Kentucky, where Hoffman's character instantly counts the box of spilled toothpicks, and St. Anne's Convent in Melbourne, Kentucky, which is the institution where Hoffman's character lives. Other less prominent sites include the Dixie Terminal downtown, which became a bank in the movie; the Suspension Bridge, which Hoffman's character hums his way across; and Terminal C at the airport (now destroyed as part of an airport expansion), where Hoffman announces his fear of flying.

— continued on next page

Fresh Horses, a 1988 romantic drama, stars Molly Ringwald and Andrew McCarthy. The Serpentine Wall downtown was the location for the opening scene. UC's Nippert Stadium is the backdrop for a tailgate party, while Kings Island (as it used to be) was dressed for the winter in the closing setting.

Tango and Cash is a 1989 action-comedy starring Sylvester Stallone and Kurt Russell. The Workhouse, a castle-like prison that is now demolished, is the setting.

An Innocent Man, filmed in 1989, stars Tom Selleck. Selleck's character is wrongfully imprisoned at The Workhouse. The Powell Valve Co., on Spring Grove Avenue in the West End, is a prison machine shop.

Dedicated to the One I Love was a 1991 CBS After-School Special.

Little Man Tate, a 1991 comedy-drama, stars Jodie Foster and Harry Connick Jr. The Hebrew Union College in Clifton is transformed into the Grierson Institute, the Tau Kappa Epsilon fraternity at Miami University in Oxford doubles as a family home, the Roanoke apartment building on Ludlow Avenue in Clifton serves as a home, and the Washington Park Demonstration School in Over-the-Rhine is Eisenhower Elementary.

A Rage in Harlem was mostly filmed in Over-the-Rhine, where the historic buildings resemble old Harlem. Local 1207 became Braddock's Bar for the action-comedy, filmed in 1991 with Gregory Hines, Forest Whitaker, Robin Givens and Danny Glover.

Lost in Yonkers, a Neil Simon comedy-drama filmed in 1992, stars Richard Dreyfuss and Mercedes Ruehl. Ludlow, Kentucky, becomes Yonkers, New York, for the film. The movie palace where the two characters meet is the 77-year-old Murphy Theatre in Wilmington, Ohio. Brookville Lake in southeastern Indiana portrays the Hudson River for a night swimming scene.

A Mom for Christmas, a made-for-TV holiday fantasy film starring Olivia Newton-John, was shot here in 1991. The Lazarus department store on Race Street downtown became Milliman's Department Store.

City of Hope, a 1991 mystery-drama, was directed by John Sayles. Arnold's Bar and Grill on Eighth Street downtown was DeLillo's Bar, where the mayor tried to compromise a councilman. The construction site of what is now the Chemed Center on Fifth and Sycamore downtown was the location for the opening and closing scenes.

The Public Eye, in which Joe Pesci debuted as a leading actor, was filmed in 1992. The mystery-drama, starring Barbara Hershey, was filmed mainly on Main Street north of Central Parkway, which became Little Italy in the 1940s. The Hamilton County Courthouse also was a hospital in the movie.

Milk Money, a 1993 film starring Melanie Griffith and Ed Harris, includes scenes of the soccer fields, gym and a couple of classrooms at Kilgour School in Mount Lookout.

Airborne is a 1993 teen Rollerblade skating film that prominently features Riverfront Stadium and Mehring Way. Pompilio's, which became famous in *Rain Man*, was transformed into a teen hangout for this film. The fictional Central High is really Western Hills High School. The Krohn Conservatory in Eden Park is where stars Shane McDermott and Brittany Powell have their first date.

Cut! That's a wrap, everybody.

A&J Art Gallery
8113 Connector Dr., Florence, Ky.
• **(606) 371-2578**

A&J is an authorized Bradford Exchange Dealer and features originals, limited-edition prints and more. It is open 9 AM to 5 PM Monday through Friday.

Gary Akers Gallery
10100 Meiman Dr., Union, Ky.
• **(606) 384-3464**

The original works of Gary Akers are shown here 10 AM to 5 PM Tuesday through Saturday and by appointment. Akers' work is best described as Rural Realism, with paintings of scenes typical of the rural Kentucky location of his studio.

Anasazi Gallery
10725 Old Pond Dr., Montgomery • 489-9708

Contemporary Southwestern and Native American art fills this gallery. Hours are by appointment.

ArtisTree Studios
6818 Ohio 128, Miamitown • 353-2100

Exhibits include artwork in a variety of media by a cooperative of Tri-state artists. Handmade gifts and seasonal decorations, in addition to oil and watercolor paintings, are displayed. Hours are 11 AM to 5 PM Monday through Sunday.

Arts Consortium
1515 Linn St. • 821-9027

The Arts Consortium has a dual focus of education and presentation. The center, which recently renovated and expanded its facility, offers photography and art exhibits at its gallery. Recent exhibits have included works by Annie Ruth and Michael Thompson in conjunction with the Consortium's 25th anniversary. Hours are 1 to 8 PM Tuesday through Thursday and 1 to 5 PM Friday and Saturday.

Attic Gallery
8th and York Sts., Newport, Ky. • (606) 491-2787

The Attic Gallery is in the highly popular York Street Cafe, so you can sip exotic coffees while you tour the art. The gallery rotates exhibits in a variety of media and is open 8 PM to midnight Monday through Saturday and 1 to 5 PM Sunday.

BASE Art Gallery
1311 Main St. • 721-2273

Two display areas offer works in different media in each exhibit space. The gallery is open 1 to 9 PM Thursday through Saturday, noon to 4 PM Sunday and by appointment.

Mary Baskett Gallery
1002 St. Gregory St. • 421-0460

This gallery features contemporary Japanese ceramics and other modern art. One recent exhibit featured engravings by Cincinnati's Henry Farny. Hours are by appointment only.

Bear Graphics and Illustration Gallery
105 E. Main St., Mason • 398-2788

Original illustrations by C.F. Payne, Jerry Dowling, John Maggard and 50 other local illustrators are displayed here. Hours are noon to 4 PM Tuesday through Saturday or by appointment.

Toni Birckhead Gallery
1985 Madison Rd. • 533-1123

This gallery features the newest art from around the region and regularly rotates its exhibits, which vary in styles and artists, although most are contemporary. Hours are 10 AM to 4 PM Monday through Friday and Saturday by appointment.

Bluerock Gallery
1707 Blue Rock St. • 541-8110

Bluerock displays works by a number of local artists. Hours are noon to 6 PM Wednesday through Saturday and by appointment.

Carey Galleries
1135 St. Rt. 125, Anderson • 753-7617

Carey Galleries is the exclusive dealer of P. Buckley Moss art. It also offers limited-edition prints and a wide variety of Cincinnati scenes. Hours are 10 AM to 6 PM Monday through Wednesday and Friday, 10 AM to 8 PM Thursday and 10 AM to 5 PM Saturday.

Carnegie Visual and Performing Arts Center
1028 Scott Blvd., Covington, Ky. • (606) 491-2030

The Carnegie Arts Center offers four galleries that change exhibits on a regular basis. It is one of the largest galleries in the

INSIDERS' TIP

For the latest in what's happening now in the arts, call the Dial-the-Arts hotline, 751-ARTS.

area and one of Northern Kentucky's premier art centers. The building, which includes a 750-seat theater, is itself a work of art, built in 1902 with funds from Andrew Carnegie and now on the National Register of Historic Places.

Chelsea Gallery
1420 Sycamore St. • 784-9311

For a truly artistic experience, the Chelsea combines a coffee shop with a rotating display of prints and paintings by local artists. You can sip while you browse. Hours are 8 AM to 6 PM Monday through Thursday, 8 AM to 9 PM Friday and by appointment.

Chidlaw Gallery
Art Academy • 562-8777

Students of the Art Academy of Cincinnati exhibit their work here. Once a year the gallery has exhibits that feature a well-known Cincinnati artist who studied or taught at the Art Academy. Hours are 9 AM to 9 PM Monday through Thursday, 9 AM to 5 PM Friday and noon to 5 PM weekends.

Cincinnati Art Galleries
635 Main St.• 381-2128

The gallery, which sits adjacent to the Aronoff Center, offers the country's largest Rookwood pottery auctions and displays Rookwood along with 19th- and 20th-century sculptures and paintings. Hours are by appointment.

Cincinnati Artists Group Effort
1416 Main St. • 381-2437

CAGE is a nonprofit, artist-run organization. Its gallery presents the best displays from local artists and is considered one of the premiere alternative spaces in the country. The gallery is open noon to 8 PM Friday, noon to 6 PM Saturday and noon to 4 PM Sunday.

Clermont College Gallery
4200 Clermont College Dr., Batavia
• 732-5223

The works of artists from Clermont County and the surrounding region are displayed here in rotating exhibits throughout the year. Hours are 8 AM to 6 PM Monday through Friday.

Closson's
401 Race St. • 762-5510
7866 Montgomery Rd., Kenwood
• 891-5531

These galleries are among the area's most esteemed. The downtown gallery has been in business for 131 years, making it one of the oldest continuously operating art galleries in the country. The two galleries feature regional and local works, 19th- and 20th-century American paintings, Far Eastern and West African art and prints by local artists John Ruthven and John Stobart. Most of the works are upscale and expensive. Hours are 10 AM to 6 PM Monday through Saturday.

FYI

Unless otherwise noted, the area code for all phone numbers listed in this guide is 513.

Sharon Cook Gallery
1118 Pendleton St. • 579-8111

The works in this gallery range from serene transitional to wild abstract. The gallery represents Phoenix Art Press and Winn-Devon. Hours are 9 AM to 5 PM Monday through Saturday.

DAAP Gallery
University of Cincinnati • 556-2839

Works from the UC School of Art are featured in this gallery on the eighth floor of the Design, Architecture, Art and Planning Building. Hours are by appointment.

FreeMan Gallery
406 Central Ave. • 579-0005

The FreeMan Gallery in the Old Town His-

INSIDERS' TIP

Looking for a cheap but sophisticated date? Tickets are marked down to half-price at noon the day of the performance for Playhouse in the Park and the Symphony. Or, try the Ballet's half-price matinees on Saturday afternoons.

toric District specializes in African-American art. It offers rotating exhibits of local, national and international artists. Tom Feeling's original illustrations for Maya Angelou's *Now Sheba Sings the Song* have appeared here. Hours are 4 to 7 PM Friday, 1 to 6 PM Saturday and by appointment.

Gallery at Wellage & Buxton Inc.
1431 Main St. • 241-9127

This gallery features a rotating display of artists of different styles. Recent exhibits have included works by Aaron Butler. Hours are 10 AM to 5 PM Tuesday through Friday and 10 AM to 3 PM Saturday.

Glendale Gallery
27 Village Square, Glendale • 771-1660

Situated in the town's tony village square, Glendale Gallery offers rotating exhibits. A show of landscapes and mystical paintings by Ned Stern is an example of recent exhibits. Hours are 10 AM to 5 PM Tuesday through Saturday and by appointment.

Golden Ram Gallery
6810 Miami Ave., Madeira • 271-8000

This is another gallery that rotates the works of various artists throughout the year. Its hours are 10 AM to 6 PM Monday, Tuesday, Thursday and Friday; 10 AM to 8 PM Wednesday; and 10 AM to 5 PM Saturday.

Marta Hewett Gallery
1209 Main St. • 421-7883

Exceptional works by contemporary artists and preeminent studio craftsmen working in glass, ceramic, metal and wood are displayed here noon to 5 PM Tuesday through Saturday and until 8 PM Friday

Hiestand Gallery
Miami University, Fine Arts Bldg.
• (513) 529-1883

The Hiestand is the Miami University stu-dent gallery, although outside works are generally brought in during the first semester. Hours are 8 AM to 5 PM Monday through Friday.

Machine Shop Gallery
Emery Bldg., Walnut St. at Central Pkwy.
• 556-2839

University of Cincinnati's Design, Architecture, Art and Planning school students exhibit their work in a rugged industrial space. It has the ambiance of New York's SoHo district. The gallery is open from 11 AM to 2 PM Tuesday through Saturday.

Malton Gallery
2709 Observatory Ave. • 321-8614

Abstract and realist images by local and nationally known artists are the heart of Malton's collection. More than 100 painters, printmakers and sculptors are represented, some emerging, others well-established. Hours are 10 AM to 5 PM Monday through Saturday.

Maritain Gallery
127 W. Loveland Ave., Loveland
• 683-1152

Exhibits by various local artists rotate through this gallery, which is open from 1 to 5 PM Sunday through Friday.

Masterpiece Gallery
2944 Markbreit Ave. • 531-8280

Various artists exhibit their work on a rotating basis here. Recent exhibits have included art by M.P. Wiggins. The gallery is open 10 AM to 8 PM Tuesday through Friday and 10 AM to 5 PM Saturday.

Miller Gallery
2715 Erie Ave. • 871-4420

The Miller has one of the largest collections of 20th-century American and European art works in the city. You can view a variety of styles, from art glass to paper compositions. Recent exhibits have included works by John

---

INSIDERS' TIP

Billboard **magazine was born in Cincinnati 100 years ago at a Vine Street saloon. William Donaldson and James Hennegan, whose family still operates a local printing company, began the publication that is now the music industry's charting guide.**

Photo: Cincinnati Symphony Orchestra

The Cincinnati Symphony Orchestra dazzles audiences year round with concerts at Music Hall and Riverbend.

Michael Carter. Hours are 10 AM to 5:30 PM Monday through Saturday.

Northern Kentucky University Gallery
NKU, Fine Arts Bldg., Highland Heights, Ky. • (606) 572-5148

Two galleries of works by NKU students, faculty, local and regional artists are open from 9 AM to 6 PM Monday through Friday or by appointment.

only artists
1315 Main St. • 241-6672

The appropriately named only artists gallery features contemporary folk art, including paintings, carvings and objects by more than 30 nationally recognized folk and local artists, many of whom never went to art school. The gallery is open noon to 5 PM on Wednesday, Thursday and Saturday, noon to 8 PM on Friday.

Laura Paul Gallery
49 E. Fourth St. • 651-5885

You can find numerous one-of-a-kind works (mostly contemporary) at this downtown gallery, which is in the arcade of the historical Dixie Terminal. Recent exhibits have included works by Enrico Embroli, Roger Muhl, David Kessler and Oliver Delhoume. It's open from 10 AM to 4 PM Tuesday through Friday, 10 AM to 3 PM Saturday or by appointment.

Pendleton ArtCenter
1310 Pendleton St. • 241-4020

More than 70 artists working in a variety of mediums house their studios in this beautifully renovated building. Studios are open for Final Fridays from 6 to 10 PM or by appointment. You can catch a free shuttle from downtown parking lots.

Ran Gallery
3668 Erie Ave. • 871-5604

Progressive exhibits by varying artists are featured here. You can view the displays from 10 AM to 5 PM Monday through Thursday and 11 AM to 4 PM Saturday.

Raymond Gallery
3508 Edwards Rd. • 871-9393

This gallery features original cartoons by Cincinnati's Pulitzer Prize-winning editorial cartoonist Jim Borgman, as well as original drawings from his comic strip, *Zits*. The gallery is open from 10 AM to 5 PM Tuesday and Thursday through Saturday, 10 AM to 8 PM Monday and Wednesday.

Row House Gallery
211 Main St., Milford • 831-7230

The excellence of John Ruthven, Mill Pond Press, Wyscoki and Greenwich Workshop art is the focus here. The gallery occupies two old row houses. Hours are 10 AM to 5 PM Monday through Friday and 10 AM to 4 PM Saturday.

Schaff Gallery
17 E. 8th St. • 421-2787

The Schaff Gallery features traditional and contemporary paintings and ceramics and offers art classes. Recent exhibits have included works by New England artists E.W. and E.M. Leary, Frank Strazzulla and Ron Johnson. Hours are Tuesday through Saturday 10 AM to 5 PM or by appointment.

Carl Solway Gallery
424 Findlay St. • 621-0069, 632-5822

Sculpture and works by local artists form the core of this avant-garde collection. The gallery, open for more than 30 years, is well-known outside of the area and draws considerable interest. It is a member of the Art Dealers Association of America. Hours are 9 AM to 5 PM Monday through Friday and Saturday by appointment.

Square Gallery
401 Main St., Hamilton • 868-7926

You can purchase limited-edition prints by Ruthven, Doolittle, Frederick and others at this gallery, which is open from 9 AM to 5 PM Monday through Friday.

Studio San Giuseppe
College of Mount St. Joseph, Ziv Art Bldg., 5701 Delhi Rd., Delhi • 244-4314

Works by Mount St. Joseph students are featured here along with outside work that the college brings in to parallel its curriculum. Hours are 10 AM to 5 PM Monday through Friday and 1:30 to 4:30 PM weekends.

Tangeman Fine Art Gallery
Tangeman Center, University of Cincinnati • 556-2839

The Tangeman is located in the UC student union building and is well-attended by students and nonstudents alike. It features work from all of the university's fields as well as from the community. Hours are 10 AM to 5 PM Monday through Friday.

Thomas More College Art Gallery
Thomas More College, 333 Thomas More Pky., Crestview Hills, Ky.
• (606) 341-5800

This is the gallery for the college's students. It's open 8 AM to 9 PM Monday through Friday, noon to 4 PM Saturday and 4 to 8 PM Sunday.

Toon Art Gallery
441 Vine St. • 651-3500

Cartoon cells, a different kind of art, are on display in the Carew Tower downtown. The gallery is open 10 AM to 6 PM Tuesday through Saturday and Monday by appointment.

Patricia Weiner Gallery
9393 Montgomery Rd., Montgomery
• 791-7717

This gallery focuses on 19th- and 20th-century American and European paintings as well as contemporary art. You may view the exhibits from 11 AM to 5 PM Tuesday through Saturday or by appointment.

WCET Gallery
1223 Central Pky. • 381-4033

WCET-TV (channel 48) has been donating its lobby walls to local artists for 20 years in exchange for one piece of art that it sells as part of its annual Action Auction fund-raiser. Hours are 9 AM to 5 PM Monday through Friday.

INSIDERS' TIP

Every year the area gets Parrothead fever when Jimmy Buffett comes to town. It was in Cincinnati that Buffett first began calling his fans parrotheads, recorded a live CD and sold out five consecutive shows during one stay.

Wentworth Gallery
7875 Montgomery Rd., Kenwood Towne Centre, Kenwood • 791-5023

The Wentworth has the distinction of being in the most popular mall in Cincinnati and as a result gets a lot of visitors. Varying artists' works are exhibited on a rotating schedule. The gallery is open 10 AM to 9 PM Monday through Saturday and noon to 6 PM Sunday.

Weston Gallery
7th and Walnut Sts. • 977-4165

One of the newest galleries in the city, the Weston sits inside the Aronoff Center for the Arts and exhibits a variety of art styles by local, regional and national artists. Hours are 10 AM to 6 PM Tuesday through Saturday (except on performance evenings, when it is open until 8 PM) and 1 to 6 PM on Sunday (except on performance evenings, when it is open until 7 PM).

Wolf Gallery
708 Walnut St. • 381-3222
41 W. Fifth St. • 241-2004

The central attraction at these two downtown galleries is the architectural photography of Cincinnati by J. Miles Wolf, although other exhibits are displayed on a rotating basis. You can view his work from 9 AM to 5 PM Monday through Friday.

Woodbourne Gallery
9885 Montgomery Rd., Montgomery • 793-1888

Works by a variety of local and regional artists are shown here on a rotational basis. Recent exhibits have featured works by local artist Robert Hasselle and the Cincinnati Craft Guild. Hours are 10 AM to 8 PM Monday through Thursday, 10 AM to 6 PM Saturday and noon to 5 PM Sunday.

Xavier Art Gallery
3800 Victory Pky., Xavier University • 745-3811

The works of Xavier University students are on display here in addition to local and regional exhibits. The gallery, which is located in the Cohen Center, is open from noon to 4 PM Monday through Friday.

The annual Cincinnati Flower Show is the largest, most prestigious open-air flower and garden festival in the country.

Annual Events

Greater Cincinnati is rich in tradition and heritage, precipitating a calendar full of annual activities that run the gamut from festivals for kids and pets to major sporting events. The Christmas holiday celebrations are enough to wear out even the most jovial of Yule Tiders.

With that said, allow us, please, to make this bit of a disclaimer: There are far too many annual events to list here in any sort of practical way. Nearly every small community in Greater Cincinnati has its own "Taste Of" or "Day Of" celebration, so we tried to stick with the major events. For a listing of the smaller annual and onetime events, check *Cincinnati Magazine*'s monthly "Calendar" section or the *Post*'s or *Enquirer*'s weekend sections. Or call one of the following activity hotlines:

Greater Cincinnati Convention and Visitors Bureau Activity Line, 528-9400, offers area-by-area events information.

Downtown Council Hotline of Events, 579-3199, has information on downtown goings-on.

Citylink, 333-6888, offers detailed accounts of downtown activities, including special weekly events, future events, sporting events, "I Do Downtown" specials, arts and entertainment activities, and things for kids and family; it even has information on dining, shopping, and parking and transportation.

During Christmas, a special **Ho-Ho Hotline** (333-6888) is set up to keep track of everything that's happening during the holiday season.

A note: Be sure to read about Tall Stacks, the world's largest gathering of steamboats, in our River Fun chapter. Staged every three or four years (next in October 1999), this nationally renowned event and its accompanying festivities are a Cincinnati tradition.

January

Bridal Show
Sabin Convention Center, Fifth and Elm Sts. • 352-3750

Preparing for a June wedding? Browse the hundreds of booths and exhibits at the Bridal Show for ideas and services to help your wedding run smoothly and make it that much more special. Fashion shows feature the latest and most glamorous wedding gowns. You can interview photographers, DJs, bands, and bakers and find the best bridal registry, all in one place. And nearly every booth offers some sort of giveaway, including honeymoon trips to exotic locations. Admission is $6. Grooms are welcome.

Travel Sports & Boat Show
Sabin Convention Center, Fifth and Elm Sts. • 352-3750

This is one of the most popular events held at the Convention Center each year. While the snow falls outside, the midmonth show gives you a chance to get away — or at least spend a week dreaming about burying your toes in some sandy beach, photographing exotic animals in the wilds of Africa, or zooming across the water in a new boat. Travel agencies give away trips, and you can watch hunting and fishing demonstrations or buy a boat or most any kind of sports equipment. Admission is $7 for adults, $2 for children 13 and younger.

February

CFA Championship Allbreed Cat Show
Sabin Convention Center Ballroom, Fifth and Elm Sts. • 244-1152

For 42 years the nation's coolest cats have gathered in this ballroom to compete for top honors as the best of their breed in this prestigious national event. More than 20 breeds compete. Vendors and exhibitors from all over the country create a supermarket of cat-related products designed to make you laugh or make your tabby purr just a little louder. Tickets are $5 for adults, $4 for seniors and $1 for children 15 and younger.

FYI

Unless otherwise noted, the area code for all phone numbers listed in this guide is 513.

Cavalcade of Customs
Sabin Convention Center, Fifth and Elm Sts. • 352-3750

The finest to the funkiest in automotive creations will show up for this weeklong event: dragsters, classic cars, model cars, street rods, monster trucks — just about anything with four wheels. Television and music personalities make appearances, signing autographs and posing for pictures. Admission is $8, $3 for children 12 and younger.

Fine Arts Funds Sampler
Various venues • 871-2787

Enjoy a smorgasbord of cultural samplings at this event, where all the area's cultural and arts organizations team to show off their wares and kick off their annual fundraising campaigns. More than 70 events take place in more than 30 locations throughout the area during the two-day, midmonth celebration. The symphony, ballet, May Festival Chorus, opera and School for the Creative and Performing Arts all perform. The Art Museum, Playhouse in the Park and Contemporary Arts Center open their doors. Guitar-a-thons, short films, plays, hands-on art lessons and other smaller events fill out the weekend. All activities are free, with most lasting less than an hour. It's a great way to get an idea of what's available in terms of culture.

Scubafest
11863 Solzman Rd. • 829-1480

Although Cincinnati is usually under snow in February, thoughts at the annual Scubafest are of being underwater. The midmonth show at the Kings Island Resort & Conference Center features more than 60 displays and exhibits of equipment, resorts, dive shops and scuba organizations. A room filled with artifacts and treasure hauled up from scuba trips is on display, and a Discover Scuba program is offered in the hotel pool to nondivers who want to give diving a try. More than 50 workshops and speakers take part in the event, which is presented by the Gavia Scuba Club. Underwater video and photography competitions are also held.

Tickets are $50 per person for the full weekend package, $15 for a two-day exhibits and presentations package, $10 for a one-day exhibits and presentations package, $10 for the Discover Scuba diving program, and $20 for a series of advanced diving workshops on such topics as underwater photography and drysuit maintenance and repair. A Buccaneer Banquet Ball is also held, with tickets at $39.

Valentine's Day Exhibit
Krohn Conservatory, 1501 Eden Park Dr. • 352-4086

Flowers, chocolate and romance dominate the atmosphere during the middle of the month in the Krohn's giant greenhouse, which has its own cocoa tree with beans from which chocolate is made. One whole wing of the giant greenhouse is dedicated to the season of love, and the flowers on display are for sale after the event — if your love can wait that long.

March

Antiques Show and Sale
Sycamore High School, 7400 Cornell Rd., Sycamore • 793-7524

More than 80 dealers gather at the high school to show and sell antiques. We're talking high-quality, top-of-the-line antiques here, not flea market goods. The weekend event is sponsored by the Montgomery Women's Club. Admission is $5.

Cincinnati Heart Mini-Marathon
Downtown • 281-4048

It's not the Boston Marathon, but the 5K and 15K races draw big crowds. The races begin and end at Fountain Square. The event, which benefits the Heart Foundation, also offers a fitness expo, speakers and a kid fun run. A 10K walk and a 20K skate are also held. It's free; pulled muscles cost extra.

Folk Art & Craft Show
11355 Chester Rd., Sharonville
• 771-7744

More than 100 of the nation's most talented traditional artisans display their fine crafts, folk art, furniture, wood carvings, baskets, quilts, jewelry and more. Admission is $5 for both days of the show, and an opening collectors' preview is $7.

Good Friday Stair Climb
30 Guido St., Mount Adams • 721-6544

For over 135 years, more than 10,000 Catholics have climbed the 356 steps from the foot of Mount Adams to Immaculata Church, praying the rosary on each step and accepting communion at the top. Even though the church closed in 1996, the annual climb continues and the brothers who ran the church return to offer communion.

Home & Garden Show
Sabin Convention Center, Fifth and Elm Sts. • 352-3750

This popular weeklong show runs in early March, just about the time you're beginning to realize spring isn't too far away and it's time to once again begin planting and working in the yard. Collect bulbs, perennials, annuals, seeds or just ideas. Water gardens, landscaping, decks, shrubs, trees, anything that has to do with homes and gardens can be found at the show. Admission is $6.75 for adults and $2.50 for children 12 and younger.

International Wine Festival
Sabin Convention Center, Fifth and Elm Sts. • 241-3434

Seminars, luncheons and, of course, (hic!)

tastings are featured in this three-day event, which is held at the beginning of the month. Hundreds of wines from around the world compete for a gold medal. If you want to learn more about wine, choose from seminars such as "The ABCs of Wine — and More" and "Blending Food and Wine." The festival benefits the classical music station WGUC. Admission packages are $50 for two Grand Tasting events, seminars, and parties and $40 for one tasting event and all the rest. Individual prices for seminars and tastings are also available.

Jim Beam Stakes
Turfway Park, Florence, Ky.
• (606) 371-0200

"The Beam," as it's known, is the richest Kentucky Derby prep race in the country. The $600,000 race is run five weeks before the Derby and regularly features at least one Triple Crown race winner, such as Lil E. Tee and Prairie Bayou. Like the Derby, fancy hats are the order of the day for women. An admission fee of $3.50 gets you into the track. Seating is extra, with varying prices depending on how good the seats are. What you spend at the betting window is up to you.

Maple Syrup Festival
Farbach-Werner Nature Preserve, Poole Rd. and Colerain Ave., Colerain
• 521-7275

One weekend each March, park rangers tap trees, cook up some flap jacks, lead hikes, set up a model Indian camp and show films. It's a fun, educational treat for kids, who can also satisfy a sweet tooth or two. Admission is free, but a $3 Hamilton County Park pass or a $1 daily park pass is needed.

Negro Spiritual Festival
Music Hall • 621-1919

College choirs from around the country compete for a $5,000 prize by singing spirituals a capella. Tickets for the event, which has been held for nearly 15 years, are $5.50, $16 and $25.50.

New Car Show
Sabin Convention Center, Fifth and Elm Sts. • 352-3750

Go car shopping without the pressure of

salespeople. Check out the latest models as well as a few futuristic models offered by all of the major manufacturers under one roof. If you ever wanted to sit in a Jaguar but didn't want to go to a dealership, now's your chance. And it smells really good. Admission is $7 for adults and $2.50 for children 12 and younger.

St. Patrick's Day Parade
Downtown • 251-2222

Although Greater O'Cincinnati has a decidedly German heritage, the area's St. Patrick's Day parade is reportedly the second largest in the country — no blarney. Arrive early in order to claim a prime street-side viewing location, as sidewalk space can be hard to find. Lawn chairs, coolers and leprechauns welcome.

www.insiders.com

See this and many other **Insiders' Guide®** destinations online — in their entirety.

Visit us today!

April

Cincinnati Flower Show
Ault Park, Mount Lookout • 579-0259

This is the largest, most prestigious open-air flower and garden festival in the country, and the only North American flower show endorsed by the Royal Horticultural Society of Great Britain. Martha Stewart likes it. *Good Morning America* says it is "one of the most beautiful events in the world." Growers, florists and designers from around the world display exhibits and give clinics and seminars plus an afternoon tea. About 35,000 people flock to the show, which runs the last weekend in April. General admission is $10, with free admission for children 12 and younger. There may be an additional admission charge for some seminars and clinics.

Cinergy Field Opening Day
Cinergy Field • 421-4510

Nowhere in the world is there anything like the Reds' opening day in Cincinnati. More work is missed than on any other unofficial holiday. A festive atmosphere permeates downtown as everyone wears red, dons baseball caps — even with business suits — and catches the Findlay Market Parade, which is an event unto itself. The parade rolls through the streets of downtown before the Reds game and includes two teams of giant Clydesdales pulling wagons, bands, marchers and former Reds players.

Hoop-It-Up
Coney Island, Anderson • 929-2140

The NBA-sanctioned three-on-three basketball tournament gives local hoopsters a chance to show their stuff. Different categories — for former college players to middle-aged, overweight bald guys who only play on weekends — keep the competition field level. Entrance fee is $88 per team.

Krohn Conservatory Easter Display
Krohn Conservatory, 1501 Eden Park Dr. • 352-4086

If Easter is a time of hope, the special display in the Krohn's giant greenhouse creates hope for those eager for spring. One whole wing of the cross-shaped greenhouse is reserved for the display, in which hundreds of blooming lilies are placed before a backdrop of lush greenery. Fountains, with water trickling down carefully placed rocks, add audible pleasure to the wonderful sights and smells. The display lasts the entire month. Admission is free, and the flowers are for sale when the display is over.

Police Auction
Sabin Convention Center, Fifth and Elm Sts. • 352-3750

Ever wonder what happens to all of the confiscated property the police collect from criminals? It gets auctioned off one day each year at bargain-basement prices. And there are bargains galore, especially since the police get to collect property from drug dealers. Some of the nicest, luxury-packed cars you've ever seen go for, well, a steal.

WCET Action Auction
Televised on Channel 48 • 381-4033

This event, which raises more than $1 million for WCET, is a combination of a

Photo: Lexington Herald Leader

The Serpentine Wall along the Ohio River downtown is one of the best places to watch the annual Riverfest fireworks show during the Labor Day weekend.

Sotheby's auction and the Home Shopping Network. A variety of merchandise — some of it quite valuable — is contributed by local residents interested in benefiting the public television station. All kinds of great bargains can be had.

May

Appalachian Festival
Coney Island, Anderson • 451-3070

They don't make things like they used to, except for the Appalachian Festival, the largest Appalachian craft show in the nation. For nearly 30 years now, festival-goers have found themselves taken back to another era by 150 exhibitors who show how things were done in the hills. There's handmade furniture, stained glass, copper water fountains, quilts, braided rugs, leather goods, dolls,

broom-making and woodworking demonstrations, music, storytelling and lots of down-home food, all during one weekend in the middle of each May. Three stages provide endless entertainment to go with the shopping. Admission is $5 for adults, $3 for seniors 65 and older and $1 for children 12 and younger. Tickets for some of the concerts are separate. Parking is $2.

The Delta Queen's Annual Spring Return
Public Landing • (800) 543-1949

During the first week in May since 1946, the giant *Delta Queen* steamboat has returned to her home port of Cincinnati to be greeted with festivities, people in period costume and Dixieland bands. The ship docks at the Public Landing and fills the air around downtown with calliope music. Check with your travel agent if you'd like to go for a spin.

Indianapolis 500
Indianapolis Motor Speedway,
Indianapolis, Ind. • (317) 484-6700

"The Greatest Spectacle in Racing" is just two hours away, and many race fans — and non-race fans who are just looking for a great big party — make the drive along Interstate 74 to the western side of Indy for the Memorial Day weekend event. It is much more than just the race, trust us. Ticket for reserved seats range from $30 to $140 and must be ordered at least one year in advance unless you want to purchase them from a scalper — then the price is up to you. General admission tickets never sell out. They cost $20 and can be purchased up to and including the day of the race.

Jammin' on Main
Court and Main Sts. • 744-8820

Cincinnati's two-day street music festival celebrates the diversity of musical styles that have flourished here. More than two dozen jazz, rock, gospel, blues and bluegrass bands perform on several stages along the front part of the Main Street entertainment district. There's plenty of food, drinks, music and people. A well-known national act such as Barenaked Ladies, Lonnie Mack, or Seven Mary Three usually caps off both nights on the main stage. Admission to the street show is $12 the day of the show and $9.50 in advance. Several entertainment establishments along the street also take part in the festivities (and also charge admission for their shows).

Jewish Folk Festival
University of Cincinnati, Shoemaker Center • 221-6728

This 21-year-old festival goes beyond the celebration of Cincinnati's Jewish heritage by featuring entertainers such as Gary Lewis and the Playboys and Lesley Gore. A children's village of activities, arts and crafts, and "A Kosher Taste of Jewish Cincinnati" are also offered. Admission to the event is free.

Kentucky Derby
Churchill Downs, Louisville, Ky.
• (502) 636-4400

For those who just can't resist wild hats and mint juleps in May, Greater Cincinnati is only two hours from Louisville and the first leg of the Triple Crown. A parade of cars can be found each Derby weekend heading down Interstate 71 towards Kentucky.

Kilgour Carnival
Kilgour Elementary School, 1339
Herschel Ave. • 533-6330

For 57 years, Kilgour has held the largest public school carnival in Cincinnati, offering rides, music, games, food, an auction, bingo and a flea market. Admission to the weekend-long event is $5.

Maifest
MainStrasse Village, Sixth and Main Sts.,
Covington, Ky. • (606) 491-0458

The village's celebration is a nod to the German tradition of welcoming the first spring wines. It's held every third weekend in May, with plenty of food and entertainment at hand. Admission to the village is free but food is not.

Mason-Dixon Steeplechase
Turfway Park, 7500 Turfway Rd.,
Florence, Ky. • (606) 371-0200

Equestrians and anyone else who likes a horse race interspersed with graceful jumps will appreciate this event. The steeplechase draws horses from all over the world, including some from England's royal stables.

May Festival
Music Hall, 1241 Main St. • 381-3300

You'll hear great sounds at the oldest continuing choral and orchestral music festival in the country, dating back to 1873. The all-volunteer May Festival Chorus is made up of 250 average Joes and Josephines (that is, nonprofessional singers) with great voices who perform to the accompaniment of the Cincinnati Symphony Orchestra. Top-name opera singers are brought in as soloists, along with the University of Cincinnati Conservatory of Music Choir and Chorale, the Conservatory's Children's Choir and the Cincinnati Boychoir. The festival is spread over two weekends. Pre-concert buffet dinners ($20) and pre-concert recitals (free) are also part of the fun. Full subscriptions are $32 to $108; either weekend subscriptions are $19 to $65; any four concerts cost $64 to $90; and single tickets are $10 to $36.

Mayor's 801 Plum Concert Series
801 Plum St. • 381-6868

This series of concerts, held in the council chambers at City Hall, features classical and jazz music. It's perhaps the best thing happening in council chambers. Tickets are $10 at the door. The concerts are held one Friday a month May through August.

Spring Home and Garden Tour
Newport, Ky. • (606) 581-6634

Tour some of Newport's historic Victorian homes and distinctive gardens during the first weekend in May. Tickets are $5 in advance and $6 the day of the tour.

Taste of Cincinnati
Garfield Park, Fourth and Pike Sts.
• 333-6888

Taste of Cincinnati, held every Memorial Day weekend, is the oldest continuously running food-tasting event in the nation, starting back in 1979. More than 50 of the best restaurants in Cincinnati set up booths along Central Parkway downtown and offer a smorgasbord of their finest fares, with items costing between $1 and $2.50. More than 400,000 people try everything from prime rib to lobster to a dozen different types of cheesecake and listen to continuous live music on three different stages. Some even work off their samplings in the Fork in the Road Run 5K race. No one, though, leaves hungry.

June

A Day in Eden
Eden Park, Eden Park Dr. • 352-6144

The area's most beloved park packs in thousands of revelers who picnic under a tree, visit the dozens of neighborhood-run food booths, and watch local bands perform at several stage locations scattered throughout the park. You can visit the Art Museum, Krohn Conservatory and the Playhouse in the Park for some culture and beat the early summer heat by dabbling your toes in Mirror Lake, a reflecting pool and fountain that is usually off-limits to waders. The

event is free, and admission to the museum and conservatory is free on this day, too.

Cincinnati Regatta
East Fork Lake State Park, 250
Williamsburg-Bantam Rd., Afton
• 734-4323

The best collegiate, high school and youth club rowing teams in the county gather on calm Harsha Lake in East Fork Lake State Park for one of the top sculling competitions in the country. Admission to preliminary events is free. Tickets for the championship rounds are $10 for adults and $5 for children 10 and younger. Tickets to the finish-line grandstand are $25 for adults and $12.50 for children. Proceeds benefit Children's Hospital.

Concours D'Elegance Car Show
Ault Park, at the end of Observatory Ave.
• 271-4545

This isn't your average car show. Every Father's Day for the last 20 years, 200 of the rarest, most exotic and most valuable cars from around the country have gathered for this highly regarded event. An art auction, art show, brunch and countryside tour round out the activities. Cost is $10 for adults, $5 for children 12 and younger. Proceeds go to the Arthritis Foundation.

Frontier Days
111 Race St., Milford • 831-2411

The 33-year-old festival offers four days of food, rides and entertainment. More than 150,000 spectators take themselves back to the days when Milford was the wild frontier. Admission is free.

Greek Panegyri Festival
7000 Winton Rd., Finneytown • 591-0030

Each mid-June the area gets a taste of Greek music, food and religion at the Greek Panegyri Festival at Holy Trinity-St. Nicholas Greek Orthodox Church. Art shows and other festival activities fill in the time between gyro eating and Greek dancing. Look for the "I've fallen and can't reach my ouzo!" T-shirts. Admission is $1.

Homearama
Various subdivisions • 851-6300

Each year the Homebuilders Association

Riverfest is a Labor Day Blast

Without a doubt, the biggest annual event in Cincinnati is Riverfest, which includes the Toyota/WEBN Fireworks display. The Labor Day weekend blast has evolved from a small fireworks display into a giant party, with 500,000-plus people jamming the riverfront to have fun and bid farewell to summer.

The fireworks celebration has grown extensively over the years, so much so that city officials were forced to rein it in to maintain control. As a result, alcohol is no longer permitted on either side of the river, and security crews search the coolers, bags and purses of those who watch from the riverfront to make sure alcohol is not sneaked into the area. Still, plenty of fun can be had. Folks toss Frisbees and footballs on whatever green space isn't covered by blankets and beach towels. Every type of food imaginable is offered. Stages set up in strategic locales feature live bands of various musical persuasions. Stunt planes and skydivers perform overhead. If you're into people-watching, you'll find such an incredibly diverse array that you may be able to earn a Ph.D. in sociology by taking notes. And a half-hour of nonstop fireworks exploding overhead is best described as, well, a blast.

To some people, the fireworks is an all-day event. They get there early in the morning to stake claims to prime viewing territories and they flow in continuously throughout the day. Then they all leave at once. Traffic leaving the riverfront after the grand finale is worse than at a Reds game, Bengals game, snowstorm, rock concert and Friday afternoon wrapped into one. TANK and Metro offer special shuttles to the riverfront to help ease parking and traffic congestion, but it's still bad. So plan on taking a few hours to get home.

Where to watch the fireworks is a strategy unto itself. Unless you are up close, you can't see some of the show, such as the waterfall of white sparks that run off the side of one of the bridges and into the river. If you aren't that close, the fireworks are synchronized with music, and WEBN (102.7 FM) broadcasts the event live from a barge on the river so you can still keep track of what is going on. To help, we've compiled "The Insiders' Eight Great Places To Watch the Fireworks From":

On the waterfront. Hundreds of boats pack the river — almost to the point of being hazardous. But if the front row is where you want to be, you can't get a whole lot closer. Some house boats even arrive days ahead of time and anchor along the shoreline to ensure their spot. Watch for falling ashes, though.

Along the riverfront. Most viewers line the shore on both sides of the river. The Cincinnati side offers the Serpentine Wall and Bicentennial Commons, complete with food and drink concession stands and all the attractions of the park. The Kentucky side offers a soft, grassy hillside that actually serves as a flood wall but makes for an ideal spot to lie back and look up at the show.

Waterfront bars, restaurants and nightspots. Squeeze into one of these places and you'll not only be on the river, but you'll have people catering to you for as long as you are there. When the show begins, the rush of people on the floating clubs who want to get a good spot causes the boats to lean heavily to one side.

A downtown office with a view of the river. Parties, sometimes extravagantly catered affairs, are going on in offices all over downtown.

Mount Adams. Any of the many bars with a view of downtown and the river is a good option. Even better is one of the many hillside homes overlooking the river. You're in a

— continued on next page

Riverfest's fireworks display is one of the most spectacular in the entire country.

comfortable setting above the crowds, you don't have to stand in line for the restroom, there are more entertainment options and you can sit back and relax afterward while the masses exit.

A hotel room with a river view. The Embassy Suites in Covington and the Comfort Suites in Bellevue are the best. They are often booked up a year in advance for the show, though. As with a home in Mount Adams, watching from the comfort of a hotel room is advantageous.

Any other hillside with a river view. Some good choices include Devou Park in Northern Kentucky, the Newport and Covington hillsides, some parts of Mount Auburn and Price Hill, and Eden Park. Although they are farther away from the heart of the action, these areas are still jammed with people. Most hillside-watchers want to see the fireworks but don't want to deal with the people and traffic.

Television. Yep, the fireworks are so big a local television station holds a special two-hour program that concludes with the fireworks. The music is the same, and, with cameras spread out around the area, viewers can see things they might otherwise miss. The atmosphere doesn't translate, though, and the explosions from the fireworks leave dots and streaks on the picture for several seconds, much like what happens with your eyes when a flashbulb goes off.

---

of Greater Cincinnati stages a Street of Dreams, with builders from around the area purchasing a lot in an upscale subdivision and designing a home in the $500,000 to $1 million range. Landscapers and interior designers compete for honors as well. The homes, many of which are sold by the time of the show, are then open to the public for a week of tours. Cost is $6 if you're 13 or older or $700,000 if you buy a house while you are there.

Juneteenth Celebration
Eden Park, Eden Park Dr. • 489-1025

This family festival celebrates the end of slavery in America. Historical exhibits, re-enactments, entertainment and organized activities for children fill the park. More than 50 vendors sell art, books, clothing, crafts, jewelry and food. The event is "free to the freedom-loving public."

Kids Fest
Sawyer Point • 352-4001

For nearly 20 years the Cincinnati Recreation Commission has put together a festival just for kids, with hundreds of hands-on activities, from water balloon battles to computer games to milking cows to making slime. Ooooh, how fun! Admission is free.

Mayor's Summer Concert Series
Various sites • 352-4000

The Cincinnati Recreation Commission organizes a series of free concerts during June, July and August featuring popular local acts. The shows are announced in the local papers and on radio stations.

Oldiesfest
Festival Park, New Richmond • 321-8900

Every spring, radio station WGRR (103.5 FM) brings back good old rock 'n roll by importing greats from the past, such as Chuck Berry, Jan and Dean, Frankie Valli and the Four Seasons, the Mamas and Papas, Brenda Lee, the Rascals and more for a free concert along the riverfront in New Richmond. The trip back to the '50s and '60s is free, although a ticket is needed to get through the gate (contact WGRR at 321-1035).

FYI

Unless otherwise noted, the area code for all phone numbers listed in this guide is 513.

P&G Concert Series
P&G Pavilion, Bicentennial Commons • 352-4000

In conjunction with local radio stations, Procter & Gamble and the Cincinnati Recreation Commission organize a series of free concerts at the P&G Pavilion in Bicentennial Commons beginning in June. The groups are smaller national acts and vary in style depending on the radio station sponsoring that week's concert.

Ribfest
Bicentennial Commons • 261-1233

More than a dozen local restaurants offer sample-size portions of barbecued ribs at this annual affair. Check out the entertainment venues when you've finished eating. Admission to this weekend event is free, although there's a small fee for the samples.

Strawberry Festival
Main St., Metamora, Ind.
• (317) 647-2109

This tiny Indiana canal town is filled with log buildings from the 1800s that have been turned into retail stores. When the strawberries begin to ripen, the town throws a party, with strawberry pies, jams, jellies, tarts and every other product imaginable made from strawberries. Admission to the festival is free, but how much you spend on strawberries is up to you.

Summerfair
Coney Island, Anderson • 531-0050

More than 250 of Greater Cincinnati's best artists gather here to display and sell their paintings, sculptures and crafts, while country, jazz and pop bands fill the air with music. Great bargains can be had. Special shows and art lessons are available for children during the weekend affair. The whole fair takes place around the already-entertaining venues at Coney Island, so if the mid-June heat bogs you down, take a dip in the pool or a ride on the pedal boats. Restaurants and arcade games are also available. Admission is $5.

Taste of Northern Kentucky
MainStrasse Village, Sixth and Main Sts., Covington, Ky. • (606) 261-4677

The best restaurants in Northern Kentucky set up booths along the streets of MainStrasse for a whole weekend and offer nibbles (just large enough to tempt the taste buds) of their best dishes. Admission to the street fair is free, although each restaurant charges for its samples.

Used Book Sale
Fountain Square • 369-6900

It's hard to imagine used books drawing such attention, but for the last 26 years they've become one of the city's main summer attractions. The main public library takes over Fountain Square, setting up huge tents full of tables filled with hardbacks, paperbacks, magazines and records. Thousands of people jam elbow-to-elbow around the assortment of textbooks, fiction, nonfiction, classics, romance and more, searching for — and in some cases fighting over — books at giveaway prices. On the final day of the five-day event, the library sells large shopping bags for $5 and allows shoppers to fill the bags with whatever is left. Great for bookworms or casual readers, the sale offers wonderful bargains and raises money for the library.

Photo: Skip Tate

Taft Museum hosts many of the city's annual events.

July

Clermont County Fair
Owensville, off U.S. 50 • 732-1657, 732-0522

All the fun and activities you associate with a county fair converge on the fairgrounds the last week in July. The fair, which is held a month earlier than other county fairs in the area, is free the first Sunday it opens. After that, admission is $6 per day or $18 for a weekly pass. Children 12 and younger get in for $1 per day or for $5 with a weekly pass

Coors Light Jazz Festival
Cinergy Field • 352-6333

This festival is the jazz equivalent of Woodstock, only it's held every year. The top names in soul, rhythm and blues and jazz perform for three straight days in Cinergy Field, attracting concert-goers from states in every direction. Patti LaBelle, Luther Vandross, George Benson, Gladys Knight, Grover Washington and Frankie Beverly have all performed at the festival. It draws the largest attendance of any such event in the country. One-day and two-day ticket packages are available, with prices ranging from $25 to $50. Other related events such as post-concert parties, river cruises, block parties, exhibits and free miniconcerts take place before and after the festival at various locations downtown.

HomeFest
Location varies, Northern Ky. • (606) 331-9500

This is the Northern Kentucky equivalent of Cincinnati's Homearama. Each year, about

35,000 people visit a subdivision in Northern Kentucky in which area homebuilders create a street of dream homes (which sell for as much as $1 million) compete for a series of honors. Interior designers and landscapers also get to show off their best work. The tour costs $6; children 12 and younger go free with an adult.

It's Commonly Jazz
Swifton Commons Mall, Reading Rd. and Seymour Ave. • 351-9415

Every Thursday from July through September you can catch some of the best free jazz concerts around in one of the most unusual settings. For the last 11 years, a stage and chairs have been set up in the parking lot of Swifton Commons Mall, and local and regional jazz artists perform for free between 6 PM and 8 PM.

LaRosa's Parties in the Park
Bicentennial Commons • 579-3199

These huge outdoor parties are held every week for five weeks, alternating Wednesday nights with the Q102 Parties at the Point (see below). The festivities begin at 5 PM, just as the work crowd is loosening the ties and packing up the briefcases. The Parties in the Park take place near the Serpentine Wall and feature musical entertainment and refreshments.

Old Timers Day
Old Crosley Field, Blue Ash • 745-8586

For those who prefer baseball the way it was played in the good old days, former Reds players get together each year for an old-timers game at Old Crosley Field in Blue Ash. The field and scoreboard of the Reds' former home have been reconstructed in exact detail near the Interstate 71 and Interstate 275 interchange. About 5,000 people flock to old Crosley each summer for the game and autographs.

Picnic on the Point
Bicentennial Commons • 352-4000

This early-July event features entertainment at the P&G Pavilion, a volleyball tournament and roving entertainment throughout the park. Fireworks cap the event at 10 PM.

Pioneer Days Rendezvous
Caesar Creek Pioneer Village, 3999 Pioneer Village Rd., Waynesville • 897-1120

The lifestyle of the early settlers is recreated and celebrated at the Caesar Creek Pioneer Village during Pioneer Days. Costumed pioneers roam throughout the 1800s village. The event is free. Food or gifts purchased at the many booths will cost you, though.

Q102 Parties at the Point
Bicentennial Commons • 763-5686

The Q102 parties alternate Wednesday nights with the LaRosa's Parties in the Park (see above). Bands play in the P&G Pavilion and refreshments are served beginning at 5 PM.

St. Rita School for the Deaf Summer Festival
1720 Glendale-Milford Road, Evendale • 771-7600

This event during the first weekend of the month is the crown prince of the nearly 30 Catholic church festivals held throughout the year in the area. More than 100 booths are set up on the school campus, with local celebrities leading emceeing events and working the booths. Prizes totaling more than $40,000 are given away.

Sawyer Point Cinema
Bicentennial Commons • 352-4000

The Cincinnati Recreation Commission hosts four movie nights at the Schott Amphitheater at Bicentennial Commons beginning in early July. The free movies are geared toward kids and begin around 9 PM.

Sunfest
MainStrasse Village, Sixth and Main Sts., Covington, Ky. • (606) 491-0458

Just to celebrate summer, a giant party is held on the third weekend in July at MainStrasse Village, with live entertainment, food, and arts and crafts. Admission to the event is free.

Taste of Ebone
Fifth St., • 961-1332

This festival brings together some of the best chefs in the area and from out of town, who offer a wide variety of ethnic cuisine. Admission is free, but nibbling will cost you. Booths open late morning and stay open until 3 AM.

U.S. Air and Trade Show
Dayton International Airport, Dayton, Ohio • (937) 255-4704

The home of the Wright brothers and birthplace of aviation (no apologies to North Carolinians) goes supersonic each year with its air show. The Blue Angels, the Army's Golden Knights precision parachute team, wing walkers, stunt pilots, endless flybys — that's just what's going on in the air. On the ground are hundreds of military planes spanning several generations. Parking at the U.S. Air Force Museum at Wright-Patterson Air Force Base and stopping in for a tour before catching a shuttle bus makes for an even greater aviation experience. Admission is $12 for adults, $8 for seniors 65 and older and kids 6 through 11. Shuttle rides are $2. The show is only an hour north of Cincinnati off Interstate 70.

August

All About Kids Convention
Sabin Convention Center, Fifth and Elm Sts. • 684-0501

Kids and health are the focus of the three-day convention, which turns the Convention

Center into a giant playground featuring inter-active sports, arts, computers, gymnastics, museums and more in 17 themed play pavil-ions. The convention is held in early August. Admission at the door is $6 for adults, $3 for children 2 through 18. Free children's tickets can be picked up at Kroger pharmacies (maxi-mum of three tickers per adult).

ATP Championship
Sports Center at Kings Island, Mason • 651-0303

During the first two weeks in August the tennis world turns to Cincinnati for the $1.8 million Great American Insurance ATP Cham-pionship. The event regularly draws the sport's top-10 men players, as well as massive crowds of nearly 400,000 during its weeklong stay in Cincinnati. A separate four-day $100,000 Leg-ends Tournament, which features well-known players of the past such as Rod Laver and Ilie Nastase, is held the week before the ATP. Ticket prices vary.

Black Family Reunion
Bicentennial Commons • 569-8582

This massive celebration of African-Ameri-can heritage, culture and pride draws people from all over the region. The two-day event, which is organized by the National Council of Negro Women, features a parade, food, fes-tivities and national and local entertainment celebrating the legacy of the African-Ameri-can family. The midmonth event, which draws 250,000 people along the riverfront, is free.

Cincinnati Playhouse House Party
Playhouse in the Park, Eden Park, 962 Mt. Adams Dr. • 421-3888

The Playhouse gets a jump-start on its sea-son with a bash that includes music, comple-mentary food, theater tours, strolling entertain-ment, tarot card readers and wine tastings. Admission is $7 at the door or free with the purchase of a season subscription.

County and State Fairs
Various sites

You'll find just about everything you ever wanted in a fair — tractor pulls, grandstand entertainment, demolition derbies, rides, car-nival events, animal exhibits, arcades and

plenty of food — at any of the area's abundant events. They include the Ohio State Fair in Columbus; Kentucky State Fair in Louisville; Hamilton County Fair in Carthage; Boone County Fair in Burlington, Kentucky; Kenton County Fair in Independence, Kentucky; and Campbell County Fair in Alexandria, Kentucky.

Delhi Skirt Softball Game
5125 Foley Rd., Delhi • 956-7000

For nearly 20 years, cigar-chomping, beer-chugging members of the Delhi fire and po-lice departments and Delhi Athletic Associa-tion have dressed in skirts and played a soft-ball game against teams such as the Bengals cheerleaders to raise money for Delhi families in need. The hilarious event raises nearly $20,000 annually.

Great Inland Seafood Festival
Yeatman's Cove in Bicentennial Commons along Pete Rose Way • 291-6572

Greater Cincinnati is 14 hours away from the ocean. Still, more than 20 top local restau-rants show how good area seafood dishes can be at this festival. Live entertainment joins the culinary extravaganza, which attracts about 150,000 people. Admission is free; nibbling will cost you. Food runs from $1 for a sam-pling to $8.95 for a full lobster dinner.

Lytle Jazz Series
Lytle Park, Fourth and Pike Sts. • 579-3191

Four free happy-hour jazz concerts are staged by the Downtown Council in the relax-ing setting of Lytle Park. The concerts are held each Thursday during the month.

Morning Glory Ride
Yeatman's Cove in Bicentennial Commons along Pete Rose Way • 749-9717

For 17 years hundreds of bicyclists have participated in this 20-mile predawn bike ride. Starting downtown at 4 AM, they ride through Eden Park, Hyde Park and Covington before returning for a breakfast at dawn along the Cincinnati riverfront. Rollerbladers also take part in the event. Cost is $25 for the ride and breakfast, $12 for the ride only.

Renaissance Festival
Ohio Hwy. 73, Waynesville • 897-7000

Belly up to the Round Table for a leg of mutton and a goblet of wine every weekend between late August and mid-October. Jousting, 16th-century costumes, strolling minstrels, shows on five stages, more than 130 craft booths, food and drink fit for a king and everything from the Renaissance period except the crown of Henry VIII go into the festival. Tickets are $12.95 for adults, $6 for children ages 5 through 12 and free for children younger than 5.

River Days
New Richmond Riverfront • 553-6161

Rides, arts, crafts, entertainment and plenty of food are part of the river celebration in this old river town. A 5K run, the largest fireworks display in Clermont County and hydroplane races on the river top off the two-day event, usually held at the end of the month.

September

Applefest
Downtown Lebanon • (513) 932-1100

Pick your own Granny Smith, Jonathon, or Delicious apples. Sample apple pies, apple juices and other apple treats as you stroll through the farmers market or craft and antique stores.

Celtic Music and Cultural Festival
**Ault Park, at the end of Observatory Ave.
• 533-4822**

For two days the arts and culture of the Celtic lands — Ireland, Scotland, Wales, Brittany and Galicia — are celebrated with bagpipe bands, Irish and Scottish dancers and traditional foods in Ault Park. More than 200 dance and instrumental competitions draw as many as 500 performers. The feis (pronounced "fesh"), the Irish word for festival, is organized by the Cincinnati Irish Cultural Society. Admission is free, although a do-

nation of $3 per person or $6 per family is suggested.

Comair Mini-Grand Prix
Fifth St. • 271-4545

Local companies race 5-HP go-carts around downtown streets to help raise money for the Arthritis Foundation. To enter, call the Arthritis Foundation at the number above, if it doesn't call you first, looking for your support.

DamFest
Neilan Blvd., Hamilton • 867-2287

This two-day festival along the banks of the Great Miami River in Hamilton, just 30 minutes north of Cincinnati, includes championship water skiers, rubber-duck races, boat rides, entertainment, a hot air balloon race and more than 90 booths of food and games. Admission is free.

Kroger Senior PGA Classic
**Golf Center at Kings Island, Mason
• 398-5742**

Every September the golf greats of yesterday return to the area to play in the $900,000 Kroger Senior Classic at The Golf Center at Kings Island. (See our Spectator Sports chapter for more details.)

Felicity Gourd Festival
Ohio Hwy. 33, Felicity • 876-2859

This 20-plus-year-old festival features a quilt and flower show, gourds of all sorts and a parade. The day is capped off with fireworks. Admission is $1 adults and 50¢ for children 12 and younger.

Harvest Festivals
Various venues

The Greater Cincinnati area has a rich farming heritage, and the harvest is still celebrated with several festivals, including those at Sharon Woods Village, Caesar Creek Pioneer Village in Waynesville and the Cincinnati Zoo. The events feature folks in period costumes, hayrides, Appalachian music, clogging, lumber-

Photo: Cincinnati Celtic Music and Cultural Festival

The McGing Irish Dancers perform a ceili dance at
the Cincinnati Celtic Music and Cultural Festival.

jacks, crafts and, of course, food. The most famous festival event of all may be the 22-year-old Harvest Home Fair Parade held in Cheviot. More than 200 displays take more than three hours to make their way through the streets of the small town. People put their chairs out along the parade route days in advance to save their viewing place. And nary a politician has ever missed a chance to be seen in the parade.

Honey Festival
High St., Hamilton • 683-2220

Remember those pesky bees during the summer? Well, all their work can be seen at the Honey Festival the last weekend in September. The free festival features honey-covered ham, barbecue with honey buns, strained honey, honeycombs, honey cream and non-honey activities such as the car show, tractor pull and someone who grows a beard of bees.

Kitchen Bath & Design Show
Sabin Convention Center, Fifth and Elm Sts. • 751-6161

Pick up some great home decorating and renovation ideas for the two most popular areas of the house. The fanciest toilets and tubs imaginable are on display. Admission is $6.

Oktoberfest-Zinzinnati
Downtown • 333-6888

Everybody's German during Oktoberfest-Zinzinnati. More than 500,000 people jam six blocks downtown during mid-September to sing, dance, stuff themselves with sauerkraut, bratwurst, schnitzel and strudel, and wash it all down with thousands of gallons of beer. In 1994, revelers consumed 168,000 mettwurst and bratwurst.

Six entertainment stages, 50 food vendors and a children's area keep the whole family busy for two days. It is the nation's largest authentic Oktoberfest, dating back to 1976. Although the event is free, food prices range from 75¢ to $6. A 10K Volksmarch helps walk off some of the strudel.

And if that isn't enough, an Oktoberfest in MainStrasse Village in Covington, Kentucky, takes place during the first week after Labor Day. Still want more? Check out the Lawrenceburg Strassefest in Lawrenceburg, Indiana.

Riverfest
On the Ohio River, downtown
• 352-4000, 684-4945

For more than 20 years 500,000 people have jammed the riverbanks on both sides of the Ohio each Labor Day weekend to bid farewell to summer with an outdoor celebration that is capped by the Toyota/WEBN fireworks. Food, activities and nationally known entertainment on numerous stages set up on both sides of the river make this one of the best annual events in the area. An air show was also recently added to get party-goers used to looking up in the sky before the big bang. Admission is free, except in Newport, where there's a $1 charge along its riverfront. Read more about Riverfest in our Close-up in this chapter.

Valley Vineyards Wine Festival
2276 E. U.S. Hwy. 22, Morrow,
• 899-2485

Try your hand at making your own vintage in the amateur wine-making contest, or let your feet's creative juices flow in the grape-stomping contest. The three-day event extends over a Thursday, Friday and Saturday. Plenty of food is available to go with the wine, especially at the steak cookouts on Friday and Saturday. Admission is free, but wine tastings and food are extra.

October

BooFest
Museum Center at Union Terminal
• 287-7000

The Cincinnati Historical Society serves up a treat for Halloween by turning the Museum Center at Union Terminal into a giant jack-o'-lantern and offering Halloween-themed activities such as The Haunted Museum, the Eerie Express, Marketplace on the Landing, and The Haunted Neighborhood. Everyone leaves with a treat. (See our Attractions chapter for more details.)

Cincinnati Antiques Festival
Sharonville Convention Center, 11355 Chester Rd. • 871-9543

Nearly 50 nationally recognized antique dealers bring out the best of the past at this show, which is in its 33rd year. Only the best-quality antiques are found at the show. Admission is $8 for the weekend-long event.

Gold Star ChiliFest
West Court St. • 579-3191

What would Cincinnati be without a chili festival? For more than 15 years more than 20 chili vendors have served up almost two dozen types of chili, from mild to "Someone Call 911." The weekend festival, appropriately, is on West Court Street near the Cincinnati Fire Museum. A country music stage provides music to go along with other events, such as the International Chili Society Cook-off and demonstrations by the Cincinnati Fire Division. The event is free, but prices for chili samplings vary. A jalapeño-eating contest is also held, with a record of 15 peppers eaten in the two-minute time limit. The winner no doubt burped fire for the next two days.

Haunted Houses
Various venues

Dozens of haunted houses can be found around the Halloween season, ranging from non-scary for small children to those good enough to qualify for an Oscar. The most popular ones are held at St. Rita School for the Deaf, 1720 Glendale-Milford Road, Evendale; Immaculate Heart of Mary, 7820 Beechmont Avenue, Anderson; Phillips Chapel CME Church, 282 Main Street, Addyston; Fountain Square, where the city puts on the Scare on the Square; Forest Fair Mall, I-275 and Winton Road, Forest Park; and the U.S.S. *Nightmare*, Covington Landing, Covington, Kentucky.

Light Up Cincinnati
Downtown • 579-3191

Downtown buildings turn their lights on, making the skyline sparkle. A photo contest is held by radio stations and camera stores with divisions for amateurs and professionals. Prizes are cash and cameras, and outstanding photos of the city have resulted.

Ohio Sauerkraut Festival
Main St., Waynesville • 897-8855

Since 1969 Waynesville, a 19th-century English village with more than 35 antique shops, has paid homage to one of the tastiest of festival foods: sauerkraut. During the second weekend in October 250,000 people flock to the small city to enjoy the more than 400 arts and crafts exhibitors, entertainment and sauerkraut served every imaginable way. It's better than it sounds.

Run Like Hell/Party Like Hell
1507 Dana Ave. • 533-9300

For a different twist to Halloween, the Run Like Hell is a 5K race that starts at 7:30 PM and travels through the Walnut Hills Cemetery. The run is followed by a party with food, beer and a costume contest. The $18 pre-race or $22 day-of-the-race entry fee benefits the Cystic Fibrosis Foundation.

Simply The Best
Union Terminal • 421-4300

All of the restaurants voted best in *Cincinnati Magazine*'s annual "Best and Worst" edition gather in the rotunda of Union Terminal and cook up samples of their award-winning fare. The $25 admission fee covers parking, drinks and samples, and the proceeds go to charity. A true social scenario in casual clothes, the late-month event also offers other "bests" from the magazine, such as massages and golf lessons.

Taste of Findlay Market
Elder St. • 241-0464

Over 8,000 people show up to sample the fares at the 26 booths that line the inside of the historic marketplace. Samples cost from 50¢ to $2.50. Entertainment on two stages, crafts and interactive booths for youths can also be found. Admission and parking are free and a shuttle bus is available.

November

Festival of Lights
Cincinnati Zoo, 3400 Vine St. • 281-4700

Live reindeer, a nativity scene with live animals, Santa, holiday shopping, Hanukkah activities and 2 million Christmas lights turn the zoo into a winter wonderland. The show runs mid-November through the first week in January. Special events such as Happy Zoo Year and Lights, Camels, aaand Action are held throughout the month. Zoo admission is $6.50 for adults and $4 for kids 2 through 12 and seniors 62 and older.

Holiday Caravan
Sabin Convention Center, Fifth and Elm Sts. • 221-0981

This is one of the best ways to kick off the Christmas shopping season. The Civic Garden Center offers 70 exhibit booths filled with unique, handmade holiday gifts, jewelry, dolls and decorations. An auction allows bidders a chance at great values. Admission is $5 for the show, which is held the weekend after Thanksgiving. Get there early, though, as a line forms outside the entrance an hour before the doors open.

Holiday in Lights
Sharon Woods, Sharonville • 287-7103

Animated storybook characters, Santa and his reindeer, snowball-throwing snowmen and more take shape from 80,000 lights. This drive-through display features a special holiday soundtrack that can be tuned in on the car radio. The cost is $7 per carload and benefits the Ruth Lyons Children's Christmas Fund. The show runs mid-November through January 1.

Honda Starlight Celebration
Sawyer Point • 684-4945

The Cincinnati Recreation Commission strings 300,000 lights throughout Bicentennial Commons, giving the park holiday cheer. You can take a free carriage ride through the park on Saturday nights while strolling carolers fill the air with Christmas tunes. The show runs from mid-November through January 2.

International Folk Festival
Sabin Convention Center, Fifth and Elm Sts. • 352-3750

In mid-November, some 30 ethnic groups gather and turn Cincinnati into an international showplace. Eat everything from egg rolls to baklava, and buy merchandise from all over the world.

Krohn Conservatory Christmas Display
Eden Park, access from Kemper Ln., Victory Pkwy. or Gilbert Ave. • 352-4086

The Crib of the Nativity manger scene with live animals outside of the conservatory is one of the big attractions of the holiday season. Inside, chrysanthemums and poinsettias bloom and you can enjoy them for free.

'Tis The Season In The City
Fountain Square • 684-4945

Beginning in late November, Fountain Square is transformed into a holiday wonderland, with an ice-skating rink, hot chocolate stands, a Santa's Workshop, live reindeer, a romantic gazebo, old-fashioned street lamps and the Fountain itself, which glows with thousands of miniature lights. Oh, and, of course, Santa has a special chair where good little boys and girls can tell him what's on their wish list. Various onetime events are scheduled. Skating admission is $1. Skate rental is also $1.

FYI

Unless otherwise noted, the area code for all phone numbers listed in this guide is 513.

Toys For Adults Show
Sabin Convention Center, Fifth and Elm Sts. • 793-2233

From jet helicopters and furs to virtual-reality games and expensive cars, the Toys For Adults Show offers fun things for big kids — with fat wallets. Most of the items are outside the affordable range for most folks, but fun to look at. Admission is $6.50 for adults and $3 for toy-lovers 12 and younger.

December

A Christmas Carol
Playhouse in the Park, Eden Park, 962 Mt. Adams Dr. • 421-3888

Another artistic favorite of the Christmas season is the performance of Charles Dickens' *A Christmas Carol* at the Playhouse in the Park. Tickets, which range from $26 to $36, are very hard to come by, but well-worth the effort, even for Scrooges. The show runs all month.

Boar's Head and Yule Log Festival
Christ Church, 318 E. Fourth St.
• 621-BOAR

The Boars Head Festival is one of the oldest continuing festivals of the Christmas season, held since 1940. It tells the story of the birth of Christ symbolically through a medieval feast. More than 250 actors, jesters, singers and musicians perform the story representing the victory of the Christ child over evil. Admission is free, but tickets must be obtained at the church in advance.

Carolfest
Music Hall, 1243 Elm St. • 621-1919

Get in the spirit of the season by listening to the booming, high-quality harmonies of the May Festival Chorus, the Youth Chorus and other guests as they belt out holiday favorites during the first week of the month. Tickets are $9 for adults and $4.50 for children 12 and younger. Fa-la-la-la-la, la-la . . .

Cinergy Train Display
Fourth and Main Sts. • 421-9500

One of the world's largest portable O-gauge miniature railroads is displayed every December, taking up a majority of the lobby in the Cinergy Building. More than 200,000 people view the display, which has been an annual event for more than 50 years. If the viewing line is long, some of the display can be seen at the window on Fourth Street. The trains roll for the entire month.

Reindog Parade
Mount Adams • 381-8696

Mount Adams goes to the dogs the first week of each December. Dogs are dressed as reindeer, complete with antlers and a red nose, if the dog doesn't mind. A tail-wagging contest and parade top off the event.

Rudd's Christmas Farm
1205 Cassel Run Rd., Blue Creek
• (937) 544-3500

Carl Rudd turns his farm into a Christmas story with more than a half-million lights celebrating the season. A steady stream of sightseers flood the farm between 5:30 and 10:30 nightly during the month. Admission is free. Take Ohio 32 east to Ohio 247, go south to West Union, Ohio, and turn east on Ohio 125 to Blue Creek, Ohio.

The Nutcracker Ballet
Music Hall • 621-1919

Every year the Cincinnati Ballet performs *The Nutcracker*. This holiday favorite has instantly sold out for the last 24 years, so be prepared to stand in line as soon as tickets go on sale. The performance, which runs for two weeks, is well worth the effort to get tickets, though.

World's Largest Office Party
Hyatt Regency, 151 W. Fifth St.
• 579-1234

One of the social events of the season, with dozens of celebrity bartenders and live bands, is held in the middle of the month at the Hyatt Regency Hotel. The after-work affair benefits a local children's agency. Admission is $8.

New Year's Events

Greater Cincinnati offers hundreds of options for New Year's Eve, depending on how you like to celebrate — wild and crazy or dressed up and dignified. All the downtown hotels offer New Year's parties, as do the nightclubs on the Riverfront. Prices of the events vary greatly depending upon how gala the event is. Those parties thrown by radio stations are very popular. The black-tie event held by the symphony is one of the most luxurious and includes a concert and dinner (call 621-1919.)

The United States Air and Trade Show, held each July in Dayton, is fast becoming one of the most important aviation events in the world, attracting more than 250,000 visitors a year.

Daytrips

We've spent all this time convincing you that Cincinnati is such a great place that you'd never want to leave. Now, we're going to tell you how to get away. Go figure.

Actually, you'll find plenty of good reasons to leave Cincinnati, at least for a day. Because the city is centrally located in one of the nation's most densely populated regions, it's just a short drive to many attractions. And not all of these trips are to other urban areas — by driving an hour or two, you also can find a variety of small-town pleasures and nature preserves.

This chapter organizes daytrips by the four cardinal directions. We've limited ourselves to trips you can make in roughly two hours or less by car. And even at that we couldn't include everything. For shorter excursions within the Greater Cincinnati area, see listings in our other chapters, including Attractions, Parks and Recreation and River Fun.

Here's one simple rule for this chapter: If an attraction in a nearby town is duplicated just as well in Cincinnati, you won't read about it here. And one word of warning: If you're taking daytrips north or west, take along a hot cup of joe or someone to keep you alert. The scenery along Interstates 74 and 75 north and west of Cincinnati is not exactly invigorating, though the destinations are worthwhile. Heading south or east you're more likely to enjoy the rolling hills.

Happy trails.

North

Dayton

It's getting harder all the time to tell where Cincinnati ends and Dayton begins along I-75, as West Chester to the south and Warren County to the north make their inevitable trek toward urban convergence. But once you hit the Interstate 675 interchange, you're in Dayton for sure. That's also the road you'll want to take to some of Dayton's chief attractions.

Dayton's greatest claim to fame, of course, is being the home of the Wright brothers. Orville and Wilbur had the sense to take a nice trip to the far more picturesque Outer Banks of North Carolina to make their historic flight, and somehow their airplane has made it onto North Carolina license plates, but never Ohio's. Nonetheless, that first airplane was designed in Dayton at the Wright Brothers Bicycle Shop. Aviation is today the source of Dayton's principal attraction — the U.S. Air Force Museum — and much of its economy, as the home of Wright-Patterson Air Force Base, still the largest Air Force base in the world and the primary aerospace research and development center for the U.S. Air Force.

Daytonians also invented the cash register (John Patterson), the automatic ignition for cars (Charles Kettering) and the daytime talk show (Phil Donahue). Please, stop them before they invent again! But the area's chief attractions harken back mainly to the Wright brothers. So swoop on in for some high-flying adventures. For more information, contact the **Dayton Area Chamber of Commerce**, 1 Chamber Plaza, Dayton 45402, (937) 226-1444 or the **Dayton Visitors' Bureau**, (800) 221-8234.

Carillon Historical Park
2001 S. Patterson Blvd. • (937) 293-3412

You can't miss the giant Deeds Carillon (that's a bell tower), which is Ohio's largest. But the park is also home to an interesting collection of historical exhibits, including an old lock that was part of the original Miami & Erie Canal, the Newcom Tavern (Dayton's oldest building), a one-room schoolhouse, a grist mill and a covered bridge. A replica of the Wright Brothers' bicycle shop and a plane the brothers built in 1905 — two years after the Kitty Hawk flight — also are on display. The park is open April through October, 10 AM to 6 PM Tuesday through Saturday and 1 PM to 6 PM on Sunday. A carillon concert takes place on Sunday afternoon. Admission is $1 for adults, free for those 17 and younger.

Cox Arboretum
6733 Springboro Pk. • (937) 434-9005

A stunning green sanctuary with dozens of herb and water gardens, Cox Arboretum is full of meandering streams and picturesque walking bridges. A popular spot for weddings (which explains those hikers in tuxedos), Cox Arboretum is open daily; admission is free.

Dayton Museum of Discovery
2600 DeWeese Pky. • (937) 275-7431

The Dayton Museum of Discovery, part of the city's Natural History Museum complex, is full of hands-on children's play exhibits, mazes, giant sandboxes and more. Hours are 9 AM to 5 PM Tuesday through Saturday; 9 AM to 9 PM Friday; and noon to 5 PM Sunday (closed Monday). Adult admission is $3, $1.50 for children 16 and younger.

FYI
Unless otherwise noted, the area code for all phone numbers listed in this guide is 513.

Paul Lawrence Dunbar House
219 N. Paul Lawrence Dunbar St.
• (937) 224-7061

This Victorian residence was home to one of America's most famous black poets and authors. Dunbar was born of former slaves in Dayton in 1872 and rose to prominence in American literature before he died in 1906 at age 33. The house holds Dunbar's library, manuscripts and personal effects. Hours are 9:30 AM to 4:45 PM Wednesday through Saturday and noon to 4:45 Sunday from Memorial Day through Labor Day. Fall and winter hours vary, so call ahead. Admission is $1.50; $1 for ages 6 through 12.

SunWatch
2301 W. River Rd. • (937) 268-8199

SunWatch is a reconstructed prehistoric American Indian village of the 13th century. It includes an audiovisual presentation in the visitors' center that explains the history of the excavation at this site and how most archaeologists work, which is surprisingly somewhat different from how Indiana Jones did it. Here you'll find displays that include a thatched roof council house, a typical dwelling, numerous artifacts, replicas of Indian clothing and a scale model of the village that shows how SunWatch worked as a sun calendar for its inhabitants. Hours are 9 AM to 4:30 PM Tuesday through Saturday, noon to 5 PM Sunday. Admission is $4, $3 for ages 6 through 17 and 65 and older. SunWatch is closed from December 1 through March 15.

Trapshooting Hall of Fame and Museum
601 W. National Rd., Vandalia
• (937) 898-1945

Vandalia is one tough place to live if you're a clay pigeon. Here is where you'll find exhibits that trace trapshooting history and honor such famous markspersons as Annie Oakley. It's the only known museum in the world devoted to the sport. Admission is free. Hours are 9 AM to 4 PM Monday through Friday. The museum is closed weekends and holidays. The Amateur Trapshooting Association, at the same address, holds its annual Great American World Trapshooting Tournament here each August.

United States Air and Trade Show
Dayton International Airport, I-75 at Exit 63 • (937) 898-5901

This show is held each July (on the 18th and 19th in 1998) and is the most international thing about the Dayton International Airport. Started in 1975, the show has fast become one of the most important aviation events in the world, attracting more than 250,000 visitors a year. Daring stunts and displays of state-of-the-art aircraft make this a must-see for anyone even remotely interested in flight. Call ahead to find out the time and day of precision stunt performances by the Air Force Thunderbirds.

U.S. Air Force Museum
Wright-Patterson Air Force Base, Area B
• (937) 255-3284

Pigs are about the only thing you won't find flying around here. This is the largest aviation museum in the world, holding more than 200 aircraft, missiles and other sorts of identified flying objects. *Un*identified flying objects and their inhabitants are kept in the deep freeze elsewhere on the base, according to legend.

But, seriously, you'll find plenty of real-life aircraft to keep you busy all day. Displays include early models built by the Wright Brothers, such famous World War I craft as the Sopwith Camel and B-29 Superfortresses from World War II, including the plane that dropped an A-bomb on Nagasaki in 1945. Other aircraft of special interest include a German V-2 rocket that fell short of Britain and into the North Sea, a German Junker and presidential airplanes. Video loops help illustrate several of the displays. An auditorium shows three films about flying. The museum has a good mix of hands-on and hand-off exhibits. Best of all, it's free.

The IMAX theater is a relatively recent addition that gives you the experience of an actual space flight through its six-story screen. Call (937) 253-IMAX for show times. Admission is $5, $4.50 for seniors 59 and older, $3.50 for students and $2.25 for kids 3 through 7.

This place is big. Be prepared to do some walking, and bring a stroller for the little ones. Hours are 9 AM to 5 PM daily except Thanksgiving, Christmas and New Year's Day.

Wright Brothers Bicycle Shop
22 S. Williams St. • (937) 443-0793

Come here, and the next time you're stacked up in the air over Atlanta, you'll know who to blame. The Wright Brothers Bicycle Shop is where it all began when Orville and Wilbur started piecing together that first flying machine. They took it on a 120-foot trip in Kitty Hawk, North Carolina, in 1903. Maps are available to help you on a self-guided driving tour along other outposts on the Aviation Trail. Admission is free.

Lebanon

Every region has its classic small town. Here, it's Lebanon, Ohio, chock-full of Americana and nostalgic quaintness. Lebanon is also a great shopping and dining experience — you could easily make a day of it. Here, you'll find The Golden Lamb, Ohio's oldest

eatery and inn (see our Restaurants and Hotels and Motels chapters for details).

The town itself is very handsome, full of tree-lined streets and imposing regal homes. The shopping district features one of the region's largest collection of antique and art shops and you'll discover streets just packed with other eclectic and exciting stores, as well as the publishing offices of *The Western Star*, the oldest newspaper west of the Alleghenies. Of particular note along the brick sidewalks and pavements are the following shops.

A Gentler Thyme
7 N. Broadway • 933-9997

A visit to A Gentler Thyme is an aromatic adventure. The store sells dried flowers of every conceivable sort.

Liberty Western
23 W. Main St. • 933-0900

Okay, Ohio isn't exactly the open prairie. But, hey partner, if you want to round up the cattle for a drive, head here first to outfit yourself in a complete line of Western hats, boots and clothing. Giddyup.

Pines Pet Cemetery
764 Riley Wills Rd., just off U.S. 48 • 932-2270

On the drive out of town, consider a stop at Pines Pet Cemetery, where more than 10,000 of our only-slightly-other-than-human friends rest in peace. We're talking goldfish, skunks and horses, too, as well as at least three people who chose to rest for eternity beside their beloved Fido and Tuffy. The fascinating grave markers and monuments alone are worth the stop.

Signs of Our Times
2 S. Broadway • 932-4435

Specializing in early and mid 20th-century toys, this is the shop where you'll find that nostalgic chemistry set or Captain Rocket toy for junior.

Type-tiques
20 S. Broadway • 932-5020

The age of Macs and desktop publishing put old-time letterset printers out of business. But fear not. The folks at Type-tiques recycle those nostalgic printer's type drawers and wooden printing blocks into innovative, one-of-a-kind mementos and wall hangings.

Whimsey & Nostalgia
31 W. Main St. • 932-0046

Whimsey & Nostalgia is the area's prime source for lace and finery, plus all the crafty sewing advice you could ask for.

Oxford

If Andy Hardy had gone to college in Ohio, he would have picked the charming university town of Oxford. Its traditional red brick buildings blend with a quirky modern downtown to form what is truly one of the area's most pleasant daytrips. The scenery on the way is certainly bucolic enough, with lots of rolling hills peppered with soybean and corn fields, but the true payoff is the impressive architecture that awaits in town. Poet Robert Frost once called the Miami University campus the prettiest academic institution he ever saw, and it is. (Transplants from New England will want to head here pronto to get a Yankee fix.)

Nearby is the tiny hamlet of Millville, the birthplace of Kenesaw Mountain Landis, the first commissioner of Major League Baseball, best known for banning eight White Sox players (including Shoeless Joe Jackson) for conspiring to fix the 1919 World Series with the Cincinnati Reds. We hasten to point out that White Sox players, not Reds players, were involved in the scandal and that Pete Rose was nowhere in sight. The frame house where Landis was born in a living room is still there, at 2705 Ross-Hanover Road.

Greene County

Just east of Dayton, Greene County offers a number of interesting attractions that are worth a trip or two of their own.

Blue Jacket
Stringtown Rd., Xenia • (937) 376-4358

This summertime outdoor drama at Caesar's Ford Park Amphitheater may not be exactly accurate historically. But it's an interesting show, featuring the story of Marmaduke van Swearingen, a white boy allegedly captured by the Shawnee at age 17 who became war leader for the Indian nation. Regardless of his ancestry, Blue Jacket was a crackerjack strategist who beat Gen. Arthur St. Clair in Indiana. Show times are 8 PM nightly June through Labor Day. Tickets are $12 Tuesday through Thursday, $14 Friday, Saturday and Sunday, and $8 for children 12 and younger every night. The amphitheater is 5 miles east of Xenia. Take U.S. 42 northeast from Cincinnati or I-71 north to U.S. 68 and follow the signs to Blue Jacket.

Clifton Mill
75 Water St., Clifton • (937) 767-5501

Six miles southeast of Yellow Springs on Ohio 72 is the largest operating gristmill in the United States, with an 18-foot waterwheel. Originally built in 1802, the mill has burned down twice. The current structure dates from 1869. The Millrace Restaurant on site serves breakfast and lunch daily, and you can eat pancakes from flour ground at the mill while you sit on the deck and watch the mill grind some more. Tours take you through the inner workings of how water is harnessed to operate the mill. A gift shop offers a wide variety of flour and pancake mixes to help you remember your visit.

John Bryan State Park
3790 Ohio 370 • (937) 767-1274

This 750-acre park 2 miles east of Yellow Springs is possibly the most beautiful in the western part of Ohio. The highlight is Clifton Gorge, a steep limestone gorge overlooking the Little Miami River. We do mean steep. Though the gorge's rim trail offers some great hiking, several young hikers who have strayed off the trail to try some rock climbing or gorge jumping never came back. One who did was Cornelius Darnell, a member of a party of men led by Daniel Boone who were captured by the Shawnee. He escaped his captors by jumping the 22-foot-wide narrows. You are advised not to try to duplicate this historic event. Abun-

The Kentucky Horse Park features horse shows, polo matches and world championship events.

dant natural springs and a towering old hardwood forest are among the other attractions that make this park worth the drive.

National Afro-American Museum and Cultural Center
1350 Brush Row Rd., Wilberforce
• (937) 376-4944

Opened in 1988, this museum draws researchers from across the United States. The permanent exhibit here details black history during the 1950s and early 1960s, and several temporary exhibits focus on special issues or earlier periods. Just off U.S. 42 in Wilberforce, the museum is adjacent to Central State University on the site of the old Wilberforce University campus. Hours are 9 AM to 5 PM Tuesday through Saturday and 1 PM to 5 PM Sunday. It's closed major holidays except for Martin Luther King Jr. Day. Admission is $4 for adults, $1.50 for students.

Yellow Springs
I-70 and U.S. 68

This is the closest thing you'll find to a 1960s theme park. This tiny village is home to Antioch College, a small liberal arts college with the emphasis on liberal. It has a reputation for excellent education and as a place where the revolutionary '60s meet the politically correct '90s. Not so many years ago, the college instituted a code of conduct requiring express verbal permission prior to each phase of the courtship process. Ohio's very conservative Republican senator Mike DeWine actually grew up on the outskirts of town, but lists his home town as Cedarville. Such is Yellow Springs' reputation.

Politics aside, this place is fun, with some good restaurants and specialty shops. **The Kings Yard**, in the 200 block of Xenia Avenue, is a collection of interesting specialty stores, including **No Common Scents**, featuring spices, scents, teas and gifts from around the world; **Yellow Springs Pottery**, focusing on the work of several area artists; and the **Rita Caz Jewelry Studio**. For lunch, try **Winds Cafe**, 215 Xenia Avenue, which serves meat, pasta and vegetarian dishes from around the world.

Glen Helen Nature Preserve, 405 Corry Street, is adjacent to the Antioch campus and across the road from downtown. Along the 26 miles of trails in this 1,000-acre preserve, you can find the Yellow Spring itself, plus Yellow Spring Gorge and the Little Miami River, a national scenic river that's a little more scenic here than along stretches near Cincinnati. A trailside museum, gift shop, Raptor Center and Riding Center are among other attractions.

On the outskirts of town, you won't want to miss **Young's Jersey Dairy**, 6880 Springfield-Xenia Road, a regional institution. The ice cream is great, and afterward you can go out back and thank the good cows responsible for it.

Champaign County

Cedar Bog Nature Preserve
Woodburn Rd. (between Springfield and Urbana) • (937) 484-3744

Cincinnatians may see no need to drive almost two hours to find a place that has stubbornly resisted the march of time. But we're talking natural history here, not social history. Cedar Bog is a freak of nature that merits a special trip.

The bog was left behind by the retreat of the glaciers after the Ice Age and has managed to maintain its cool, damp, boggy climate ever since. The preserve covers about 100 acres in a natural depression. Cold, alkaline spring water helps keep the bog unusually chilly, and the cold air is held in by a flow of warm air currents overhead, like an invisible serving-dish lid.

The result is a collection of plant and animal life found few other places and includes 100 rare and endangered species that couldn't survive outside the bog. Two species of spiders were found here years after they had been declared extinct. Cedar Run, which runs through the bog, is the only stream in Ohio cold enough to support brook trout. Needless to say, they won't be building an outlet mall here anytime soon. In fact, new four-lane U.S. 68 stops abruptly at Cedar Bog's fringe. The project was bogged down (sorry, couldn't resist) by a public outcry to save the corner of the bog it would have claimed.

A one-mile boardwalk traverses the bog and lets visitors look around without sinking into the muck. Two-hour tours are conducted Saturday and Sunday starting at 1 PM and 3 PM April through September. The bog is also open from 9 AM to 5 PM Wednesday through Sunday if you want to go it alone, but the tour is recommended, as the naturalist provides some good insights. You also can phone to arrange tours at other times of the year, but do be patient — the bog has one staff member. Admission is $2, $1.60 for ages 65 and older and $1 for kids 6 through 12.

Take U.S. 68 north to a left on Woodburn Road, which dead-ends at the edge of the bog parking lot and naturalist's quarters.

Columbus

If you haven't been to Columbus in about 10 years, you're in for a surprise. The "Cowtown" label put on this place in the 1970s by a local alternative newspaper no longer fits so well. For example, the trendy Short North district on High Street was several years ahead of Cincinnati's Main Street. And the Columbus City Center is bigger and flashier than Cincinnati's Tower Place.

Keep in mind that this boom has been financed in no small part by the taxpayers of the rest of Ohio, thanks to the ever-growing state government. As long as we're paying for it, we may as well stop in and enjoy it once in a while. Some highlights are listed below. The Columbus Visitors Center at Columbus City Center, (614) 221-CITY or (800) 345-4FUN, can provide more information on these attractions.

Center of Science and Industry
280 E. Broad St. • (614) 228-COSI

Four floors of interactive hands-on exhibits explore science, health, technology and history. Highlights include a Foucault pendulum, a planetarium and an electrostatic generator. Outside in Science Park is a high-wire cycle ride 20 feet off the ground on a one-inch rail (they swear you can't fall off). The rat basketball show is popular with kids. The center is open 10 AM to 5 PM Monday through Saturday and noon to 5:30 PM Sunday. Admission is $5, $3 for individuals 55 and older, kids 3 through 18 and students with ID.

Columbus City Center
111 S. Third St. • (614) 221-4900

This tri-level, 135-shop urban mall is a cut above Cincinnati's Tower Place, with such retailers as Marshall Fields, Abercrombie and Fitch, Jacobson's and a New York Metropolitan Museum of Art Store. The mall is open 10 AM to 9 PM Monday through Saturday and noon to 6 PM Sunday.

Franklin Park Conservatory and Botanical Garden
1777 E. Broad St. • (614) 645-TREE

Housed in a 12,500-square-foot glass structure built in 1895 in the style of London's Crystal Palace are a simulated tropical rain forest, Himalayan Mountains habitat, desert, Pacific island water garden and tree fern forest. Other displays include a bonsai garden and an orchid collection. It's open Tuesday through Sunday and holiday Mondays 10 AM to 5 PM. It's closed from Thanksgiving through Christmas. Admission is $4 for most folks, $3 for individuals 61 and older and students, and $2 for kids ages 4 through 11.

German Village
Off I-71 Exit 100B • no phone

Settled by Germans in the 1800s, this 233-acre restored village is MainStrasse Village but larger. You'll find lots of nice shops and scrumptious German restaurants. You can't leave Columbus without sampling a Bahama Mama, a giant sausage on a bun, at Schmidt's Sausage Haus on 240 E. Kossuth Street.

Ohio Historical Center and Ohio Village
I-71 and Seventh Ave. • (614) 297-2310

This is the core museum of the Ohio Historical Society, open year-round 9 AM to 5 PM Monday through Saturday and 10 AM to 5 PM

on Sundays and holidays except Christmas, New Year's Day and Thanksgiving, when it's closed. The best attraction here is the Ohio Village, a re-created Civil War-era town that represents a typical county seat during the 1860s. The village is open January through November 9 AM to 5 PM Wednesday through Saturday. Admission is $4, $3.20 for those 62 and older, $1 for kids 6 through 12, and half-price on Monday and Tuesday.

Ohio State Capitol
Broad and High Sts. • (614) 466-2125

After seeing sausages made in German Village, head north a few blocks to the State Capitol and see laws being made. Then decide which is worse. Actually, there's no visitors gallery, so you can't see laws being made here, but you can check out the architecture in the newly refurbished Statehouse, which is considered one of the best examples of the Doric style in the United States. A painting of the Great Seal of Ohio is in the center of the rotunda dome. There's also a collection of historical documents and portraits of Ohio's noted governors and U.S. presidents.

The rotunda is open 7 AM to 7 PM Monday through Friday and 11 AM to 5 PM Saturday and Sunday. The Senate chamber is open Monday through Friday 9 AM to 4:30 PM when the Senate is not in session. Admission as a visitor is free — if you want to come here as an elected representative, it will cost you plenty.

Ohio State Fair
717 E. 17th Ave. • (614) 644-3247

Held each August, this century-old fair is among the biggest and best in the country. Actually, it is the biggest and the best, if those folks in Texas, who think they need to have the biggest everything, would just concede. Here you'll find daily live entertainment by big-name performers and all the usual fair stuff — only more of it.

Santa Maria Replica
Batelle Riverfront Park, Marconi Blvd. and Broad St. • (614) 645-8760

This is a museum-quality, full-scale replica of the flagship of the city's namesake. Visitors get a feel for the life of a 15th-century shipmate. It's open March through December,

Tuesday through Sunday 10 AM to 5 PM (and until dusk Friday through Sunday from Memorial Day through Labor Day). Admission is $3.50, $3 for adults 60 and older and $1.50 for kids 5 through 17.

Holmes County

Amish Country
Amish Country Visitors Bureau,
• (330) 893-3467

Holmes County features one of the largest settlements of Amish in America, and indeed, a trip to this hilly farm community is like a journey back in time. Horse and buggies, barn raisings, community quilts, they're all here. Towns such as Berlin and Charm feature quaint craft, quilt and furniture shops. While in Charm, stay at the Charm Countryview Inn, owned by a Mennonite family, and dine at the delightful Der Dutchman in nearby Walnut Creek, serving up family style meals. Don't miss the town of Sugarcreek, known as the Switzerland of Ohio for its 13 cheese factories and homes styled after Swiss chalets.

South

Lexington

Hold your horses. Or ride them if you wish. But if it's horses you like, run, don't trot, to Lexington. You won't be alone. Queen Elizabeth II, sheiks from Dubai and other assorted royalty like to visit to check out the equestrian action. We've included several excellent horse farm tours as well as other outstanding attractions.

The Greater Lexington Convention and Visitors Bureau can provide you with more information. Contact them at 430 W. Vine Street, Suite 353, Lexington 45407; (606) 233-1221.

American Saddle Horse Museum
4093 Iron Works Pike • (606) 259-2746

Gen. Robert E. Lee rode a saddlebred horse, and Mr. Ed was one. Those are two good reasons why horse lovers will want to check out this museum, dedicated to

Kentucky's only native breed and the oldest registered American breed of horse. The museum offers a variety of multimedia presentations and exhibits, plus horse shows and scenic trail rides atop saddlebreds. The museum is open 9 AM to 6 PM Memorial Day through Labor Day and 9 AM to 5 PM September through May. Admission is $3 for adults, $2 for seniors 62 and older and children 7 through 12.

Claiborne Farm
Winchester Rd., Paris • (606) 233-4252

One of America's most famous horse farms, this is where mile record-holder Secretariat retired to stud and is buried. His memory lives on in more than 300 offspring. Tours are available 9 AM to 2 PM.

Historic & Horse Farm Tours
3429 Montavesta Dr. • (606) 268-2906

This tour company has a monopoly on Calumet, the farm with the red-trimmed white barns that produced eight Kentucky Derby winners. The normal tour hits Calumet, the Keeneland race track and a brood mare farm. A tour van picks up visitors at most hotels in the area. Daily tours start at 8:30 AM and 1:30 PM and the cost $18. Do call in advance because there's sometimes a wait of two weeks or more. And be forewarned that tourgoers are generally restricted to the van.

Keeneland Race Course
4201 Versailles Rd. • (606) 254-3412

Yes, they also race horses in Lexington. In fact, you'll find many travel agencies in Cincinnati that are keenly aware of this fact and offer group tours during Keeneland's scant six weeks of racing each year — three in April and three in October.

Keeneland has been called the most beautiful horse track in the world, with its manicured grounds and dogwood-shaded paddock. It also lacks a PA system, giving it something of an old-world charm. A dozen Derby winners have been acquired through Keeneland's July and September yearling sales, another big draw for serious horse traders and wannabes.

The spring season generally opens the second Saturday in April and runs six days a week (all but Monday). The fall season opens the second Saturday in October and runs five days a week (Monday and Tuesday off). General admission is $2.50. Reserved seats vary by day and season. The rails and paddock are preferred areas for people-watching, so consider the general admission ticket. If you want to eat at the Keeneland restaurant, make your reservations far in advance.

Kentucky Horse Center
3380 Paris Pike • (606) 293-1853

Not to be confused with the Kentucky Horse Park, this is a working thoroughbred training complex with a 1-mile training track and 900-seat sales pavilion. A one-hour tour gives visitors a behind-the-scenes look at the industry. Tours are offered at 9 AM, 10:30 AM and 1 PM Monday through Friday from April 1 through October 31. Cost is $10, $5 for kids 10 and younger.

Kentucky Horse Park
4089 Iron Works Pike • (606) 233-4303

The only equestrian theme park in the world, the Kentucky Horse Park's lush, rolling 1,032 acres provide a good look at the importance of the horse in Kentucky and worldwide. Man 'O War is buried beneath a statue of himself at the park entrance.

After viewing wide-screen films at the information center, visitors can tour the park on foot, aboard a shuttle or, of course, on horseback or by horse-drawn carriage. Exhibits include a working horse farm, representatives of more than 30 breeds in the Breeds Barn and Parade of Breeds, and tributes to great horses in the Hall of Champions. A 3,500-seat arena is also the site of many annual world championship events, plus regular horse shows and polo matches.

The park is open 9 AM to 5 PM daily except from November 1 through mid-March, when it's closed Monday and Tuesday. One-day general admission is $7.50 for adults and $4.50 for children 7 through 12. A combination ticket costing $9.75 for adults and $5.25 for children also gets you into the nearby American Saddle Horse Museum (see listing above). A 50-minute guided trail ride on the outskirts of the park costs $10 a person.

Mary Todd Lincoln House
585 W. Main St. • (606) 233-9999

This recently restored home is the first site in America to honor a first lady. The house offers a unique look into the early years of the wife of Abraham Lincoln. The house was originally a brick tavern constructed in 1803 and was renovated into a family dwelling by Mary's father in the 1830s. The house contains many period furnishings and personal effects of Mary's. Public tours are offered April 1 through December 15, Tuesday through Saturday, 10 AM to 4 PM. Admission is $4 for adults, $1 for children 6 through 12.

Rupp Arena
430 W. Vine St. • (606) 233-4567,
Ticket Information • (606) 233-3566,
Charg-A-Tick • (606) 233-3535

They also like their basketball in Lexington, and this is where it's played. In fact, some people think that the basketball world revolves around this 23,000-seat arena. But you'll also find Cincinnatians taking the trip down I-75 for major concerts.

Shaker Village of Pleasant Hill
U.S. Hwy. 60, 25 miles southwest of Lexington • (606) 734-5411

Pleasant Hill is the largest restored Shaker village in the United States, with 33 19th-century buildings on 2,700 acres of farmland. It was established in 1805 by a group of the United Society of Believers in Christ's Second Coming, otherwise known as the "Shakers" because of the dances that were part of their religious ceremonies. A re-creation of a Shaker service here provides a demonstration.

With the exception of a handful of people in New Hampshire, there are no more living Shakers. That's largely because the sect believed in segregation of the genders. Their rather stringent rule of no offspring put a crimp in growth of the church. The only time Shaker men and women congregated was during church services, and one of the minister's duties was to make sure nothing untoward took place during those energetic dances.

The Shakers also believed in a simple, economical lifestyle, demonstrated by the unadorned simplicity of their furniture and housewares. Little did they know these items would become hip and trendy a century later. Alas, the Shakers themselves died out and the village was closed in 1910, well before they could profit from their flair for design. The village was restored in the 1960s and today is open for tours year-round.

A self-guided tour of the whole village takes about two hours. Included are working furniture, weaving, candlemaking and broommaking studios. You can also take a trip aboard the *Dixie Belle* sternwheeler. Meals featuring generous helpings of authentic Shaker and Kentucky country cuisine are well worth the $7.50 a head for breakfast, $6.50 to $9.50 for lunch and $13.25 to $17.75 for dinner. Lodging is also available in 15 restored buildings.

The village is open year-round except Christmas Eve and Christmas Day, 9:30 AM to 5 PM. Some exhibition buildings are closed November through March. Admission is $6 for adults, $4 for kids 12 through 17, $2 for kids 6 through 11. The family rate is $22. Combination tickets that include the riverboat excursion are $11.50 for adults, $6 for youths, $3 for children and $30 for families.

Shopping

Many Cincinnatians will find it hard to believe, but they do things in Lexington besides raise horses and play basketball. The **Civic Center Shops**, 410 W. Vine Street in the heart of downtown, is a favorite stop, featuring three levels of specialty shops. **Victorian Square**, 401 W. Main at Broadway, is a downtown area of 16 restored Victorian buildings with more than 20 shops featuring upscale clothes and other specialty items. And the **Market Place**, 325 W. Main Street, is another tri-level shopping complex anchored by a carousel.

Three Chimneys Farm
Old Frankfort Pike • (606) 873-7053

Seattle Slew, the 1977 Triple Crown winner, stands stud at this picturesque farm. Call for times when the farm is open to the public.

Louisville

The Kentucky Derby at Churchill Downs is clearly the big draw, but there's more to Louisville than mint juleps and fast horses. Note, the "s" in Louisville is silent. So are all the vowels when natives pronounce it. The correct pronunciation is "Louie-ville" for out-of-towners and "Lou-a-vull" for natives.

While in town, check out the **West Main Street Historic Cultural and Arts District** between the 500 and 900 blocks downtown. This is the largest collection of 19th-century cast-iron storefronts this side of Soho in New York City.

You can contact the **Louisville Convention and Visitors Bureau** at (800) 626-5646 or, in Kentucky, (800) 633-3384.

FYI

Unless otherwise noted, the area code for all phone numbers listed in this guide is 513.

Churchill Downs
700 Central Ave. • (502) 636-4400

Lexington may have all the horses, but Louisville's got the big race. The Kentucky Derby, the first and foremost leg of the Triple Crown, is run the first Saturday of each May. The derby has been run on this course since 1875. The track hosts other thoroughbred races from the last week in April to the first week in July and from the end of October to the end of November.

The waiting list for Kentucky Derby tickets is very long, but you can always join the throngs in the infield. Your best bet for a grandstand seat is any day but Derby day. Admission is $3 for clubhouse, $2 for grandstand. Reserved seats are $2 extra. And parking is $2.

The **Kentucky Derby Museum**, (502) 637-1111, is adjacent to Gate One at the racetrack and houses numerous racing artifacts and a 360-degree audiovisual re-creation of the Derby. The museum is open daily 9 AM to 5 PM except on Derby weekend, Thanksgiving and Christmas. Admission is $6, $5 for those 55 and older and $2 for kids 5 through 12.

INSIDERS' TIP

If you're going to Columbus, save some time for shopping on the way there or back. A popular stop is the outlet malls at the Jeffersonville exits off Interstate 71.

Photo: United States Air Force Museum

More than 200 flying machines are featured at the U.S. Air Force Museum.

Colonel Harland Sanders Museum
1441 Gardiner Ln. • (502) 456-8352

If you were a chicken, you probably wouldn't think this was such a great place to visit. But here's the place to get the lowdown on the whole Col. Sanders story, even though it actually started in Corbin, not Louisville. What are the 11 herbs and spices? And how did he keep that suit so white when he was handling chicken all day? Exhibits include the Colonel's original pressure cooker. It's free and open

Monday through Thursday 8 AM to 4:45 PM and Friday 8 AM to 3 PM.

Falls of the Ohio State Park and National Wildlife Conservation Area
Clarksville, Ind. • (812) 280-9970

Heading across the river from Louisville will take you back in time, back even farther than when you started out in Cincinnati, some 350 million years in fact. This is the largest exposed fossil bed in the world. It's best viewed from the

Indiana shore, where parking is available along Riverside Drive near the upper gates of the McAlpine Dam. Accessibility to the beds is best from August through October, the dry months, when the Ohio River is at its lowest. But the beds aren't always visible because the river, like the weather, is a little erratic around these parts.

The beds are part of a 950-acre park that also contains a coral reef of geological import. The interpretive center is open 9 AM to 5 PM daily and every 30 minutes shows a film on the history of the falls.

Hadley Pottery
1570 Story Ave. • (502) 584-2171

In historic Butchertown, this pottery makes handpainted stoneware using designs created by Mary Alice Hadley in the 1940s. Free guided tours are given Monday through Friday at 2 PM, if the temperature is not hotter than 85. The pottery is open for business Monday through Friday 8 AM to 4:40 PM and Saturday from 9 AM to 12:30 PM.

John Conti Coffee Museum
4023 Bardstown Rd. • (502) 499-8602

This is the only coffee museum in the country and contains displays of 1,500 coffee-related items, including antique grinders, roasters and tins. Makes you a little jittery just thinking about it, eh? The museum is free and open Monday through Friday 9 AM to 5 PM.

Kentucky Art & Craft Gallery
609 W. Main St. • (502) 589-0102

Many examples of the region's rich craft tradition are displayed in this gallery. It's free and open Monday through Saturday 10 AM to 4 PM.

Louisville Slugger Tour
**Hillerich & Bradsby Co., 1525
Charleston-New Albany Rd.,
Jeffersonville, Ind. • (502) 585-5229
ext. 227**

It could be! It may be! It is! It's the one and only place where they manufacture Louisville Sluggers. The only point of confusion is that the factory is actually in Indiana, just across the Ohio River from Louisville in Jeffersonville. It was moved from Louisville in 1974. This stop will surely clear the bases for any baseball fan in your household. If you played baseball as a kid, you probably went through your share of Louisville Sluggers. That is, unless you were a post-1970 aluminum bat kid and you didn't, like Robert Redford in *The Natural*, hand-turn your own bat out of a tree felled by lightning. So there's nostalgia galore here, including a museum featuring a bat used by Babe Ruth.

The plant is open free to the public Monday through Friday, with tours at 8, 9, and 10 AM and 1 and 2 PM. But it's closed the first two weeks in June, the first two weeks of July and Christmas week.

Louisville Stoneware
731 Brent St. • (502) 582-1900

The home of the famous handpainted dinnerware offers free tours Monday through Friday 10:30 AM to 2:30 PM. The sales room is open Monday through Saturday 8 AM to 4:30 PM.

East

Adams County

Adams County may be one of Ohio's poorest in money terms, but it's among the state's richest in attractions and natural beauty — including one of the nation's largest and most elaborate prehistoric Indian mounds, southwest Ohio's most beautiful nature preserve and one of the region's favorite getaways.

Blake Pharmacy
**206 North Market St., West Union
• (937) 544-2451**

This unpretentious drugstore houses one of the state's few remaining authentic soda fountains. Ask and they'll gladly prepare you a raspberry or vanilla Coke, made the way our parents remember it. Some 30 weddings have been performed in the aisles of this drugstore, if for no other reason than it's the most notable tourist attraction in sleepy West Union.

Edge of Appalachia
Nature Preserve
**19 Abner Hollow Rd., Lynx
• (937) 544-2880**

Stephen Ostrander, formerly of the Ohio Department of Natural Resources, rates this the all-around best nature preserve in Southwestern Ohio in his book, *Natural Acts Ohio*. This group of 12 preserves totals more than 10,500 acres about 10 miles east of West Union and along the actual geographic edge of the Appalachian Plateau. Of the 12 preserves, Lynx Prairie, Buzzardsroost Rock and The Wilderness carry the designation of National Historic Landmark from the U.S. Department of Interior. Only Lynx Prairie and Buzzardsroost are open to the public.

Buzzardsroost has the steepest topography in Ohio and provides what Ostrander calls one of the state's best natural panoramic views. This windswept roost of turkey vultures also served as a lookout for Native Americans. Overall, the preserve protects about 100 rare or endangered plants and animals. Take Ohio 125 east to Lynx, then turn south on Tulip Road for a half-mile to East Liberty Church.

Lewis Mountain Herbs
2345 Ohio Hwy. 247, West Union • (937) 549-2484

Judy and John Lewis have been tending their herb farm for well over a decade now. Their greenhouse complex and gift shop feature hundreds of well-known and exotic fresh herbs for cooking, medicinal purposes and just plain nibbling. The farm is located atop a hillside (you'll know you're near it when you pass the volunteer firehouse) and is a perfect spot for a picnic or Kodak moment.

Murphin Ridge Inn
750 Murphin Ridge Rd., West Union • (937) 544-2263

This country inn in a restored 1810 house is one of the best quick getaways from the Cincinnati area or a good place to stop in for a meal while visiting the area's other attractions. Only nine years old, it has quickly become a popular stop for guests from throughout the region.

The inn has 10 rooms, two with fireplaces and all furnished with antique reproductions by The Workshops of David T. Smith, the Cincinnati area's foremost maker of reproduction furniture. One room is used as an art gallery to show the work of Adams County artists. Nearby on Wheat Ridge Road are a quilt shop and Miller's Bakery and Furniture, with Amish

baked goods and crafts. Innkeepers Sherry and Darryl McKenney can direct you to other craft and food stores.

The setting is quiet and pastoral, with plenty of privacy and three hiking trails on site. More modern amenities include a pool and tennis court. Meeting rooms are available, and the entire inn can be reserved with sufficient notice. Meals are good Amish country cooking and moderately priced. But keep in mind that the county is dry.

Make reservations before you go and make them several months in advance of fall foliage season in mid-to-late October.

Serpent Mound
Ohio Hwy. 73, 4 miles northwest of Locust Grove • (937) 587-2796

Atop a ridge along Brush Creek, this mound, in the shape of a snake with an egg in its mouth, is nearly ¼-mile long and as high as 5 feet in spots. The best view is from the observation tower, but keep in mind that the prehistoric Indians didn't have this luxury when building the mound. A museum and picnic facilities also are on site. The park is open daily 9:30 AM to 8 PM Memorial Day through Labor Day. From April 1 through the day before Memorial Day and from Labor Day through October 31 it's open Monday through Friday 10 AM to 5 PM and 10 AM to 7 PM Saturday and Sunday. Admission is $4 per private vehicle, $3.20 if the passenger is 65 or older.

Highland County

Fort Hill State Memorial
Ohio Hwy. 41, a half-mile south of Ohio 753 • (937) 588-3221

The ancient Hopewell Indians are believed to have built the earthworks that form this "fort" centuries before Europeans arrived in this area. Though this Highland County site is owned by the Ohio Historical Society, it's also one of southwest Ohio's most beautiful nature preserves, according to Ostrander (see listing for Edge of Appalachia Nature Preserve above). It's a great place for birding and has one of Ohio's best botanical collections.

The 2-mile Fort Trail is a fairly easy hike and gets you to the earthworks, the main attraction for history buffs. The 4.5-mile trail that leads to Baker Fork Gorge and the earthworks is far more challenging, with numerous geological wonders. Even deeper are the Deer and Buckeye Trails, which branch from the Baker Fork Gorge trail and include a 350-foot ascent during a half-mile stretch.

Admission to the park is free and it's open daily, dawn to dusk.

Augusta, Ripley and Maysville

Augusta and Maysville in Kentucky, with Ripley tucked in-between on the Ohio side of the river, make up a triad of picturesque river towns along a 20-mile span of the Ohio, and they're well worth a trip.

You can visit each of these cities separately over time, or, if you're ambitious, you can hit them all in a day. Follow U.S. 52 and its parallel highway on the south shore of the river, Kentucky. 8. You can cross the river via the bridge between Aberdeen, Ohio, and Maysville or via ferry ($5 each way) between U.S. 52 just west of Higginsport and Augusta. The ferry is the only river crossing in the 63 miles between Cincinnati and Maysville. Keep a keen eye on the road for a sign that says "Augusta, KY, 1 Mile" and points toward the river. The ferry runs 8 AM to 6 PM Monday through Friday and 9 AM to 6 PM Saturday and Sunday.

Augusta

This pretty river town in Kentucky, which dates to 1780, was inadvertently built on the burial ground of an ancient vanished race of unusually large Indians. Residents regularly unearth shards of pottery and arrowheads when they plant their begonias.

Augusta is also home to a variety of antique shops. Of special interest is the **Pied-**mont **Art Gallery**, 115 W. Riverside Drive, a restored home that houses the works of regional artists and artisans. It's open year-round noon to 5 PM Thursday through Sunday or by appointment. Call (606) 756-2216.

While in town, eat at **The Beehive**, 101 W. Riverside Drive, a restored 1796 building with a fantastic restaurant operated by Cuban native Luciano Moral.

Ripley

Ripley, believe it or not, is Ohio's only burley tobacco market. As you drive in on U.S. 52, you'll pass row after row of the deadly weed planted all the way to the river. Annual auctions are held here from morning to early afternoon from mid-November to January, except for Christmas week.

This is also home to the **John Rankin House** (follow the signs off U.S. 52 on the west side of town), where the Rev. John Rankin, in cahoots with a farmer on the Kentucky shore, helped more than 2,000 slaves to freedom during the 1850s and 1860s. Documentary evidence confirms an account in *Uncle Tom's Cabin* of a runaway slave girl, Eliza, who escaped pursuers to the Rankin House by leaping from ice floe to ice floe along the Ohio River with a baby in her arms. That is what you call motivated. The Rankin House is open noon to 5 PM Wednesday through Sunday from Memorial Day through Labor Day and the same hours on weekends only during September and October.

Make time for a stop at **Moyer's Winery**, a scenic winery and (just as notably) a restaurant about 15 miles past Ripley in Manchester [3859 U.S. 52, (937) 549-2957]. Ken and Mary Moyer have been growing the grapes and serving up regional American cuisine on the Ohio River for a quarter-century. There are lots of gazebos and porches on which to sip wine, or lemonade if you're the designated driver. Open Monday through

---

INSIDERS' TIP

Kentucky may hold the record for offbeat museums, from the Colonel Sanders Museum and the John Conti Coffee Museum in Louisville, to the Patton Museum of Cavalry and Armor in Fort Knox, Museum of Coca-Cola Memorabilia in Elizabethtown and the National Corvette Museum in Bowling Green.

Thursday 11:30 AM to 9 PM and Friday and Saturday 11:30 AM to 10 PM.

Maysville

One of the oldest settlements on the Ohio River, Maysville was settled in 1784 by the Virginia legislature as a supply point for settlers coming down the Ohio River. Daniel Boone's family operated a tavern here for a while, and some of his relatives are buried behind the **Maysville Public Library**, 221 Sutton Street.

While in Maysville, you'll want to try transparent pie, a pudding-like dessert peculiar to this area. Transparent pie central is **Magee's Bakery**, 212 Market Street, open Tuesday through Saturday 8:30 AM to 5 PM.

Burley tobacco is big here too. In fact, it's the world's second-largest burley market after Lexington. Auctions are conducted from mid-November through mid-January, except Thanksgiving and Christmas weeks.

Antique shops, galleries and boutiques dot the center of this charming little river town. The place to eat is **Caproni's**, at the foot of Rosemary Clooney Street next to the railroad depot.

For more information, call or write the **Maysville-Mason County Chamber of Commerce**, 15½ W. Second Street, Maysville, Kentucky 45106; (606) 564-5534.

West

Nashville, Indiana

Nashville, the county seat of Brown County, is one of the Tri-state area's major arts and crafts centers, with more than 90 specialty shops, seven antique stores, 10 art galleries, 16 restaurants and a dozen ice-cream and candy stores. It's a pretty sweet life for the town's 700 inhabitants, who cater to thousands of visitors who flock here mainly from Cincinnati and Indianapolis. Of particular culinary interest is **The Ordinary**, a restaurant that is anything but (try the pheasant and other Colonial dishes).

Fall foliage season in mid-to-late October is peak season. And the town is packed. Late spring and summer are the best times to visit if you just want to check out the art and entertainment. Holiday shopping season is also popular without being quite as hectic as October.

Horse-drawn carriage rides are available from **Alexander Carriage Rides** on the N. Van Buren Street main drag. Two country music halls also beckon fans from miles around. The **Country Time Music Hall**, a mile east of town on Indiana 46, is in a hand-pegged barn. The **Little Nashville Opry**, three-quarters of a mile southwest of town on Ind. 46, brings in big name acts from March to November.

For more information, contact the **Brown County Chamber of Commerce** at 37 W. Main Street, Nashville, Indiana 47448; (812) 988-6647.

Brown County Art Gallery Association
1 Artist Dr. • (812) 988-4609

The association presents excellent art exhibits featuring artists from Nashville's earliest art colony days of the '20s and '30s. It's open 10 AM to 5 PM Monday through Saturday and noon to 5 PM on Sunday.

Brown County Art Guild
Van Buren St. • (812) 988-6185

Here's another of the better galleries on the Van Buren Street main drag. The art is for sale and admission is free. The gallery is open March through December from 10 AM to 5 PM Monday through Saturday and noon to 5 PM Sunday. It's open weekends in January and February, 10 AM to 5 PM Saturday and noon to 5 PM Sunday.

Brown County Playhouse
Van Buren St. • (812) 988-2123

Indiana University students perform Broadway musicals, dramas and children's plays here from June through October at 8 PM daily. Call for ticket prices.

Brown County State Park and Abe Martin Lodge
Ind. 46 • (812) 988-7316

Located two miles east of Nashville, this park and lodge are popular stops for visitors. Cabins are basic, but family cabins have cooking facilities. Rates are very reasonable. Book way in advance for the fall foliage season.

John Dillinger Historical Museum
Corner of Van Buren and Franklin Sts.
• (812) 988-7172

What is probably the most macabre museum in Indiana is a must-see. The notorious bank robber hailed from these parts; exhibits include wax figures, the trousers Dillinger wore the night the FBI gunned him down, and even a replica of the bullet-ridden corpse. The museum is open daily 10 AM to 6 PM, closed major holidays. Admission is $3 and well worth it.

FYI

Unless otherwise noted, the area code for all phone numbers listed in this guide is 513.

The Story Inn
Ind. 46 • no phone

The tiny hamlet of Story (pop. 7), about 10 miles from Nashville, features a wonderful restaurant housed in an old tin-sided general store. Antique tools and toys line the shelves, but the real star of the place is its regional American menu; the fare is delicious and modestly priced.

Indianapolis, Indiana

Some folks in Cincinnati may kiddingly use the term "Indianoplace." But let's face it. This is the closest place for NBA basketball. Its children's museum is one of the best in the United States. And, of course, there's that race they have here.

Children's Museum
13th and N. Meridian Sts.
• (317) 924-5431

Sure, Cincinnati's got one, too. But this is perhaps the biggest and best children's museum in the world. Next to the Indy 500, it's the city's biggest draw. Major attractions include the SpaceQuest Planetarium and the Lilly Center for Exploration, designed by teens for kids to explore a variety of topics. Dinosaur replicas, full-scale and model trains, a carousel with goats, giraffes and lions in addition to horses, and a performing arts theater are other big attractions.

The museum is open 10 AM to 5 PM Monday through Saturday (until 8 PM Thursday, when it's free from 5 to 8 PM) and Sunday noon to 5 PM. It's closed Monday from September through May, plus Thanksgiving and Christmas. Admission is $6, $5 for those 60 and older and $3 for ages 2 through 17. Admission is free between 5 and 8 PM on Thursday and on Martin Luther King Jr.'s birthday and President's Day. The planetarium costs an extra $2, and the carousel is 50¢ a go-round.

Eiteljorg Museum of American Indian & Western Art
500 W. Washington St. • (317) 636-9378

The Western collection includes works of Georgia O'Keeffe, Frederic Remington and members of the original Taos, New Mexico, art colony. The Indian collection includes crafts and artifacts from throughout North America. The museum is open June through August from Monday through Saturday 10 AM to 5 PM and Sunday noon to 5 PM. The rest of the year it's closed on Monday. Admission is $3, $2.50 for those 65 and older and students, and $1.50 for kids 5 through 17. The family rate is $10. Admission is more during special events.

Indianapolis Motor Speedway
4790 W. 16th St. • (317) 481-8500

You may have heard of the Indianapolis 500. Every year on the Sunday before Memorial Day, around a half-million people jam this 2.5-mile oval to watch cars going around in circles very fast. Time trials in early May are

INSIDERS' TIP

There are other burgs named Cincinnati, of course, should you tire of this one (horrors!). There's Cincinnati, Arkansas (pop. 401), and Cincinnati, Iowa (pop. 363). But the only Cincinnati within easy driving distance of Cincinnati, Ohio, is Cincinnati, Indiana (pop. 25), which has a church, a library and "a neat little lookout tower."

another big draw — you can see the cars without so many other people around. There's also an 18-hole golf course inside and around the track, but forget tee times on Memorial Day weekend.

Call April 1 for a ticket order form for the Indy 500. Return the form ASAP, as ticket availability is based in part on how early you apply. Prices range from $30 to $100 (for the paddock penthouse).

The **Auto Racing Hall of Fame and Museum**, appropriately enough, is here too, displaying many of the winning cars and related memorabilia. A film about the track's history and highlights is shown every half-hour. The museum is open daily 9 AM to 5 PM. Museum admission is $2, free for those 15 and younger. A bus tour of the track is another $2.

Madame Walker Center
617 Indiana Ave. • (317) 236-2099

This restored four-story theater is embellished with the African and Egyptian motifs loved by Madame C. J. Walker, America's first female self-made millionaire, who also was black. This was once the place where Louis Armstrong and Dinah Washington performed and today is the center of a district of small jazz clubs. "Jazz on the Avenue" takes place here every Friday evening. Tours are available by appointment. Admission is $2, $1 for students.

Market Square Arena
300 E. Market St. • (317) 639-2112

The Pacers play here. Call the number above for tickets, which aren't particularly hard to come by unless the Pacers are playing the Chicago Bulls.

RCA Dome
100 S. Capitol Ave. • (317) 262-3410

One of the few air-supported domed stadiums in the United States, this one is home to the Colts and site of numerous concerts and conventions that draw Cincinnatians. It also houses the National Track and Field Hall of Fame. Check local papers for a list of events.

Metamora, Indiana

Whitewater Canal State Historic Site
U.S. 52, just south of town
• (317) 647-6512

Once a booming canal town, Metamora declined with the advent of the railroad. In the past four decades, however, the town's old gristmill has been restored, log cabins built and a 14-mile section of the canal reopened as a tourist attraction. The **Whitewater Canal State Memorial** is on the National Register of Historic Places.

The *Ben Franklin*, a replica canal boat, takes visitors on a 25-minute ride for a $2 admission fee (free for kids 3 and younger). The restored 1845 gristmill is open Tuesday through Saturday 9 AM to 5 PM and Sunday 1 to 5 PM from mid-March through mid-December. Admission is free.

Two good country-cooking restaurants also await here. The **Hearthstone Restaurant** is on the east end of town on U.S. 52 and **The Mounds** is 11 miles east of Metamora on U.S. 52.

Madison, Indiana

This 19th-century town, a major river port in the Old Northwest Territory, now attracts thousands of tourists with its bountiful historic homes and churches. The **Madison Area Visitors Center**, 301 East Main (800) 559-2956, offers a variety of walking tours and maps. Of particular note on the tour is the **J.F.D. Lanier Mansion and Gardens,** a National Historic Landmark. The town has history aplenty: Visit a vintage tavern or the office of a frontier physician, or watch tinsmiths and broommakers at work. The area also abounds in waterfalls and towering limestone cliffs.

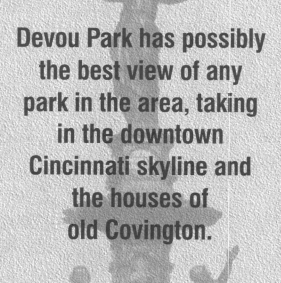

Devou Park has possibly
the best view of any
park in the area, taking
in the downtown
Cincinnati skyline and
the houses of
old Covington.

Parks and Recreation

You need never be bored in Greater Cincinnati! There are plenty of recreational opportunities — indoor and out. We've included in this chapter an overview of parks, water activities, sports, health clubs, and lots of other fun things to do and places to go.

Parks and Nature Preserves

Though it's one of the nation's oldest and most developed industrial areas, Greater Cincinnati is blessed with an abundance of well-preserved natural beauty, thanks to some forward-thinking local governments and private philanthropists. In addition to numerous parks with extensive recreation facilities, you'll find thousands of acres of nature preserves that offer limited access to humans so as to offer unlimited access to the flora and fauna. Besides locally run parks, the Cincinnati area is home to at least five state parks. Combined, these green spaces provide the opportunity to enjoy just about every outdoor pursuit imaginable, including backpacking, biking, canoeing, Frisbee golf, hunting, fishing, downhill and cross-country skiing, and more.

Foresight obviously was once a hallmark of the City of Cincinnati and Hamilton County governments, since this most densely populated portion of the Tri-state area has some of the best and most extensive parks and parkland. Taxpayers in the surrounding counties are a little tighter with a buck, and their governments got into the parkland acquisition game later, when land was more expensive. The outlying counties do have parks, certainly.

But most of the parkland outside Hamilton County is owned by the states of Ohio or Kentucky. The Cincinnati Nature Center, one of Clermont County's largest parks and one of the most beautiful nature preserves in the area, is privately owned.

Once upon a time in Cincinnati, there was an invisible barrier between the East Side and the West Side. And nowhere was this barrier more evident than in the park system. You were no more likely to find an East Side family picnicking at, say, Farbach-Werner Nature Preserve in Colerain than you were to find a West Side couple strolling at Woodland Mound in Anderson. It simply took too much time and hassle to drive cross-county.

All that changed in late 1997 with the opening of the last leg of the Ronald Reagan Cross-County Highway, which links Colerain in the far West with Montgomery in the East and makes it possible, for the first time, to cross Hamilton County in 17 minutes instead of the 50 minutes it took on stop-and-go city streets. Now the invisible wall is down . . . far-East Siders can zip to the wiffleball fields at Triple Creek in just a few minutes, while far-West Siders can flock to the fishing boats at Lake Isabella in mere moments. Call it park parity. Wherever you choose to live in Cincinnati, you can now call every preserve your neighborhood park.

Surprisingly, this new concrete roadway is having a positive impact on the environment — or at least, on the park system. The highway passes directly by the entrances of many of the region's green spaces (Sharon Woods, Winton Woods, Lake Isabella, Kroger Hills Prairie, Richardson Forest Preserve, for example) and provides links to many more.

Greater Cincinnati has many more parks than we could possibly cover here. So what follows is a listing of the best parks in Ohio and Northern Kentucky — ones you might drive out of your own neighborhood or out of your way to visit. Unless otherwise noted, parks are open to the public year-round, dawn to dusk.

FYI

Unless otherwise noted, the area code for all phone numbers listed in this guide is 513.

Ohio

Cincinnati

The City of Cincinnati alone has 138 parks comprising more than 5,000 acres and ranging from one-square-block playgrounds to 1,466-acre Mount Airy Forest, the largest municipal park and first municipal forest in the United States. Call the City of Cincinnati Parks Board at 352-4080 to reserve park facilities.

Airport Playfield
Beechmont and Wilmer Aves.
• 321-6500

You can watch the planes take off from Lunken Airport as you walk or bike along the park's 6.5-mile trail or play the par 3 golf course and driving range. Bike rental is available if you don't want to bring your own. Children will love the "Land of Make Believe," one of the more extensive playgrounds in the area.

Ault Park
End of Observatory Ave. • no phone

The pavilion at this 143-acre park is a Hyde Park landmark. The attractively landscaped park is a great place for walks, Frisbee tossing and picnics. Each May it also becomes the site of the Greater Cincinnati Flower and Garden Show, the nation's largest outdoor garden show, and it hosts the city's premier Celtic Festival each September.

Bicentennial Commons, Sawyer Point, and Yeatman's Cove
Between the Ohio River and Pete Rose Way • no phone

These adjacent parks offer the best all-around recreation facilities of any city park. Among the attractions at the 22-acre Bicentennial Commons, opened during the city's 200th anniversary in 1988, are a superior playground, a dozen tennis courts, the famous/infamous flying pigs sculpture, fishing piers, a rink for roller-skating and ice-skating, a boathouse and rowing center, and the Procter & Gamble Performance Pavilion, site of free summer concerts (check the entertainment section in local newspapers for shows).

The Serpentine Wall along the edge of Yeatman's Cove is a great place for warm-weather lolling, frolicking and river-watching. Parking costs $2, but it's well worth the investment. Or you can park for free at the Public Landing at the western edge of the parks.

Burnet Woods
Clifton Ave. and Dr. Martin Luther King Dr. • no phone

Across the street from the University of Cincinnati and Hebrew Union College, this park is a natural favorite with college students. But the 89-acre park is also popular with locals for its hiking trails, picnic shelters, small lake and nature center. It's wise to avoid this particular park after dusk, however.

Eden Park
Access from Kemper Ln., Victory Pky. or Gilbert Ave. • no phone

The park's name came from the land's original owner, Nicholas Longworth, who called it the Garden of Eden. One trip here and you'll see why. Though it's not loaded with recreation areas, this 186-acre Mount Adams park is one of the most beautiful urban parks in the United States. Eden Park gets four stars as a place to take a date for a picnic.

The park also is the center of the city's cultural life, as home to the Playhouse in the Park, Seasongood Pavilion, Krohn Conservatory and Cincinnati Art Museum. (See our Arts and Attractions chapters.) The pavilion band shell is the site of frequently packed summer concerts in the Mayor's Summer Concert Series. (Check the entertainment listings in local newspapers for times and details.) Krohn Conservatory, one of the nation's largest public greenhouses, offers a tropical rainforest, a rushing 20-foot waterfall, plus orchids, floral displays, a cacti exhibit and more.

Mirror Lake here is the most picturesque place in Cincinnati for winter ice-skating. And an adjacent playground is one of the best in the city park system.

Mount Airy Forest
5083 Colerain Ave. · 352-4094

This 1,466-acre park is the largest municipal park in the United States and became the first municipal forest when established by the City of Cincinnati in 1911. Today it's a natural haven and playground for West Siders, with miles of hiking trails, a Frisbee golf course, numerous picnic shelters and play areas. Mount Airy Arboretum features displays of azaleas, flowering crab apples, lilacs and rhododendron. The forest itself boasts a million hardwoods and conifers. A giant "medieval castle" in Mount Airy Forest is actually a masonry wall that hides 14 water towers sitting atop the highest point in Hamilton County.

Mount Echo Park
Off Elberon Ave. · no phone

This park offers one of the best views of the city. With several shelters, it's a great place for family outings and picnics. There's a small playground and basketball and tennis courts.

Hamilton County

Hamilton County deserves some hearty thanks for its generosity from residents of the other relatively park-poor Ohio counties and the rest of the Tri-state. Not only does Hamilton County operate 16 parks totaling nearly 13,000 acres, but it charges the same annual $3 parking fee to residents and nonresidents alike ($1 for a onetime pass). What's more, the county's biggest and best parks — Miami Whitewater Forest, Winton Woods, Sharon Woods and Woodland Mound — are quite convenient for residents of Dearborn, Butler, Warren and Clermont counties, respectively. All parks are open dawn to dusk, 365 days a year (some gift and nature shops are closed holidays). Pets on leashes are permitted in all parks.

The county also offers an extensive program of special events and enrichment activities at the parks. Watch for the park district's "Evergreen" insert, which comes out in *The Cincinnati Enquirer* every two months. For other scheduling or event information, call the Hamilton County Park District at 521-PARK, Ext. 67.

Juilfs Park
8249 Clough Pike, Anderson · 474-0003

This Anderson park, which also attracts its fair share of folks from the west side of Clermont County, has one of the East Side's best playgrounds, plus soccer and baseball/softball fields and a walking trail. Watch the papers or call for times for the summer movies here, which are free. Nice deal.

Miami Whitewater Forest
Access from New Haven, Dry Fork and Oxford Rds., Harrison · 367-4774

This 3,906-acre park is the largest in the Hamilton County Park District. In addition to over 3 miles of nature paths, it has a 7.8-mile multipurpose jogging/bicycling/skating/walking trail, a 1.2-mile inner loop for the less adventurous, horseback riding trails, a boathouse and lake, boat fishing, campground, Frisbee golf course, playgrounds, a visitors center, gift shop and snack bar. Pirate Cove is a fun "sprayground," with a cascading waterfall and water cannons. Located in northwest Hamilton County, the park is also easily accessible to residents of Dearborn County, Indiana, just off Exit 3 of I-74.

Sharon Woods Park and Sharon Woods Village
U.S. 42, Sharonville · 521-7275

One of the larger and better-equipped Hamilton County parks, Sharon Woods is also popular with visitors from Butler and Warren counties. The 755-acre park is a great site for fossil hunting . . . but don't take them home with you. Other attractions include a hiking and biking trail around the lake, a fitness trail, a boathouse and many picnic areas. The gorge trail provides a good 1.25-mile nature hike past small waterfalls. The water park includes an elephant fountain and pedal boats.

Also within the park is Sharon Woods Village, which has restored 19th-century buildings brought from other parts of Southwest

Ohio, including a medical office exhibiting Civil War medical equipment and a barn with period equipment. The village is open Wednesday through Friday 10 AM to 4 PM and Saturday through Sunday 1 to 5 PM from May through October. Admission is $5 for adults, $3 for adults 62 and older, $2 for kids 6 through12, and free for kids 5 and younger.

Winton Woods
Winton Rd. and Lake Forest Dr., Greenhills • 521-7275

This 2,628-acre park, which completely surrounds the city of Greenhills, is the biggest and most popular park in the Hamilton County Park District. Because it's only a few minutes from the county line, it's also popular with Butler County residents.

The park has a 3-mile paved hike/bike trail (bike rental is available), a bridle trail and a riding center on the south side of Winton Lake, along with a dozen picnic areas, a 1-mile fitness trail, a boathouse, nine shelters, an 18-hole Frisbee golf course and a regular golf course.

Parky's Farm, a combination play farm and petting zoo, is a great attraction for kids, with goats, pigs, chickens, horses and other farm animals in abundance. Horse rides ($1) and an indoor playground inside a barn (admission $1.50) are also available. (See our Kidstuff chapter.)

Woodland Mound Park
Access from Kellogg Ave. or Nordyke Rd., Anderson • 474-0580

Stephen Ostrander, author of *Natural Acts Ohio*, rates the view from Woodland Mound among the best scenic overlooks in Ohio. But there's more to do here than look around. The park has a great playground, two low-key hiking trails of 1 mile and 0.5 mile, a well-regarded golf course, an outdoor concert area where the Cincinnati Symphony Orchestra and the Cincinnati Pops hold occasional free concerts, ballfields and a snack bar. Because it sits on a steep hillside over the river, Woodland Mound almost always has a good enough breeze to fly a kite.

The Seasongood Nature Center includes nature exhibits, wildlife viewing windows and a gift/bookshop.

Butler County

Hueston Woods State Park and Nature Preserve
Ohio 732, College Corner
• (513) 523-6347

This 3,596-acre forest straddles the Butler and Preble county line just off Ohio 732, north of Oxford. It has a popular lodge and restaurant, golf course, picnic areas, camping, fishing, swimming pools, a nature center and a pioneer farm museum. A 200-acre nature preserve within the park is a great place for hiking and bird watching (150 species have been spotted here). The park also has a lake for boating. Boat rentals are available.

Clermont County

Cincinnati Nature Center
4949 Tealtown Rd., Glen Este
• 831-1711

The beauty of this private, nonprofit nature preserve inspired the 1969 book *The Inland Island* by Josephine Winslow Johnson. Today that name is more apt than ever. The 1,425-acre preserve is an oasis of nature encircled by rapid development in western Clermont County.

Hiking is the main activity here, since the center is dedicated purely to conservation and outdoor education. You can choose from 15 miles of trails that range from the wheelchair-accessible Stanley Rowe All Persons Trail to some fairly long and steeply sloped trails. Scenery runs the gamut from open meadows to fairly deep woods, though most of the center is a relatively young second-growth forest. Do pick up a trail map at the Rowe Building, because it's not hard to get lost in the winding trails. Take it from one who knows.

The Nature Center is of special interest to birders, who have sighted 153 species of birds here. Rare (to this area) badgers and coyotes also have been spotted. And the park is home to the endangered Indiana bat and the blue-spotted salamander. Novice gardeners will enjoy the Herb Wall, a collection of well-labeled cultivated herbs. You'll find 237 kinds of wildflowers blooming here at various times of the year.

The nature center and gift shop in the Rowe Building have perhaps the area's best collection of nature books. The nature center is open Monday through Sunday. Admission is $3 for adults, $1 for children. Members get in free; membership is $30 a year and includes a 10 percent discount at the gift shop.

A scenic walkway leading from the Rowe Building along Powel Crosley Lake is a favorite gathering spot for families with kids, who feed bread crumbs to always-hungry fish and turtles.

East Fork State Park
Intersection of Ohio 125 and Ohio 222, between Amelia and Bethel • 734-4323

East Fork is a large (8,420-acre) but relatively underdeveloped state park in eastern Clermont County. The public beach is covered with fine pebbles rather than sand. There are picnic shelters, a campground, hiking trails, a 5-mile mountain bike trail, and bridle paths. The lake, with its five launch ramps, offers bountiful bass fishing and boating opportunities. Open daily May through September.

Stonelick State Park
2895 Lake Dr., just east of Milford in Wayne • 625-7544

This is the smaller and lesser used of the state parks in Clermont County. The 1,058-acre park offers picnicking, hiking trails, swimming and a snack bar. Stonelick also has an innovative Rent-a-Camp program: For $26, you get a campsite complete with tent, foam sleeping pads, cots, cooler, and other necessities for your night in the forest. Restrooms and hot water are available so you don't have to rough it entirely. Reservations are a must. Nature programs are presented at the park amphithe-ater. Stonelick Lake offers boating and fishing (bass, bluegill and crappie). Open daily May through September.

Union Park
Glen Este-Withamsville Rd. and Clough Pike, Eastgate • no phone

This is by far the best equipped of the locally run parks in Clermont County. It includes a walking trail (no bikes, puuhh-lease), a playground and basketball courts. Look for the Vietnam-era helicopter at the corner of the park, which is part of a Vietnam veterans memorial.

Warren County

Caesar Creek State Park
4020 N. Clarksville Rd., Waynesville • (513) 897-1050

One of the largest and best developed parks in Ohio, Caesar Creek's 10,771 acres feature a large man-made lake with a boat ramp, a campground, hunting and fishing opportunities, numerous picnic areas, hiking and bridle trails and scenic overlooks. The Visitors Center displays fossils and Indian artifacts from the site and provides information about the area's history. An original log cabin from 1807 located on this site became the anchoring attraction for Pioneer Village, a collection of other (mostly Quaker) homesteads from the late 1700s and early 1800s that have been rebuilt or relocated from other parts of the park.

Northern Kentucky

Big Bone Lick State Park
3380 Beaver Rd., Union, Ky. • (606) 384-3522

We knew you must be wondering, so here's how this park got its name: Archaeologists found a bunch of big bones of prehistoric animals who were drawn to the salt lick here. Today, this 525-

---

INSIDERS' TIP

Lake Isabella, a 28-acre lake stocked with adult channel, blue and shovelhead catfish, and rainbow trout, is ideal for the first-time fisherman. You pay to fish ($7 and up, plus boat rental) but an Ohio State Fishing License is not required.

acre state park off U.S. Highway 42 and Ky. Highway 338 is the site of mock archaeological excavation sites that help recount the real archaeological work that was done here. Trails lead to dioramas of prehistoric beasts and a view of a herd of buffalo on the park grounds.

A museum at the site displays some of the bones and other items uncovered during the digs. Museum hours from April through October are 10 AM to 6 PM Monday through Thursday and 8 AM to 8 PM Friday through Sunday. The rest of the year (except January, when it's closed), hours are 9 AM to 5 PM Monday through Thursday. Admission is $1 for adults and 50 cents for children.

This nicely developed park also has miniature golf, tennis, hiking trails, a campground and fishing.

Devou Park
Access from Western Ave. or Ky. Hwy. 1072, Covington,Ky. • (606) 431-2577

Another great urban park, Devou has possibly the best view of any park in the area, taking in the downtown Cincinnati skyline and the houses of old Covington. Devou's playground has the most beautiful view you can get while pushing a kid on a swing. The 550-acre park also has a golf course, tennis courts, a lake and picnic areas. The Behringer-Crawford Museum features exhibits about Northern Kentucky's natural and cultural heritage, including a fascinating collection of dinosaur era fossils and Ice Age artifacts.

Retreats

Although parks are great for communing with nature, retreats are becoming a more and more popular option for recharging the batteries in a pristine environment. Below are some of the area's more popular nature retreats.

Grailville
932 O'Bannonville Rd., Loveland • 683-2340

Owned and operated by The Grail, a private nonprofit organization with its origins in the Grail women's movement in prewar Europe, Grailville is open to anyone, but its literature specifically notes that "nature lovers" will appreciate the 300 acres of organic gardens and

fields, the pond and pine grove, creeks and the nature trail for hiking. Overnight accommodations and meals can also be arranged.

Marydale
945 Donaldson Hwy., Erlanger, Ky.
• (606) 371-4224

Marydale offers retreats on contemplative living, healing and more. The facilities are available for all religious and nonprofit groups as well as individuals by special arrangement.

Milford Spiritual Center
5361 S. Milford Rd., Milford • 248-3500

The center offers individual and group retreats at its complex on the banks of the Little Miami River. Opened by the Society of Jesus in 1927, it promotes quiet solitude via nature walks and other programs.

Biking

In addition to the public bike trails listed below, some of the region's more considerate communities cater to bicycle riders. Blue Ash and Madeira have a bermside bike trail along Kenwood Road, and Indian Hill has an extensive network of on- and off-street trails intended for horseback riding (maps are available at the Indian Hill Rangers Station, 6525 Drake Road, 561-7000).

Early (very early!) one Sunday morning every August, the streets of Cincinnati and Covington — which include some extremely challenging hills — become a bike route as part of the 20-mile Morning Glory Ride (see our Annual Events chapter; for more detailed information, check out newspaper calendars or your local bike shop). Bike shops also can provide information and application forms for the Cincinnati Cycle Club and maps of local trails.

Airport Playfield
Beechmont and Wilmer Aves. • 321-6500

This park next to Lunken Airport features a 6.5-mile walking/biking trail. Watch out for low-flying Cessnas, though.

California Junction Trail
5400 Kellogg Ave. • 231-8678

This pleasant bike trail runs through California Woods Nature Preserve for about one

Photo: Greater Cincinnati Convention and Visitors Bureau

The Beach Waterpark offers 35 acres of summer activity, including waterslides, a favorite way to keep cool in the city.

mile. Mountain bikers and in-line skaters use the trail as well. The nature preserve has naturalists on hand to tell you what flora and fauna is in season at the time you're choosing to bike the trail.

Little Miami Scenic Trail
22 miles through numerous counties
• no phone

By far the longest and best bike trail in the region is the Little Miami Scenic Trail, a paved bikeway that runs nearly 22 miles along a former railroad track from Milford in Clermont County through Loveland in Hamilton County and into Morrow in Warren County. Construction is underway to extend the trail past Morrow and into Greene County. Also under construction, and scheduled for opening in spring 1998, is the Fort Ancient State Memorial, a museum honoring the Fort Ancient prehistoric mounds, which are a National Historic Landmark.

Construction at Fort Ancient ended, oh, say 2,000 years ago. But it began again in 1997 to expand the Fort Ancient Museum to four times its original size. The $3.5 million project is expected to be completed in mid-1998, with the museum encompassing the entire prehistory of the Ohio Valley. The com-

plex will feature dioramas, computer interactives, even a 15,000-square-foot garden featuring the crops grown by the early cultures.

The gently rolling trail here has some beautiful deeply-wooded sections and some extremely ugly industrial and post-industrial sections. The prettier sections are between Miamitown and Kings Mill, where you're almost assured of spotting at least one bluebird (once rare to this area) during a summer trip. Sections where you'll want to keep your head down and just concentrate on pedaling include parts of the trail between Milford and Miamitown and between Kings Mill and Morrow.

The best staging areas are in downtown Loveland and at The Schoolhouse Restaurant, 8031 Glendale-Milford Road, Camp Dennison, which graciously lets bikers use its parking lot, located adjacent to the trail (and it's not fussy about serving meals to sweaty bikers). The Schoolhouse is about a mile from the Milford end of the trail, and it's easier to start here than to fight the traffic from wherever you can find to park on Milford Road. Bikes for the bikeless are available for rent at stores along the trail in Loveland and Miamitown. Note that although biking is the primary use of this trail, it's also for hiking, in-line skating and horse-back riding. Bikers need to be alert for all these slower-moving users and prepared to dodge the occasional horse pie.

Shaker Trace Trail
Miami Whitewater Forest, Dry Fork and Oxford Rds., New Haven • 367-4774

You can rent bicycles as well as tandem and in-line skates at the visitor's center. One particularly nifty feature for cyclists on the 7.8-mile trail is the "courtesy cart" that patrols the trail and is outfitted with emergency patch kits for flat tires and offers first aid and cool drinking water.

Boating

If it floats, Cincinnatians love it. You'll find plenty of outlets for sailing, canoeing, rafting, tubing, kayaking and other boating sports on the region's abundant lakes and rivers. The season is generally May through September, but many boat rental outlets will open early or stay open through October if the weather's nice. (Be advised: Although boat rental outfits are plentiful, few if any rent powerboats or Jet Skis because of liability and insurance considerations.)

Between sunrise and sunset, powerboaters and Jet Ski riders on the Ohio River are subject to a no-wake zone between Interstate 75 and Interstate 471. There's no specific speed limit, but law enforcement agencies from both sides of the river will use common-sense judgment to determine if water craft are making too many waves. No-wake zones are in effect 24 hours a day near floating marinas, riverfront restaurants and other riverfront businesses. Offenders can be fined $65 in Ohio and $15 to $100 in Kentucky.

Operating a boat while under the influence is illegal and punishable by fines and jail time similar to those for DUIs.

Ohio requires boat licenses and registration, with fees ranging from $10 to $48. Your boat dealer can arrange for the license. Boat trailers must be licensed through state license agencies. Kentucky requires boat licenses, which range from $15 to $28 and are sold by the County Clerk's office in the county where the boat is docked. You only need a license from one state — the one where the boat is docked.

Need access to a boat launching site? Fee ramps include the **Riverside Public Ramp**, the **California Ramp** and **Yeatman's Cove Public Landing** in Cincinnati, the **New Richmond Public Ramp** in New Richmond, and the **Foster Public Ramp** in Foster.

The following listings include outfitters (offering everything from rentals to guided tours) as well as boating locations.

FYI

Unless otherwise noted, the area code for all phone numbers listed in this guide is 513.

Bruce's Loveland Canoe Rental
200 Crutchfield Pl., Loveland • 683-4604

The place to go for canoeing and tubing on the peaceful Little Miami River. Rustic river trips start at $20 for canoes, $8 for rubber inner tubes.

Caesar Creek State Park
4020 N. Clarksville Rd., Waynesville • (513) 897-1050

A large manmade lake offers a scenic day of boating or fishing. Waterskiers and powerboat enthusiasts, in particular, flock to this 2,800-acre lake designed for unlimited horsepower watercraft (there are no wake zones). There are five launch ramps around the shoreline, the two largest just near the park office near the entrance. The park does not rent boats, so bring your own.

Cincinnati Kayaks Downtown
255 McCormick Pl. • 421-3671

This outfitter offers Ohio River kayak cruises and adventures on the serene Licking River ($20 and up). Boat rental includes an experienced guide and safety instructions.

Coral Reef Diving Encounters
9859 Cincinnati-Columbus Rd., West Chester • 755-6200

Coral Reef carries diving and snorkeling equipment and offers instruction in the basics as well as the new "re-breather" technique. It also has folding kayaks designed for rock quarry diving.

East Fork State Park
Intersection of Ohio 125 and Ohio 222, between Amelia and Bethel • 734-4323

East Fork's lake offers bountiful bass fishing and boating opportunities. The 2,100-acre manmade reservoir has five launch ramps, with the largest near the park office. There are no boat rentals.

Fort Ancient Canoe Rental
219 Mill St., Morrow • 899-3616

You'll find dozens of canoes for rent here. Prices vary seasonally and are quoted on request.

Kincaid Lake
Rural Rt. 1, Falmouth, Ky.
• (606) 654-3531

The Kentucky State Park system manages this 183-acre lake, which features a dock with 38 slips, launching ramps and rental fishing boats and pontoons ($7 a day and up).

Lake Isabella
Off Loveland-Madeira Rd. • 791-1663

This 28-acre lake features a full-service boathouse with rowboat rentals ($6.13 and up), a pier and canoe access to the Little Miami River.

Miami Whitewater Forest Lake
Access from New Haven, Dry Fork and Oxford Rds., Harrison • 367-4774

Miami Whitewater Forest Lake is an 85-acre man-made body of water, built in 1971 by damming a woodland creek. A boathouse rents rowboats, pedal boats and canoes, for fishing and other recreational activities. The cost is $4.01 for a half hour up to $11.32 for the entire day.

Rivers Edge
3928 Ohio 42, Waynesville
• (937) 862-4540, (800) 628-2319

Rivers Edge rents both canoes and kayaks for journeys on the Little Miami River. The kayaks are of the touring variety, vs. the more familiar whitewater version, and are perfectly suited to the easier-going Little Miami (easier-going, that is, compared to the Colorado rapids). Experts provide instruction at the shore before departure, and there's also a video to watch about safe kayaking. Rivers Edge does not, however, provide guides for your river trip. Rental fee is $16 per kayak for up to six hours. Canoe rental varies on how long you have it out, but for a four-hour trip, for instance, the cost would be $26.

Sharon Woods Lake
U.S. 42, Sharonville • 521-7275

Sharon Woods Lake was constructed in 1936 by damming Sharon Creek. A boathouse rents rowboats, canoes, pedal boats and hydrobikes for recreational activities. The cost is $4.01 for a half hour up to $11.32 for the entire day.

Stonelick State Park
2895 Lake Dr., just east of Milford in Wayne • 625-7544

Stonelick Lake — a long and smooth 181-acre body of water — offers boating and fishing, with extensive stocks of bass, bluegill and crappie. It's one of the area's quietest lakes, thanks to a policy of no gas motorboats (small sailboats and electric motors are allowed, as are canoes or rowboats). Two small launch ramps are located at either end of the lake. The park office plans to rent paddleboats and canoes for the first time in the summer of 1998, but no prices had yet been set at press time.

Strictly Sail Inc.
10766 Kenwood Rd., Kenwood
• 984-1907

Strictly Sail rents out more than 50 types of sailboats, from 10-footers up to 30-footers, including Hobie Cats, Catalinas, Capris, plus kayaks and paddleboats. Sailing lessons are also offered. Prices vary with the size of the boat.

Winton Woods Lake
Winton Rd. and Lake Forest Dr., Greenhills • 521-7275

This 188-acre lake is undergoing an extensive restoration project, so call first for the status on boating. The new boathouse — due for completion in mid-1998 — will rent rowboats, canoes, pedal boats and hydrobikes for recreational activities. The cost is $4.01 for a half hour up to $11.32 for the entire day.

Spring Grove: America's Cemetery

It's not a park in any formal sense of the word. It has lawns, yes, and trees, but also—um—its own certain esprit d'corpse.

It's Spring Grove Cemetery and Arboretum, but it's not what you think of when somebody says cemetery. People regularly get married here (renting the chapel costs $450), and year-round Spring Grove offers a busy social calendar featuring nature walks, jogging runs, ice cream socials, big band concerts and more.

Welcome to Spring Grove, which, at 733 acres, is the nation's second largest cemetery. "Funny thing about cemeteries," observes Dr. Joan Howison, a University of Cincinnati professor who teaches a "Who's Sleeping With Whom?" course on area resting places. "People either love 'em, or hate 'em. Half the people won't even go into them unless they absolutely have to."

But if you are gonna go, this is the place. Spring Grove is the cemetery of the rich 'n' famous, chock-full of historical landmarks and lush gardens, fantastic crypts and awesome headstones. Of particular note among the architectural wonders is the Dexter Mausoleum. Built in 1869, it's a Gothic Revival chapel complete with flying buttresses. There's more than graceful architecture, of course. The rolling hills and lush forestry make for a wonderful day amid natural beauty. And, of course, everything is quite quiet.

We got to digging, and unearthed these fascinating facts about Spring Grove:

Among those buried here are a Speaker of the House of Representatives, a Secretary of the Treasury under Lincoln, a Chief Justice of the Supreme Court, nine Ohio governors, 25 Cincinnati mayors, the parents of two U.S. presidents, 36 Union

— continued on next page

Photo: Sean Hughes

The Dexter Mausoleum is just one of the architectural wonders at the Spring Grove Cemetery.

generals, a grocer (Bernard Kroger, who founded Kroger's), and two guys named William Procter and Joseph Gamble (they ran a soap company you may have heard of). Still debated is whether Agnes Lake Thatcher is actually buried here. Never heard of her? She went by the moniker of "Calamity Jane."

And yes, you too can finally rest here. Expect to pay around $2,000 for a plot. Just walking around the place, fortunately, is free.

Bowling

Cincinnatians will constantly argue about the better place to live: East Side or West Side. If you're a bowler, however, there's no contest. The West Side, with its traditional family values and working class origins, has spawned the city's finest bowling lanes. Below are our favorites (from both sides). A complete list of area bowling centers (they no longer refer to themselves as alleys) is available from the Greater Cincinnati Bowling Association, 761-3338.

Brentwood Bowl
9176 Winton Rd. • 522-2320

Around since the '60s, Brentwood Bowl offers 48 lanes as well as multiple leagues for men, women, seniors and children. Some 200 kids, ages 3 to 7, bowl every Saturday morning. On Saturday afternoons, the Bowl hosts what may be the area's largest league for the mentally and physically disabled. Billiards, video games and a restaurant round out the experience. There's a nursery for any toddlers too young to pick up a ball.

Cherry Grove Lanes
4005 Hopper Hill Rd., Cherry Grove
• 528-7888

What doesn't Cherry Grove have? There's a pro shop, sand-lot volleyball, billiards, arcade, darts, a sports bar and an outdoor bar and grill. And, oh yes, 34 lanes with automatic scoring.

Glenmore Bowl
3716 Glenmore Ave. • 661-5394

One of the area's oldest lanes, Glenmore opened its doors in 1927. A sense of history, yes, but the Bowl's 10 lanes are state-of-the-art, refitted synthetic lanes. A neat bar, too.

King Pin Lanes
7735 Beechmont Ave., Anderson
• 231-8010

Little kids and their parents flock to King Pin, with its terrific "Bumper Ball" leagues on 48 lanes. Your 3-year-old (and his/her older siblings) can join the junior league.

Madison Bowl
4761 Madison Rd. • 271-2700

All 32 lanes at Madison are open 24 hours a day. A lounge, snack bar and restaurant means you never have to leave.

Princeton Bowl
11711 Princeton Rd. • 671-7222

Princeton features 50 lanes, plus the full array of video games and a grill restaurant.

Strikes & Spares
8032 Blue Ash Rd., Deer Park • 891-9355

Twelve lanes, with leagues playing every night. There's a restaurant, bar and video games.

Super Bowl
I-75 at Commonwealth Ave., Erlanger, Ky. • (606) 727-2000

There's billiards, games, a pro shop in addition to 64 lanes. It's where Kentuckians go to bowl.

Western Bowl
6383 Glenway Ave. • 574-2222

The promised land. Or promised lane. The Western Bowl stands above all the rest. It bills itself as Cincinnati's largest bowling center and is host to the Hoinke Classic, a tournament that lasts 10 months a year, attracts 50,000 entrants and gives away $2 million in prize money. It's open 24 hours a day, with free nursery care.

Fishing

Local anglers fish the lakes and rivers of the region throughout the year, even if it means cutting a hole in the ice. To fish from a boat on the Ohio, you need a special Ohio River fishing license, which is only issued by the State of Kentucky (Kentucky claims all but a few feet of the river on the Ohio side as its property). A three-day fishing license is $12.50, a 15-day license is $20. They can be obtained at sporting goods and fishing tackle retailers. If you want to fish from the Ohio shore, all you need is a regular Ohio driver's license. Or, if you want to fish from the Kentucky side, all you need is a regular Kentucky driver's license.

Fish are more numerous and healthier in the Ohio now than in the 1970s. But all three states warn to steer clear of eating walleye, carp, channel catfish, white bass or paddlefish caught in the river. High levels of chlordane and PCBs are sometimes found in these bottom feeders.

Other assorted rules and regs: Snagging is generally illegal for all fish except carp and select forage fish. Poisons, firearms, electricity and chemicals as fishing devices are prohibited by all three states (as are, we presume, tactical nuclear weapons). It is illegal to release exotic species of fish into the Ohio or its tributaries. Frogs may not be shot except with a bow and arrow. Turtle traps must be marked with the name and address of the owner. It is unlawful to possess more than 100 crayfish unless you are a licensed bait dealer. And lastly, anglers may use no more than two fishing lines.

All that said, here are a few places where you can spend a great day throwing out a line. We've indicated where boat rentals are available.

Caesar Creek State Park
4020 N. Clarksville Rd., Waynesville • (513) 897-1050

Caesar Creek's sizable 2,800-acre lake features lots of coves, inlets and bays that promote bountiful bass fishing. Saugeye and walleye are also stocked annually. Caesar Creek is open 6 AM to 11 PM year round, but the lake is open 24 hours a day for those who like to get in the boat well before dawn. On a state park lake, no fishing license is required for anglers 16 and younger. Adults can obtain a fishing license at Wal-Mart, Kmart or a local fish and tackle store. There is no fee for fishing at the lake. Parking is free.

East Fork State Park
Intersection of Ohio 125 and Ohio 222, between Amelia and Bethel • 734-4323

East Fork's 2,100-acre reservoir is a favorite of local bass anglers, especially from shore in the spring. East Fork is open 6 AM to 11 PM year-round. No fishing license is required for anglers 16 and younger. Fishing licenses can be obtained at Wal-Mart, Kmart or a local fish and tackle store. There is no fee for fishing at the lake, and parking is free.

Kincaid Lake
Rural Rt. 1, Falmouth • (606) 654-3531

Kincaid Lake covers 183 acres and is stocked with crappie, bluegill and more.

Lake Isabella
Off Loveland-Madeira Rd. • 791-1663

This 28-acre lake is stocked with adult channel, blue and shovelhead catfish, and rainbow trout. It's ideal for the first-time fisherman or fisherwoman, because an Ohio state fishing license is not required and friendly staff members are on hand to help you learn the ropes. The lake is a pay-fishing lake ($7 and up, depending on how many trout you bag).

Miami Whitewater Forest Lake
Access from New Haven, Dry Fork and Oxford Rds., Harrison • 367-4774

Fishing is by rental boat only and electric trolling motors are permitted. You can rent a rowboat, pedal boat or canoe. The cost is $4.01 for a half hour, with a maximum of $11.32 for the entire day. There's also a bait and tackle shop. Bank fishing is allowed only in the cove adjacent to the visitor's center. In the winter, ice fishing is allowed.

Sharon Woods Lake
U.S. Hwy. 42, Sharonville • 521-7275

Fishermen say this 35-acre lake has the best bass fishing of any county-owned lake in the region. Fishing is by rental boat only, and electric trolling motors are permitted. A boathouse rents rowboats, canoes, pedal boats and hydrobikes. The cost is $4.01 for a half hour, up to a $11.32 maximum for the day. There's also bank fishing along the pier.

Stonelick State Park
2895 Lake Dr., just east of Milford in Wayne • 625-7544

Stonelick Lake offers bountiful bass, bluegill and crappie. The lake is relatively small for a state park, just 200 acres, and quiet (gas motorboats are forbidden). Stonelick is open 6 AM to 11 PM year round.

Winton Woods Lake
Winton Rd. and Lake Forest Dr., Springfield • 521-7275

This 188-acre lake is undergoing an extensive restoration project, so call first for the status on fishing. The new boathouse — due for completion in mid-1998 — will rent rowboats, canoes, pedal boats and hydrobikes. The cost is $4.01 for a half hour up to $11.32 for the entire day. Bluegill, crappie, bass and channel catfish are stocked.

Frisbee Golf

The Tri-state is home to some great Frisbee golf courses. The 18-hole Frisbee course at Woodland Mound is the area's most attractive; although the holes aren't long, they can be unforgiving. City and county parks with notable Frisbee golf facilities are:

Miami Whitewater Forest, access from New Haven, Dry Fork and Oxford roads, 367-4774

Mount Airy Forest, 5083 Colerain Avenue, Mount Airy, 352-4094

Winton Woods, Winton Road and Lake Forest Drive, Springfield, 521-727

Woodland Mound, access from Kellogg Avenue or Nordyke Road, Anderson, 474-0580

Hiking/Backpacking

There are literally dozens of options for both the amateur and the seasoned hiker in the region. Wherever you choose to hike, do pick up a trail map at the various visitors centers or park offices, because it's not hard to get lost on some of the more winding trails. Other warnings: There are two poisonous snakes in the Tri-state area, the copperhead and the timber rattler. Neither is aggressive, and in fact there are no reports a backpacker has ever been bitten. Still, it's wise to hit the encyclopedia if you don't know what these two snakes look like, and to pack a snake bite kit. Those with an abnormal fear of snakes, venomous or otherwise, should wait until after the first frost in fall — you won't see a single slithering creature.

Caesar Creek State Park
4020 N. Clarksville Rd., Waynesville • 897-1050

Caesar Creek has 43 miles of easy to rugged trails, all excellently maintained. The terrain is incredibly varied, ranging from meadows to gorges. A handicapped trail begins near the dam overlook. The Little Miami Trail can also be accessed near Corwin, north of the park. The most notable landscape features are waterfalls, as well as Caesar Creek Lake and Caesar Creek Gorge, formed by glacial meltwater and over 180 feet deep. The Gorge Trail is tough; for easier hikes, consider the Flat Fork Ridge/Wellman Meadows Trail. Day-issue permits are available for fossil collecting from the Visitors Center.

Cowan Lake State Park
729 Beechwood Rd., Wilmington • 289-2105

A perfect park for the beginner. There are 5 miles of trails; the Emerald Trail is considered easiest, the Lotus Cove Trail moderate. The terrain, shaped by a glacier 10,000 years ago, varies from shale to lily ponds. Fossils abound. There are 200 campsites on four loops located on the north side of Cowan Lake. Conveniences include rest rooms and shower stations, as well as a park.

Cincinnati Nature Center
4949 Tealtown Rd., Glen Este • 831-1711

Hiking is the main activity at this 1,425-acre nature preserve. You can choose from 15 miles of trails that range from the wheelchair-accessible Stanley Rowe All Persons Trail to some fairly long and steeply sloped trails.

Terrain ranges from open meadows to fairly deep woods. Note to bird watchers: Some 150 species of birds have been spotted here. You also can find 237 kinds of wildflowers blooming here at various times of year.

East Fork State Park
Intersection of Ohio Hwys. 125 and 222, between Amelia and Bethel • 734-4323

East Fork has 40 miles of trail showcasing the park's fascinating rock formations, stone terraces and meandering streams. Several sites of both the Adena and Hopewell Indian cultures remain, dating back some 3,000 years. All vestiges of the gold mines that once operated here in the 1860s, however, are gone. As is, we presume, the gold. There are no lodges or cabins, but select campgrounds do feature electricity and hot showers. Park rangers on horseback patrol the trails, a security feature unavailable at some of Ohio's other state parks. Carrying your own drinking water supply, or a purifying system, is a must. Wear bright clothes, to discourage any confusion a hunter might have between you and a buck.

To decide which of the trails to hike (many favor the Back Country Trail, a three-day adventure) and where to access them, call first. Oh, if you're wondering who the Steve Newman Worldwalker Perimeter Trail is named after, Cincinnati's Newman recently walked around the globe and wrote a book about it called *Worldwalker*.

Fort Thomas Landmark Tree Trail
S. Fort Thomas Ave. at Carmel Manor Dr., Fort Thomas, Ky. • no phone

The Fort Thomas Tree Commission can be thanked for preserving the city's most beautiful old-growth forest. It's 1.1-mile trail winds across lush green slopes, offering views of wood bridges and at least 15 different species of trees (including buckeyes), plus wildflowers and numerous birds. Bikes are not permitted on this trail.

Hueston Woods State Park and Nature Preserve
Ohio 732, College Corner • (513) 523-6347

A National Natural Landmark, the pre-serve offers all the amenities: lodge, campsites, cabins and more. Hit the rest rooms and drinking fountain at the start of Big Woods Trail. Terrain is tall timber, primarily beech trees and sugar maple — don't miss autumn here if you like to gawk at colorful leaves. And if you visit at the end of winter, you're sure to be offered some freshly tapped maple syrup. The 200-acre nature preserve within the park is a great place for hiking and bird-watching. One hundred and fifty species of birds have been spotted here including plenty of hawks and woodpeckers. Wildflowers put on amazing displays in almost every season.

Little Miami Scenic Trail
22 miles through numerous counties • no phone

The best bike trail in the region is also a walking and hiking trail. The Little Miami Scenic Trail is a paved bikeway that runs nearly 22 miles along a former railroad track from Milford in Clermont County through Loveland in Hamilton County and into Morrow in Warren County. Watch out for fast-moving bikes.

Miami Whitewater Forest
Access from New Haven, Dry Fork and Oxford Rds. • 367-4774

At 3,906 acres, this is the largest park in the Hamilton County Park District. There are 3 miles of nature paths, a 7.8-mile walking trail, and a 1.2-mile inner loop for the less adventurous.

Mount Airy Forest
5083 Colerain Ave. • 352-4094

Though city parks aren't often known for their hiking trails, the one at Mount Airy is superb. At 1,466 acres, it's the largest municipal park and forest in the nation. There are miles of hiking trails through a forest that boasts a million hardwoods and conifers.

Shawnee Lookout Park
Miamiview Rd. just outside of Cleves • 521-PARK

The park's self-guided trails are marked with numbered stakes that are keyed to brochures, which are available by calling ahead. Terrain is hills, woods, ravines, creeks, with some terrific overlooks offering a panoramic view of three states as well as the Ohio and Great Miami rivers. Both the Little Turtle and Blue Jacket trails offer rest rooms and drinking water, and are good for the beginning hiker. Archaeology buffs will appreciate the 12-acre fort built by an ancient people, with walls built atop sleep slopes.

Stonelick State Park
2895 Lake Dr., just east of Milford in Wayne • 625-7544

Stonelick includes shelters, a modern campground with tent sites, and 7 miles of foot trails. Warning: Much of the hiking trails are on level, poorly-draining soil. During the late winter and spring, it's soggy, but it's one of the best places to spot butterflies or wildflowers, if you're so inclined. Terrain is primarily flat forest.

Horseback Riding

Cincinnati may not quite be in Bluegrass horse country, but equestrian pursuits are still quite popular. The village of Indian Hill is known for its extensive network of horse trails (maps of which are available at the village offices, 6525 Drake Road, 561-6500) in addition to its palatial mansions. See the Parks section above for public parks offering horse trails.

The following stables offer lessons and, where we've so noted, trails open to the public for a fee. Specific age cut-offs for lessons for children are also noted, but most teach riding to any child able to mount a pony and stay seated without the aid of a parent. A horse is a horse, of course, of course, but we do offer this caveat nonetheless: The hours of these stables vary incredibly, depending on what month of the year it is, whether they are running pony camps, and other seasonal factors. So it's best to call first. All do stay open year round, but in some months, only for boarding purposes.

Choco-Ridge Equestrian Center
8511 U.S. Hwy. 42, Florence, Ky. • (606) 384-4433

Choco-Ridge offers centered and dressage lessons for kids to adults, beginners to ad-

Volleyball is just one of the recreational opportunities available during the warm summer months.

vanced. Private lessons are $30 an hour. Semi-private lessons are $20 an hour.

Cross Creek Farm
2031 Millville-Shandon Rd., Hamilton • 738-4142

For $25 an hour for private lessons or $20 for an hour with a small group, you can learn dressage, jumping, combined training and basic western. Private lessons with a British Horse Society instructor are $35 an hour. The summer pony camps for kids are $175 for a week-long series of lessons in which they learn basic riding, horse care and even take a field trip to the Kentucky Bluegrass country.

East Fork Stables & Lodge
2215 Snyder Rd., Batavia • 797-7433

East Fork Stables teaches English saddle, western and endurance saddle riding lessons for kids and adults, beginners to advanced. Fifteen hours of lessons are available for $175. The week-long summer pony camps for kids teach all aspects of riding, grooming and horse care for $175. Members of the public can also hop a horse and ride East Fork's 50 miles of trails for $20 an hour. There's an overnight camping lodge and cabins available for $55 to $60.

Engle Equine Center
2675 Carriage Gate Ln., Landen
• 398-3399

The Engle Equine Center offers beginners and advanced western and English riding lessons for kids and adults. Private lessons are $30 an hour, group lessons are $20 an hour.

Fox Chapel Stables
6111 Kyles Station Rd., Hamilton
• 777-8848

Fox Chapel Stables offer lessons for kids and adults at all levels in western, English, saddle seat, hunt seat and jumping. The cost of a one-hour lesson is $15.

Green Township Stable
2840 Delhi Rd., Monfort Heights
• 481-6347

Green Township Stable has beginners and advanced lessons for all ages in western and English riding. Half-hour lessons are $15, a full hour is $25.

Have Fun Acres
6846 Cozaddale Rd., Morrow • 899-2839

Have Fun Acres teaches dressage to kids and adults, beginners and advanced. Lessons are $30 an hour, cross-country schooling lessons are $35 an hour.

Greystone Farm
15412 Wilson Creek Rd., Lawrenceburg, Ind. • (812) 926-2223

Greystone Farm offers basic riding lessons for beginners age 12 and up and advanced lessons. A one-hour lesson costs $25.

Lakewood Stables
9974 S. Ohio Hwy. 48, Loveland
• 677-2109

Lakewood Stables has classes for all ages and levels. Lessons can be held in the inside arena or outside on the 100-acre grounds. Private or semi-private lessons are $30 an hour.

Little Miami Scenic Trail
22 miles through numerous counties
• no phone

The Little Miami Scenic Trail runs nearly 22 miles along a former railroad track from Milford in Clermont County through Loveland in Hamilton County and into Morrow in Warren County. Although primarily a trail for bikers and hikers, horseback riding is also encouraged.

Old Stone Riding Center
2920 Minton Rd., Hamilton • 868-3042

Old Stone Riding Center offers dressage, hunter and other lessons on its 70 acres for all ages and levels. The costs are $110 for five group lessons or $45 an hour for private lessons.

Red Fox Stables
1342 U.S. Hwy. 50, Milford • 831-5010

Red Fox Stables teaches jumping to kids to adults at all levels. The cost is $25 an hour.

Trails of Fiddlers Green
3096 Fiddlers Green Rd., Miami
• 941-8977

Trails of Fiddlers Green offers basic riding lessons for all age groups at all levels. Group lessons are $90 for six weeks or $20 a lesson. Private lessons cost $150 for six weeks or $25 a lesson. Summer pony camps, which introduce kids to horseback riding and essential horse care, are $150.

Trena Lenger Stables
10830 Big Bone Church Rd., Union, Ky.
• (606) 384-2974

Trena Lenger Stables offers all levels of hunter, jumper and equitation lessons for kids and adults for $30 an hour.

Win Row Farm
1177 Cook Rd., Lebanon • 398-4679

Win Row Farm teaches basic riding skills to kids and adults at all levels. Semi-private lessons are $25 an hour, private lessons are $35 an hour.

Winterwood Farm
5465 Day Rd., Dunlap • 385-6511

Winterwood Farm offers all levels of hunter and jumper lessons to all age groups. Lesson prices are quoted on request.

YMCA Western Ranch Camp
Camp Ernst, Boone County
• (606) 586-6181

The YMCA Western Ranch Camp is a summer riding camp for youngsters ages 9 and older. Camp is $310, with a $25 discount for Y members, and is offered at various times during the summer.

Mall Walking

Just about every mall in the area has a walking program. Call the mall office nearest you for details (see our Shopping chapter). By far the most challenging and popular mall walk is at the 1.8 million-square-foot Forest Fair Mall (at the Forest Park Exit off Interstate 275). In this vast expanse, mall walkers can be found all day, not just in the early morning hours.

Rowing

Cincinnati Rowing Center
Bicentennial Commons at Sawyer
• 241-2628

Thanks in part to the collegiate rowing championships held at East Fork State Park in Clermont County each June, rowing is a popular sport here. The Cincinnati Rowing Center at Sawyer Point offers classes and facilities.

Skiing

In addition to the Tri-state's two downhill skiing resorts with man-made snow, you can try cross-country skiing at three Cincinnati parks. Trails at **Mount Airy Forest**, 5081 Colerain Avenue, are available for free to cross-country skiers on the weekends. The **Neuman Golf Course** at 7215 Bridgetown Road and **California Golf Course** at 5920 Kellogg Avenue offer cross-country skiing and equipment rental when the snow is four inches or deeper.

Perfect North Slopes
19640 Ind. 1, Lawrenceburg, Ind.
• (812) 537-3754, 381-7517 in Cincinnati

With 70 acres of tree-lined trails and wide open slopes, Perfect North is the region's top skiing facility. There are four chairlifts and seven rope tows, a ski school, a "slow skiing" zone for nervous novices, and much more. The pro shop can outfit you with any equipment you might need, available for

rental or purchase, and also specializes in boot repair, waxing and binding. The resort, which uses man-made snow when Mother Nature doesn't cooperate, also offers skiing all day and night, racing clinics and racing camps. Season passes are available for $400 (a second family member can be added to the pass for another $300, a third can be added for $235, and after that, each additional family member is an extra $140). A single lift ticket on weekends is $30.

Ski Butler
Ky. 227 • (502) 732-4231

Ski Butler, 2 miles southeast of Carrollton, Kentucky, provides man-made snow on 25 acres of slopes. There are three chairlifts, a skiing school for newcomers to the sport, ski shop with rental equipment, nine ski runs and a full array of lodge and cottage accommodations. It's generally open from mid-December through March.

Skydiving

Waynesville Skydiving
Waynesville Airport, 4925 N. Ohio Hwy. 42 • 897-3851

If throwing yourself out of a plane is your idea of a good time, Waynesville is the place to do it. Waynesville Skydiving offers skydiving for the experienced or novices.

Soccer

Cincinnati has more soccer players per capita than anyplace else in the United States. Youth soccer is extremely popular, but it's not the whole story. Here are some very active soccer leagues and centers in the Greater Cincinnati area.

Beechmont Soccer Club, 474-0919

Girl's Southeast Cincinnati Soccer Association, 474-5939

Kolping Society, 10235 Mill Road, New Burlington 851-7951

Northern Kentucky Youth Soccer Association, (606) 371-6674

Ohio Youth Soccer Association, 231-9400

Soccer World, 2115 Schappelle Lane, 742-4442

Photo: Skip Tate

The foot-deep wading pool at Sawyer Point offers a cool
pick-me-up when wilting weather sets in.

Softball

Softball is so big in Cincinnati that an estimated 1,200 softball teams are fielded each year — and that's probably a conservative estimate. The Cincinnati Recreation Commission (805 Central Avenue, 352-4000) organizes some mighty good amateur baseball leagues that may include former minor and major leaguers. Local recreation commissions (see next section), employers, churches, and bars organize softball teams, or can help set you up. The following softball complexes also organize leagues:

Amateur Slow-Pitch Softball, 10400 Hamilton-Cleves Highway, 738-3636

Cincinnati Softball Center, 10701 Campbell Road, Harrison, 367-0266

Softball City Sports Complex, 620 Mason Road, Taylor Mill, Kentucky, 581-0510

Queen City Softball Complex, 9267 Cincinnati-Dayton Road, West Chester, 777-8638

Swimming

Check the Yellow Pages under "Swimming Pools" for public and private swim clubs, and see the listings for recreation centers and YMCAs below.

Recreation Centers and Commissions

Greater Cincinnati is a hotbed of softball, soccer and volleyball. Call or visit one of the local recreation centers listed below for information on their specific programs.

Ohio

Cincinnati

Bush, 2640 Kemper Lane, Walnut Hills, 281-1286

Camp Washington, 1201 Stock Street, 681-6046

Clifton, 320 McAlpin Avenue, 961-5681

Corryville, 116 Piedmont Avenue, 281-3401

Dunham Complex, 4320 Guerley Road, Price Hill, 251-5862

Ebersole, 5701 Kellogg Avenue, California, 231-6617

English Woods, 1976 Sutter Avenue, Fairmont, 481-7264

Evanston, 3204 Woodburn Avenue, 861-9414

Hartwell, 8275 Vine Street, 821-5194

Hirsch, 3630 Reading Road, North Avondale, 751-3393

Kennedy-Woodford, 6065 Red Bank Road, Kennedy Heights, 631-5625

Krueck, 270 W. McMillan Avenue, Clifton, 861-6572

LeBlond, 2335 Eastern Avenue, East End, 281-3209

Lincoln, 1027 Linn Street, West End, 721-6514

McKie, 1655 Chase Avenue, Northside, 681-8247

Millvale, 3303 Beekman, Cumminsville, 681-7223

Mount Auburn, 270 Southern Avenue, 381-1760

Mount Washington, 1715 Beacon Street, 232-4762

North Avondale, 617 Clifton Springs Avenue, 961-1584

North Fairmount, 1660 Carll Street, 471-3727

Oakley, 3950 Paxton Avenue, 871-9180

Over-the-Rhine, 1715 Republic Avenue, 381-1893

Pleasant Ridge, 5915 Ridge Avenue, 731-7894

Price Hill, 959 Hawthorn Avenue, 251-4123

Sayler Park, 6720 Home City Avenue, 941-0102

Westwood Town Hall, 3017 Harrison Avenue, 662-9109

Winton Hills, 5170 Winneste Avenue, 641-0422

Suburban Areas

Anderson Park District, 474-0003

Blue Ash Recreation Center, 4433 Cooper Road, 745-8550

Blue Ash Sports Center, 11540 Grooms Road, 745-8586. A replica of the old Crosley Field was rebuilt on this site using the original seats.

Cheviot Recreation Commission, 3837 Carrie Avenue, 481-2835

Crescentville Recreation Center, 12153 Crescentville Road, 671-2191

Evendale Recreation Center, 10500 Reading Road, 563-2247

Forest Park Recreation Department, 595-5258

Glendale Lyceum, 865 Congress Street, 771-8383

Green Township Parks and Recreation, 6303 Harrison Avenue, 574-8832

Greenhills Recreation Department, 11000 Winton Road, 589-3581

Greenhills Golf & Tennis Club, 14 Enfield Road, 589-3585

Hamilton (City) Parks and Recreation, 868-5874

Hamilton County Park District, 10245 Winton Road, 521-PARK, Ext. 67

Mariemont Swimming Pool, 6000 Mariemont Avenue, 272-0593

Mariemont Tennis Courts, 3928 Plainville Road, 561-8711

Montgomery Park, information and reservations, 891-2424

Montgomery Swimming Pool, 7777 Sycamore Avenue, 791-0148

North College Hill Pool, End of Grace, 522-5488

Norwood Recreation Commission, 2605 Harris Avenue, 531-9798

Sharonville Recreation Department, Adult & Youth Sports, 563-9072; Sports Hotline, 563-4257

Springdale Parks & Recreation Department, 11999 Lawnview Avenue, 671-6260

Northern Kentucky

Boone County Recreation Department, (606) 334-2117

Petersburg Community Center, 6517 Market Street, (606) 586-8318

Covington Recreation Department, (606) 292-2151

Covington Community Center, 1008 Lee Street, (606) 491-2220

Florence World of Sports (Sports Complex), 7400 Woodsport Drive, (606) 371-8255

Fort Mitchell Parks & Recreation, 267 Grandview Drive, (606) 331-9118

Fort Thomas Recreation Department, Armory Recreation Center, 950 S. Fort Thomas Avenue, (606) 781-1700

Newport Recreation Department, (606) 292-3686

YMCAs

In addition to city recreation centers and commissions, community YMCAs are the other major source of year-round activities for kids and adults. Two dozen YMCAs serve the Tri-state. Virtually all of them offer whirlpools, saunas and child care for adults using the facilities. Amenities and special fitness equipment for each Y are listed below.

Ohio

Hamilton County

Blue Ash YMCA
5000 YMCA Dr. • 791-5000

The Blue Ash Y has two indoor pools and one outdoor pool in addition to Nautilus equipment, free weights, an indoor running track and a basketball court. The ambitious tots exercise program features Pee Wee Play, Gym Tots, Pre-Tumbling. For kids 3 to 5, there are Little Leagues for indoor soccer and other sports, plus arts and crafts and, if you can believe it, basic cooking classes for 5-year-olds. For older children, there is the usual hockey, football and gymnastics, but lessons in ballet and tap dancing are offered too.

Central Parkway YMCA
1105 Elm St. • 241-5348

This well-equipped downtown Y has two indoor pools, Nautilus and Hammer Strength equipment, free weights, two gyms, an indoor track, four racquetball courts, handball courts, an indoor golf driving room and free parking for members. It also has massage therapists and personal weights instruction available by appointment. Suburban Y members can work out for free here three times a year; after that, it costs $5 a visit. Classes are offered in step aerobics, powerfit and such esoteric activities as cardio boxing, ninjutsu and scuba diving.

Clippard YMCA
8920 Cheviot Rd. • 923-4466

The Clippard Y has a nice mix of indoor and outdoor amenities. Inside are a pool, full gym, health and wellness room with cardiovascular workout equipment, Nautilus equipment and free weights. Outside are pools for adults and kids, two tennis courts and a sand volleyball court.

Columbia Parkway YMCA
Columbia Pky. and Delta Ave. • 871-4594

A small Y, this one includes a gymnasium, senior center and teen center. A recent addition is a fitness center with cardiovascular and weight-training equipment, plus a locker room and showers.

Powel Crosley Jr. YMCA
9601 Winton Rd., Springfield • 521-7112

An indoor and outdoor pool, three outdoor tennis courts, two outdoor sand volleyball courts, six racquetball courts, a one-fifth-mile walking-running trail, gymnasium and Universal and Nautilus equipment are available at this large and popular Y.

Gamble-Nippert YMCA
3159 Montana Ave., Westwood • 661-1105

Both indoor and outdoor swimming pools are available at this West Side Y, along with three tennis courts, a racquetball court, Nautilus equipment and free weights.

Walter L. & Nell Gross YMCA
9940 Springfield Pike, Woodlawn • 771-9622

This small Y has a Nautilus room, free weights and a gym. Pools are available at the Powel Crosley Jr. Y nearby.

Lincoln Heights Center YMCA
1100 Lindy Ave. • 563-6822

You'll find a gymnasium, weight room and outdoor pool here.

M.E. Lyons YMCA
8108 Clough Pike, Anderson • 474-1400

This very active Anderson Y has both indoor and outdoor pools, a family fitness center with cardiovascular workout equipment, an indoor track, Nautilus equipment and free weights, six tennis courts, five racquetball courts and a gym. There's a full range of swim, gymnastics and wrestling classes, plus the more unusual tae kwon do, scuba diving, and the hot new sport in town, in-line hockey.

Madisonville YMCA
6100 Desmond St. • 271-4879

This is smaller Y that has only a weight room and gymnasium.

Melrose YMCA
2840 Melrose Ave. • 961-3510

Facilities here include a gymnasium, an indoor pool, Universal and Nautilus equipment, free weights, a youth recreation center, a multipurpose room and two club rooms.

Richard E. Lindner YMCA
Sherman and Walter Aves. • 731-0115

The Norwood Y has an indoor pool, outdoor pool, gymnasium, racquetball courts, Nautilus equipment and free weights.

University YMCA
270 Calhoun St. • 556-4937

Serving the University of Cincinnati campus and surrounding area, this Y offers Nautilus equipment and a gym in addition to a wide variety of programs that include ballroom dancing and self-defense.

West End YMCA
821 Ezzard Charles Dr. • 241-9622

The West End Y has a weight room, gymnasium, game room and Nautilus equipment. There's no pool, but there are a host of youth programs in this youth-oriented facility.

Williams YMCA
1228 E. McMillan • 961-7552

The Williams Y serves the university area with Nautilus equipment, a basketball court, indoor swimming pool, indoor track, racquetball court, stretching area and boxing program.

Butler County

Fairfield YMCA
785 Nilles Rd. • 829-3091

Facilities here include an indoor pool, full gymnasium, free weights and Nautilus equipment.

Hamilton Central YMCA
Second and Market Sts., Hamilton • 887-0001

This Y has an indoor pool, Cybex machines and two indoor tracks.

Hamilton West YMCA
1307 N.W. Washington Blvd., Hamilton • 869-8550

The Hamilton West Y has an indoor pool, Cybex machines and an indoor track.

Clermont County

Camp Felicity YMCA
1349 Lenroot Rd., Amelia • 876-4473

An outdoor pool and running track are among the features at this camp.

Clermont YMCA
2075 Frontwheel Dr., Afton • 724-9622

Indoor and outdoor pools are available here, along with an outdoor playground, indoor track, full gymnasium, Universal and Nautilus equipment, free weights and multipurpose room.

Warren County

Countryside YMCA
1699 Deerfield Rd., Lebanon • 932-1424

This is by far the biggest and best-equipped Y in the region. The building, which of itself occupies 5 acres, sits on 126 acres of land. Outdoor amenities include two heated pools, tennis courts, a sand volleyball court, a 1.5-mile nature trail, baseball and soccer fields, a half-mile track, a picnic pavilion, three playgrounds and garden plots available to members at no extra cost.

Inside are Nautilus equipment, free weights in a light weight room and a heavy weight room (for serious grunting and groaning), a circuit training room, three pools, a track, racquetball courts, tennis courts, a game room with a pool table and table tennis, a regulation dance floor, three gymnasiums and a snack bar.

Northern Kentucky

Camp Ernst YMCA
7615 Camp Ernst Rd., Burlington, Ky.
• **(606) 586-6181**

An operating Western ranch, Camp Ernst has a well-regarded summer camp for boys and girls, ages 9 through 16. Among the gigantic playthings are a harness Zip Line and a giant bouncing balloon on the lake.

Campbell County YMCA
**1437 S. Fort Thomas Ave.,
Fort Thomas, Ky.**
• **(606) 781-1814**

This Y has indoor and outdoor pools, Nautilus equipment, free weights and racquetball courts.

Kenton County YMCA
5262 Madison Pike, Independence, Ky.
• **(606) 356-3178**

An outdoor-only facility, the Kenton County Y has a pool and volleyball, tennis and basketball courts.

Tri-City YMCA
212 Main St., Florence, Ky.
• **(606) 371-4680**

This Boone County Y has indoor and outdoor pools, outdoor tennis courts, a sauna, soccer and baseball fields, a gymnasium, a Nautilus and free-weight room and a full set of cardiovascular fitness equipment.

Wade YMCA
1806 Scott Blvd., Covington, Ky.
• **(606) 431-8140**

Although this facility is small, it offers league basketball, indoor soccer, plus preschool tumbling and other classes for kids.

Southeastern Indiana

Dearborn County YMCA
23596-C Jeb Dr., Lawrenceburg, Ind.
• **(812) 637-0800**

The Dearborn Y offers classes in schools throughout the Dearborn area in aerobics,

youth sports, tumbling, day camp programs and sports leagues. Call for sites and details.

YWCAs

Although area YWCAs are nowhere near as extensive as YMCAs (one reason being that YMCAs have always been open to women), they are nonetheless a potent force in terms of their aggressive stand on women's health issues (breast cancer awareness, domestic abuse counseling and shelters, and so on). The YWCAs also offer a number of services and recreational opportunities for both men and women.

FYI

Unless otherwise noted, the area code for all phone numbers listed in this guide is 513.

Ohio

Hamilton County

Downtown Center YWCA
898 Walnut St. • 241-7090

The downtown YWCA offers a pool, health club facilities, gym, sauna and indoor walking track. The Fitness Center offers classes in health and wellness as well as self-defense. There are girls' basketball and volleyball leagues.

Clermont County

Clermont Center YWCA
55 S. Fourth St., Batavia • 732-0450

The Clermont YWCA offers a variety of recreational and educational opportunities and classes, for both children and adults. There are no pool or exercise facilities on site, however.

Health Clubs and Sports Centers

Area residents tend to pick their health club based on geographic convenience. Local Yellow Pages list hundreds of such clubs. For tourists and travelers who are in town for only a few days, we've culled a short list of clubs that don't require monthly or annual membership, although you may need to belong to an affiliated

Photo: Skip Tate

When downtown, take a break with a dip in the fountain.

club or association. We've included hotels that have major health and fitness facilities for their guests. (See our Health Care chapter for fitness facilities run by and at local hospitals.)

Bally Total Fitness

4780 Cornell Rd., Blue Ash • 469-0090
9700 Colerain Ave., Colerain • 385-5522
9675 Montgomery Rd., Montgomery
• 984-4811
3694 Werk Rd., Western Hills • 922-1731

Each of these clubs has an indoor swimming pool and track, weight training equipment, racquetball courts and stair machines. Child care is available. You must have a Bally membership, but it can be to any club in the United States.

Carew Tower Health & Fitness Club

441 Vine St. • 651-1442

This is certainly the most conveniently located health club to major downtown hotels such as The Westin, Omni Netherland Plaza and Hyatt. The club offers a 40-foot lap pool, Cybex machines, free weights, an aerobics room and a full set of cardiovascular workout equipment, such as stationary bikes, stair machines, NordicTrack and rowing machines. There's also a steam room and sauna. Nonmembers can spend the day for $10.

Cincinnati Sports Club

3950 Red Bank Rd., Fairfax • 527-4550

The Cincinnati Sports Club is a full-feature health club: cardiovascular-vascular fitness center, Cybex machines and free weights, indoor and outdoor pools, one-fifth-mile indoor running track, and basketball, squash, racquetball and tennis courts. The club is part of the Sports Mall, a multipurpose sports facility with two indoor soccer fields, five indoor batting cages, a snack bar, a retail sporting goods store, a rehabilitation/sports medicine clinic, gymnastics training and aerobics classes. Nonmembers must be-

long to the International Racquetball and Squash Association in order to use the facilities.

Comfort Suites Riverfront

420 Riverboat Row, Newport, Ky.
• 291-6700

Cincinnati's newest major hotel offers its guests a fitness room with lifecycles, stair steppers, treadmills and Nautilus equipment.

The Drawbridge Estate

I-75 at Buttermilk Pk., Fort Mitchell, Ky.
• (606) 341-2800

Certainly the place for exercise buffs to stay if they want to be near the Cincinnati/Northern Kentucky International Airport. It offers no less than three swimming pools (one indoors), tennis courts, sand-lot volleyball, a fitness room, a whirlpool, a sauna and more.

Embassy Suites RiverCentre

10 E. RiverCentre Blvd., Covington, Ky.
• (606) 261-8400

This facility provides an indoor pool, a sauna and a fully outfitted fitness center. Even better, for joggers, it's next to the riverfront and beautiful Riverside Drive.

Hyatt Regency Cincinnati

151 West Fifth St. • 579-1234

Use the indoor pool and in-house health club at the Hyatt or take a quick stroll to any number of downtown health clubs, such as Moore's (listed below) and Carew Tower (listed above).

Mid-Town Athletic Club

5400 Kennedy Ave. • 351-3000

A bargain $9 per day allows nonmembers the full use of Mid-Town's facilities, which include a wide range of virtual reality bikes, cardiovascular workout equipment, racquetball and squash courts, Nautilus equipment, free

---

INSIDERS' TIP

We don't have killer bees, but we do have two flying nuisances: yellow jackets and cicadas. The yellow jackets swarm in early fall, especially around park picnic tables. Cicadas are huge insects that wake up every decade or so from their underground hibernation. They're harmless, but ugly with a capital U.

weights and tanning beds. Mid-Town is a quick 10-minute drive from downtown, right up Interstate 71. The club lives up to its motto, "Fitness With a Personal Touch," by offering seniors' programs, weight reduction programs, healthy lifestyle classes, massage, injury recovery programs, and personal trainers and a staff exercise physiologist.

Moore's Fitness World
On the Skywalk (next to the Regal Cincinnati Hotel) • 381-2323
8790 Colerain Ave. • 923-3399
Forest Fair Mall (next to Bigg's), Forest Park • 671-0888
10681 Loveland-Madeira Rd., Loveland • 697-9797
2241 E. Sharon Rd., Sharonville • 771-1022
496 Patterson Blvd., Fairfield • 867-0923
613 Ohio Pike, Cherry Grove • 753-6700
7827 Tanners Ln., Florence, Ky. • (606) 525-6666

With one in practically every major Cincinnati neighborhood, you're never far from a Moore's. These large clubs feature Nautilus equipment and free weights, a full array of recumbent lifecycles, cardiovascular workout equipment, racquetball courts, indoor pools, seniors' programs, and babysitting. Of particular note for travelers is the Moore's on the Skywalk downtown; it's right next door to the Regal Cincinnati Hotel and is easy walking (or jogging) distance from the other downtown hotels. It's $10 a day for nonmembers ($3 for Regal guests). Of course, members of Moore's 500 affiliates nationwide are welcome at all clubs for free.

Omni Netherland Plaza
35 W. 5th St. • 421-9100

You'll find an indoor pool and a health club offering free weights, an aerobics room and a full set of cardiovascular workout equipment, including stationary bikes, stair machines and rowing machines.

Regal Cincinnati Hotel
150 West 5th St. • 352-2100

The Regal offers a full-service health club for its guests, plus the use of the outdoor rooftop pool (in season). Even better, Regal guests get in at the Moore's next door for just $3 (see Moore's listing above).

Victory Lady Fitness Center
9351 Colerain Ave. • 923-3334
433 Ohio Pike, Anderson • 528-2434

A women-only health and fitness center, Victory Lady caters to women who want to work out without getting checked out. Facilities include an indoor swimming pool, free weights, Hammer Strength equipment, lifecycles, stair machines, electronic treadmills, personalized programs and private showers. Nonmembers can get one free visit if they mentioned they've seen the club's ad in the Yellow Pages. Members of the International Racquetball and Squash Association or any of the 400 Allied Health Association clubs nationwide get unlimited access.

The Westin
Fountain Square • 621-7700

The Westin hotel's fitness center has a year-round pool, tanning beds and a workout room.

Diehard golfers can find a place to tee off in Greater Cincinnati — even in February!

Golf

"Fore!" and many other four-letter words are screamed a lot during the warm weather months in Greater Cincinnati. Not because we're that bad at golf, mind you, but because golfers are as abundant here as politicians and chili parlors. The area is a duffer's delight, with nearly 100 nine- and 18-hole courses spread throughout the Tri-state, most of them within a 25-minute drive from downtown.

No logical explanation has been found as to why the area is so rich in golf courses. It isn't particularly a golfer's destination like Hilton Head or Palm Springs, and there's no long list of well-known professionals who grew up here (baseball players, yes — golfers, no). Perhaps we just like the feeling of frustration. Who knows?

Everybody seems to play, though. Don't be surprised if you can't get in touch with certain business executives in their offices during the first few warm spring days. Plenty of local business takes place on the links. And if you need a building inspected, check the back nine. That's where a local television station found then-county building inspectors a few years ago, teeing it up on taxpayer time.

Some of the courses are private, most are public. And a surprising number are part of a residential golfing community. It seems you can't build a housing development around here these days without including a golf course. (See our Neighborhoods chapter.) Some of the private clubs are also liable to be Old Boys Clubs, which isn't good news if you are, oh, say, a woman. One local woman filed — and won — a discrimination grievance against one country club where the membership form lists "gentlemen" and "wife's name," and where spouses of "regular" members must wait until 12:30 PM before teeing off. The club appealed the order to end discrimination against women and the case is now in court. Another club recently changed its tee time restrictions for women because of the discrimination suit and

built a new dining area for both men and women.

We've put together a comprehensive list of public courses in Greater Cincinnati by area, with basic information about each one. The distances and par are from the back tees.

Putt well.

Central

Avon Fields Golf Course
4081 Reading Rd. • 281-0322

Owned by the City of Cincinnati, this 80-year-old course is the oldest municipal golf course west of the Allegheny Mountains. Located in the heart of the city, it is accessible from all parts of town. The 5051-yard, par 66 course offers straight and simple fairways played over a rolling terrain. There are no par 5 holes on the course, with the longest hole being a 432-yard par 4, one of 12 par 4s the course has to offer. Although the course can be played by beginners, the small target greens make the course more of a challenge for more experienced players. The greens and fairways are bentgrass.

The greens fee is $16.50 every day, and the cart fee is $21. Reservations are required for weekend tee times until noon and must be made at least 24 hours in advance. A driving range and pro shop are available.

Beech Creek Golf Club
1831 Hudepohl Ln. • 522-8700

Beech Creek is one of many nine-hole courses in Greater Cincinnati that can be adapted to an 18-hole course through the use of different tees. The course measures 3000 yards through nine holes, so it's good if you're looking for a quick game or don't want to walk long distances. The course has its challenges, though, such as a waterfall that sits behind the green on the 2nd hole and a grove of beech trees in the middle of the fairway on the 5th hole. Both are scenic, but demand good shooting. The greens fee is $12.50 for 18 holes, and the cart fee is $15. Reservations are suggested.

Blue Ash Golf Course
4040 Cooper Rd., Blue Ash • 745-8577

This scenic course is owned by the City of Blue Ash and is playable at all levels of ability. The course is tree-lined and well-bunkered by both sand and water. Water hazards, in fact, come into play on nine holes (including No. 1 and No. 18), which can make for a terrible (or a wonderfully ego-boosting) way to begin and end a round. Hole No. 1 requires a drive over two creeks that cut through the fairway, while hole 18 is a 525-yard par 5 that ends at a creek that cuts right in front of the green. Hole 6 may be the toughest because of the lake that sits next to the green. The par 72 course runs 6643 yards, with four par 5s.

The greens fee is $22 every day, and the cart fee is $22. Reservations can be made seven days in advance by Blue Ash residents and five days in advance by nonresidents. Practice greens and practice bunkers are available.

Glenview Golf Course
10965 Springfield Pike • 771-1747

Glenview has been recognized as one of the country's 50 outstanding public golf courses according to *Golf Digest*. The course is owned by the City of Cincinnati and located in a rural setting with beautiful bluegrass fairways and bentgrass greens. It has five tees on each hole. From the back tees, the course plays 7024 yards with a par of 72. An additional nine holes were recently added, giving the course 27 holes, each a par 36, each with two par 5s, but each with its own characteristics. The East Course ends with a 563-yard par 5. The West Course and South Course each have two almost identical holes that play over water hazards, one just 181 yards and the other 205 yards in length.

Greens fees are $23.50 weekdays and $26 weekends and holidays. The cart fee is $11

per person. Reservations can be made seven days in advance. A pro shop and driving range are available.

Golden Tee
I-75 and Sharon Rd., Sharonville • 771-0933

This nine-hole, par 27 course is just 1548 yards long and good for beginners in that it is as basic as courses get. The holes range from 66-yard No. 6 to 150-yard No. 4. The greens fee is $7 every day. There are no carts and no reservations, with tee times on a first-come basis. A 66-tee driving range (30 tees are sheltered and heated) is open until midnight, and pool tables and video games are available in case it's too cold for golf. Two 18-hole miniature golf courses are also available.

Greenhills Village
14 Enfield St., Greenhills • 589-3585

This tiny par 3 nine-hole course runs just 2214 yards, but it's a mature course with lots of large trees and hilly terrain. All the greens are elevated, adding to the challenge by making approach shots critical. Greenhills Village is a great course for beginners who are developing their skills, though, or for those in search of a very quick round of golf. The greens fee is $11. There are no carts.

Lake Gloria Golf Center
10511 Pippin Rd. • 825-9900

A tiny par 3 course of just 1100 yards over nine holes, Lake Gloria is good for beginners, seniors or anyone in search of a very quick round. It is as basic as courses get. The greens fee is $9.50. There are no carts.

Sharon Woods Golf Course
1355 Swing Rd., Sharonville • 769-4325

Sharon Woods is the oldest of the seven courses owned by the Hamilton County Park District, dating from 1938. The par 70 course runs 6403 yards, with the 468-yard 4th hole running uphill all the way. As one might gather from the name, the course is carved out of a heavily wooded section of a local park, making mature trees a regular hazard. The round ends with a 535-yard par 5, the course's longest hole. The greens fee is $18 every day. The cart fee is $11. Reservations can be made five days in advance.

Winton Woods/Meadow Links
10999 Mill Rd., Greenhills • 825-3701

This course in Winton Woods is owned by the Hamilton County Park District. The nine-hole, midlength course, which features bluegrass fairways and bentgrass greens, stretches over 2110 yards, with a par of 31. The course is spread out wide, which is good for players who by choice or by chance spread the ball all around the fairways. It is more of a challenge than most nine-hole courses, though. Water is in play on four of the nine holes, including the 150-yard No. 9 hole, where water sits just off the tee. Because the course sits in the middle of a local park, mature trees abound.

The greens fee is $10 every day, and the cart fee is $5.25 per person. Reservations can be made five days ahead of time. A pro shop, driving range and lounge are available.

Also offered at Meadow Links is the Golf Academy, with a 49-station covered and heated driving range, a natural turf practice area of different course scenarios, an indoor auditorium and learning center, special programs that are free to the public and a complete lesson program for all skill levels.

Winton Woods/Mill Course
1515 W. Sharon Rd., Greenhills • 825-3770

This long, rolling course sits in Winton Woods park and has bentgrass fairways and greens and five water hazards. The Mill was renovated in 1993 and includes a new clubhouse for the challenging 6376-yard, par 71 course. Its No. 2 hole is a 513-yard par 5 that makes a sharp 90-degree turn to the left. The No. 11 hole is a 409-yard par 4 that travels over water.

The greens fee is $17.75 every day, and the cart fee is $10.75. Reservations are accepted five days ahead of tee times.

Wyoming Golf Club
81 Mount Pleasant Ave., Wyoming • 821-8226

Although it has only nine holes, the course at this 82-year-old private club fools newcomers with its difficulty. It is not a pitch-and-putt course — a creek runs through five holes and there are three par 5 holes, including one 465 yards long and another 555 yards long. The course is somewhat exclusive, although not to the point where nonmembers can't find a member to host them for a round. The course is 3160 yards long with par 36. The greens fee is $25, and the cart fee is $10. A driving range, practice areas, swimming pool and platform tennis courts are also available.

East

California Golf Course
5920 Kellogg Ave. • 231-6513

This 60-year-old course, which is owned by the City of Cincinnati, is edged with heavy woods, and the trees spill over into the narrow fairways, creating the need for precise aim. The course is played over a rolling terrain and is built around two massive holding basins for the city's water works, which offer water hazards along with a beautiful setting. It sits high above the Ohio River, too, creating scenic overlooks of the Kentucky hills. The par 70 course is 6236 yards long, but straightforward with only one par 5 — the 480-yard No. 2 hole — and one hole with a dogleg. The back nine has only one par 3.

The greens fee is $17.75 every day, and the cart fee is $22. Reservations can be made seven days in advance. A restaurant and pro shop are available.

INSIDERS' TIP

The Golf Center at Kings Island was designed by golfing legend Jack Nicklaus and, until 1994, was known as the Jack Nicklaus Golf Center. Not surprisingly, the course record was set by Nicklaus himself, a nine-under 62 shot in 1973. J.C. Snead tied the record at the 1996 Kroger Seniors Classic.

Deer Track Golf Course
6160 Ohio Hwy. 727, Goshen • 625-2500

This 6352-yard, par 71 course features one of the area's few island greens. One of the course's 16 lakes surrounds the green on the par 3, 157-yard 15th hole. The course also has 47 sand traps. Permanent weekend tee times are available. Weekday specials offer twosomes a chance to ride 18 holes for $48 or $24 each. The weekend greens fee is $20 for 18 holes. The cart fee is $10.

Eagles Nest Golf Course
1540 Ohio Hwy. 28, Goshen • 722-1241

Eagles Nest is flat, easy to walk and offers open fairways, elevated greens and a sampling of all hazards, including so much water that scuba gear may be necessary. The 156-yard No. 7 hole isn't much more than a tee, a lake and a green. The 299-yard par 4 No. 3 hole also goes over a lake. The toughest hole may be No. 9, which has water off the tee and water around the green, forcing a good drive and a good approach shot. The course features rye and bluegrass and runs 6100 yards with a par of 71.

Greens fees are $17, and the cart fee is $10 per person. Reservations are accepted seven days in advance. A pro shop and driving range are available.

Hickory Woods Golf Club
1240 Hickory Woods Dr., Loveland • 575-3900

The course is short, just 6105 yards long, but deceiving. The front nine holes are fairly open, but the back nine combine hills, woods and streams on just about every hole. Par is 70. Bluegrass and rye grass are combined on the fairways, while greens are bentgrass. Hole No. 8 seems to stretch on forever, doglegging left and right, with 580 yards between the tee and the green. Possibly ruining the day, the 18th hole is a 472-yard par 5 that requires a drive over water. The greens fee is $31 and includes a cart. Reservations can be made seven days in advance.

Indian Valley Golf Course
3950 Newtown Rd., Newtown • 561-9491

Sitting along the banks of the Little Miami River, this 6284-yard, par 72 course is flat and ideal for older golfers or beginners. The holes range from the 130-yard, par 3 No. 5 to the 523-yard, par 5 No. 14. Water comes into play on two holes, 3 and 15. The greens fee is $17. The cart fee is $20. No reservations are required.

Little Miami Golf Center
3811 Newtown Rd., Newtown • 561-5650

Owned by the Hamilton County Park District, Little Miami offers two nine-hole courses, both of which are flat, simple, short and great for beginners. The larger course is a par 35 that stretches 3204 yards and features a 592-yard, par 5, two par 3s and 15 par 4s that range from 314 to 400 yards. One of the par 3s is only 66 yards long. The smaller course is 845 yards with a par of 27. The holes, however, do offer some challenges, such as the 90-degree turn on the 274-yard No. 9 hole.

The greens fees are $5.75 for the par 3 and $9.75 for 18 holes. The cart fee is $5.50 per person. Reservations are needed for weekend mornings only and can be made five days in advance. A pro shop and driving range are available.

O'Bannon Creek Golf Club
6824 Ohio Hwy. 48, Loveland • 683-9100

This private course features rolling terrain and plenty of trees along 6513 yards, offering a par of 70. Greens fees are $28 weekdays, $38 weekends. The cart fee is $11. A driving range and practice green are available.

Reeves Golf Course
Beechmont and Wilmer Aves. • 321-2740

The 40-year-old Reeves course is owned by the City of Cincinnati and is part of the Lunken Airport playfield, so it's not uncommon for corporate jets, private planes, helicopters or even the Goodyear blimp to go flying by overhead. The course is level, easy to walk and offers no water hazards, except in the spring when the course, which is near the Little Miami River, becomes flooded. It is usually closed for a time each spring because of the flooding, and when it reopens the low-

www.insiders.com

See this and many other Insiders' Guide® destinations online — in their entirety.

Visit us today!

lying areas are usually still under water, creating temporary hazards. The par 70 course, with rye fairways and bentgrass greens, is 6371 yards long and features elevated greens that make approach shots critical. Almost all of the holes are straight and not exceptionally long, with the 471-yard No. 10 and the 477-yard No. 4 its longest.

The greens fee is $16.75 every day, with a cart fee of $21. Reservations can be made a day ahead of time. A lighted practice area and heated driving range stalls are available. Tennis courts and softball fields are nearby.

Vineyard Golf Course
600 Nordyke Rd., Anderson • 474-3007

The Vineyard is the "resort course" of the seven owned by the Hamilton County Park District. It features bentgrass tees, fairways and greens in a rolling, scenic and heavily wooded setting in Woodland Mound Park. The par 71 course has three lakes that come into play on six holes and 45 white sand bunkers running throughout its lengthy 6789 yards. Some holes, such as the No. 2, which stretches for 553 yards, is protected by all three hazards: lake, trees and bunkers.

The greens fee is $24.75 every day, and the cart fee is $11. Reservations can be made five days ahead. The golf shop is rated as one of the country's 100 best by *Golf Digest*.

West

Circling Hills Golf Club
10109 Carolina Trace Rd., Harrison • 367-5858

This course on the far western edge of Cincinnati added a second nine holes during the summer of 1997. It remains a flat, links-style course with two lakes and numerous bunkers spread over 6523 yards. It is easily walkable, although a couple of holes seem to go on forever. The 434-yard No. 3 hole doglegs to the left and is followed by the 559-yard par 5 No. 4 hole, which requires a chip shot over a creek to make the green.

The greens fee is $17 daily, and the cart fee is $10. A driving range, pro shop and practice greens are available. Reservations can be made seven days in advance.

Delhi Hills Golf Course
1068 Ebenezer Rd., Delhi • 941-9827

This small par 3 course covers just 2600 yards and has no sand traps but plenty of hills. It has been family owned and operated since 1958 and is excellent for practicing iron shots. The greens fee is $5 and there are no carts.

Dunham Golf Course
4400 Guerley Rd. • 251-1157

The City of Cincinnati owns this course, which sits along the banks of the Little Miami River and is ideal for juniors or beginners. It stretches just 1396 yards, with a par of 29, so it's also convenient for those looking for a fast game or looking to work on their short game. Hills and valleys make each hole unique, with holes ranging from the 83-yard No. 3 to the 259-yard No. 9. Five of the holes are less than 116 yards.

The greens fee is $6.25 every day for nine holes, with carts $10 and reserved for seniors only. Reservations are not taken, with play on a first-come basis.

Fernbank Golf & Tennis Club
7036 Fernbank Ave., Saylor Park • 941-9960

This nine-hole, executive-style course runs 2198 yards with flat, wide-open fairways and a par of 31. The course is easy to walk and good for beginners, with two holes less than 92 yards. The 391-yard No. 8 and 419-yard No. 9 holes are exceptions to the short course. Greens fees are $7 weekdays and $9 weekends. There are no riding carts, although pull carts can be rented for $2. Play is on a first-come basis.

Hartwell Golf Club
Caldwell Dr. and May St. • 821-9257

The nine-hole course at this private club offers tight, tree-lined fairways covering 2480 yards. The hilly terrain helps push par to 34. Rye fairways and bentgrass greens are featured. The No. 3 hole is the course's longest, stretching 408 yards. Greens fees are $13 weekdays and $15 weekends. Cart fees are $10 weekdays and $15 weekends per person.

Hillview Golf Course
6954 Wesselman Rd., Mack • 574-6670

This scenic, family-owned course sits atop a hill on the city's west side and features several lakes. The par 71 course is 5435 yards long. Greens fees are $11 before 1 PM weekdays and $13 after 1 PM weekdays and on weekends. The cart fee is $16.

Miami View Golf Club
8411 Harrison Ave., Whitewater
• 353-2384

The first two holes of this private course are a 477-yard par 4 and a 435-yard par 4, possibly making for a long day for short hitters. The rest of the par 71 course features rolling hills and three lakes through its 6469 yards. Fees are $25 weekdays and $30 weekends. The club also has a driving range, putting green, practice fairway and chipping green.

Miami Whitewater Forest Golf Course
8801 Mount Hope Rd., Harrison
• 367-4627

A lot of wildlife roams this scenic, Hamilton County-owned par 72 course. It sits adjacent to a lake, but that simply adds to the beauty of the course because water does not come into play on any of the holes. The course is straight-forward and good for beginners, but it is long, stretching 6780 yards. None of the par 4 holes is less than 350 yards, and four are more than 400 yards long. The greens fee is $17.75 every day, and the cart fee is $11. A pro shop and driving range are available.

Neumann Golf Course
7215 Bridgetown Rd. • 574-1320

Neumann is the most popular course in Greater Cincinnati, with an estimated 95,000 rounds played here each year. The 30-year-old course, which is owned by the City of Cincinnati, features three nine-hole courses: Red, 2943 yards long, par 35; White, 3046 yards long, par 36; and Blue, 3172 yards long, par 35. The 27 holes are all over rolling, wooded terrain. The Red Course features a 465-yard par 5 that bends to the right around a grove of trees, forcing golfers to either go over or around it. The White Course includes one of the few holes with water, the 307-yard No. 2, which has water just off the tee. The Blue Course has two of the toughest back-to-back holes, with a 390-yard No. 7 that goes over water, followed by a very long 612-yard par 5.

Greens fees are $17 or $27.50 with a cart. A practice range, driving range and pro shop are available. Reservations can be made no more than two days in advance.

Pebble Creek Golf Course
9799 Prechtel Rd., Bevis • 385-4442

Trees and bentgrass tees, greens and fairways make this rugged, hilly course lush. The course runs just 5848 yards, although it includes four par 5s, with the longest hole the 520-yard No. 12. Greens fees are $20 weekdays and $25 weekends for the par 71 course. The cart fee is $10. Reservations can be made four days ahead of tee time.

Shawnee Lookout Golf Course
2030 Lawrenceburg Rd., North Bend
• 941-0120

You can see three states from the 12th tee of this scenic, hilly Hamilton County-owned course that overlooks the Ohio River. Deer and other wildlife roam the heavily wooded course. No holes on the front nine of this par 70, 6001-yard course extend beyond 365 yards. The holes, though, are crooked as can be, with dogleg and Z-shaped fairways throughout. A small creek runs through the course, coming into play on half the holes, and a small lake complicates the 159-yard par 3 No. 5 hole.

INSIDERS' TIP

A good way to learn the game is by attending the Meadow Links Golf Academy in Winton Woods. The academy is run by the Hamilton County Park District and offers a 49-station covered and heated driving range, a natural turf practice area of different course scenarios, an indoor auditorium and learning center, special programs that are free to the public and a complete lesson program for all skill levels. Call 825-3701.

The greens fee is $15 every day, and the cart fee is $11. Reservations can be made five days in advance.

Woodland Golf Course
5820 Muddy Creek Rd. • 451-4408

Woodland is a short, nine-hole course but is hilly and features a little bit of all types of hazards that require accurate tee shots. The 2449-yard, par 34 course is owned by the City of Cincinnati, has only two par 3 holes and includes two par 5 holes at 597 and 575 yards. The greens fee is $9, and the cart fee is $5. Reservations are required for holidays and weekends only. The old barn clubhouse adds to the rustic atmosphere.

North

Photo: Cincinnati Recreation Commission

Public, private and residential golf courses provide plenty of putting opportunities.

Fairfield Golf Club
2200 John Gray Rd., Fairfield • 867-5385

This 6290-yard, par 70 course is flat and easily walkable, but almost half its holes have water hazards. Hole No. 16, a 393-yard par 4, features a green surrounded on three sides by water, while water and trees pack the 543-yard par 5 No. 3. The greens fee is $19 every day, and the cart fee is $11. Reservations can be made seven days in advance for weekends and holidays. Putting greens and tennis courts are nearby.

Hueston Woods Golf Course
6961 Brown Rd., Oxford • 523-8081

Situated in Hueston Woods State Park, this course is filled with mature trees. Featuring bluegrass fairways and bentgrass greens, it is a very long 7005 yards, with a par 72. Water comes into play on three holes, but two of them — the 208-yard No. 16 and the 201-yard No. 18 — require drives over the drink. The 11th hole is the longest, stretching a whopping 567 yards.

Greens fees are $16.50 weekdays and $22.50 weekends. The cart fee is $11.50 per person. Reservations can be made the Monday before the tee time. A pro shop and driving range are available.

Pleasant Hill Golf Club
6847 Hankins, Middletown • 539-7220

This flat, open course is used a lot by leagues and senior golfers. It features shorter par 5s and longer par 4s on its 6586 yards. Par is 71. Greens fees are $15 weekdays and $16 weekends. The cart fee is $16. A driving range, pro shop and practice areas are available.

Potters Park Golf Course
417 Hamilton-New London Rd., Hamilton • 868-5983

A tight, undulating course, Potters Park features small greens, few bunkers and long par 3s over its 5449 yards. Par is 69. The greens fee is $15.50 every day, and the cart fee is $19.

Vista Verde Golf Club
4780 Millikin Rd., Hamilton • 868-6948

Eight miniature ponds sit within this 5900-yard, par 73 course, which features elevated tees and no bunkers. All greens are surrounded on three sides by trees or placed on hills and are sand-based for quick drainage. The greens fee is $26 every day and includes a cart. You can see fox, deer, pheasant and geese in abundance on the course.

Weatherwax Golf Club
5401 Mosiman Rd., Middletown • 425-7886

Weatherwax, which was designed by Arthur Hills and has been rated by *Golf Digest* as one of the top 75 public courses in the country, has four nine-hole courses — Woodside, Meadows, Valley View and Highlands — that can be arranged six different ways. Each course has three sets of tees, creating 18 different ways to play the course. The two main courses, Woodside and Meadows, combine for a very long 7174-yard par 72 from the back tees. Valley View and Highlands combine for a lengthy 6756-yard par 72.

The course just completed a $2.2 million renovation that included a switch from bluegrass to bentgrass fairways, elevated tees and new sand traps. The greens fee is $20 every day, and the cart fee is $17. A driving range and practice area are available, along with a limited pro shop.

Wildwood Golf Club
5877 Ross Rd., Fairfield
• 874-3754

Wildwood is a semiprivate club built inside a residential community. It offers restricted hours for public play. The course is a regulation length nine-hole, 3160-yard, par 35 course. It has two sets of tees on each hole, though, creating the option to play 18 holes. The 396-yard No. 4 becomes a 459-yard No. 13 with the second tee. The 489-yard No. 9 becomes a 399-yard No. 18. The course, which has bluegrass fairways and bentgrass greens, is tight and hilly. The greens fee is $19, and the cart fee is $10. Check for availability of public play.

Northeast

Crooked Tree Golf Course
3595 Mason-Montgomery Rd., Mason
• 398-3933

Crooked Tree is one of the newer courses in the area, built around plenty of mature trees, lakes and rolling terrain that make the course picturesque. The 6415-yard course, which features bentgrass throughout, starts off with a 535-yard par 5 that doglegs to the right and then back to the left. The turn is made after a 540-yard par 5 in which a creek runs down the middle of the fairway and wraps around the green. There are four par 5s in the par 70 course, and drives must be made over a lot of

rough on several holes before reaching the fairway.

The greens fee is $23 every day for the par 70 course. The cart fee is $10. Crooked Tree, which is part of a residential development, also has one of the largest pro shops in the area. Reservations can be made seven days ahead. A driving range and clubhouse restaurant and bar are also available.

Golf Center at Kings Island
6042 Fairway Dr., Mason • 398-7700

The Golf Center at Kings Island is everything you could imagine in a day of golf, giving amateur golfers a chance to see how they might fare against the pros. It is home to the annual PGA Seniors tournament and has hosted 25 professional championships since it was built. It has two 18-hole courses: the larger Grizzly and the smaller Bruin, both designed by Jack Nicklaus.

The championship Grizzly course runs 6731 yards and cuts no slack throughout. Mature trees and dozens of sand bunkers are spread throughout the course and there's water on six holes. And, as a final exam, the course ends with a 546-yard par 5 that doglegs left over a large lake that has eaten up more than its share of pro players. Greens fees, which include a mandatory cart, are $51 Monday through Thursday, $52 on Fridays and $60 on weekends and holidays.

The Bruin is a 3428-yard, par 61 midlength course, with seven par 4s and 11 par 3s. Water comes into play on just one hole of the Bruin, which is flatter, straighter and much more direct than the Grizzly. Greens fees for the Bruin are $12.50 weekdays, $13.50 weekends. Carts, which are mandatory, run $13.50.

Reservations for both the Grizzly and the Bruin can be made seven days in advance. Eight tennis courts, a driving range with grass tees and practice bunkers are available. The upscale restaurant and bar is a good place to wrap up the day.

Harmon Golf Club
314 S. East St., Lebanon • 932-9067

This semiprivate course, just two blocks from historic downtown Lebanon, has bentgrass fairways, numerous trees and bunkers. It runs 6064 yards with a par 71. Greens fees are $17 weekdays and $20 weekends. The cart fee is $9. Check for availability of public play.

Kingswood Golf Course
4188 Irwin Simpson Rd., Mason
• 398-5252

A large lake and rolling fairways are featured on the squeezed 5834 yards at Kingswood. The course has a par of 71, and water comes into play on three holes. The 454-yard par 4 No. 2 hole is wedged between Nos. 3 and 8, requiring precision placement or a trip onto a neighboring fairway. Greens fees are $17 weekdays and $18 weekends. The cart fee is $20. Reservations can be made seven days in advance.

Shaker Run Golf Club
4361 Greentree Rd., Lebanon
• 425-5530, (800) 721-0007

Just about every shot in the bag is needed to work through this 6965-yard Arthur Hills-designed course, which *Golf Digest* has ranked as the top public course in Ohio. The course is heavily wooded throughout and dotted with water hazards on 11 of the 18 holes. Bring your trunks, because you'll go for a swim at least once. It is, quite possibly, the most challenging course outside of Kings Island. It opens with a 567-yard par 5, and if that doesn't get you off to a bad start (well, it would us — you might be a better golfer), the par 3 No. 5 requires a drive that carries 240 yards over water onto a green that hugs the water. The turn is made after a 435-yard par 4 No. 9 that follows the water's edge before turning right, carrying over more water and onto a green that is just about an island. The round ends with a 420-yard par 4 that drives over water in order to reach the fairway. Par is 72.

Greens fees are $60 weekdays and $70 weekends, with the cart included. Reservations can be made seven days in advance, and a 48 hour cancellation notice is required.

Twin Run Golf Course
2505 Eaton Rd., Hamilton • 868-5820

This par 72 course stretches a lengthy 6677 yards over rolling farmland but is playable by golfers at all levels. A clubhouse with a snack bar and pro shop was recently added. The greens fee is $15.50, and the cart fee is $19. Reservations are taken a week in advance.

Western Row Golf Course
Mason-Montgomery Rd., Mason
• 398-8886

Western Row is one of the most highly played clubs in the area because of its flat hazardless course. With the par 72 course running a lengthy 6746 yards, it has its challenges, particularly the four par 5s, all of which are more than 500 yards. Those seeking tee times sometimes have to compete with leagues and outings. Greens fees are $16 weekdays and $17 weekends. The cart fee is $18. Reservations are required for weekends only.

Northern Kentucky

AJ Jolly Golf Club
U.S. 27, Alexandria • (606) 635-2106

Campbell County owns this scenic par 71 course, which features an abundance of water hazards, including a 250-acre lake. The par 71 course, which stretches out over 6200 yards, includes a lengthy 558-yard par 5 on the No. 9 hole. The greens fee is $17 and a cart is $10. Reservations can be made up to eight days in advance.

Boone Links Golf Course
19 Clubhouse Dr., Florence
• (606) 371-7553

This 27-hole course is owned by Boone County and is open from February until December for diehard golfers who don't mind cold weather. The course is straightforward, with no tricky holes, although five par 5s can be found through the 27 holes, including a 490-yard par 5 on the first hole. The course runs 6600 yards and can be played with three different configurations.

The greens fee is $20 and a cart is $20. Reservations can be made seven days in advance. A pro shop and restaurant are available.

Devou Park
1344 Audubon Rd., Covington
• (606) 431-8030

Devou Park's course is part of a larger city

park that offers great views of the downtown Cincinnati skyline. With the recent addition of nine new holes, it can now be played over 6000 yards with a par of 70. The fairways are a combination of rye and bluegrass, while the greens offer bentgrass. The course is straightfoward and playable by all levels. It has just one par 5, the 523-yard No. 4, although the hole is straight.

The greens fee is $18 every day, and the cart fee is $10 per person. A pro shop, restaurant and bar are available. Reservations can be made only three days in advance.

Kenton County/Fox Run
3908 Richardson Rd., Independence
• (606) 371-3200

One of three courses owned by Kenton County that share a common clubhouse, Fox Run is the largest and nicest, heavily wooded with bentgrass tees and greens and nine holes with water hazards. The rolling terrain stretches 7055 yards, including a 558-yard 18th hole that doglegs right and left and then requires a good approach to the green, which sits behind a lake. Par is 72. That can make for a tough ending to a day on the links.

The greens fee is $18 every day, and the cart fee is $10.50. Fox Run offers a driving range, a warm-up range and a putting green. Kenton County residents can make reservations 10 days in advance; nonresidents must wait until seven days out.

Kenton County/Pioneer
3908 Richardson Rd., Independence
• (606) 371-3200

The Pioneer is the original of the three courses owned by Kenton County and is the most playable by the average golfer. Fairways are wide, and only three holes have water hazards. Water on the 202-yard par 3 No. 13, though, leaves no room for error, and the water on the 369-yard par 4 No. 4 forces drivers to either do their best Tiger Woods impersonation or pull up short and hit an iron over the water. Bentgrass tees and bluegrass fairways mark the course, which has only one par 5, and that isn't until the 17th hole.

The greens fee is $18 for the 6059-yard par 70 course. The cart fee is $10.50. Kenton

County residents can made reservations 10 days in advance; nonresidents, seven.

Kenton County/Willows
3908 Richardson Rd., Independence
• (606) 371-3200

A very demanding back nine highlights this Kenton County-owned course. Six holes on the front nine feature water. The par 72 course runs 6791 yards, and the 398-yard No. 4 hole is played over water twice. The greens fee is $18 every day, and the cart fee is $10. As with the other course, Kenton County residents may schedule tee times 10 days in advance and nonresidents, seven.

Lassing Pointe Golf Course
2260 Double Eagle Dr., Boone County
• (606) 384-2266

Bentgrass tees and fairways highlight the long 6742 yards of the par 72 Lassing Point, which has been rated as the best public course in Kentucky by *Golf Digest*. The course has some of the largest greens in the area, with four to six sets of tee boxes for each hole. The day starts with the course's longest hole, a 555-yard par 5.

The greens fee is $36 and includes a cart. Reservations can be made seven days in advance for weekdays, nine days for Saturdays, and 10 for Sundays. A fully stocked pro shop, practice range and short-game center are available.

Meadowood Golf Course
5353 Limaburg Rd., Burlington
• (606) 586-0422

Four lakes and postage stamp-size greens are featured in this short, 5200-yard, par 69 course. Four of the holes are less than 150 yards. Even though the course is short, it does have three par 5s, including the 515-yard No. 13. The greens fee is $15 every day, and the cart fee is $10. Reservations are required for weekends only. A driving range and pro shop are available.

Twin Oaks Golf Course
E. 43rd and Michigan, Covington
• (606) 581-2410

After 85 years, Twin Oaks is undergoing a slow renovation after being purchased out of bankruptcy. Its flat course with wide Bermuda grass fairways stretching over 6396 yards attracts 190-plus corporate outings every year. Large trees, three lakes and numerous bunkers make the par 70 course challenging, though. There are only two par 5s in the 18 holes: a 560-yard hole at No. 16 and a 516-yard hole at No. 5. The back nine runs along the Licking River.

The greens fee is $16 every day, and the cart fee is $21. Reservations for weekend tee times can be made beginning the previous Monday.

World of Sports
7400 Woodspoint Dr., Florence
• (606) 371-8255

The par 58 executive course at this fitness center offers 14 par 3s and 4 par 4s for quick rounds. The greens fee is $18. The cart fee is $9 per person. No reservations are required.

Southeastern Indiana

Elk Run Golf Club
Soap Hill Rd., Aurora • (812) 926-1747

This small, nine-hole course runs just 2480 yards but has only two par 3 holes. It is a good course for beginners. The greens fee is $9 for 18 holes, with a cart fee of $8. Tee times are on a first-come basis.

Grand Oak Golf Club
370 Grand Oak Dr., West Harrison
• (812) 637-3943

A premium is placed on accuracy on this tight, target course. Elevated tees and bentgrass fairways run throughout the scenic, par 71 course, which stretches 6400 yards through mature trees. Five holes include water hazards. The course begins with a 390-yard par 4 that requires play over water, which can start the day with a splash. The 555-yard par 5 No. 16 is actually U-shaped, requiring some tricky shooting.

Greens fees are $21 weekdays and $26 weekends. The cart fee is $11 per person. Reservations are accepted seven days in advance. A driving range and short game center are available, and club repair is handled in the pro shop.

Indian Lakes
7234 E. Ind. Hwy. 46, Batesville
• (812) 623-GOLF

The emphasis in the name is on lakes. All nine of the course's holes are over water — and not just a stream or trickle, but a lake. Rolling hills and tree-lined fairways also help make the course difficult, as well as scenic. The large greens help ease the strain. Greens fees at the course, which is part of a residential resort, are $18 weekdays and $23 weekends. Carts are free for resort members and $10 per person for non-members.

Sugar Ridge Golf Club
2010 State Line Rd., Lawrenceburg
• (812) 537-9300

The course at Sugar Ridge is very hilly and long (at 7000 yards it is one of the longest courses in the area) with a par of 72 and secluded fairways. Heavily wooded, it is named after the abundance of sugar maples around the course. A lot of wild animals wander around the course, which offers four sets of tees on each hole. The 16th hole is a 600-yard par 5 with a green surrounded by bunkers, one of four par 5s; it's followed by a 180-yard par 3 that is over water. Greens fees, which include a cart, are $32 weekdays and $39 weekends. Reservations can be made up to two weeks in advance.

Vineyard Golf Club
Ind. 250, Rising Sun • (812) 594-2627

This small, nine-hole course runs 3100 yards with a par of 36, but it may be difficult for beginners. The 250-yard par 4 17th, for instance, leads to a peninsula green. Greens fees are $12 during the week and $15 on weekends. The cart fee is $10.

Cincinnati sportscasters Marty Brennaman and Joe Nuxhall are so popular they have their own brand of potato chips.

Spectator Sports

As a city, Cincinnati may be small compared to other major metropolises. As a sports city, though, we can stand toe-to-toe and slug it out with any city in the country. In fact, sports are a dominant characteristic of the area's makeup. Major league baseball, for instance, is not only played here, it started here. The city supports a professional football team, two college basketball teams that often rank among the top 25 in the country and two minor league hockey teams, and hosts one of the top nine tennis tournaments in the world, a seniors golf tournament and the richest Kentucky Derby prep race in the country. Seeing the Goodyear blimp buzzing around the sky is no big deal.

Plus, numerous onetime events are frequently held in the area. Figure skating and gymnastics are hugely popular. We've hosted world and national skating and gymnastic championships and just about every post-Olympic event that skates or tumbles. Our sports scene includes the NCAA basketball tournament, the NCAA hockey tournament, Olympic hockey team exhibitions, NBA basketball and NHL hockey games and even the rodeo, indoor motorcycle racing, monster truck tractor pulls and professional WWF big-time wrestling with Texas cage, to-the-death, last-man-in-the-ring, world championship, no-holds-barred, heavyweight title matches — assuming you consider these activities sports.

There's even an attempt to get the ultimate onetime event, the Olympics, held in Cincinnati. Former city councilman Nick Vehr quit his city job and took up an effort to convince the U.S. Olympic Committee that Cincinnati is the place to hold the Summer Games in 2012. We aren't holding our breath, but anything is possible.

Not only are sporting events vital to the immediate area's economy and psyche, they are probably our major regional attraction. Fans regularly travel hundreds of miles from Indiana, Kentucky, Ohio, West Virginia and even Tennessee to watch the Reds and Bengals play.

We must admit, though, that regionalism and unity of community don't hold true with all sports. In some instances, allegiances tend to stop at the borders. Few Kentuckians, for example, care about Ohio State football. Few Ohioans follow University of Kentucky basketball. And don't try telling anyone in Indiana that there's another team — particularly another basketball team — besides Indiana University's.

If you're new in town, here's what you can expect in terms of spectator sports in Greater Cincinnati. If you want to play, you had better be darned good, or check our Parks and Recreation chapter for a more suitable activity.

Baseball

Cincinnati Reds
Cinergy Field • 421-4510, (800) 829-5353

Baseball and Cincinnati are synonymous in the minds of local residents. This is the place where the professional game originated, where the first night game was played after President Franklin Roosevelt threw a switch at the White House to turn on the ballpark lights, where hometown hero Pete Rose became the all-time hits leader, and where Opening Day each April is an unofficial holiday celebrated with a parade.

It is the place where the Big Red Machine once dominated the game, winning six Western Division titles, four National League titles and two World Series. It is the place where five World Series trophies rest, where the first National League team to go wire-to-wire, staying in first place every day of the season, resided and where some of baseball's greatest players and managers call home. In fact, as summarized by Lonnie Wheeler and John Baskin in their book *The Cincinnati Game*, "If there is one city whose removal from the face of baseball history would disfeature it beyond recognition, it is Cincinnati."

When the Reds (née the Red Stockings) began playing professionally in 1869, the team put together a 130-game winning streak before suffering its first loss, setting high standards for the game and particularly for Cincinnati. We didn't like to lose then, and that's still true today. The team continued to roll until 1871, when it was discontinued by the owners for six years because of (does this sound familiar?) increased salary demands.

By 1919, though, the Reds were back on top of the baseball world, winning their first World Series over the Chicago White Sox, a team that became better known as the Black Sox because some team members accepted bribes from gamblers to throw games. Although a cloud and a question mark hung over that World Series title, the Reds didn't let it stop them in their search for glory, playing in eight more World Series (1939, 1940, 1961, 1970, 1972, 1975, 1976 and 1990) and winning four of them. During those years, some of the game's all-time greatest players wore a Reds uniform: Rose, Johnny Bench, Frank Robinson, Joe Morgan, Tom Seaver, Ernie Lombardi, Ted Kluszewski, Buck Ewing.

The area's contribution to major league baseball is not limited to just Reds' players; almost 250 Greater Cincinnati natives have made it to the major leagues, either as players or managers. Today, more than a dozen local players are in the majors, including Barry Larkin, David Justice, Ken Griffey, Jr., Jeff Russell, Tim Naehring and Lance Johnson. Put them all on one team and you'd have the beginnings of another Big Red Machine.

Former greats Buddy Bell, Dave Parker, Leon "Bull" Durham, Ewing, Joe Nuxhall, Jim Bunning, Kent Tekulve, Walter Alston, Jim Frey and Don Zimmer and others helped the area collect 32 national amateur baseball titles and more than 50 state high school baseball championships.

Today, baseball in Cincinnati revolves around the current edition of the Reds, which

FYI

Unless otherwise noted, the area code for all phone numbers listed in this guide is 513.

has had its struggles. Free agency, high salaries, a depleted farm system, a small market, player strikes, and even questionable decisions by a wacky owner have forced the team to constantly try to make more out of less. It's been tough. Gone are the days of Big Red Machine stability, and what each new season will bring is a great unknown. The team is on its seventh manager since 1989 and it's truly become a situation where you can't tell the players without a scorecard. A revolving door ushers in high-priced free-agent players each year and then ushers them out just as quickly. Interestingly, some of the players that have come through the doors have been second-generation Reds, such as Eduardo Perez, son of Tony Perez, and Pete Rose Jr., son of, well, you know. About the only solid core the team has had in recent years has been Larkin, who was the Most Valuable Player in the National League in 1995.

Sometimes, though, the team still manages to overcome the obstacles and finds itself in the playoffs, or at least in the running ("The Hunt for Reds October" is a common cry). The 1990 World Series team is still fresh in our memory, as are such teams as the 1995 edition, which made it to the National League Championship Series.

Unfortunately, even the successes on the field tend to get overshadowed by all the action off the field. The topics of where the team will play in the future and who will be its leader are grabbing newspaper headlines and filling hours of sports talk shows.

Marge Schott, the tough-as-nails, dog-loving, sometimes admirable, sometimes embarrassing owner of the team was suspended as the team's chief executive officer through the end of the 1998 baseball season by fellow owners for repeatedly making racial, ethnic and sexist comments. (Read more about Marge in our Close-up.) She has been suspended before for making such slurs, but she returned after a year. This time, though, people are wondering if she will come back at all.

In the meantime, she is concentrating on getting the team a new place to play. She doesn't think the team's current home, Riverfront Stadium (now known as Cinergy

Photo: Greater Cincinnati Convention and Visitors Bureau

The Cincinnati Bengals play at home in the 60,000-seat Cinergy Field.

Field), is suitable for baseball and is negotiating with the county for a new baseball-only ballpark — one of those retrofit parks like Jacobs Field in Cleveland and Camden Yards in Baltimore that seem to be in vogue these days. The citizens of Hamilton County approved a sales tax increase in November 1995 to fund a new stadium (as well as one for the city's football team, the Bengals) but the particulars are still being hammered out. The new ballpark would feature something that is desperately missing from Cinergy Field — a place to honor Cincinnati's great contributions to the sport, with Reds statues, plaques, souvenirs and perhaps a Reds Hall of Fame.

Despite the escalating costs associated with the sport, the Reds remain the least-expensive baseball team to watch, with $1 hot dogs, $2 beers and affordable tickets. Marge was quite proud of the relative inexpensiveness of a day at the ballpark and hadn't changed ticket prices in four years, but with

her out of the picture, things were bound to change. And they did, although in some cases for the better. In 1997, ticket prices for two premium lower-level seating sections increased, but the price of seats in the upper parts of the stadium actually decreased, making the cheap seats even cheaper.

Ticket prices are currently $14 for blue level, $11 for green and yellow reserved levels, $8 for green level, $9 for red reserved level, $6 for red level and $3 for "top six" tickets in the top six rows of the stadium. Tickets can be ordered by calling the numbers listed above or purchased with a service charge from any TicketMaster outlet in the country. Locally, TicketMaster's number is 749-4949. In Cincinnati, when the team is out of town, tickets for future games may be purchased without a service charge at the northwest ticket window on the plaza level of Cinergy Field (between gates 11 and 13) between 9 AM and 5 PM. When the team is in town, ticket windows are open be-

Football

tween 9 AM and the end of the fifth inning. Tickets and other memorabilia are also available at The Reds Dugout gift shop in the lobby of the Westin Hotel at Fifth and Vine streets downtown.

Catching the Reds games on television can be a bit confusing. Three local stations split the contract to air the games, so on some nights the games might be found by tuning in WSTR (channel 64), or WKRC (channel 12), or Time Warner's Fox Sports Ohio. WLW radio (700 AM) provides outstanding Reds coverage, with Marty Brennaman and Joe Nuxhall telling it like it is — good or bad, whether anyone likes it or not. They've been called to the league's offices for their unbiased comments and have faced the wrath of the Reds' front office.

Marty and Joe, who are so popular they have their own brand of potato chips, also provide a fix for diehard baseball fans during the long winter months between the World Series and spring training with a periodical "Hot Stove League" talk show on WLW that concentrates on baseball only. And, if you think there is nothing more disappointing than a rain delay, you're in for a pleasant surprise if you're within earshot of a radio. Marty and Joe fill in the time with entertaining and hilarious stories about the game and take questions on what they refer to (for reasons known only to themselves) as the Banana Phone.

For those who prefer baseball the way it was played in the good old days, each year former Reds players who grew up in Cincinnati and players from around the country get together for an old-timers game at a replica of old Crosley Field in Blue Ash. See our Annual Events chapter (July) for more details.

Cincinnati Bengals
1 Bengals Dr. • 621-3550

Welcome to The Jungle. During football season, that's what Cincinnati becomes: the home of the Bengals. For sixteen Sundays each fall the city puts on its orange and black stripes, picks up a football and starts chanting, "Who dey think gonna beat dem Bengals?" Throngs of 65,000 or so faithful march down to Cinergy Field (a.k.a. The Jungle when the Bengals are playing there) to cheer the team on, which, honestly, hasn't been an easy thing to do lately. After twice making it to the Super Bowl in the 1980s, the Bengals somehow lost their bite and have accumulated the worst record in football in the 1990s.

But while fans have becoming increasingly frustrated, they are very thankful they still have a team to root for. The city went through a scary period in which it looked as if the Bengals might become the latest team to pick up and relocate to another city — an issue that overshadowed everything the team was doing on the field. In 1997, the team agreed to stay in Cincinnati for the next 25 years, and the city's white knight turned out to be none other than the man who had been talking about leaving, president and general manager Mike Brown.

For years Brown was looked upon by some as a tight-fisted monarch, king of the family-owned business, who was unwilling to dip into the free-agent market and sign high-priced players or spend money on some genius general manager or a huge scouting staff — actions that most fans believed (and many still believe) were necessary to produce a

INSIDERS' TIP

The hottest ticket in town each winter is for the annual Crosstown Shootout basketball game between the University of Cincinnati and Xavier University. The two schools are regularly among the top 20 teams in the nation, and their campuses are only a few miles apart. Emotions run high in these games.

winning team. Brown's approval rating was worse than most politicians'.

Suddenly, though, the fans' perception of Brown began to change. Sometime in late 1995 he became an honest and fair businessman whose wallet wasn't padlocked and whose primary interest wasn't increasing his personal wealth. What changed their mind? Taxes, for one thing. The Cleveland Browns, for another. Browns owner Art Modell packed up the team and moved it to Baltimore in exchange for a $40 million upfront cash incentive, along with the keys to the city, all the crab cakes he could eat and the family jewels. Meanwhile, back in Cleveland, 70,000 faithful Browns fans who had packed the stadium for every game were left out in the cold, screaming for Modell's head on a platter.

But Baltimore, as Cincinnati learned, had first approached Mike Brown. It could have been the Bengals who moved to Baltimore, but Brown turned down the deal, saying his first priority wasn't to make as much money as he could, and that he was committed to Cincinnati. Before he would ever move the team, he said, he would first give the people of the city a chance to do whatever was necessary to keep the team in town — which meant passing a tax levy to pay for the construction of a new football-only stadium. Wow, the fans thought, maybe Brown wasn't such a bad guy after all. In the world of professional sports, where the dollar seems to be almighty and owners regularly offer their teams to the highest-bidding city, here was someone who was committed to us first.

So, in November 1995, the fans matched Brown's commitment by overwhelmingly passing a sales tax increase. Construction of the new ultramodern Paul Brown Stadium is under way along the riverfront, three blocks west of The Jungle.

Some fans still have ill feelings about Brown's management skills. The team has never had a winning season while he has been general manager, but of late Brown and the team seem to at least be trying to make major strides toward winning. They've tried to sign veteran free agents and made commitments to some of the team's top players, such as quarterback Jeff Blake. Blake's abili-

ties were discovered by accident in late 1994 when Blake, then the team's third-string quarterback, was forced into the game because of injuries to the first two quarterbacks. What looked like a disaster waiting to happen turned out to be a blessing in disguise. Blake ended up taking control of the offense and getting it to play like it hasn't played in years, hitting speedy receivers such as Carl Pickens and Darnay Scott for touchdowns and digging the team out of back-to-back 3-13 seasons in 1993 and 1994. By 1995, his first full year as a starter, Blake was in the Pro Bowl and hopes were revitalized.

Plus, in 1995, for the first time in its history, the team traded up in the draft — all the way to the No. 1 position, in fact — where it picked running back Ki-Jana Carter. Brown opened his wallet and gave Carter a $7.125 million signing bonus. (This bonus, the largest ever in the team's history, was about the same amount the Brown family paid for the franchise rights back in 1968.) A year later the team drafted offensive lineman Willie Anderson, and then began opening its wallet, signing several other experienced players, and edging its payroll near the salary cap . . . a place the team previously had chosen to stay a good distance away from.

Although it's still a long way away, our thoughts are starting to drift toward the playoffs and — could it be? — a return to the Super Bowl. The Bengals have twice made it to the Super Bowl, losing each time to the San Francisco 49ers, darn it, in two of the closest Super Bowls games ever. Some of the greatest players ever to wear Bengals stripes played in those Super Bowls, including Boomer Esiason, Tim Krumrie, Isaac Curtis, Ken Anderson and Anthony Munoz, the first Bengal ever to make it into the Hall of Fame. Future greats may lead the team back to the big game, and the city will be thankful they are ours.

Ticket prices for 1998 Bengals' games at Cinergy Field are $34 for the upper deck, $38 for field level, $42 for the good seats and $46 for the really good seats. Ouch! If you prefer to see the team play for a lot less, summer camp is at Georgetown College in Georgetown, Kentucky, about 70 miles south of Cincinnati, near Lexington, Kentucky.

That's Marge!

All you need is one name, like Madonna or Cher. Just say "Marge" in Cincinnati and everyone immediately knows who you are talking about: Marge Schott, the colorful if controversial owner of the Cincinnati Reds.

People in Cincinnati love Marge. Or hate her. Or both, depending on what she has said or done most recently. And there's no telling what that might be.

Marge is a double-edge sword and sometimes a contradiction unto herself. She's Dr. Jekyll and Mrs. Schott. She's well known for treating people harshly and insensi-

tively, but she graciously signs autographs for the fans who line the aisle next to her seat behind home plate. She has admitted to being such a tightwad she checks employees' garbage cans to make sure they're using both sides of scrap paper, but if she finds a cause she

believes in she will spend money like she's intent on going broke.

She is probably, for better or worse, Cincinnati's single most identifiable personality. People who know nothing about the city have heard of Marge. She's the one who gave the Pope a Reds jacket. She's the one who lets her dog run around the field before games. She's the one who has so embarrassed the sport of baseball with her racial and ethnic slurs she's been suspended from her position as the Reds' chief executive officer twice, most recently through the end of the 1998 season. And, whether we like it or not, she is ours.

For now, we don't have to worry so much about what Marge might say or do next. The suspension is keeping her out of the spotlight — at least as much as Marge can possibly be kept out of the spotlight. Center stage is a place she loves to be. And although she has temporarily turned over the day-to-day operations of the team to someone else while suspended, she is still overseeing the team's direction both on the field and off, which at times is a bigger story than what is going on down on the field.

We should have been able to see what we were getting with Marge back on December 1, 1984, the day she bought the team. She was brash, open, and spoke her mind, which was a stark contrast and a refreshing break to the previous owners, the Williams brothers, who were nearly invisible in their ownership. "I'm really, really lousy at 'no comment,' " she said at the time.

We already knew. During one losing season before she bought the team, she hired a plane to fly over the stadium trailing a banner that read, "Tony (Perez), Pete (Rose), Joe (Morgan). Help — Love, Marge." The response from one of the Williams brothers, William, was, "Sometimes she does or says something on the spur of the moment that she regrets later." Or, as author Mike Bass wrote in his biography of Marge, *Unleashed*, "She simply has no filter between her brain and her mouth."

For a while, it was cute. She called everybody "honey" so she wouldn't have to remember names. She once called former Reds' general manager Bill Bergesch "Whatchmadoodle." Over time, though, the cute wore off, starting in early 1992 as her prejudices and racial and ethnic views surfaced. Before anyone knew it, the stories were tumbling like an avalanche out of control.

After being suspended for a year by other team owners and ordered to undergo sensitivity training, it looked as if everything would remain quiet, or at least relatively so, although there were still the stories of treating workers poorly and the unwillingness to spend money — how she would give employees leftover candy bars as Christmas

— continued on next page

Photo: Mark Bowen

Red's owner Marge Schott is one of baseball's most controversial figures.

bonuses; how she would take their lunches from the refrigerator and feed them to her dog, Schottzie; how she refused to pay $300 a month for the wire service that provided out-of-town scores that were shown on the scoreboard; how she limited press notes to one page so she could save $5 in copying costs; how she refused to chip in even a penny to help pass a tax levy that would generate the money necessary to build new stadiums for the Reds and Bengals; how she would not trade a player because he was good-looking; or how she would not sign a manager because he lived with his fiancee before they got married.

Then, as the 1996 season got underway, it started again. Umpire John McSherry died on the field on Opening Day, halting the game, and Marge said she "felt cheated." Two days later, she sent the rest of the umpires recycled flowers that someone had sent to her the day before, just changing the note card. It was good material for Leno and Letterman, but embarrassing to Cincinnati. Then, in May, a reporter from ESPN asked her if she still owned the Nazi arm band, the item that opened the Pandora's Box of her discriminatory views. "Hitler was right in the beginning, everyone knows that," she told the reporter, "he just went too far." She still had it.

The ESPN interview was followed a few weeks later by an honest and unflattering look at Marge in *Sports Illustrated,* in which she was not only depicted as a lonely old

— continued on next page

woman, but one who continued to openly insult African-Americans, Asian-Americans and even working women. "Schott Happens" became a popular phrase. "Marge was good in the beginning, but she just went too far" became a popular joke. Renowned sports sociologist Dr. Harry Edwards said, "Look, Marge is an old woman who smokes. The problem will take care of itself." The other team owners finally had enough, though, and suspended her again.

Why she doesn't just stop giving interviews seems to be the biggest question. Most of the problems would go away if she would just keep quiet. But she just keeps talking. She gives interviews like she smokes cigarettes — endlessly. "The quickest way to get hurt," Pete Rose once said, "is to come between Marge and a microphone."

People in Cincinnati react less than others to Marge's antics. Perhaps it's because we like to protect our own. Perhaps it's because we're so used to hearing and seeing what she says and does we've become numb and it doesn't faze us that much anymore. Many people here see Marge and her views as a dinosaur, something antiquated and from another time. "That's just Marge," they'll say. "Those were the views of her generation and she just never changed." But most people don't accept these excuses, particularly for someone in such a public position and in charge of a business that projects an image of the city to the world.

But, as we mentioned, Marge isn't just about being cheap and making slurs. She has other sides, both business and personal, that few see. When she found out that the infant son of Jim Bowden, now the team's general manager, was near death, Marge arranged to have the baby flown across town to Children's Hospital where doctors, in a last-ditch effort, administered a drug that had been legalized just eight months earlier. It worked, saving the baby's life. She lets kids run around the field and takes them down to the dugout before and after games.

Marge also owns a local car dealership — Schott Buick — and other out-of-town businesses. Many of these businesses were inherited from her late husband, Charles, following his death in 1968. Mostly a socialite prior to his death, Marge was forced to become a hard-boiled business executive in order to keep hold of the businesses, and she remains one today. If you want to work for Marge, you only need to know her one rule: Everything is done her way. Period. No exceptions. No apologies.

The world of business was never totally foreign to Marge, though. While she was growing up, she spent a lot of time with her father, Edward Unnewehr, a second-generation manufacturer who made a fortune in cigar boxes and lumber. Marge was the second of five daughters and, lacking a son, was the one her father saw as the heir-apparent to the family business. "Butch," he called her. She would spend her days at the factory, running the machines and doing whatever needed to be done.

Her family was what she called "Achtung! German." Her father would ring a bell to call her mother. The children weren't allowed to eat with the adults until they were old enough to behave. When she wasn't at the factory, Marge attended private school, wore white gloves, took 12 years of French, and learned how to behave like a lady.

Parts of that starkly contrasting upbringing still show, others don't. She revealed to *Sports Illustrated* that she no longer buys her own clothes, but wears whatever someone sends her. The discipline and strict values, though, haven't changed. She admitted to videotaping players as they got on and off of planes to make sure there wasn't any "cutsey-pooing" going on between them and their girlfriends.

Love it or hate it, that's just the way she is. That's Marge.

College Sports

University of Cincinnati
2624 Clifton Ave. • 556-2287

Basketball tends to dominate the sports scene at UC, with the Bearcats regularly ranked in the Top 20 teams in the nation. UC once dominated college basketball around the time Oscar Robertson walked the campus, winning the NCAA tournament twice in the early 1960s. The Bearcats then fell into a long drought, but under the leadership of fiery head coach Bob Huggins, it has become a formidable power once again. With his "play harder longer" motto, Huggins has led his teams to the top of college basketball polls and made them regulars in the NCAA tournament. He even took his team to the NCAA Final Four in his third year at the helm.

He hasn't done so without a bit of color and controversy, though. Huggs, as he is known locally, has a give 'em hell attitude on the court. He isn't the least bit hesitant about screaming at his players or officials during games, and he has gained such a reputation for his temper that TV cameras often focus on him as much as on the court action.

Off the court, though, Huggins is calm and so soft-spoken he's sometimes hard to hear. He also supplies the area with a dash of color through his fashionable attire. His dapper suits and bright ties have garnered so much attention that a local men's clothing store began supplying him with ties for each game. The ties are then auctioned off during Huggins' weekly radio show, with the proceeds going to charity.

Personality aside, the Bearcats play hard for Huggins, and the team has risen to the level where not winning a game is bigger news than winning one. And many of his players have gone on to the professional ranks, including Danny Fortson and Nick Van Exel.

UC plays at the 13,000-seat Shoemaker Center, and tickets for the games are very difficult to come by. There has been talk of trying to expand seating at the facility to squeeze in more fans, but it hasn't happened yet. The university has a somewhat unusual arrangement with its season ticket policy, whereby those who want season basketball tickets must also buy season football tickets. The ticket trick was a way to boost attendance and support for the football program, although coach Rick Minter has turned the football team around to where getting football and basketball tickets together may soon be a bargain.

Minter came to UC in 1994 after serving as the defensive coordinator at Notre Dame and improved what had been a lackluster program struggling to shed its losing ways. By the 1997 season, the team was playing in a post-season bowl game. Fans of Bearcats football have nothing but high hopes for the future. The team plays in the newly created Conference-USA, which recruited schools from a variety of other conferences and became one of the country's most competitive conferences from its inception. Games are played at Nippert Stadium on the UC campus.

Xavier University
3800 Victory Pky. • 745-3411

The Muskies of Xavier University, a private Jesuit college of just 6,300 students, has become one of college basketball's elite powerhouses. And it has done so with class, remaining free of NCAA sanctions and graduating every player who played as a senior since 1986.

Starting with coaches Bob Staak and Pete Gillan and continuing with current head coach Skip Prosser, Xavier has taken its program up a notch on the success ladder each year and now finds itself regularly named one of the Top 20 teams in the country (and no longer overshadowed by its state-supported neighbor, UC).

The Muskies, who play in the powerful Atlantic 10 Conference, offer an exciting, fast-paced game with plenty of fast breaks and a lot of in-your-face pressure defense. This strategy has served the team well, taking it as far as the Elite Eight in the NCAA Tournament and sending players such as Brian Grant and Tyrone Hill into the NBA.

Currently, Xavier plays its home games off-campus at the 10,000-seat Cincinnati Gardens, although a new 10,000-seat $40 million convocation center is in the process of being built on the Xavier campus and should be ready for 1999. Tickets are becoming harder to get, as more than 6,500 people have purchased 1997-

98 season tickets — a record for XU — leaving only a handful after students, faculty and alumni scoop up most of the remaining ones.

Miami University
Oxford • (513) 529-3924

Miami is known in the football world as the Cradle of Coaches, with coaching legends Bo Schembechler, Woody Hayes, and Ara Parseghian, among others, getting their start in Oxford. The RedHawks — known as the Redskins until political correctness prevailed — haven't had much luck with coaches or winning on the gridiron in a while, though. But a trip to the beautiful Miami campus and Yeager Stadium is a great way to spend a fall afternoon.

The university's basketball program gets overshadowed by UC's and Xavier's but is a strong program. Under new coach Charlie Coles, the RedHawks have had four straight 20-win seasons and three trips to the NCAA Tournament in six years, and they continue their winning ways. The RedHawks often make a run for the Mid-American Conference title. They play at Millett Hall on the Oxford campus.

Other colleges

The success of the area's basketball teams doesn't stop at the Division I level. **Northern Kentucky University**, (606) 572-5193, has been the runner-up in the NCAA Division II Tournament for the last two years and is desperately trying to shake the bridesmaid business and win it all.

It's been a long, hard struggle for the NKU Norsemen to make it to that level. Just a few years ago, they were perpetual strugglers, always fighting to overcome. The Lady Norse, in fact, were a dominant team on the Division II level and often attracted more attention than the men's program. That has changed, though,

and now both programs find themselves celebrating March Madness. It's some of the best basketball most people never see.

NKU has taken a hard look at starting a football program, but has not made the commitment yet.

Thomas More College, (606) 341-5800, sports a Division III program. Both the Saints' football and basketball programs tend to get overshadowed by all of the high-powered teams in the area, but they're contenders in their own right. The basketball program has done so well, in fact, it has drawn players talented enough to go on to the professional ranks in Europe or to the Continental Basketball Association. One of its most famous recruits was a local player from Covington Latin High School named David Justice, who decided to stop playing basketball and concentrate on playing baseball and is now one of the best players in the major leagues.

Thomas More just started its football program in 1990 and found immediate success, although the team struggled in 1997, its first non-winning season at 5-5. It regularly competes with the **College of Mount St. Joseph** in the Bridge Bowl. Mount St. Joseph (244-4311), which also plays on the Division III level, also started its football program in 1990. Both schools are small (and academically challenging), and the games don't draw much of a crowd, but they have started a good little annual rivalry.

Fans in the area really pay more attention to what happens with **Ohio State University** football. When OSU plays at home, I-71 is jammed with Greater Cincinnati residents, who beat a path to Columbus to watch the Buckeyes (the fanaticism stops at the river, though). Trying to get a ticket to the Horseshoe, a.k.a. Ohio Stadium, is a tough task, but a call to (800) GO-BUCKS is worth the try.

> # FYI
> Unless otherwise noted, the area code for all phone numbers listed in this guide is 513.

INSIDERS' TIP

A cheap way to see a Reds game: Buy a Top Six ticket (seats in the top six rows of the upper deck) for $3.00 when they go on sale two hours before the game and then stand around or find an empty seat in one of the lower decks.

And the craze that the entire state of Kentucky — minus a small contingent in Louisville that is an island unto itself — has for the 1996 NCAA Champion **University of Kentucky** Wildcats trickles over a little bit into Ohio. Local radio stations carry the UK games, and when local sports talk shows say something bad about UK the phone lines are flooded by defensive Big Blue supporters who believe it is impossible for the Wildcats to do anything wrong. It takes good connections or a friendly scalper to get a ticket to Rupp Arena for a Wildcats game. To try, though, call (606) 257-1818.

Hockey

For years Cincinnati tried repeatedly, and failed repeatedly, to support a hockey team. The Mohawks, the Wings, the Swords, the Firebirds, the Stingers, the Tigers, the Stingers again all got their teeth knocked out and were sent to the showers. Now we have two teams — arguably more than we know what to do with. Both teams are battling for fans, and only time will tell who will win that game of attraction.

The Cyclones
The Crown, 200 Pete Rose Way
• 531-PUCK

The storm created by the Cyclones when they first came to town in 1990 is growing, thanks in part to the success the team has had on the ice. It is regularly a playoff contender and usually in the fight to make it to the Turner Cup Finals, the height of heights in the International Hockey League.

The team started out in the East Coast Hockey League, the bottom of the professional ranks. Now it sits one notch below the National Hockey League as part of the IHL. The Cyclones are a farm team of the NHL's Florida Panthers, who made it to the Stanley Cup Finals in 1996. Players are sometimes called up to the NHL during the season, but the team has a core of players who keep it from being a group of unknowns, including team captain and fan favorite Don Biggs.

Although the hockey is good, sometimes the entertainment at the games gets a little out of control: fireworks, player introductions with the lights off and spotlights following the players as they enter the ice and tacky intermission exploits. The entertainment facet is largely attributable to the fact that one of the team's founding owners, Ron Fuller, graced the professional wrestling circuit in the 1970s under the name The Tennessee Stud. Games are not as gaudy as World Wrestling Federation matches, but purists might be shocked. Together, though, the hockey and the "show" fit together to form a very entertaining package. And the rabid — almost cult-like — fans are making Cyclones merchandise as popular in local stores as Bengals and Reds merchandise.

Ticket prices are $15, $12, $10 and $6, with a $2 discount for students and children 12 and younger, and obtaining tickets shouldn't be a problem now that the team plays in the 22-year-old Crown coliseum, a 16,000-seat venue right next to Cinergy Field downtown. After seven years at the Cincinnati Gardens, promptly dubbed "The Hockey Barn of Bedlam," the Cyclones owners decided to pump $14 million into renovating the deteriorating and sometimes disgusting Crown facility (known then as Riverfront Coliseum) and move the team in.

The Mighty Ducks
2250 Seymour Ave., Norwood • 562-4949

When the Cyclones departed for The Crown, the owners of the 10,300-seat Cincinnati Gardens decided they didn't want those turnstiles to stop spinning, so they went out and bought their own hockey team, which they nicknamed the Mighty Ducks. The Ducks, who played their inaugural season in 1997, are named after their parent club, the Anaheim Mighty Ducks of the NHL. Cincinnati's version plays in the American Hockey League, the starting point for young players as they try to skate their way up the ladder. With some marketing help from the Disney Company, which owns the Anaheim team and the Mighty Ducks name, Cincinnati's Mighty Ducks' merchandise has also become popular in stores around town.

Ticket prices for Ducks games run $14, $11, $9 and $5. Kids 2 through 12 can join the Mighty Ducklings Kids Club and purchase any available seat in the Gardens for $5 when accompanied by a full-paying adult.

Horse Racing

Railbirds and rookies alike are happy with area horse racing. We have two thoroughbred tracks and a harness racing track. And when the ponies or trotters aren't running locally, which isn't often, the TV screens at Turfway Park and River Downs simulcast — and accept wagers on, of course — races at other parks across the country.

Furthermore, Greater Cincinnati is only two hours away from Louisville, and a parade of cars heads down Interstate 71 each Kentucky Derby weekend.

Turfway Park
7500 Turfway Rd. (just off I-75), Florence, Ky. • (606) 647-4700, (800) 733-0200

Turfway Park in Northern Kentucky holds meets in September and October and December through March. Turfway likes to think it offers "Major League Horse Racing" and for good reason: It's the 11th most lucrative racetrack in the country, according to *Thoroughbred Times Statistical Review*, with an average daily purse of $206,000. Those statistics by themselves are major league, but the track also hosts special events such as the Jim Beam Stakes, the richest Triple Crown prep race in the country. This $600,000 race is run five weeks before the Kentucky Derby and five of its last eight winners — Lil E. Tee, Prairie Bayou, Hansel, Summer Squall and Serena's Song — have gone on to win a Triple Crown race.

The track was purchased by its current owners in 1986 and renovated from an old track where the grandstand roof leaked and the toteboard was falling down into a first-class facility with a plush, climate-controlled grandstand. The track also houses the area's largest restaurant (reservations are suggested),

with a very good menu, tables that overlook the track and personal TV monitors at each table for close-ups of the race or for watching simulcast races.

A recently added $5 million section known as The Race Book is for serious bettors and includes more than 200 TV monitors to keep up with what's going on at other tracks around the country. The track also goes to extremes to help beginners, with a free "Beginner's Guide" pamphlet, a free "ABC's of Handicapping" booklet, free how-to seminars and special beginners-only mutuel betting windows.

Admission prices are $3.50 for the grandstand, $5 for the clubhouse and $1.50 to the Blinkers Sports Bar. Reserved seating in the grandstand and clubhouse is $2, while cocktail seating in the fourth-floor lounge is $2.50. A $1.25-per-seat charge is required for the dining room, with a $7 minimum. Parking is free.

River Downs
6301 Kellogg Ave., Anderson • 232-8000

River Downs has been offering thoroughbred racing for nearly 70 years, running every day except Thursdays from mid-April through the summer and again in late fall. The best local horses can be seen regularly, but twice a year River Downs draws horses from around the country with the $150,000 Bassinet Stakes and the $200,000 Miller Highlife CradleStakes.

The track, which sits along the riverfront and next to Old Coney Island and Riverbend Music Center, underwent a $14 million renovation a few years ago and now offers an enclosed, air-conditioned grandstand in which lunch and cocktails can be ordered. Since the track runs during the warmer months, most of the track's seating is in an outdoor grandstand, where bettors can see, feel and smell the action.

INSIDERS' TIP

The best way to enjoy a Reds game is to take along a portable radio and listen to Marty and Joe broadcast the play-by-play on WLW (700 AM). The best way to watch the Reds on TV is to turn down the sound and listen to Marty and Joe on the radio (even though Marty does do the TV broadcasts in innings four through six).

Photo: Greater Cincinnati Convention and Visitors Bureau

Cinergy Field is the home of the Cincinnati Reds and Bengals.

The track also offers simulcasts of seven races from Thistledowns in Cleveland as well as the Triple Crown races, and it just opened the River Downs Race Book betting area, in which races from around the country are simulcast.

Admission prices are $3 for the clubhouse and $2 for the grandstand. Upper grandstand seating is free. Parking is free in designated areas.

Lebanon Raceway
Ohio Hwy. 63, Lebanon • 932-4936

Lebanon Raceway is open for harness racing from January through May and September through December. You can watch the trotters from a glass-enclosed, climate-controlled clubhouse. Check with the track for post times. To get to the track take the Lebanon Exit off I-75 and go east about 1 mile. Admission to the clubhouse is $20, the grandstands are free and parking is $1.50.

Auto Racing

Auto race fans can find plenty of speed at the area's two small oval tracks or its long drag strip. Or, the greatest spectacle in racing, the Indianapolis 500, is just two hours away, and hard-core race fans and speed novices alike often spend Memorial Day weekend each year in Indianapolis watching the race.

Florence Speedway
12234 U.S. 42, Florence, Ky.
• (606) 485-7591

Florence Speedway in Northern Kentucky offers short-track racing for sprint cars, modifieds and late-model stock cars. The track is 9 miles west of I-75 on U.S. 42 in Florence and runs early spring to late fall, weather permitting. Ticket prices vary depending on the event.

Lawrenceburg Speedway
U.S. Highway 52, Lawrenceburg, Ind.
• (812) 367-5444

Lawrenceburg Speedway in Southeastern Indiana offers sprint cars, modified stocks and pro stock cars, with ticket prices ranging between $10 and $15. Children 12 and younger are admitted free. The track runs early spring to late fall, weather permitting. Take I-275 west to U.S. Highway 52 and go west 2 miles.

Edgewater Sports Park
4819 E. Miami River Rd. • 353-4666

Edgewater Race Park offers local drag racing when the weather permits between February and November. Admission is $5 on Friday night and $8 Saturday night. Take I-74 to Rybolt Road and go west 2 miles.

FYI

Unless otherwise noted, the area code for all phone numbers listed in this guide is 513.

Soccer

According to the Soccer Industry Council of America, Cincinnati has more amateur soccer players than any other city. And that interest is filtering up to Cincinnati's two professional teams.

The Silverbacks
The Crown, 200 Pete Rose Way
• 458-KICK

The owners of the Cyclones started an indoor soccer team, the Silverbacks, which plays in the National Professional Soccer League. The team's 50-game season lasts from October to March. Matches are played at The Crown. Ticket prices range from $5 to $18.

Tennis

Great American Insurance ATP Championship
250 E. Fifth St., Suite 1830 • 651-0303

During the first two weeks in August, the tennis world turns to Cincinnati for the $2.2 million Great American Insurance ATP Championship. The event is one of the Mercedes Super 9 tournaments, along with tournaments in Monte Carlo, Paris, Rome, Toronto, Hamburg, Toronto,

Stuttgart, Indian Hills and Key Biscayne, making it one of the showcase events on the ATP tour and a regular stop for the sport's Top 10 players, including Pete Sampras, Michael Chang, Goran Ivanisevic and Andre Agassi. The ATP Championship is also the only non-Grand Slam tournament — Wimbledon and the U.S., French and Australian opens — with a center court and two large grandstand courts. These large seating areas make it a great place to watch tennis and are highly popular with the players because more fans get to see them play. Massive crowds of about 200,000 people pack the courts during the weeklong event.

A separate four-day $100,000 Legends Tournament, which features well-known "senior" players such as Rod Laver and Ilie Nastase, is held the week before the ATP.

Much more than tennis goes on during the tournaments. Dozens of corporate hospitality tents and vendors with every type of specialty tennis product imaginable pack the grounds around the stadium.

Individual single-day tickets cost $14 for the first day of the tournament on Monday and increase to $16 on Tuesday, $22 on Wednesday, $24 on Thursday, $28 on Friday, $32 on Saturday and $36 for the finals on Sunday. Individual tickets are only available for the upper section of the stadium. All seats in the lower section are sold as part of series packages. A weekend package of five sessions, including the finals on Sunday, is $150. A package for the Legends Tournament and qualifying rounds of the main tournament is $208. A package for both tournaments is $236.

You can become one of the 1,000 volunteers who work the tournament each year. The ATP is run by a nonprofit organization, Tennis for Charity Inc., and the proceeds from the tournament — in the $250,000 range — are donated each year to Children's Hospital in Cincinnati and the Tennis for City Youth.

Met Tennis Tournament
Lunken Playfield, Beechmont and Wilmer Aves. • 321-1772

For tennis on a smaller scale, the city's annual Met Tennis Tournament is held each summer at Lunken Playfield on the east side. The tournament determines the city's amateur champions.

Golf

Kroger Senior PGA Classic
6062 Fairway Dr., Kings Mill • 398-5742

Arnie's Army still marches onward. Chi Chi still swashbuckles invisible foes with his putter. Lee Trevino still keeps the galleries rolling in laughter. Every September the golf greats of yesterday return to the area to play in the $900,000 Kroger Senior Classic. This Seniors PGA event draws thousands of duffers and dreamers to The Golf Center at Kings Island to see the sport's legends, who may have lost a few yards on their drives but can still play the game.

The Classic is played on a Friday, Saturday and Sunday, although other events fill out the week. Monday and Tuesday are for practice rounds, and a $10,000 Skin's Game is played Tuesday afternoon. On Wednesday and Thursday a pro-am tournament is held, with four amateurs — often local celebrities — and one pro per team.

Practice rounds and the Skin's Game are free. Tickets for events Wednesday through Sunday are $25 each day. A weekly grounds-only badge costs $50. A weekly badge for grounds and the clubhouse is $60. Children 15 and younger get in free with an adult. All prices include parking.

For a smaller spin, each year The Met Golf Tournament determines the city's local amateur champion. Call 352-4000 for information.

Other Sports Events

Each June the **National Collegiate Rowing Championship** is held on Harsha Lake in East Fork Lake State Park. The event brings in top collegiate rowing teams from around the country. Proceeds from the event benefit Children's Hospital. Call 753-7211 for information.

Also, in nearby Madison, Indiana, high-powered hydroplanes gather each summer for the **Madison Regatta** on the Ohio River. It's like the Indy 500 on water. The race is run in June, weather permitting. An occasional late-spring flood sometimes pushes the date back to later in the summer. General admission tickets are $15 in advance and $20 the weekend of the race, VIP passes are $110 with parking and $90 without, and pit passes are $20. Call (812) 286-5000.

Prefer a sport designed more for, say, kings? Riders saddle up at the **Cincinnati Polo Club** for a few chukkers each Sunday during the spring and summer. The fields are at Wilshire Farm in Warren County, near Kings Island. For information call Wilshire Farm at 398-0278. You can watch the matches for free.

The most distant suburbs in the Greater Cincinnati area are only a 25-minute drive from downtown Cincinnati.

Neighborhoods and Real Estate

Like a ripple in the water, Greater Cincinnati is getting larger and spreading out in all directions. It now comprises eight counties in three states: Hamilton, Warren, Butler and Clermont counties in Ohio; Kenton, Boone and Campbell counties in Kentucky; and Dearborn county in Indiana. Within this 77-square-mile area is a diversity of community types: subdivisions, neighborhoods, villages, townships and even cities. What mainly binds them together is a work force that commutes between downtown Cincinnati and other business districts and homes in the "suburbs."

New neighborhoods and homes are being developed at a rapid pace in what were once tiny farming communities on the area's outer edges. By the year 2000, nearly 2 million people will live in Greater Cincinnati according to a study by the Hamilton County Regional Planning Commission. This figure represents a 3.3-percent increase from 1990, and almost all those newcomers will head for the spaciousness of the outer 'burbs. Urban areas such as downtown, the central communities, and Covington and Newport in Northern Kentucky can actually expect a 6 percent *decrease* in population according to the study. Meanwhile, out in the fringes, only 2 percent of the land mass in Sycamore, for instance, remains undeveloped. Symmes, which was the fringe in 1980, is now 70 percent developed.

One reason for the expected population increase is that people are discovering Greater Cincinnati is a good place to raise a family, especially compared to other large cities. That's one reason *Places Rated Almanac* ranked Greater Cincinnati as America's Most Livable City in 1993 and the suburb of Blue Ash was listed in *50 Fabulous Places to Raise A Family* in 1993 and 1996. It's why so many sports figures who come to play for the Reds or Bengals end up staying here, even though their careers take them to another city during playing season.

And it's cheaper. The median price for a house is 14 percent lower than the national average. Meaning you get a lot more house in Cincinnati than you would in other parts of the country. A home that costs $172,000 in Boston or $177,000 in San Diego, for instance, is only $92,000 here.

Greater Cincinnati offers a wide variety of house styles, from ultra-contemporary to historic, and an equally wide variety of neighborhood types. Some river communities have hardly changed since the days of paddlewheelers. Some neighborhoods are like their own small town. There are golf course communities and enclaves of Victorian and antebellum homes on streets with gaslight lamps. But best of all, even the most distant suburbs are only 25 minutes from downtown, allowing residents to be near the city but still live in a very rural setting. And none of the neighborhoods are far from community or county parks, churches or shopping.

Greater Cincinnati also has a wide variety of schools from which to choose, with 50 public school districts and more than 250 private schools. There are schools that place a heavy emphasis on religion and those that place a heavy emphasis on the arts. There are preparatory schools that require students to take Latin, while others have strong vocational programs. There are schools for the deaf and schools for the learning disabled. Wherever you live in Greater Cincinnati, you won't be far from a school that meets your children's needs.

The most important thing to know if you're looking for a home in Greater Cincinnati is that the East Side and the West Side (Vine Street is the dividing point) are as polar-opposite communities as any one city could have. The West Side is the working-class side, with lunch buckets, bowling balls, old homes handed down for generations, people who drink Hudepohl 14K beer and grill burgers on the back porch while listening to the Reds on the radio, where everyone went to school with each other and where there's a church and/or bar on just about every street corner. The East Side is the suit-and-tie side, with art galleries and upscale shopping centers, where people drink imported beers on the back deck of their new and expensive homes and where they can afford Bengals tickets and drive BMWs. People joke about the differences between the two sides of town, but we're all really just one big happy family. Sort of.

FYI

Unless otherwise noted, the area code for all phone numbers listed in this guide is 513.

A real estate agent should be able to help you find what you are looking for. Many agencies in Greater Cincinnati belong to the Multiple Listing Service, a computerized listing of all the homes for sale in the area.

If you want to get a head start finding a home, check the homes section in *The Cincinnati Enquirer*, one of the local real estate magazines or TV shows, or even the World Wide Web. Many families like to first find an area they would feel comfortable in and then search for a home within that area. The **Greater Cincinnati Relocation Services**, 271-4900, helps locate fully furnished apartments for a day, week or month if you want to take your time looking. (Also see our Hotels and Motels chapter for furnished apartments and extended-stay options.)

Although we couldn't possibly mention all the multitudes of communities that comprise Greater Cincinnati — some communities, such as O'Bryonville, in fact, aren't even recognized by city officials — we've tried to give a brief description of most of the larger communities in the area. The Greater Cincinnati and Northern Kentucky maps in the front of this book will help you locate some of these communities.

Neighborhoods

In the City

There are more than 2,000 residential units **downtown**, ranging from apartment flats and townhouses to luxury condominiums. And more units are being built annually as the city tries to lure life back from the suburbs. More than 200 rental units were recently built along Piatt Park in the northwestern section of downtown, for instance, and a rundown office building was converted into 36 loft apartments. Plus, ground has been broken for a community of townhomes adjacent to Bicentennial Commons on the southeastern side of town.

Because of the higher price of real estate, however, living downtown is typically more expensive than in the suburbs. Small, one-bedroom apartments will begin renting for around $600 a month. The new townhomes are expected to begin at around $100,000. Luxury condos start at $350,000 and can go up to $1 million. With Interstates 75, 71 and 471 all intersecting downtown, residents have easy access to other parts of town. There's been talk for several years of building a large grocery store downtown, but for now residents must go outside the area for all but minor grocery shopping. Still, if living in the center of the city is your dream, with arts and entertainment within a short walk, downtown is where you should be.

One of the up-and-coming areas in the heart of the city is historic Betts-Longworth in West End on the western edge of downtown. Although most of West End remains lower income, efforts by city officials to create moderate-income housing in the area has created a mini-boom of renovations and new construction. Old, historically significant single-family houses with detailed woodwork are being restored, and clusters of single-family row houses are being built. The city, which offers financial incentives to both builders and buyers, likes to feature these homes in an annual parade of inner-city homes known as Cityrama. Some of the first homes built in the area — along Central Avenue north of Ninth Street — now sell in the $110,000 range, more than double their original value.

Mount Adams, which is Cincinnati's entertainment district, offers one of the city's more unique urban settings. Located just east of downtown, the neighborhood features tall, thin houses and apartment buildings wrapped tightly around an L-shaped hillside that offers views of either downtown or the river. Other homes, all loaded with charm and character, line the neighborhood's narrow, winding streets and steep hills and mix seamlessly with the numerous trendy restaurants, bars, boutiques and arts and crafts shops. Residents of this lively community have the luxury of being connected to large and beautiful Eden Park, which offers not only lush greenery but also many of the area's arts centers.

Like the rest of the communities in the central part of the city, Mount Adams is in the Cincinnati Public Schools District. Few families live in Mount Adams, though; many of the residents are empty nesters, young business executives who like to walk to work, or people who want to be in the center of the entertainment action. Vidal Sassoon has a home here. His wife is from Greater Cincinnati and his hairstyling products are manufactured by Procter & Gamble. The average home price here is $225,000 but can range up to $500,000 and more, depending on the quality of the view and the size and condition of the house.

Over-the-Rhine, which has the largest collection of Italianate buildings in the country, adjoins downtown to the north and is fast becoming one of the city's trendiest places to live. With its incredible 19th century architecture, the entire Over-the-Rhine area has earned a listing in the National Register of Historic Places; in fact, it's the largest national historic district in the nation. Once the home of thousands of German immigrants, the community is reminiscent of a turn-of-the-century neighborhood. It earned its name because residents had to cross over the canal that ran through downtown, which reminded them of the Rhine River in their homeland.

Over-the-Rhine is also a local historic district, which means that architectural controls and guidelines can make the restoration of buildings more difficult and slow. Advocates of low-income housing, who fear that a rush of new development would force the poor from their homes, are also slowing the process, but the city is working on creating a zoning plan that would make the community a mixture of lower-income to upper-middle income homes. Much of the area is currently low-income housing, although artistically renovated apartments and flats in the $70,000 to $250,000 range are slowly becoming available on the eastern side of the neighborhood, especially around Main Street, where coffee houses, art galleries and trendy nightclubs abound.

The **Liberty Hill** area includes small two- and three-bedroom homes built on a tree-lined hillside that offers a unique overlook of downtown and is still within walking distance of the central business district. The homes have become popular with do-it-yourself types, who buy them for as little as $50,000 and modernize them, adding large windows and decks to take advantage of the view.

Central Suburbs

Mount Auburn, immediately north of downtown, offers an abundance of frame and brick homes built sturdily upon a hillside. Many homes in this older neighborhood, which was one of the area's original hilltop suburbs, have views of downtown and the river. Although some homes have not been properly maintained over the years, their affordability and character are making them very popular with do-it-yourselfers and are leading to a rebirth of the community. Homes here average $55,000, but can quickly increase in value. Mount Auburn is served by the Cincinnati Public Schools system.

Walnut Hills, which sits east of Mount Auburn and is also in the Cincinnati Public School system, is one of the area's oldest and most fashionable communities. In the early days, this splendid neighborhood was home of the city's "upper crust," and some majestic mansions still remain in the eastern portions of Walnut Hills. Many of the old, elegant buildings, especially those near Eden Park and in east Walnut Hills, have been renovated and are in superb condition. One of the more intriguing homes here is a 1952 Frank Lloyd Wright-designed home that has 492 windows and a gold-leaf ceiling in the bedroom.

Overall, though, the community offers diverse home styles and attracts a wide variety of residents with its ancient trees, wide streets and large lawns. The average price of a home is $109,000, although some sections of the community, which are targeted by those with lower incomes, offer more modest homes on small lots. In fact, prices can range from as low as $40,000 to in the millions for a mansion.

Clifton is another of Cincinnati's landmark historic neighborhoods and is home to some of the area's oldest upper-class families, University of Cincinnati professors, and many physicians who practice in "Pill Hill," the area's nearby medical community. Clifton, which sits about 10 minutes north of downtown, is dominated by the elegant stone mansions built by 19th-century business barons looking to move away from the masses. But more moderate frame and brick homes also fill the neighborhood's wide streets, most of which are lined with large, stately trees and lit by old-fashioned gas lamps. Modern condominiums and single-family residences can also be found, particularly around The Windings, which is a converted massive, castle-like home that belonged to William Neff, who amassed a great fortune in pork packing. The Windings became a girls' school after Neff left and is now divided into six luxurious condominiums, with newer multilevel homes surrounding it.

Homes here, which are serviced by the Cincinnati Public Schools, average $135,000, although prices can range up to around $650,000. Residents can relax in majestic Mount Storm Park, which was also once a private residence, or Burnet Woods. Or they can visit the community's business district, which includes several trendy restaurants and nightclubs as well as the Esquire Theater, an old-time movie house that brings in art and cultural films that can't be found at the megaplexes.

Corryville is dominated by the University of Cincinnati, and many of the large but less stately homes built near the campus in eras past have since been turned into affordable multiunit rentals or fraternity or sorority houses. Many entertainment businesses geared toward the college crowd line sections of Corryville. Still, those who prefer to live with the young, hip crowd can find home bargains that average just $53,000 in this neighborhood.

Avondale is also one of the area's early 1900s "gaslight" communities and is highly popular because of its central location and easy access to the interstates. The community sits between I-71 and I-75 and just south of the Norwood Lateral and offers single- and two-family homes in a wide range of prices and architectural styles. Like some of the other older and larger communities in the area, Avondale has split into two distinct sections: north and south. The northern section has older, well-kept homes and has maintained its European characteristics, quaint charm and turn-of-the-century feel. Beautiful landscaping and a strong and active neighborhood association keep the area attractive to families and young professionals. Homes average $99,000, but can range from $45,000 to $600,000, and children attend Cincinnati Public Schools. The southern half of the community, which is anchored by the Cincinnati Zoo and its proximity to the area's medical community, has fallen on harder times, although efforts to build this section of Avondale back up are ongoing.

Perhaps the greatest community rebirth story in the area belongs to **Norwood**, one of the largest independent cities in Greater Cincinnati. Once a center for Greater Cincinnati's industrial and manufacturing businesses, the community fell on hard times when many of its older plants closed their doors in the 1970s and 1980s. Some thought was given to incorporating Norwood into the city of Cincinnati, which surrounds it on all sides. Norwood, though, worked to rebuild itself, and has gone, as one headline put it, "from fizzle to sizzle in eight years." It is now home to an upscale retail center, numerous professional business parks and hundreds of homes fashionable enough to attract young families looking for nice, modest two- and three-bedroom homes. Although older, most homes have been well maintained by the blue-collar owners who worked at the factories, and they now sell for around $66,000. The 24,000 residents in the 3-square-mile city also benefit from nine city parks, easy access to both I-75 and I-71, and their own school system.

Like Norwood, **Pleasant Ridge** is a comfortable, old community dating back to 1795 and offers many affordable homes. Pleasant Ridge also includes several mansions and stately homes that once belonged to Cincinnati's aristocratic families, but the community remains unpretentious and the homes moderately priced, averaging $88,000. First-time buyers find the central location, convenient highway access, neighborhood shopping and the community swimming pool major assets.

Just north of Pleasant Ridge along I-71 are the middle-class communities of **Deer Park** and **Silverton**. Both offer modest ranch and Cape Cod-style single-family homes, averaging around $74,000. Many first-time buyers stay on once they discover the conveniences of the business district, the central location and the down-to-earth benefits and lifestyles each community affords. Deer Park maintains its own school district, while Silverton children attend Cincinnati Public Schools.

Farther north along I-71 is **Blue Ash**, the area's second-largest business district, with nearly 2,000 businesses and a daytime population of more than 70,000. But when the workers leave, less than 13,000 people and a great little community remain. As we noted above, Blue Ash was once listed as one of the *50 Fabulous Places to Raise A Family*. And for good reason. The city collects an abundance of taxes from the businesses and then turns around and spends the money on improving the community. The city's Community Center has an Olympic-size swimming pool, a whale-shaped children's wading pool, and twisting tube slides. A scale replica of Crosley Field, the former home of the Reds, is in the Blue Ash Sport Complex, along with 10 baseball fields and six soccer fields. The community common areas are always lush with greenery. The city also offers residents a nature park,

amphitheater park, their own golf course — one of the best public courses in the country — and even an airport. There are free special events in the town square and memorial park.

Once people move into Blue Ash they don't want to leave, so finding a home in the 7.7-square-mile city can be difficult. Almost all of the homes are new and contemporary, and sell for an average of $177,000. Children attend the highly regarded Sycamore schools. The Raymond Walters College branch of the University of Cincinnati is also located in Blue Ash.

Sharonville, which sits along I-75 just south of the I-275 interchange, is best-known for its business and entertainment district. This community of 13,200 just added a 56,000-square-foot convention center to go with its hotels, retail areas and nightclubs, making it a frequent destination for travelers. Residents, though, like the area for its quiet subdivisions, which feature many newer multilevel homes that are valued around $112,000. Home prices can range from $50,000 all the way to $200,000, though. Residents take great pride in keeping their homes nicely landscaped with well-trimmed hedges and flower gardens.

The focal point of nearby **Springdale** is its shopping district. Residents with shopping on their mind are thrilled by the abundance of retail options in the area, which is anchored by the massive Tri-County Mall and includes hundreds of small and large stores in the smaller plazas and strip malls that branch out along its heavily travelled retail corridor. And, if that's not enough, Forest Fair Mall sits just five miles away and Northgate Mall just 10 miles away. A wide mixture of residential properties also can be found within Springdale's six square miles. Homes here sell for around $90,000 and are popular with families, who are attracted by the town's proximity to the I-75 and I-275 interchange, its location within the Princeton School District and its community center, which offers a pool and tennis courts to the community's 10,700 residents.

Southeast of Springdale is the tony village of **Glendale**, one of the area's most distinctive neighborhoods. Glendale was the first planned community in the area and one of the first in America. Laid out in 1851, it is today the only national landmark community in Ohio.

Glendale looks like it still belongs in the 19th century. This splendid community has worked hard at maintaining its parklike setting, with gas street lamps on winding lanes and distinctly elegant homes with stone walls or white rail fences surrounding the large, beautifully landscaped lawns with well-established foliage. Even new homes are built on larger lots and are required to keep within the architectural parameters set by the community's original plan. Many of the homes are older — in fact, some of the original homes are still standing and sell for around $248,000, which tends to be higher than comparable homes in other neighborhoods. Prices generally start around $100,000 and extend up to $500,000. But residents benefit from Princeton schools and the community's beauty.

Farther south on I-75 are **Arlington Heights** and **Lincoln Heights**, both lower-income communities. Both of these neighborhoods have a wide range of single- and two-family homes, most of which are offered as rental properties. Currently only 30 percent of the homes in Lincoln Heights are owned by their occupants, although there are concerted efforts to increase home ownership through grants, discounts, guidance from a business specializing in home rehabbing and through the coordination of the Lincoln Heights Housing Committee. Homes can be purchased for around $32,000 in Lincoln Heights and for roughly twice that in Arlington Heights.

The middle-class communities of **Evendale**, **Reading** and **Lockland** all sit just off I-75, offering residents easy access to the rest of the area. These towns were once part of a burgeoning industrial valley and feature many well-built brick and frame houses that were home to generations of hard-working families who earned livings in the local industries. Those houses are now attracting young families who are looking for affordable first homes.

Evendale, which is best-known as the location of General Electric Aircraft Engines, placed very strict limitations on new development from the early 1950s until the 1980s, creating a demand for land from which it is now benefitting. Sixty percent of the homes in Evendale are less than six years old, while the remaining 40 percent are 25 to 35 years old. Prices range from $80,000 up to $450,000.

The Reading area was once farmland but is now being developed with spacious new homes that average around $80,000. Prices are bolstered by the town's numerous historic homes, located particularly in the northern section known as Reading Heights. Reading has its own school system.

Lockland, which has suffered the most from the loss of industry, has sturdy homes in the $50,000 price range. Lockland residents are very proud of their schools, which they fought hard to maintain through the down times.

Amberley Village takes its name from a village in England and is one of the area's most distinctive and prestigious communities. Carefully planned by its citizens and government, Amberley works hard to preserve its rural, wooded characteristics and spacious atmosphere. Just 3,200 residents live within its five square miles. Professionals and executives are attracted to this quiet and peaceful neighborhood located 12 miles north of downtown. Many of the homes in this elegant community were built on at least one acre of land and are secluded behind plush landscaping, tall hardwoods and well-established foliage, but you can also find contemporary, custom-built estates. Rollman Estates subdivision was a recent Homearama site (see our Annual Events chapter). Home sales here average $226,000, but can reach the $1 million mark.

The communities of **Bond Hill**, **Paddock Hills** and **Roselawn** are some of the most centrally located communities in the area, and

INSIDERS' TIP

Getting a new puppy to go along with your new home? Ohio law requires that dogs three months and older be licensed. Cincinnati law also requires dogs to be on a leash if they are outside of your yard. And a pooper-scooper law is enforced locally, meaning you have to immediately clean up any calling cards your pooch leaves in your neighbor's yard or the local park.

are anchored by their proximity to Cincinnati Gardens, the arena for Xavier University basketball games and Mighty Ducks hockey games. Much of Bond Hill and Paddock Hills is middle to lower-income and offers a wide range of single- and two-family homes (averaging around $65,000) and apartments. The Old Bond Hill section of Bond Hill, though, still features Victorian and Queen Anne-style homes set in wooded areas. Roselawn is a well-kept community, featuring many English and Early America styles of homes on beautifully landscaped lawns that sell for an average of $108,000.

St. Bernard and **Elmwood Place**, which are located along the western edge of I-75, were originally developed for families working at nearby businesses such as P&G's Ivorydale and Nu-Maid margarine, in the heart of industrial Mill Creek Valley. Homes here average $67,000 and are still popular among those working in the area.

Of all the communities in Greater Cincinnati, neighboring **Winton Place** and **Winton Hills** comprise the largest land area, but only a small portion of it is for homes. Just 2,600 residents live in Winton Place, while just 6,000 reside in Winton Hills, where small two- and three-bedroom homes average $48,000. The communities offer a little of everything — residences, industry, commercial businesses — although much of the area is taken up by the ELDA landfill, which was closed and capped in 1998. The massive and elegant Spring Grove Cemetery also rests within the two communities, lending beauty to the neighborhood (see the Close-up on Spring Grove Cemetery in our Parks and Recreation chapter).

Carthage and **Hartwell** are the northernmost communities within the city limits of Cincinnati and offer homes in a wide variety of sizes and architectural styles. Much of the development of these two communities came in the years following World War II, when families built homes to be near the local industries. The area still maintains a somewhat commercial and industrial nature, although it has some rural aspects. For instance, squeezed between the homes and businesses in Carthage, where houses average $49,999, is the Hamilton County Fairgrounds. Homes in Hartwell, which offers some hilly areas with

spectacular views of the residential valley below, average $69,000.

The historic village of **Wyoming** traces its roots back to 1861, and more than 300 homes in this splendid community are listed on the National Register of Historic Places. Comprising just two-and-a-half square miles, Wyoming is one of the most distinctive neighborhoods in the area, with old, Victorian homes — some with carriage houses — sitting back off the wide streets edged with ancient trees. The area's 8,300 residents take great pride in the community's school system, which is one of the best in the state, and neighbors frequently get together for civic club activities and community-wide social events. Home prices average $171,000 and are easily accessible from I-75 and the Cross County Highway.

Finneytown is an attractive, family-oriented neighborhood of 13,000 residents who maintain an independent school system and are active in the affairs of the community. A mixture of homes can be found here, most dating back 30 to 35 years and ranging from a modest $55,000 to $210,000. A central location and proximity to I-75 and the Cross County Highway make it easy for residents to get to all other parts of town.

Mount Airy is a quiet neighborhood with smaller homes, many of which were built in the late 1940s. The homes are still in good condition and are moderately priced, although newer, higher-priced homes in the area have bumped the average price of a house to near $100,000. Mount Airy, which sits on one of the highest hills in the area, includes massive Mount Airy Forest, where residents and people from all over the city come to hike through its hills and towering hardwoods.

College Hill and neighboring **North College Hill** trace their roots back to the days when two colleges were located on their hilltop, which was then far enough away from the city to allow for proper studying. These now-densely populated areas have many older homes in a variety of sizes, as well as many pleasant apartments. Many young families are drawn here by the abundance of attractive and sturdy starter homes. Homes in North College Hill tend to be a bit smaller and sit on smaller lots; the average price is $61,000. College Hill homes average $80,000. Residents also find the proximity to Interstates 75 and 74 attractive, as well as the busy business district and the community school district.

Energetic residents of **Greenhills** and **Forest Park** love their proximity to Winton Woods, the 2,400-acre county park that offers numerous recreational opportunities, including golf, fishing and baseball fields. For those residents who prefer shopping to sports, Forest Fair Mall is nearby. Both communities also offer their residents historical places to live.

Greenhills was created in the 1930s as one of 25 experimental residential developments around the country established by the federal government as a means of easing problems brought on by the Great Depression and to study the relatively new concept of community planning and design. The government based its plans for the 1.5-square-mile community on the garden cities of England. Although most of the homes are of a size more typical of the 1930s, they are still in good shape, averaging $87,000, and are highly attractive to young couples searching for ideal starter homes.

Forest Park also began as a planned community and has since developed into the third-largest city in Hamilton County. Houses on the classic older tree-lined streets average $84,000, but homes can be found to match every taste and budget. In addition to having Winton Woods in its midst, Forest Park also offers its 18,600 residents several public parks and recreational facilities within its 5.5 square miles.

Residents of both communities are served by the Winton Hills School District, the culmination of a merger in the early 1980s of the Forest Park and Greenhills school districts.

Eastern Suburbs

One of the city's oldest and most prestigious neighborhoods is **Hyde Park**. Most of the homes in this lovely community are older and full of character and personality, with leaded and stained glass windows and doors, intricate woodwork and lush landscaping. Massive, castle-like stone mansions from eras past sit back on secluded hillsides. But houses of every size and style can be found here, and even the simplest of frame houses seem to exude a bit more character in Hyde Park. Homes tend to be higher-priced than in other areas, averaging $214,000 but with some selling in the millions of dollars.

Along with churches, day care centers and shopping areas, Hyde Park offers some of the area's most interesting specialty shops and trendy restaurants. Residents frequently browse the town square's stores on warm days, stop by Graeter's for ice cream and sit on tree-shaded park benches near the gently flowing fountain. They are also surrounded by two of the area's largest parks, Alms Park and Ault Park, which are packed on summer days by young families and health enthusiasts.

Neighboring **Mount Lookout** is similar, with a fashionable town square and many large, old homes. Singles, young professionals and even families find the many remarkable older homes and rowhouse condominiums in this area attractive. The average home price is $192,000. Mount Lookout's town square offers a glimpse of the diversity, style and tastes of the community, with everything from an old-fashioned deli and grocery shop that has been in the same location for decades, to trendy coffee houses, used book stores and even a movie theater/restaurant where moviegoers are shown current films while being served dinner at tables. This is where you'll find one of the area's favorite "dives," Zip's, which serves arguably the best hamburger and fries in the city.

Mount Lookout also has the distinction of being the home to the area's only observatory. Operated by the University of Cincinnati, the observatory was relocated from Mount Adams in order to give astronomers a clearer view of the heavens. (For information on the Mount Lookout Observatory, see our Attractions and Kidstuff chapters.)

Down fashionable Delta Avenue toward the river is **Columbia-Tusculum**, once a steamboat manufacturing town. This riverside community is one of the oldest in Greater Cincinnati, and is well known for its renewal and restoration of the old, sturdy frame houses from the steamboat era. Some of the homes are even decorated with steamboat themes to match the area's history. Young couples love the Victorian homes — "painted ladies," as they are known because of their colorful exte-

Many of Cincinnati's neighborhoods retain the charm
and architectural heritage of another era.

riors. Not all of the homes in the community
have been renovated, though, so houses are
available for around $75,000, although beau-
tifully built bargains in need of some work can
be found for less than that. A few contemporary homes and modern rowhouse condominiums, some of which offer river views, can also
be found.

The focal point of **Mount Washington**, located on the easternmost fringe of the city of
Cincinnati, is its massive water tower. Sitting
on the highest point on the East Side, the
tower, with its revolving beacon, can be seen
from all parts of Greater Cincinnati. During the
Christmas season, rows of lights are strung
down its smooth sides, creating a beautiful
sight. Beechmont Avenue, one of three main
thoroughfares into downtown Cincinnati from
the East Side, slices its way through Mount
Washington and its business district, which is
lined with old-fashioned stores and modern

new retail establishments. Many small apartment buildings and large complexes can be
found along Beechmont, which is served by
all of the major East Side bus routes.

On the narrow streets off of Beechmont sit
an assortment of homes, many built in the
1940s after World War II and occupied by the
same families for several decades. Homes here
can be found for around $96,000, a price that
is increasing regularly as young couples seeking to be near desirable but more expensive
Anderson are moving in. Children here are
served by Cincinnati Public Schools and can
play Frisbee or swing in nearby Stanberry Park.

Anderson is one of the fastest-growing
communities in the area, thanks to good
schools, access to interstates and major thoroughfares, proximity to major retail areas, availability of large tracts of land, the presence of
Mercy Hospital Anderson and a commitment
by township leaders not to sacrifice the town's

natural beauty for the sake of more development. In an effort to preserve its rural, wooded character and prevent the desire for development from spinning out of control, township officials set aside more than 200 acres of land as a natural setting. This unique foresight has made Anderson one of the most beautiful communities in which to live. Homes and even entire subdivisions seem to be carved into scenic hills and virgin woodlands rather than being built on them.

Anderson's 38 square miles were mostly modest farmland as little as 15 years ago. Most of the homes here are new, but they come in a wide variety of architectural styles, prices and sizes. The average sale price is $180,000, but custom homes are being built regularly and selling for $500,000 and above.

Many of the 42,000 residents in this family-oriented community regularly get together to enjoy the abundance of activities offered throughout the year, such as free family movies shown on a large screen at two local parks during the summer and an annual festival put on by the fire department. The Forest Hills school system, one of the best in the state, serves the Anderson area. Residents also enjoy the township's seven local parks and three upscale golf courses. Shoppers are close to Beechmont Mall, which includes nearly every type of store imaginable and is the focal point of the Anderson shopping experience.

Nearby **Newtown** offers the benefits of small-town living with the benefits of a larger community. Founded in the early 1700s, Newtown remains in many ways a quaint little village, with a gas station and a popular ice cream stand on the village's main corner. Within its three square miles are many small, older homes, but there's also an abundance of large estate homes, most of which are in the sprawling Ivy Hills subdivision. The village's schoolhouse is still standing, but children now attend the highly regarded Forest Hills schools.

Greater Cincinnati's growth has overtaken two rural communities in Clermont County: **Batavia** and **Amelia**, which are becoming increasingly popular because of their remoteness but easy accessibility from I-275.

Batavia's history can be traced back to the 1830s when it was a gold-mining town, albeit a short-lived one. Still, the historic old village survived and now offers residents the beauty of a small town in the country that is not too far removed from civilization. The town's 2,000 residents live in a mixture of historic homes — some nearly 200 years old — in the heart of town and in newer homes with acreage built in subdivisions on the town's fringes. Residents are served by the growing West Clermont School District and enjoy the availability of the University of Cincinnati's Clermont County branch.

Amelia, too, is a small town that has become a popular destination for those looking to get away from city life. Many young families have moved into the town's three square miles, buying older, historic homes or newer multilevel houses in recently built subdivisions.

Residents of **Union** are attracted by its proximity to local interstates, its mix of historic homes and new-home subdivisions, and abundant shopping options. The township includes the ever-growing Eastgate community, Glen Este, Mount Carmel and Withamsville. Homes in Mount Carmel, which sits immediately west of Anderson, now average $100,000, while those in Eastgate average $102,000. Much of the growth in these areas has occurred over the last 10 years in conjunction with the development of the Eastgate shopping area, a booming retail mecca anchored by Eastgate Mall and including hundreds of large discount stores, specialty shops, restaurants and hotels. Residents of Union are also blessed with the presence of the Cincinnati Nature Center, one of the most serene sites in all of Greater Cincinnati.

Milford traces its roots back to 1788 when early settlers fell in love with the area, which sits snuggled between the Little Miami River and East Fork River. It still remains a somewhat rural community, but with easy access to I-275 and U.S. 50 it has become popular with those who like the seclusion of country living. New homes and condominiums have created a variety of housing options for the 6,100 residents, with properties available for around $130,000. Milford is an exempted village, outside the governing influences of the county, and as a result has its own school system and its own governing council made up of community leaders who have protected the small-town feel by maintaining three municipal parks and a preserve along the Little Miami River for hiking and picnicking.

Indian Hill is unquestionably the most upscale community in Greater Cincinnati. This onetime farming community still has working dairy farms, but they share the village's 20 square miles with $3 million estates. Homes here are second to none in Greater Cincinnati, and many sit back from the roads on rolling, heavily wooded hillsides. Houses with their own tennis courts and pools and even their own horse stables are not uncommon. Horse-crossing signs are posted throughout the community, and it is not unusual to see residents horseback riding along its narrow, winding roads.

Indian Hill's 5,000 residents take great pride in living here and work hard at preserving their community's rural and secluded character. Most actively participate in the village's activities and operations. Although a full-time village manager handles day-to-day operations, most decisions are made by an elected council of community residents. Seven garden clubs help keep the common areas beautifully landscaped year-round and Indian Hill Exempted Village Schools, one of the best school systems in the state, always has an abundance of parent volunteers.

Indian Hill is home to many of Greater Cincinnati's wealthiest families, and it shows in the average sale price of residences, which is around $510,000. Homes in the village, though, can range from $350,000 to $3 million and more. *Worth* magazine, a national financial publication, ranked Indian Hill as No. 102 on its list of America's 300 Richest Towns in 1996 — no surprise to most Cincinnatians.

The scenic Little Miami River splits Indian Hill and neighboring **Terrace Park**, which is reminiscent of a New England village, with its stately trees, Colonial homes and neatly divided streets that are named after famous colleges. The village covers just 1.5 square miles and is one of the most sought-after communities in which to live. Offering a strong histori-

cal flavor, old-world charm and highly regarded Mariemont schools, many of the 2,100 residents don't want to leave Terrace Park once they locate here. Homes range from $90,000 to $400,000.

Mariemont is another quiet, peaceful community whose homes are in high demand. This tiny, 1-square-mile community, which is one of the area's earliest planned communities, is listed on the National Register of Historic Places. It is an English-style village, complete with an all-English Tudor town square, and filled with Colonial and Georgian-style homes. Most homes here are priced around $162,000, but this community of 3,100 has become so popular that housing is very difficult to find. Although small, the village is served by its own school system, which is one of the best in the state.

The communities of **Oakley** and **Madisonville** are becoming two highly popular areas with young couples and singles because of their affordable housing options and their proximity to restaurants, shopping and some of the trendiest parts of town. These suburban communities remain mostly middle- to lower-income, but many attractive homes with charming features such as hardwood floors and front porches can be found for moderate prices. Housing in Madisonville is priced around $50,000, while in Oakley, which has experienced a great jump in housing values, home sales average $82,000.

Another small but popular community is **Madeira**. The community, which covers just 3.5 square miles, tries hard to maintain its small, country-town atmosphere. Its focal points are a tiny railroad depot from the days when trains regularly stopped here and a busy business district, which houses cozy restaurants and interesting specialty shops. Madeira is very much a family-oriented community that takes great pride in its school system. The area's 9,000 residents enjoy a mixture of home styles and sizes (most of which sell for around $125,000) and take an active part in the protecting the quality of the community by strictly controlling development, virtually prohibiting commercial projects, and restricting exterior signs — including real estate "sold" signs.

Just north of Madeira is **Kenwood**. The pulse of this affluent community is its upscale retail area, which features Sycamore Plaza and the Kenwood Towne Centre, the area's most upscale and most popular mall. Kenwood features much more than shopping though, with mature trees, well-landscaped lawns, and homes of all styles and sizes, all of which seem to spill over with charm and personality. It is easily accessible via I-71 and is a favorite with families in the middle and upper-middle income brackets. Homes here typically sell for around $143,000. School children are served by one of four school districts — Madeira, Indian Hill, Deer Park and Cincinnati Public Schools — depending on which section of the community they live in.

Neighboring **Montgomery**, which stretches north to I-275, offers homes in a spacious environment that the community's residents have worked hard to preserve through high standards and strict zoning requirements. The 9,800 residents who live within its five square miles enjoy a wide variety of home sizes and architectural styles, and feel good about sending their children to Sycamore schools. Homes in this upscale family community can be found for around $205,000. Montgomery's city square, known as Olde Montgomery, sets the standards with its English Tudor buildings and 19th-century-village feel, and the flavor and quality carry over to the rest of the community. Olde Montgomery offers residents some of the most interesting upscale shops and restaurants, including the original Montgomery Inn Restaurant (see our Restaurants chapter).

Loveland is a mecca for active residents, with the luxury of having within its borders one of the area's busiest and most beautiful exercise areas. The Loveland Bike Path stretches for 24 miles along the shoreline of the Little Miami River, offering runners, walkers, bikers and rollerbladers a beautifully scenic setting in which to exercise. This community of 6,000, which sits just northeast of the I-275 and I-71 interchange, is one of Greater Cincinnati's fastest-growing, and it takes great pride in its abundance of green spaces and its location next to the scenic Little Miami River. Housing here comes all price ranges and sizes — there's even a castle (see our Attractions chapter) — but homes generally can be purchased for around $154,000. Primary and secondary

school children are served by the town's own school system.

Along the riverfront on the East Side are two original river towns: **New Richmond** and **Moscow**. New Richmond is in many ways still reminiscent of an old river town, with historic buildings and old woolen mills that still operate. Park benches underneath large shady trees line the riverbanks along the village's downtown business district. And the 2,500 residents have carefully planned the community's growth, accepting new developments while making sure not to upset its image as a "uniquely historic river town." Home prices range from $45,000 all the way to $500,000. And New Richmond residents are quite proud of their independence. The village is an exempted village, meaning it is exempt from county influences, both political and educational. Its school system, New Richmond Exempted Village Schools, is one of the richest in the state. Residents here are never far from recreational opportunities, with eight municipal parks in the town.

Moscow is perhaps best known as the location of the Zimmer Power Plant, which was originally designed to be nuclear powered but was converted at great expense to coal power before the first atom was split.

Western Suburbs

Immediately west of downtown is the historic community of **Price Hill**, one of the first hillside communities settled as the city's affluent citizens fled from the smoky downtown basin to the scenic hills. Like its eastern counterpart, Mount Adams, J-shaped Price Hill offers great views of the river and downtown, and many of its distinctive 19th-century houses are now being renovated after years of wear. Today, Price Hill is home to 40,000 residents, mostly middle-class and many of whom have had homes in the community through several generations and can trace their roots back to the time when 60 percent of the neighborhood was made up of German-Catholic or Irish-Catholic families. Many brick, frame and Victorian homes with large front yards and large front porches are available for around $52,000. Price Hill, which is served by Cincinnati Public Schools, is fully developed, so there are no new homes in the area.

Mount Echo Park sits on Price Hill's southeastern hilltop and offers splendid views of the river, Northern Kentucky, downtown and miles of Cincinnati. A few newer condominium developments can be found in Covedale, one of the smallest communities in town, but one that also offers Victorian homes. Homes within Covedale's 73 acres average about $75,000.

The community of **Delhi** is well known for its gardens. For some unknown reason, more commercial greenhouses are located in Delhi (pronounced by locals as Dell-high) than any other section of Cincinnati, and many of the homes in this bedroom community have lovely, well-kept flower gardens. Many of the homes here are older, with mature trees and foliage. In addition, there are several higher-income subdivisions on the western side, some offering wonderful vistas of the river and Northern Kentucky. Homes here sell for an average of around $97,000 and are served by the Oak Hills School District. The 30,000 residents within Delhi's 10 square miles also work hard at protecting their community, and have stuck together strongly in their battles with the airport about overhead flight patterns. Delhi also has the distinction of being the home of the College of Mount St. Joseph, one of the oldest colleges in the area.

North of downtown and to the west of I-75, **Camp Washington** is home of some of the city's oldest industrial businesses, and **Fairmount** has many less expensive homes and two of the city's low-income housing developments.

Nearby **Cheviot** and **Westwood** are older neighborhoods dominated by Cincinnati's German-Catholic heritage. Residents of Cheviot take great care of their splendid little community through an independent municipal government that is filled by elected officials from within the community. Founded in 1818, this simple, conservative neighborhood of just one square mile sits high on the western hillside and offers its 9,600 residents a small-town atmosphere with mature trees and well-preserved colonial-style homes that are available for around $70,000. Neighboring Westwood has a wide variety of distinctive older homes dating back to the late 1800s that average around $75,000, as well as some more expensive multilevel homes built in newer

subdivisions. The streets in Westwood are clean and secluded, and shopping, churches and day care are close by, as is Mount Airy Forest, Cincinnati's largest and most beautiful wooded area. Both communities are served by Cincinnati Public Schools.

Western Hills is well known as the area's baseball breeding ground, with 10 Western Hills High School graduates playing in the major leagues, including Pete Rose, Don Zimmer and Russ Nixon. But residents like the 12.5-square-mile community for the charm of its older homes, its community offerings such as two parks and a swimming pool, and its strong German heritage, which is still evident today. The area's 30,000 residents live in affordable homes that cover a variety of architectural styles and sizes, with many of the homes sitting on larger lots. The Western Hills section of Glenway Avenue serves as the main retail district for the entire West Side. The community is served by Cincinnati Public Schools, but parts of Western Hills extend outside Cincinnati city limits and into Miami, Delhi and Green, which can have an impact on taxes.

White Oak and **Monfort Heights** are growing rural communities, where the rolling hills that just a few years ago were farmland are beginning to sprout new multilevel homes priced at around $109,000. Both of these peaceful communities are served by Northwest Schools and adjoin parts of Mount Airy Forest. Monfort Heights has just 8,100 residents within its six square miles, while White Oak is a shade smaller, with 7,400 residents on six square miles.

Colerain Avenue, one of the largest and busiest retail districts in Greater Cincinnati, is the heart of **Colerain**. The district is anchored by massive Northgate Mall and contains hundreds of specialty stores spread throughout dozens of strip malls, plazas and freestanding buildings for several miles in both directions. Colerain, which is located to the west of I-275 at U.S. 27, is the largest geographic township in Ohio at 45 square miles, although most of the residential development is south of I-275. Many traditional and contemporary homes as well as a number of houses in older subdivision are priced around $96,000. Although a few larger estates and many farms are located on the gently rolling hills north of I-275, that area has yet to be mass-developed by home builders, although it's just a matter of time. Northwest Schools serve Colerain's 57,000 residents. It must be noted that Colerain is the repository for much of Greater Cincinnati's trash. The Rumpke landfill, or "Mount Rumpke" as it is known, is the highest man-made peak in Ohio, and it hasn't even reached capacity yet, although it is expected to in the not-too-distant future.

Harrison sits as close to Indiana as possible while still remaining in Ohio. Many people find this area highly attractive because of the affordability of homes, some of which are brand new and others that date back to the 1800s, and the great care the community takes in preserving its rural, wooded character. Some parts of the community, which are served by Southwest Schools, have minimum acreage requirements for homes. The city maintains four recreational playfields and two pools. Just 12,000 people live within Harrison's 12.5 square miles.

Like Cincinnati itself, many smaller river towns were founded in the area's early developmental period and are now West Side communities of Greater Cincinnati. These include **Sedamsville**, **Riverside**, **Sayler Park**, **Fernbank**, **Addyston**, and, perhaps most notably, **North Bend**. North Bend is the final resting place of President William Henry Harrison and the birthplace of President Benjamin Harrison. Although some new estate homes with wonderful vistas of the Ohio River are being built in these communities, most remain small towns with older homes, many dating back to the 1800s. All of the communities are served by Three Rivers Schools, and are near Shawnee Lookout Park. Home prices range from $40,000 to $100,000.

Northern Suburbs

Fairfield is a medium-size town of 44,000 residents that Greater Cincinnati expanded out to and is now connected to, but like several other local independent communities, it's very much its own entity. Many residents of Greater Cincinnati are attracted to this city, which is 18 miles north of downtown, and its population has more than doubled in the past 10 years. An abundance of new apartments and single-family homes that average around $114,000 have been built within its 20.5 square miles to meet the demand. Billed as the "City of Opportunity," Fairfield gives its residents an opportunity to get involved, and they usually do, with 20 community organizations keeping the city clean, well run and well cared for. The city has four parks and is close to Mercy Hospital Fairfield. Residents can find most everything they want at the hundreds of restaurants, businesses, retail stores and hotels that line both sides of U.S. Route 4, which slices through the core of the city. Fairfield has its own city schools, which are highly respected and have recently expanded to meet the growth.

About 15 miles north of downtown, north of the I-75 and I-275 interchange, is **West Chester**, one of the fastest-growing and most prestigious areas in Greater Cincinnati. The soft, rolling hills that were farms just 10 years ago now feature some of the most luxurious estate home developments in the area. Home prices in this distinctive community average $155,000, although homes can be found near the $1 million range. This 35-square-mile area has become so popular and grown so fast, its highly regarded Lakota School District had to build two new high schools and turn the old high school into a junior high in order to meet the demand.

Like most of the northeastern suburbs, **Mason** has become a development site for upscale homes, with an incredible 1,500 new homes ranging from $100,000 to $800,000 built between 1991 and 1995. Residents and town officials, though, have kept the secluded, 14-square-mile community from becoming overdeveloped by maintaining more than 190 acres for parkland, four parks, two lakes, baseball and soccer fields and hiking trails. The area's 15,000 residents send their children to Mason Schools, and thrill-seeking residents love having Kings Island in their backyard.

Northeastern Suburbs

Symmes lies northeast of the I-71 and I-275 interchange. The area's 13,000 residents have seen an explosion of growth in recent years, and the township's 9.7 square miles are now 70 percent developed. Still, large, upscale single-family homes continue to be built here and it has been the site of several recent Homearama shows. Estate homes, townhomes and condos are all under construction, as are retail and commercial developments. School options can be puzzling, as three school districts — Sycamore, Indian Hill and Loveland — service different parts of the township. All three school systems, though, are outstanding, so residents can't lose. Older homes can be found for as little as $35,500, while newer ones can cost as much as $400,000. Most, though, sell for $100,000 to $175,000.

Within Symmes is Landen, a planned community designed in 1975 that is a mecca for nature lovers, as it is centered around a heavily wooded 100-acre park that includes an 8-acre lake and a network of hiking and biking trails. The homes in this remarkable community are mostly custom-built and located in the Kings School District. Homes prices here average $120,000 but can top $500,000.

Lebanon is an old city, founded in 1796, that is being rediscovered as the suburbs push outward. Residents love the rustic, small town charm and its turn-of-the-century main street, which is packed with dozens of antique stores and the highly popular The Golden Lamb restaurant and hotel (see our Restaurants and Accommodations chapters). The city even has its own train, adding to its 19th century atmosphere. Distinctly elegant homes from the 1800s can be found here, as well as some newer homes, most priced around $118,000. Although located 29 miles north of downtown, residents find the area very accessible off I-71. About 11,000 people make their home here, including astronaut Neil Armstrong.

Northern Kentucky

Covington is by far the largest city in Northern Kentucky and, with a population of 41,000, is the third-largest city in the state behind Louisville and Lexington. This river city is located directly across the Ohio from downtown Cincinnati and is connected by the historic Roebling Suspension Bridge. Towering office buildings and luxurious hotels that carry the Cincinnati business environment across the river distinguish Covington's downtown area from all others in Northern Kentucky and give it the look and feel of a true city.

Covington has all of the markings of a city its size, too, with businesses, retail districts, and nightlife spots, including Covington Landing, one of Greater Cincinnati's prime riverfront entertainment areas (see our Nightlife chapter). Its residential communities are one of its key attractions, though. Historic Victorian homes can be found throughout the older sections of the city, where rehabbing of the stylish homes, with their turn-of-the-century charm, is common. Many of the homes are on the National Register of Historic Places, including most of those in the Historic Riverside Drive District, which is filled with antebellum Southern mansions, 130-year-old row houses and Civil War-era homes. New upscale condominium complexes are also being built in Covington, particularly on its hillsides, which have fantastic views of Covington's river basin and downtown Cincinnati. The MainStrasse area in Covington is also very popular because of its quaint setting, its German village feel and a retail district that offers numerous specialty shops and cozy restaurants (see our Attractions and Shopping chapters).

Being such a large city, Covington has its share of middle-income and poorer areas as well, so homes average around $87,000 but can range in price from $30,000 all the way up to $300,000. Families here are served by Covington schools. The city's west side includes Devou Park, a 704-acre playground with an 18-hole golf course, picnic area and one of the area's best overlooks of downtown Cincinnati and downtown Covington. Several other golf courses are located in the southern parts of Covington. St. Elizabeth Medical Center is also located in the city.

Large mansions can be found in neighboring **Newport**, another landmark historic neighborhood that sits directly across the river from downtown Cincinnati. Three bridges connect Newport to Cincinnati, so residents on the north side of the river flow into Newport to enjoy all its entertainment spots. Newport's reputation as the area's "Sin City," garnered in the 1930s when it was more popular than Las Vegas for gambling and prostitution, is waning as a result of the community's efforts over the last 15 years to clean itself up and turn itself around. The entertainment hotspots now center around "Riverboat Row," a lineup of floating and land-based restaurants and bars. Diners flock to Riverboat Row year-round to grab a bite to eat, watch the boaters on the river and catch the spectacular vistas of the Cincinnati skyline. Two other major entertainment attractions are also under construction in Newport: a $41 million aquarium and a 1,234-foot Millennium Tower, which should be open sometime in 1999.

Some of the city's many residential neighborhoods feature remarkable Victorian, Queen Anne, Italianate and Colonial Revival homes that are more than 100 years old. The Mansion Hill and Gateway districts of the city are both listed in the National Register of Historic Places. Most residents, though, live in smaller homes that can range in price from $50,000 all the way to $200,000. Newport has its own school system.

Adjacent to Newport is **Bellevue**, a small town whose roots date back to its founding in 1870. This charming river town of 6,300 is centered around its old-fashioned business district, which runs right along the river and includes a generations-old pizza parlor and a candy store where they still make all of the sweets by hand. A number of homes in this one-square-mile town date back to the early century, particularly in the fashionable Bonnie Leslie area, which offers well-maintained brick houses with large trees and river and city views. Homes here, most of which are 50 and 60 years old, can be found in the $35,000 to $80,000 range. Residents of Bellevue are particularly proud of their schools, displaying banners that read "Tiger Town" (in honor of their sports teams) on street lights around town.

Dayton, next in the string of small river towns, also offers old-time charm, with numerous patio-styles homes, some of them located on a hilltop that offers wonderful river views. Dayton is one of the area's older communities and its 6,000 residents are a combination of lifelong residents and new families. Some new families live in apartments that were built in the town's old high school.

One of the most exclusive communities in Northern Kentucky is **Fort Thomas**, which sits on the hill above the Ohio River and was a longtime military outpost. Known as the "City of Beautiful Homes," Fort Thomas offers houses in a wide variety of sizes and architectural styles, all well maintained with mature trees and plush landscaping. Many have panoramic vistas of the river and the eastern side of Cincinnati. Homes here, some of which are more than 120 years old, are priced around $95,000, and it's not unusual to find a $60,000 two-bedroom home sharing a narrow, winding street with a large $200,000 home. Nor is it unusual for a home to sell before it's even listed; word of mouth is often enough to attract a buyer. The 15,000 residents of this quiet, peaceful community are quite proud of their schools, which are some of the most competitive in sports in the state, and are comforted by the presence of St. Luke Hospital East located in the city.

Northern Kentucky University is the focal point of **Highland Heights**, which sits at the southern end of I-471. The community has grown by 50 percent in the last six years, and the smaller, 40-year-old Cape Cods and ranch style homes that sell for around $60,000 are now being mixed with newer multilevel homes that range up to $180,000. Many condominiums are being built in the area, as well as a large number of retail establishments along U.S. 27, which cuts through the heart of the city. The city's Civic Center provides residents with a wide variety of activities.

Nearby **Wilder** was found to be the fastest-growing community in Northern Kentucky in the most recent census. More than 2,500 residents now live in the tiny community along the Licking River because of the boom in con-

INSIDERS' TIP

Mount Adams got its name from former president John Quincy Adams, who in November 1843 traveled 1,000 miles for the dedication of the Cincinnati Observatory. The 76-year-old Adams delivered a two-hour history of astronomy. Locals were so impressed they changed the site's name from Mount Ida to Mount Adams.

dominium and apartment communities. Most homes sell for around $65,000 to $150,000 but can range upward to $300,000. **Southgate** is also becoming an attractive area, particularly with first-time buyers because older, more traditional homes are available for moderate prices — between $80,000 and $140,000.

Twelve miles south of downtown on U.S. 27 in Campbell County is **Alexandria**, a growing city of 7,100 residents. Established in 1856, Alexandria is becoming one of the area's fastest-growing communities, thanks to the recently completed AA Highway connecting Alexandria (the only town in the Greater Cincinnati area the highway touches) to the East Coast. East of Alexandria, large tracts of land can still be bought inexpensively, and a small-town atmosphere is still very pervasive. Homes here are available from $60,000 to $400,000. Alexandria is also home of the Campbell County Schools District, which serves most of the county's residents, as well as A.J. Jolly Park, where residents can enjoy golf, baseball, swimming, camping and fishing.

Area residents are also discovering **Cold Spring**, a tiny community of 3,400 along U.S. 27 that is sprouting an abundance of new subdivisions and condominiums. Homes can range from $70,000 to $250,000.

Florence, located just off I-75, has quickly become the second-largest community in Northern Kentucky, with nearly 20,000 young individuals and large families attracted to its proximity to the Cincinnati/Northern Kentucky International Airport, businesses and the largest retail district south of the river. The Florence Mall is the heart of the retail district, and it is surrounded by hundreds of smaller and medium-size stores and large, big-box users such as Sams, Wal-Mart and Target. Almost all of the homes in this area have been built within the last 15 years, and are available for around $114,000. Homes range from $70,000 to $400,000, and numerous condominiums and apartments are also available. Florence is in the Boone County School District.

Erlanger is also one of Northern Kentucky's largest cities, as well as one of its oldest. Sitting along I-75, this community of 17,000 has its own independent school system and the largest movie theater south of the river, the Showcase. Many older homes are spread around town and sell for $50,000 to $125,000.

Crestview Hills, on the south side of I-275, is a smaller, more rural, but certainly not sleepy community. Crestview Hills Mall, anchored by McAlpin's, is located within the community's three square miles, as is Thomas More College, one of the most exclusive private colleges in the area. The neighborhood's 2,500 residents live in a mixture of older homes with mature trees and newer single-family home in subdivisions, ranging in price from $90,000 to as much as $600,000.

Many young families are attracted to **Edgewood**, a relatively new community at the bottom of the I-275 circle freeway. The community's 8,500 residents enjoy newer homes built on spacious lots. Most homes sell for $120,000 to $200,000, but homes that sell for as much as $1 million can be found here. St. Elizabeth South Hospital is located within the community's four square miles.

Fort Mitchell is a highly desirable neighborhoods in Northern Kentucky. Located off I-75, it has many well-cared-for older homes priced around $152,000, as well as estate communities with custom-built houses. Children attend Beechwood Independent Schools, which are some of the best in the state. Fort Mitchell also offers a wide variety of dining and entertainment options, and is the home of the Drawbridge Estate, a highly popular hotel, convention and entertainment complex that features several restaurants, nightclubs and a microbrewery.

Next to Fort Mitchell is small — just two square miles — but quite tranquil **Lakeside Park**, with its six lakes spread out among 14 residential developments. This lovely neighborhood offers its 3,000 residents a wide variety of classic older homes, as well as some newer homes that have been built to match the classic tradition of the rest of the community. Most homes are priced around $152,000. Residents are quite active in keeping the community beautiful through a civic association, and even hand out awards to residents who do the most to beautify their property.

Villa Hills was rated the area's most livable neighborhood in a study by *Cincinnati Magazine* in 1994 and has adopted the slogan

"A special place to live." This is easy to understand, as the small community, which overlooks the river on the western side of Kenton County, provides its 7,400 residents with distinctive new homes, wonderful views of the Ohio River and one of the lowest crime rates in the area. It is also a favorite neighborhood for sports stars and other personalities. Homes here are mostly priced around $112,000, which is a bargain.

Fort Wright and **Park Hills** are small communities, but they feature beautiful, large traditional homes (valued at around $112,000) on wooded hillsides, and they adjoin Devou Park. **Crescent Springs**, to the south, has smaller traditional homes that are attracting many younger families. More than 3,600 residents now live in this small town along I-75, whose history dates back to the 1850s.

Many other smaller, older towns can be found along the river in Northern Kentucky: **Bromley**, **Ludlow**, **Silver Grove** and **Melbourne**. Homes in these communities tend to be older, and the towns truly small towns, with families who have lived there for several generations.

Southeastern Indiana

Southeastern Indiana includes a number of small river towns, including **Lawrenceburg** and **Aurora**. Lawrenceburg's 4.5 square miles are being converted into a major tourist attraction because of the opening of a gambling casino on its riverfront (see our River Fun chapter). The 4,000 residents are expecting 3 million visitors to the casino each year. Homes in Lawrenceburg are priced around $76,000, while in nearby Aurora they average around $60,000.

Just outside of Lawrenceburg is **Hidden Valley Lake**, a planned residential development built around a 150-acre lake and an 18-hole golf course. It's becoming an upscale bedroom community for business executives who seek to get away from the city. **Brookville Lake**, **Greendale** and **Bright** are attractive communities for those who don't mind the commute because they all offer a lot of land for development, outstanding property values and a very rural setting. Homes here generally start around $80,000 and range upward to $250,000.

Golf Course Communities

Golf and Greater Cincinnati seem to be intertwined, although we aren't sure why. (If you doubt it, see our Golf chapter and count the number of courses for yourself.) Realizing this — and it didn't take long — developers began building whole communities around golf courses. The risk of a broken window from an errant tee shot is easily outweighed by being able to walk out the back door and onto the back nine. Or, as is the case with some diehard duffers, the justification for owning your own golf cart.

Wynnburne Park, now **Western Hills Country Club**, was the area's first country club community, chartered in 1912 and platted in the 1920s. The developer boasted it was "only a mashie shot away" from the golf course. Many courses followed, and many more will. The area still has enough large tracts of inexpensive farmland available that developers can afford to build both homes and a golf course.

If living on the links is what you're looking for, ask your real estate agent to give you a tour of one of the following subdivisions: **Ivy Hills** in Newtown; **Coldstream** in Anderson; **The Oasis** in Loveland; **Wildwood** in Fairfield; **The Golf Center at Kings Island**, **The Heritage Club**, **Fairway at Pine Run**, **Eagle View** and **Crooked Tree** in Mason; **Beckett Ridge** and **Wetherington** in West Chester; **Waldon Ponds** in Indian Springs; **Shaker Run** in Lebanon; **Deer Run** in Miami; **Pebble Creek** in Colerain; **The Traditions** in Burlington, Kentucky; **Triple Crown** in Union, Kentucky; and **Hidden Valley Lake** in Dearborn County, Indiana.

All these communities offer upper-income single-family residential properties and a few

INSIDERS' TIP

Not a land lover? Living on a boat along the riverfront is not uncommon.

The Historic District in Covington, Kentucky, is filled with antebellum, Southern mansions, 130-year-old row houses and Civil War-era homes.

have multifamily residential, condominium and landominium properties.

Living On The Water

The Ohio River may not be the Carolina coast, but it is water. And for those who don't like to be landlocked or who like to sleep on a real water bed, the river is the only place to reside. Twelve harbors along the river have slips that allow for full-time residence on houseboats. The slips, with individual electrical and water hookups, can be rented by the season or by the month. Prices vary depending on the harbor. Of course, if you live on a houseboat and don't like where you are, it's a heck of a lot easier to pack up and move.

Four Seasons Marina, 4609 Kellogg Avenue, 871-4354, and **Watertown Yacht Club**, 1301 4th Avenue, Dayton, Kentucky, (606) 261-

8800, are two of the newest marinas. They offer shelter from the noise and traffic of the river as well as electrical hookups, fuel and a parking lot for those excursions inland.

Builders and Developers

Greater Cincinnati has an abundance of home builders and developers who can provide everything from small, modular homes to custom homes that begin at $1 million.

If you're into that rustic atmosphere, you can choose among several log home builders who offer different styles: hand-cut, hand-hewn logs, machine cut and smoothed logs, and on . . . . If you're looking for a custom-built home, a good place to see the work of several builders at the same time is the annual Homearama show in Cincinnati or the HomeFest show in Northern Kentucky. Builders and developers purchase lots in a newly developed, very upscale subdivision and try to one-up each other with amenities, luxury, landscaping and decorating.

If you have questions about a certain builder or developer, try checking with the Home Builders Association of Greater Cincinnati, 851-6300.

Many new subdivisions will have a model home or two and an on-site agent who can tell you all about the community and help you purchase a home there. Be aware, though, that on-site agents work for the builder or the real estate company that is marketing the community, although by law they must treat you fairly and honestly. However, if you want someone to represent your best interests, get your own real estate agent.

Real Estate Agencies

In addition to the major franchises, Greater Cincinnati has dozens of small or independently owned real estate agencies — far too many to list here. The following list is an overview of the area's real estate offices.

Biederman Realtors
4741 Cornell Rd., Blue Ash • 530-5222

Biederman Realtors has been serving Cincinnati since 1979 and has two offices in the area to meet home buyers' needs. One office is on Cornell Road in Blue Ash, which makes it convenient not only to communities on the East Side, but also the rapidly growing northeastern suburbs. Its other office is on the heavily travelled North Bend Road on Cincinnati's West Side, where it monitors the buying and selling activities of the older communities on that side of town.

Bischoff Realty Inc.
3620 Glenmore Ave., Cheviot • 662-1990
1004 Harrison Ave., Harrison • 367-2171

This small but rapidly growing real es-

tate company has carved out a niche for itself by becoming an expert on homes on the West Side of Greater Cincinnati and in Southeastern Indiana. The Cheviot office provides expertise in the heavily residential areas of the near West Side, and the Harrison office, near the Indiana border, extends their range of expertise.

Century 21 Champions
11421 Chester Rd., Sharonville
• 772-7733, (800) 543-3007

Champions is one of seven local independently owned and operated Century 21 offices and it features a relocation department.

Century 21 Complete Realty
600 Columbus Ave., Lebanon
• 621-9599

Complete Realty has relocation and auction departments in its office. It's UIP Referral Network links it to the thousands of offices in the Century 21 chain nationwide, making relocation easier.

Coldwell Banker West Shell
4555 Lake Forest Dr., Blue Ash
• 733-0900, (800) 552-3251

Coldwell Banker became the dominant real estate company in Greater Cincinnati in October 1997 when it bought West Shell Realtors, which had been the area's largest firm with more than 10,000 transactions and $1.3 billion a year in sales. Coldwell had been the third largest firm in town; the combined agencies will account for 15,000 transactions and nearly $2 billion in sales. When the consolidation of offices and shifting of agents is completed, CBWS will have around 25 offices spread throughout Greater Cincinnati. The national presence allows for easy communication with people relocating from another city with a Coldwell Banker office. It also offers mortgage services and publishes its own monthly *Real Estate Guide* magazine.

INSIDERS' TIP

Many, but not all, suburban communities give you credit for local income taxes you pay where you work. Check with your city hall to make sure you don't have to pay taxes in both places.

Coletta & Associates
9810 Montgomery Rd., Montgomery
• 984-1150
2691 Madison Rd., Norwood • 871-1600
This small, two-office boutique agency focuses on the area's East Side. It has become a popular alternative to the large agencies.

Comey & Shepherd Inc.
6901 Wooster Pike, Mariemont
• 561-5800
Comey & Shepherd has a network of nearly 200 sales associates who offer city-wide service. Its "Home Tour" television program is a visual tour of local homes that airs every day on the local cable network (Time Warner Cable channel 20 and Coaxial Cable channel 7). Comey also offers PropertySource, 271-HOME, a telephone listing service that gives detailed descriptions of each of its listings. Relocation services, an in-house mortgage assistance group and a home warranty program are available. In addition to its Mariemont headquarters, Comey & Shepherd has offices are in Anderson, Hyde Park, Montgomery and West Chester.

First Agency Group
618 Buttermilk Pike, Crescent Springs,
Ky. • (606) 578-8200
First Agency Group has been serving Northern Kentucky home buyers and sellers since 1979 with auctions, consulting and For Sale By Owner plans. Its Crescent Springs office covers the western side, including Florence, Villa Hills, Fort Mitchell and other communities in Boone and Kenton counties. Its Fort Thomas office is located in one of the most desirable communities in Northern Kentucky and serves all of Campbell County and parts of Kenton County.

Jim Huff Realty Inc.
2332 Royal Dr., Fort Mitchell, Ky.
• (606) 344-4616
Jim Huff Realty has been the dominant home seller in Northern Kentucky for the last 20 years and has more than 270 professional sales associates. This family-owned agency is the fourth largest in Greater Cincinnati, with more than 2,700 transactions in 1996 and $186 million in sales. In addition to the Fort Mitchell headquarters, there are offices in Dry Ridge, Erlanger, Florence and Fort Thomas. Jim Huff also just entered the Cincinnati market with an office on Montgomery Road in Symmes.

Jordan Realtors
7658 Montgomery Rd., Kenwood
• 791-0281
3960 Montgomery Rd., Norwood
• 531-4740
This small agency was founded in 1966 and concentrates on the East Side. Still family-owned, the offices' 30 agents offer "professional services with a personal touch." Although its two offices are on the same road, they are far enough apart to allow agents to cover a wide portion of the East Side. The agency also offers marketing analysis, relocation services and home appraisals.

Mike Parker Real Estate Inc.
71 Cavalier Blvd., Florence, Ky.
• (606) 647-0700
Mike Parker Real Estate covers all three counties in Northern Kentucky, with homes ranging from less than $50,000 all the way to more than $1 million. Mike Parker, the agency's founder, is a longtime Northern Kentucky Realtor, most recently for RE/MAX, where he was that agency's top broker in Northern Kentucky for five years before setting out on his own. Parker also helped start the real estate channel on TKR Cable (channel A9), and has a 30-minute program of his listings on the channel that airs six times a day. The agency offers a true team approach to buying and selling homes, with all three of its agents involved in each transaction. Parker handles the listing and selling aspects of the transaction while another agent focuses solely on the marketing and a third agent concentrates strictly on the closing aspects. The agency also handles property management for upscale condominiums.

RE/MAX
11311 Cornell Park Dr., Blue Ash
• 530-2020
RE/MAX is a well-known national real estate agency with 22 independently owned and operated businesses throughout

Greater Cincinnati. Being part of a nation-wide organization allows for communication with thousands of offices around the country, making relocating to or from Greater Cincinnati easier.

Sibcy Cline Realtors
8040 Montgomery Rd., Kenwood
• 984-4100

Sibcy Cline is the second largest real estate company in Greater Cincinnati with more than 750 Realtors and 19 offices in the area. Sibcy had more than 7,700 transactions in 1996 that accounted for more than $1 billion in sales. The agency offers a wide variety of other services to help in the buying and selling process, including a guaranteed sales program, relocation and auction departments and a financial services and mortgage department. The agency publishes its own *Listings* magazine twice monthly, produces a TV show on Channel 12 and offers a ListNet site on the World Wide Web that shows interior as well as exterior pictures of listed homes. It also has The Listing Line, a telephone listing service that provides a complete description of all listings.

Signature Realtors
9118 Winton Rd., Finneytown
• 522-2900, (800) 798-3104
9560 Montgomery Rd., Kenwood
• 791-5300

Signature Realtors covers the east and north-central parts of the area from its two offices. Although not large, it offers almost all of the same services as the larger agencies, including an auction division, relocation services, an appraisal division and a commercial division.

Star One Realtors
8170 Corporate Park Dr., Montgomery
• 247-6900

Star One is one of the area's newest and fastest-growing real estate companies. It has expanded to seven offices throughout the area and gained quite a reputation for service,

quickly becoming the third-largest agency in terms of sales and transactions. In 1996 the agency completed more than 3,100 transactions for more than $400 million in sales. The offices cover all of Greater Cincinnati north of the river, and include a relocation division and a commercial division.

Real Estate Publications

Numerous real estate magazines list area properties for sale. Most of them contain listings of a variety of real estate agencies (those who pay for space), although some larger agencies print their own magazines with just their own listings. Almost all these publications are free and can be picked up at area grocery and convenience stores. In addition, several TV shows feature available properties (check local TV listings), and real estate agents Mike Rose and Michael Bastian host a radio program on various real estate topics, including listings, on WKRC (550 AM) each Saturday between 7 and 8 PM.

Coldwell Banker Real Estate Guide

Coldwell Banker publishes this magazine of its own local listings monthly. It's available as an insert in *The Cincinnati Enquirer* as well as at local grocery and convenience stores.

For Sale By Owner

This free publication, which comes out every other month, previews homes throughout the area that owners choose to put up for sale without the help of a real estate agent.

Greater Cincinnati Relocation Guide

Real estate agencies publish this glossy magazine in cooperation with the Greater Cincinnati Chamber of Commerce. It includes some community profiles, relocation information, feature articles and general information about the city. The guide is available through most real estate agencies or can be purchased at some bookstores for $8.

Harmon Homes

Harmon publishes one magazine for Ohio and Indiana and another for Northern Kentucky. Both include listings for condominiums and land and come out twice a month.

Listings

Sibcy Cline Realtors' magazine provides information on homes listed by the agency.

Real Estate Week

The Cincinnati Enquirer offers a special advertising biweekly publication with listings and articles on home maintenance and care, moving and other related topics. It's available at all Kroger grocery stores.

The Real Estate Book

This glossy publication gives clear, all-color looks at hundreds of homes for sale around the area.

Apartment Communities

Greater Cincinnati has an abundance of apartment and rental communities for those who are looking for a place to live without buying. While there are far too many to list here, we've offered a tasting of what's available in different areas. Many apartment communities are clustered with other apartment communities, so if one isn't exactly to your liking, there may be more options nearby.

You can pick up a copy of *Apartment Rental Guide of Greater Cincinnati & Northern Kentucky* for more information on the numerous apartment communities around Greater Cincinnati. Temporary and corporate housing is included in this colorful, pocket-size guide, which comes out every two months. *Apartments For Rent* also features apartment complex ads and is published every two weeks. Both publications are free and available at racks in grocery and convenience stores.

Woodridge
3977 Woodridge Blvd., Fairfield
• 874-1988

Woodridge is a combined community of four smaller communities — Woodridge Crossing, Woodridge Knoll, Woodridge Point and Woodridge Glen — that sit in a wooded setting in Fairfield, off Route 4 near the I-275 exit. Large two-bedroom apartments begin at $509 a month and include cathedral ceilings, private balconies, controlled building access, mini and vertical blinds on the windows and vanities in the master bathroom. Each building has laundry facilities, or washer/dryer hookups are available. Woodridge is near Tri-County Mall and Forest Fair Mall, restaurants, and bus routes. The communities are operated by Associated Land Group, one of the finest apartment management firms in Greater Cincinnati.

Harper's Point
8713 Harperpoint Dr., Symmes
• 489-1160

Located in one of the most desirable areas of town, Harper's Point offers one-, two- and three-bedroom townhomes with a rough-sawn look with cedar shakes, loft spaces, woodburning fireplaces, plush landscaping and duck-filled ponds. Units, which range from $600 to $1,085 a month, include vaulted ceilings, washer/dryer hookups and extra storage space. The clubhouse has a pub for parties. Short-term leases are available and pets up to 20 pounds are welcome. Residents are near the popular Shops at Harper's Point and get a discount at the Club at Harper's Point.

Summit of Blue Ash
4870 Hunt Rd., Blue Ash • 793-4090

The Summit is located in the heart of "fabulous" Blue Ash, just a short walk from Memorial Park and the city's quaint shopping district. One-, two- and three-bedroom units are available from $705 to $1,045 a month. Some two-bedroom units have two full bathrooms. Other units have wraparound balconies, built-in bookshelves, washer/dryer hookups, gas heat and oversized soaking bathtubs. Pets under 25 pounds are welcome. Parking spaces are covered. Furnished corporate housing is also available in the complex.

Williamsburg of Cincinnati
200 W. Galbraith Rd. • 948-2300

Williamsburg of Cincinnati is one of the largest and nicest apartment communities in Greater Cincinnati, offering studio, one-, two- and three-bedroom units. Within the heavily wooded 110-acre complex just one mile west of I-75, renters find three designer swimming pools for socializing or cooling off, a fitness center, tennis courts, guest rooms for visitors and washer/dryer hookups in each unit. Some units offer fireplaces, built-in bookcases and carports or garages, and heat is paid for. One-bedroom lofts include spiral staircases. Short-term leases are available. Dry-cleaning service, concierge service and an ATM are on site. Large dogs are welcome. Studio units rent for $445 a month, with one-bedroom units at $525, two-bedroom units $690 and three-bedroom units $915 a month.

Aspen Village
2703 Erlene Dr. • 662-3724

Aspen Village is two communities, both offering spacious one- and two-bedroom apartments at an affordable price, starting at $310 a month. The communities share five outdoor pools, three tennis courts, a Nautilus fitness center and picnic and playground areas. Leases as short as three months are available for apartments that include fireplaces, and heat is paid for. Pets are welcome. The communities are located off Queen City Avenue near I-75, on major bus routes.

Panorama
2375 Montana Ave. • 481-1234

Located in the middle of a large apartment area on Montana Avenue in Westwood, Panorama stands out with its luxurious amenities. All apartments have large balconies, central air and ceiling fans, and heat and hot water are paid for. Two-bedroom units have fireplaces and three-bedroom apartments have washer/dryer hookups. Panorama is on a major bus route convenient to I-74, I-75 and I-275. You can bring your cat.

Village of Coldstream
998 Meadowland Dr., Anderson
• 474-4907

Coldstream is located in a parklike setting in the highly desirable area of Anderson. It offers one-, two- and three-bedroom apartments and townhomes. The brick or stone colonial buildings, built by upscale specialists Towne Properties, have spacious floor plans, large walk-in closets, extra storage space and

washer/dryer hookups. Heat is paid for. Plenty of social activities take place at the clubhouse, tennis courts and swimming pool. Pets up to 20 pounds are welcome. Units start at $500 a month and go to $890 a month.

Eastgate Woods
4412 Eastwood Dr. • 752-2727

These English Tudor buildings sit in a beautifully landscaped and heavily wooded area adjacent to the popular Eastgate shopping area. Each building has a private entry and apartments have private balconies and extra storage space. Clubhouse facilities, a swimming pool, 24-hour emergency service and short-term leases are available. Seven different floor plans are available, with one-bedroom units starting at $375 and two-bedroom units at $465.

One Lytle Place
621 E. Mehring Way • 621-7578

One Lytle Place puts residents right along the riverfront in the heart of downtown and offers spectacular views. The 25-story building has 11 different spacious floor plans for one- and two-bedroom units, starting at $630 a month. The highly secured building also has a rooftop observatory, concierge, covered parking, hot tub and sauna, heated pool and an exercise and fitness center. Pets are welcome. Bicentennial Commons park sits at the building's back door. A free access shuttle is available to drive residents around downtown or to nearby shopping areas.

Paddock Club
8000 Preakness Dr., Florence, Ky.
• (606) 282-7444

Paddock Club is right in the middle of one of the busiest areas in Greater Cincinnati — just west of the Florence Mall and its surrounding retail district and just south of Turfway Park race track. The one-, two- and three-bedroom apartments start renting at $569 a month and offer decorator wall coverings, washer/dryer hookups, gas log fireplaces and garages with automatic door openers. Community areas include a clubhouse, hot tubs, sauna, tanning beds, indoor racquetball courts, weight room and swimming pool. Small pets are welcome.

Highland Ridge
1400 Highland Ridge Blvd., Highland
Heights, Ky. • (606) 781-2900

This newly developed community has one-
and two-bedroom units with three distinctive floor
plans, woodburning fireplaces, washer/dryer
hookups and extra storage. A fitness center and
clubhouse are available to residents, as well as
a pool and sundeck, guest apartment for visitors
and away-from-home services. Pets are welcome
and short-term leases are available.

Utility Services

Gas and Electric

Cinergy
139 E. Fourth St. • 421-9500, 287-2400
TDD-TTY

Cinergy operates the gas and electric utilities for Greater Cincinnati north of the river
and Southeastern Indiana. To report gas leak
emergencies, call 651-4466. To report power
outage, call 651-4182.

Union Light Heat & Power Co.
107 Brent Spence Sq., Covington, Ky.
• (606) 421-9500

In Northern Kentucky, Cinergy does business as **ULH&P**. For electrical problems call
651-4182 or (800) 543-5599. For gas leaks or
other problems call 651-4466 or (800) 634-4300.

Water

Boone County, (606) 586-6155
Butler County, 887-3061
Campbell County, (606) 441-2310
Cincinnati, 591-7700, 591-7900 (broken
water mains)
Clermont County, 732-7970
Kenton-Boone Counties, (606) 331-3066
Warren County, 925-1377

Sanitation and Garbage Removal

Municipalities in the Greater Cincinnati area
contract with individual companies to collect
trash. Residents are billed through user fees
or taxes. If you live in an unincorporated part
of a county, though, you may well be on your
own. Generally, the sanitation and garbage
removal in Greater Cincinnati is handled by
Rumpke, 742-2900; **BFI**, 771-4200; or **Waste
Management of Greater Cincinnati**,
242-5080.

Sewers

Butler County Sewer Department,
887-3061
Clermont County, 732-7970
**Cincinnati/Hamilton County Metropoli-
tan Sewer District**, 352-4900 days, 244-5500
nights/weekends
Warren County Water Department,
925-1377

Telephone

Cincinnati Bell
201 E. Fourth St. • 565-2210, TDD-TTY
241-2899

Cincinnati Bell is the primary telephone service in Greater Cincinnati. It offers a multitude
of additional services beyond basic phone service. For phone repair, call 611, or 566-1511
from a cellular phone or 397-9611 for TDD-
TTY hearing impaired service.

Cable TV

See our Media chapter for complete information about cable TV.

Plenty of activities and services in the Greater Cincinnati area are geared just to older adults.

Senior Services

With Interstate 75 providing a straight shot to the warm weather and sandy beaches of Florida, many of Greater Cincinnati's older adults head south upon retirement and never make the U-turn to come back. But that doesn't mean the area is left with nothing but young whippersnappers. Nearly one quarter of the area's population is older than 50, making older adults Greater Cincinnati's largest population group.

And the result is plenty of activities and services geared just to older adults. Those 60 and older qualify for a Golden Buckeye Card, a special discount card honored by thousands of restaurants, retailers and attraction sites across Ohio that entitles holders to reduced prices and special offers. Call 721-0502 for a card. Those 62 and older qualify for a Golden Age/Golden Eagle passport that offers free entry to national parks and 50 percent discounts on user fees. Call 684-3262 for a card.

Many golf courses offer senior rates during nonpeak hours. Some restaurants have special senior menus. Those 65 and older can ride the Metro for reduced fares. Banks have special accounts for people who are 50 and older. Special publications, such as *Prime Edition*, 741-6051, and *Senior Gazette*, 637-2233, are printed just for seniors and even offer personals in the back. Both papers are free and available at nursing homes, retirement centers and senior centers.

Services

The Alzheimer's Association
644 Linn St., Ste. 1026 • 721-4284

The Alzheimer's Association provides relatives and friends of those afflicted with Alzheimer's disease with information, support-group meetings and telephone counseling.

Arthritis Foundation, Southwestern Ohio Chapter
7811 Laurel Ave., Madeira • 271-4545

The Southwestern Ohio Chapter of the Arthritis Foundation is a local branch of the national organization and provides information and support for those suffering with arthritis.

Cincinnati Area Senior Services
644 Linn St. • 721-4330

The staff here has compiled a comprehensive list of services for those 60 and older. Many of the services, including a senior transportation service, make it possible for less active adults to continue living at home. The program also operates five senior centers and meal sites throughout the city. Some of the other services include the Guardianship Assistance Program (an adult protective service), medical transportation, Meals on Wheels, an adult daytime care center, a health-testing program and Alzheimer's disease information.

Clermont Senior Services
2085 Front Wheel Dr. • 724-1255

Clermont Senior Services offers a complete listing of information, resources and services such as social and recreational activities, nutrition information, residential facilities and medical programs for Clermont County residents 60 and older.

Council on Aging, Cincinnati Area
644 Linn St. • 721-7670

The statewide program helps those 60 and older with the special problems and concerns associated with the senior years.

Eldercare Locator
644 Linn St. • (800) 677-1116

This central referral service of the Area Agencies on Aging helps families access nationwide information about health, homemaking, nutrition, transportation, legal matters and other community-based services especially for older adults.

Elderlife at Deaconess Hospital
311 Straight St. at Clifton Ave.
• 559-2340

A free health and wellness program from Deaconess Hospital, Elderlife offers discounts on prescription drugs and vision, hearing and dental care, in addition to transportation, assistance with insurance claims, physician referrals and seminars for seniors. It also has an ElderHelp emergency response system that keeps members in contact with Deaconess health care professionals 24 hours a day.

Family Care Inc.
1014 Vine St. • 721-7440

This agency offers home health care via nurse's aides and companions for live-in or daily care.

First Call for Help
256 Ludlow Ave. • 221-1131

This United Way agency offers a free, confidential, 24-hour information and referral service that links callers with appropriate health and human services.

Franciscan Hospital Senior Network
2950 W. Park Dr. • 451-6100

This free resource center offers a variety of services and information for individuals 55 and older and is conducted in conjunction with the Franciscan hospitals.

Jewish Hospital of Cincinnati Inc.
3200 Burnet Ave. • 569-3582

Jewish Hospital's Semmons Center on Aging and its Center for Assessment and Referral of the Elderly (CARE) provide geriatric assessment and referral, geriatric psychiatry, physical rehabilitation, hearing tests, a continence restoration program and other health and social services for older adults.

Medicare Hotline
• (800) 282-0530

Nationwide Insurance Company provides this phone line to answer questions about Medicare.

Mercy Hospitals Goldenlife Care Program
3000 Mack Rd., Fairfield • 870-7018
100 Riverfront Plaza, Hamilton
• 867-6440
7500 State Rd., Anderson • 624-3298

This free service offers a variety of information and programs for individuals 55 and older and is conducted in conjunction with the area's three Mercy Hospitals.

Ohio Department of Aging
50 W. Broad St., eighth floor, Columbus, OH 43226 • (614) 462-6200

Write for a *Guide to Benefits and Services for Older Adults in Ohio*. Send $4 per book.

Pro Seniors Inc.
105 E. Fourth St. • 621-8721, 621-8721 legal hotline

Older persons with legal and long-term care problems can get assistance here. Pro Seniors also offers legal advice, referrals and representation and helps find nursing homes and home care for those in need. It publishes a free guide on selecting a home-care provider and investigates nursing home complaints.

Senior Services of Northern Kentucky Inc.
1032 Madison Ave., Covington, Ky.
• (606) 292-7968

Senior Services is a clearinghouse of information, resources and services for seniors living in Northern Kentucky. Topics it can provide information on include social and recreational activities, nutrition, residential facilities and meeting medical needs. It also operates 12 senior centers throughout the area and a volunteer program.

INSIDERS' TIP

For senior sportsters, the Senior Olympics has contests in the area. Call the Council on Aging, 721-1025, for information.

Social Security Administration
550 Main St., Room 2008
600 Kilgore Rd., Batavia
1710 S. Erie Rd., Hamilton
1811 Losantville Ave., Roselawn
228 Grandview Dr., Fort Mitchell, Ky.

These offices handle all inquiries regarding Social Security. The telephone number for all five offices is (800) 772-1213.

United Home Care Visiting Nurse Association
2400 Reading Rd. • 345-8080

Hospice, respite and private-duty nurses are available through United Home Care, which offers short-term care to relieve family caregivers. Sliding fees and hourly rates are offered.

Residences

Choosing a place to live is never easy. The Council on Aging Housing Coordinator, 644 Linn Street, Suite 1100, Queensgate, 721-7670, provides information on housing options for older adults, including congregate living, subsidized apartments, shared housing and home-matching opportunities. A separate Passport Program may pay for in-home nursing care and supportive services for low-income persons.

The Cincinnati Metropolitan Housing Authority, 662-7528, is the city's low-income housing unit. It offers low-income senior housing at Marquette Manor, 1999 Sutter Avenue, Fairmont, and 11 other communities within the city.

The following area facilities offer a variety of independent and assisted living options.

Amber Park Retirement Community
3801 E. Galbraith Rd., Deer Park
• 745-7600

Independent, assisted-living and temporary stays are available here. Each apartment has a balcony or terrace and full kitchen (or three meals a day and snacks are available). Amber Park is joined to the East Galbraith Health Care Center, which offers skilled nursing care; a registered dietitian on staff; physical, occupational and speech therapy; and podiatry, dental and optometry services. Housekeeping services, laundry and linen services, transportation and a full activity program are available. All utilities except telephone are included. Respite stays are available. The facility is Medicare and Medicaid certified.

Asbury Woods Retirement Villa
1149 Asbury Rd., Anderson • 231-1446

The villa is an independent-living facility with 50 one- and two-bedroom apartments. A villa van shuttles residents to preplanned social activities. A caterer serves meals once a week.

Baptist Village of Northern Kentucky
3000 Riggs Ave., Erlanger, Ky.
• (606) 727-4448

Baptist Village residents have an option of independent or assisted living in cottages on 21 scenic acres. Security is available 24 hours a day, as well as emergency services, planned activities and housekeeping. Subsidized assisted-living is also available. The community is also developing condominium units.

Batavia Nursing and Convalescent Inn
4000 Golden Age Dr., Batavia • 732-6500

This facility welcomes Medicare and Medicaid residents. Short-term care is available, along with physical and occupational therapy, skilled nursing and independent living. The center has 254 beds.

Bayley Place
990 Bayley Place Dr., Delhi • 347-5500

Residents here receive independent assistance in daily living tailored to their needs. Bayley Place's motto is "for those who don't need nursing care, but who would appreciate an occasional helping hand." In/out patient physical, occupational and speech therapy are available. Tiered pricing and short-term respite care are also available, and no admission fee is required. It is sponsored by the Sisters of Charity. It also offers The Terrace apartments for seniors with memory impairment.

Beechknoll Community
6550 Hamilton Ave., North College Hill
• 522-5516

Beechknoll offers both assisted and independent living in studio or one-bedroom apartments. Three meals are served daily. An Alzheimer's disease and dementia unit is available. The facility is Medicare and Medicaid approved. Respite stays are welcome.

Berkeley Square
100 Berkeley Dr., Hamilton • 856-8600

Berkeley is a large community with more than 80 cottage homes, completed or under construction, ranging from one bedroom to three bedrooms. Seventeen apartments are also available for rent, and a 50-bed nursing and assisted-living wing just opened. The community includes a town hall, swimming pool, whirlpool, exercise room, library, woodworking shop and dining room. One meal is served a day.

Bethesda Scarlet Oaks Retirement Community
440 Lafayette Ave.
• 861-0400

This facility, located in an upscale residential gaslight district, has operated since 1909. It offers one- and two-bedroom independent living apartments and personal support for those needing assistance. It has a 70-bed nursing unit, welcomes respite/short-term stays and has no entrance fees. It is Medicare certified and part of the Bethesda/Good Samaritan hospitals partnership.

Brookwood Retirement Community
12100 Reed Hartman Hwy., Blue Ash
• 530-9555

Residents here receive independent, assisted-living, skilled or intermediate nursing care. Brookwood is approved for Medicare and 16 Medicaid beds. Respite stays are available.

Chesterwood Village
8073 Tylersville Rd., West Chester
• 777-1400

This newly developed community offers cottages for independent living. Each two-bedroom, two-bath cottage has an attached garage and an enclosed porch. A central clubhouse for parties and community-sponsored social events is located on the grounds. Emergency response systems are monitored.

FYI

Unless otherwise noted, the area code for all phone numbers listed in this guide is 513.

Colonial Heights Retirement Community
6900 Hopeful Rd., Florence, Ky.
• (606) 525-6900

Independent and assisted living is available to residents here in five apartment sizes. Meals, housekeeping and on-site nurses are available. Utilities are paid. The facility sits on 17 acres near the Florence retail area.

Cottingham Retirement Community
3995 Cottingham Dr., Sharonville
• 563-3600

Cottingham has independent and assisted-living apartments, a skilled-nursing area, an early stage dementia center and a temporary/respite program. A beauty salon, branch bank, general store, indoor pool, cafe and chapel are all on site. Physical, occupational and speech therapy are offered. Cottingham is Medicare certified.

Deupree House East
3939 Erie Ave. • 561-6363

Deupree offers independent living in one-bedroom apartments. Health care services and security are available in addition to an active social program. It is associated with the Episcopal church and accredited by the Continuing Care Association Commission.

Eastgate Retirement Village
776 Old Ohio Hwy. 74, Eastgate
• 753-4400

Eastgate has independent studio and one- and two-bedroom apartments and two-bedroom deluxe units. A nurse's aide is on call 24 hours a day. Three meals are prepared daily; other amenities include housekeeping and laundry, a beauty salon, a health club, Jacuzzi, greenhouse, library, chapel and Sunday mass. Pets are welcome.

Evergreen Retirement Community
230 W. Galbraith Rd. • 948-2308

Another independent- and assisted-living facility, with skilled-nursing care available, Evergreen has one- and two-bedroom apartments in country cottages lining a golf course. Immediate occupancy is available with 12-

Photo: Cincinnati Recreation Commission

Cincinnati offers abundant activities for active seniors.

month leases, and no endowment is necessary. Extra storage and transportation are available.

Franciscan at St. Clare Retirement Community
100 Compton Rd., Wyoming • 761-9036

St. Clare, which is part of the Franciscan Health System of Cincinnati Inc., offers both a skilled-nursing unit and assisted and independent living facilities. Temporary stays are available. An indoor swimming pool, chapel, exercise programs, physical therapy and rehabilitation services are available. It is Medicare certified.

Franciscan at West Park Retirement Community
2950 W. Park Dr., Westwood • 451-8900

West Park's options include assisted and independent living, a skilled-nursing unit, meals, a bank, chapel, beauty/barber shop and free transportation to nearby shopping areas. Temporary stays are available. West Park is part of the Franciscan Health System of Cincinnati Inc.

Garden Court Shared Family Living Home
7111 Plainfield Rd., Blue Ash • 793-4013

Garden Court is a small, independent-living facility geared for low-income senior citizens. The on-site staff offers some assistance. Three meals, housekeeping, laundry services and access to a house car are included in the rent.

Garden Manor Extended Care Center
6898 Hamilton-Middletown Rd., Middletown • (513) 421-1289

This facility is set up for independent and assisted living, and extended care is also available. Residents live in one- or two-bedroom apartments. There are gardens to walk in, planned trips, a central dining hall, movies, bingo and a swimming pool.

Highland Crossing Retirement Community
400 Farrell Dr., Fort Wright, Ky.
• **(606) 341-0777**

Residents have the choice of assisted or independent living in studios and one- and two-bedroom units, with weekly housekeeping, two hot meals daily and 24-hour emergency assistance.

Hillrise Retirement Community
1500 Groesbeck Rd., College Hill
• **541-4268**

Hillrise offers independent- and assisted-living apartments as part of a congregate and nursing home complex. Emergency assistance is available 24 hours a day. This affordable community is centrally located and adjacent to the community business district and major bus routes.

www.insiders.com

See this and many other **Insiders' Guide®** destinations online — in their entirety.

Visit us today!

Judson Village Retirement Community
2373 Harrison Ave., Westwood
• **662-5880**

This facility on 30 wooded acres offers independent and catered living. Nursing care is available 24 hours a day. Full therapy services, a chapel, greenhouse, arts and crafts workshop, wood shop, beauty shop, barber shop and bank are also available. It is Medicare/Medicaid certified and accredited by the Continuing Care Association Commission.

Julmar Share A Home
5427 Julmar Dr., Covedale • 922-5106

Julmar offers independent-living bedrooms in a renovated convent. Three meals a day and laundry service are available, and staff is on call 24 hours a day.

Llanfair Retirement Community
1701 Llanfair Ave., College Hill
• **681-4230**

Llanfair has Cape Cod-style cottages and apartments on 14 wooded acres. Independent- and assisted-living options are available. Skilled nursing is also available, along with a supportive unit for Alzheimer's patients. Transportation, 24-hour emergency services, and activities are provided. The center is Medicare and Medicaid certified and accredited by the Continuing Care Association Commission. It offers guest stays and respite care. Although Llanfair is part of the Presbyterian retirement communities, it has an interdenominational chapel.

Mallard Cove
1410 Mallard Cove Dr., Sharonville
• **772-6655**

Residency requires no endowment or entrance fee. Mallard has studio and one- and two-bedroom apartments, a 24-hour-a-day staff, transportation and one to three meals a day and snacks. Housekeeping services, laundry and linen services, transportation and a full activity program are also available. All utilities except telephone are included. A 24-hour emergency call service is in place. Assisted-living services are also available.

Manorcare at Woodridge Retirement Communities
3801 Woodridge Blvd., Fairfield
• **874-9933**

Woodridge's services include assisted and independent living with three daily meals, nursing assistance on call 24 hours a day, housekeeping, transportation, a barber/beauty shop and chapel. It is Medicare certified. Rent is monthly, and no endowment fee is required.

Maple Knoll Village
11100 Springfield Pike, Springdale
• **782-2717**

Maple Knoll Village has operated for 145 years and was recently voted one of the top 20 continuing care retirement communities in the country. Independent and assisted living are available, as are intermediate and skilled nursing care. It offers manor homes, cottages and apartments. A health and wellness center, heated swimming pool, fitness room and whirlpool are included. Radio station WMKV operates from the village.

Marjorie P. Lee Retirement Community
3550 Shaw Ave. • 871-2090

Features here are independent and assisted living, skilled nursing care and dining and housekeeping services. It is accredited by the Continuing Care Association Commissions and is part of Episcopal Retirement Homes Inc.

Mason Christian Village
411 Western Row Rd., Mason • 398-1486

This complex has 125 cottages, 32 apartments, 60 assisted-living beds and 62 skilled-nursing beds. It is Medicare-approved and sponsored by the Christian Benevolent Association.

Mercy St. Theresa Center
7010 Rowan Hill Dr., Mariemont
• 271-7010

The center offers a congregate-living environment. Services here include personal and nursing care, subacute rehabilitation care and special care for the memory-impaired. It is Medicare certified and a member of the Mercy Hospitals Health System.

Mount Healthy Christian Home Inc.
8097 Hamilton Ave. • 931-5000

Sponsored by the Christian Benevolent Association, this home offers independent and assisted living and nursing care. It is Medicaid approved.

New England Club
8135 Beechmont Ave., Anderson
• 474-2582

Amenities and services in this new, upscale community include three meals a day, housekeeping and linen service, free transportation, paid utilities and a resident manager. No buy-in fees are required. Month-to-month rent is available.

North Hill Court Shared Family Living Home
6920 La Boiteaux Ave., North College Hill
• 931-2567

This large home has 16 rooms for independent living, with residents sharing the rest of the home. Three meals are served each day. Laundry and housekeeping are available.

Northgate Park Retirement Center
9191 Round Top Rd., Bevis • 923-3711

Residence at Northgate Park requires no entrance fee. The center has no steps or elevators. Each apartment has a kitchenette, patio and woodburning fireplace, and residents are offered a flexible meal plan, 24-hour security, transportation service, satellite TV and a beauty/barber shop.

Philada Apartments
7732 Greenland Pl., Roselawn
• 761-5544

The facility has 37 studio and one-bedroom apartments for independent living. Each apartment has its own kitchen. Laundry facilities are available. Rent is based on income.

St. Paul Lutheran Village Inc.
5515 Madison Rd. • 272-1118

Residence at St. Paul's requires no entrance fee. The facility offers independent living in a studio or one-bedroom apartment, and transportation, meals, a laundry and beauty parlor are available.

SEM Terrace
5371 S. Milford Rd., Milford • 248-1140

SEM Terrace offers independent living in a congregate environment on 55 wooded acres. Three meals a day are available. Home health care is another option. The center is on one level, and pets are permitted.

SEM Villa
201 Mound Ave., Milford • 831-3262

SEM Villa is a congregate living facility. Three meals a day, home health care, monthly rates and rental assistance are available. Pets are welcome.

Schroder Manor
1302 Millvill Ave., Hamilton • 867-1300

This center offers independent and assisted living with skilled nursing and a special Alzheimer's disease unit.

Seasons Retirement Community
7300 Dearwester Dr., Kenwood
• 984-9400

Seasons offers independent- and assisted-living options in large apartments. Skilled nursing is also available, should the need arise. The community sits near the upscale Kenwood Towne Center and Sycamore Plaza and dozens of restaurants.

Sutton Grove Apartments
1131 Deliquia Dr. • 231-0008

Residents at Sutton Grove have access to a garden, transportation, an exercise room, a chapel, an emergency call system, a beauty/barber shop and laundry facilities. Pets are welcome.

FYI

Unless otherwise noted, the area code for all phone numbers listed in this guide is 513.

Town Square Retirement Villa
4719 Alma Ave., Blue Ash
• 984-1131

Town Square is an independent-living facility with 50 one- and two-bedroom apartments within two blocks of a major shopping area.

Twin Towers
5343 Hamilton Ave. • 853-2000

Twin Towers, which sits on 125 wooded acres, was started by the United Methodist Church in 1899. Residents in this large community can choose from one-floor patio homes, all with garages, or studio and one- and two-bedrooms apartments. An indoor pool, whirlpool and craft rooms are among the amenities. Monthly rates are available. Twin Towers is Medicare and Medicaid certified and approved by the Continuing Care Association Commission.

Valley Creek Retirement Community
10620 Montgomery Rd., Montgomery
• 984-4045

Valley Creek, which sits in the heart of upscale Olde Montgomery, offers independent living in one- and two-bedroom apartments. Management is on-site. Transportation is available, and an intercom entry is required for security. Storage is also available.

Victoria Retirement Community
1500 Sherman Ave. • 631-6800

Services here include skilled nursing care and assistance with bathing, dressing and medication supervision. A nurse's aide is on call 24 hours a day. Three daily meals are served, and short-term stays can be arranged. The center offers weekly housekeeping and laundry service, daily planned activities, transportation, a beauty/barber shop and 24-hour security.

Village Eastgate Retirement Center
776 Old Ohio Hwy. 74, Summerside
• 753-4400

This independent-living center has studio, one- and two-bedroom apartments and two-bedroom deluxe units. Three meals a day are available, as are housekeeping and laundry services, a health club, greenhouse, library, chapel and beauty salon. A nurse's aide is on call 24 hours a day. Pets are welcome.

Western Hills Retirement Village
6210 Cleves-Warsaw Rd., Western Hills
• 941-0099

These independent living apartments have 24-hour security and emergency services. Residents may take advantage of daily activities and religious services, along with free cable TV, housekeeping, laundry and transportation. Covered parking is available. Skilled and intermediate nursing, and occupational, speech and physical therapy are available. The center does not require an entrance fee.

INSIDERS' TIP

Several organizations can help seniors make home repairs for discounted rates — or sometimes for free. Try Handyman Connection, 771-1122; People Working Cooperatively, 351-7921; and Handyman Housecalls, 825-3863.

Activity Centers

Greater Cincinnati and Northern Kentucky have dozens of activity centers for older adults that offer a wide range of cultural, recreational and social activities geared specifically to their age group. Seniors can try their hand at ceramics, painting, crafts and other hobby interests or get involved in aerobics or exercise programs, bowling, dancing and bingo. Programs are open to anyone 60 and older.

The City of Cincinnati Recreation Commission and the Senior Services of Northern Kentucky together have 40 senior activity centers, meaning there is probably one pretty close to where you live. To find the senior center nearest you, contact the Cincinnati Recreation Commission at 352-4000 or the Senior Services of Northern Kentucky at (606) 491-9245.

Other centers, most of which are community based, include:

Anderson Senior Center, 7970 Beechmont Avenue, Anderson, 474-3100

Cincinnati Area Senior Services Centers and Meal Sites: 1720 Race Street, 381-3007; 1820 Rutland Avenue, 731-8197; 2010 Auburn Avenue, 621-8733; 1999 Sutter Avenue, 661-5270; 3700 Reading Road, 751-8212

Colerain Senior Citizens Center, 4300 Springdale Road, Bevis, 741-8802

Green Township Senior Citizens Center, 3620 Epley Road, Monfort Heights, 385-3780

Hillrise Senior Center, 1500 Groesbeck Road, College Hill, 542-9344, 2800 Erie Avenue, 321-6816 (TDD-accessible)

Loveland Friendship Center, 227 E. Loveland Avenue, Loveland 783-7049

Maple Knoll Village Center for Older Adults, 11199 Springfield Pike, Springdale, 782-2400

Marielders Senior Center, 6743 Chestnut Drive, Mariemont, 271-5588

North College Hill Community Senior Center, 1586 Goodman Avenue, North College Hill, 521-3462 (TDD-accessible)

North Fairmont Seniors Center, 2569 St. Leo Place, North Fairmont, 921-8671

South Fairmont Seniors Center, 1860 Queen City Avenue, South Fairmont, 921-5809

Springfield Township Community Senior Citizen Center, 8791 Brent Drive, Finneytown, 522-1154

Sycamore Senior Center, 4131 Cooper Road, Sycamore, 984-1234

Volunteer, Employment and Education Opportunities

You'll find ample opportunities to get involved in volunteer activities in Great Cincinnati. Volunteering offers the double benefit of helping the community and keeping you vital and involved. We have suggested a few centers and services to get you started. Most of the agencies and organizations previously mentioned in this chapter would be other good sources to contact for specific interests. And don't overlook cultural, educational and youth-oriented groups, which are described in other chapters in this book and are always looking for extra hands.

AARP Senior Employment Services, 700 Walnut Street, 721-0717

Bethlehem Temple Learning Center, 4781 Hamilton Avenue, 542-4500

Retired Senior Volunteer Programs (RSVP) Cincinnati Area Senior Services, 644 Linn Street, 721-7900

Senior Services of North Kentucky, 1032 Madison Avenue, Covington, Kentucky, (606) 491-0522

Service Corps of Retired Executives (SCORE), 525 Vine Street, 684-2812

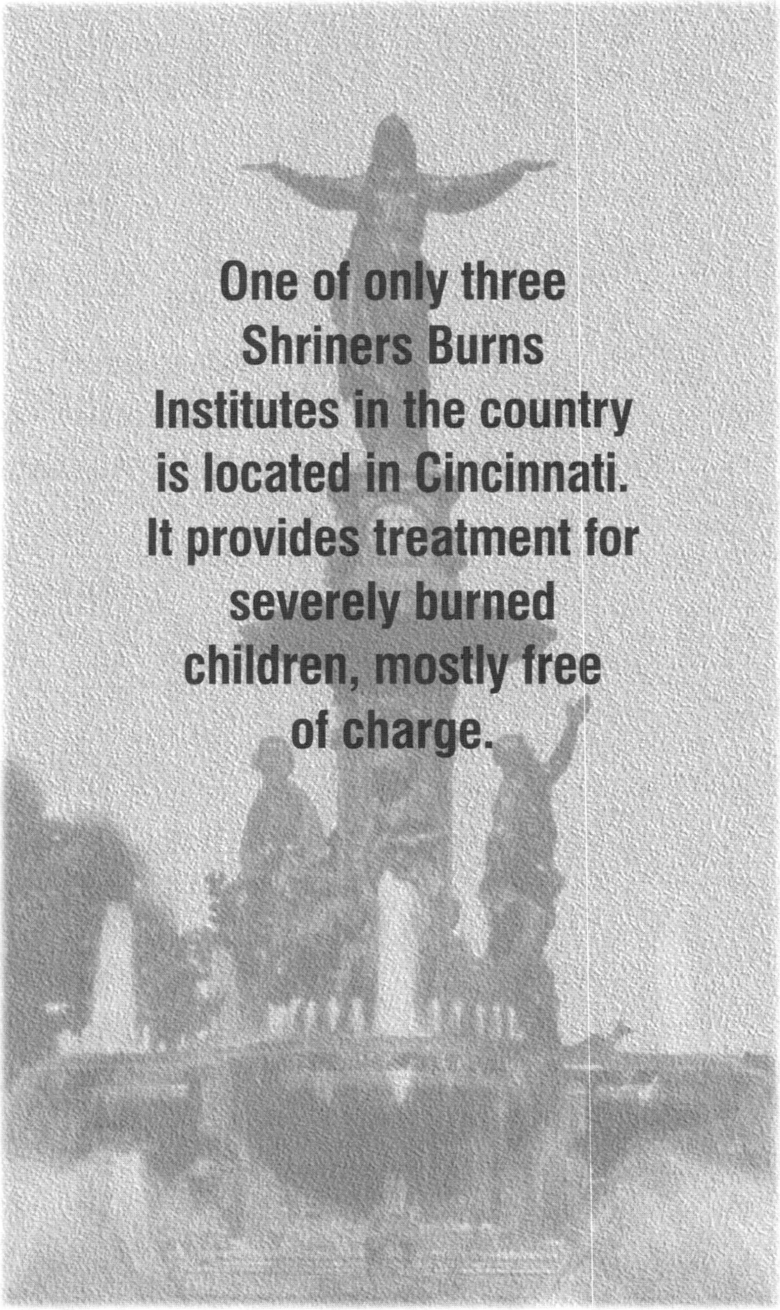

One of only three
Shriners Burns
Institutes in the country
is located in Cincinnati.
It provides treatment for
severely burned
children, mostly free
of charge.

Healthcare

If you have to get sick somewhere, the Cincinnati neighborhoods of Clifton, Mount Auburn and Avondale would be good places to do it. The area's biggest hospitals and a cluster of smaller or specialty hospitals are located in these neighborhoods north of downtown, an area collectively known as "Pill Hill" in the healthcare community. There are also plenty of other suburban and rural hospitals, including affiliates of the Pill Hill hospitals, that serve the rest of the Greater Cincinnati area.

Cincinnati hospitals are well-known regionally and nationally for quality care. University Hospital's two Air Care helicopters, for example, provide emergency service as far as 150 miles away. Cincinnati's Children's Hospital Medical Center is among the largest and busiest children's hospitals in the United States. And Cincinnati's Shriners Burns Institute is one of only three in the country and provides treatment for severely burned children, mostly free of charge.

Cincinnati also has a reputation as a cradle of medical research. Albert Sabin developed the first oral polio vaccine at the University of Cincinnati and Children's Hospital. Henry Heimlich was chief of surgery at Jewish Hospital when he developed his famous maneuver and started an institute in Cincinnati to help fund other research. O'dell Owens was among the first physicians to use frozen embryos in treating infertility. The first medical laser laboratory was established by Leon Goldman at Children's Hospital, and the first argon laser surgery in the United States was done here.

The consolidations are helping fuel the "centers of excellence" concept, in which each hospital concentrates on an area or areas of expertise. Of course, which hospitals are "centers of excellence" in which specialties remains a point of debate. Several Pill Hill hospitals lay claim to that title in such

areas as cardiac and cancer care and even rehabilitation. The descriptions below note areas where hospitals have identified their strengths. Emergency rooms and diagnostic imaging devices, such as MRIs, are available at most of these hospitals.

Bethesda Oak Hospital
619 Oak St. • 569-6111

Bethesda was opened in 1896 by seven German Methodist deaconesses to minister to the needs of the sick and poor. Today, it is part of a system of two hospitals and 18 healthcare centers and offices throughout Greater Cincinnati. It's also affiliated with Good Samaritan Hospital through Tri-Health alliance, thereby consolidating some management and health services.

Bethesda was the first Pill Hill hospital to open a suburban satellite, Bethesda North in 1970 (see listing below). Today Bethesda has probably the most extensive network of suburban offices and treatment centers of any Cincinnati hospital system. Indeed, Bethesda North Hospital has become the primary hospital in the Bethesda system under a recent reorganization. The Bethesda system includes centers in Eastgate, Fairfield and Warren County that provide diagnostic and physical therapy services. Bethesda Warren County in Lebanon also offers 24-hour emergency services (see our section on Urgent Care Centers).

A 1998 study by the Centers for Disease Control ranked Bethesda Oak's fertility center as the most successful (that is, live births relative to fertility procedures) of any in Ohio, Kentucky and Indiana.

A network of community mental health services and employee assistance program sites throughout the area is another of Bethesda's strengths. Among Bethesda's other claims to fame are having the area's first freestanding outpatient surgery center, birthing room and lithotripsy (sound-wave treatment) for kidney stones and gallstones.

Hospice of Cincinnati has moved from Bethesda Oak to a new building in Blue Ash as part of a major restructuring of the hospital to make it more patient friendly. Bethesda Oak has now added a new short-term parking lot by the front door, introduced valet parking and rearranged services into a "medical mall" that puts related care areas closer together, cutting down on confusion and long walks through the complex.

Bethesda specializes in providing health services to businesses and has nearly 3,800 corporate clients in Greater Cincinnati. Corporate services include physicals and testing services, work-site occupational nursing services, preventive health programs, a CONCERN employee assistance program and management of fitness centers for 10 companies, including Procter & Gamble and General Electric Aircraft Engines.

Bethesda North Hospital
10500 Montgomery Rd. • 745-1111

Bethesda North is the 314-bed suburban satellite of Bethesda Oak Hospital (see listing above) and serves the northeastern suburbs and beyond. It's the largest and busiest suburban hospital in the Tri-state area. On or near the Bethesda North campus are five physician office buildings and an outpatient surgery center. Bethesda North provides a full range of medical, surgical and community services, including cardiology and cardiac catheterization, outpatient surgery in an on-site stand-alone center, diabetes services, full-service operating rooms, adult day care and physical therapy services. It has the second-busiest adult emergency room in Greater Cincinnati after University of Cincinnati Hospital in Clifton.

FYI

Unless otherwise noted, the area code for all phone numbers listed in this guide is 513.

Children's Hospital Medical Center
3333 Burnet Ave. • 559-4200

When kids get very sick in Cincinnati, Children's Hospital Medical Center is usually the one to treat them. This hospital has the busiest pediatric emergency room, the most outpatient visits and performs the most surgical procedures of any children's hospital in the United States. Founded in 1883, this 300-bed hospital currently ranks fifth in overall pediatric admissions nationwide, behind only children's hospitals in Boston and Philadelphia. It also has by far the busiest emergency room of any kind in Greater Cincinnati. Children's 109 pediatric residents make its residency program one of the largest of any kind in the United States.

Children's Hospital is a regional hospital, with 15 percent of its patients coming from outside Greater Cincinnati. It's the only Level 1 pediatric trauma center serving Southwestern Ohio, Northern Kentucky and Eastern Indiana. And Children's provides specialized medical and surgical services in such areas as diagnosis of rare and complex diseases, tracheal reconstruction and laser neurosurgery. Services also include a child abuse treatment team, craniofacial and other plastic and reconstructive surgery, a lead poison clinic and bone marrow, heart, liver and kidney transplants.

In 1973, Children's Hospital united with the following six organizations to form the Medical Center: Children's Hospital Research Foundation, Cerebral Palsy Services Center, Children's Dental Care Foundation, Cincinnati Adolescent Clinic, Cincinnati Center for Developmental Disorders and Convalescent Hospital for Children.

Achievements by Children's Hospital's researchers include development of the Sabin

---

INSIDERS' TIP

The Cincinnati Health Care Plan Value Project ranks health plans for the city's largest companies. Five plans received the star "Above Average" ranking in 1997: Anthem HMP, ChoiceCare New Health, ChoiceCare Primary Access, ChoiceCare Select and UHC.

oral polio vaccine and a bubble oxygenator to make open-heart surgery possible. Current research by the hospital's 26 research divisions focuses on cystic fibrosis, prevention of premature births, kidney disorders, sickle cell disease, juvenile rheumatoid arthritis and many other conditions.

Children's Psychiatric Hospital of Northern Kentucky
502 Farrell Dr., Covington, Ky.
• (606) 578-3200

Founded in 1979, this nonprofit inpatient facility serves severely disturbed youth ages 5 to 17. The hospital coordinates treatment with outpatient mental health providers, local school special education programs, pediatricians and state social service agencies. The 51-bed main hospital is a refurbished facility originally built in the 1950s. A therapeutic living area on a wooded hillside overlooks the Ohio River valley and Cincinnati skyline.

Services include psychiatric and psychological evaluation and treatment; individual and group psychotherapy; family therapy; art, music, and recreational therapy; a year-round accredited school program; a behavior management program; aftercare coordination; and specialized treatment groups dealing with sexual abuse, loss and grief, substance abuse, social skills training, values clarification and anger/stress management.

An outpatient program involves youths in a five-day-a-week program with three hours a day of class instruction followed by three to four hours of psychotherapy and therapeutic programs.

The Christ Hospital
2139 Auburn Ave. • 369-2000

The Christ Hospital was founded in 1889 through the philanthropy of Procter & Gamble cofounder James Gamble and the work of Methodist missionary Isabella Thoburn. It is still a regional health center, treating more patients from outside Hamilton County than any other Pill Hill hospital. But it treats plenty of Cincinnatians too.

The Christ Hospital was ranked among the top 100 superior performing hospitals in a 1997 study published by HCIA Inc. and William M. Mercer Inc.'s Health Care Provider Consulting Practice. The hospital has placed in the top 100 for two of the four years the studies have been conducted. The Christ Hospital was also identified in 1997 as one of the most preferred providers of health services in the nation, according to a national survey conducted by National Research Corporation.

The 550-bed hospital is part of the Health Alliance of Greater Cincinnati, which also includes the University of Cincinnati Hospital, the Jewish Hospitals on Pill Hill and in Kenwood, and the St. Luke hospitals in Northern Kentucky. The goal of the alliance is to reduce operating and administrative costs and better use technology and facilities. The Christ Hospital's specialties include heart disease, women's health, internal medicine, cancer care, advanced orthopedics, surgical specialties and behavioral medicine.

Facilities include cardiac catheterization and endoscopy labs and Greater Cincinnati's first — and as of 1995 only — positron emission tomography (PET) scanner. The PET scanner differs from CAT and MRI scanners in that it shows the biochemical processes involved in disease. The hospital also has outpatient testing facilities in Delhi, Mason and Blue Ash.

The Christ's Hospital Cardiovascular Research Center has performed research on the blood clot-dissolving drug TPA, an angioscope that sees inside the beating heart, a catheter that opens blocked coronary arteries and a new laser for heart surgery. In fact, The Christ bills itself as "Cincinnati's Heart Hospital."

Two floors of the hospital are dedicated to women's health. Obstetrics and gynecology make up about 30 percent of the hospital's patient care. It's Center for Reproductive Studies offers several infertility treatments, including high-tech in vitro fertilization and gamete intrafallopian transfer (GIFT).

The Christ Hospital's psychiatric program is the largest in a private hospital in Ohio and includes an eight-bed psychiatric intensive care unit and a 16-bed senior adult mental health unit specializing in care for patients 60 and older.

Clermont Mercy Hospital
3000 Hospital Dr., Batavia • 732-8200

A 151-bed general, medical/surgical acute-care hospital founded in 1973, Mercy offers diagnostic and imaging services, intensive care treatment, cardiac rehabilitation, laser surgery, one-day surgery, psychiatric inpatient and outpatient units for adult and adolescent treatment, and physical, respiratory and occupational therapy.

Clermont Mercy was among the first in Greater Cincinnati to perform laproscopic (laser) gall bladder surgery. The hospital is also known for its inpatient psychiatric care programs, psychiatric day treatment programs for adolescents and the elderly, comprehensive cancer treatment/linear accelerator, and physical/occupational health therapy services. It is one of four Mercy Health System hospitals in the Greater Cincinnati area.

Although it's the only hospital in Clermont County, Clermont Mercy does not have a maternity unit. Nearby Mercy Hospital Anderson and other hospitals in Hamilton and Brown counties provide maternity care for Clermont County residents.

Deaconess Hospital of Cincinnati
311 Straight St. • 559-2100

Deaconess was founded in 1888 when the ministers of several German American Protestant denominations founded the Deaconess Society. Today, this 265-bed hospital on Pill Hill provides a wide range of medical, surgical and health services.

On-site specialty centers include Deaconess' Arthritis Center, Back Treatment Center, Breast Care Center, Cardiac Care Center, Cincinnati Joint Replacement Center and Cincinnati Laser Center. Other specialized programs include sports medicine, asthma and allergy treatment, and Elderlife, a senior membership health and wellness program.

Deaconess also specializes in treating patients on Medicare, deriving more than 70 percent of its revenues from that program and working with several health plans to develop Medicare HMOs.

Dearborn County Hospital
600 Wilson Creek Rd., Lawrenceburg, Ind. • (812) 537-1010

Dearborn County is a 144-bed hospital founded in 1959 that serves residents of southeastern Indiana through its central Lawrenceburg facility and medical office buildings in Rising Sun, Dillsboro and Milan. Its medical and surgical services include diabetes education and support classes, hospice, laproscopic and laser surgery, lithotripsy for kidney stones and gallstones, and a full range of diagnostic and imaging services. Other services include a "Sitter Sense" teen baby-sitting program and an infant/child safety program.

Drake Center
151 W. Galbraith Rd. • 948-2500

Drake Center fills the gap for patients who are too sick for nursing homes but don't require the services of an acute-care hospital. Affiliated with the University of Cincinnati Hospital, and through that link with the Health Alliance of Greater Cincinnati, Drake Center is one of only a handful of hospitals in the nation dedicated solely to providing rehabilitation and long-term skilled nursing care.

Funded largely by a special Hamilton County tax levy, Drake offers a sort of long-term care safety net to Hamilton Countians that few people in the United States have. If you have a severe accident or injury and you live in Hamilton County, Drake will be there to provide rehabilitation, whether you can pay or not.

Drake has special multidisciplinary teams to treat spinal cord and brain injuries and the area's largest ventilator unit to treat persons with severe respiratory conditions. Services include occupational therapy, physical therapy, therapeutic recreation and speech-language pathology, psychological counseling and independent living and community re-entry assistance.

Facilities include an aquatic therapy pool and on-site living areas to help patients adapt to disabilities in a home setting before leaving the hospital. Rehabilitation engineers are available to help patients adapt their homes to their disabilities before discharge. A Behavioral Medicine Program at Drake combines several disciplines to help persons learn to cope with or overcome chronic pain and return to work.

Drake also offers support groups to help families cope with arthritis, Guillain-Barre syndrome, Huntington's disease, head injuries, spina bifida, respiratory conditions that require ventilators and other conditions.

Fort Hamilton-Hughes Memorial Hospital
630 Eaton Ave., Hamilton • 867-2000

Memorial is a 307-bed hospital that provides a full range of medical and surgical services to residents of southern Butler County, including cardiac catheterization and rehabilitation, full diagnostic and imaging services, laser surgery, a cancer treatment center and occupational and physical therapy. Its Comprehensive Childbirth Center is the only maternity unit in southern Butler County and offers traditional labor and delivery and alternative obstetrical care from certified nurse midwives.

The hospital also has a freestanding SurgiCenter for outpatient surgery, a cocaine-specific treatment program and an employee assistance program and employer-sponsored sick-child care program.

Franciscan Hospital (Mount Airy Campus)
2446 Kipling Ave. • 853-5000

This Mount Airy hospital was founded in 1971 to serve residents of northeastern Cincinnati and nearby suburbs. It is one of two hospitals operated by the Franciscan Health System of Cincinnati.

The hospital's "Comeback Team" rehabilitation unit and Cardiac Care Unit offer extensive diagnostic, surgical and rehabilitation services. Inpatient and outpatient cancer care is provided in a hospital-based cancer program and a freestanding radiation therapy facility that have received joint accreditation by the American College of Surgeons.

The Franciscan Pain and Work Rehabilita-

tion Center uses a behavioral approach to ease chronic pain without reliance on medications. Surgical services include use of laser equipment in orthopedic, eye, gynecological and other surgical procedures.

Franciscan Hospital (Western Hills Campus)
3131 Queen City Ave. • 389-5000

The 267-bed Western Hills member of the Franciscan Health System of Cincinnati provides the western neighborhoods of Cincinnati and Hamilton County with emergency, rehabilitation, surgical and cardiovascular services, cancer treatment, and Lifespring, a mental health program for persons 65 and older.

Good Samaritan Hospital
375 Dixmyth Ave. • 872-1400

Good Samaritan is the largest private hospital in Greater Cincinnati and has more licensed beds (673) and births per year than any other single hospital facility in the area. It's affiliated with the Bethesda hospitals through an alliance in which it has consolidated administrative and some medical services. Founded in 1852, it's also among the oldest hospitals in the area.

Good Sam has one of only four local Level 1 neonatal intensive care units. And besides having the busiest maternity unit, it also offers a comprehensive array of prenatal programs for siblings and fathers plus a "Shaping Up for Motherhood" class for moms.

The hospital lists its Comprehensive Heart Center as another center of excellence. The 70-bed center includes a coronary care unit, intensive care unit, two cardiac catheterization labs, two open-heart surgical suites, a pacemaker clinic, a vascular lab, diagnostic testing facilities and full cardiac rehabilitation services.

Good Sam also has a Level 1 Trauma Center — one of two (along with Children's Hospital) in Greater Cincinnati verified by the American College of Surgeons. The Trauma Center has specialists in all areas of bodily injury. The hospital also has developed a Fast Track service to treat patients who come to the emergency room for nonemergency care, primarily indigent patients who use the ER for routine care.

Alternative Health Care: The Road to Wellville

What began in the monasteries of China and the streetfront shops of Clifton Heights is now going mainstream. Alternative medicine is being practiced to an ever-greater extent by Greater Cincinnati's hospitals and doctors; in fact, it's become a big money-maker for the medical establishment: Call it I-Ching meets "cha-ching."

Almost all local hospitals now offer some form of alternative healthcare treatment (massage therapy and biofeedback, for example). But some hospitals are taking it one step further. In Anderson, Mercy Hospital Anderson just opened (in June 1998) the nation's third largest "wellness center," the massive Mercy Center for Health and Wellness (a.k.a. "The Healthplex"), directly across the street from the hospital. There's more. Mercy Hospital Fairfield is opening (in July 1998) what will be the fourth largest wellness center in the country. In Blue Ash, there's the Tri-Health Fitness & Health Pavilion. Run jointly by Good Samaritan and Bethesda hospitals, it's the seventh largest wellness center in the nation. In Western Hills, the Franciscan Health System is building its new wellness center. And on Pill Hill, the University of Cincinnati Medical Center recently established its Massage Therapy Center.

The wellness complexes offer the usual fitness basics: weight rooms, exercise machines, treadmills, spas, pools and other traditional gym fare. It's the holistic aspect — treating the mind and spirit as well as the body — that makes these centers different from Joe's Gym down the road. The wellness program at Mercy Hospital Anderson, for instance, offers anything from biofeedback and full-spectrum light therapy (to combat seasonal affective disorder, migraines and PMS) to reflexology and therapeutic touch.

There's a whole lot of wellness shaking down. Behind it all, say local doctors and nurses, is this simple philosophy: The cure to certain ailments lies within yourself, not inside a pill bottle — that perception and attitude can indeed triumph where pharmaceuticals fail — and a three-pound organ, the brain, is at the crux of many a cure. Of course, keeping it in perspective, much of this "alternative" medicine isn't all that new or New Age; it's Far Eastern medicine that predates "traditional" Western medicine by as much as 50 centuries.

As the line between orthodox and unorthodox medicine continues to blur, some hospitals prefer to call "alternative" medicine "complementary" medicine. They don't like the implication of an "either/or" situation, that patients must somehow choose between going with a traditional or an alternative treatment. Certainly when it comes to a major medical crisis — emergency room treatment, surgery, trauma — the services of a trained M.D. are a must. Hospitals are merely acknowledging with these wellness centers that when it comes to the everyday aches and pains of life (as well as certain chronic diseases such as arthritis), you might do better to seek solutions outside the hospital corridors.

By one estimate, at least one Cincinnatian in three is trying some form of alternative medicine. Some local employers' medical plans will even cover acupuncture, chiropractic, reflexology, yoga and some equally unusual forms of care. Greater Cincinnati also has dozens of shops and outlets where you can learn more about your options, most notably Whatever Works Wellness Center & Bookstore in Silverton (a wonderful store full of resources and supplies and especially notable for its aromatherapy collection), Spatz's Natural Life Health Food downtown, and New World bookshop in Clifton. (See the writeups on all three in our Shopping chapter.)

— continued on next page

The Mercy Center for Health and Wellness is the third-largest wellness center in the country.

The most popular forms of alternative medicine in Greater Cincinnati? We compiled this list with the help of hospitals, the Academy of Medicine and other sources.

Acupuncture. A linchpin of Chinese medicine for centuries, it's based on the premise that inserting needles at various points in the body will, through energy meridians, influence the course of certain diseases. Studies have indeed shown that acupuncture provides short-term relief of pain by releasing endorphins (naturally produced substances that resemble morphine). It's also been shown to alleviate asthma. There are many acupuncturists listed in the local Yellow Pages.

Aromatherapy. This is a relatively new term for the ancient practice of using aromatic herbs and fragrances to treat illness. The Egyptians whipped up a perfume of cinnamon and clove to ease stress. Muslims in the 12th century inhaled sandalwood to relieve migraines. The Greeks favored cypress odor to overcome depression. The theory: The part of the brain that receives and processes smells, the limbic system, also controls vital body functions, including hormone secretion. Certain odors can stimulate the release of certain hormones. Whatever Works in Silverton is an excellent outlet if you're considering aromatherapy.

Biofeedback. "Biofeedback teaches you how your body works. It helps deal with panic attacks, stimulates relaxation response, and we see just phenomenal results with high blood pressure," says Anita Schambach, a registered nurse at Mercy Hospital Anderson. Essentially, biofeedback allows you to gain voluntary control over normally involuntary body functions by observing electronic sensors that let you measure and, ideally, control heart rate, skin temperature and blood pressure. Call Mercy for more information.

Biomagnetics. According to Jeff Bathiany, whose Fort Thomas practice is "attracting" all sorts of attention, biomagnetics is simply the theory that magnets, placed on the body for lengthy periods of time, ease the aches of carpal tunnel syndrome and other ills. (His catalog offers magnetic necklaces, bracelets, watchbands, belts, even foam insoles for foot pain.)

Chelation. Championed by Cincinnati's own Jane Heimlich (wife of Dr. Henry

— continued on next page

Heimlich), this therapy involves dripping a synthetic amino acid into a vein to remove toxins. The method, as well as ozone therapy (a combination of ozone and oxygen to combat disease) are outlined in Jane Heimlich's book, *What Your Doctor Won't Tell You*, a guide to alternative medicine.

Chiropractic. This is a medical practice based on the belief that misaligned vertebrae can impair the nervous system and lower the body's resistance to disease. Spinal manipulation, hence, can cure various ailments and aches. Consult the Yellow Pages for a list of chiropractors.

Chunging (pronounced chun-ging). This Korean regimen of simple exercises and breathing techniques will help what ails you, even serious diseases such as diabetes, according to Dr. Yungjo Chung, the Cincinnati-based author of *Chunging: The Cleansing Side of Medicine*. Chung should know; he struggled with diabetes until he came across this method, which stresses getting bad things (pills) out of the body (in contrast with traditional Western medicine, which is largely drug-based).

Hypnotherapy. As a therapy, the belief is that hypnosis enables a patient to gain direct control of normally involuntary bodily responses and functions (such as the immune system). The Yellow Pages lists hypnotherapists.

Qigong (pronounced ki-gong). Once the quiet regimen of monks in China, the practice of this 5,000-year-old healing method is spreading. Proponents say the daily routine of movements can battle arthritis, depression, heart disease and other chronic illnesses. Translated, qigong simply means a long period of daily effort of holding postures that employs exercise, visualization (or imagery) and affirmation/prayer, according to Luke Chan, the Cincinnati-based author of *101 Miracles of Natural Healing* and the area's leading authority on qigong.

Rubenfeld Synergy. It's all about talking and touching says Candee Lawson, a certified Rubenfeld Synergist who runs a Mount Healthy practice. Ilana Rubenfeld developed this body-mind method, which blends compassionate touch and psychotherapy, to deal with her own debilitating back spasms. The Rubenfeld Synergy Method combines elements of Gestalt therapy, hypnotherapy, Alexander Technique and Feldenkrais Method. "RSM accesses stored emotions and memories in the body which may result in energy blocks, tensions and imbalances," says Lawson.

The 40-bed inpatient Rehabilitation Center, one of the largest in Cincinnati, is certified by the Commission on Accreditation of Rehabilitation Facilities in comprehensive inpatient rehab, spinal cord injury, brain injury, outpatient medical rehab, work hardening program, infant and early childhood development program and residential/supervised living.

Other programs and services include a Molecular Diagnostics Center that develops new tests based on the latest developments in recombinant DNA technology, an occupational health program, a comprehensive cancer program, locked and open inpatient psychiatric units, neurosurgery and outpatient assessment and membership programs for seniors.

Healthsouth Corp.
201 Medical Village Dr., Edgewood, Ky.
• **(606) 341-2813**

Known as the Northern Kentucky Rehabilitation Hospital before a 1995 acquisition, this hospital provides a range of inpatient and outpatient rehabilitation services to treat spinal cord and brain injuries, multiple trauma, cerebral palsy and multiple sclerosis, arthritis, amputation, hip fractures, stroke, joint replacement and other conditions requiring long-term rehab.

Healthsouth treats patients who require more intense and comprehensive services than those offered in most traditional hospital rehab units or nursing homes. Services include physical and occupational therapy, orthopedic rehabilitation, personal and family counseling, nutrition counseling, respiratory therapy, cognitive retraining, behavior therapy, recreational therapy and speech and language pathology.

The Jewish Hospital
4777 E. Galbraith Rd., Kenwood
• 745-2200

With the recent closing of the original Jewish Hospital on Pill Hill, this has become Jewish's primary patient facility. The origins of Jewish Hospital date to the cholera epidemic of 1849, which convinced Cincinnati Jews of the need to raise money for a hospital to treat indigent Jews. The founders also wanted to make sure no Jew would be buried without another Jew there to say Kaddish, the prayer for the dead, and prevent deathbed conversions to Christianity by Jews anxious to receive some kind of religious rite.

Today, Jewish Hospital remains one of Greater Cincinnati's most respected hospitals, treating persons of all religious faiths. Among its medical and surgical services and facilities are a coronary care unit, a diabetes management program, outpatient surgery and a recently added maternity unit. Senior citizen care services include an osteoporosis diagnostic center, geriatric counseling service and a senior wellness program. Jewish also provides adolescent outpatient chemical dependency services.

Jewish has expanded its services to the suburbs in recent years, opening a same-day outpatient surgical and imaging center at the Evendale Medical Building, 10475 Reading Road, 554-3800. For urgent care, there is also a Jewish Hospital Downtown Medical Center at 417 Vine St., 241-3322.

Mercy Hospital (Anderson)
7500 State Rd., Anderson • 624-4500

Residents of Anderson, Newtown, Mount Washington and southeastern Clermont County are served by this 186-bed hospital located just north of Beechmont Mall off Five Mile Road. The hospital shares a CEO with Clermont Mercy and other administrative services with the other three Mercy hospitals in Greater Cincinnati, but it is for the most part administratively separate from the others.

Among medical and surgical services and

facilities are the Cancer Center, which offers an extensive range of outpatient cancer therapies and counseling; the Family Birthing Center with birthing suites; and the Cardiovascular Training Center, offering comprehensive cardiac rehabilitation and a full range of diagnostic and emergency cardiac care services.

The hospital's Holistic Health and Wellness Center puts an interesting twist on the wellness programs widely offered by area hospitals. The program's menu of services includes massage therapy, biofeedback, meditation classes and tai chi in addition to exercise classes, smoking cessation, stress management, and weight-loss and support-group programs. The hospital has affirmed its commitment to this approach by announcing plans for a new stand-alone building for the center, scheduled to open in June 1998.

Mercy Hospital (Hamilton)
100 Riverfront Plz., Hamilton • 867-6400

Jointly managed today with Mercy Hospital Fairfield, Mercy Hamilton was founded in 1892 and serves residents of Hamilton and southeastern Butler County. Medical services include cardiac diagnostic and rehabilitation services, a senior membership program, complete diagnostic imaging services, industrial medicine programs, a Sleep Disorders Center in Springdale (1275 E. Kemper Road, 671-3101) and a sick-child care program. Mercy Hamilton also offers long-term care beds in its Progressive Care Center.

Mercy Hospital (Fairfield)
3000 Mack Rd., Fairfield • 870-7000

Built in 1978, Mercy Hospital Fairfield provides the same medical services as Mercy Hamilton (see listing above) in addition to an executive fitness program, CancerCare center and a pulmonary rehabilitation program. The hospital recently added a Family Birth Center, featuring 15 birthing suites, each with a Jacuzzi, TV and VCR, two operating rooms for C-sections, a Level 1 nursery for stabilizing high-risk infants, and 24-hour anesthesia and neonatal coverage.

The Mercy Ambulatory Surgery Center next to Mercy Hospital Fairfield is one of the most highly used, freestanding surgery centers in the country. Utilizing the latest in techniques and equipment for outpatient surgery (endoscopy, pain management, laser procedures), it enjoys a 99 percent satisfaction rate from patients.

Middletown Regional Hospital
105 McKnight Dr., Middletown
• (513) 424-2111

Serving central Butler County, this 310-bed hospital was founded in 1917 and has the third-busiest adult emergency room in Greater Cincinnati. Services include a maternity center with birthing suites, cardiac catheterization and rehabilitation, industrial medicine, a fast-track emergency department for noncritical care, a geriatric acute care unit and the only infertility treatment program in Butler County.

Pauline Warfield Lewis Center
1101 Summit Rd. • 948-3600

This state psychiatric hospital provides acute, intermediate and long-term residential care. Services include a full range of psychiatric and psychological therapy, plus medical, occupational therapy, religious and social services. The Lewis Center has been the focus of controversy in recent years over security problems that have permitted frequent escapes by patients. Area residents also have protested the state's decisions to place violent, criminally insane offenders here. As a result, security has been tightened and some of the most violent offenders have been placed elsewhere by court order.

St. Elizabeth Medical Center North
401 E. 20th St., Covington, Ky.
• (606) 292-4000

Founded in 1861 and managed jointly with St. Elizabeth Medical Center South in Edgewood, Kentucky (see listing below), this facility is part of Northern Kentucky's largest hospital system in terms of licensed beds, budget and emergency room visits.

Employee job satisfaction here is greater than at any hospital in an independent survey that included several Pill Hill hospitals. St. Elizabeth notes that employee turnover in the combined hospital system has been consistently lower than the average for Greater Cincinnati hospitals.

Services provided at St. Elizabeth North include inpatient and outpatient chemical dependency treatment, Northern Kentucky's only inpatient hemodialysis unit and a long-term skilled nursing care unit. The hospital also offers a wide range of diagnostic and imaging services, a diabetes management program and a general medical and surgical inpatient unit and includes the following facilities:

Kentucky Diagnostic Center, 2904 Foltz Road, Edgewood, Kentucky, (606) 341-3333, a freestanding MRI center serving both the North and South hospitals;

The **Employee Assistance Center**, 211 Grandview Drive, Suite 144, Fort Mitchell, Kentucky, (606) 331-3275; and

Saint Elizabeth Grant County, 238 Barnes Road in Williamstown, Kentucky, (606) 823-5051, a rural acute care hospital.

St. Elizabeth Medical Center South
1 Medical Village Dr., Edgewood, Ky.
• (606) 344-2000

St. Elizabeth South, founded in 1978, has Northern Kentucky's only open-heart surgery program and manages a busy cardiac catheterization program for the St. Elizabeth hospitals and St. Luke East and West hospitals. The Cancer Care Center at St. Elizabeth South is the largest outpatient cancer treatment program in Northern Kentucky. The Family Birth Place here is also the busiest maternity unit

FYI

Unless otherwise noted, the area code for all phone numbers listed in this guide is 513.

INSIDERS' TIP

Firearms are the leading cause of accidental injury or death in Greater Cincinnati, accounting for 25 percent of all cases. Poisoning and falls are the next likely culprits to land you in the hospital emergency room, followed by car crashes and bicycle accidents. Just wear a helmet at all times.

south of the river, with more than 2,600 births annually. All the rooms at The Family Birth Place allow mom and baby to stay in the same room from delivery until they go home. Other services include a Work Rehabilitation Center, hospice program, a women's wellness center and candela laser surgery for removal of skin lesions.

St. Luke Hospital East
85 N. Grand Ave., Fort Thomas, Ky.
• (606) 572-3100

St. Luke East is a 310-bed general medical and surgical acute care hospital. It is part of an alliance that includes its St. Luke West affiliate in Florence, Kentucky, and The Christ Hospital and University of Cincinnati Hospital in Pill Hill.

Services and facilities at St. Luke East include inpatient and outpatient alcohol and chemical dependency treatment, birthing suites, a comprehensive cancer treatment center (the first in the region to be recognized by the American College of Surgeons), cardiac diagnosis and rehabilitation, infertility services, employer-sponsored sick-child care, and centers for sleep disorders, diabetes, skilled nursing and women's healthcare.

St. Luke Hospital West
7380 Turfway Rd., Florence, Ky.
• (606) 525-5200

St. Luke West, affiliated with St. Luke East and allied with The Christ Hospital and University of Cincinnati Hospital, is a 177-bed hospital whose services include cardiac diagnosis and rehabilitation, cancer care, an employee assistance program, psychiatric inpatient care, day treatment and partial hospitalization programs, a sleep disorders center and a work conditioning program for rehabilitation.

Shriners Burns Institute
3229 Burnet Ave. • 872-6000

One of only three Shriners Burns Institutes in the United States, this is a regional referral hospital providing acute and rehabilitation care free of charge for severely burned children primarily from a 1,000-mile radius around Cincinnati. It was founded in 1964 and opened its current facility adjacent to Children's Hospital Medical Center in 1992.

The 30-bed hospital is funded primarily by a Shriners Hospitals for Crippled Children endowment fund, which also pays for transport of children to the hospitals. Patients, who must be referred by a physician, have come to the hospital from 35 states and 16 nations.

Research programs at the hospital have helped improve survival rates of severely burned children nationwide. When the program began, a child with 40 to 50 percent total body surface burn had only a 50 percent chance of survival. Today a child with burns on 85 percent of his or her body has the same chance of living. A patented high-calorie diet for burn victims was developed here and is now available everywhere.

The hospital also provides occupational therapy, reconstructive surgery, a school re-entry program and summer camp program for former burn patients. An on-site Parent House provides lodging for parents of long-term patients.

The University Hospital
234 Goodman St. • 558-1000

The oldest of all Greater Cincinnati hospitals, University Hospital is by most measures the biggest too. Founded in 1823, it is one of the area leaders in number of licensed beds (662), number of adult emergency room visits annually (more than 65,000) and number of inpatient admissions (nearly 22,000).

The hospital's announcement that it will sever ties with the university and become a private, nonprofit hospital, has generated controversy. Hospital officials say the move is needed to remove the burden of expensive state regulations and cut costs to remain competitive. Critics, including employee unions and the Hamilton County Democratic Party, see the move as a way to shed employee benefits and a step that could endanger care for the poor. University has been the primary provider of indigent care, funded through a Hamilton County hospital levy.

University Hospital's alliance with The Christ Hospital links the two largest hospitals in the city with The Jewish Hospital in Kenwood and the St. Luke Hospitals. University Hospital physicians also regularly provide service to rural areas through relationships with hospitals in southwestern Ohio and southeastern Indiana.

University's cardiovascular care program includes research, education and clinical care, the Heart Emergency Room, a cardiac transplantation/heart failure program and an adult congenital heart disease program. The neurosciences center at University treats patients referred from all over the world for brain tumors, stroke, epilepsy and aneurysms. And the University Hospital Trauma Center was the region's first Level 1 trauma centers. The hospital provides round-the-clock physician coverage in every surgical specialty, anesthesia and intensive care. Since 1984, the University Air Care two-helicopter medical team has transported nearly 9,000 patients within a 150-mile radius.

University provides probably the most comprehensive range of services of any Greater Cincinnati hospital, including cancer prevention, treatment and research services; liver and pancreas transplantation; a birthing center that provides obstetrics and gynecology for high-risk moms and babies; family planning services through Nurse-Midwifery Associates; infertility services; an AIDS-related disorders center; an inpatient burn care unit; a sensory disorders center; ear and eye banks; a mobile crisis team; a stroke ER; and a sickle cell center.

The University Hospital was ranked among the top 100 superior performing hospitals in a 1997 study published by HCIA Inc. and William M. Mercer Inc.'s Health Care Provider Consulting Practice. The hospital has placed in the top 100 for two of the four years the studies have been conducted. And, in late 1997, *U.S. News & World Report*, in conjunction with the National Opinion Research Center, conducted an objective assessment of hospital care nationwide in 17 specialities. The report listed The University Hospital as a top-40 performer in 10 of those specialties.

An extensive research program at University Hospital includes a $7.8 million, five-year research program on congestive heart failure funded by the National Institutes of Health and a $2.5 million NIH-funded program to study the effects of progestogens on bone density and memory during menopause.

Veterans Affairs Medical Center
3200 Vine St. • 861-3100

Founded in 1954, this hospital serves United States military veterans. Special services include an AIDS clinic, an amputee prosthetic clinic team, biofeedback, a chronic pain program and a women's clinic.

Urgent Care Centers

A step down from hospital emergency rooms, these urgent care centers generally offer minor emergency treatment and off-hour medical care for nonemergency illness.

Bethesda Warren County, 1618 Deerfield Road, Lebanon, 745-1436; a full-scale, freestanding around-the-clock emergency room.

Children's Urgent Car at Outpatient North, 9560 Children's Drive, 559-6800; open 6 AM to 10 PM Monday through Friday and noon to 7 PM Saturday and Sunday.

Franciscan MediCenter at Harrison, 10400 New Haven Road, 367-2222; open 24 hours a day.

Immediate Care Center, 8200 Beckett Park Drive, West Chester, 860-9292; open 5 PM to 9 PM Monday through Friday and 9 AM to 9 PM Saturday and Sunday.

Jewish Hospital Downtown Medical Center, 417 Vine Street, 241-3322; open 8 AM to 6 PM Monday through Friday.

Mercy Medi-Center Eastgate, 4404A Glen Este-Withamsville Road, 752-9610; open 8 AM to 6 PM Monday through Friday, 9 AM to 5 PM Saturday and noon to 5 PM Sunday.

Mercy Urgent Care-Mason, 10500 Mason-Montgomery Road, Mason, 870-7000 (scheduled to open in summer 1998).

West Mitchell Avenue Medical Center, 64 W. Mitchell Avenue, 641-2010; open 8 AM to 5 PM Monday through Friday.

Hospice Care

Home Health Plus Hospice, 625 Eden Park Drive, 421-2273

Hospice of The Christ Hospital, 2415 Auburn Avenue, 665-3000

Hospice of Cincinnati, 4310 Cooper Road, Blue Ash, 891-7770

Hospice of Middletown, 4414 Lewis Street, Middletown, 424-0282

Hospice of Northern Kentucky, 1419 Alexandria Pike, Fort Thomas, (606) 441-6332

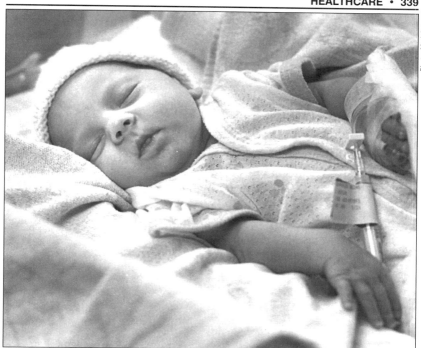

Photo: Mark Lyons

New additions are part of everyday life at Good Samaritan Hospital.

Hospice of Southeastern Indiana, 370 Bielby Road, Lawrenceburg, (812) 537-8192

Physician Referral Services

These services are popular with newcomers seeking physicians in a particular specialty in their area of town. Physician referral lines in some cases will also refer you to physicians based on the type of insurance they accept. A listing of Greater Cincinnati physician referral services and their sponsoring hospitals (when not already in the name) follows.

The Appointment Book (Jewish Hospitals), 569-2100

Ask-A-Nurse (Bethesda and Good Samaritan), 569-5400

Ask-A-Nurse (Bethesda and Good Samaritan), Lebanon number 932-5410

Deaconess Healthlink Physician Referral, 559-2255

Health Match (Franciscan Health System), 389-5110

MedExchange (The Christ Hospital), 369-2601

Mercy Med-Line, 271-8600

Nurse On Line (Fort Hamilton-Hughes), 867-2222

Pediatrician Referral Service, (Children's Hospital), 559-4724

Physician File (St. Elizabeth), 292-4444

Medicaid and Other Insurance

How do you pay for all this healthcare? If you're lucky, you're covered by an employer health plan. But, as is true just about everywhere, finding insurance coverage for individuals is tricky business in Greater Cincinnati.

Many insurers in the area offer health insurance for individuals, but there are some caveats. If you or a family member has a history of medical problems, you will either be turned down or pay a very steep rate. In Ohio, HMOs are required to allow individuals to enroll once a year regardless of their medical history or employment status. But rates are high.

The Greater Cincinnati Chamber of Commerce offers one of the best and most affordable "group" plans around, provided you're self-employed or own a business, are healthy and join the Chamber. (The same goes for many smaller chambers such as the Anderson Area chamber.) A good rate on the coverage generally more than makes up for the Chamber's $315 annual membership fee, even for a one-employee business. The Chamber plan includes Choice Care coverage. A similar plan is available to non-Chamber members through Anthem Blue Cross and Blue Shield, the Chamber's former insurance provider.

Medicaid is available to qualified unemployed persons and administered through county human services departments throughout Greater Cincinnati.

Human Services Departments

These county human services departments handle adoption, food stamps, Medicaid, foster parents programs and welfare.

Boone County, (606) 371-8832
Butler County, 887-4000
Campbell County, (606) 292-6733
Clermont County, 732-7111
Hamilton County, 946-1000
Kenton County, (606) 292-6340
Warren County, 925-1420

FYI

Unless otherwise noted, the area code for all phone numbers listed in this guide is 513.

Community Health Resources

Public clinics that charge patients on a sliding scale based on income are also available for routine medical care. The Cincinnati Health Department operates six such clinics.

Ambrose H. Clement Health Center, 3101 Burnet Avenue, Corryville, 357-7300

Braxton F. Cann Health Center, 5919 Madison Road, Madisonville, 271-6089

Elm Street Health Center, 1525 Elm Street, Over-the-Rhine, 352-3092

Millvale Health Center, 3301 Beekman, 352-3192

Northside Health Center, 3917 Spring Grove, 357-7600

Price Hill Health Center, 2136 W. Eighth Street, 352-2538

Elsewhere in the Greater Cincinnati area:

Boone County Health Center, 7505 Burlington Pike, Florence, Kentucky, (606) 525-1770

Campbell County Health Center, 12 E. Fifth Street, Newport, Kentucky, (606) 431-1704

Dearborn County Health Department, 215-B W. High Street, Lawrenceburg, Indiana, (812) 537-8826

Hamilton Health Clinics, 647 East Avenue, Hamilton, 868-5984

Kenton County Health Center, 912 Scott Street, Covington, Kentucky, (606) 581-3886

Warren County Health Department, 416 S. East Street, Lebanon, 677-6228

In or near Clermont County, the Southern Ohio Health Services Network, operates five health clinics that charge patients on a sliding scale.

Batavia Family Practice, 2245 Bauer Road, 732-0870

INSIDERS' TIP

The most common reasons for hospitalization in Greater Cincinnati? Circulatory diseases, pregnancy, neonatal problems, respiratory disease and digestive disease. Heart failure accounts for only 2.9 percent of all hospital stays, suggesting a lower stress factor in Cincinnati than in the rest of the country.

Batavia Obstetrics and Gynecology, 2245 Bauer Road, 732-0700

Batavia OB/GYN Anderson Office, 7691 Five Mile Road, Anderson, 624-9400

Goshen Family Practice, 1507 Ohio Highway 28, 575-1444

New Richmond Family Practice, 1050 Old U.S. Highway 52, 553-3114

Emergency Numbers

Emergency police, fire or medical aid, 911

American Red Cross, 579-3000

Battered Women's Crisis Line, 381-5610

Battered Women's Helpline, 753-7281

Battered Women's Hotline, 241-2757

Child Abuse Hotline, (Hamilton County Department of Human Services) 241-KIDS

Cocaine Hotline, (800) COCAINE

Drug and Poison Control, 558-5111, (800) 872-5111; in Northern Kentucky, (800) 722-5752

Elderly Abuse Hotline, 421-LIFE

Family Violence Hotline, 421-HELP

Psychiatric Emergency Services, 558-8577

Rape Crisis Center/Women Helping Women, 381-5610

Runaway Shelter, 961-4080; in Northern Kentucky, (606) 581-1111

Suicide/Crisis Intervention Hotline, 281-CARE

Women's Crisis Center of Northern Kentucky, (606) 491-3335

YWCA Amend (batterer's treatment), 221-6363

YWCA House of Peace Helpline (Clermont County), 753-7281

YWCA Dove House (Butler County), 863-7099

Other Important Numbers

Here's a list of other health-related numbers that could be of help.

Adoption Connection, 793-3366

Adult Children of Alcoholics, 771-4071

Adult Day Care, 721-7900

AIDS Counseling and Information Hotline, (800) 590-2437

AIDS and Sexually Transmitted Disease Information, 357-7350

AIDS Volunteers of Cincinnati, 421-2437; 421-5030 TDD/TTY

AIDS Volunteers of Northern Kentucky, (606) 341-0696

AlaTeen, 771-4071

Alcoholics Anonymous, city 861-9966; suburbs 791-6219; Northern Kentucky, (606) 491-7181

Alzheimer's Association, 721-4284

American Cancer Society, 559-1050

American Diabetes Association, 281-0002

American Heart Association, 281-4048

American Lung Association, 724-1156

Arthritis Foundation, 271-4545

Barrett Center for Cancer Prevention, Treatment and Research, 558-3200, (800) 750-0750 TDD/TTY

Cancer Family Care, 731-3346

Central Intake for Home Care, Cincinnati Health Department, 357-7400

Cincinnati Center for Developmental Disorders, 559-4648

Cincinnati Comprehensive Sickle Cell Center, 559-4541

Community Cancer Information Center, 624-4921

Council for Epilepsy, 281-2368

Drug and Poison Information Center, 558-5111, (800) 872-5111

Leukemia Society of America Inc., 891-9666

March of Dimes, 772-3553

Mental Retardation and Development Disabilities Information and Referral, 821-5060

Nutrition Hotline, 721-7900, 762-7250 TDD/TTY

Planned Parenthood, 721-7635

Prenatal Care, 772-3560, 762-7250 TDD/TTY

Psychiatric Emergency Services, 558-8577, 558-8157 TDD/TTY

Suicide Prevention, 281-2273, 281-2273 TDD/TTY

Teen Pregnancy/Parenting, 721-SUMA

Wellness Community for Cancer, 791-4060

St. Rita School for the Deaf is the nation's only privately funded school for the deaf.

Schools and Child Care

Greater Cincinnati has more than 50 public school districts and more than 260 private schools. Perhaps nowhere in the country are schools changing as profoundly as they are here.

In Ohio, legal skirmishes over public schools and how they should be funded boiled over in 1997. Traditionally, the public school system has been funded by local property taxes. Critics and school officials have long challenged the fairness and equity of funding that relies on variable local property values as well as the good will of the electorate to pass school levies. In mid-1997, the Ohio Supreme Court finally agreed, ordering the legislature and governor to — within one year — replace reliance on property tax with some other funding system (almost certainly more state monies and a corresponding tax increase). The long-term effect? In theory, poorer urban school districts will gain equal footing with posh suburban districts.

For newcomers to Ohio, the issue has some very real and unsettling implications. If you move to an area that has an impressive and well-funded school district today, things could change dramatically overnight. Funding may be cut or you may have to come up with supplemental local monies to maintain current school spending. At the same time, many districts that are cash-poor today will be in for a windfall when reform is implemented in the next year or so. Stay tuned.

On the Kentucky side of the river, changes already are in motion. The Kentucky Education Reform Act, now in its seventh year of implementation, has helped equalize funding among school districts and launched a host of controversial educational reforms. The verdict by the national media on KERA is overwhelmingly positive, but polls show a majority of Kentuckians view it negatively. Largely, opposition centers around multigrade grouping and nontraditional teaching methods instituted as part of the reform.

Private schools are numerous and strong in the region. One in four students in Hamilton County attends a private school, a higher proportion than in any metropolitan area in the state and two-and-a-half times the national average. Enrollment in non-diocesan private schools is growing four times faster than in public schools in the Tri-state. And enrollment in diocesan Catholic schools is growing twice as fast as in public schools. With 57,000 students, the Archdiocese of Cincinnati already runs the ninth-largest Catholic school system in the nation. It's also the biggest school system of any kind in Greater Cincinnati, with 6,000 more students than Cincinnati public schools. Another roughly 12,000 students attend schools run by the Diocese of Covington.

If you are considering home-schooling your child, the following organizations can help you through the hurdles: **Homeschool Network of Greater Cincinnati,** 772-9579; **Home Education Association,** 661-7396; **Holy Family Catholic Home Educators,** 671-2633; **Christian Home Educators of Cincinnati,** 398-5795; **Teaching Homes in Northern Kentucky,** (606) 525-2520; and **Northern Kentucky Catholic Homeschoolers,** (606) 283-0610.

The choices are obviously many. What follows are highlights of some of the best, biggest and most popular public and private schools in Greater Cincinnati.

Public Schools

In the following listings we've included per-pupil spending, student/teacher ratio, average daily attendance rate, dropout rate, student body size and other factors parents will want to consider. For Ohio school districts, we've also included the most recent results (released in 1998) of the Ohio Ninth Grade Proficiency Test; because a student must pass all five sections of this test (writing, reading, math, science and citizenship) in order to receive a high school diploma, this is a closely watched barometer of a district's academic standing. Students have 11 chances to pass the test, and may even continue taking the test after finishing their senior year of high school.

many Ohio schools is the state's property tax rollback system. Under this system, a school tax levy always raises roughly the same amount of money as when first passed, even as property values increase later. Only new development can actually increase school funding without a new levy. As a result, all but a handful of lucky school districts must constantly come back to voters for new levies as inflation increases their costs but not their tax revenues.

Despite the complexity and inequity of its funding system, Ohio still manages to have some pretty good schools. And Greater Cincinnati has some of the best schools and school districts in the state. An impressive five of nine school levies passed in the city's 1997 elections, right on par with voter support across the state (statewide, voters approved 119 of 194 school issues, a solid 60 percent support).

Ohio

Funding for Ohio's school system is, for the moment at least, based mostly on property taxes, though a few school districts have passed income taxes to partially fund their budgets. The current system favors districts with strong industrial tax bases or pricey residential real estate. Poorer school districts, particularly rural districts, fare much worse. Though it's technically supposed to help equalize per-pupil spending, the state funding formula actually adds to the inequities in some cases because it grandfathers in funding levels from decades ago. Challenges to similar funding systems have prevailed elsewhere in the country, including Indiana and Kentucky.

The solution usually involves a system in which one mill (1/1000th of a dollar) of property tax generates the same revenue for a school district regardless of the value of real estate there. State funding makes up the difference for poorer school districts. In Ohio such a system would mean that to keep state funding at current levels, state support for many of the richest school districts would have to be eliminated.

Adding to the current financial woes of

Hamilton County

Results of the latest Ohio Ninth Grade Proficiency Test, released in 1998, reflect that Cincinnati public schools, the area's largest public school system, posted significant academic improvement over scores in previous years, including a 9 percent jump in writing scores.

Cincinnati public school students, however, continue to lag behind those in the more affluent suburban districts (as well as behind most of those in Ohio's larger cities, trailing all but Cleveland and Dayton). Top scorers among the area's suburban districts in 1998 included Wyoming City School District (with a stunning 99 percent of its 9th graders passing reading and writing), the Sycamore Community School District and Milford Exempted Village School District.

Cincinnati Public Schools
230 E. Ninth St. • 475-7000

With 50,000 students spread among nine high schools, eight junior high schools, 61 elementary schools and five special schools, the Cincinnati public schools make up by far the largest public school system in the area. Give the Cincinnati public schools an A, or at least a high B, for effort. Unfortunately, this is still an urban district, with all the problems associated with big urban school districts.

The district has tried to alleviate these problems by inviting the business community to take the lead in telling the district how to solve its problems. Specifically, the Cincinnati Business Committee, a group of 27 heads of some of the city's major public and private companies, has taken an active role in advising the district, if not in actually sending any of their children there. The CBC appointed the Buenger Commission, which recommended some fairly fundamental reforms in the management of the school district. Most of the major recommendations have been carried out, including:

• Reducing central school administration by 70 percent;

• Hiring a private sector executive to run nonacademic, i.e., business, operations;

• Establishing greater accountability for teachers, principals and administrators — this has been done through more frequent job appraisals and a pay-for-performance system, in which employees of schools that improve graduation rates and test scores can get up to 4 percent merit raises;

• Upgrading vocational education programs; and

• Establishing a training academy for educators.

The district also still faces some major problems in funding much-needed repairs of aging buildings (supposedly, money is coming as part of the deal to build the new Bengals football stadium; voters approved a levy that included an attachment for school funding).

Academically, the district has some big challenges. Overall performance numbers paint a very mixed picture. Districtwide, about half of Cincinnati students go on to college — not bad for an urban district. And at Walnut Hills High School, the district's college preparatory academy, teacher Sharon Draper was named National Teacher of the Year in 1997. Yet, the percentage of 9th graders who passed the most recent proficiency tests was 75 for writing, 77 for reading, 37 for math, 55 for citizenship and 46 for science.

Also noteworthy is that, in Cincinnati, the middle school concept is being phased out.

Instead, students will be grouped in grades K-3, 4-6 and 7-8 in order to link students with the same teachers over a longer period of time. The student/teacher ratio is 18.5 to 1, daily attendance is 83 percent and the dropout rate is 11 percent. Despite its funding woes, it should be noted that the Cincinnati district's per-pupil spending is a very respectable $6,692. Of course, much of that goes for such things as crosstown transportation, which suburban districts don't have. And the expenses of magnet programs (more on these below), which might seem like frills, are part of a court-mandated desegregation program.

Despite a relatively attractive pay scale (starting salary is $27,600), Cincinnati public schools still often get the last pick of teachers. This isn't just because it's an urban district with urban troubles, but also because Cincinnati is often the last district in the area to hire new teachers each year. Enrollment levels are either so unpredictable — or so poorly predicted — that many teachers are hired in September or October, weeks after the school year has begun.

Going into 1998, there was some concern over the impending retirement of long-time Superintendent Michael Brandt. Brandt led the Cincinnati public schools through the Buenger Commission changes, and his tenure is generally seen as a high mark in the recent history of the school system. There is understandable nervousness over who his successor will be, and what changes he or she might bring.

Now, a word about the Cincinnati public schools' magnet program. And that word is "terrific." These specialty schools attract children from across the city and include The Academy of World Languages, Hughes Center (a communications school that also offers math, science, Paideia and a Zoo Academy), Jacobs Center (math and science), Fairview (teaching German), Clark (Montessori), Schiel (arts), Quebec Heights (math and science), Withrow (international studies) and the School for the Creative and Performing Arts (think of the movie *Fame*).

Magnet schools are a desegregation tool, so acceptance is somewhat determined by a child's race and sex. Withrow's international studies program also has stringent academic requirements, and the School for the Creative and Performing Arts requires auditions.

In addition to these citywide schools, there are magnet programs in select neighborhood public schools (primarily Montessori, Paideia, language and college prep programs); entry to the neighborhood programs is limited to those living in certain parts of the city.

Because these magnet schools (so named for their "attraction") are so highly regarded, there is understandably a scramble to win a place on waiting lists. Generally, the school system announces a signup day on one Saturday in midwinter. But it doesn't announce the *location* of the registration tables until 7 AM of that Saturday, via local TV and radio. Why? Because when the school system announced the location ahead of time, eager parents would camp out at the doors Friday night, no small indication of the popularity and respect for the magnet schools. For more information on individual magnet schools, call 475-7099.

Deer Park Community Schools
8688 Donna Ln., Deer Park • 891-0222

This blue-collar school district northeast of Cincinnati is one of the smallest in Hamilton County, with 1,600 students in three elementary schools and one junior-senior high. The community has traditionally been a hard sell on more money for schools, but it did pass a levy in 1995. The student/teacher ratio is 21 to 1, daily attendance is 95 percent and the dropout rate is 6.6 percent. The percentage of 9th graders who passed the most recent proficiency tests was 91 for writing, 89 for reading, 65 for math, 73 for citizenship and 67 for science.

Finneytown Local Schools
8916 Fountainbleu Ter. • 728-3700

Finneytown has traditionally been one of the best school districts on the west side of town and, by the numbers, one of the most productive districts in the state. The 1,950-student district has three elementary schools, one junior high and one senior high school. Community support is strong: Both school levies that have appeared on the ballot since 1989 have passed, as did a bond issue in 1996 for renovation and expansion. Per-pupil spending is $5,569. The student/teacher ratio is 19.5 to 1, daily attendance is 94.5 percent and the dropout rate is 2.3 percent.

The percentage of 9th graders who passed the most recent proficiency tests was 90 for writing, 90 for reading, 75 for math, 81 for citizenship and 74 for science.

Forest Hills Local Schools
7550 Forest Rd., Anderson • 231-3600

This 8,000-student school district is one of the larger and better-known suburban districts in Greater Cincinnati and one of the more efficient. It has six elementary schools and two high schools. Per-pupil spending is a mere $4,820. The student/teacher ratio is 22.4 to 1, daily attendance is 95.5 percent and the dropout rate is 2.5 percent. The percentage of 9th graders who passed the most recent proficiency tests was 94 for writing, 90 for reading, 82 for math, 89 for citizenship and 80 for science.

Science teacher John Farmer of Ayer Elementary was chosen as a finalist for the 1997 Presidential Award for Excellence in Teaching; with that award comes grants to the school from the National Science Foundation. Anderson High School was among seven schools in the state to be honored by the prestigious Blue Ribbon Schools Secondary School Recognition Program in 1996.

Both Forest Hills high schools have extensive advanced-placement and honors programs, and the district has computer writing

---

www.insiders.com

See this and many other **Insiders' Guide®** destinations online — in their entirety.

Visit us today!

centers in all schools. In sports, both high schools are known for soccer, and the rivalry is intense. Both schools also generally field strong teams in other sports as well.

Because of rapid growth in Anderson and because the district's reputation attracts families with kids, Forest Hills passed a bond issue in 1996 to build a new 1,400-student school for grades 7 and 8 at the former site of Nagel Park. That school is currently under construction.

Indian Hill Exempted Village Schools
6855 Drake Rd., Indian Hill • 272-4500

Indian Hill is Cincinnati's wealthiest, and one of the nation's poshest, school districts — home to Carl Lindner and other top executives of Cincinnati's major companies. Not surprisingly, the schools aren't too shabby. Per-pupil spending of $8,002 is among the highest in Greater Cincinnati.

The student body is a fairly exclusive group of 2,000 in three elementary, one junior high and one high school. The student/teacher ratio is 16 to 1, daily attendance is 96 percent and the dropout rate is 1.5 percent. The percentage of 9th graders who passed the most recent proficiency tests was 98 for writing, 99 for reading, 87 for math, 89 for citizenship and 87 for science.

Lockland City Schools
210 N. Cooper Ave., Lockland • 563-5000

A small, 881-student, working-class school district in north central Hamilton County, Lockland has two elementary schools and one junior-senior high. Lockland is generously endowed with an industrial tax base, thanks to GE Aircraft Engines. Per-pupil expenditure is a hefty $7,653. With revenues from GE dwindling, Lockland passed a levy to maintain its independence. Given the spending figures and the output in terms of student achievement, it would be easy to argue that this is not money well spent and that a school district smaller than some elementary schools elsewhere in the Tri-state is not terribly efficient.

The district's attendance rate, 92 percent, is below average. Its dropout rate of 11.3 percent is one of the worst in Hamilton County. The district does offer a special tutoring and remedial program for at-risk primary students and Saturday work/study programs for junior and senior high students who need special help. The student/teacher ratio is 20 to 1. The percentage of 9th graders who passed the most recent proficiency tests was 92 for writing, 84 for reading, 62 for math, 77 for citizenship and 71 for science.

Loveland City Schools
757 Lebanon Rd., Loveland • 683-5600

This 3,600-student school district in northeastern Hamilton County also crosses into parts of Clermont and Warren counties. Student population at the district's three elementary schools, one junior high and one senior high has grown steadily, up about 30 percent overall in the past five years. But the administration has done a good job of planning for it, and voters have funded the needed expansion.

Loveland lacks the cachet of such nearby districts as Sycamore and Mariemont, but it still manages some pretty good results on a lean budget. Per-pupil spending is $4,764. The student/teacher ratio is 23 to 1, daily attendance is 95 percent and the dropout rate is 3.1 percent. The percentage of 9th graders who passed the most recent proficiency tests was 93 for writing, 96 for reading, 83 for math, 90 for citizenship and 87 for science.

Madeira City Schools
7465 Loannes Dr., Madeira • 791-0016

The Madeira school district has a mix of longtime residents, newer families with kids and middle- and upper-income residents. The 1,400 students attend two elementary schools, one middle school and one high school. The student/teacher ratio is 18.7 to 1, daily attendance is 96 percent and the dropout rate is 1.6 percent. Per-pupil spending is $6,446.

Academically, Madeira enjoys a very above-average reputation. Sellman Middle School was among six in the area honored by the U.S. Department of Education's Blue Ribbon Recognition Program in 1997. The high school has an extensive array of advanced-placement courses, reflecting the college orientation of the student body. And the district has been a leader in setting up Internet accounts to permit students to get familiar with online research. The percentage of 9th graders who passed the most recent proficiency tests was 92 for writing, 93 for reading, 87 for math, 88 for citizenship and 87 for science.

Mariemont City Schools
6743 Chestnut St., Mariemont • 272-2722

The villages of Mariemont, Fairfax and Terrace Park make up this 1,660-student district, which includes a mix of upscale and blue collar residents. The combination of affluent housing in Mariemont and Terrace Park and a good industrial tax base in Fairfax helps make for strong funding. So does the willingness of voters to support tax levies; all three levies on the ballot since 1989 have passed. Thus, Mariemont schools have a per-pupil budget of $6,938.

Another sign of good schools: People with kids are flocking here. Enrollment has grown 25 percent in the past five years, leading to the conversion of a leased-out school building to a second junior high school. The system also has two elementary schools and one high school. The student/teacher ratio is 19.4 to 1, daily attendance is 96 percent and the dropout rate is slightly under 1 percent. The percentage of 9th graders who passed the most recent proficiency tests was 96 for writing, 92 for reading, 82 for math, 85 for citizenship and 80 for science.

Mount Healthy City Schools
7615 Harrison Ave., Mount Healthy • 729-0077

Combine an aging population and falling enrollment and you get the roots of financial trouble for any school district. This 4,000-student district in a working class area on the west side of town has had trouble passing levies in recent years, but finally passed one (by a very slim margin) during a special election in 1998. School officials hoped to eventually restore bus service and sports programs that were cut in early 1998, as well as several teacher positions that had been eliminated after the November 1997 levy failed.

The district has increased staff development and graduation requirements in recent years. Other pluses are active parent booster groups for extracurricular activities. Per-pupil spending is $6,133. The student/teacher ratio

is 19.4 to 1, daily attendance is 92.4 percent and the dropout rate is 9.9 percent. The percentage of 9th graders who passed the most recent proficiency tests was 87 for writing, 78 for reading, 43 for math, 56 for citizenship and 42 for science.

North College Hill City Schools
1498 W. Galbraith Rd., North College Hill • 931-8181

This 1,600-student blue-collar school district does a good job with the resources at its disposal. Per-pupil spending is $5,162. The student/teacher ratio is almost 23 to 1, daily attendance is 93 percent and the dropout rate is just over 6 percent. The percentage of 9th graders who passed the most recent proficiency tests was 88 for writing, 96 for reading, 53 for math, 80 for citizenship and 63 for science.

The district's primary schools have multi-age, multi-disciplinary classrooms. Voters failed to support a school levy in the 1997 elections.

Northwest Local Schools
2760 Jonrose Ave., Groesbeck • 923-1000

With nearly 11,000 students, this is the second-largest school district in Hamilton County and one of the largest in the area. It encompasses nine elementary schools, three middle schools, two senior highs — Colerain and Northwest — and two vocational schools. The student/teacher ratio is 22.6 to 1, daily attendance is 94 percent and the dropout rate is 4.8 percent. Per-pupil spending is $4,749. The percentage of 9th graders who passed the most recent proficiency tests was 92 for writing, 92 for reading, 71 for math, 83 for citizenship and 75 for science. Northwest voters backed a school levy in the 1997 elections, a healthy sign of community support.

Norwood City Schools
2132 Wilms Ave., Norwood • 396-5523

The largely urban, 3,300-student Norwood district has struggled through some tough times coping with the loss of tax revenue from the closing of a General Motors assembly plant some years ago. The city still has a reasonably good tax base, however, and per-pupil spending is a healthy $6,622. Students attend one primary school, four elementary schools and one middle and one high school. The student/teacher ratio is 22.5 to 1, daily attendance is 93 percent and the dropout rate is 2.9 percent. The percentage of 9th graders who passed the most recent proficiency tests was 88 for writing, 92 for reading, 64 for math, 89 for citizenship and 69 for science.

Oak Hills Local Schools
6479 Bridgetown Rd., Mack • 574-3200

Here's a hard-working school district in the best of the West Side tradition. The community has been a hard sell on providing more funds, though a levy did pass in 1994 after five tries. The 8,300-student district has five elementary schools, two junior highs and one high school. Per-pupil spending is $4,498. The student/teacher ratio is 23 to 1, daily attendance is 95 percent and the dropout rate is just under 4 percent. The percentage of 9th graders who passed the most recent proficiency tests was 91 for writing, 93 for reading, 79 for math, 80 for citizenship and 80 for science.

Princeton City Schools
25 W. Sharon Rd., Glendale • 771-8560

Princeton's 6,700-student district, with nine elementary schools, one junior high and one senior high, is among the most economically diverse suburban districts in the city. It enjoys extremely good funding thanks to an industrial tax base, with expenditure per pupil at nearly $8,187, one of the highest in the Tri-state. Facilities have traditionally been very good here, including a swimming pool at the high school, and the district boasts highly ranked sports teams. The student/teacher ratio is 14.7 to 1, daily attendance is 93 percent and the dropout rate is 3.3 percent. The percentage of 9th graders who passed the most recent proficiency tests was 85 for writing, 82 for reading, 56 for math, 73 for citizenship and 65 for science.

Reading Community City Schools
Bonnell and Halker Aves., Reading • 554-1800

This small, middle-class 1,400-student district with two elementary schools and one junior-senior high enjoys strong community support. When the district went to voters in 1994 with its first levy request in 13 years, the levy passed the first time, and Reading voters backed a school levy in the 1997 elections. Per-pupil spending is $6,868. The student/teacher ratio is 19 to 1, daily attendance is 94 percent and the dropout rate is 6.7 percent.

The percentage of 9th graders who passed the most recent proficiency tests was 94 for writing, 89 for reading, 64 for math, 76 for citizenship and 65 for science. Reading Junior/Senior High also was among six Ohio schools nominated for the Blue Ribbon Schools Secondary School Recognition Program in 1997.

St. Bernard-Elmwood Place
105 Washington Ave., St. Bernard • 641-2020

With 1,300 students, this is one of the smaller school districts in Hamilton County. This working-class district enjoys a strong industrial tax base that permits per-pupil spending of an impressive $7,224. In early 1998, voters approved a five-year emergency renewal levy to pay for operating expenses. And school officials have doggedly tried to avoid filling any position that has become vacant in the past four years, in anticipation of tough times. The tough times, of course, may never come, depending on the outcome of the state funding debate.

The student/teacher ratio here is 18.5 to 1, daily attendance is 93 percent and the dropout rate is 7.3 percent. The percentage of 9th graders who passed the most recent proficiency tests was 85 for writing, 90 for reading, 71 for math, 80 for citizenship and 66 for science.

The district provides a wide range of special programs, including extended-day kindergarten for at-risk students and after-school enrichment for gifted students.

Southwest Local Schools
230 S. Elm St., Harrison • 367-4139

Southwest's 4,000 students attend six elementary schools, one junior high and one senior high school. Per-pupil spending is

Cincinnati private schools showcase some of the city's finest architecture.

$4,822. Even given this low spending rate, the district was recognized by *Redbook* magazine for excellence. The student/teacher ratio is 24 to 1, daily attendance is nearly 94 percent and the dropout rate is 5.4 percent. Parent involvement includes a rarity: an Academic Boosters Club. The percentage of 9th graders who passed the most recent proficiency tests was 85 for writing, 87 for reading, 71 for math, 76 for citizenship and 73 for science.

Sycamore Community Schools
4881 Cooper Rd., Blue Ash • 791-4848

Sycamore's 6,000-student district covers the upscale suburbs of Blue Ash, Montgomery and Sycamore and is generally recognized as among the best in Greater Cincinnati. The five elementary schools, one junior high and one senior high have all the hallmarks of an affluent community — including high parental involvement. Per-pupil spending is $7,095. The student/teacher ratio is 19 to 1, daily attendance is 95 percent and the dropout rate is 1.2 percent. The percentage of 9th graders who passed the most recent proficiency tests was 97 for writing, 98 for reading, 92 for math, 94 for citizenship and 92 for science.

Three Rivers Local Schools
92 Cleves Ave., Cleves • 941-6400

This 2,300-student district on the far western side of Hamilton County faces the fortunate dilemma of an influx of upscale residential development that is filling three elementary schools to capacity. The district has one middle and one high school. Per-pupil spending is $6,050. The student/teacher ratio is 23 to 1, daily attendance is 93.4 percent and the dropout rate is 5.3 percent.

The percentage of 9th graders who passed the most recent proficiency tests was 93 for writing, 94 for reading, 71 for math, 88 for citizenship and 78 for science. Despite its relatively small size, the district offers several high school advanced-placement classes and extended-day kindergarten for at-risk students.

Winton Woods City Schools
1215 W. Kemper Rd., Forest Park
• 825-5090

Winton Woods is a large, 4,500-student district with six elementary schools, one middle school, a 9th-grade school and a senior high. In early 1998, voters finally approved a school levy during a special election, after voting down ballot issues twice in 1997. Even so, the district is planning to cut $1.2 million from its 1998-99 budget.

Per-pupil spending here is $5,881. The student/teacher ratio is 20 to 1, daily attendance is 94 percent and the dropout rate is 3.1 percent. The percentage of 9th graders who passed the most recent proficiency tests was 84 for writing, 84 for reading, 52 for math, 68 for citizenship and 57 for science.

Wyoming Public Schools
100 Pendery St., Wyoming • 761-7857

Wyoming is generally regarded as among the best — if not the best — school districts in Greater Cincinnati. It straddles the east-west line geographically but clearly has East Side demographics, serving as home to many top executives, including Procter & Gamble CEO John Pepper. The district has one primary school, three middle schools and one high school.

The numbers back Wyoming's stellar reputation. The dropout rate, a stunning zero percent, is the best in the city. The student/teacher ratio is 18 to 1, and daily attendance is 97 percent, one of the best attendance rates in the city. Per-pupil spending is $6,289. The percentage of 9th graders who passed the most recent proficiency tests was a remarkable 99 for writing, an equally remarkable 99 for reading, 90 for math, 93 for citizenship and 86 for science.

The high school's curriculum includes 15 advanced-placement courses despite the relatively small size of the 1,800-student district. Foreign language is taught through immersion programs in junior and senior high.

Butler County

Nearly every school district in this fast-growing area of Greater Cincinnati has spending levels well below the state average. Still, it turns in decent results and keeps attracting new students.

Fairfield City Schools
211 Donald Dr., Fairfield • 829-6300

This middle-class community has a fairly wide range of income levels and expectations for its schools. Growth and funding are problems in this large system, with 8,800 students, four elementary schools, one middle school, a freshman school and a senior high school. Per-pupil spending is $4,915. The student/teacher ratio is 24 to 1, daily attendance is 94 percent and the dropout rate is 6.3 percent. The percentage of 9th graders who passed the most recent proficiency tests was 86 for writing, 86 for reading, 65 for math, 76 for citizenship and 69 for science. Fairfield voters backed a school levy in the 1997 elections.

Lakota Local Schools
5030 Tylersville Rd., West Chester
• 874-5505

Serving the rapidly growing West Chester community, this is one of the largest and fastest-growing suburban school districts in Ohio. Enrollment has risen 38 percent in five years. With more than 13,000 students, it's the 10th-largest district in Ohio, so it has plenty of capacity to offer a wide range of curricula to suit diverse needs.

The district has eight elementary schools, two junior highs, one freshman school and two high schools. Per-pupil spending is $4,336. The student/teacher ratio is 23.5 to 1, daily attendance is 95.5 percent and the dropout rate is 2.1 percent. The percentage of 9th graders who passed the most recent proficiency tests was 95 for writing, 96 for reading, 83 for math, 90 for citizenship and 87 for science.

Ross Local Schools
3371 Hamilton-Cleves Rd., Ross
• 863-1253

Mostly rural and working-class, the Ross

FYI

Unless otherwise noted, the area code for all phone numbers listed in this guide is 513.

school district has 2,600 students in the southwestern corner of Butler County. The district turns in an all-around good performance. The student/teacher ratio is 22 to 1, daily attendance is nearly 95 percent and the dropout rate is 3.2 percent. The percentage of 9th graders who passed the most recent proficiency tests was 91 for writing, 95 for reading, 76 for math, 82 for citizenship and 82 for science.

Clermont County

Clermont County schools get a bad rap that is in many ways a bum rap. They suffer in comparison to schools serving upscale communities just across the border in Hamilton County. A look at the numbers tells a somewhat different story. Clermont County schools serve largely working class and rural communities that are similar income-wise to districts in western and less affluent parts of eastern Hamilton County. Despite slim budgets, Clermont schools turn in respectable numbers on state reports.

Batavia Local Schools
800 Bauer Ave., Batavia • 732-2343

Batavia's small 1,600-student school district is growing, with one elementary school, one junior and two senior highs that serve a fairly diverse community of blue- and white-collar residents in an area that's next in line for big-time suburban sprawl. A Ford transmission plant here helps provide a sizable tax base, so property taxes have been kept fairly low.

Per-pupil spending is $5,145. The student/teacher ratio is 19 to 1, daily attendance is 93.5 percent and the dropout rate is 5.5 percent. The percentage of 9th graders who passed the most recent proficiency tests was 93 for writing, 87 for reading, 67 for math, 83 for citizenship and 77 for science.

Bethel-Tate Local Schools
200 West Plain St., Bethel • 734-2238

This 2,100-student rural/blue-collar district in eastern Clermont does a good job with the basics in its three schools — elementary, middle and high — despite limited means at its disposal. Per-pupil spending is $4,579. The student/teacher ratio is 23 to 1, daily attendance is 93.6 percent and the dropout rate is 3.6 percent. The percentage of 9th graders who passed the most recent proficiency tests was 93 for writing, 91 for reading, 62 for math, 74 for citizenship and 72 for science.

Clermont Northeastern Local Schools
Main St., Newtonsville • 625-5478

For the past several years, Clermont Northeastern has been a school district in crisis, as repeated levy failures resulted in deep cuts and state loans. Passage of a 1 percent income tax levy in 1995, the first levy passed in nine years, has helped. This far-flung district has been the site of increasing suburban development. There are 2,200 students in two elementary schools, one middle and one high school.

Per-pupil spending is $4,803. The student/teacher ratio is 22.5 to 1, daily attendance is 92.5 percent and the dropout rate is 7.3 percent. The percentage of 9th graders who passed the most recent proficiency tests was 83 for writing, 84 for reading, 64 for math, 77 for citizenship and 70 for science.

Felicity-Franklin Local Schools
415 Washington Rd., Felicity • 876-2111

This 1,300-student rural and blue-collar district has an elementary school, a middle school and a high school. Per-pupil spending is $5,172. The student/teacher ratio is 22 to 1, daily attendance is 93.5 percent and the dropout rate is 8.3 percent. The percentage of 9th graders who passed the most recent proficiency tests was 72 for writing, 81 for reading, 55 for math, 60 for citizenship and 46 for science.

Goshen Local Schools
6785 Goshen Rd., Goshen • 722-2222

Goshen is a blue-collar suburban/rural district in northern Clermont that serves 2,700 students in three elementary, one junior high and one high school. Per-pupil spending is $5,018. The student/teacher ratio is nearly 23 to 1, daily attendance is 93 percent and the dropout rate is 8.2 percent. The percentage of 9th graders who passed the most recent proficiency tests was 86 for writing, 84 for reading, 54 for math, 74 for citizenship and 64 for science. Although the district had trouble passing levies in the late 1980s, four of six levies on the ballot in recent years have passed. Voters failed to support a school levy in the 1997 elections.

Milford Exempted Village Schools
525 Lila Ave., Milford • 831-5100

Milford's 5,700-student district has four elementary, a middle school, a junior high and a high school and is the biggest and wealthiest district in Clermont County in terms of community demographics. But it's the latest of the Clermont County school districts to be sucked into the vortex of levy failures and school-community strife.

School levy attempts have failed by hefty two-to-one margins three times since 1995. Nevertheless, a fairly well-equipped high school includes a pool and media studio. The student newspaper is popular and well-staffed, and advanced-placement offerings are extensive compared to other districts in Clermont County.

Per-pupil spending is $5,103. The student/teacher ratio is 22.5 to 1, daily attendance is 95 percent and the dropout rate is 5.3 percent. The percentage of 9th graders who passed the most recent proficiency tests was 95 for writing, 96 for reading, 80 for math, 89 for citizenship and 88 for science.

New Richmond Exempted Village Schools
1139 Bethel-New Richmond Rd., New Richmond • 553-2616

This wide-ranging 2,800-student district covers most of southern Clermont County, with three elementary, one junior high and one senior high school. It is the wealthiest of the Clermont County districts in terms of tax base, thanks to two power plants — the Beckjord and Zimmer stations. Per-pupil spending is $6,947. The student/teacher ratio is 18.5 to 1, daily attendance is 93 percent and the dropout rate is 7.6 percent. The percentage of 9th graders who passed the most recent proficiency tests was 86 for writing, 82 for reading, 60 for math, 73 for citizenship and 64 for science.

West Clermont Local Schools
4578 E. Tech Dr., Amelia • 528-0664

Passage of a levy in 1994 meant restoration of high school bus service and extracurricular activities and ended a lengthy levy struggle. An $11 million expansion covering four of the district's eight elementary schools, its two junior highs and two high schools is expected to be completed by June 1998.

Increasingly, West Clermont is becoming two communities in one school district. An influx of upscale housing in the schools feeding Glen Este High School is making that area more like neighboring Anderson. The area surrounding Amelia High School remains closer to its rural/Appalachian roots, though that area, too, is seeing continued residential growth.

Overall, the 9,200-student district delivers some relatively strong returns. Per-pupil spending is $4,500. The student/teacher ratio is 23 to 1, daily attendance is 94 percent and the dropout rate is 5.1 percent. The percentage of 9th graders who passed the most recent proficiency tests was 87 for writing, 89 for reading, 68 for math, 74 for citizenship and 68 for science.

Clough Elementary, in particular, has earned honors for its programs and become known for one of the best special education programs in the area.

Williamsburg Local Schools
145 W. Main St., Williamsburg • 724-3077

Williamsburg's 1,200-student school district has room to grow thanks to passage of a bond levy and renewal of an operating levy in

INSIDERS' TIP

The most closely watched barometer of a school district's academic progress is the Ohio Ninth Grade Proficiency Test. All Ohio students must pass the five sections of the test (writing, reading, math, science and citizenship) in order to receive a high school diploma.

1995 for this rural/blue-collar district. Students attend one elementary school and a combined middle/high school. Per-pupil spending is $4,970, and the student/teacher ratio is 20 to 1. The percentage of 9th graders who passed the most recent proficiency tests was 93 for writing, 92 for reading, 65 for math, 76 for citizenship and 67 for science.

Warren County

Warren is a pretty good county for schools. Funding levels are similar to those in Clermont County, and Warren has the same combination of rapid population growth and largely tax-abated industrial development as Clermont.

Kings Local Schools
5620 Columbia Rd., Kings Mills
• 459-2900

The Kings Local district has had a good record of community support, with five of six money issues passing in recent years. The student body of this 3,400-student district is up about 25 percent in the past five years, and a just-completed building program includes a new elementary school and expanded junior and senior high schools. Per-pupil spending is $5,322. The student/teacher ratio is 22 to 1, daily attendance is 95 percent and the dropout rate is 5.3 percent. The percentage of 9th graders who passed the most recent proficiency tests was 96 for writing, 95 for reading, 83 for math, 89 for citizenship and 82 for science.

Lebanon City Schools
25 Oakwood Ave., Lebanon
• 932-0999

Instead of neighborhood schools, this fast-growing 4,200-student district comprises three elementary schools, one intermediate (grades 4 and 5), one middle and one high school. Per-pupil spending is $4,248. The student/teacher ratio is 23.5 to 1, daily attendance is 94 percent and the dropout rate is 3.4 percent. The percentage of 9th graders who passed the most recent proficiency tests was 89 for writing, 94 for reading, 76 for math, 79 for citizenship and 83 for science.

Little Miami Local Schools
5819 Morrow-Rossburg Rd., Morrow
• 899-3408

Little Miami voters backed a school issue in the 1997 elections — good news for this scrappy school district. Per-pupil spending here is $5,145. The student/teacher ratio is 19 to 1, daily attendance is 93.5 percent and the dropout rate is 5.5 percent. The percentage of 9th graders who passed the most recent proficiency tests was 91 for writing, 92 for reading, 79 for math, 91 for citizenship and 80 for science.

Mason City Schools
211 N. East St., Mason • 398-0474

Mason's 3,300-student district has two elementary schools and a high school. This rapidly expanding district is having some growing pains, and a bond levy to build a new school failed in 1996. Per-pupil spending is $4,686. The student/teacher ratio is 21.5 to 1, daily attendance is 95 percent and the dropout rate is 6.4 percent. The district enjoys a strong reputation for its special education programs. The percentage of 9th graders who passed the most recent proficiency tests was 97 for writing, 97 for reading, 88 for math, 96 for citizenship and 90 for science.

Kentucky

The Kentucky Education Reform Act has dramatically improved the image of Kentucky schools nationally. Kentucky has always exerted considerable control over its local school districts and, under KERA, state micromanagement of local school affairs has grown. Some elements of the reform are almost universally applauded, such as safeguards that prevent the nepotism and favoritism once prevalent in many rural districts. Distribution of school funds among districts too is now clearly more equitable. However, some conservative Christians equate KERA with moral relativism, humanism and other creeping ills of modern society.

In terms of teaching methods, KERA has brought about a virtual cultural revolution. Formal lecture formats are discouraged. The teacher's role has become that of a facilitator of education rather than the funnel through which all education flows. In multi-age, ungraded elementary schools, older peers also serve as teachers for the younger. Much of the day is spent in unstructured, individually guided activity. This has made not only conservatives but also many teachers quite uncomfortable. Critics denounce what they call "unproven" teaching methods (although they generally don't spend much time talking about what a great job the old "proven" methods were doing).

The state testing program also has been controversial. It relies on open-ended essay and problem-solving questions that, while undoubtedly making students think more, are harder to grade objectively. Substantial parts of the state's evaluation of students and schools also are based on evaluation of a portfolio of the students' work and other subjective factors.

If nothing else, KERA has Kentuckians talking about and paying attention to their schools as never before, though the same poll that showed that a majority of respondents disapproved of KERA also showed that more than half of respondents had never heard of it. Anything that focuses more attention on education has its merits.

Here's one non-KERA issue to keep in mind about Kentucky schools: Average daily attendance rates tend to be higher than in Ohio because the schools get their state funding in part based on average daily attendance and go to great lengths to maximize it. As a result, Kentucky schools close at the slightest hint of snow and log a great many more snow days than schools across the river.

Beechwood Independent Schools
50 Beechwood Rd., Fort Mitchell, Ky.
• (606) 331-3250

This small district, with fewer than 1,000 students, has both its schools — a K-6 elementary and a 7-12 secondary school — in the same location. Beechwood Independent serves a relatively upscale suburban Fort Mitchell community. Every classroom, as well as the computer labs and libraries, have Internet access. The football team has won state championships five out of the last six years. Per-pupil spending is $3,460. The student/teacher ratio is 17 to 1, daily attendance is 96 percent and the dropout rate is zero percent.

Bellevue Independent Schools
215 Center St., Bellevue, Ky.
• (606) 261-2108

Bellevue's 1,000-student district includes an elementary school and a high school. Per-pupil spending is $4,188. The student/teacher ratio is 17 to 1, daily attendance is 94 percent and the dropout rate is about 1 percent.

Boone County Schools
8330 Ky. 42, Florence, Ky.
• (606) 283-1003

Boone County Schools is a rapidly growing district that serves 12,000 students in nine elementary schools, four middle schools, three senior highs — Boone, Conner and Ryle — and one vocational school. This is a district with growing pains, as a rapidly increasing population strains budgets. Aggravating the problem is that Boone County Schools, with one of Kentucky's stronger tax bases, lost money under KERA, resulting in spending cuts. Per-pupil spending is $4,026. The student/teacher ratio is 17.5 to 1, daily attendance is 95 percent and the dropout rate is 1.1 percent.

Campbell County Schools
101 Orchard Ln., Alexandria, Ky.
• (606) 635-2173

A new high school opened in 1995 in this 4,800-student district, which also includes five elementary and four middle schools. The district places an emphasis on parental involvement, with a chairperson at each school in charge of recruiting adult volunteers to aid teachers and a community-assisted reward program for kids with good grades and attendance records. The school board is spending millions on updating classroom technology as well as adding a new performing arts center. Per-pupil spending is $4,255. The student/teacher ratio is 17 to 1, daily attendance is 95 percent and the dropout rate is 3.5 percent.

Covington Independent Schools
25 E. Seventh St., Covington, Ky.
• (606) 292-5854

Covington is an urban district facing urban challenges. This 5,000-student district was one of those involved in the state lawsuit that brought about KERA, and it has benefited from the reform. Spending per pupil in the district is now greater than in neighboring Northern Kentucky districts. Although the district hasn't qualified for rewards under KERA, its state evaluation scores did go up.

Serving the needs of this community means having such special schools as the James E. Biggs Early Childhood Education Center and the Covington Adult High School for adult students returning to complete their education. Per-pupil spending is $4,552. The student/teacher ratio is 15 to 1, daily attendance is 93.5 percent and the dropout rate is 5 percent.

Dayton Independent Schools
200 Clay St., Dayton, Ky.
• (606) 491-6565

The Dayton school district serves 1,400 students with an elementary and a high school. Per-pupil spending is $4,508. The student/teacher ratio is 14 to 1, daily attendance is 94 percent and the dropout rate is 1.5 percent.

Erlanger-Elsmere Independent Schools
500 Graves Ave., Erlanger, Ky.
• (606) 727-2009

This 2,200-student district puts the emphasis on community schools. The four elementary schools are small and within walking distance for the children they serve. This largely blue-collar district also has one middle school and one high school — Lloyd. Per-pupil spending is $4,145. The student/teacher ratio is 15 to 1, daily attendance is 95 percent and the dropout rate is 1.3 percent.

Fort Thomas Independent Schools
2356 Memorial Pkwy., Fort Thomas, Ky.
• (606) 781-3333

Fort Thomas' 2,400-student district has the parental involvement and high expectations that go along with one of Northern Kentucky's most upscale communities. Each classroom in the three elementary schools, one middle school and one high school (with more schools to come soon, district officials promise) has at least a half-dozen computers. Per-pupil spending is $4,072. The student/teacher ratio is 18.5 to 1, daily attendance is 95 percent and the dropout rate is 1 percent.

Kenton County Schools
20 Kenton Lands Rd., Erlanger, Ky.
• (606) 344-8888

With more than 12,100 students, this is one of Northern Kentucky's largest school districts. It has an open enrollment policy, allowing students to enroll in district schools outside their neighborhoods. Those schools include 12 elementary schools, three junior highs and three high schools — Dixie Heights, Scott and Simon Kenton.

This district is growing and faces a tightening budget, although neither the growth nor the budget woes has been as pronounced as in Boone County. The district is in the midst of a $70 million expansion program for which no new taxes have been sought. A new elementary and middle school complex should be completed some time in 1998.

The district has been open to experimentation, with recently added alternative, after school and international baccalaureate programs. The National Alliance of Restructuring Education has two experimental programs in the district. Per-pupil spending is $4,550. The student/teacher ratio is 18.5 to 1, daily attendance is 95 percent and the dropout rate is 2.9 percent.

Ludlow Independent Schools
525 Elm St., Ludlow, Ky.
• (606) 261-8210

This 1,100-student urban river-town district has one elementary, one junior high and one high school. Per-pupil spending is $3,971. The student/teacher ratio is 18 to 1, daily attendance is 95 percent and the dropout rate is under 1 percent.

Newport Independent Schools
Eighth and Washington Sts., Newport, Ky. • (606) 292-3004

Newport's 3,000-student district serves an urban community with three elementary, one junior high, one high school and special schools that include a vocational school and an adult learning center. Seventy percent of the district's students are classified as at-risk, so this district has its work cut out. Special programs to address these needs include an alternative high school, mentoring and a day-treatment drug program. Per-pupil spending is $4,527. The student/teacher ratio is 14 to 1, daily attendance is 93 percent and the dropout rate is 8.5 percent.

Private Schools

Many of the schools listed here have waiting lists and competitive entrance requirements. Kicking and screaming, the Ohio schools were forced to take the state proficiency tests. Scores for individual schools are not released by the Ohio Department of Education but, overall, private schools in Ohio posted these results in 1998: 98 percent of private school 9th graders passed the writing section, 99 percent passed the reading section, 93 percent passed the math section, 95 percent passed the citizenship section, and 94 percent passed the science section.

Some private schools are all male or all female. We indicate in the listing when this is the case.

Ohio

Adath Israel School
3201 E. Galbraith Rd., Amberley Village • 792-5082

Adath Israel is a conservative Jewish religious school associated with Adath Israel Synagogue. It serves 180 students from preschool to 7th grade. Although a majority of the students are of the conservative Jewish faith, there is some mixture of reform and orthodox in the student body according to school officials.

Archdiocese of Cincinnati
100 E. Eighth St. • 421-3131

The Archdiocese runs the largest school system of any kind in Greater Cincinnati, the ninth-largest system of Catholic schools in the United States and one of the few parochial systems nationwide that is still growing (the addition of a 13th high school is a distinct possibility). Interestingly, at least 10 percent of its students are not Catholic.

The Archdiocese (an exception to the above statement about private schools not re-

leasing test scores) reported in 1998 that 96 percent of its 9th graders passed the writing section, 97 percent passed the reading section, 83 percent passed the math section, 90 percent passed the citizenship section, and 84 percent passed the science section.

The district operates 72 elementary schools and 12 high schools. We've listed the high schools here.

Badin High School, 517 New London Road, Hamilton

Elder High School, 3900 Vincent Avenue (male)

Fenwick High School, 3800 Center Road, Middletown

LaSalle High School, 3091 North Bend Road, Monfort Heights (male)

McAuley High School, 6000 Oakwood Avenue, College Hill (female)

McNicholas High School, 6536 Beechmont Avenue, Mount Washington

Moeller High School, 9001 Montgomery Road, Kenwood (male)

Mother of Mercy High School, 3036 Werk Road, Westwood (female)

Mount Notre Dame High School, 711 E. Columbia Avenue (female)

Purcell Marian High School, 2935 Hackberry Street, East Walnut Hills

Roger Bacon High School, 4320 Vine Street, St. Bernard

Seton High School, Glenway & Beech, Price Hill (female)

Cincinnati Christian Schools
7350 Dixie Hwy., Fairfield • 874-8500

This independent, nondenominational Christian school was formerly associated with, and is still next to, the Tri-County Assembly of God Church in Fairfield. The 300-student school covers kindergarten through 12th grade with a Bible-based curriculum.

Cincinnati Country Day School
6905 Given Rd., Indian Hill • 561-7298

One of the most expensive and most prestigious private schools in Greater Cincinnati, this 860-student school has classes for early childhood classes through high school. Admission is competitive except for the developmental preschool program. Tuition assistance and scholarships are available.

Recreational opportunities abound even for the youngest Cincinnatians.

Cincinnati Hills Christian Academy
11300 Snider Rd., Symmes • 247-0900

The Academy is an increasingly popular nondenominational Christian school with 900 students in kindergarten through 12th grade. Scripture is integrated into the curriculum through classwork and weekly religion classes. Advanced-placement courses are available in English, chemistry and biology. The first class of seniors graduated in 1995. New facilities include a fine arts center and tennis complex. The school was among six in the area honored by the U.S. Department of Education's Blue Ribbon Recognition Program in 1997.

Cincinnati Waldorf School
745 Derby Ave. • 541-0220

Emphasizing multisensory learning and movement activities in all subject areas, this is one of 500 Waldorf schools in the United States and the only one in Greater Cincinnati. Fine arts programs are integrated throughout the curriculum. The school has 100 students in preschool through the 4th grade.

Holy Trinity Episcopal School
7190 Euclid Rd., Madeira • 984-8400

This small (20 students) Episcopal school specializes in education for students with diagnosed neurological disorders, particularly ADD/hyperactivity disorder, in preschool through 6th grade. Individually guided education is tailored to each student's needs.

Landmark Christian School
500 Oak Rd. • 771-7050

Landmark is a Baptist school that emphasizes Bible training and personal responsibility in traditional classes. The school has 300 students in kindergarten through the 12th grade and offers intervention for at-risk students and enrichment programs for gifted students.

Marva Collins Preparatory School
7855 Dawn Rd. • 761-6609

Famous Chicago educator Marva Collins of the Westside Preparatory School was a consultant in establishing this 200-student school, which covers preschool through the 8th grade. She is not involved in running the school now, but the staff follows her philosophy that no student is a failure, and teachers use a variety of teaching styles to pique curiosity.

Montessori Schools

Montessori schools, which stress individually guided instruction through discovery, are very popular for preschool and primary education in Greater Cincinnati. Below are three of the more popular programs. In addition, some magnet elementary schools in the Cincinnati public school system offer Montessori programs.

Mercy Montessori Center, 2335 Grandview Avenue, 221-4999

The New School, 3 Burton Woods Lane, 281-7999

Xavier University Montessori Lab, 3800 Victory Parkway, 745-3521. Xavier is one of the few colleges in the country to offer a master's degree in Montessori education, and this is the lab school that helps train

Montessori educators. The lab school has a long waiting list.

Regional Institute for Torah and Secular Studies
7617 Reading Rd., Reading • 761-0995

This is the region's only Jewish girls school, and the high school draws boarding students from outside the area as well. The Judaic curriculum is conducted in Hebrew. The school, which has about 50 students, offers two years of calculus and four other advanced-placement courses.

St. Rita School for the Deaf
1720 Glendale-Milford Rd., Evendale • 771-7600

St. Rita serves 165 students from preschool through 12th grade, providing comprehensive education from birth on for deaf students. It's the nation's only privately funded school for the deaf. Small classes combined with one-on-one instruction permit highly individualized instruction. The school uses a total communication approach that includes sign language, lip reading, speech and auditory enhancement. Tuition is on a sliding scale. St. Rita's annual summer festival is perhaps the city's best-known fund-raiser, attracting thousands.

St. Ursula Academy
1339 E. McMillan St. • 961-3410

St. Ursula's is an independent female Catholic school, with 500-plus students in grades 9 through 12. It places strong emphasis on community service and preparation for college.

St. Xavier High School
600 North Bend Rd. • 761-7600

This all-male Jesuit school, known as "St. X" by most Cincinnatians, is the city's oldest and largest private school in addition to being one of its most prestigious. Classroom instruc-

---

INSIDERS' TIP

The hottest ticket in town, at least when it comes to school programs, is the Walnut Hills Alumni Lecture Series. And why not? The spring series ($50 for four lectures) highlights such big-name Walnut Hills alumni as TV producer Douglas Cramer (*The Love Boat* and *Dynasty*) and yippie Jerry Rubin.

tion for its 1,400 students remains traditional, but the school uses interdisciplinary offerings and team teaching. Recently updated facilities include a new computer center, remodeled library and 10 new classrooms.

Schilling School for Gifted Children
7200 School Rd. • 489-3999

Schilling is a new school and claims to be the only one in Ohio serving gifted children (defined by the admission requirement of an IQ of 130 or higher). Current classes include K-9, and the school expects to expand to 12th grade by 2001. School officials stress multi-age grouping and individualized instruction for the approximately 60 students. Of 11 faculty members, seven have at least a master's degree.

The Seven Hills School
5400 Red Bank Rd. • 271-9027

Insiders may jokingly call this the "Seven Bills School," but it's actually only the third-most expensive private school in Greater Cincinnati. The 970-student school consists of preschool through 12th grade. About 15 percent of its student body receives financial aid. The school boasts having students from 60 Cincinnati ZIP codes. The emphasis is naturally on college prep, with special concentration on fine and performing arts and global education.

The Springer School
2121 Madison Rd. • 871-6080

Springer has 200 students in grades 1 through 8 and provides a comprehensive program for children with learning disabilities who nonetheless show above-average potential. Customized programs include work with a variety of professionals. This is the most expensive private school in Greater Cincinnati, but financial aid and grants are available, and most children return to traditional classrooms in community schools after three years.

Summit Country Day School
2161 Grandin Rd. • 871-4700

This 1,000-student school is another of the area's most prestigious private schools and has the only independent Catholic K-12 program in the city. The high school has a com-

prehensive array of advanced-placement programs. Foreign language instruction begins in the Montessori kindergarten and continues through grade 12.

Ursuline Academy of Cincinnati
5535 Pfeiffer Rd. • 791-5791

Ursuline is the girls' equivalent of St. X. This 609-student college-preparatory independent Catholic high school places emphasis on leadership and decision making. The school has been honored for excellence by the U.S. Department of Education.

Yavneh Day School
8401 Montgomery Rd., Kenwood • 984-3770

With a student body of 400, preschool to 8th grade, Yavneh serves conservative, reform, orthodox and nonaffiliated Jewish students. The school stresses an academic program of general education and Judaic studies.

Kentucky

Diocese of Covington
947 Donaldson Hwy., Covington, Ky. • (606) 283-6230

The Covington diocese operates a system with 11,500 students in 31 elementary and 10 secondary schools. Value-based education, with an emphasis on traditional instruction along with technology and cooperative learning, are hallmarks.

Covington Latin School
21 E. 11th St., Covington, Ky. • (606) 291-7044

This is a unique college prep program for academically talented students, who usually enter in the 6th or 7th grade and graduate by age 16. The program compresses junior and senior high into four years. Begun as a boys school in 1923, it now has a coed enrollment of about 200 students.

Villa Madonna Academy
2500 Amsterdam Rd., Villa Hills, Ky. • (606) 331-6333

A relatively small school with 130 students, this 90-year-old college prep program for grades 1 through 12 is nonetheless notable for being run by Benedictine sisters, known for the quality of their teaching, and for its academic consistency. Tradition doesn't necessarily mean old-fashioned: The nuns' computer curriculum, with Internet access for all, is nationally recognized.

Child Care

Finding reliable, competent child care in any city is a challenge. In Greater Cincinnati, that challenge is made all the more formidable by a confluence of factors beyond the control of the average parent. The U.S. Census reports that 45,552 Greater Cincinnati children under the age of 6 live in homes where both parents (or the only parent) works. Yet in the entire Tri-state, there are only about 45,000 available slots for children in day-care settings. In other words, this is a tight market for finding available child-care openings. And it's going to get tighter.

In a national survey published in *Working Mother* magazine in 1997, day cares in Ohio, Kentucky and Indiana all won lackluster ratings — Ohio the lowest of all. Furthermore, a 1997 day-care study shows area child-care workers can only expect to earn $7.18 an hour before taxes — about what a McDonald's fry chef earns here on average.

Child-care centers must be licensed by the state in Ohio, Kentucky and Indiana. That said, in Ohio especially, the loopholes are infamous. And since the far majority of the area's day-care centers are found on the Ohio side (Hamilton County alone has about 1,300 child-care centers and home providers, with slots for 18,000 children and 2,000 infants), this is a problem worth addressing in some depth. Understand that Ohio is still in the midst of the Republican revolution that swept the nation a few years back. Conservative legislators and the governor are cutting, or at least certainly not increasing, funds for children's services. And services such as inspections of day-care facilities are a "luxury" the administration can't afford. Yes, the Ohio Department of Human Services is required by state law to inspect all day-care centers in Greater Cincinnati and

FYI

Unless otherwise noted, the area code for all phone numbers listed in this guide is 513.

elsewhere twice a year. At least one of those two inspections must be unannounced. However, a recent study published in the *Enquirer* showed numerous centers do not receive the two inspections and that, indeed, the state keeps no record of how often this requirement is met.

The Department of Human Services, for its part, counters that it is struggling to keep up with inspecting a burgeoning number of day-care centers (4,000 in Ohio, as opposed to 3,000 just a decade ago) with no increase in its staff of 38 inspectors statewide. Department officials claim the lack of inspections doesn't affect safety although, mystifyingly, no Ohio state office is actually required to keep statistics on accidents and deaths in child-care centers.

Ohio is currently one of six remaining states that does not regulate home-based day care (as long as it involves six children or less). The six-pack rule effectively means the vast majority of the state's home day-care providers don't have to meet any requirement, regulation or inspection — not even a Health Department checkup on kitchen and sanitary facilities.

The only time home care is regulated is if the home is "certified" — which it must be if the care is subsidized by a state or federal program — or licensed, a requirement only if seven or more children are watched at one time. Action for Children, a nonprofit watchdog organization, estimates that three-fourths of children in home-based day care here are under unregulated care.

The demand for child care in the region is expected to increase even more as more single parents move into the workplace. And that will certainly happen under the Welfare Reform Law that took effect in late 1997. How many families are we talking about? More than 47,000 Tri-state children currently live in homes where one or both parents are on welfare. What happens next, and the impacts on the quality and availability of child care in the area, is an open question. Certainly, as the laws of supply and demand take hold, costs will rise. (Right now, child care in Greater Cincinnati runs about $123 on average per week for infants, $100 for toddlers, $89 for preschoolers and $80 for school-age children.)

In Kentucky, as a result of the welfare reform legislation and its looming consequences, the state is actively contracting with churches and other religious organizations to operate child-care facilities. Kentucky city, county and state governments can funnel tax money to nonprofit corporations set up by churches as long as the funds are used for child care and other nonreligious purposes. The upshot: If you're looking for child care in Kentucky, consider calling local churches. You do not have to become a member of the church or denomination in order to have equal access to these state-funded care centers.

For live-in nannies or au pair options, consider contacting such firms as **Child Care Professionals,** 561-4810, or the Cincinnati office of **Au Pair in America,** 221-7248.

Baby-sitting services are few and far between, with the Yellow Pages listings being largely devoted to pet sitters. Among the few sitters of the human variety are **Professional Sitting Services,** (606) 291-0941, and **Jack & Jill Babysitter Service,** 731-5261. Your best bet may be to canvass your own neighborhood or post notices at local groceries, schools and churches. Also consult your local weekly's classified advertising section, as many teens in need of extra cash advertise there.

There are a number of organizations and support groups for parents in Greater Cincinnati. MOMS (Moms Offering Moms Support) Club, 459-8855, organizes playgroups and lunch outings for at-home moms and their kids. Support for Single Parents, 231-6630, runs weekly support groups for moms or dads on their own. Parents Anonymous, 961-8004, offers weekly support groups for moms and dads struggling with parenting issues. The Mothers of Twins and More Club, 858-2709, aids moms of multiples.

And Cincinnati has a full complement of youth organizations to help keep your kids busy after school, in the evenings or on weekends. They include the Boy Scouts, 961-2336; Girl Scouts, 489-1025; Campfire, 242-0584; and the Boy's/Girl's Club, 421-8909. It's also worth contacting Big Brother/Big Sister, 421-4120, for details on its mentoring program.

That's the overview of child care in Greater Cincinnati. Here are some nuts and bolts about resources to locate quality child-care providers. The very first phone call you make should be to **Comprehensive Community Child Care,** better known in the area as the 4Cs, 221-0033. Funded by local businesses and the United Way, the 4Cs assists families on both sides of the Ohio River in finding child care options. In its 26th year of operation, the agency will help you sift through the possibilities of au pairs, home providers and day-care centers. The agency refers to 398 area centers, 665 home providers, 622 preschools and 582 after-school programs. The 4Cs has also launched a Quantum Leap Campaign, with a goal of helping create and accredit 75 new day-care centers by the year 2000 as well as adding 200 home providers to its accredited registry.

Some of the larger chain care centers in the area include **Children's World Learning Centers, Kinder Kare Learning Centers, Biederman Education Centers, Bright Horizons, The Goddard Schools, Youthland Academy** and **Little Red School Houses.** You can find a complete listing of commercial ventures under "Child Care Centers" in the Yellow Pages. The *Cincinnati Business Courier* publishes an annual listing of the largest child-care centers in the area in their annual list directories.

In Ohio as well as Kentucky, church-run day nurseries and preschools are another option. The long lines of parents who traditionally wait to sign up for such programs are a solid indication that the child care programs run by the region's churches are equal or sometimes superior to commercial ventures. Check under "Churches" in the Yellow Pages.

The **YMCA of Greater Cincinnati** is the largest day-care provider in the region, operating 85 care centers of both sides of the Ohio River for kids 2 months through 12 years of age, and is well worth a phone call. (See our Parks and Recreation chapter for the number of your nearest Y.)

Many parents turn to Montessori schools for their infants, toddlers and preschoolers. There are dozens in the area, though you should know that only a select few such as **The Children's Center,** 891-6665, the **Springs East Montessori School,** 793-7877, and **Terry's Montessori School,** 821-7227, accept infants. For a comprehensive list of Montessori schools and the age groups they encompass, contact the **Cincinnati Montessori Society** at 631-1602.

A number of public and private schools offer extended day care as part of their curriculum. Keep in mind, however, that a major shift in how Ohio's schools are funded is on the horizon (as we noted in the introduction to this chapter), and these latchkey programs may be among the first to feel the ax in the 1998-99 school year. That said, Ohio school districts currently offering extended care include: Cincinnati Public Schools, Deer Park, Fairfield, Finneytown, Indian Hill, Lockland, Mariemont, Milford, Mount Healthy, Northwest, Norwood, Oak Hills, Princeton, Reading, St. Bernard, Sycamore and Wyoming. In Kentucky, school districts offering latchkey programs include Beechwood, Bellevue, Boone, Campbell, Covington, Erlanger, Fort Thomas, Kenton and Ludlow.

In addition to public schools, many private schools offer after-school care programs. They include Cincinnati Country Day, Cincinnati Hills Christian Academy, Cincinnati Waldorf School, St. Ursula Villa, The Seven Hills School, Summit Country Day and Villa Madonna Academy, as well as many Catholic Archdiocese grade schools. (See our Schools listings earlier in the chapter for contact numbers for all these district, diocesan and private schools.)

During the summer, of course, many of these schools are closed. Consider options such as the **Cincinnati Recreation Commission,** 352-4000, which will care for the children of working parents all day during the summer. The children must be between the ages of 6 and 12. The care takes place in the community recreation center nearest the child's school. Other summer options include the area's many day camps, many run by the Cincinnati Park Board (including Nature Camp, Preschool Discovery Morning and Adventure Camp), the Hamilton County Park District, the Cincinnati Nature Center, and any number run by the YMCA. (See our Parks and Recreation chapter for contact numbers for the various park boards and districts as well as Ys.)

Your best summer resource may well be *All About Kids*, a free monthly magazine avail-

able in most grocery stores. Its March issue each year is devoted largely to a comprehensive and up-to-date "Summer Camp Directory," which includes most day, overnight, sports, special needs and academic camps as well as art, music and dance camps.

If you're moving to town to work for a major corporation, you may be in luck. Companies such as Procter & Gamble, Chiquita and Kroger have taken the lead in making sure their employees' children are properly looked after. And six area employers — AT&T, Deloitte & Touche, GE Capital Services, IBM, Citicorp and Ethicon Endo-Surgery Inc. — have pooled $640,000 to improve day-care options for their workforces, believing that worry-free employees are productive employees. If you're not working for one of the Fortune 500 companies, you still ought to inquire with your firm's human resources director about any company child-care plans (or subsidies) that might exist.

In addition to Fortune 500 firms, most area hospitals, universities and the locals arms of federal agencies such as the Internal Revenue Service offer their employees some kind of onsite center or other resource. United Way also funds a number of day-care centers, including Fairmount Day Care Center, Madisonville Day Care Center, Wesley Child Care/Infant Toddler Center and New Beginnings Child Care Inc. The United Way requires all centers it funds to be accredited by the 4Cs.

Even if you find a satisfactory day-care or home-care situation, you child will inevitably get sick. A number of agencies in Greater Cincinnati will care for a moderately sick child while the parent is at work. **AM & PM Health Care,** 941-2663, **American Nursing Care,** 731-4600, and **Parkes Cares for Kids,** 771-2600, will care for mildly ill children. For more serious illnesses, consider contacting your local hospital. **St. Luke Hospital,** in Fort Thomas, Kentucky, 572-3610, for instance, has a program in which nurses will care (during the daytime only) for kids affected by such contagious disease as strep or measles. **Bethesda Oak Hospital**'s program, 569-5400, even allows for nurses to care for sick children in the child's own home.

Here are some practical first steps you can

take as you actually begin to weigh the value of one day-care center against another. State law in both Ohio and Kentucky does require that inspection reports be posted in visible locations at day-care centers for parents to see. You can also write the agency and obtain a report of any given day-care center. In Ohio, write the Ohio Department of Human Services, 65 E. State St., Columbus, Ohio 43215. In Kentucky, contact the Cabinet for Human Resources, Office of the Inspector General/Division of Licensing and Regulations, 275 E. Main St., Frankfort, Ky. 40621. Neither state agency encourages telephone queries.

As you consider day-care centers, be aware that in addition to state and 4Cs accreditation, about 10 percent of local child-care centers go to the trouble of becoming accredited by the National Association for the Education of Young Children, an important distinction.

Knowing a day care is licensed or accredited is all well and good, but it doesn't absolve you of the need to check out the child-care provider yourself. The best way to shop for child care is to call ahead to arrange for a visit the first time, then make a second visit unannounced. Any center or provider that has a problem with unannounced visits is probably one to avoid. On any visit, watch how staff members speak to the children; see if they are more concerned with a smudged wall than with comforting an unhappy child. Are emergency fire procedures in place? Find out which is the nearest hospital and the neighborhood's average 911 response time (this is public information published regularly in the local papaers).

Ask the center about its ratio of child-care workers to the number of children in a class. Find out how, and how often, staff will formally communicate to you (either by oral or written report) on your child's socialization success and other benchmarks.

Check with the Cincinnati Better Business Bureau for a record of complaints. Also check the public library's newspaper database to see if favorable, or unfavorable, stories have appeared about a child care center you are considering.

Finally, be aware that "day care" and "preschool," in this region at least, are nowhere near the same thing. A private day-care center, even one that claims to offer some kind of "preschool" program, doesn't have to conform to any state educational requirements. If you want your child to attend a licensed, legitimate preschool, make sure it's one accredited by the state Department of Education.

Good luck. And may the 4Cs be with you.

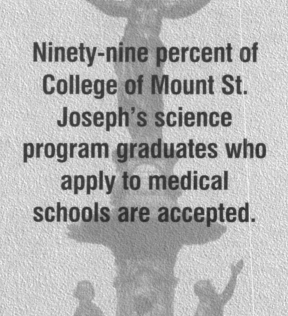

Ninety-nine percent of College of Mount St. Joseph's science program graduates who apply to medical schools are accepted.

Higher Education

The largest employer in Cincinnati isn't Procter & Gamble or Kroger or even Chiquita Banana. It's the University of Cincinnati, and that fact alone says volumes about how vital higher education has become in the mindset of Greater Cincinnati. The area offers everything from a huge state institution to a midsize Jesuit university to a dozen smaller colleges, both public and private. You can choose from a full range of campuses: urban, suburban, even rural. And the quality and breadth of majors and academic study paths are as diverse as the student populations themselves.

Xavier University and the College of Mount St. Joseph, in particular, are notable academic institutions. Both were recently singled out in *U.S. News & World Report*'s "America's Best Colleges." The schools ranked 8th and 12th respectively among 123 Midwestern colleges and universities. In the academic reputation category, Xavier tied for third best in the Midwest, while the Mount (as it's known locally) scored fourth in the region for "best college value" (where students get the most value for their money). Miami University of Ohio, meanwhile, was named fifth "most efficient" university in the country, meaning it offers high academic quality at a relatively low cost.

No discussion of higher education in Cincinnati can go very far without delving into what the University of Cincinnati — the second largest educational institution in Ohio — has to offer. And that's a lot. For years, UC was stuck with the reputation of being a mediocre state school with a pretty darned good basketball team. Coach Bob Huggins' Bearcats still stand tall in the national rankings, but now so do the academic programs. UC continues to lead as a nationwide pioneer in cooperative education, giving students valuable on-the-job training and contacts while they're still in school. And now the campus is going high tech; engineering students, for instance, participate in interactive lectures with NASA researchers thousands of miles away.

Meanwhile, the research arm of the university continues to, if you'll pardon the expression, expand. Thanks to its budding Center for Obesity and Nutrition Research (funded by $1 million annually in federal grants), UC recently assembled a star team of scientists who may transform "America's 8th fattest city" into a national center for obesity research.

You should know, however, that the state university system is in the midst of a revolution instigated by Ohio Gov. George Voinovich's demand "to work harder and smarter and do more with less." Public higher education has borne 40 percent of the total state budget cuts made by Voinovich, some $270 million. The state still spends $2 billion a year on higher education, but it wants even less waste and greater efficiency. UC, for its part, is finding new sources of income, including patents. It's now 25th among universities in the nation in terms of patent and licensing income on inventions by its faculty.

All this said about budget cuts, the State of Ohio offers many economic incentives for students to study here rather than fleeing to one of the coasts. You can purchase tomorrow's tuition at today's rates under Ohio's Prepaid Tuition Program. Created by an act of the state legislature a few years back, it allows you to prepay your child's 2018 tuition, for instance, in 1998. Tax-free "tuition units" are $43 each, with 100 units buying a full year at any Ohio public university, no matter what it may actually cost in 2018. (For details, call 1-800-AFFORDIT.) Another incentive: Ohio high school students, even if they don't plan to attend one of the local colleges after graduation, are permitted to take college courses free during their junior or senior years and receive dual high school and college credit. (See our Schools and Child Care chapter for more information.)

The area's state schools also offer some special bargains, one being the reciprocity agreement between UC, Cincinnati State Technical and Community College and Northern Kentucky University that allows Ohio residents in Hamilton, Butler, Warren, Clermont and Brown counties to attend Northern Kentucky at Kentucky-resident rates and Northern Kentucky residents to attend UC or Cincinnati State at Ohio-resident rates. To qualify, Ohio students must complete associate's degree programs in their home state, then transfer. (Excluded from the reciprocity deal are electronics, engineering technology, industrial technology-construction, manufacturing engineering technology, nursing, and social work majors.) Students from southeastern Indiana may also qualify for in-state resident rates at these Ohio and Kentucky institutions. Admissions offices can provide more details.

Branch campuses of UC and Miami offer lower tuition rates than the main campuses, and they provide classes that in most cases transfer to four-year degrees at the main campuses. Cost per quarterly credit hour at UC's Clermont College is less than 80 percent of the cost at the main campus, and the cost at UC's Raymond Walters campus in Blue Ash is less than 90 percent. At Miami's Middletown and Hamilton branch campuses, annual undergraduate tuition is about a third lower than at the main campus in Oxford. All Miami branch campus credits transfer to the main campus, but you need to check the course listings for UC's branch campuses to see which credits will transfer there.

A further advantage if you choose to study here: Cincinnati's institutes of higher learning do cooperate with each other. The Greater Cincinnati Consortium of Colleges and Universities allows students at the 13 member private and public schools to take courses at any of the other schools if they're not offered at their home institutions. Consortium members include the Art Academy of Cincinnati, Athenaeum of Ohio, Cincinnati Bible College & Seminary, Cincinnati State, Chatfield College, College of Mount St. Joseph, Hebrew Union College/Jewish

FYI

Unless otherwise noted, the area code for all phone numbers listed in this guide is 513.

Institute of Religion, Miami University, Northern Kentucky University, Thomas More University, University of Cincinnati, Wilmington College and Xavier University.

Greater Cincinnati colleges are also long on convenience. Many of them offer evening and weekend programs. Chatfield College and the Cincinnati branches of Wilmington College have centered their entire programs around working adults.

Chances are you can study at a Cincinnati university without spending much on gas either. Even the campuses of UC have branches at some area high schools and off-site office centers, including a new one in Lebanon. Chatfield College offers classes in Lower Price Hill. And UC, Xavier University and Mount St. Joseph also offer classes at the Downtown University Center, 617 Vine Street, 241-7996.

Everyone, in fact, seems to be branching out. The newest and fastest-growing satellite campuses can be found on the far East Side, and that's not surprising, since the East Side — along with the northern suburbs — boasts some of the fastest-growing residential communities in the Tri-state. Wilmington College just added an East Side branch in the Eastgate Mall area near Anderson, for instance. And Clermont College in Batavia, a satellite of UC, just launched a massive expansion program with an eye toward the next millennium. Enrollment at Clermont, already up 40 percent since 1989, is sparking construction of a $10 million complex housing 43,000 square feet of additional classroom space.

The listings in this chapter cover the major traditional colleges in the area along with some alternatives to traditional colleges — among them, Cincinnati State, Communiversity and The Union Institute, perhaps the nation's most innovative alternative education institution. You'll also find a section on continuing adult education.

The area also offers numerous trade and technical schools that offer associate or certificate programs in a bewildering variety of specialties. Listings for these can be found under the Schools heading in the Yellow Pages.

In short, whatever your educational need,

whatever your timeframe and financial constraints, you'll find the solution at one of Greater Cincinnati's numerous houses of higher education. Read on.

Colleges and Universities

Art Academy of Cincinnati
1125 St. Gregory St. • 721-5205

Located at the Cincinnati Museum of Art in Eden Park, the Art Academy of Cincinnati is one of five museum schools in the United States (the academy actually predates the museum). It was founded in 1869 as the McMicken School of Art, an early department of what would become the University of Cincinnati in 1873. But the founders felt the art school should be separate from the university and affiliated with the art museum when the museum opened in 1885. The academy gained use of the old Mount Adams Public School on nearby St. Gregory Street in 1979, and classes are now held at both locations.

The Art Academy offers associate's and bachelor's degrees in design and fine arts and is the only college offering the Bachelor of Fine Arts degree in the area. Of its roughly 200 students, more than 80 percent attend full time.

The Academy is a member of the Alliance of Independent Colleges of Art and Design, which includes such prestigious schools as the museum schools in Washington, Chicago and Boston, the Rhode Island School of Design and the School of the Visual Arts in New York. Academy students are eligible to spend a semester in a similar program at other member schools for credit.

Athenaeum of Ohio/Mount St. Mary's Seminary
6616 Beechmont Ave. • 231-2223

The Athenaeum of Ohio is an accredited center of education providing programs of preparation for and development in ministry within the Roman Catholic tradition. It was inaugurated in 1829 by the first bishop of Cincinnati (along with Xavier University, which later split to form its own Jesuit-run campus).

The Athenaeum is authorized by the Ohio Board of Regents to offer master's degrees in divinity, theology, biblical studies, religion and pastoral counseling. It also offers certificates in lay ministry. About 70 percent of its more than 200 students attend full time.

The mission of Mount St. Mary's Seminary of the West is to prepare candidates for the ministry as ordained presbyters in the Roman Catholic church.

Chatfield College
20918 Ohio Hwy. 251, St. Martin • 875-3344

The mission of Chatfield College is to make a liberal arts education available to people who might never be able to attend college if Chatfield did not exist. Most of the 270 students, whose average age is 31, are first-generation college students from Cincinnati and Appalachian counties east of the city. The private three-year college offers the Associate of Arts degree with concentrations in business, health and human services, child development, commercial art and liberal arts. In addition to classes at its main campus, Chatfield offers four courses each semester at Lower Price Hill Community School, 2104 St. Michael Street, 244-2214.

The college has an open admissions policy, accepting any student who has a high school or college transcript or a GED certificate. Classes usually meet only once a week during daytime or evening hours to accommodate work schedules. The academic year includes two 15-week semesters during fall and spring and a shorter summer session. Yearly tuition at this private school is less than that at UC or Miami.

Cincinnati Bible College & Seminary
2700 Glenway Ave. • 244-8100

Cincinnati Bible College & Seminary prepares students who will take full-time ministries within their local churches or who want ministry-related careers or want to be volunteer leaders in their churches. The private college, supported by Christian churches and Churches of Christ, was created in 1924 by the merger of institutions in Cincinnati and Louisville, Kentucky.

Situated on the highest hilltop overlooking downtown Cincinnati, the 40-acre campus includes a mix of modern buildings and traditional structures from the 1870s. Faculty members have studied at more than 80 universities, and more than 60 percent have or are working toward doctorates. Of the nearly 900 students, two-thirds attend full time.

The college offers associate's, bachelor's and master's degrees. Programs include Bible, general studies and church music, plus emphases on youth ministry, ministry to the deaf, early childhood education, teacher education, music education, journalism and psychology. This is another private school with budget-minded tuition, which runs about $1,000 less than the state universities in Ohio.

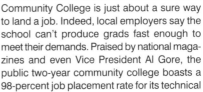

www.insiders.com

See this and many other **Insiders' Guide®** destinations online — in their entirety.

Visit us today!

Cincinnati College of Mortuary Science
3860 Pacific Ave. • 761-2020

Housed in the Cohen Center on the campus of Xavier University but not affiliated with Xavier, the Cincinnati College of Mortuary Science is the oldest college of mortuary education in the United States. It was founded in 1882 by Joseph H. Clarke and has grown to have an international reputation. CCMS is accredited by the Ohio Board of Regents and is authorized to offer instruction leading to the Bachelor of Mortuary Science and the Associate of Applied Science degrees.

The college's approximately 160 students come from 30 states and several foreign countries. After graduation, many pursue employment as funeral directors and embalmers, but others take jobs in such areas as pathology, anatomy, forensics, grief counseling and mortuary science education.

Cincinnati State Technical and Community College
3520 Central Pkwy. • 569-1500

Attending Cincinnati State Technical and Community College is just about a sure way to land a job. Indeed, local employers say the school can't produce grads fast enough to meet their demands. Praised by national magazines and even Vice President Al Gore, the public two-year community college boasts a 98-percent job placement rate for its technical graduates in fields ranging from laser electro-optics and civil engineering to health care and aviation maintenance.

Cincinnati State, formerly known as Cincinnati Technical College, offers a wide range of associate's degrees and an extensive cooperative education program. Among the most popular degrees are dental hygiene and environmental technology. Of the college's more than 5,700 students, more than 60 percent attend part time.

College of Mount St. Joseph
5701 Delhi Rd. • 244-4400

This coeducational Catholic liberal arts college was founded in 1920 by the Sisters of Charity of Cincinnati. "The Mount," as it's known by many Cincinnatians, offers career-oriented programs for traditional and nontraditional students in day, evening and weekend schedules. About half of the college's nearly 2,300 students are nontraditional, meaning they are older than 23 and more than five years out of high school. More than half attend part time and more than two-thirds are women. The percentage of freshmen who graduate in five years is 66 percent, well above the national average of 48 percent.

Students may choose from more than 13 associate's degrees, 42 bachelor's degrees, two master's degrees, eight pre-professional programs and several certificate programs. Ninety-nine percent of science program graduates who apply to medical schools are accepted. Physical therapy is another rapidly

INSIDERS' TIP

You can purchase tomorrow's tuition at today's rates under the state of Ohio's Prepaid Tuition Program. Created by an act of legislature, it allows you to prepay your child's 2018 tuition, for instance, in 1998.

Photo: Miami University

Miami University students stroll by academic buildings on this historic campus.

growing major at the college. And cooperative education programs are available to full-time students in all majors.

The college offers several outreach programs. Project EXCEL provides support services to help students with learning disabilities succeed at the college. Project SCOPE is a summer program of college orientation and enrichment for black high school students. The college also offers a summer residency program for high school women to introduce them to career opportunities in math and sciences and prepare them for college study in these fields.

The College of Mount St. Joseph is about 7 miles southwest of downtown Cincinnati on a 325-acre site overlooking the Ohio River and across from the Greater Cincinnati/Northern Kentucky International Airport. A $4.5 million student center is now under construction as part of a campus-wide retrofit and renovation.

Communiversity
Class locations vary • 556-6932

Communiversity is the region's most ambitious alternative education program, coordinated by UC's Department of Continuing Education. It's where "community meets university" through a variety of noncredit classes meeting at such far-flung locations as the Cincinnati Observatory, area gardens and parks, art galleries, downtown stock brokerages, Music Hall, even Sharon Woods Golf Course. Hundreds of courses are offered each year in the broad categories of art, astronomy, business and career, communications and literature, computer skills, culinary arts, fitness, home and garden, language, law and finance, music, needle arts, sports adventures, studio arts and handicrafts, theater and dance, and travel.

Area and national experts are recruited from traditional faculty resources to teach the classes. Recent courses have included "Celtic

Art and Ornaments" (taught by the city's most notable Celtic artist, Cindy Matyi), "Writing To Sell" (taught by Tom Clark, the editor of *Writer's Digest* magazine), "Travel Agent Training," "The Joy of Soy Cooking," and "Rock Climbing for Beginners."

You must be 18 or older to attend Communiversity classes. Course costs range from $20 to $200, but most classes are free to senior citizens. The easiest way to get a listing of Communiversity courses is through local branch libraries, which display course brochures.

Hebrew Union College–Jewish Institute of Religion
3101 Clifton Ave. • 221-1875

Hebrew Union College was established in 1875 by Rabbi Isaac Wise, the founder of American Reform Judaism, as the first institution of Jewish higher education in the United States. It has been an intellectual center of Reform Judaism ever since and houses the Reform movement's library and archives collections. HUC is also a leading center for study, training, research and publication in the Bible, ancient Near Eastern languages, Hellenistic studies, rabbinics, Jewish religious thought and philosophy and modern Jewish history. The campus' Skirball Museum-Cincinnati Branch exhibits art and artifacts from 4,000 years of Judaic cultural tradition. And, not least among its roles is offering master's and doctoral programs to more than 120 students of Jewish and other faiths.

Although it is one of the area's smaller colleges, HUC has a prominent place in the history of the city and the world. During the Holocaust, HUC literally saved the lives of many European Jewish scholars who faced death in Nazi-occupied Europe by bringing them to the Cincinnati campus. It also became a successor to many of the Jewish institutes of higher learning destroyed in Europe. In 1972, HUC participated in the ordination of the first female rabbi. Today, about 50 percent of the college's rabbinic students are women. The college also trained the first Reform Rabbi in Israel, ordained in 1980, and the first Israeli woman rabbi, ordained in 1992.

Recent research milestones for HUC include using computer analysis to unlock secrets of the Dead Sea Scrolls and rescuing from near extinction the ancient Aramaic language, the original language of several books of the Bible and the Talmud and of Jesus Christ and his apostles.

The college merged in 1950 with the Jewish Institute of Religion in New York, where a second campus of the college remains. The merged school opened a Los Angeles campus in 1954 and a Jerusalem campus in 1963. In conjunction with the University of Cincinnati, HUC also operates the Center for Ethics and Contemporary Moral Problems, where international scholars research and debate ethical issues. A program analyzing ethics in the media (or the lack of them) has garnered national attention.

Ivy Tech State College
575 Main St., Lawrenceburg, Ind.
• (812) 537-4010

This Lawrenceburg campus is part of a network of 22 two-year technical colleges in Indiana that provide college-level, job-oriented training in both certificate and associate's degree programs. Of the more than 800 students on the Lawrenceburg campus, over two-thirds attend part time, and the average age is 30.

Programs include accounting, business administration, computer information and systems technology, industrial technology, manufacturing technology, medical assistant training, a practical nursing certificate, and an associate's degree in nursing.

Annual tuition is among the lowest of any community or four-year college in the state. Residents of the Kentucky counties of Boone, Carroll, Gallatin and Trimble counties also pay Indiana in-state rates.

Miami University
Roudebush Hall, Oxford • 529-1809

Founded in 1809, Miami has a reputation as one of the best deals in college education. It was recently ranked the fifth most cost-efficient university in the nation by *U.S. News & World Report* and 35th on *Money* magazine's annual list of the top 100 best college buys. Students at the Hamilton branch, 1601 Peck Boulevard, 863-8833, and the Middletown branch, 4200 E. University Boulevard, 424-4444, get an even better deal their first two years — about two-thirds of the main campus tuition rate. Enrollment is about 20,500 overall, with 2,200 on each of the branch campuses. More than 100 students also attend Miami's John E. Dolibois European Center in Luxembourg.

This state school's reputation as a "Public Ivy" has helped make it one of the most popular state campuses and the toughest to get into. The middle 50 percent of enrolled freshman ranked in the top 7 to 23 percent of their high school classes.

Renowned for its beauty, the heavily wooded main campus is dominated by the modified Georgian style popular in the 19th century. Miami's King Library, which owns more than 2 million volumes and is the largest building on campus, just underwent a $2 million renovation.

Miami places an emphasis on senior faculty teaching undergraduates, including freshman and sophomore courses. Eighty-five percent of freshman classes are taught by faculty who hold the highest degrees in their fields. More than 82 percent of all students graduate in five years and 75 percent in four, both well above national averages. More than 76 percent of graduates who apply to medical or law schools are accepted.

Among the best recognized of a comprehensive array of programs and majors are accounting, English, environmental and life sciences, history, international studies, paper science (one of eight such programs in the country) and political science. Miami's School of Interdisciplinary Studies, known as the Western College, allows students to design their own major. The program's 240 students live and study together in an historical section of the campus.

Miami is also the only primarily non-commuter campus in the Cincinnati area, so it provides the option of "going away" to college without having to go very far. About two-thirds of Miami students come from Ohio, the rest from 42 other countries and other parts of the United States. Though less than an hour's drive from downtown Cincinnati or Dayton, Miami dominates the tiny college town of Oxford — population score: students, 16,000, townies, 8,500. (One word of caution. "Tiny" isn't always synonymous with "safe"; the Oxford campus, in some years, has had as many rapes and assaults as the urban UC campus. And the university was recently taken to task by no less judicial body than the U.S. Supreme Court for obfuscating its campus crime reports.)

Northern Kentucky University
Nunn Dr., Highland Heights, Ky.
• **(606) 572-5100**

NKU offers deep-discount pricing in the Greater Cincinnati college market, with state-resident undergraduate tuition less than half that of state institutions across the river. And since many Ohioans in Greater Cincinnati can pay in-state rates at NKU, at least for their last two years of college, many do.

Of course, NKU isn't just cheap. It also offers a solid education in a wide range of programs and all classes are taught by faculty, not student assistants. Programs include aviation administration (one of the few programs in the country), education, information systems, journalism and radio/television, management, marketing, mathematics and computer science, nursing and theater. The college also offers pre-professional programs in dentistry, engineering, law, medicine, pharmacy, physical therapy, veterinary, and wildlife management in conjunction with the University of Kentucky at Lexington.

Of particular note is the communications department, which has a state-of-the-art Macintosh computer lab, an award-winning weekly paper and, most notably, WNKU-FM, a public radio affiliate where news reporting students can obtain some real-life newsroom experience.

At the graduate level, NKU offers its well-respected Salmon P. Chase College of Law, an MBA program, a combination juris doctor/MBA program, and public administration and nursing degrees.

Founded in 1968, NKU is the newest of Kentucky's eight public universities. Of NKU's 12,000 students, more than 60 percent attend full time, but the university caters to large numbers of nontraditional students from both sides of the river.

Among the wide range of intercollegiate athletic programs — baseball, softball, tennis, cross country, men's golf, men's soccer, women's volleyball and others — are NKU's

Division II men's and women's basketball programs, which compete as the Norse in the Great Lakes Valley Conference.

Thomas More College
333 Thomas More Pkwy., Crestview Hills, Ky. • (606) 341-5800

Thomas More College is a Catholic liberal arts college affiliated with the Diocese of Covington, Kentucky. The campus is just minutes from downtown Cincinnati.

Thomas More was founded in 1921 as a teacher training school for young women and became coeducational in 1945. The college offers 23 bachelor's and 23 associate's degree programs. Through the Thomas More Accelerated Degree Program (TAP), students with 60 credit hours of previous college work can obtain a bachelor's degree in business administration in 18 to 20 months by attending class one day per week and a small group meeting one day per week. More than 60 percent of the 1,200-plus students at Thomas More attend full time.

Students tend to come out of their programs well prepared, as demonstrated by one graduating class where 83 percent of the accounting graduates passed the CPA exam on their first attempt, 100 percent of the nursing graduates passed the National Council Licensure Examination and 100 percent of education majors taking the National Teachers Examination were successful.

The Union Institute
440 E. McMillan St. • 861-6400

The Union Institute is a private university that offers bachelor's degrees and Ph.D.s (but no master's degrees). Most of the 2,200 students are in their 30s and 40s, and the flexible "university without walls" offers these busy working professionals the chance to complete a degree while maintaining a career. The institute uses the word "learner" rather than student to emphasize its objective of active rather than passive learning. Tutorial-guided study options and a minimum number of residential seminar meetings throughout the year permit flexible scheduling.

Students, who are as likely to be from across the world as across town, work one-on-one with faculty, primarily by phone and computer modem. Notable grads include author Rita Mae Brown (author of *Rubyfruit Jungle*), pioneer child care author Grace Mitchell (who's also the mother of attorney F. Lee Bailey), and Clarissa Estes, author of the bestselling *Women Who Run With Wolves*.

Located in an historic Tudor building in Walnut Hills, the Union Institute was founded by 10 college presidents in 1964 as a vehicle for educational research and experimentation and has focused its efforts on programs for the highly motivated adult learner. As you might have guessed, the curriculum and students alike are nontraditional, with an emphasis on self-directed study. In fact, when *U.S. News & World Report* compiled a list of schools with the highest proportion of classes with less than 20 students, The Union Institute ranked No. 1 (99 percent of its classes), beating out Yale and Harvard.

The graduate school in Cincinnati confers only doctorate degrees. Undergraduate programs for Bachelor of Arts or Bachelor of Science degrees are also offered here and in Miami, Florida, Sacramento, California, and Los Angeles. Both graduate and undergraduate students generally enter as mature adults. Admission for graduate school, in fact, is conditional upon demonstration of extensive prior learning from work or other experience or study. A learner's committee may grant credit for that prior learning. Up to 25 percent of the total credits toward a degree may be from prior "experiential" learning.

For undergraduates, programs in 50 areas of concentration are individually designed with the help of a full-time professor who serves as academic advisor. Courses emphasize active problem solving in a seminar rather than passive note-taking in class. "Learning Agreements," which include group agreements and individual agreements, outline specific academic goals and objectives. Instead of letter grades, students receive narrative evaluations of work performed under these agreements. An undergraduate's entire degree plan culminates in completion of a senior project that

FYI

Unless otherwise noted, the area code for all phone numbers listed in this guide is 513.

can take many forms but is expected to include an oral presentation to a final review committee.

The graduate school likewise requires individually tailored plans. There are no prescribed courses. Each learner's program is developed in consultation with faculty and advisers. A faculty committee helps evaluate learners' past and present learning to ensure the work is of doctoral quality.

No credits are counted. Rather, learners move through a series of stages, with faculty members serving as facilitators. The unique program includes an entry colloquium during which learners, faculty and consultants live and work together for 10 days away from their normal routines. Over the following 24 months or longer, learners choose from among 50 seminars offered annually.

During the program, learners must spend 10 days in peer meetings and 15 days at seminars. The rest of the work is faculty-guided independent study based upon each individuals Learning Agreement. The process culminates in a Project Demonstrating Excellence, which may be a formal dissertation or take other forms.

Tuition for the private university is moderate and within 20 to 30 percent of what UC and Miami charge.

University of Cincinnati
2624 Clifton Ave. • 556-6000

The University of Cincinnati made its first major mark on U.S. education in 1906, when it created the first cooperative education program in the country through its College of Engineering. UC counts among its alumni former president and later Chief Justice William Howard Taft, author Thomas Berger and sports greats Sandy Koufax and Oscar Robertson and among its faculty Albert Sabin, developer of the oral polio vaccine, and Neil Armstrong, the first man on the moon.

In a candid assessment as part of his recent review of the university, President Joseph Steger summed up UC's contributions this way: "UC is not a renowned center of theory. We have become good at turning great ideas into something useful. . . . We're known in education for starting cooperative education. . . . We're known in music for performance.

We're known in the classics for archaeology. We're known in the arts for design. We're known in the life sciences for medicine."

UC's College of Law was ranked one of the top 50 law schools in the country in a 1998 *U.S. News & World Report* study. The magazine, which placed the UC college among the likes of Stanford and Columbia, cited it's 93 percent passage rate for bar exams as well as the rate of grads employed nine months after graduation — 94 percent. The college is the fourth oldest continually operating law school in the country, after Harvard, Yale and the University of Virginia.

UC also has a top-notch engineering school and industrial design program. Its undergraduate business and MBA programs, while lacking the prestige of Ivy League or other major programs around the country, have gained national attention for their own spin on cooperative education — having students act as consultants for small businesses and providing in many cases very successful solutions. And the College of Design, Architecture, Art and Planning is arguably one of the finest in the country.

In all, UC offers 87 doctoral, 122 master's, 146 bachelor's and 90 associate's degree programs in a wide range of disciplines, most with an eye toward landing students a job in the real world. For its part, Procter & Gamble, the largest company in Cincinnati, recruits heavily from the UC campus, primarily in the chemistry and health research departments.

UC traces its origins to 1819, when the Cincinnati College and the Medical College of Ohio were founded. In 1870, the City of Cincinnati founded the University of Cincinnati, which later absorbed the medical college and several other institutions. For years, UC was the second-oldest and second-largest municipal university in the country, until it became a state university in 1977.

This largely commuter school has more than 34,000 students, slightly less than two-thirds of whom attend full time. Only about 3,000 students live on campus and another 750 live in nearby sorority and fraternity houses. That puts parking at a premium in the tightly packed Clifton neighborhood north of downtown, UC's location.

Another addition to the fray: The campus is

constantly being renovated and expanded (students joke that UC actually stands for Under Construction). A decade-long expansion plan includes a $22 million student center, a new hotel and conference complex, a concert amphitheater and, thankfully, more green space in the form of grass quads. Right now, wrecking cranes and yellow tape are the order of the day, and entire departments are often moved overnight. Nothing is where you think you left it yesterday. Check the daily student paper, the *News-Record*, regularly for updates.

UC's branch campuses — Clermont College, 4200 Clermont College Drive, Batavia, 732-5200; and Raymond Walters College, 9555 Plainfield Road, Blue Ash, 745-5600 — offer both two-year associate's degrees and programs that can lead to four-year degrees either at UC's main campus or elsewhere. There are 3,600 students at Raymond Walters and 2,300 at Clermont, so neither branch is what you'd call small. Surprisingly, many branch campus students find that their credits transfer more easily to NKU than to UC's main campus. Among the popular programs at the branches are allied health and veterinary assistant training at Raymond Walters and criminal justice at Clermont College.

The 130-year-old College Conservatory of Music at UC, already one of the top conservatories in the country, is undergoing a $56.8 million renovation and expansion. It alone has an enrollment of 1,200 students, plus 1,800 in preparatory programs, and offers 100 degree programs. Among its alumni and former attendees are the appropriately named opera diva Kathleen Battle, Suzanne Farrell (one of the century's great ballerinas), legendary trumpet player Al Hirt and the late popular musicians Tennessee Ernie Ford and Frank Zappa. CCM ensembles have made acclaimed tours in recent years to New York, Europe and the Far East. Closer to home, CCM events number nearly 900 annually.

UC is also known for research. The Carnegie Commission ranks it as one of only 75 Research I universities among 5,000 institutions of higher learning in the United States. Among firsts developed whole or in part at UC are the first antihistamine, Benadryl, by George Reiveschl; the first electronic organ, by Winston Koch; the first YAG laser to remove brain tumors; the first baccalaureate degree program in nursing; the first emergency medicine residency program; and the first degree program offered via satellite (health planning).

UC has a notable intercollegiate sports program, especially Division I football and basketball. The basketball program ended its two decades in the wilderness of mediocrity between the Oscar Robertson era and current successes when fiery Bob Huggins was named basketball coach in 1990. Since then, UC has made Final Four and Final Eight appearances in back-to-back years. The football program has suddenly proven itself no slouch, either. Coach Rick Minter led his team to victory in the 1997 Humanitarian Bowl, the football team's first bowl appearance in 47 years.

Wilmington College
3 Triangle Park Dr., Sharonville
• 772-7516

The focus of the Cincinnati branches of Wilmington College is the adult working student. The Sharonville campus is a branch of a private four-year liberal arts college established in 1870 by the Religious Society of Friends in Wilmington and is less than an hour's drive to the northeast. The college has just added an East Side campus in the Eastgate Mall area near Anderson.

Of the Sharonville campus' nearly 400 students, more than 90 percent attend part time. All services, including admissions and registration, are handled at times designed to mesh with work schedules. Offices are open until 8 PM Monday through Thursday and 8:30 AM to noon Saturday. Faculty and administrators strive for flexibility in coping with absences due to work or family demands. And as many

INSIDERS' TIP

A recent survey showed the highest annual tuition in the area is at Xavier University ($13,650). Tied for lowest are Northern Kentucky University ($2,120) and Cincinnati State ($2,718). In between are UC ($4,359), Miami ($5,406), Thomas More ($11,250), and Mount St. Joseph ($11,900).

as 30 credit hours may be earned through the College-Level Examination Program (CLEP), Advanced Placement (AP), proficiency examinations or experiential learning assessment.

The branches offer programs leading to Bachelor of Arts degrees in accounting and business administration with marketing or management concentrations. Students able to take courses on the main campus too may choose from additional majors.

Xavier University
3800 Victory Pkwy. • 745-3000

Xavier University was established in 1831 by the first bishop of Cincinnati, Edward Fenwick, and named the Athenaeum. After the first Jesuits arrived to staff the school in 1840, the name was changed to St. Xavier College. Originally in downtown Cincinnati, St. Xavier College moved to its present location in 1919. In 1930 the name was changed to Xavier University, reflecting the school's new growth and development.

Today Xavier offers associate's, bachelor's and master's degrees in a wide range of programs, with strength in such areas as communications arts, business administration, education, psychology and pre-med/vet studies in life sciences. Seventy-eight percent of Xavier grads who apply for medical or veterinarian school get in. Xavier prides itself on its small class sizes, averaging 23 students. It is primarily a commuter school, half of whose roughly 6,000 students attend full time and half part time.

As a private school, tuition is naturally steeper here than at surrounding public institutions, but 80 percent of students receive some form of financial aid. Service scholarships also provide some top students with full rides in return for regular weekly service to the community. For that matter, most Xavier academic programs contain some service component, in keeping with Xavier's Jesuit tradition. At the graduate level, Xavier students are sometimes surprised to find that they don't pay that much more than state school students when they take into account that Xavier's graduate programs tend to be less bloated with needless course requirements.

In sports, Xavier is known for its basketball team, which moved to the Atlantic 10 Conference in 1995 to face such big-time competition as the University of Massachusetts. Xavier hasn't been nearly as successful on the court as UC in recent years. But it has been a winner in the crosstown integrity shoot-out. Faced with a choice between doing the right thing and or the winning thing prior to Xavier's last NCAA appearance in 1995, Coach Skip Prosser chose the right thing. He suspended two players caught in a barroom scuffle just before the first-round game. Xavier lost the game but gained a moral victory.

Workers broke ground in 1998 for the Xavier Convocation Center, a $44 million complex that will become the biggest building on campus and the heart of the university's social life. The facility, when it opens in early 2000, will expand the campus by 20 percent. It will accommodate such events as graduation and homecoming, which are currently held at The Crown and Union Terminal, respectively, because of space constraints.

Xavier's top-ranked basketball team will again be able to play "at home" in the Center's 10,000-seat arena (since 1984, the team has had to schlep across town to the Cincinnati Gardens). Workshops, reunions, career fairs, concerts, even huge Catholic weddings are among the events Xavier officials foresee for the complex, which will also serve as the central dining area for students.

Adult Continuing Education

Besides offering credit courses, many of the colleges and universities listed in this chapter also offer adult continuing education, as do many of the larger suburban public school districts and vocational school districts. Other resources to check include:

Anderson High School, 7560 Forest Road, 232-2772

Diamond Oaks Career Development Campus, 6375 Harrison Avenue, Dent, 574-1300

Grant Career Center, 3046 Ohio Park, Bethel, 734-6222

Great Oaks Institute for Professional Development, 3254 E. Kemper Road, 771-8925

Live Oaks Career Development Campus, 5956 Buckwheat Road, Mount Repose, 575-1900

The newly created Magazines and Newspapers section at the main downtown library subscribes to 15,300 newspapers and periodicals.

Libraries

If all Greater Cincinnati government services worked as well as the libraries do, world leaders would be flocking here to see how they could bring Utopian bliss to their people. Well, okay, maybe the libraries aren't quite that perfect . . . but they're pretty close.

The area's libraries are a model of regional cooperation, thanks to the Greater Cincinnati Library Consortium, a group of 40 college and university, public, school and special libraries with more than 10 million books and 50,000 periodicals. A library card from any member library allows you to borrow materials directly from any of the others. Then you can return what you borrowed to the closest member library, and it will get routed back to the right place.

At least part of the local library system's success is due to the fact that Hamilton County early on consolidated all its libraries into one system, avoiding duplication of staff and expenses. (By comparison, Cleveland's Cuyahoga County has nine public library systems.)

Library systems in the surrounding suburban counties have branch systems of their own. Anyone with library cards from these systems also can obtain a free Hamilton County library card, and an estimated 9 percent of the Hamilton County system's circulation is attributable to noncounty residents.

At the center of the region's public library system is the Public Library of Cincinnati and Hamilton County, the oldest public library west of the Alleghenies. It was founded in 1853, 16 years before the Reds, which gives you an idea of its lofty place in Cincinnati history. Nationwide, it ranks second in per-capita circulation among major public library systems in the nation and fourth in total collection overall. While the library's per-capita circulation ranks it ahead of the New York and Chicago public libraries (and many others), local librarians are

nonetheless upset with their No. 2 slot — for 17 years, you see, the Cincinnati/Hamilton County library consistently placed No. 1, until Denver claimed the top spot in the most recent 1998 ranking. There was, to say the least, much weeping and gnashing of pocket protectors.

If you plan to use the Public Library of Cincinnati and Hamilton County, get ready to enter the information age. The card catalog is computerized, using CINCH (Computerized Information Network for Cincinnati and Hamilton County). The CINCH number, 369-3200, accesses NEWSDEX (an index to local newspapers that is updated daily) and more than 50 electronic databases, including the ABI/INFORM business database and newspaper abstracts, *Books in Print*, Select Phone (a searchable database of nationwide phone listings), INFOTRAC (a general index of 1,100 periodicals that serves as a sort of electronic *Reader's Guide to Periodical Literature*), and American Business Information (a searchable database of business phone listings). You can access all these databases for free if you have a library card.

The heart of the 42-library system is the main branch downtown, which holds 8.8 million books, periodicals, maps, books on tape, CDs and CD-ROMs. You can also research your family tree in one of the nation's largest — and from all appearances most heavily used — genealogy centers.

A new, block-long annex to the downtown branch, opened in 1997 at a cost of $44 million, offers a plethora of services. The newly created Magazines and Newspapers section subscribes to 15,300 newspapers and periodicals, and the new Public Documents and Patents section is one of only three at U.S. libraries to offer the complete U.S. census records. The dazzling Children's Learning Center includes dozens of computers and free Internet access (see our Kidstuff chapter for more details). The Library for the Blind and Physically Handicapped offers a full range of services for the disabled, including CINCH workstations with voice and Braille capability. This annex is connected to the main library by a skywalk.

With a card from most public libraries, you can check out or even order books and materials in collections of local college libraries. (College libraries are covered in the Colleges and Universities chapter.)

Public Libraries

Aurora Public Library
414 Second Street, Aurora, Indiana, (812) 926-0646 (Please note that at press time the library was closed for extensive renovations. Call first.)

Boone County (Ky.) Public Library
Main Branch, 7425 U.S. Highway 46, Florence, (606) 371-6222

Lents Branch, 3215 Cougar Path, Hebron, (606) 586-8163

Campbell County (Ky.) Public Library
Main Branch, 3920 Alexandria Pike, Cold Spring, (606) 781-6166

Fort Thomas Branch, 1000 Highland Avenue, (606) 572-5033

Clermont County Public Library
Main Branch, 180 S. Third Street, Batavia, 732-2128

Amelia Branch, 58 Maple Street, 752-5580

Bethel Branch, 111 W. Plane Street, 734-2619

Goshen Branch, 6678 Ohio Highway 123, 722-1221

Milford Branch, 1099 S.R. 131, 248-0700

Union Branch, 4462 Mount Carmel-Tobasco Road, 528-1744

Williamsburg Branch, 594 Main Street, 724-1070

Kenton County (Ky.) Public Library
Main Branch, 502 Scott Street, Covington, (606) 491-7610

FYI

Unless otherwise noted, the area code for all phone numbers listed in this guide is 513.

Erlanger Branch, 3130 Dixie Highway, (606) 341-5115

Independence Branch, 6477 Taylor Mill Road, (606) 363-0200

Lane Public Library System
Main Branch, N. Third and Buckeye Streets, Hamilton, 894-7156

Fairfield Branch, 701 Wessel Drive, Fairfield, 858-3238

Lindenwald, 2121 Pleasant Avenue, Hamilton, 893-4691

Oxford, 15 S. College Avenue, 523-7531

Smith Library of Regional History, 15 S. College Avenue, Oxford, 523-3035

Lawrenceburg (Ind.) Public Library
123 W. High Street, (812) 537-2775

Lebanon Public Library
101 S. Broadway, 932-2665

Mason Public Library
200 Reading Road, 398-2711

Public Library of Cincinnati and Hamilton County
Main Branch, 800 Vine Street, 369-6900

Anderson, 7450 State Road, 369-6030

Avondale, 3566 Reading Road, 369-4440

Bond Hill, 1703 Dale Road, 369-4445

Bonham, 500 Springfield Pike, Wyoming, 369-6014

Cheviot, 3711 Robb Avenue, 369-6015

Clifton, 351 Ludlow Avenue, 369-4447

Corryville, 2802 Vine Street, 369-6034

Covedale, 4980 Glenway Avenue, 369-4460

Cumminsville, 4219 Hamilton Avenue, 369-4449

Deer Park, 3932 E. Galbraith Road, 369-4450

Delhi Hills, 5095 Foley Road, 369-6019

Elmwood Place, 6120 Vine Street, 369-4452

Green Regional, 6525 Bridgetown Road, 369-6095

Greenhills, 7 Endicott Street, 369-4441

Groesbeck, 2994 W. Galbraith Road, 369-4454

Harrison, 300 George Street, 369-4442

Dark Deeds and Dandy Detectives

Cincinnati loves a mystery. The Queen City landscape is littered with literary murders and at least a half dozen nationally published mystery authors reside here or use the city as the setting for their tales.

You can learn a great deal about the city's foibles and felons by reading works by  these writers because spread in amongst the fiction is a great deal of fact. A quick survey:

D.B. Borton — Her series of novels begins with *One for the Money* and is currently in a sixth entry, *Six Feet Under*. Her hero is Cat Caliban, a Northside grandmom who's raised three kids and has now settled down to snoop. Borton wonderfully weaves real-life Cincinnati politicos and media types into her private eye narrative.

Jim DeBrosse — After toiling in the trenches at both *The Cincinnati Post* and *The Cincinnati Enquirer*, DeBrosse decided to turn the tables on the local papers and write a series of novels loosely based on his Cincinnati journalism experience. His fictional reporter, Rick Decker, exposes shady dealings and the foibles of the press beginning in *The Serpentine Wall*, and later in *Hidden City* and *Southern Cross*. *Hidden City* is particularly notable for its fascinating details about Cincinnati's long-abandoned subway system.

Lynn S. Hightower — Granted, she lives just down the road in Lexington, but she chooses to set her grim police procedurals in the Queen City. Her heroine, Sonora Blair of the Cincinnati Homicide Division, investigates the bizarre underground life of the town. Start with *Flashpoint* and move on in the series of books.

Cathie John — Actually, she is a she and a he: the husband-and-wife writing team of John and Cathie Celestri. Their murder mystery novels feature Cincy detective Kate Cavanaugh. *Add One Dead Critic*, the first book in the series, was about the nasty murder of a nasty restaurant critic. The second culinary mystery, *Beat A Rotten Egg to the Punch* is set at the Taste of Cincinnati food fest.

— continued on next page

Photo: Sean Hughes

Mystery writer Albert Pyle oversees the Mercantile Library.

A.M. Pyle — Also known as Albert Pyle (see our listing for the Mercantile Library), he has turned out a riveting series starring Detective Cesar Franck. Start with *Murder Moves In* and *Trouble Making Toys*, then graduate to *Pure Murder*.

Jonathan Valin — Valin is the honorary granddad of Cincinnati mystery novelists. His Harry Stoner novels, starting with *Lime Pit* and *Final Notice* and moving on to *Fire Lake* and *The Music Lovers*, have received national kudos and have even been turned into TV movies. Stoner is a throwback, Sam Spade kind of detective but with some modern twists.

A footnote: Although not a mystery novel per se, Judge Deidra Hair's *No Shoes, No Shirt, No Trial* is an hilarious look inside the city's criminal court system. The recollections include portraits of some of the town's most colorful characters, most notably streetperson Fifi Taft Rockefeller, who claims Elvis Presley among her romantic conquests.

Hyde Park, 2747 Erie Avenue, 369-4456

Lincoln Park, West End, 805 Ezzard Charles Drive, 369-6026

Loveland, 649 Loveland-Madeira Road, 369-4476

Madeira, 7200 Miami Avenue, 369-6028

Madisonville, 4830 Whetsel Avenue, 369-6029

Mariemont, 381 Pocahontas Avenue, 369-4467

Miami, 8 N. Miami Avenue, 369-6050

Mount Healthy, 608 Hamilton Avenue, 369-4469

Mount Washington, 2049 Beechmont Avenue, 369-6033

North Central Regional, 11109 Hamilton Avenue, Pleasant Run, 369-6068

Northern Hills, 1400 W. North Bend Road, College Hill, 369-6036

Norwood, 4325 Montgomery Road, 369-6037

Oakley, 4033 Gilmore Avenue, 369-6038

Parkdale, 655 Waycross Road, 369-4478

Pleasant Ridge, 6233 Montgomery Road, 369-4488

Price Hill, 3215 Warsaw Avenue, 369-4490

Roselawn, 7617 Reading Road, 369-6045

St. Bernard, 4803 Tower Avenue, 369-4462

Sharonville Regional, 10980 Thornview Drive, 369-6049

Sycamore, 4911 Cooper Road, 369-6051

Symmes Regional, 11850 E. Enyart, 369-6001

Valley, 301 W. Benson Street, Reading, 369-4465

Walnut Hills, 2533 Kemper Lane, 369-6053

West Fork, 3825 W. Fork Road, Monfort Heights, 369-4472

Westwood, 3345 Epworth Avenue, 369-4474

Salem Public Library
535 W. Pike Street, Morrow, 899-2588

Private Libraries

In addition to a vast array of public libraries, Cincinnati has an interesting assortment of private libraries to which the public has at least limited access. Here are a few.

Cincinnati Historical Society Library
1301 Western Ave. • 287-7020

Surely the most valuable resource in town if you're interested in anything to do with Cincinnati history or heritage. Upstairs in Tower A is the nation's largest library devoted to railway history.

Cincinnati Stake Family History Library
5505 Bosworth Pl., Norwood • 531-5624

This library is operated by the Church of Jesus Christ of Latter-day Saints for family history research and is open to the public.

Civic Gardens Center of Cincinnati Library
2715 Reading Rd. • 221-0981

You should find the answer to most any gardening question you may have in this collection of noncirculating books. A $25 annual membership entitles you to full use of the library, plus gives you access to the newsletters, lectures, classes and workshops offered by the Civic Garden Center.

Frank Foster Library
2115 W. Eighth St., Price Hill • 251-0202

The City of Cincinnati's Urban Appalachian Council runs this research library, which contains the largest collection of books and materials on Appalachia outside of Appalachia. It is open to the public.

www.insiders.com

See this and many other **Insiders' Guide®** destinations online — in their entirety.

Visit us today!

Lloyd Library
917 Plum St. • 721-3707

The works of John Uri Lloyd (1849-1936), a prominent Cincinnati pharmacist and author, are housed here. Lloyd wrote hundreds of articles for medical and scientific journals on the chemical properties of plants and books on pharmacology. More than 50 years after his death, the library is still a major center for scholars researching the history of pharmacology.

Lloyd also wrote in 1895 one of the world's first science fiction/fantasy novels, *Etidorhpa* (that's Aphrodite spelled backward), in which the protagonist is kidnapped and taken into the center of the earth, where he is guided through bizarre crystal forests by an eyeless humanoid. It was one of the more offbeat things ever to come out of Cincinnati and made a few folks wonder if Mr. Lloyd was sampling what he studied. But the book became a cult classic and has remained popular. An endowment from Lloyd's family keeps his legacy alive in this library, which is open to the public for research.

Mercantile Library
414 Walnut St. • 621-0717

This historic library in the Mercantile Library Building downtown, just reopened after a major face-lift, is a sort of book-lined home-away-from-home for its members, says executive director Albert Pyle. You can do things here you just can't do at other libraries, such as bring your lunch and eat it as you read. (Gasp! Don't tell the cops!)

The elevator to the 11th floor seems something of a time machine that transports visitors to an era and place far removed from the modern bustle of downtown Cincinnati. You can relax in a leather-and-wood booklover's paradise, replete with an extensive collection of statuary that seems to invite leisurely perusal. The library literally reeks of history, with that musty smell that can only come from an accumulation of volumes that goes back to when the library opened at this site in 1835 (some books in the rare-book collection date from well before then).

The general public is welcome to visit. Membership in the Young Men's Mercantile Library Association (also open to women, of course) costs $45 a year ($15 for students) and entitles you to borrow materials, plus you get first dibs on frequently filled-to-capacity lectures by renowned writers. Among the authors who have appeared here are Ralph Waldo Emerson, Herman Melville, Tom Wolfe, John Updike and Ray Bradbury.

Hours are 9 AM to 5:30 PM Monday through Friday, with occasional weekend hours for lectures and concerts.

No matter what kind of music you like, from Big Band to urban contemporary, you'll find it on one of Greater Cincinnati's 40 radio stations.

Media

News junkies have an easy time of it in Greater Cincinnati. The area boasts five daily newspapers (two in Cincinnati, two in Northern Kentucky and one in Hamilton), 35 community weeklies, two business papers, two alternative papers, a dozen or so special interest papers, four magazines, 40 radio stations and 10 TV stations. That's a lot for a city the size of Cincinnati and enough to drive you crazy trying to keep up with it all. But if you want still more, out-of-town newspapers are available at many larger bookstores and *The New York Times* and *The Wall Street Journal* can be home-delivered.

The two biggest local news sources are *The Cincinnati Post* and *The Cincinnati Enquirer*, which are published under a joint operating agreement. Because of this agreement, many people think they are one and the same paper, but that is far from the truth. A daily comparison of the two makes that abundantly clear. The agreement simply means that the two papers maintain separate editorial voices, but they save money by sharing costly business operations, including advertising, distribution and printing. The larger *Enquirer* handles all the business-related items. Profits are shared, albeit unevenly, between the two papers. In fact, the *Post*, sadly, will probably join the growing list of dead daily newspapers when the agreement expires on December 31, 2007.

With such an abundance of news sources, one might expect the news outlets, both broadcast and print, to try to out-scoop each other on stories. And they do. But Cincinnati isn't Washington, D.C. when it comes to big news, and the lack of hard-hitting local stories means that the media often step into the "investigative" arena for their exclusive reports — sometimes with mixed results.

The *Enquirer* occasionally runs an extensive series of articles on topics such as racism in Greater Cincinnati or teenage pregnancy.

The *Post* recently did a series on drugs in the area and ended up making the news itself when someone shot at the reporter and photographer working on the series. WCPO-TV (Channel 9) has a special "I-Team" that concentrates on these types of stories, although the stories only run during "sweeps week." The I-Team has gained a reputation, though, thanks to a few early successes, such as exposing county building inspectors who clock in and then go golfing and the county pothole repair crews who park their trucks on side streets and then sit around eating doughnuts and reading the newspapers.

But occasionally the media stumble. One reporter was caught placing a hidden camera in a courtroom. Several reporters have done their training here and run off to such highly acclaimed journalistic programs as *Inside Edition* and *A Current Affair*.

On the radio side, the face of the Cincinnati market is changing, and it looks a lot like Jacor Communications Inc. The media giant, now the third-largest radio ownership company in the country with more than 170 stations, recently maneuvered its way through the local market and now owns five radio stations, including the highly popular WLW (700 AM) and WEBN (102.7 FM). In the process, it bought out or eliminated much of its competition. Plus, by teaming with a friendly partner, it controls the operations of three other local stations.

Jacor also owns the rights to broadcast most of the major sports events in town — the Reds, Xavier, and University of Cincinnati games — with the exception of the Bengals, Cyclones and Mighty Duck games. The Bengals games were on the list, but the comments and controversy sparked by some of Jacor's on-air personalities didn't sit well with the Bengals management, so when the time came to renew, the Bengals took their broadcast rights and sold them to the much smaller combination of WUBE (105.1 FM) and The Bob (1160 AM).

Jacor isn't the only national media giant in town. The E.W. Scripps Company is also headquartered in Greater Cincinnati and, collectively, the two own 23 daily and weekly newspapers, more than 170 radio stations and nine TV stations across the country, in addition to numerous cable franchises, a newspaper syndicate, an entertainment production company and a news service. That's a lot of national media influence coming out of Cincinnati.

Much of Cincinnati's electronic media presence dates back to Powel Crosley, who manufactured affordable tabletop radios in the 1920s and who founded WLW radio in 1922 and WLWT-TV (Channel 5) in 1945. WLWT-TV was the first television station to go on the air in Ohio. In its early days, WLW radio broadcast at 500,000 watts. It had to cut back to 50,000 watts, though, after complaints that it was drowning out stations from here to Cuba and that the signal was so strong people were picking it up in the metal fillings in their teeth. The station remains a clear-channel station, meaning it is the only station that broadcasts at its 700 kilocycle (AM) frequency.

FYI

Unless otherwise noted, the area code for all phone numbers listed in this guide is 513.

Daily Newspapers

The Cincinnati Enquirer
312 Elm St. • 721-2700

The morning *Enquirer* is a staple in the area; local residents are addicted to it, along with their coffee and toast. And if ever that was in question, it became decidedly clear during the summer of 1996 when the paper attempted to change its delivery system after 155 years. Rather than selling its papers to wholesalers, who acted as independent businesses, "owned" specific routes and were responsible for deliveries, the paper tried to do everything itself, buying out the wholesalers and hiring its own delivery crews.

It didn't work out as planned, at least not initially. People who were supposed to get papers didn't. People who weren't supposed to get papers did. Whole streets went without, while other whole streets got papers. It was such a mess and so many people called to complain about not getting their paper, Cincinnati Bell had to shut down the phone line for fear of overload. One minister's sermon on the virtues of patience cited not getting the *Enquirer* as an exception. Although frustrating to the public, the experiment confirmed the powerful position the *Enquirer* holds in the area.

The *Enquirer* offers a decidedly conservative editorial slant, paralleling the views of most area residents. Its editorial views are now more clearly spoken following a senior-level management transformation in 1992 that included a new publisher, editor and editorial page editor. The very conservative opinions of editorial page editor Peter Bronson, though, are written with a light and humorous style that less conservative readers can also appreciate.

The paper's conservative editorial nature is often offset by the more liberal work of Pulitzer Prize-winning editorial cartoonist Jim Borgman. Borgman won the paper's only Pulitzer in 1991 for his humorous and well-stated editorial drawings. (See our Close-up on Borgman in this chapter.)

In addition to Borgman's cartoon, which is a daily must-see, popular columnists include Laura Pulfer and Cliff Radel on the metro pages, gossip columnist Jim Knippenberg in the "Tempo" section, television columnist John Kiesewetter, and dueling sports columnists Paul Daugherty and Tim Sullivan.

The paper sometimes struggles, though, with its position as the area's source for national and international news and its desire to also be a community paper. Even though it can't do everything, it tries. The paper added more community news with zoned "Hometown" news pages each day. It also added a "Let's Go!" weekend entertainment guide each Friday in an attempt to better cover the local entertainment scene, with reviews of local bands and nightlife. It expanded its business section, placing it on the back of the "Metro" section and adding special columns and features each day. Other regular sections include "Wheels" and

"At Home" on Saturday, and "TV Week," "Real Estate," "Taste," "Job Market," and "USA Weekend" on Sunday.

The *Enquirer* was first published on April 10, 1841 and was the first newspaper nationally to publish a Sunday edition, beginning in 1848. The paper has gone through a handful of different owners through the years. In 1952, the paper's owner intended to sell the *Enquirer* to then rival *Times-Star*, but employee investments, wealthy sponsors and bonds sold by brokers raised $7.5 million for a counteroffer and kept the paper alive as an employee-owned operation.

In 1956, Cincinnati-based E.W. Scripps Company purchased a majority interest in the *Enquirer* from the employees but never exercised control. A court order in 1971 forced Scripps, which also owned the afternoon *Post*, to divest its ownership in the *Enquirer*. Scripps eventually sold its shares to American Financial Corporation, a privately owned company controlled by Cincinnati's self-made millionaire Carl Lindner, who became the paper's publisher. Lindner kept the paper for four years before selling to Combined Communications Corporation, a diversified media company that merged with Gannett Company Inc. in 1979. The paper is now one of the largest daily papers in the company's chain, with a daily circulation of 205,000 and a Sunday circulation of 355,000.

Subscription rates are $195 a year daily and Sunday, $114.40 a year daily only and $96.72 a year Sunday only.

The Cincinnati Post
125 E. Court St. • 352-2000

The *Post* has been a Cincinnati staple since 1883 when E.W. Scripps bought control of *The Cincinnati Penny Paper* and renamed it *The Penny Post*. At that time, Cincinnati had seven English and five German newspapers. In 1956, the *Post* purchased its afternoon rival, *The Times-Star*, and made Cincinnati a two-newspaper town. The *Post* became the cornerstone for Scripps, which also owns WCPO-TV (Channel 9) in Cincinnati as well as numerous newspapers, television stations, publishing and production companies, syndicates and cable companies nationally.

As with many afternoon papers, the *Post* has a difficult time maintaining subscription levels, which have dropped below 90,000, down by more than half from when it entered into a joint operating agreement with the *Enquirer*. More than half of those sales are in Northern Kentucky, where its Kentucky version, *The Kentucky Post*, reigns. And that is translating into reductions in its editorial efforts. The *Post* has been forced twice in recent years to offer buyout or early retirement packages to its employees, resulting in the loss of veteran reporters. Add to that a hiring freeze and the no-longer-uncommon occurrence of reporters jumping over to the *Enquirer* for the sake of job security, and the effectiveness and reporting ability of the paper continue to be hurt.

The *Post* offers a more liberal editorial viewpoint than the *Enquirer* and devotes more space and effort to covering local issues and high school sports. Despite its lagging circulation and loss of staff, it often scoops the *Enquirer*. Essentially, it must provide better reporting, since the *Enquirer* controls its destiny outside of the newsroom.

Popular columnists include David Wecker, who provides an offbeat and lighthearted approach to life in the "Living" section; Connie Yeager, who offers an entertainment tipsheet in "Living"; Nick "Father of George" Clooney, who writes about life in Cincinnati; sports columnist Bill Koch; Joyce Rosencrans, who offers food advice on Wednesdays and home advice on Saturdays; and TV critic Greg Paeth.

Small-business columnist Howard Zuefle and editorial cartoonist Jeff Stahler recently published books of their best works. In addition to appearing daily on the *Post*'s editorial page, Stahler's cartoons are often featured in *Newsweek* and other national magazines. The *Post* is also the only newspaper in town where you can read "Peanuts" and "Dilbert." (The E.W. Scripps Company also owns United Media, which syndicates and licenses the rights to "Peanuts" and "Dilbert" and all of their merchandise.)

Special sections include "Marketwise" on Tuesday, "Food" on Wednesday, "Timeout" weekend entertainment guide on Thursday, "TV Magazine" and "Living at Home" on Saturday. The *Post* also operates free lines for weather, 241-1010, and sports scores, 721-0700. A subscription is $90 a year.

The Kentucky Post
421 Madison Ave., Covington, Ky.
• (606) 292-2600

The Kentucky Post is a one- or two-section paper that is "wrapped" over the early edition of *The Cincinnati Post* and distributed to Northern Kentucky residents. *The Kentucky Post* covers Northern Kentucky issues in depth and dominates Northern Kentucky's news coverage, which is becoming increasingly important as more and more businesses and residents locate south of the river.

Its staff gives particular attention to the area's sporting interests, which tend to differ from those north of the river. The paper gives detailed coverage of the University of Kentucky and local high school sports, which are highly popular in Northern Kentucky.

The Kentucky Post is also responsible for more than half of *The Cincinnati Post*'s total circulation. A subscription is $107.40 a year.

The Kentucky Enquirer
226 Grandview Dr., Fort Mitchell, Ky.
• (606) 578-5555

The Cincinnati Enquirer recently began making a more concerted effort to cover the news of Northern Kentucky by opening a Northern Kentucky bureau and publishing *The Kentucky Enquirer*. The staff concentrates strictly on events south of the river and produces a separate front page and "Metro" section. As a result, the paper is making a small dent in the virtual monopoly on Kentucky news that *The Kentucky Post* once had. Subscription rates are $182 a year daily and Sunday, $101.40 a year daily only and $96.72 a year for Sunday only.

Hamilton Journal News
Court St. and Journal Sq., Hamilton
• 863-8200

The *Journal News* offers some national and international news but concentrates on the news and events in Hamilton, Fairfield and surrounding northern communities. A subscription is $130 a year.

Community Newspapers

Press Community Newspapers
4910 Para Dr. • 242-4300

Press Community Newspapers publishes 21 zoned newspapers that cover virtually all of Cincinnati's and Northern Kentucky's suburban communities. The papers are more professional than many local weekly newspapers and offer detailed coverage of the local news, most of which is considered "too small" to be covered by the daily papers. Town and village council meetings are covered, as are school board meetings. The papers are usually so on top of happenings in the communities that they are often one step ahead of the daily newspapers on larger suburban issues as well.

These papers are the best place to find out what's happening in your particular neighborhood: road repairs, business openings or closings, area residents who did something noteworthy, school honor rolls. The papers are also well-read for their classified ads, police reports and school lunch menus.

The papers are delivered free to homes every Wednesday, and individuals must contact the papers' offices in order *not* to get a paper. The papers include: *Delhi Press*, *Hilltop Press*, *Northwest Press*, *Price Hill Press*, *Tri-County Press*, *Western Hills Press*, *Bethel Journal*, *Clermont Community Journal*, *North Clermont Community Journal*, *Western Clermont Community Journal*, *Mason Community Press*, *Eastern Hills Journal*, *Forest Hills Journal*, *Loveland Herald*, *Milford Advertiser*, *Northeast Suburban Life*, *Suburban Life*, *Campbell County Recorder*, *Boone County Recorder*, *Kenton County Recorder* and *Erlanger Recorder*.

Clermont Sun
465 E. Main St., Batavia • 732-2511

This weekly paper publishes every Thursday and is available through subscription only for $12 per year in Clermont, Brown and Hamilton counties.

EastSide Weekend
394 Wards Corner Rd., Loveland
• 248-7111

After operating independently for more than seven years, *EastSide Weekend* was purchased in 1997 by Press Community Papers. This weekly entertainment, home, dining and features publication is distributed free each Thursday to about 50,000 homes in the more affluent sections of the eastern side of Cincinnati. Although the publication's name indicates an East Side distribution area, it is also available downtown in street-corner boxes or by subscription for $19.95 a year. The publication operates from Community Press' East Side office.

Journal News Weeklies
5120 Dixie Hwy., Fairfield • 829-7900

Hamilton Journal News publishes four community weeklies: *Fairfield Echo*, *Oxford Press*, *Mason Pulse-Journal* and *West Chester Press*. The *Echo* is inserted in the *Journal News* each Wednesday; nonsubscribers to the *Journal News* receive the *Echo* free at their door. *Oxford Press* is available through subscription, while *Pulse-Journal* and *West Chester Press*, which was just purchased from Press Community Newspapers, are available through voluntary payment (that is, the papers are free but you can throw money at the nice kids who throw the paper on your lawn).

Mt. Lookout Observer
1203 Herschel Woods Ln. • 321-3280

This monthly paper is a publication of the Mt. Lookout Civic Club and is in its 70th year. It covers church, school, social and business news and is distributed free to local residents on the second Monday of each month.

Living Publications
179 Fairfield Ave., Bellevue, Ky.
• (606) 291-1412

Living Publications publishes seven papers in the suburban Cincinnati and Northern Kentucky communities of Blue Ash, Hyde Park, Indian Hill, Oakwood, Wyoming, Fort Mitchell and Fort Thomas. The papers run

wedding and engagement announcements, birth announcements, retirements and "anything that you think might be something people would like to know and read about." Distribution of the papers is staggered throughout the month. Residents of the communities receive the publications free through the mail. Residents outside of the communities can subscribe for $14 a year.

Alternative Newspapers

CityBeat
23 E. Seventh St. • 665-4700

CityBeat, the newest of the city's two alternative papers, was started by the former editor of its rival, *Everybody's News*, and has quickly made a name for itself in the arts, entertainment and news arenas. Like most alternative papers, it reviews the arts, movies, records, bands, nightclubs and events, but it also offers an alternative look at the major news issues around the city. It often tackles news stories not covered by the daily and suburban papers. For instance, it recently ran a midterm look at the promises made by local politicians and whether they've been kept. It also ran a story by a heroin addict on what it's like to be addicted to the drug.

Alternative lifestyles, arts and entertainment, though, are its staple. Its movie and music reviewers are so popular they are also heard on various radio stations. And the paper frequently cosponsors entertainment events and puts its alternative spin on them. At one event, it provided on-the-spot tattoo artists and body piercers.

This free weekly paper publishes every Thursday and can be found in sidewalk racks around downtown, Clifton and Over-the-Rhine. It's also available at the entrance of many restaurants and bars throughout the city and in all Kroger grocery stores.

Everybody's News
1310 Pendleton St. • 381-2606

Everybody's News is "Greater Cincinnati's First Alternative News, Arts and Entertainment Weekly," offering an alternative look at Cincinnati issues. It concentrates heavily on issues important to GenXers and the arts and enter-

Pulitzer Prize-Winning Borgman Draws on Wit

Jim Borgman sits in his 19th-floor corner office, leaning over his drawing board, putting the finishing touches on the cartoon that will run on the editorial page of *The Cincinnati Enquirer* the next day. The target du jour is a debate raging in the city about some nightclub strippers who appeared on the cable access channel. He checks the cartoon over carefully, nods with approval and sends it to the paper's printing plant several miles away.

Tomorrow afternoon it will be the same scenario but a different topic.

Every day, Borgman loads up his paint brush with a single bullet and takes aim at  whatever is in the news. Usually, the shot hits its target dead center with a combination of wit, biting political or philosophical statements, humorous caricatures and under-appreciated artistic skills. His marksmanship earned him the Pulitzer Prize in 1991. It also earns him regular scorn from the paper's readers. Despite being arguably the most prominent and well-liked media personality in the city, 90 percent of the letters that arrive in his small office are negative, taking him to task for his viewpoints.

Borgman is a bit of a paradox to the city — part comic editorialist, part fly in the ointment of Cincinnati's conservatism. His cartoons sometimes directly contradict his paper's editorial view, and he often stands alone as a liberal island in a sea of right-wing thought. He draws former vice president Dan Quayle as a stick figure. He still blasts former presidents Bush and Reagan for building the deficit.

When the city became outraged over a local arts center showing homoerotic photos as part of an exhibit by photographer Robert Mapplethorpe, Borgman was one of the few to side with freedom of expression, defending the rights of the arts center and lambasting those who were against the show. He drew a cartoon of sheriff Simon Leis, former prosecutor Art Ney and former police chief Larry Whalen pulling a statue of Michaelangelo's "David" into the courthouse saying, "Your honor, we found this clown parading around in a homoerotic pose." He identified Art Ney as "Art? Ney!"

Under the headline "Great Moments in American Thought," he showed a patriot from 1776 screaming, "I may not agree with what you say, but I will defend to the death your right to say it," followed by a 1990 citizen of Cincinnati with his fingers in his ears saying, "Go away!"

"I rebel against the constrictive attitudes of this city to kind of close down and suffocate my right to make reasonable choices, so I am always fighting for the elbow room," says Borgman, who insists he is conservative in many ways despite the public's perception. "But I think I am more contrarian than anything else. I think if this was a more liberal city I would be picking apart those tenets. It is no big deal to preach to the choir, particularly here. You have a conservative reader and a conservative newspaper, and to be a conservative and confirm all their biases is no big trick. But to do something else and challenge them

— continued on next page

in a way that I at least hope I do and still have them appreciate me is something I am proud of."

One of the great attractions of Borgman's work and what keeps him on the good side of those whom he offends is that he doesn't spend every day taking a stand on one issue or another. Much of his work is spent applying a curious, quirky, ironic twist to a subject. As the Berlin Wall fell and the Soviet Union broke apart, Borgman summed up the whole topic by drawing some average Joe sitting in his La-Z-Boy, Sunday paper spread all around his feet saying, "Now that Communism is dead I think I'll take a nap."

"A cartoonist friend of mine said that he thought the trick to my work was it was warm at the same time as being provocative," Borgman says. "That kind of hangs with me. People say that in different ways to me — 'Well, I may not agree with what you say, but I like looking at your work' or 'I can tell you're not mean.' I take that to mean they see something warm and human and compassionate in it, and even if they don't agree with the bottom line they don't mind listening to the voice."

Borgman has tried taking a hard-line stand on issues day after day like some of his peers, Herb Block, Paul Conrad, Pat Oliphant, but couldn't sustain what he says is the anger — that fire in the belly that's needed to be so adamant about something every day. The lighthearted, isn't-life-funny? child inside of him kept creeping out and into his work.

As a youth growing up in Price Hill on the blue-collar West Side of Cincinnati, Borgman sat around for hours admiring the works of Mort Drucker of *Mad Magazine* and Warner Brothers animator Chuck Jones and would then amuse his friends by drawing caricatures of teachers in the margins of his high school notebooks. When an underground newspaper started, he used the forum to lampoon the school's administration. In grade school, his renditions of Popeye and Olive Oyl were praised on a local television show. Even as far back as 4th grade at St. William Elementary he dabbled in his future profession, prompting one of the school's nuns to scold him, "Don't waste your talent on cartoons."

"It was always pretty clear I would end up in art somewhere," he says, looking back. "My dad was a frustrated artist. Sign painting was as close as he got to his artistic destiny, but there were always a lot of art materials and cardboard and paints around our house. We were probably one of the few households in Price Hill where growing up and being an artist was entertained along with every other possibility."

— continued on next page

Borgman graduated summa cum laude in 1976 from Kenyon College in Gambier, Ohio, with a degree in fine arts. Following the advice of the nun, whom he still affectionately refers to as "The Prune," it wasn't until his senior year that he broke away from more formal art forms and actually created his first editorial cartoon for the school paper. A few months into that first semester of his senior year, with a grand total of 13 cartoons to his name and the courage of the naive, Borgman applied for the vacant editorial cartoonist spot at the *Enquirer*. Former editorial page editor Thomas Gephardt, who now looks like a genius with amazing foresight, hired him based upon Borgman graduating.

The job was pure hell for a while. Borgman was still trying to define his style and was not used to being yelled at by angry adults. The experience gave him the beginnings of an ulcer and contributed to the patches of gray that now run through his curly, shoulder-length hair. He evolved quite nicely, though. He is now one of the paper's highest-paid employees, and he supplements that income with payments from the syndication rights, the sale of his original drawings at a local art gallery for prices that push the $800 range, and his latest creation, a daily cartoon strip, "Zits," that is syndicated nationally as well.

What impressed Gephardt and the growing group of area residents who have a collection of original Borgman cartoons in their homes was his art skills. "Sometimes I think very grandly it's sort of a higher form of art," Borgman says with all sincerity while trying not to sound aloof. "It involves writing, humor, good drawing, communicating philosophically and politically what you stand for in life. I don't know of any art form that takes on any more than that as its goal. I don't want to make it sound highfalutin, but tell me why it's not? Everything I learned in composition, drawing, print-making, painting, all my art classes goes into this as well as things I learned in theater, literature, history, even science. Things pop up in the news and you have to at least understand a little bit about what they are talking about. You have to have some context to put it in. Charles Schulz said a cartoonist has to be a B student in everything. I think that is kind of true. There isn't anything that comes up in the news you have to have some idea how to wrap your mind around in order to deal with it.

"I'll also never understand why when you inject humor or pile humor on top of everything else you are accomplishing it suddenly denigrates it in people's minds that you are not a serious person. To me that jacks the whole thing up one more notch."

— continued on next page

" IT'S THE NEW SHERIFF, BOYS! HIDE THE GIRLIE MAGAZINES! "

The humor as well as the artistic skills are not lost to his peers. In addition to the Pulitzer, Borgman has won the National Cartoonist Society Best Editorial Cartoonist for three straight years and the Thomas Nast Prize, named for the 19th-century father of editorial cartooning, in which the winner is awarded his weight in cases of wine. Most recently he won The Reuben, in which his peers voted him the country's best cartoonist, ahead of runners-up Garry Trudeau and Lynn Johnston.

One of his cartoons hangs in the home of Gen. Norman Schwartzkopf (a drawing of Schwartzkopf standing next to Iraqi president Saddam Hussein who is dubbed "Dummkopf"). Another hangs in the White House. When President Clinton invited a group of editorial cartoonists to the White House for a visit, Borgman walked into the bathroom off the Oval Office and, much to his surprise, there above the toilet was one of his cartoons from the campaign.

"Truthfully, I thought it was a forgettable cartoon," he says. "I forgot about it as soon as I drew it. I don't know why he took to it or how he got a hold of it." The cartoon shows a doctor examining Clinton, who is cut up and scattered in pieces around the floor. "He's still breathing, so he must be our candidate," it says.

Borgman has a picture hanging in his office of when he met former President Reagan at a White House luncheon. "With Reagan, it was an awkward meeting," he says. "It was in the Cabinet Room, and we were all sitting around the table the Cabinet meets at. I was sitting in the secretary of agriculture's chair or something. I don't think Reagan quite grasped who we were, though. He may have been busy or preoccupied. He talked most of the time to Bill Mauldin, who was a great World War II cartoonist. They swapped old war stories. Neither of them had actually been in the war, but they fancied they had."

To Borgman, whose honesty, humbleness and down-to-earth nature are a refreshing break from the loud "Notice Me!" style of others at the top of their fields, the whole idea of meeting with presidents, being honored and being recognized around the country is beyond anything he ever imagined. When he was awarded the key to the city in 1991, he blushed.

"To me, my dad was as big of a person as you could get in the world, which is to say head of the parish council and a big player in the PTA," he says. "I never thought I would ever be more important than that."

— continued on next page

Four times a week, Marian Borgman catches a bus to downtown from her Price Hill home and goes to work for her famous son. When King Features began syndicating his cartoons to about 200 newspapers around the country in 1980, Borgman was told to find someone to work a few hours a day making copies, stuffing envelopes and mailing the cartoons to the papers. Wondering where he might find someone, he asked his mom if she knew of anyone.

"As soon as I brought it up her eyes got real wide, and she said she wanted to do it," he says. "You would never think that would work. The minute I said OK I began to regret it. I kept thinking, 'How can this work — my mother coming in and working with me?' She's the greatest person in the world to work with, though, quiet as a mouse, never interferes. Even when she is stuffing a cartoon I know she disagrees with she never opens her mouth." She occasionally tosses out an idea, he admits, but generally stays out of the daily grind.

Borgman is responsible for six cartoons a week, four of which must be of national interest for the papers that subscribe to the syndicate. Creating a daily editorial cartoon is truly a nonstop process, Borgman says, that involves twisting everything you see or hear into a possible cartoon idea. Generally, though, it takes the better part of a full workday to envision, develop and draw a cartoon. Borgman, usually dressed in jeans and rarely wearing shoes while he is drawing, starts collecting ideas in the morning by listening to National Public Radio during his commute, jotting down ideas on Post-it notes. He thumbs through the *Enquirer* and the *Post* and a few other newspapers and magazines, trying to keep up with the events of the world before settling on a topic. If an idea isn't in hand by 1 PM, a mild panic sets in.

"For me, the whole process is pretty hard. Forgive my saying it, but I try to play the game at a pretty high level. I think if all one tries to do is make a joke about something that happened in the news yesterday, it wouldn't be that hard. Jay Leno spouts out 20 of those in a night's monologue. If you are really trying to make a commitment to life and where you would like to see the country go and what you think is right and wrong, then you've got a bigger role for yourself. In my own mind I've carved out a pretty big mission. There have been a lot of laughs along the way, but, yeah, I work at it pretty hard."

Granted, he says, some of his opinions have changed over the years. He makes no apologies. And there may even be contradictions in his beliefs. Still, no apologies. Sometimes his opinions are very philosophically clear. "I'm for a lot of forms of gun control. I've always been for fiscal responsibility, which I think comes from my Price Hill roots. I can't imagine us racking up bills we are not intending to pay and leaving them for somebody else. That's a conservative streak."

Other times his beliefs aren't clear. In a cartoon about abortion he had a woman say, "Seems to me everybody has rights in this, but nobody has all the rights. The truth is I'm pro-life and pro-choice," at which time she was stoned by both sides.

"I'm sorry to say my profession is full of people these days who do nothing more than a gag a day about something in the news and over the course of a decade don't make a significant statement about what they believe in or what they really feel," he says. "So I'm kind of weird that way. I'm probably more serious about that than I should be. I probably should take some easy shots and amuse folks in doing it but it just isn't what I think I need to get good and stay good."

Borgman's corner office includes a large glass window that overlooks the Ohio River and a smaller one that looks across to his native West Side. He was surprised when he found out he was getting the office. He thought he was going to get a cubicle in the newsroom along with the rest of the staff. His shelves are full of books by other cartoonists. A boom box sits on one end of a long row of filing cabinets and a Reds hat sits on the other. Pictures of his meetings with presidents Reagan and Clinton hang on

— continued on next page

the walls alongside drawings by his kids. "The one is of me and I think the other is a dog," he says of his kids' drawings.

The most prominent wall space by his desk is taken up by framed drawings sent to him by "Calvin and Hobbes" creator Bill Watterson, who began his career as Borgman's counterpart at *The Cincinnati Post*, and editorial cartoonist Jeff MacNelly, who draws the cartoon "Shoe." The front page of the *Enquirer* announcing his Pulitzer hangs behind the door. The Pulitzer announcement from Columbia University is on a far wall.

It's a fine office, modest and unassuming, the best part of which may be the door that allows him to shut out the squawking of police radios and chatter from the next-door newsroom. He can handle the noise while he is drawing, but not while he is creating. The creative ideas that propel one to the Pulitzer level have small voices that can't be heard above the din. "You tend to come up with this stuff in the dark corners of your mind, and there just can't be a lot of commotion around," he says. "There is a core one-to-two hours a day when I really need to be alone. If I was in a cubicle I would just die. I took a personality test one time and came up as an extreme introvert, which doesn't surprise me at all. Most of the cartoonists I know are fairly solitary people. You get good at cartooning and gravitate toward cartooning because you're the kind of person who goes to your room and draws at night instead of working on cars or playing basketball. The expectations are you will be the life of the party, a stand-up comedian only on paper and it's a real different type person who is attracted to cartooning."

These expectations are creating one of the real dilemmas in Borgman's life. Since winning the Pulitzer in 1991, he is inundated with requests for everything from giving a commencement speech at the University of Cincinnati, which he did in 1991, to people wanting him to come to a party. "That's the great friction in my life," says Borgman, who is still uncomfortable with his celebrity despite the numerous awards. "This is much more of a public-type job than I am suited to. I like the part that involves putting the lines down on paper, but I don't like the part that people would like to meet you or have you come talk to them. That is the toughest part. I enjoy one-on-ones with people, but in any kind of larger group I'm just very shy. I don't like that kind of situation. I have to do a certain amount of it, I know, but it doesn't come natural to me at all."

— continued on next page

His office phone will ring about 30 times a day. He set up a detailed voice mail message that answers most questions, but still feels the need to make himself available and answers it himself 50 percent of the time.

"If you're not careful your daydreaming time can get eaten up, and that's probably your most valuable part of the day," he says. "That's when you're really doing what people really need you for — brainstorming on ideas and trying to come up with lively ones. And if you're not careful you can turn into the cartoon corporation and just churn out work."

He has a studio set up at home and could easily do more work from there, he says, but he likes the office environment. Besides, when he is at home he prefers just being with his family and wrestling with his kids in the living room rather than wrestling with the muses in his studio. Not all work escapes his home, though. His wife, Lynn, taught herself the publishing business 12 years ago and has published four collections of Borgman's work to date.

The Borgmans have two children, Dylan and Chelsea, who don't seem to be overly affected by their father's profession, at least not yet. They don't ask him to teach them to draw, and, so far, their friends seem to view him with more of a star status than someone whose political views they might not agree with. Borgman laughs now, knowing that will change. "Oh, as their friends become more politically aware they will no doubt suffer their share of grief over my stuff," he says.

tainment crowds, and its news stories often take a hard slant against the city's conservative policies and beliefs. Issues of freedom of speech and freedom of choice are of particular interest to the publication.

The paper also offers local features and reviews of the arts, movies, records, bands, nightclubs and events and, like its counterpart, *CityBeat*, frequently sponsors events popular with the alternative crowd. Other regular columns offer an entertaining look at the alternative lifestyle. The paper is also well read for the syndicated and very amusing "News of the Weird," as well as the adults-only section of entertainment and personal classified ads in the back of the paper. This free weekly paper publishes every Friday.

Business Newspapers

Cincinnati Business Courier
35 E. Seventh St. • 621-6665

The *Business Courier* created some of the biggest business news of 1996 when in a surprise move it acquired the assets of its long-

time competitor, the *Greater Cincinnati Business Record*. The purchase ended a nine-year battle between the two business weeklies, in which snipes and skirmishes of the publishing variety were of common order. The *Business Record* was actually the larger of the two papers, but the *Courier* is part of a large chain of business weeklies that were purchased by Newhouse Publishing in New York, whose owners wanted full control of this market and made the owners of the *Record* a financial offer they couldn't refuse.

Many of the reporters and editors of the *Business Record* moved over to the *Business Courier,* allowing the paper to incorporate the best of both worlds. The paper usually offers more in-depth analyses of the major business stories of the day than what is found in the business sections of the daily papers, in addition to dozens of smaller business stories that the daily papers don't have space for.

Each week, the *Business Courier* offers an in-depth look at the financial portfolio of a publicly-held Cincinnati company and examines a local privately-held business. This is a great source of information for job-seekers looking for background on a business they may be interested in working for or interviewing with.

The *Courier* also offers mutual fund listings, stock reports and numerous other financial data on Cincinnati-based businesses. A section of the paper is devoted to "Business Leads," featuring people who've accepted new positions, as well as new incorporations, lawsuits and liens filed against businesses. Additional special sections on real estate, healthcare and small business, for example, rotate on a weekly basis each month. The paper also runs a popular weekly listing in which it takes topics such as executive compensation or publicly-held companies and ranks them in order from greatest to smallest. It then compiles the listings into an annual *Book of Business Lists*.

The *Courier*, which began publishing in Cincinnati in 1983, publishes on Friday. Newsstand price is $1.50. Subscriptions are $57 a year.

Small Business News
635 W. Seventh St. • 357-8500

Small Business News covers issues and events relating specifically to smaller businesses in Greater Cincinnati. Business owners receive complimentary subscriptions. Others can subscribe for $20 for 12 issues.

Other Weekly Papers

Cincinnati Herald
354 Hearne Ave. • 961-3330

The *Herald* serves Cincinnati's African-American community with news, arts, sports, entertainment and religion articles focusing on the city's African-American lifestyle and issues. It offers a different perspective from that of any of the area's other newspapers.

The paper has been in the news itself quite a bit recently, most notably regarding its recent sale. Sesh Communications, a Cincin-

nati-based media company that also owns *NIP* magazine, purchased the *Herald* from Porter Publishing Co., which was having financial difficulties. Just a few months earlier, those difficulties forced the 25,000-circulation *Herald* to miss its publication date for the first time in 42 years. Like many newspapers, it was having a difficult time generating enough advertising to pay for the high price of newsprint and printing. Not even a firebombing of its editorial offices in 1994, in retaliation to a controversial editorial, had managed to stop the paper from making it to the news stands on time. Since the purchase by Sesh, though, the paper has turned around and is quickly becoming a "must read" for everyone, not just the African-American community. Prices are 50¢ an issue or $20 annually.

The Downtowner
128 E. Sixth St. • 241-9906

The Downtowner is a free publication that focuses mostly on the positive issues, events, business news and people of downtown, with regular feature columns mixed in. One of the most popular columns in this weekly paper is "Speaking of Sex," a sex advice column written strictly from a clinical perspective by a local psychologist. The paper also runs "Mr. and Ms. Downtowner," which gives a brief profile of two downtown workers. *The Downtowner* can be picked up at a number of news racks around downtown. It is common lunchtime reading.

Out-of-Town Newspapers

Out-of-town newspapers can be found at the following outlets:

Fountain News, Fifth and Walnut streets, 421-4049

Joseph-Beth Booksellers, 2692 Madison Road, Norwood, 396-8960

Barnes & Noble, 3802 Paxton Avenue, 871-4300; 7800 Montgomery Road,

Kenwood, 794-9440; 9891 Warston Boulevard, Deerfield, 683-5599; or 7663 Mall Road, Florence, Kentucky, (606) 647-6400

Little Professor Book Center, 8537 Winton Road, Finneytown, 931-4433; Forest Fair Mall, Forest Park, 671-9797; 814 Main Street, Milford, 248-2665; 7844 Cox Road, West Chester, 777-0220

Duttenhofer's Treasures 214 W. McMillan, 381-1340.

FYI

Unless otherwise noted, the area code for all phone numbers listed in this guide is 513.

Magazines

Applause!
7710 Reading Rd. • 761-6900

The magazine "for Cincinnati's black lifestyle" offers profiles of the area's highly prominent African-Americans and features on places of special interest to the area's African-American community. This bimonthly magazine publishes special editions during the year that focus on Cincinnati's African-American business community, as well as a calendar of events.

The magazine is perhaps best known and highly respected for its annual Imagemaker Awards, which honors exceptional achievements of African-Americans and names local African-American pacesetters. A one-year subscription is $13.95.

Cincinnati Magazine
One Centennial Plaza • 421-4300

Cincinnati Magazine began as a publication of the Chamber of Commerce but is now wholly independent and offers a much more in-depth look at people, places, events and issues in the news around Greater Cincinnati than you will find in most area publications. The monthly publication offers short tidbits in its "Observer" section, along with medium-length "Department" stories and full-length features, all written in a light, easy-to-read style.

The magazine is well-known for its dining critiques and restaurant listings, including its annual "Dining Out Guide," which provides a complete list of area restaurants. (To make things easier, though, just flip back to our Restaurants chapter.) A separate "Schools Guide" provides a look at all of the area's schools and day care

facilities. Four times a year it publishes a "Homes" section, which is inserted in the magazine and allows a peek into some of the area's most unbelievable and unusual homes. Other special sections on a variety of topics are published each month.

Cincinnati Magazine is perhaps best known, though, for its annual "Best and Worst" picks, in which it takes a light-hearted look at the events of the past year, in addition to some businesses and restaurants that are — or aren't — worthy of a visit. Subscriptions are $18 annually.

NIP
354 Hearne Ave. • 961-3331

NIP is an acronym for news, information and photos. The magazine focuses on the news, social life and entertainment of the African-American community in the Cincinnati region. The magazine is also available in Dayton, Columbus, Indianapolis, Lexington and Louisville. Subscriptions are $16 annually, $30 for two years and $42 for three years.

St. Anthony Messenger
1615 Republic St. • 241-5615

This 102-year-old national magazine for Catholics is headquartered in Cincinnati. Articles focus on issues and people of the modern world, including highly controversial topics such as abortion, racism, and the sexual revolution and how they mix with Christian values and beliefs. The monthly magazine costs $2 per issue or $19 per year.

Other Publications

50 Plus!
1077 Celestial St. • 684-0501

The publishers of *All About Kids* magazine have added to the list of specialty publications in the area by starting a free monthly paper that deals with health and lifestyle issues facing older Cincinnatians. *50 Plus!* profiles prominent Cincinnatians and includes articles about living, adventure, health, love, money and a wide variety of topics geared specifically for people over 50. A calendar of events is included. The magazine also sponsors seminars — including one last year that featured Ralph Nader — and an annual Over 50 Expo. You can pick up a copy free at newsstands and local libraries.

All About Kids
1077 Celestial St. • 684-0501
All About Kids is a free monthly paper that deals with family issues, some of them controversial. Psychologist Earladeen Badger publishes the paper, which is an Award of Excellence winner from Parenting Publications of America. You can pick up a copy at newsstands and local libraries.

The American Israelite
906 Main St. • 621-3145
A weekly paper centering around the area's Jewish community, this is the oldest English-Jewish weekly in America, established in 1854 by Isaac M. Wise. Subscriptions are $24 a year. Newsstand price is 50¢.

Antenna Magazine
2515 Fairview Ave. • 287-6518
Antenna is a monthly arts magazine that provides features, reviews and details about all of the area's art establishments and organizations, including those outside the major venues. The magazine also carries classified ads for artist-related needs. The magazine is available at arts venues throughout the city, or a basic subscription is $22 annually.

Bengals Report
6629 Muddy Creek Rd., Blue Ash
• 941-9021
This is required reading for diehard Bengals fans. The paper offers game recaps, profiles, stats, analyses and opinions about the Bengals and the National Football League. The publication comes out 15 times a year — biweekly August through December and monthly in January, April, May and July. A subscription is $26.95 annually.

Catholic Telegraph
100 E. Eighth St. • 421-3131
The Archdiocese of Cincinnati began publishing this weekly paper, which focuses on the area's Catholic community, in 1831. Subscriptions are $22 a year.

Cincinnati Court Index
119 W. Central Pky. • 241-1450
The *Cincinnati Court Index* details Hamilton County's daily legal activities, including legal notices and scheduled trials and hearings and provides a full list of the previous day's municipal, common pleas, district and bankruptcy court filings. The paper is directed toward the legal community and interested businesses. Subscription price is $85 for one year or 75¢ per issue.

EastWord
6320 E. Kemper Rd. • 469-0166
Started by the former editor of *EastSide Weekend*, *EastWord* survived as an independently owned publication until 1996, when it was purchased by the Thomson Newspaper chain, which has since beefed up the paper. Touted as the "Magazine For People Who Care," it includes features and regular articles on home, business, money and travel topics. Delivery is free by mail to 26,000 homes on Cincinnati's East Side.

The Employment News
1172 W. Galbreath Rd. • 728-4000
This free weekly publication offers local job listings along with local and national articles on searching for a job. The paper is available in newsracks downtown.

Entertainer Magazine
2314 Iowa Ave. • 281-5544
Entertainer Magazine publishes articles and listings of events, activities and establishments around the Tri-state 26 times a year. It is free and can be found on newsstands and at restaurants, bars and nightclubs throughout the area.

Equine Edition
4910 Para Dr. • 242-4300
This monthly paper serves horse enthusiasts in Ohio, Kentucky and Indiana — and there are many, especially as you near Bluegrass country. Articles on horse health, training, competitions and stables are among the offerings. The subscription price is $12.95 per year.

Express Cincinnati
771-5088
Express Cincinnati is a monthly newspaper chronicling the activities of the city's upscale social scene. Photos and articles of pre-

vious events, stories about upcoming events, columns, a calendar and even Blue Book wedding announcements are detailed. The publication can be found at newsstands around the city and at select fund-raising events or by subscribing for $15 a year or $28 for two years.

Sports & Fitness Cincinnati
4719 Reed Rd., Columbus
• **(614) 451-5080**

Sports & Fitness publishes magazines throughout the state of Ohio offering suggestions, helpful hints, opportunities and places in which people may participate in sports and fitness activities. The Cincinnati version, which comes out 12 times a year, has a mix of local and statewide articles. The magazine can be picked up at newsracks throughout the city and in many grocery stores or can be purchased through a subscription of $18 a year.

Reds Report
1350 W. Fifth St., Columbus
• **(614) 486-2202, (800) 760-2862**

For diehard Reds fans, *Reds Report* offers game recaps, profiles, stats, analyses and opinions regarding the Reds and baseball. The paper comes out monthly, with subscriptions costing $27.95 a year.

Television

Major Local Stations

WLWT Channel 5 (NBC)
WCPO Channel 9 (ABC)
WKRC Channel 12 (CBS)
WPTO Channel 14 (PBS)
WXIX Channel 19 (Fox)
WBQC Channel 25 (Independent)
WKOI Channel 43 (Independent)
WCET Channel 48 (PBS)
WCVN Channel 54 (PBS)
WSTR Channel 64 (WB)

With a good antenna you can also pull in Dayton stations 2, 7, 22 and 45.

Cable TV

If you have a complaint relating to your cable operation, Greater Cincinnati has outlets to help

you. Cable subscribers within Cincinnati city limits can call the city's Office of Cable Communications at 325-3721. Subscribers in the suburbs can call the Intercommunity Cable Regulatory Commission of Southwest Ohio at 772-4272. In Northern Kentucky, call the Kenton-Boone Counties Cable Television Board at 261-1300.

Coaxial Communications of Southern Ohio
3416 Ohio Hwy. 132 • **797-4400**

Coaxial fills in the gaps in Greater Cincinnati not covered by Time Warner and some of the larger cable systems. It serves many multiunit dwellings. Coaxial has two packages: basic and standard. Prices differ depending on the location.

Frontiervision
1272 Ebenezer Rd. • **941-7000**

This company serves rural areas on the extreme western side of Greater Cincinnati, including Delhi, Miami, Whitewater, Cleves, Addyston and North Bend. Frontiervision offers only a basic package of 38 channels for $22.58 per month (you can order additional premium channels separately).

TCI Cablevision of Ohio
4117 Hamilton-Middletown Road, Hamilton • **868-2569**

TCI serves Butler County. It offers basic and expanded packages beginning at $10 per month.

Telesat Cable TV
11 Spiral Dr., Florence, Ky.
• **(606) 283-6780**

Telesat serves only the city of Florence with one package of 42 channels for $19.80 per month.

Time Warner Cable
11252 Cornell Park Dr. • **469-1112**

Time Warner serves Cincinnati and most of Hamilton County, offering three cable packages — basic, expanded and standard — from $16 per month for 38 channels to $31 per month for 56 channels. It is in the process of upgrading its lines from coaxial to fiber optic, which allows for even more channels. That upgrade is not available in all locations yet, though. Call to find out if your area has been upgraded. Warner also has a $9 reception package that offers just the public stations that anyone can pick up but without the worry of poor reception.

Time Warner Cable of Green Township
3290 Westburn Dr., Bridgetown
• **451-6730**

Time Warner, which just took over from Metrovision, serves Green and Cheviot on the area's West Side. Basic service for 13 channels is $7.89 per month. The Preferred package offers 42 channels for $20.34 per month. It also offers two additional tiers of five channels each that can be added on to the Preferred package.

TKR Cable of Northern Kentucky
717 Madison Ave., Covington, Ky.
• **(606) 431-0300**

TKR serves all of Northern Kentucky with two levels: Basic (26 channels) and Advantage (more than 50 channels). Prices for the Basic package differ depending on the location.

Radio Stations

Adult Contemporary
WRRM 98.5 FM

Big Band
WPFB 910 AM (Middletown)
WMUB 88.5 FM
WOBO 88.7 FM
WMKV 89.3 FM (and wellness for seniors)

Country
WOBO 88.7 FM (also Big Band and ethnic)
WYGY 96.5 FM (young country)
WSCH 99.3 FM (Aurora, Ind.)
WRBI 103.9 FM (Batesville, Ind.)
WUBE 105.1 FM
WPFB 105.9 FM (Middletown)
WNKR 106.5 FM (Dry Ridge, Ky.)

Jazz
WMUB 88.5 FM
WVXU 91.7 FM
WVAE 94.9 FM
WNOP 740 AM

National Public Radio
WMUB 88.5 FM (Miami University, Big Band, jazz)
WNKU 89.7 FM (Northern Kentucky University, folk)
WGUC 90.9 FM (University of Cincinnati, classical)
WVXU 91.7 FM (Xavier University, jazz, talk)

News, Talk, Sports
WKRC 550 AM
WLW 700 AM
WBOB 1160 AM
WUBE 1230 AM
WAZU 1360 AM (CNN Headline News)
WMOH 1450 AM (Hamilton)
WVXU 91.7 FM (Xavier University, jazz, NPR)

Oldies
WUBE 1230 AM
WMMA 97.3 FM
WGRR 103.5 FM
WSAI 1530 AM

Religious
WAKW 93.3FM
WNLT 104.3 FM (contemporary Christian)
WIOK 107.5 FM (Falmouth, Kentucky, Southern gospel)
WTSJ 1050 AM (Christian)
WCVG 1320 AM (gospel)
WCIN 1480 AM (and classic oldies)
WCNW 1560 AM

Rock
WOFX 92.5 FM (classic)
WOXY 97.7 FM (alternative)
WEBN 102.7 FM (album-oriented)
WAQZ 107.1 FM (modern)
WVMX 94.1 FM (classic)

Top 40 and Pop
WKRQ 101.9 FM

Urban Contemporary
WIZF 100.9 FM

Varied
WAIF 88.3 (hip-hop to blue grass to foreign to urban contemporary)

Cincinnati teenagers
who violate the city's
teen curfew are taken to
rec centers for holding
until their parents
come get them.

Law-Abiding Cincinnati

Cincinnati is changing its ways.

For decades, we've been famous as an uptight, Puritan town. We threw out Larry Flynt and his *Hustler* magazine (the subject of the Hollywood opus, *The People Versus Larry Flynt*, set in Cincinnati) and we arrested an art museum director for exhibiting Mapplethorpe photographs.

Yes, we're changing our ways. Now we're an uptight, Puritan town that allows, however reluctantly, the sale of *Hustler* and other X-rated magazines. Flynt himself cut the ribbon on the first downtown news shop to offer his skin mag. *Hustler* aside, though, don't come to Cincinnati expecting a booming sex industry. Local law still forbids X-rated movies (even art films) or peep shows. Outside of the occasional strip club way out in the farmlands or an isolated video shop in Clermont County that dares to carry anything above an R, we are the proverbial Mr. Clean.

Never mind the fact that we've got a street downtown named after a certain convicted felon who also happens to hold the record for hits by a major league baseball player. And forget for a minute that we have two new buildings — the Aronoff Center for the Arts and the Aronoff Center for Art, Architecture and Planning at the University of Cincinnati — named after a state legislator who pleaded guilty to a misdemeanor charge in connection with accepting illegal payments for making speeches.

To become a law-abiding citizen here, it's helpful to understand that there is no single Greater Cincinnati Book of Laws. The region includes three states with three state legislatures busily enacting separate (and often conflicting) rules and regulations, plus at least eight counties and the ensuing flurry of county restrictions. But add to this confusion that, within those three states and eight counties, Greater Cincinnati is a hodgepodge of some 200 towns, small cities, villages, hamlets, urban neighborhoods, townships, municipalities and unincorporated areas. Some burgs have their own police departments (such as the Rangers in ritzy Indian Hill), while others make do by asking coverage from a neighboring town. Of course, none of the 200 communities looks at crime in the exact same way: an aggravated assault in sensitive Mariemont might be written off as a simple bloody nose in a tougher place such as Cleves.

The incidence of serious crime is actually relatively low here (with the puzzling exception of arsons), according to the most recent FBI survey. The homicide rate in 1997 was the lowest in a decade, half that of Cleveland and Columbus and even below that of much smaller Dayton.

We seem to have a problem with serial killers, nonetheless. Charles Manson was born here. The Cincinnati Strangler terrified the city. And nurse's aide Donald Harvey became the Midwest's most prolific serial killer by dispatching 37 hospital patients, most of them elderly or terminally ill, during the '80s.

Where does the serious crime occur? A *Cincinnati Magazine* survey of one year's police records says downtown Cincinnati, Over-the-Rhine, Queensgate, Laurel Homes, West End, Covington, Cleves, Lincoln Heights, Newport, Hamilton and Woodlawn are all areas where you should be particularly careful. The safest neighborhoods? Terrace Park, Crescent Park, Silver Grove, Bromley, Aurora, Crestview

Hills, Lakeside Park, Southgate, Villa Hills, Indian Hill and Wilder. An unusually high number of serious crimes in Greater Cincinnati occur in August, by the way, so plan accordingly.

Greater Cincinnati boasts a rather interesting, if peculiar, set of laws and enforcement practices. If you're going to live here, or even visit, you should know about some of them.

X Marks the Spot? No Way. If you came to Cincinnati looking for an X-rated video or peep show, you've come to the wrong place. Of course, you probably didn't come here looking for those things — not only because you're not that sort of person, but also because Cincinnati's aggressive antipornography enforcement is by now well-known nationwide. To some Cincinnatians, this is a claim to fame. To others, it's an embarrassment. Either way, it's a fact of life, so you need to get used to it. Most convenience stores and even bookstores have voluntarily removed such magazines as *Playboy* and *Penthouse* from their shelves and from behind the counter (even though neither has been prosecuted in Cincinnati) in response to pressure from anti-porn forces. (The aforementioned *Hustler* shop downtown is an exception to the rule.)

The most famous — or notorious — incident involved the 1990 prosecution of the downtown Contemporary Arts Center for an exhibition of the photographic works of Robert Mapplethorpe. Now, many people probably wouldn't want some of these photos in a coffee-table book. But, then again, you don't find a lot of unsuspecting minors hanging around the CAC galleries. The prosecution helped forever cement in the national psyche Cincinnati's reputation as the capital of blue-nosed repressiveness. Lost in the publicity was the fact that a Cincinnati jury found the CAC and its director not guilty.

Whether Cincinnatians are really more conservative than other people about these issues is debatable. Much of the crackdown on porn results from pressure by a few very powerful people and interest groups. Cincinnati financier Carl Lindner, the wealthiest man in

the city and among the wealthiest in the United States, backs and bankrolls much of the local effort. The influence of Lindner and his friends has been known to make public anti-porn advocates out of people known to have very little private sympathy for the issue. One of the genuine generals in the anti-porn fight was a Lindner protege, Charles Keating, who founded the Cincinnati Decency League and spearheaded the anti-porn drive here for many years before he moved west and became famous for other things, such as his starring role in the S&L crisis and fraud conviction. Keating's brother, William, was for many years publisher of *The Cincinnati Enquirer.*

The new generation of porn fighters is headed by Phil Burress, president of the Citizens for Community Values, who sits on the Clermont County Library Board and is a nonstop crusader against porn throughout the Tri-state area. Hamilton County also has had a series of prosecutors who are very tough on pornography. Most prominent among them is former prosecutor Simon Leis, now Hamilton County sheriff. Leis cut his anti-porn teeth in the 1970s on Flynt. He also prosecuted the producers of *Oh, Calcutta!*, a Broadway musical from the 1970s known for its large number of singing naked people, among other things. Even to this day, anytime someone gets naked on stage in Cincinnati, you can expect someone from the vice squad to be in the audience, making sure the naked actor is not appealing to any prurient interests.

Even First Amendment purists and other opponents of pornography prosecutions have to admit some benefits have resulted from our Puritan mindset. You won't find a red-light district or "combat zone" in Cincinnati. However, sections of Covington and Newport, Kentucky, and most recently Monroe in Butler County, are known for clubs that feature nude or nearly naked dancing. But the sleaze factor is greatly reduced in the area as a whole, and that contributes to an overall feeling of safety. Street prostitution, though far from gone, has trouble finding places to thrive without red-light districts, so it has not become the sort of obvious blight found in other cities.

FYI

Unless otherwise noted, the area code for all phone numbers listed in this guide is 513.

Plum Street, downtown Cincinnati, is the site of impressive
City Hall, designed by Samuel Hannaford.

Gambling Fever. Wagering is generally illegal in Ohio, Kentucky and Indiana. Just ask Pete Rose. That said, there are some major exceptions. Riverboat gambling is legal in Lawrenceburg and Rising Sun, both Indiana river towns (see the Close-up in our River Fun chapter). Racetrack gambling is legal and thrives at River Downs in Anderson and Turfway Park in Florence, Kentucky. Church bingo is a big business in the Tri-state area (though it's taken a hit from the new riverboat casinos).

And, of course, all three states sponsor lotteries. To play Hoosier Lotto, pick six numbers from 1 through 48. Match six of six and win the jackpot (odds are 12,271,512 to 1). If you're feeling that lucky, you'll certainly want to purchase an Ohio Super Lotto ticket — fewer numbers to pick from (1 through 47) and the odds are more favorable (10,737,573 to 1). Lotto Kentucky is better yet: still fewer numbers (1 through 42) and the odds are a mere 5,246,000 to 1. Lottery tickets are available in all three states at some grocery stores and most liquor stores. The payoff varies, though the lucky employees at a Fort Thomas real estate office split $28 million off a $5 ticket — which they pooled to buy.

E-Check Blues. It's baaaack. E-Check, Ohio's auto emissions test program, which was suspended soon after it began in 1996 because of massive implementation problems, resumed in early 1998. Ohio motorists are now required to drive to one of 13 regional centers and fork over $19.50 for the test. Even-number model year vehicles must be tested in 1998, during whichever month the registration expires. Odd-numbered model years get their E-check in 1999. Exceptions: Cars less than 24 months old and titled to the original owner and cars older than 25 years (presumably "classic" collector cars). E-Check stations are open 7:30 AM to 7 PM Monday through Friday and 7:30 AM to 3 PM on Saturday and you can only pay with cash or a check. Call (800) CAR-TEST for the testing center nearest you. Yes, there will be long lines after work on weekdays and on Saturdays, so plan according. And speaking of emissions . . .

Wanna Smoke? Hope You Like the Great Outdoors — and We Don't Mean Cinergy Field. OK, Mark Twain, here's at least one area where Cincinnati was not 10 years behind the rest of the world. Cincinnati has been a national leader in restricting smoking in public places. Restaurants in the city are required to provide nonsmoking sections. Offices in the city have been required for several years to provide a smoke-free environment for nonsmokers. Although few people ever get ticketed for smoking violations, two who did were on-air personalities for WLW-AM who blew smoke in the face of local antismoking crusader Ahron Leichtman in the studio.

Smoking is now banned in Cinergy Field. And it is kind of nice, if you're a nonsmoker, not to have to smell the ubiquitous cigar and cigarette smoke for nine innings on a muggy night. But this smoking ban came as bad news to Reds owner and noted chain-smoker Marge Schott, who was taped blatantly defying the ban from her front-row seat. Schott rallied fans to overturn the ordinance, but to no avail.

Smoking is tolerated much more in areas east and south of the city, where people have been known not only to consume tobacco but also to grow it in large quantities. One of the all-time great politically incorrect moments in Greater Cincinnati history occurred when Marge Schott served as grand marshal of the Ripley Tobacco Festival parade east of Cincinnati.

Not Exactly Enlightened. Cincinnati has a charter amendment that bars any kind of protection for gays and lesbians against discrimination based on sexual orientation. Effectively, this means if you are black and living in the City of Cincinnati, you can't be denied housing or a job based on your race. If you are gay or lesbian, you are plain out of luck. The charter amendment, approved by the voters as Issue 2 and decried by gay-rights activists nationwide, has since been upheld by the Sixth U.S. Circuit Court of Appeals.

It's 10 PM. Do You Know Where Your Children Are? If you don't, there's a good chance they're being detained at a Cincinnati recreation center. Cincinnati has a curfew for teenagers — 10 PM for teens 15 and younger and midnight for 16- and 17-year-olds — unless they're accompanied by parents. Wayward teens are taken to rec centers for holding until their parents come get them. Norwood, Newtown and Golf Manor have adopted similar curfews, as has Forest Fair Mall. Other areas may follow suit under a state law allowing townships to pass curfews.

Hey, Pipe Down! Noise ordinances have become increasingly popular throughout the Tri-state area. For instance, Cincinnati prohibits car stereos played so loud that they bother people 50 feet away or any other noise that annoys within that same range. Similar laws are on the books in Batavia, Edgewood, Florence, and Ludlow. Covington prohibits any noise that can be heard 25 feet from a structure any time and 10 feet from a structure between 11 PM and 7 AM. You'll generally get off with a warning, unless you're a repeat offender.

No Pit Bulls, Lions or Giraffes. It's illegal for individuals to keep pit bulls or any kind of exotic animal in the city of Cincinnati. A good rule of thumb is that if it can eat a small child, you're not allowed to keep it as a pet.

No Tailgating. This doesn't mean failure to maintain an assured clear distance behind the driver ahead of you, though this is also illegal. This law means you can't open up the tailgate of your station wagon and pop open a few cold ones before the next Bengals or Reds game. City Council considered amending this law in its never-ending crusade to make Cincinnati a more fun place — and heaven forbid anyone should have to face even the first quarter of a Bengals game sober. But the city couldn't find any way around an Ohio law prohibiting open containers of alcoholic beverages in public places.

. . . But You Can At Least Scalp Your Ticket. Strange as it may seem in a place where so many other things are illegal, you are allowed to scalp tickets to sporting or entertainment events in Cincinnati. So, if you're a smoker and you just can't go another nine innings without lighting up, feel free to sell your season tickets at a sizable markup.

There are, of course, a few regulations regarding this practice. You need a permit from the city if you plan to scalp tickets on a regular basis. You can't scalp tickets on city property, including walkways, ramps and the concourse leading to the stadium. Sidewalks leading to the stadium are OK, but you can't obstruct traffic. And you can't use placards advertising that you're selling tickets. In case you were wondering, all those folks with signs that say "I Buy Tickets" would really much rather sell you tickets. Some storefront agencies also do a booming trade in secondhand tickets.

Hot Dog Vendors, Street Musicians, Beware. Cincinnati police have relented of late in their once-relentless battle to keep dangerous types like hot dog vendors and street musicians behind bars where they belong. Actually, you just need the proper city permit to sell hot dogs. And you can play music in the street, provided you aren't annoying anyone

in an office too much. But you would be well advised not to whip out a tuba in the courtyard of the Procter & Gamble headquarters, except during Oktoberfest, of course, when you can engage in all the oompah you want.

Feed a Meter: Go to Jail. It's illegal to feed someone else's expired parking meter in Cincinnati. Just ask the grandmother who got caught feeding meters in Clifton. A cop gave her a ticket, charged her with resisting arrest when she got "unruly," cuffed her and put her in jail. She even got a sprained arm in the process. It seems the local merchants were concerned about people parking on the street too long. When the story hit the international wire services, it was just one more example to the world of Cincinnati's steadfast commitment to law and order. So, please, keep those humanitarian impulses in check.

No Jaywalking. Cincinnati police do enforce jaywalking laws, though usually only when someone nearly causes an accident or is obviously drunk. It's not quite like Columbus, where tickets for jaywalking are more common than Buckeye fans.

U May B 4 UK, But Keep It to Yourself If You're in Ohio. Ohio requires that you put a license plate on both the front and the back of your car. That means transplanted Kentuckians with "IAM4UK" front license plates may be in for a rude awakening and a ticket, particularly if a cop who is 4UC or 4XU happens to see it. Seriously, police in some revenue-hungry areas of the city will enforce this law — if it's an Ohio car.

Red and Yellow Badge of Shame. There's another vanity plate you definitely don't want on your car in Ohio: the dark yellow plates with red letters and borders that signify a repeat DUI offender who only has driving privileges during work hours.

Halt! Drop That Paint Brush and Put Your Hands in the Air! If you live in parts of Montgomery or Mariemont, you might want to think twice before painting your house purple

INSIDERS' TIP

Amazingly, alcoholic beverage sales are prohibited until after the polls close on Election Day in all three states. Yes, that means the electorate was actually sober when it put some of these folks in office.

or adding a sun room. Both cities have historic districts that restrict your ability to make alterations not in keeping with the historical character of the neighborhood. Feel free, however, to paint your house purple or salmon in Cincinnati's Columbia-Tusculum neighborhood, where the vibrant "painted ladies" are an aesthetic treat for passersby on Columbia Parkway.

Halt! Drop That Yard Sign! Can you believe political yard signs are a hot topic in Greater Cincinnati and the subject of much legal wrangling. (Now yard geese are another matter — no law could possibly be too restrictive.) Perhaps it's because yard signs began to get so large. One homeowner painted a sign the size of her house. Perhaps it's because Cincinnatians just get too enthused about a political campaign. At any rate, current laws restrict "Vote for Joe" signs to a maximum of 8 square feet. Signs, however, no longer have to be 10 feet back from any street or right of way. You can plant those suckers right next to the roadway, as long as they're still on your property.

Maybe Just Leave 'Em on the Grass. You can't put your grass clippings, leaves or other yard waste out on the curb for trash pickup anymore in Cincinnati or most of the rest of the Ohio communities in the Tri-state area. You can just leave the stuff on your lawn, where it probably belongs in the first place, or if you live in Cincinnati or several other communities, you can call Rumpke (742-2900) or BFI (771-4200) to haul your yard waste away to giant compost heaps for 75¢ a bag. Many suburban communities routinely sweep, mulch and compost leaves piled at curbside in the fall for free and will take away other yard waste for a fee or for free the rest of the year. Call your local community government for details.

That'll Be $1,000 for Your License Plates, Please. If you're moving to Kentucky and you bought your car somewhere else, you'd better have proof you paid sales tax. Kentucky assesses a 6 percent tax on the current market value of your vehicles when you go to get your new Kentucky plates, which you must do within 15 days of setting up housekeeping there. That's $600 per $10,000 of car. But any sales tax you can show you paid when you bought the car is credited against that amount.

You'll also need to show proof of liability insurance plus your title for the car, which also must be converted to a Kentucky title. Kentucky residents may also be required to buy city stickers for their cars. Check with your city government.

After this, you'll still owe personal property tax on your vehicle, which can be rather steep. In Campbell County, for instance, rates run from 1.3 percent in unincorporated areas to 2.1 percent in Bellevue. That's up to $420 a year for a $20,000 car.

In Ohio, you have 30 days to get new plates, and in Indiana you have 60 days. Ohio's annual license charges are $42 for cars, $57 for trucks, $47 for motor homes, $21 for motorcycles and mopeds (additional charges may apply depending on the community you live in). You must also transfer the title to Ohio, which costs another $19.50, plus $10 more if you have a loan. It gets easier and cheaper after the first time because you can get annual renewal stickers by mail (you'll be notified by mail and get the form when the time comes).

As in Kentucky, plates in Indiana also can be very steep, ranging from $22 up to $1,000 or more, depending on the year and model of the car. You have 60 days to get your new Indiana plates and title. You'll need your old auto title and your auto liability insurance policy number. You get your plates at one of several local license bureaus in Ohio or Indiana.

While You're At it, Get a New Driver's License. Folks from Ohio will tell you that people from Kentucky and Indiana don't drive right, but all three states actually require drivers to have licenses and pass the same more-or-less rigorous written and driving tests. At 16, you can get a temporary permit by passing a written test in any of the three states. Once you're licensed anywhere, you can get a new license in the Cincinnati area fairly easily.

A new law in Ohio, passed by the Ohio General Assembly and effective July 1, 1998, allows teenagers to get temporary permits that allow them to drive at 15 1/2, if accompanied in the car by their parent or guardian. At 16, the teen can drive if accompanied by any licensed driver 21 or older. At 17, the teen can obtain full driving privileges after passing an exam. The law now also requires drivers under age 17 in the State of Ohio to be off the street between 1 AM and 5 AM unless accompanied by an adult or guardian.

In Ohio, newcomers have up to 30 days to get a new driver's license after moving. You'll generally only have to take a written test and simple eye exam, but an examiner may require a road test at his or her discretion. You'll need your driver's license from your old state and Social Security card, plus $10. Licenses are good for four years and expire on your birthday. Licenses are available at any license bureau.

In Kentucky, it's pretty much the same deal, except you only have 10 days and the cost is only $8. Indiana gives you 60 days to get a new license and you only pay $6. Also, remember to bring your birth certificate for the new Indiana license.

Don't Pass Those Stopped School Buses. Like just about everywhere else, Ohio, Kentucky and Indiana require drivers to stop in both directions for a stopped school bus with its red lights flashing. An exception is on four-lane highways, where drivers are still required to stop in the same direction as the bus but not in the opposite direction.

Park Free on Weekends. To help boost the city's economy, Cincinnati lets you park free at meters on Saturday and Sunday. You still have to pay to park in city garages, of course.

Turn Right on Red. You may turn right on red anywhere in the Tri-state area after coming to a full stop unless a sign at the intersec-

tion says otherwise. You also can turn left on red at intersections of two one-way streets with the same restrictions. Right turns on red are prohibited at most downtown intersections but allowed everywhere else. Do, however, be mindful of pedestrians and be aware of when left-turn arrows on the other side of the intersection may create opposing traffic from an unexpected direction.

Skinny Kids Cannot Slip Through the Cracks. Ohio, Kentucky and Indiana all have laws requiring child safety seats in cars. In most places, a child 4 and older, 40 pounds or over, or at least 40 inches tall no longer needs to be in a seat. However, in Ohio a child must be 4 years old, weigh 40 pounds AND be 40 inches tall to get sprung from the seat. Kentucky exempts children riding in pickup trucks from the safety seat law, provided they're in the cab with an adult.

Go Light on the Gas in Ohio. Speeding is illegal everywhere but more so in Ohio. The Ohio Highway Patrol has a nationwide reputation for giving people speeding tickets, and folks from out-of-state are disproportionate victims of their vigilance. You do get a 10-mph benefit of the doubt, generally. You can see drivers speed up a notch as soon as they cross the line into Kentucky or Indiana, where enforcement is not so vigorous. Don't get cocky, though, especially on I-471 in Northern Kentucky, where local police occasionally do issue tickets. Places to be particularly mindful of include any highway in Cincinnati, particularly the small stretch of I-275 just north of the Ohio River, and on I-275, I-71 and I-75 in Springdale, Sharonville and Montgomery. Also watch out for small towns and villages such as Milford and Terrace Park, which are known for their rabid enforcement of speeding laws. The Beechmont Levy in Mount Washington is also a famous local speed trap. And across the region, fines are doubled in construction zones, so be especially cautious there.

In Ohio, driving scofflaws better pay up or get off the road. The Hamilton County Clerk of Courts has announced a crackdown on drivers who haven't paid their fines or have missed court dates: they lose their driver's licenses. A thousand drivers had their licenses suspended in the last half of 1997 for an array of traffic violations. The driver's license is unsuspended when the offender pays the original fine plus an additional $15 fee.

Try to Only Pay the Piper Once. Every municipality in the Tri-state area charges income tax of some sort , ranging from as low as 0.5 percent to as high as 2.5 percent in Newport and Covington. But if you live in one city and work in another, you could end up paying income tax in both unless your city credits taxes paid to other cities or has a reciprocity agreement with that city. Fortunately, most suburbs don't force you to pay twice, but some do. So before you move, check it out with the city government where you plan to live. Ohio, Kentucky and Indiana honor the tax rates of the employment site for cross-state workers.

Graduated income-tax rates range from 0.743 percent to 7.5 percent in Ohio and 2 percent to 6 percent in Kentucky. In Kentucky, the top rate kicks in for anyone with an income greater than $8,000, while in Ohio, the top rate applies to incomes of more than $200,000. Indiana has a flat income tax rate of 3.4 percent on all income.

Drowning Your Sorrows, By the Book. Though you might expect a place that frowns upon so many other things to be fairly tough on alcohol consumption, Greater Cincinnati's alcoholic beverage laws are relatively lenient. In fact, Cincinnatians have something of a tradition of hoisting a few, what with their city having been at one time home to numerous breweries. If you can believe it, the Cincinnati Reds even got drummed out of the National League back in the last century because the team insisted on continuing to sell beer during games when the rest of the league prohibited it. Today, however, Cincinnati is pretty much in line with the rest of the country in its alcohol tolerance. The minimum drinking age, for instance, is 21 throughout the Tri-state area. In Ohio, restaurants, bars and other licensed establishments can sell alcoholic beverages from 5:30 AM to 1 AM Monday through Saturday, and 1 PM to 11 PM on Sunday. Kentucky

Photo: Skip Tate

Sawyer Point Park offers an impressive view of the downtown Cincinnati skyline.

restaurants, bars and other licensed establishments can sell alcoholic beverages from 6 AM to 1 AM Monday through Saturday and 1 PM to 11 PM on Sunday. In Indiana, licensed restaurants and bars can sell alcoholic beverages from 7 AM to 3 AM, Monday through Saturday. Alcoholic beverage sales are prohibited in most Indiana establishments on Sunday, except for some restaurants that are permitted Sunday sales until midnight.

Having an open container of an alcoholic beverage in public is a no-no everywhere, except during festivals, fairs and other events with the appropriate open-air permit (Riverfest, the Labor Day weekend fireworks extravaganza on the Riverfront, no longer permits alcohol sales or consumption of any kind).

Laws on sales of alcoholic beverages at retail stores are a little more complex in Ohio. Blue laws still haunt us, so you can't buy even a six-pack of beer before noon on Sunday. Some, but certainly not all, grocery and convenience stores now sell hard liquor, thanks to the ongoing privatizing of the Ohio State Store system. This switch from state clerks to private vendors has done wonders for such things as customer service and extended hours (most state stores used to close at 6 PM.). The bad news is, the price and brand selection is still mandated by the state. So if Bacardi introduces a new rum, you won't find it on Ohio shelves for quite a while — not until state bureaucrats OK the new brand, a painfully slow process that no doubt involves many, many fact-finding junkets to San Juan.

Given Ohio's mandated prices and selection, privately owned liquor stores in Kentucky and Indiana do a brisk business catering to Ohio residents who buy booze in bulk there and illegally smuggle it across the border. Alcoholic beverage taxes are lower in those states, and many Ohioans take advantage of the price difference. Since Ohio still maintains an undefended border with these barbarians to the south and west, enforcement of laws against alcohol smuggling is pretty much nonexistent.

Vote, Vote, Vote! To vote in Greater Cincinnati, you must be a U.S. citizen, 18 years or older by Election Day, have been a resident of Ohio, Kentucky or Indiana for 30 days, and be a resident of the county and precinct where you intend to vote. You can register to vote at the Board of Elections, any office of the Bureau of Motor Vehicles, or at public libraries. To maintain your registration, you must vote at least once every four years.

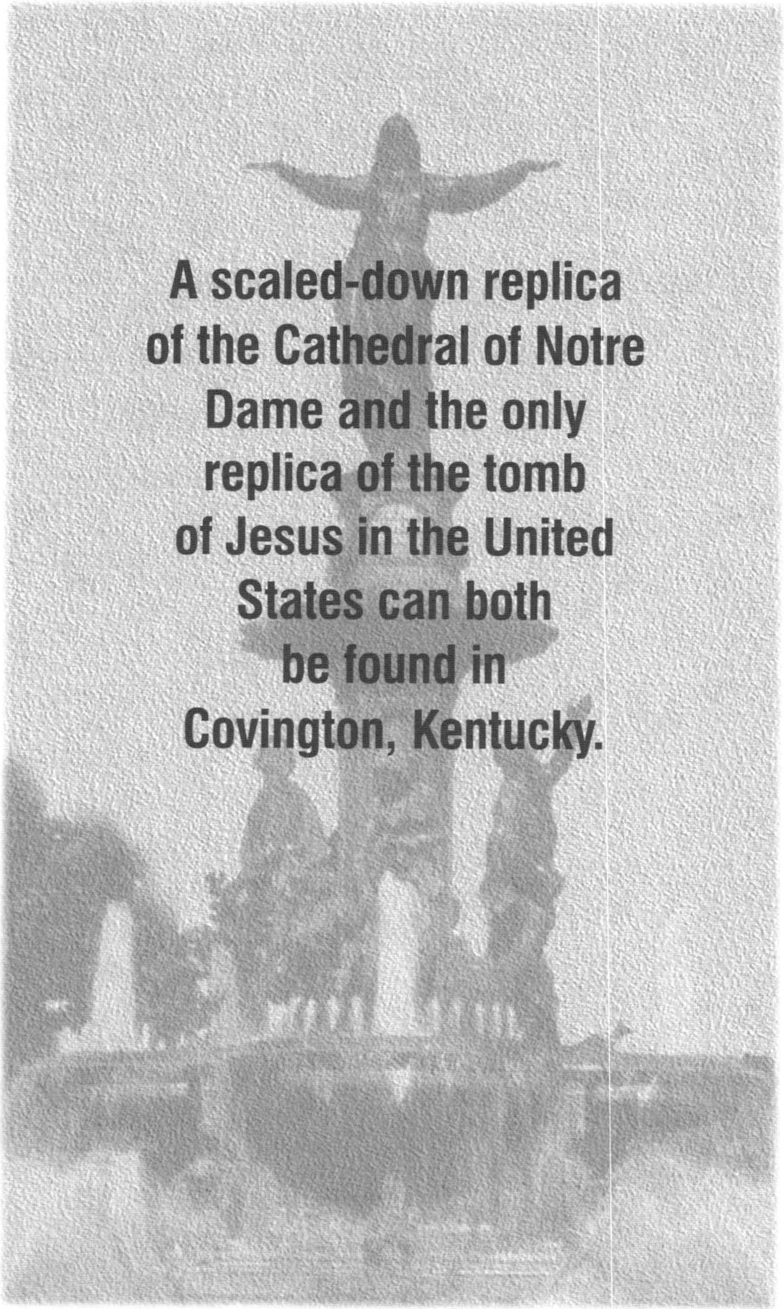

A scaled-down replica
of the Cathedral of Notre
Dame and the only
replica of the tomb
of Jesus in the United
States can both
be found in
Covington, Kentucky.

Worship

Religion has always held a place of significance in Greater Cincinnati, which is obvious from the area's buildings, history and activities. If it seems like there's a church around every corner, there's a good reason. More than 1,000 churches, synagogues, temples, chapels, mosques and meeting places of all denominations fill Greater Cincinnati.

Obviously, it would be impractical to write about each and every house of worship, so we've put together a very broad overview of the religious scene, mentioning some churches because of their historical and/or architectural significance. Check the Yellow Pages for lists of churches, synagogues and mosques in the area. The Saturday religion pages of *The Cincinnati Post* and *The Cincinnati Enquirer* carry specifics about times of worship.

Among the more noteworthy churches is Cathedral Basilica of the Assumption, which features a French Gothic design with gargoyles and flying buttresses, mural-size oil paintings by renowned artist and parishioner Frank Duveneck and the largest stained-glass window in the world. The church's architectural beauty has earned it the title of "basilica," meaning it has been singled out for its special religious or historical significance. It is one of only 31 basilicas in the country.

St. Francis DeSales church claims the largest swinging bell in the world, a 17-ton, E-flat monster named Joseph (in honor of the gentleman who provided the funding). The first time "Big Joe" was rung, the vibrations shattered windows for several blocks around. It was never rung again.

The smallest church in the world is Monte Casino, on the grounds of Thomas More College in Crestview Hills, Kentucky. The church was used for prayer by monks working in the vineyards. The vineyards are gone now and the church sits at the entrance to the college,

where it is still used on occasion, even though it can only accommodate two people at a time.

The only replica of the tomb of Jesus in the United States, which includes trees and plants mentioned in the Bible, is in Covington's Garden of Hope.

The first Jewish cemetery west of the Allegheny Mountains is located in the West End.

Greater Cincinnati has been the home of many noted theologians. The Rev. Lyman Beecher headed the Lane Theological Seminary for 18 years, beginning in 1832. Although the most powerful preacher of his day, The Rev. Mr. Beecher was eventually surpassed in recognition by his daughter, Harriet Beecher Stowe, who used her experiences in Cincinnati to help write *Uncle Tom's Cabin*. Isaac M. Wise founded the Reform Judaism in America movement after coming to Cincinnati in 1854. Joseph L. Bernardin, who later became a cardinal in the Catholic church, was named archbishop of the Cincinnati diocese in 1972.

Greater Cincinnati doesn't have a local ministerial society of association of churches. Individual denominations seem to go their own way. On occasion, though, religious leaders will get together — frequently for political reasons. Several ministers from the area's predominately African-American churches have formed a coalition known as the Black Ministers Conference. Although only a few years old, the conference has become a rather influential political entity within the city, regularly voicing an opinion on issues affecting the city's African-American community, and even creating the grass roots movement that led to the defeat of the "strong mayor" campaign in 1995 (see our Area Overview chapter).

But the mixing of church and state doesn't stop there. Each holiday season, religion seems to dominate the news, which may not be too surprising except when the Ku Klux Klan and American Civil Liberties Union get involved. Several years ago, the Jewish Federation began erecting a large menorah on Fountain Square to celebrate Hanukkah. Offended, a local chapter of the KKK decided that because the menorah was in a public place, a giant wooden cross should be erected as well, and the KKK should be the ones allowed to build it. The battle over the legality of the idea raged between the KKK and the city, eventually ending up in the courts, where the KKK, with the ACLU's help, won the right to put up a cross. And it does so every year, over the protests of local churches and citizens.

On a more peaceful note, every Good Friday more than 10,000 Catholics from the area and from other states walk the 356 steps up a steep hillside to Immaculata Church in Mount Adams, pausing on each step to pray a bead of the rosary. And, on occasion, huge masses of people gather in suburban Norwood, where sightings of the Virgin Mary have been reported.

The Catholic Community

The Greater Cincinnati area has a sizable Catholic community (292 parishes in 1995, according to a study conducted by *Cincinnati Magazine*), which includes Roman and Anglican Catholics. Cincinnati became the eighth diocese in the United States, established by Pope Pius VII in 1821. As of 1996, the diocese included more than 500,000 parishioners and was the 26th largest in the country.

In addition to those mentioned above, many of the area's Catholic churches are quite interesting. Downtown's St. Xavier church is on the National Register of Historic Places. The church was built in 1860 but burned on Good Friday 1882, only to be rebuilt. Xavier University and St. Xavier High School both had their beginnings as part of the church.

FYI

Unless otherwise noted, the area code for all phone numbers listed in this guide is 513.

Old St. Mary's church is the oldest Catholic church in Cincinnati and is a National Historic Site. Built in 1842 by German immigrants in Over-the-Rhine, the church features Bavarian-style stained-glass windows and offers Latin, German and English masses. Immaculate Conception in Norwood, Sacred Heart in Camp Washington and St. Gertrude the Great in Sharonville also offer traditional Latin services.

St. Peter in Chains cathedral downtown became the second permanent cathedral in the country when it was built in 1845. It now holds regular worship sessions — including one in which the service is signed for the hearing impaired — and all the liturgical functions of the archdiocese.

Cincinnati's Jewish Heritage

Rockdale Temple was the first Jewish congregation west of the Allegheny Mountains, chartered on January 8, 1830. The temple, which was previously on Rockdale Avenue, is now at Cross County Highway and Ridge Road.

In 1846, German-born Jews, unhappy with the English-born Jews at Rockdale Temple, established a new congregation, B'nai Yeshurun. They brought in Isaac M. Wise in 1854 to lead the congregation, which later became the foundation of the Reform Judaism in America movement. The congregation began constructing its own temple in 1866, after a two-year delay due to the Civil War. Now named after Isaac Wise, who led the congregation until his death in 1900, the temple is still the main sanctuary of the congregation. Members split worship services between this temple and the one in Amberley Village, also named after Wise.

INSIDERS' TIP

Looking for a different way to spend a lunch hour downtown? The First Presbyterian Church at Elm Street and Garfield Place offers a mini-service each Wednesday with hymns and a sermon, followed by a $3 buffet lunch. Food for the soul *and* the body.

The interior of the main temple, which is illuminated by 1,100 light bulbs, is stenciled with Hebrew inscriptions in color and gilt. When the temple underwent a $2 million restoration in 1995, more than 65 colors and 135 different stencils were used to paint the interior. During the renovation, a prayer book and newspaper dated 1890 were found behind a wall. All of the pews and sanctuary furniture are original to the building, including an 1866 pipe organ. The temple is a National Historic Landmark.

Isaac Wise also founded the first rabbinic school in America, Hebrew Union College, in Cincinnati in 1876. The college now has additional campuses in New York, Los Angeles and Jerusalem. The Cincinnati campus includes an extensive museum of Jewish art, history and culture. HUC continues to make contributions to the Jewish religion: It graduated the first woman rabbi in 1972 and its scholars are leading the way in piecing together and translating fragments of the Dead Sea Scrolls.

Greater Cincinnati now has 23 synagogues. The Jewish Federation of Cincinnati includes the Cincinnati Board of Rabbis and the Rabbinical Council of Cincinnati.

A Place for Everyone

Regardless of your religious affiliation, you will most likely find a house of worship in the Greater Cincinnati area.

Cincinnati Magazine's 1995 study found 239 local **Baptist** churches in the area. The Columbia Baptist Church was the first Protestant church west of the Alleghenies, organized on January 20, 1790. The Columbia Baptist Cemetery, across from Lunken Airport, holds the remains of area pioneers, including Maj. Benjamin J. Stites, who led the first group of settlers to the area (they established homesteads in what is now the Columbia-Tusculum neighborhood). Union Baptist Church is the second oldest predominantly African-American congregation in the state.

The area has 25 **Episcopal** churches, including Christ Church Cathedral, which was erected in 1835. The Boar's Head and Yule Log Festival, one of the oldest continuing festivals of the Christmas season, has been held here since 1940. (See our Annual Events chapter.)

Methodist denominations include Free Methodist and United Methodist. Milford United Methodist Church was founded in 1797, followed by Armstrong Chapel Church in 1798. For 120 years Armstrong Chapel was the only church in Indian Hill. The Korean Madisonville United Methodist Church offers services in both Korean and English.

Presbyterians founded Covenant-First Presbyterian Church in 1790. Lyman Beecher, one of the best-known preachers in the country in his day, served at the church. The Korean Presbyterian Church has a Korean School for its parishioners.

Among the area's 40 **Lutheran** churches is Concordia Lutheran Church, which still offers services in German.

Although many **Quakers** stayed in the eastern part of the state, three congregations made their way here, including the Friends Meeting, which was established in 1813, making it one of the oldest congregations in the area.

Six **Mormon** churches are spread throughout the area, including Cincinnati Stake Center in Fort Mitchell, Kentucky, and Cincinnati North Stake Center in Sycamore.

The large **Islamic** mosque built in 1995 in West Chester serves the 3,000 to 5,000 Muslims in Southwestern Ohio. Although **Buddhists** comprise a small segment of the population, their needs are met at the Yoseikan Zen Buddhist Center in Covington, Kentucky.

In addition to those mentioned above, many other religions and denominations are represented in the Greater Cincinnati area. There are also churches that offer services in Chinese, German, Latin, Spanish, Arabic and sign language for the deaf, and even churches that speak the language of today's youth — the New Life Church in Symmes boasts that it is "where the flock likes to rock." Geared toward "Generation Xers," the church band plays contemporary Christian music, allows casual dress and shows Christian music videos and film clips. The area also has more than 25 nondenominational churches.

Index of Advertisers

Index

Symbols

50 Plus! 398

A

A Christmas Carol 216
A Gentler Thyme 221
A La Carte Charter Services 150
A Show of Hands 114
A&J Art Gallery 191
A&M Farm Orchard 116
A&W Root Beer 118
A.B. Closson Jr. Co. 108
AARP Senior Employment Services 325
Abercrombie & Fitch 115
Abigail Cutter Theater 178
Access Shuttle 27
Acorn 111
Action for Children 362
Adath Israel School 358
Addyston 304
Adoption Connection 341
Adrica's 111
Adult Children of Alcoholics 341
Adult Continuing Education 377
Adult Day Care 341
Aglamesis Brothers 56, 113
AIDS & Sexually Transmitted
        Disease Information 341
AIDS Counseling and Information Hotline 341
AIDS Volunteers of Cincinnati 341

AIDS Volunteers of Northern Kentucky 341
Airport Playfield 167, 238, 242
AJ Jolly Golf Club 271
Alamo 29
AlaTee 341
Albee, The 41
Alcoholics Anonymous 341
Alexander Carriage Rides 233
Alexander House, The 92
Alexandria 307
All About Kids 168, 399
All About Kids Convention 210
All About Kids Show 168
Alliance of Independent Colleges
        of Art and Design 369
Allison House 97
Allyn's Cafe 73
Alms Park 298
Alzheimer's Association 317, 341
AM & PM Health Care 364
Amateur Slow-Pitch Softball 254
Amateur Trapshooting Association 220
Ambar India 44
Ambassador Carriage 29
Amber Park Retirement Community 319
Amberley Village 296
Ambrose H. Clement Health Center 340
Amelia 300
American Cancer Society 341
American Diabetes Association 341
American Heart Association 341
American Israelite, The 399

Going Somewhere?

Insiders' Guide presents 48 current and upcoming titles to popular destinations all over the country (including the titles below) — and we're planning on adding many more. To order a title, go to your local bookstore or call (800) 582-2665 and we'll direct you to one.

Adirondacks

Atlanta, GA

Bermuda

Boca Raton and the Palm Beaches, FL

Boulder, CO, and Rocky Mountain
National Park

Bradenton/Sarasota, FL

Branson, MO, and the
Ozark Mountains

California's Wine Country

Cape Cod, Nantucket and
Martha's Vineyard, MA

Charleston, SC

Cincinnati, OH

Civil War Sites in the Eastern Theater

Colorado's Mountains

Denver, CO

Florida Keys and Key West

Florida's Great Northwest

Golf in the Carolinas

Indianapolis, IN

The Lake Superior Region

Las Vegas

Lexington, KY

Louisville, KY

Madison, WI

Maine's Mid-Coast

Minneapolis/St. Paul, MN

Mississippi

Myrtle Beach, SC

Nashville, TN

New Hampshire

North Carolina's Central Coast
and New Bern

North Carolina's Mountains

Outer Banks of North Carolina

The Pocono Mountains

Relocation

Richmond, VA

Salt Lake City

Santa Fe

Savannah

Southwestern Utah

Tampa/St. Petersburg, FL

Tucson

Virginia's Blue Ridge

Virginia's Chesapeake Bay

Washington, D.C.

Wichita, KS

Williamsburg, VA

Wilmington, NC

Yellowstone

Insiders' Publishing Inc. • P.O. Box 2057 • Manteo, NC 27954
Phone (919) 473-6100 • Fax (919) 473-5869 • www.insiders.com